Business, Society and Global Governance

Business, Society and Global Governance is a thoroughly revised and updated new edition of *Building Business–Government Relations: A Skills Approach* to ensure this successful book continues to be the go-to textbook introducing US business–government relations in the institutional context of the United States. Written from a practitioner's perspective, it provides historical, descriptive, and comparative accounts of the public and private sectors, the different roles government plays with business (including several conceptual models to contextualize the two sectors), and various economic policies associated with business. Business–government relations are considered through three different social economic contexts: the socio-political arena, local economic development, and the global market.

This new edition includes:

- Extended coverage of the role of nonprofits
- The Trump "era" and effect of the Biden presidency
- The positive and negative effects of technology in society and the increasing role of disinformation
- COVID and the role of government in crises.

In the course of discussion, a set of skills, such as searching government jobs, starting a business, analyzing stakeholders, ethical reasoning, advancing a business agenda, leveraging public resources, contracting with government, interpreting global trends, doing business abroad, and leveraging international resources, are introduced and exercised.

Anna Ya Ni is the Associate Dean and Professor of public administration at the Jack H. Brown College of Business and Public Administration at California State University, San Bernardino. She has published over 20 research articles in journals, such as *Public Administration Review*, *Journal of Public Administration Research and Theory*, *American Review of Public Administration*, and *International Journal of Educational Technology in Higher Education*. She serves on the Board of American Society of Public Administration

(ASPA), Section of Science and Technology in Government (SSTIG), and the Inland Empire Chapter.

Montgomery Van Wart is a Professor in the Department of Public Administration at California State University, San Bernardino. He served as Chair of his department and Dean of the College of Business and Public Administration. He has authored 11 books including *Dynamics of Leadership*, *Leadership in Public Organizations*, *Administrative Leadership in the Public Sector* (with Dicke), and *Human Resource Management in Public Service* (with Berman, Bowman, and West). He has over 100 publications and has been a distinguished visiting professor at KU Leuven, the University of Hong Kong, Rutgers, and the University of Ireland.

Business, Society and Global Governance

A Skills Approach

Second Edition

Anna Ya Ni and Montgomery Van Wart

NEW YORK AND LONDON

Cover image: © Getty Images

Second edition published 2023
by Routledge
605 Third Avenue, New York, NY 10158

and by Routledge
4 Park Square, Milton Park, Abingdon, Oxon, OX14 4RN

Routledge is an imprint of the Taylor & Francis Group, an informa business

First edition published by Routledge 2015

ISBN: 978-1-032-01439-5 (hbk)
ISBN: 978-1-032-01432-6 (pbk)
ISBN: 978-1-003-17862-0 (ebk)

DOI: 10.4324/9781003178620

Typeset in Times New Roman
by codeMantra

Contents

Preface

The textbook you hold in your hands, *Society, Business and Global Governance*, has been crafted in such a manner as to be a comprehensive read for both upper- and lower-division undergraduate business students. It offers the reader a thorough understanding of government's roles with business and the skills necessary to create and maintain successful relations with government. At the same time, it defines the roles business can play with government that are compatible with its own needs to achieve corporate objectives and fulfill corporate responsibilities. This book approaches business–government relations from the practitioner's perspective and is intended for both private and public professionals.

Having taught business and government students at various universities over the course of many years, the authors have observed that there is both an aversion to theory and a strong desire to learn "how to" skills. Although theory will help students understand the complex social interactions between the two sectors, the applied nature of the field demands mastering the practical skills required to make informed choices and manage complex activities.

There are a few overarching themes that drive the content of the manuscript: a practical approach integrates the political, economic, and social theories with business and government practices; an interdisciplinary perspective reflects reality in practice; and of course, a concentration is evident on the much-wanted skill-building.

Our overall approach to this book is to intrigue readers into resolving practical problems, each of a different nature in the field. We introduce these as the text progresses, after general historical, institutional, and theoretical knowledge is acquired.

The contents of this textbook have been taught and exercised in a series of upper-division undergraduate business classes with proven success. Regardless of whether you are a business, public administration, history, or biology major, the knowledge and information you find in this book will be valuable as a citizen and probably in your career as well.

Acknowledgments

Many persons have contributed to the preparation of this book. We would like to give special acknowledgment to Paul Suino, our close working partner, for his invaluable editorial assistance in writing the book. We are indebted to the Department of Public Administration at California State University, San Bernardino, where the book was conceived, nurtured, and supported. Special thanks to contributing authors, such as Jonathan Anderson, Marc Fudge, Ann Johnson, Alexandru Roman, Tom McWeeney, Sharon Pierce, and Joshua Steinfeld, for their expertise and cooperation in conforming to our shared specifications. Anna Ya Ni thanks her mother Lihua Ma, her brother David Ni, and Wallace Heuser, for their support and encouragement throughout this endeavor.

Introduction

Part I (Chapters 1–4) provides you with the historical, descriptive, and comparative accounts of the public and private sectors, the different roles government plays with business, including several conceptual models to understand the social interactions between the two sectors, and various economic policies associated with business. The skill of researching government institutions and their functions and the skill of identifying and analyzing business stakeholders are introduced. Starting in Part II, business–government relations are considered through three different social economic contexts: sociopolitical, local political economic, and global.

Part II (Chapters 5–8) focuses on building business–government relations in the sociopolitical arena, in which government's role as agent of business interest groups and its limited role as social architect are introduced. Chapter 5 discusses the various government protective regulations for business stakeholders, be they consumers, employees, investors, or the planet. The skill learned in this section is to leverage public policies to protect your stakeholders while advancing your business. Chapter 6 concentrates on the limitations of government in promoting social values and business's responsibility to society. This section introduces a progressive business ethics model and an analytical framework for resolving ethical dilemmas in business scenarios. The skill of ethical reasoning is defined and exercised. Chapter 7 explores the policy-making process, the various business interest groups, and government's role in advancing business agenda in the American political system. The skill of advocating for a business and promoting an agenda is introduced. Chapter 8 examines the third or nonprofit sector with its various roles as society's heart as well as the promoter of special interests.

Part III (Chapters 9–11) depicts the interaction between government and business in economic development, in which government acts as a promoter of, partner with, and buyer from business. This section starts by introducing the various government economic development strategies and funding mechanisms. Chapter 10 focuses on the industrial recruitment strategy in which business and government interact intensively through bargaining for economic and social good. Chapter 11 explores the role of government as public entrepreneurs for economic development through partnering with business, and discusses the various privatization tools of government used in the current political economy, with an emphasis on government's role as buyer, contractor, and partner to business. The skills introduced include how to leverage public resources, how to negotiate, partner, and contract with government, and how to interact with the public for the interest of your business.

Part IV (Chapters 12–14) provides the audience with the global context and introduces the various governing institutions of the global economy. It focuses on government's role as promoter of domestic business in the global market. Chapter 12 introduces government trade policies in the context of globalization. Chapter 13 examines the political economy of two different and critical political and economic bodies—China and the European Union. The discussion of China focuses on its economic development policies and their impacts, while that of the European Union emphasizes its governing structure and its economic and political implications. Chapter 14 introduces the three international trade and financial institutions—the WTO, IMF, and WB—and their purpose, governing structure, and roles played in the global political economy. The skills learned are how to interpret global trends, how to do business in a different political/economic system, and how to leverage trade policies and international institutions to advance your business agenda.

Key characteristics of this book include:

- Opening scenarios: Each of the chapters begins with a story of Zach and Zoey, their family members, or friends. The scenario presents a central topic that will be featured in the ensuing chapter, and poses a question of skill or a dilemma needing to be resolved. The chapter ends by returning to the sentiment of the opening scenario, introducing a practical business skill dealing with business–government relations.

- Chapter introductions: Each chapter opens with a presentation that lays out the main ideas to be covered therein. The introduction often relates these ideas to the content of other chapters.
- Boxed examples and case discussions: These materials highlight particular ideas and encourage class discussion and debate.
- Graphics and illustrations: A number of graphs and pictures are provided to help you better visualize the subject matter.
- Chapter summaries: A concise list of the main ideas and points covered is given at the end of each chapter. Each compendium offers the reader a useful review of, and a correct focus for, the chapter content.
- Key terms: A list of useful terms at the conclusion of each chapter highlights important concepts and helps strengthen your growing vocabulary. The terms are italicized and defined in the text.
- Study questions: The review questions at the end allow you to test your understanding of content, to think critically and develop your arguments, and to apply what you've learned to real problems.

Welcome to Society, Business and Global Governance. Let's get started!

Part I

Introduction to Business–Government Relations

1 Comparing the Roles of Business and Government

Chapter Contents

Case 1 Scenario

Zoey Considers Her Options

Zoey is at the student union, enjoying a soda in between classes at college. She is about to get her degree in business administration at a regional state university. She has majored in accounting and will graduate with a high GPA. However, in trying to maintain good grades and work part time at the university, Zoey has not really focused on what she would do after graduation until now. The reality is beginning to sink in—she will soon be out of school! She picks up her soda can, takes a sip, and begins to really consider her options.

DOI: 10.4324/9781003178620-2

Although she is good with numbers, it is not her passion. She has come to realize that she is happy to have it as a powerful tool, but making a lot of money is not her first priority at this point in her life. More important to her is an interesting job that will provide her with experience and an opportunity to use her analytic skills to develop her other interests into a true career.

Zoey has a horse named Happy, now 22 years old but still rideable. It is her most deeply loved possession. As she ponders what she could do with her life, she realizes that working with animals is not a passing fancy. However, it is not the skillset she has developed, so it is not likely that she can pursue that directly, at least for the time being.

Zoey also considers the political science classes she has taken during her undergraduate career. She found them fascinating and would have majored in it, except that practically, she knew job opportunities would be highly limited with a general liberal arts degree. Now she wonders if she might work for a government. She could consider working for her local city, county, or state, or even the federal government. She understands that many government jobs pay well, and the training that they provide is generally excellent. Indeed, maybe she could get a job that involves both animals and the government!

To explore a few of these options, Zoey takes her laptop out of her backpack and begins Googling various sites. She starts by searching for government jobs in her state. One of the top listings is USAJOBS, which turns out to be the electronic federal job center. Her state has two job locations, one for private sector employment (called the state job bank) and one for jobs in state government. There is also a *city-jobinfo* site with a*.gov* suffix. While there are third-party sites for government jobs, Zoey does not think it wise to use them until she has exhausted the direct search prospects first. She doesn't see county jobs high in the Google listing, so she types that in and goes directly to the available jobs in the counties close to her. She is amazed at the number of prospects. She sees opportunities to use her accounting skills, which she may rely on for her first job or two. One of her professors told her that having worked in both a government and private sector job provides great experience and makes you much more marketable in both sectors. In this area, Zoey sees far more opportunities than she expected. However, she does not find any jobs with her specific interest in working with animals. A little saddened, Zoey wonders if her boyfriend Zach has any ideas that could help. Frustrated, Zoey grabs a few dollars and heads to the snack bar to buy some chocolate chip cookies.

When she then Googles government jobs with animals, Zoey finds few options. There is a government veterinarian position at the federal level in her area and one working for animal control at the county level. She is not qualified for one and not interested in the other. Zoey would like to continue her job search, but it is time to go to one of her last classes. Well, in just a half hour she learned a lot. She resolves to return to her research about opportunities working with government soon.

Defining Business–Government Relations in the US

Business–government relations are affected by how the public and private sectors interact in their numerous complementary, cooperative, and conflicting roles. These relationships vary extensively from country to country because of the type of government, the nature of the business environment, and the types of mechanisms and strategies used by each sector in various aspects of their relationships. Prominent features of business–government relations are the following societal choices:

1 The particular mix of *strategies used for implementation* of public policy: government ownership, partial ownership (government corporations or government-backed corporations), public–private partnerships, contracting out, procurement, tax incentives, and regulation, among others (e.g., the US oil industry is private, while over 80 percent of the oil production and profits around the world is owned by their respective governments[1]).
2 The *monetary policy* pursued (e.g., the control over the supply of money and interest rates as is done by the Federal Reserve) which affects the short- and long-term business environment.
3 The *fiscal policy* followed (e.g., the amount of taxes collected and the way they are spent, such as defense versus education, as well as the role and size of debt which is largely controlled by Congress), which affects the short- and long-term business environment.
4 The amount of *government protect* of the society's most vulnerable (e.g., welfare), of individual rights (e.g., due process rights; transparency), and of social responsibilities such as the environment, product safety, etc. (e.g., the resources provided to the Environmental Protection Agency (EPA), Occupational Safety and Health Administration (OSHA), Food and Drug Administration (FDA), etc.), which have direct and indirect effects on the economy and thus business.
5 The amount of *business regulation* to ensure commonly accepted business standards (e.g., building codes), aesthetic standards, tax levels, level playing-field competition, etc.

6 The amount of *promotion of the business sector* domestically (e.g., economic development) and internationally (e.g., trade policies and promotion).

The amount of *prohibition of government competition* (e.g., against entering markets, non-compete clauses in laws,[2] legal prohibitions against price negotiation[3])

7 The *influence of the private sector*, especially big business and Wall Street, on government policy-making (e.g., through lobbying, campaign contributions, advisory committees, special access, drafting legislation, fielding political candidates, high-level appointees such as at the Treasury Department, and other means) and administrative actions.

The US model, for example, has shown minimal management of overarching industry strategies and a more regulatory approach to social and individual responsibilities. Asian countries such as Japan, China, and South Korea have demonstrated a much more corporatist approach, with government steering industry strategies and choosing areas of the economy to emphasize. The European approach has historically been more of a limited socialism model since World War II, ensuring broader inclusiveness of the population and less economic disparity. The European model has been shifting toward the US model for some time, however, even as the US has taken small steps toward the European model, such as with prescription-drug expansion for Medicare in 2003 and the comprehensive health reform (the Patient Protection and Affordable Care Act, or Obamacare) enacted in 2013. On the other hand, the US government has been robust in its role in monetary and fiscal policy in order to keep the economy balanced and a preferred "safe harbor" for world capital. However, as Exhibit 1.1 illustrates, sometime basic US government–business principles conflict in rather dramatic ways.

Harvard business scholar Roger Porter (2002) has summarized the context of business–government relations in the US over time with a useful list of factors. His list of those factors is found in Exhibit 1.1, along with contemporary examples of those trends.

Exhibit 1.1

Examples and counter examples of long-term trends in US government–business relations since 2000

Overarching US Business–Government Positions	*Recent Examples of Long-Term Positions*	*Some Recent Countervailing Examples*
Private ownership of capital and public enterprise over public ownership	While the US government provided extensive research funding for COVID-19 vaccines, drug companies created and owned their vaccines. For example, Pfizer did not accept government funds and earned about $5 billion in profits the first year. On the other hand, Moderna was almost entirely dependent on government support and therefore made a smaller profit due to its prior agreements.	Airport security was locally administered by airports themselves in most cases before 2000. After the 9/11 event destroying the Twin Towers, the Transportation Security Agency was formed in 2001, nationalizing airport security.
Use of regulation more than government ownership	Regulation (and deregulation) of oil and gas industries rather than state ownership which is very common around the world. Two-thirds of Federal US government labs are run by the private sector.	Creation of eight, relatively small, new national parks since 2000.
Reliance of the market over central planning by government	China relies on the country's three state-run telecom operators to provide massive 5G infrastructure improvement. By contrast, the US worked through the private sector but had more-fragmented 5G coverage in its rollout as well as uneven speeds.	COVID-19 vaccination: the Trump administration used the Defense Production Act 18 times to aid vaccine development. Health care initiatives (e.g., Affordable Care Act and Medicaid Expansion) aim to coordinate health care industry somewhat for better efficiency and effectiveness.

Overarching US Business–Government Positions	*Recent Examples of Long-Term Positions*	*Some Recent Countervailing Examples*
Anti-trust policies (to break up or regulate monopolies) versus complete laissez-faire policies	Rigorous DOJ and Federal Trade Commission oversight and enforcement of mergers and acquisitions to limit market distortions. An example of a DOJ price fixing enforcement action occurred when the former CEO and President of Bumble Bee Foods was sentenced to 40 months in jail and a criminal fine of $100,000 in 2020 for conspiracy to fix prices of canned tuna.	The consideration of major anti-trust suits against tech and marketing giants Facebook, Google, and Amazon faces uphill battles in courts.
Openness and use of judicial mechanisms to solve issues rather than reliance on interpersonal trust or interlocking networks (e.g., Japanese keiretsu, Korean chaebol, or Chinese state-owned enterprises)	There are millions of business lawsuits every year, mainly routine debt collection, contract disputes, and landlord–tenant disputes. Although tort claims are a tiny percentage, they often get high visibility such as the too-hot-coffee successful lawsuit against McDonalds; they are more prevalent in the imagination of the public than in the courts themselves.	A number of business areas are immune to tort and even breach of contract lawsuits by law. Famously, gun manufacturers and sellers are not legally responsible for how their products are used. Innumerable cases involving harm and negligence do not go to court because employees, clients, or customers had signed legal waivers that weaken successful litigation.
Distribution of power through levels of government and within branches of government	The government regulates the activities of businesses in areas such as advertising, labor, environmental impact, privacy and health, and safety at the federal, state, and local levels. Often broad regulation occurs at the federal level and is expanded at the state and local levels. However, some regulations are local or state only, such as zoning.	Anti-trust litigation is handled almost exclusively at the federal level because of the size and economic power of the defendants.

A stable, two-party government with power sharing	In spite of losing the popular vote, George W. Bush and Donald Trump became president because of their electoral college victories. The losers of those elections, Al Gore and Hilary Clinton, nonetheless attend the victors' inaugurations.	President Trump disputes overwhelming election results in 2020. He loses by 74 electoral votes, 4.4 percent of popular vote (over 7 million fewer votes than candidate Biden). Approximately 35 percent of the American electorate believes the "big lie" and polls indicate an increased willingness to use violence to settle political differences.
A highly differentiated business community including umbrella business associations and trade organizations that can lobby government versus a national economy based on just one or two powerful industries	Supreme Court in "Citizens United" (2010) ruled that corporations and other outside groups can spend unlimited money on elections (example of business lobbying power). The enormous US Chamber of Commerce takes expansive, long-term economic views versus many narrower professional and advocacy organizations (example of variety and complexity of business organizations).	The gun lobby continues to be so powerful that it can defy strong national sentiment for better gun regulation, even with missteps by the NRA, and in the face of a gun death rate dwarfing all other advanced democracies (e.g., the gun death rate in the US is about 100 times greater than in the UK).
Stability of economic, legal, and institutional framework	The US avoided a depression in 2008; instead, the US only experienced a Great Recession (2007–2009 with lingering effects for several years) despite the enormity and extensiveness of the economic meltdown). Continuing implicit belief in maintaining judicial precedents for long periods of time. Transition of power from Trump to Biden despite allegations of widespread election fraud.	Economy endangered by historically high public debt levels. Partisanship is the highest since the Civil War. The US Capitol was stormed in 2021 and Congress had to be evacuated. The event led to five deaths, 140 injuries, and over 700 arrests. Nonetheless, Congress itself has struggled to agree on a bipartisan commission to investigate it.

Why Government at All?

The philosopher Thomas Hobbes pointed out that government is more than a fact of life; it is a necessity. As the foundation of modern social contract theory, from which business contract theory flows, he asserted that without it, there would be no place for industry, no navigation, no significant buildings, no heavy instruments for travel or agriculture, no knowledge of the face of the earth, no account of time, no arts and letters, and indeed, no society beyond small clans; "and which is worst of all, continual fear, and danger of violent death; and the life of man, solitary, poor, nasty, brutish, and short" (Stanford Encyclopedia of Philosophy 2002). To build a society, he argued, people must not only work together, but there must be a consistent system of rules to motivate people to want to be productive beyond their daily survival needs. Indeed, the great things of society are a product of complex coordination. While some utopians have asserted that life without government is possible, examples beyond small communes exercising direct democracy or very sparsely populated societies are largely absent.

So most of us accept that not only is government necessary, and in modern times it tries to ensure that our nation is secure and we have laws and police for security, that our drinking water is pure and our airplanes safe, that our money will not lose its value, that our roads, bridges, tunnels, and harbors are well maintained, that we are provided basic education, and that we can have a say in our policies through the political system. It should be apparent that this list can go on and on.

Of course, governments, like the people they represent, are imperfect, and can themselves become the cause of problems and misdeeds. As the great statesman William Burke noted, "Among a people generally corrupt liberty cannot long exist." So at their worst, governments can launch wars of aggression, become captive to small oligopolies, demotivate progress, interfere in people's personal freedoms, and impose harsh societal norms. Fortunately, as the founder of Pennsylvania noted, "if men be good, government cannot be bad," and Americans have been fortunate to have a government whose social conscience has evolved with society. Examples of that evolution include the expanded understanding of the meaning and scope of the Bill of Rights, the emancipation of slaves, the inclusion of women in the political system (i.e., giving women the franchise to vote), the expansion of current-day civil rights and substantial efforts to improve the environment.

Pragmatically, we know that government not only is the place where rules are authoritatively made for the entire economy, but that government itself directly constitutes about one-third of the economy. Business people need to know the rules, such as zoning codes, and frequently want to try to influence the rule-making process, such as in zoning variances. Government provides a large market for goods such as office furniture and airplanes, offers a vast array of services useful to business, for instance trained workers and employment services, and manages business investment at the local level by making it more or less strict and expensive to develop businesses or residential construction. It also manages international trade agreements through organizations such as the World Trade Organization, and global finance as it flows through the International Monetary Fund and World Bank. On the whole, business has a compelling need to influence the development and implementation of public programs and to ensure that government performance contributes to growth and prosperity.

Two Purposes of This Book

There are two fundamental assumptions that underlie this book. The first is that business–government relations constitute a necessary skillset for modern business people because government in modern society is large and thoroughly integrated into our lives. Understanding how governments operate and the democratic processes that they must follow, what services they offer, and how to work well with government officials and personnel has become as vital a function as accounting, finance, marketing, human resource management, or management of information systems.

The second assumption is that we have a duly established, contract-based government that contributes enormously to the highest quality of life that the world has ever experienced. Nonetheless, all governments, including governments in the US, function better or worse depending on a variety of circumstances related to the quality of policy-making, decision-making, leadership, and implementation. Reasonable people can disagree on the areas that government should emphasize or avoid, or on the overall size of government, and it is not the purpose of this book to assert, for example, that more or less government is good or bad. However, it *is* the purpose of this book to describe what government actually does, to report on its record even when it has not been successful, and, most importantly, to provide analytic tools to understand where government is more or less likely to be successful and to fairly evaluate and criticize its performance. Furthermore, it is a fundamental purpose of the book to distinguish between the policy-making branches and functions of government, and public administration which is intended to be the neutral, effective, and efficient implementation of those policies. Appropriate policies and careful crafting of those policies should not be confused with good and poor implementation of those policies. Therefore, the book aims at a better understanding of, and better tools for, the appreciation *and* critique of government policies and implementation, especially as it deals with business. Also, to the degree that we implicitly evaluate the record, strengths, and weaknesses of business, we will strive to offer the same fair-handed, but candid, treatment.

In this chapter, we next move to the debate about the roles of government, tackle a critical analysis of government functions, review private and public sector reform, and then end with a rapid recap of government structure. These topics are further expanded upon in the following chapters of Part I.

Part II focuses on business–government relations in the sociopolitical arena related to interest-group politics and ethics, Part III covers economic development, and Part IV covers business–government relations in the global context.

The Debate about the Role and Size of Government

Since the nation's founding, it has been debated how much of a role the government should play in business affairs. The first Secretary of the Treasury, Alexander Hamilton crafted immensely important policy reports laying down the no-default principle on debt, the need for a national bank, the need to steer the country toward a better balance of agriculture and trade, and a strong system of tariffs, To this day, the design of the nation's political and economic institutions reflects a clash, yet also a creative blending, of two distinct theoretical ideas: a free market philosophy and an active government doctrine (Lehne 2006). In this section, we will first look at the history of the debate, and then we will look at some contemporary statistics that discuss the size of government in three different important dimensions in absolute and proportional terms. We will then look at the explanations for the size of government. We also introduce the roles of government in this section.

Historical Debate: Laissez-Faire versus Activist Government Approaches

A free market economy (also known as market economy, or laissez-faire approach, a French term that means "leave it alone") refers to an economic system in which decisions regarding investment, production, and distribution are based on supply and demand. The prices of goods and services are determined in a free price system. The idea was preached by Adam Smith, a Scottish social philosopher and a pioneer of political economy. In the same year that the Continental Congress declared independence, Adam Smith published his classic work: *An Inquiry into the Nature and Cause of the Wealth of Nations* (1776), generally simply known as *The Wealth of Nations* (Smith 1937), which laid the foundation of modern economics. Smith praised the advantages of freely operating markets, in which "an invisible hand" could help to promote not only the individual interest, but also the public interest. Smith believed the less government intervened in economic matters, the better, as government could neither have appropriate knowledge nor be impartial to manage a nation's economy effectively.

Smith's *Wealth of Nations* was a critique of the economic theory of mercantilism, which was a prevailing thought that dominated public policy-making in colonial times. Mercantilism had encouraged European expansion and guided British policy toward its colonies since the sixteenth century. According to mercantilism, national wealth could be gathered or even plundered from neighbors or colonies. To ensure the prosperity and military security of the state, government should manage substantial aspects of economic activity, especially foreign trade and tariff protection for domestic industries. Mercantilists' ideas were embraced by Alexander Hamilton. In his *Report on the Encouragement and Protection of Manufacturers* (1791), Hamilton advocated an active role of government in economic affairs, especially in protecting domestic industries through federally funded assistance and tariffs. Newer versions of this activist government philosophy are popular today in continental Europe (Siaroff 1999) and East Asia (Hau and Hasmuth 2013).

When the founding fathers debated the design of governmental institutions for the new nation, they drew insights from both intellectual ideas: free market theory and the active government doctrine associated with mercantilism. On the one hand, they wanted to limit the role of government, worrying that a government actively involved in the details of the economy might overshadow liberty and lead to economic tyranny; yet on the other hand, they saw the necessity of retaining government power in certain economic and trade policies to protect their fledgling industries. Throughout the history of the US, these two intellectual ideas, although framed using various terms, have constantly been adjusting the institutional design of government and shaping public policies of the day.

The nation started with a very limited government. During the Industrial Revolution (1820–1870), American government started to pursue a moderate control of certain aspects of the economy. The Industrial Revolution made the US a leading global industrial power by the late nineteenth century. Despite the gradually expanded government roles in the nation's economy, America's commitment to free market theory was extremely high in the late nineteenth and early twentieth century. The end of slavery, as well as the surge of immigration, created a large market of inexpensive labor. New technologies in iron and steel manufacturing, new communication tools such as telegraph and telephone, the emergence of corporations as the dominant form of business organization, vast infrastructure improvements, and a readily available supply of natural resources all fueled the engine of capitalism. Powerful industrialists such as Andrew Carnegie, Jay Gould, and John D. Rockefeller, known as "robber barons" by their enemies, held great wealth and power. This period of cutthroat competition for massive wealth accumulation, known as the "Gilded Age," eventually created the call for reform both in the private sector and in government (which was thought to have become corrupted by big money interests) simultaneously, thereby segueing into a new period called the "Progressive Era." The Progressive Era (1880–1920) saw the reform of the private sector by means of "trust-busting," or anti-monopoly laws, and the reform of local government (e.g., making it less partisan in many places) and the Congress, by means of restructuring the Senate with the Seventeenth Amendment.

Exhibit 1.2

Adam Smith (1723–1790)

Source: Wikimedia Commons (1787). James Tassie.

The Great Depression, which began in 1930 largely as a result of market excess and the devastating economic collapse that worsened over four years, introduced an era of active government controls that are associated with Keynesian economics (Blinder 2008). John Maynard Keynes was a British economist, one of the founders of modern macroeconomics, and considered the most influential economist of the twentieth century. In his book *The General Theory of Employment, Interest and Money* (1936), Keynes introduces the idea that some private sector decisions could lead to overall inefficiency and could require active government policy responses. Without regulation,

Exhibit 1.3

Alexander Hamilton (1755–1804)

Source: Wikimedia Commons (1804). John Trumbull.

for example, thousands of banks could fail in a single year, wreaking havoc. During 1933 alone, over 4,000 banks did indeed fail, wiping out over $140 billion in savings. Such losses caused millions of depositors to withdraw their money, leading to the collapse of the economy for nearly a decade. Keynesian economics advocates a mixed economy, in which the private sector is predominant, but in which government also plays a role in order to

Exhibit 1.4

John Maynard Keynes (1883–1946)

Source: Getty Images/Walter Stoneman and Samuel Bourne.

prevent depressions and intervene during milder recessions. Keynesian economics served as the standard economic model in the US during the latter part of the Great Depression, World War II, and the post-war economic expansion (1945–1973).

The economy was increasingly expanding and prosperous during this post-war period, until the early 1970s. Under new foreign competition and rising oil prices, the nation experienced a period of "stagflation" featured by sluggish growth, high inflation, and high unemployment rates. Up to

Exhibit 1.5

Friedrich Hayek (1899–1992)

Source: Wikimedia Commons (2009). Mises Institute.

that time, Keynesian economists had ignored the possibility of stagflation because historical experience suggested that high unemployment was commonly associated with low inflation, and vice versa. However, when stagflation occurred, it became obvious that the relationship between inflation and employment rate could shift. Economists became skeptical of Keynesian theories, and Hayek's defense of classical liberalism regained popularity.

Friedrich A. Hayek, winner of the 1974 Nobel Prize in economics, published his classic work *The Road to Serfdom* in 1944, in which he launched a war against central planning. A planned economy is an economic system in which the government controls and regulates all aspects of economic activities, including investment, production, distribution, prices, etc. Hayek believed that government should play a limited role in the areas that most members of a free society would tend to agree should be under market control. If government's role reached into those areas where people would probably not readily or generally agree, it could create a tendency toward dictatorship and totalitarianism (the "serfdom"). Hayek's resurgent popularity introduced a worldwide movement dubbed "neoliberalism," which espouses free market economics (or economic liberalism) as a means of promoting economic development and securing political liberty (Hayek 1989). Famous proponents of neoliberalism in the US included another famous Nobel Prize winner, Milton Friedman (1962), and his colleagues at the University of Chicago. The movement is sometimes described as an effort to reinvigorate the policies of the eighteenth- and nineteenth-century classical economic liberalism preached by Adam Smith.

The emergence of neoliberalism coincided with the rise of Conservative governments in Great Britain in 1979 with Prime Minister Margaret Thatcher, and in the US in the 1980s with Ronald Reagan. Under Friedman's influence, President Reagan promised an economic revival through deregulation, tax cuts, and a reduction in the size and scope of federal programs. Reagan's economic policies led the nation through the recession that had begun in the late 1970s; however, the economic recovery was beset by a soaring budget deficit that resulted from increased defense spending, as well as reduced revenue due to the enacted tax cuts. After the dissolution of the Soviet Union in 1991, which often symbolizes the defeat of the planned economy, free market economics—under the name of neoliberalism—became the worldwide reigning economic model. Reagan's successors, both Democrats and Republicans, more or less all embraced free market doctrines.

The advent of the global financial crisis of 2008, however, led to a resurgence of Keynesian thought.[4,5] Economic policies undertaken in direct response to the crisis by both Republican President George W. Bush and Democratic President Barack Obama, reflected Keynesian theoretical underpinnings (Giles, Atkins, and Guha 2008). Bush, for instance, used government power and finances for a massive bailout of Wall Street. As the financial crisis quickly deepened, Obama continued the strong support of Wall Street and expanded it to include the industrial sector (e.g., a bailout of the auto industry), main street (along with the Federal Reserve, who pressured banks to lend to small business with extraordinarily low interest rates to big banks), and localities (stimulus funds to prevent the immediate contraction of state and local governments struggling with a precipitous loss of tax revenues).[6] Keynesian support of the economy surely kept it from plunging into a deep recession, but the price was a vast expansion of federal debt.

The worldwide COVID-19 pandemic beginning in 2020 forced governments around the world into another enormous round of deficit spending which is discussed in terms of the US later in this chapter. See Exhibit 1.6 on the virtues and traps of Keynesian and supply-side economics for a review of some of the pertinent issues. The next section looks more closely at the facts about the size and roles of government before analyzing the pros and cons of the way it functions today with regard to business.

Exhibit 1.6

The virtues and traps of Keynesian and supply-side economics

In the ideal, Keynesian economics promotes a strong and large capitalist private sector with a moderately sized government to provide a variety of ongoing national, local, and individual functions such as defense, education, and transportation. Because of the normal ups and downs of the business cycle, it also advocates strong government spending when the business cycle is down, especially in infrastructure and employment. It also advocates programs that tend to collect money over the long term, such as unemployment insurance, and that will be drawn upon more heavily in bad times. Such programs, which were absent during the Great Depression, provide economic stabilization. There is little doubt that the large Keynesian infusion of government funds into banks, select corporations, infrastructure, and state and local governments greatly softened the downfall caused by the Great Financial Crisis of 2008. Many believe that the infusion of funds, along with the programs such as the Federal Deposit Insurance Corporation (FDIC) and Social Security, averted another great depression.

Supply-side economics points out the power of a growing economy. For example, the federal government dutifully made payments on the large World War I debt and brought it down by one-third in absolute terms by 1929. However, because of economic expansion, the debt had fallen by one-half as a function of the GDP. Government revenues were also up considerably in 1929, largely owing to the expansion of the economy. The central insights of supply-side economics are that, in the long term, a stable absolute debt becomes less significant as the economy grows, and a vital private sector economy becomes more important in order to maintain that growth.

The challenge of Keynesian economics is one of being virtuous in good times. It is easy to spend money when it is flowing into the treasury, rather than save it for a rainy day. While economic discipline at the federal level was good through the 1970s, it collapsed in the 1980s. Conservatives wanted to cut government spending heavily except for a build-up in defense, and Liberals refused to eliminate programs. In the end, Conservatives were able to cut taxes and ratchet up defense spending, Liberals got to keep their programs, and so the deficit began to grow. While there was a round of sensible deficit reduction during the Clinton presidency when fiscal Conservatives pressured Clinton and the Democrats into paying down the debt during the economic boom, this resolve vanished thereafter, with neither Conservatives nor Liberals willing to make the necessary sacrifices after 2000. So *good* Keynesian economics has not been practiced by the US government in several decades, nor has either political party seriously addressed the growing fiscal debt crisis. As discussed later in this chapter, not only does such poor fiscal management saddle one or more generations with enormous debt, but it undermines the international confidence in the US economy.

The Relative Size of Government

To get a balanced sense of the size of government, there are three primary metrics that one must examine: the size of the workforce, the size of the budget, and the size of the debt.

In the earliest days of the country, the federal, state, and local governments were all relatively small. For example, less than one tenth of one percent (.007 percent) of the population was employed by the federal government (civilian) in 1800, and the bulk of those who did work in government were employed by the Post Office; state and local governments were also very small.[7] Federal civilian employment grew to .7 percent of the population in 1940, to 1.4 percent by 1970 when it reached its peak, and in 2020 it had shrunk to .7 percent of the population. The peacetime average employment for all governments (local, state, and federal) grew from 4.2 percent of the population immediately after World War II to 6.4 percent in 1970, 7.4 percent in 2000, and declined to 6.5 percent by 2021. Currently, total government employment is the smallest percent of population since the 1960s. While the current level of 15 percent of the entire workforce working for government may seem high in comparison to before World War I, when roads were largely unpaved, street lighting was minimal, public education was rudimentary, and public health coverage was primitive, the US remains at the bottom of the list of developed countries, with only Japan having a smaller percentage.[8]

Absolute government employment has grown since World War II (see Exhibit 1.7), but it has grown very differently among the various levels of government. Federal employment has been relatively flat in absolute numbers, while state government has grown moderately. Outpacing federal and state levels, local government growth has been very substantial, with its focus on service provision.

The second metric to examine for a clearer sense of the size of government is the size of budgets. The absolute size of all government budgets has been increasing at all levels since World War II. Overall expenditures have increased from $62 billion in 1950 to $8.78 trillion in 2020.[9] However, far more useful as an indication of the size of government is its scale in relation to the economy. Government has grown from approximately a 23 percent

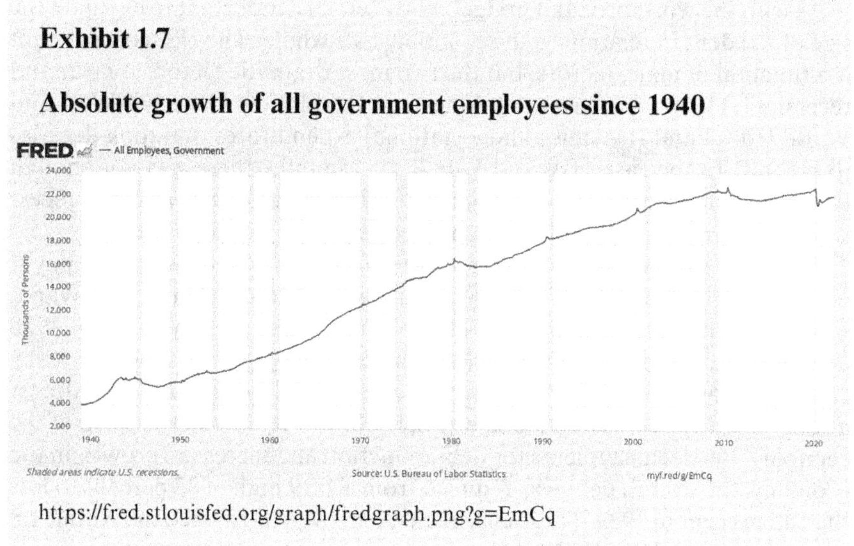

Exhibit 1.7

Absolute growth of all government employees since 1940

https://fred.stlouisfed.org/graph/fredgraph.png?g=EmCq

share of the economy in 1950 to a 36 percent average in 2010 which temporarily jumped to 41 percent in 2020 after extraordinary COVID pandemic spending.

Our third important metric when considering the size and roles of government examines how much government takes in as revenue, and how much it spends. This perspective asks whether government is living within its means, outspending its current resources, or paying off its debts. In any given year when expenditures and revenues match, the budget is said to be in balance. When expenditures exceed revenues, there is a deficit, and, it follows, when revenues exceed expenditures, there is a surplus. The amount owed in any given year that is based on unpaid deficits is called the debt. The total national debt in 2021 was approximately $30 trillion and therefore about 137 percent of GDP, representing a debt of $85,000 for every US citizen. However, since approximately $6 trillion is held in government accounts, some economists consider the national debt to be only $24 trillion, or 110 percent of GDP. The highest percent reached after World War II were 119 and 106 percent respectively, which was by far the largest in US history at the time.

Debt is generally not allowed by state constitutions as a part of the annual budget process. However, state and local governments nonetheless borrow money for long-term obligations primarily through bond measures. At one time, these bond measures were used largely for expensive infrastructure improvements in which the expense was essentially being amortized (e.g., spreading out the cost of a sewer system or bridge over a number of years). Today, local government bond issues are more frequently used for services and, occasionally, for general fund support. State and local combined debt stood at about $3.4 trillion in 2021, with Democratic-leaning states having a higher debt ratio on average than Republican-leaning states.

As with the workforce and budget, however, it is important to evaluate the size of the debt in relation to the economy as a whole. The US national debt is a function of many factors, but the two most dramatic factors are war and recession. The great wars—the American Revolution, the Civil War, and World Wars I and II—caused huge national expenditures that took decades to pay off. In the case of World War I, for example, there was not enough time to pay down the debt completely before the country was mired in recession, and so it was rolled into the costs of new national calamities.

There are two ways to bring down the size of debt. One way is to pay it off as one would do in a household or business. Thus, after World War I, subsequent Presidents and Congresses ensured that every year from 1920 through 1930, the national debt was being paid down with small but steady surpluses, to approximately 35 percent of the absolute amount. Yet almost as important as decreasing the size of the debt was renewed expansion of the economy. Between payments for debt reduction and increased growth in the economy, the overall debt was reduced from a 1919 high of 32 percent to less than 15 percent in 1929. These classic cases are well illustrated in Exhibit 1.8 for events through World War II.

Beginning in the 1980s, different economic philosophies have affected the debt cycle. Tax rates were perceived to be too high in the 1970s, and this led to tax reductions at all levels of government. Services were not reduced at the same time, however, so revenue and expenditure patterns rarely matched, pushing up annual deficits and overall debt in the same way that a war normally would. A reverse of this pattern occurred in the latter part of the Clinton Administration when a Conservative Congress and a "new Democrat" President vied with one another in an effort to reform government. One positive example was the Welfare Reform Act of 1996, which kept in place programs that ensured the very poorest children and their mothers would continue to get assistance, but that reduced excessive use and abuse of the program, in order to cut costs. The pattern was again reversed under a Republican presidency in the early 2000s, with new tax cuts and increased defense spending, raising the debt modestly (about $1.5 trillion), even though the economy was expanding rapidly. The collapse of the economy in 2008 triggered substantial new deficit spending, and the 2020 economic collapse caused by the pandemic caused yet another spike in deficit spending.

Various people have speculated about the underlying reasons for the expansion of government budgets. The earliest in modern times was German economist Adolph Wagner, who proposed a Law of Increasing State Activity to explain the growth of government in democratic states. He asserted that governments have a tendency to be given new roles over time, and are asked to perform those roles more intensively as well. As governments learn to perform these functions efficiently, they are asked to do yet more. Two researchers in the UK produced an assertion that focused on the economic dynamic that was termed the Peacock–Wiseman Hypothesis (Peacock and Wiseman 1961). They argued that the single most powerful factor of government expansion was revenue expansion. Thus, wars greatly expand revenues, which may decline slightly after the special exigencies of wartime economies, but which rarely return to their lower pre-war levels. They argued, then, that psychologically the "tax tolerance" of people is very important, and once stretched by wars and disasters, rarely completely resumes its former scope, assuming the ongoing success of the democratic-capitalist state. Also, political scientists have long pointed out that special interest groups are highly effective in getting their needs addressed in public policy processes because of their tenacity in their pursuit for a piece of the pie, however noble or self-serving, from funding for developmentally disabled children to subsidies for tobacco farmers.

Exhibit 1.8

CBO—Federal Debt trends

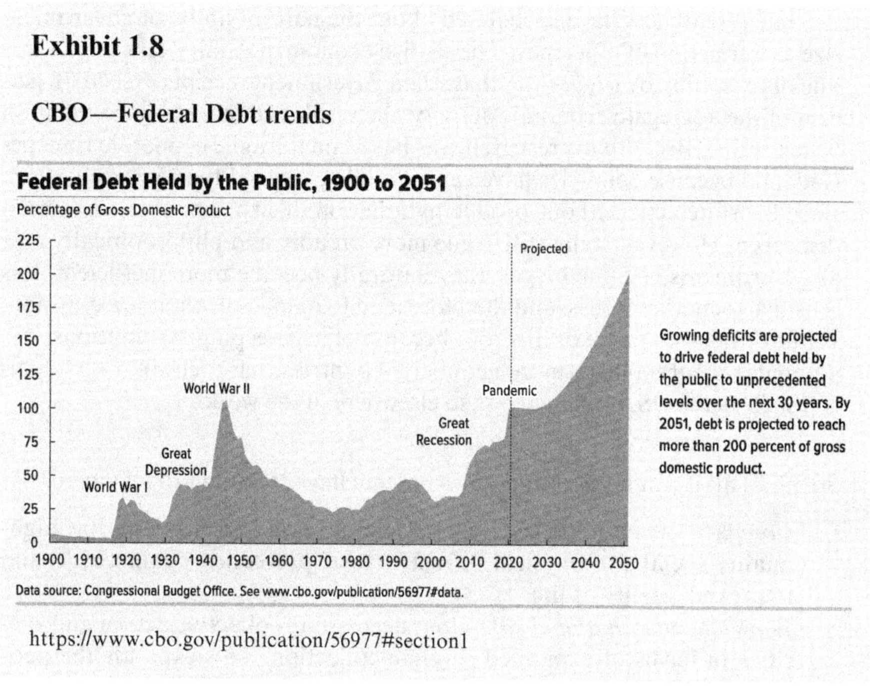

https://www.cbo.gov/publication/56977#section1

Other researchers have argued that the nature of modern society requires more public management and investment, leading to a development model of government. In particular, they argue, modern societies need mass education systems that provide the foundation for an educated workforce, and a consistently good infrastructure that provides for the transportation of goods and services. Highly developed societies need greater management of complex modern issues such as poverty and mass health care. Finally, government growth is most likely when government is perceived as a positive engine of social and economic good. For example, the US government's reputation for repairing the private sector economy of the Great Depression and winning World War II encouraged a favorable environment for it to expand into new policy areas for more than 30 years afterward.

Still, there are also powerful forces limiting the growth of government. Few things are more disliked than taxes. Daniel Defoe's famous comment about the certainty of death and taxes is relatively typical and reminds us of our resignation, and annoyance, with taxes. Complaints about taxes are a favorite with humorists, too, such as Mark Twain, who quipped: "What is the difference between a taxidermist and a tax collector? The taxidermist takes only your skin." On a more serious note, taxation without representation was a primary cause of the American Revolution. The French Revolution was in part caused by unrest over excessive taxes levied by the national government, local aristocrats, and the Church. Thus, excess or unfairness can lead to real political consequences inside and outside the normal social structure.

Some researchers have speculated about the natural limits of government size as a function of efficiency. The British economist Colin Clark began this line of reasoning by suggesting that when government receipts exceed 25 percent of the aggregate economic activity, the result will inevitably be inflation (Clark 1977). Because his research was based on a fragile economic time period, and because countries have substantially exceeded the 25 percent mark since his statement without producing inflation, his specific thesis has been disproven. However, some still argue more broadly and philosophically that as governments become bigger, they naturally become more inefficient, less sensitive to market forces, and therefore tend to damage economic expansion. While difficult to prove or disprove because of its sweeping assumptions, it is a popular theory among more neoliberal countries that focus on individualism such as the US, but much less so elsewhere in the world.

So, all in all it can be said that governments have steadily grown when:

- *Complex societies* place greater demands on government for high-quality social and physical infrastructure, protection against risk, and improved quality of life.
- *Wars and other national calamities* necessitate collective action and sacrifice in terms of expanded revenue collection. This expands the people's tax tolerance.
- Many *special interests* are successful in finding a place in the public sphere over time. These special interests are possible to dislodge, but it is very difficult to do so once they are integrated into the system.

The limits of government expansion have also been discussed, including that:

- The *natural aversion to taxes* is seemingly universal. This aversion can lead to tax revolts and even revolutions if excessive.
- As government programs expand, they often become perceived as overly bureaucratic and inefficient and are thus perceived as being arbitrary and unaccountable.

- As governments become larger and occupy more of the economy, the more they can become *political targets if they are not successfully managed.*

Two Historic Government Roles Related to Security

There are two ancient and universal roles which governments play—defense and public safety. Yet in ancient, medieval, and into modern times, public safety and national defense were often a relatively small part of the economy if the country was not at war. Policing was not a significant factor in the economy because public expectations were low and enforcement was largely provided by civic volunteers or as a part of civic duties. For example, the first modern police department was in Philadelphia, the largest US city in colonial times, and was not created until 1828, approximately 50 years after the American Revolution. Before that, policing was a publicly required private responsibility (similar to jury duty today):

> In colonial days, each of the city's wards appointed a constable, and each property owner took a turn as watchman at an assigned post. There was no coordination between the wards' constables, and while the watchmen did carry arms, they did not wear uniforms and did not even patrol throughout their ward until early in the nineteenth century. If a watchman did not appear at his assigned post on time, he was put in the stocks. Not until 1750 did constables or watchmen receive any compensation at all for their work, when the Mayor was able to hand-pick those who were to be hired.[10]

Many countries did not maintain standing armies, as was the case with the US until the 1840s, when the expansion of the West began in earnest. For example, the size of the defense department in 1805 was *proportionally* one-ninth the size and cost of today's standing army in 2000, or less than one-half of one percent of the nation's GDP. In 2020, at $725 billion, national defense is 11.1 percent of the federal budget and about 3.5 percent of the GDP. Put in international perspective, the US spends as much as the next ten countries combined in 2019; Exhibit 1.9 illustrates the proportional size of military spending. At the state and local levels, public safety constitutes a substantial percent of local government budgets, divided between police, corrections, fire, and legal services.

The Eight Government–Business Roles

Today, governments do far more than the expanded defense and public safety roles discussed above. Governments at all levels across the globe play various important roles with business. In the US, where governments are founded upon democratic and capitalistic principles, governments work to

Exhibit 1.9

Comparisons of expenditures by country

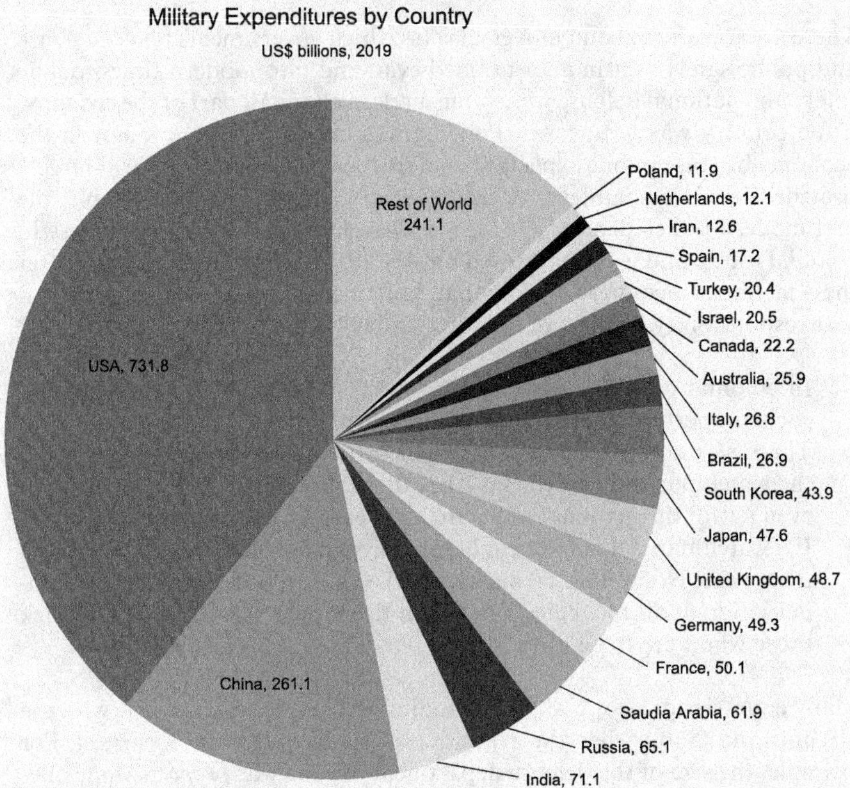

https://upload.wikimedia.org/wikipedia/commons/9/90/Military_Expenditures_by_Country_2019.svg?download

preserve the public interest, to correct market failures, and to promote a positive environment for business. Despite the popular preference of limited government throughout the nation's history, government has acquired and expanded its many roles with business, among them as a:

- *Provider of monetary and fiscal structure*: Governments manage the nation's monetary and fiscal framework, including the national currency, the amount of money in circulation, and taxes and tariffs. These policies affect currency values, interest rates, and the financial environment within which business enterprises carry out their operations.

- *Regulator*: Governments affect the activities of business through various laws, rules, and regulations to enforce business contracts, protect patents, prosecute fraudulent activities, restrict monopolies, ensure worker safety, protect the environment, preserve product and consumer safety, regulate bankruptcies, and address other public concerns. Not only do laws protect business much of the time: as importantly, they provide consistency and predictability so critical to business.
- *Safeguard against risk*: Governments provide a variety of insurance programs to protect individuals and businesses against both natural and social risks as well as offer the last resort for businesses needing bailouts in financial meltdowns. This enhances the business environment by providing consistency and predictability.
- *Provider of infrastructure*: Governments provide public infrastructure, such as vast systems of transportation, communications including regulation of the Internet, and waterways and power lines which are crucial for business operations.
- *Purchaser*: Governments purchase a large quantity of commercial goods and services from business enterprises, ranging from office supplies to military equipment.
- *Social architect*: Governments provide the basic public education system for K-12 to community colleges and state universities, and promote an enormous agenda for research and development (R&D) through both direct subsidies and tax incentives.
- *Service provider*: Governments provide a variety of services to the general public and businesses such as public safety, utilities, libraries, postal service, and human services. These services provide an environment more conducive for business to flourish in.
- *Promoter of business*: Governments utilize a wide range of economic development strategies and techniques to promote business in domestic and international markets.

These eight roles are of particular interest for this book. The historical growth of these roles in the US will be discussed more extensively in Chapter 2, but next, we look at some concrete examples of what government does well, when it tends to do poorly, and when it receives blame through no, or little, fault of its own.

From Debate to Analysis: Judging Government's Performance on Its Purpose and Merits

The private and public sectors have different purposes and merits that will affect performance. But first, let's look at some of the ways that business and executive branch government operate similarly in process and in the environment.

Both private sector companies and government agencies are types of organizations. They share many similarities in terms of general administrative functions such as planning, organizing, staffing, directing, coordinating, and budgeting. They both have competence pressures, although the private sector feels competence pressures more through the market and the public sector feels it more through laws, budget processes, legislative oversight, and the like. Both have to deal with a variety of specific legal constraints, although public agencies are much more circumscribed than the private sector. Internal or organizational politics are common to all organizations regardless of sector. Both private sector companies and government agencies provide products and services, although the type of service or product that is emphasized and how it is funded are entirely different (Rainey 2009).

The differences are as important (Perry and Rainey 1988). Typically, it is thought that the private sector prides itself on fierce competition, while the public sector is more regulated. The private sector values dynamism and the public sector tends to ensure stability. The private sector focuses on the bottom line, profits, and the interests of individuals and special groups (such as shareholders). The public sector has a strong focus on good value, reasonableness, and the interests of society and the public good. Thus, business is often perceived to be more nimble, more innovative, and very strong at providing concrete products to meet individual demand. Government, on the other hand, is often perceived to be more stable, better at assessing long-term social effects, and very strong at regulating for the common good.

Conversely, business is often perceived to have less of a comparative advantage at self-regulation, less attention to externalized costs of its actions, and less attention to society's overall needs (Markham 2006). See the ironic example of for-profit education at the end of this chapter. Government is often perceived to be excessively rule bound or bureaucratic, and to have more monopolistic elements that lead to less efficiency and service variation (Yergin and Stanislaw 1998).

The Good, the Bad, and the Ugly

Let's provide some concrete examples of the public sector in action to portray some of these comparative strengths and weaknesses, as well as to portray some times when government seems to get conveniently blamed as a scapegoat, but is really not the source of the problem. Let's start with some examples where government is generally considered to do well ("the good") (Goodsell 2004)[11]:

- The public sector is good at providing a system of money, regulating banking and trading, insuring deposits, providing protection from international market manipulation, and many other things related to the macro economy. When the economy is not well stabilized, as is the case in many developing countries, investment is generally very low and capitalist principles cannot work well because of the lack of public trust in the equity and durability of the system.

- The Constitution, a vital part of our government, is ultimately a social contract. As the basis of our political and legal systems, it provides continuity and stability. Business contracts can only flourish when the political and legal systems are strong and reliable, which is a fundamental purpose of government.
- While private charity—individual, religious, and corporate—makes a valuable contribution, public welfare for the most vulnerable has become an essential social function in modern society, especially in an age when the extended family has diminished in importance. Government can provide rule-based welfare at a scale unmatched by the private sector.
- Often, we want to share things through taxes, rather than paying for them on an individual basis. Thus, the public sector is good for providing roads, bridges, lighting, and sewers for common usage.
- Ensuring the protection of the country can be done through mercenaries or private armies, and domestic security can be largely provided by private companies, but these avenues are *not* well thought of by democratic societies who want public power to control the use of force. While we used mercenary fighters in the Afghan and Iraq Wars, and while the use of security guards is common, these measures are considered both supplemental and subordinate to the authorized use and control of power by government.
- Reducing risk is a fundamental strength of the public sector. Imagine using a "buyer-beware" attitude without any regulation of water systems, airline security, food and drug safety, offshore oil rigs, and so on.
- The public sector can also provide shared social infrastructure efficiently. Before the rise of state-supported education, illiteracy was rampant in the US. Public schools provide a foundation for wide access to quality education, from kindergarten through community colleges and state universities. At the other end of the age spectrum, destitution and severe poverty were common for the elderly 100 years ago. Today, Social Security provides resources to 65 million Americans every month and the elderly have a modest, but invaluable, safety net.

Governments do not always perform well. Indeed, sometimes they function quite poorly. Below are some of the contexts in which they do not perform well ("*the bad*").

- When governments take over completely, they tend to be corrupted by their own power, even when they believe that they are well meaning. George III of England was not nearly the tyrant he was commonly thought to be at the time of the American Revolution. However, neither he nor the Parliament of the day could conceive of the type of power sharing that the American colonies were demanding through their cries for representation. Americans, sensitive to amassed power, initially eliminated almost all central power under the Articles of Confederation, and then built both checks and balances into the national government in the Constitution, and power sharing between federal and state governments to protect it. Presidential term limits, as well as term limits imposed in many states, are a limitation on political power accumulated by long tenure in office. While the problem of true government domination can sometimes be detected in exceptional cases (e.g., the extra-Constitutional powers that Presidents have assumed during wars), it is not a significant occurrence in the American system despite the rise of "deep state" conspiracy theories (Moynihan 2020).

- More common and problematic than unitary power in the US system is the collusion of powerful interests, such as when big business and big government become too enmeshed and self-supporting. The Seventeenth Amendment (1913), requiring direct election of senators, was largely due to the fact that in many states, only the wealthiest men could buy enough votes to "win" legislative office. Today, the influence of the investment bank Goldman Sachs (and Wall Street in general), whose former employees have controlled Treasury and other important government posts, is considered a major problem by some because it has become too fused with government. At its peak, big labor was also a part of the oligopoly (from the 1950s through the 1980s), but most analysts do not consider that a significant distorting factor today outside some narrower areas such as excessive pension benefits which are received scrutiny after the Great Recession[12] and subsequently widespread reductions via higher employee contributions, higher age requirements, longer vesting terms, etc.
- Corruption is always a problem, both in the public and private sectors. Political corruption is endemic to all political systems but can be curtailed by transparency laws for elected and senior appointed officials and by sensible laws limiting conflicts of interests. Crass, non-financial vote-trading is common and difficult to prevent (i.e., when is it self-serving and when is it a sign of collegiality and compromise). However, outright corruption involving bribery or trading lucrative positions for gain is less common. Yet some political contexts have a history of corruption, such as the State of Illinois. To the State's credit, however, they shipped four of seven consecutive governors off to prison, sending a strong message of intolerance. Administrative corruption is relatively uncommon in advanced democracies, in terms of both number of incidents and scope. Because of their rarity and because of public transparency, small incidents of administrative fraud are widely reported that may only involve thousands of dollars, while private sector peccadilloes are hardly considered newsworthy if they do not involve tens or hundreds of millions of dollars.
- Part of the beauty of democratic-capitalist systems is that when they work well, society flourishes with sufficient discipline and fairness, all

while economic competition and innovation are encouraged. Sometimes the successes of government, the lapses of the private sector, or the ambitiousness of policy-makers can push governments to take on issues that they are not as well suited for. This is less of a problem for the American system, in which the government rarely takes over consumer industries such as automobiles, steel, coal, and oil, as it has been for other countries. However, by extension, excessive regulation can have the same effect, and industries that were regulated for good reason at one time may need to be deregulated in another era. For example, American Telephone and Telegraph (AT&T) was a private corporation that enjoyed a monopoly that was consolidated by strong government regulation (legalized in the Kingsbury Commitment of 1913) for 100 years. It had served the country quite well in terms of providing the most extensive, inexpensive local service, and most reliable telephone system in the world. Yet by 1984, the industry was being held back by the dominance of a single company, world class though it was. Deregulation of the industry came at a good time, in fact just before the wireless age really took off, and created a surge in innovation and market expansion that continues today.

- Another problem that the public sector can run into that limits its efficiency/value and effectiveness over the long term is escalating complexity.[13] For simplicity, we can say that an original policy is passed with limited scope and rules. Over time, the scope of that policy is expanded, and as problems are discovered, they are fixed with additional rules. Sometimes special interests get exceptions and waivers put into the regulations as time goes by. Over time, the rules can become enormous, highly sophisticated, and off-putting to the conventional user, and more convenient for special interests. Two famous examples are environmental regulation and tax filing. Environmental regulation is itself a complex issue, so it is understandable that the regulatory process would become complex in the case of industries with high pollution potential, such as those related to fuels, land use, chemicals, and wastes. Nonetheless, environmental regulation has been less burdensome on the public. Just the opposite, it is often argued, is the case in tax filing. Typical taxpayers often must resort to accountants for relatively simple returns, and small businesses are hard pressed to keep track of tax record responsibilities. On the other hand, almost all large corporations manipulate the tax code legally, with Apple Corporation, FedEx, and Pfizer being three of the corporate leaders in effective tax "dodging."[14] Warren Buffet has famously criticized a tax code that allows him to pay a lower effective tax rate than his secretary.[15]
- A related problem is special interests. Everyone is a member of special interests—parents, mortgage holders, car owners, business owners, environmentalists, the poor, the wealthy, etc.—so the problem is not the existence of special interests, but rather the undue influence in

passing policies with relatively obscure benefits to special groups, or in which special interests can dominate a public process.[16] Examples of such problems have already been cited, such as when we spoke of corporate taxation. Special interests can warp sensible policies over time, such as when some public agencies increase pension rates based on the expectation of a never-ending boom economy, or when entitlement enhancements become unrealistic for the revenue that taxpayers are willing to pay. This problem is endemic to democracy. Good policy-making eventually fixes these problems, but poor policy-making allows these problems to fester until there is a crisis.

- Finally, there is the typical organizational problem of agencies becoming inefficient over time, of their mandates becoming outdated, and of their resources needing to be reallocated. While this issue is simply called organizational change in the private sector, it is called government reform in the public sector because it generally entails a substantial political component and potentially new legislation to enact.

An increasing problem for the public sector in the last 50 years is that it is often given tasks which are nearly impossible to accomplish, or it is the target of attacks that are not based on facts. We will provide three examples—taxation levels, foreign aid, and prison responsibilities—of this unfortunate phenomenon ("*the ugly*").

- As discussed, we love to hate taxes for a number of reasons. We may be ambivalent about paying for less-observed services like national defense and police protection; we may overlook many services we have received in the past or currently receive, such as education, medical subsidies, and roads, or we may underestimate the cost of services we receive. Nonetheless, the average American breadwinner earning $100,000 has a larger family health insurance cost (albeit often largely subsidized by employers) than they do a federal tax bill.[17] Although the costs of government services are driven up by required due process rights and transparency laws, they are also reduced because of no need for profits, economies of scale, and good long-term planning. Some complain that we do not have adequate say over how our tax dollars are spent, but with approximately 89,000 governments in the US and vigorous laws requiring hearings and public input, opportunity for involvement is about as great as it can be without creating chaos. While tax complexity is a reasonable complaint, to discuss tax rates in terms of marginal rates, as is frequently done, is simply misleading; while our marginal rates are higher than many developed countries, our effective rates are among the lowest.[18] The poor often pay relatively low rates in any case; the base income for most of the middle class is paid at the lower tax rates and substantially reduced by mortgage and child-rearing deductions; and the wealthy have access to substantial tax breaks that make their effective rates a fraction of the publicized marginal rates.[19] As Oliver Wendell Holmes once stated, ironically noting how most of us neglect to appreciate the benefits of our taxes: "I like to pay taxes. With them I buy civilization."

- Americans criticize government vehemently for spending vast sums of money on foreign aid; some feel that just eliminating foreign aid could almost balance the budget. Sadly, this belief is simply ignorance of the facts.

  In poll after poll, Americans overwhelmingly say they believe that foreign aid makes up a larger portion of the federal budget than defense spending, Social Security, Medicaid, Medicare, or spending on roads and other infrastructure. In a World Public Opinion poll, the average American believed that a whopping 25 percent of the federal budget goes to foreign aid. The average respondent also thought that the appropriate level of foreign aid would be about 10 percent of the budget—10 times the current level.[20]

  Foreign aid has generally declined as a percentage of GDP in recent decades, despite the exceptional funding that has gone to post-war reconstruction in Iraq and Afghanistan, policy initiatives that were strongly supported by the American public. Even so, it is estimated that Americans spend about the cost of a single restaurant dinner for two, or about $73, on foreign aid, as opposed to $1,763 on defense.[21]
- The American people like to think of themselves as benevolent and kind. However, since the war on drugs and the get-tough-on-crime initiatives in the 1970s, the US has increased incarceration rates over 700 percent, the highest in the world. The US currently houses nearly 25 percent of the world's total prison population.[22] Government is frequently blamed for causing the rates to increase, as well as for the associated soaring economic and mental health costs involved (Montross 2020). The Eighth Amendment prevents cruel and unusual treatment, such as massive overcrowding, which has become common in middle- and low-security facilities. Government policies, enacted with strong public support, have made the US the world's leader in imprisoning its own population, and have been efficient in carrying out the public's demand for increased safety. Although we are far tougher on crime than the UK, incarcerating about four times as many people, the homicide rate in the UK is one-quarter of that of the US. So while literacy has increased in the last 100 years, morality of individuals and of the society at large seems to have fallen, when crime and society's failed reactions to it are examined. Or, as Theodore Roosevelt noted, "to educate a man in mind and not in morals is to educate a menace to society." To blithely blame government for this policy failure is to abnegate our civic responsibilities. We *are* the government.

Summary of Sectoral Differences

Although the private and public sectors—business and government—can occasionally be seen in an adversarial light, in general it is best to think of them as complementary. American society functions best with each playing a robust role and balancing the strengths—and weaknesses—of the other.

The private sector harnesses the dynamic energy of market capitalism. When it works well, individuals are incentivized to work hard, save and invest, and innovate. It is a powerful motivator for individual wealth creation, which, in turn, provides social wealth. It focuses on improving the quality of life by creating and providing products and services that are in competitive demand. It also creates demand by the use of various marketing techniques. It handles many industries, ranging from consumer products to housing to power distribution. It also shares some industries with government, such as risk reduction and private security. Risk reduction, in the form of private insurance, is hundreds of years old but was a luxury for only the wealthy until World War II when it slowly began to replace the extended family as a major source of contingency needs. Private security is also an old, formerly narrow, industry that has now expanded, with private security becoming common for housing developments, malls, and even foreign embassies. Philanthropy is part of the ideal of giving back by those who are successful in the capitalist system from which they have profited. Private charity is encouraged by the publicly shared tax system.

The public sector has the external and internal security of the state as its foundation. It is also the authorized source of minimum social norms through laws and administrative regulations. Part of its regulatory responsibility is to ensure that the market has as close to ideal and fair competition as possible, that private sector parties do not damage the common good for private gain, and that the economic environment is stable and predictable. It is natural that some private interests, in their self-absorbed pursuit, will define what is right to do as only what is required by law. Therefore, it is important to ensure that everything from major issues such as fraud, racketeering, invasion of privacy, and environmental degradation, to lesser but important issues such as zoning and code enforcement, are carefully proscribed by government. Quality of life is seen in shared or communal terms rather than individual terms. We share local services such as libraries and parks and much of our transportation system, and we even want some government regulation and standardization of communication systems in the post-"Ma Bell" world to prevent pandemonium. The government is also society's shared conscience, working in a rule-based manner to provide basic human necessities for today's most helpless citizens. In this regard, it also ensures broad educational access and conservation of the national heritage for all to enjoy. Finally, it plays a role in the promotion of business. The public sector is fierce in the promotion of favorable international trade agreements, in fighting international patent infringement, and in opening up business export and expansion opportunities. Domestically, economic development provides competition to local communities seeking to enhance their business base and provide jobs for local citizens.

These complementary functions are summarized in Exhibit 1.10, contrasting the two sectors.

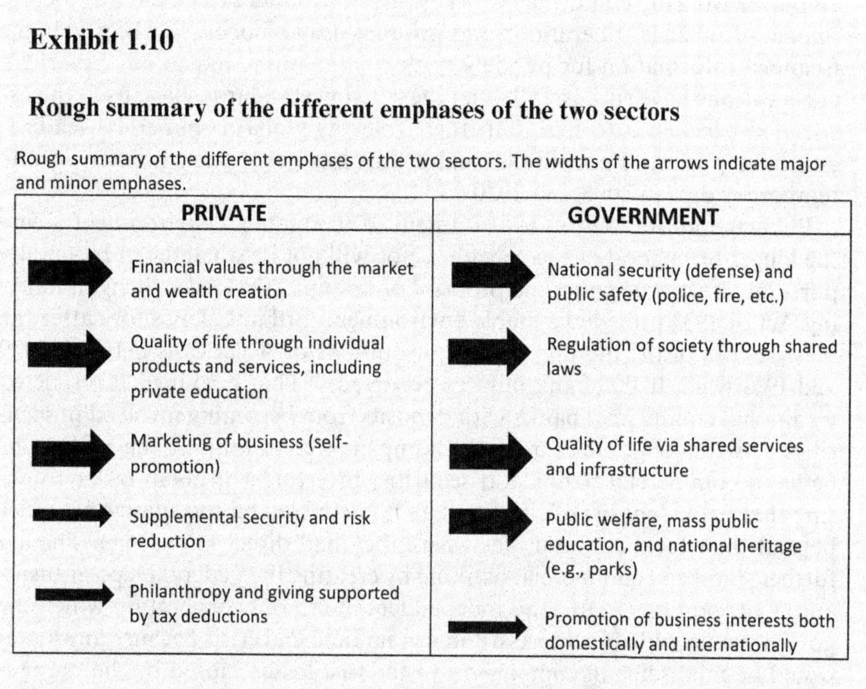

Exhibit 1.10

Rough summary of the different emphases of the two sectors

Rough summary of the different emphases of the two sectors. The widths of the arrows indicate major and minor emphases.

PRIVATE	GOVERNMENT
Financial values through the market and wealth creation	National security (defense) and public safety (police, fire, etc.)
Quality of life through individual products and services, including private education	Regulation of society through shared laws
Marketing of business (self-promotion)	Quality of life via shared services and infrastructure
Supplemental security and risk reduction	Public welfare, mass public education, and national heritage (e.g., parks)
Philanthropy and giving supported by tax deductions	Promotion of business interests both domestically and internationally

Reform of the Private and Public Sectors

Much reform in the private sector comes from the dynamics of the competitive market place. Old companies that have become less efficient may find that they need to reform because of an evolving competitive environment. Innovations must be integrated. Companies move from niche markets to broader markets and back again as they develop and are required to reinvent themselves in light of new opportunities, market conditions, and legal constraints. Whole new markets come into being while others disappear. Yet it is not just profits that drive reform. Companies sometimes seek to reform (improve) their public and internal image by acting more responsibly with regard to the environment, by minimizing the external social costs of their actions, by acting as social leaders, or by treating their employees more generously.

One of the public sector's major jobs (important for our study of business–government relations) is to externally reform the private sector through laws in the policy sphere, and through regulations and enforcement in the administrative sphere. In this sense, the public sector sets the boundaries to define unacceptable behavior and practices. Since the beginning of the twentieth century, standards for companies have increased in terms of expectations of employee working conditions, worker safety, product safety, environmental impact of business operations and product usage, honest labeling, reliable financial information for publicly traded companies, and so on. American corporations have successfully met these rising standards, have used the associated excellence to maintain their roles as global commercial leaders, and have produced corporate wealth that has never been greater despite temporary dips in 2008 and 2020.[23]

Publicly induced reform is also intended to create an environment where the longer-term good of the private sector will not be squandered by unduly pursuing short-term gains and profits. For example, the Glass–Steagall Banking Act of 1933 provided a stable environment for bank depositors after the massive loss of the lifetime savings of millions of Americans between 1929 and 1933 when 10,000 bank failures occurred.[24] That banking act restricted traditional commercial banks with deposits from becoming involved in securities activities (e.g., stock market trading) as well as limiting the affiliations between commercial banks and securities/investment firms in order to ensure that bank deposits of citizens were not gambled on speculative activities beyond their local communities where they had direct knowledge. The act further stabilized commercial banking by creating the Federal Deposit Insurance Corporation (FDIC), an independent, nonprofit corporation which the government could afford to assist in a great financial crisis because any losses would be minuscule in comparison to the vast losses caused by the unregulated banking environment of the 1920s. Because essentially every depositor in the US wanted to permanently withdraw their money from all banks by 1933, this act saved the banking industry from its own excesses and failures, and created the most stable and well-respected banking system in the world, which, in turn, led to US leadership in the world banking system.

Public Sector Reforms

The public sector also reforms itself internally. Market forces are not as significant here as they are for the private sector, but are nonetheless significant. The area in which market competition is most keenly felt is in competition for a high-quality workforce, especially since education requirements for the public sector tend to be higher on average than for the private sector. There are a number of shared industries where market competition is closely watched, such as education, utilities, garbage collection, educational TV, and others. Indirect market forces work via the authorization of budgets where legislators scrutinize the value of agency contributions in light of the fiscal context. Executive oversight induces minor reforms as it does in the private sector, but structural administrative reform must be passed as law. For example, the program that existed to protect the nation's infrastructure was upgraded by Congress into a separate agency called the Cybersecurity and Infrastructure Security Agency (CISA) with expanded resources and authority in 2018. It was created in response to increased state-sponsored attacks against US government systems and assets such as the massive breach of 22 million federal personnel files.

Externally induced reform through law occurs for the public sector, too. Low- and badly performing agencies can get new regulations. For example, after a series of Housing and Urban Development (HUD) scandals, Congress required additional measures to reduce political manipulation and outright corruption in the agency in 1989.[25] Because of the policy failures associated with intensive low-income housing projects that provided a breeding ground for crime rather than a respite for the poor, Congress required major changes in strategy during the 1990s to de-concentrate low-income housing and provide more resident responsibility.[26]

Low- and badly performing agencies can be subordinated to other agencies as well. After the attack on the US on 9/11 in which the World Trade Towers were destroyed, the Pentagon was damaged, and an airplane was hijacked to attack the White House, there was a major governmental reorganization of 22 agencies into the Department of Homeland Security to provide better coordination of international and domestic public safety agencies. These agencies had been arrayed under many departments including Treasury, Justice, Transportation, Defense, the FBI, Energy, General Services Administration, Agriculture, and Health and Human Services. The new umbrella organization also includes the formerly freestanding Federal Emergency Management Agency, which had once had cabinet-level status.

Low- and badly performing agencies also risk complete elimination. A prime recent example is the Minerals Management Service, which was disbanded in 2011 after a series of administrative debacles including the massive Deepwater Horizon oil spill in the Gulf of Mexico the year prior. It was completely reconstituted as the Bureau of Ocean Energy Management, Regulation, and Enforcement with an entirely new management team, new rules, and a reinvigorated mandate. Many agencies are created to work on crises in wars or major financial crises, but are eliminated when their work is complete. The Works Progress Administration from the Great Depression (1935–1943), the Work Production Board from World War II (1942–1945), and the Resolution Trust Corporation from the Savings and Loan Crisis (1989–1995) are examples of agencies that were abolished after successfully completing their time-limited missions.

Both internal and external types of government reforms are significant for business–government relations because the success and efficiency of the public sector should aid the private sector in ultimately doing its business better. Every year legislative bodies institute hundreds of necessary, useful, and successful reforms, and every so often, require major reform agendas in different policy areas, such as the 1933 Banking Act and other examples cited above. However, it should also be noted that the lack of necessary reform, or government reform that is badly conceived or badly implemented, creates an environment where either government draws resources from the private sector with little value added, or agencies simply work at suboptimal levels even though they create positive value overall. An example of lack of reform is the savings and loan debacle that occurred in the 1980s, causing a $250 billion bailout where only some technical issues were corrected, ultimately allowing the much greater and wider banking system meltdown in 2008. Special interests had pushed for changes in laws related to the savings and loan industry early in the decade. These changes quickly let the industry careen out of control, often with outright corruption, and led to a massive federal bailout and re-regulation of the industry (Black 2005). An example of unsuccessful reform was the California deregulation in 1996 that allowed the energy consortium Enron to use both legal and illegal means to manipulate the Western energy market, to create market shortages and reduced services, and to extort vast sums of money from ratepayers.

Paul Light categorizes four types of government reform (Light 1997). Reforms can focus on *greater efficiency* by paying attention to the principles of good administration, and by modifying structures and rules for optimal output. These reforms focus on reorganizations and process reengineering. An example of this type of legislation is the Reorganization Act of 1939, which reorganized the Office of the President, which had become unwieldy with the growth of administration.

A second type of reform focuses on *less waste*, especially when it is through negligence, incompetence, or corruption. Such reforms focus on maintaining generally accepted practices, and use audits and investigations to prevent low performance and malfeasance. A classic example of this type of reform was the 1978 Inspector General Act, which required inspectors general in all major federal agencies to reduce fraud and ineptitude.

A third type of reform focuses on *ensuring fairness*, including the balancing of rights among employees, citizens, and taxpayers. It ensures due process, access to information, and transparency. An example of this type of reform was the Administrative Procedures Act of 1946, which required the extensive rule-making and adjudication occurring in administrative agencies to follow the same principles of openness and due process that are required in legislative and judicial proceedings.

A fourth type of reform, focused on *encouraging high performance*, tends to emphasize outcomes and results, sets high standards, and inspires group goal-setting and high individual achievements. A good example of reform with this intent was the 1993 Government Performance and Results Act, which attempted to streamline the red tape hampering many federal agencies, while simultaneously requiring greater documentation of, and account ability for, policy results from those agencies.

American Government Institutions: Who Does What in Government?

Both sectors have tremendous variety, and it is useful to take a moment to review some of the basic differences in the public sector when discussing business–government relations. In terms of structure, the Constitutional democracy gives concurrent responsibilities to the federal government and state governments, dividing power among different types of functions. Defense may be a federal responsibility, for instance, but the penalty for various types of murder and most other crimes is largely determined by state governments. Negotiating treaties may be another federal responsibility, but deciding what type of building may go on a parcel of land is delegated by state governments to their local governments, which they create and control. In the early days of the Republic, individual states probably had the lion's share of responsibilities and power, but that has probably shifted in favor of the federal government due to federal grants to states and local governments, as well as the opportunity for federal preemption when supported by the Supreme Court. In addition to power sharing between the federal government and states, the Constitution sets up checks and balances to ensure that the three separate branches of federal government also share power. Essentially, Presidents implement and propose, Congress authorizes, and the courts ensure that the rules and laws of the land are followed.

In terms of size, there are 89,055 governments in the US (see Exhibit 1.11). The federal government is the largest, both in terms of employees and budget, but only in terms of budget when the federal government is contrasted with all other governments. The number of states, counties, and townships has been quite stable for the last 50 years. The number of school districts declined considerably over the last century through consolidations. At one time, essentially every high school was its own district. On the other hand, incorporated municipalities have steadily increased along with the growing population. The explosion of special districts represents the greatest change in the last 50 years. These districts provide specialized tax areas to support specific functions. In addition to schools, special districts are incorporated to address these functions: airports, air pollution control, cemeteries, community colleges, conservation, diking and drainage, emergency medical services, fire protection, flood control, health, irrigation and reclamation, libraries, mosquito and pest control (often called vector control), parks, ports, public housing, public utilities, solid waste, transportation, and water, among others. Taxes charged by each of these districts are individually small, but do add up, and are normally collected by the local county assessor, where a typical taxpayer may be required to pay for three to eight special districts. An important new type is the business improvement district, of which there are now about 1,000 in the US. For example, a portion of a downtown area may incorporate to have supplemental lighting, landscaping, and police presence, and almost always a joint marketing function.

Exhibit 1.11

Number of governments in the US in 2012

Federal	*States*	*Counties*	*Municipal*	*Townships*	*School Districts*	*Special Districts*	*Total*
1	50	3,031	19,522	16,364	12,884	37,203	89,055

Source: US Census Bureau, Department of Commerce (2012).

Note: Excludes a number of special governments such as Tribal Governments (566), the District of Columbia, five territories, independent agencies which nonetheless have considerable autonomy, etc.

Exhibit 1.12

US Federal spending

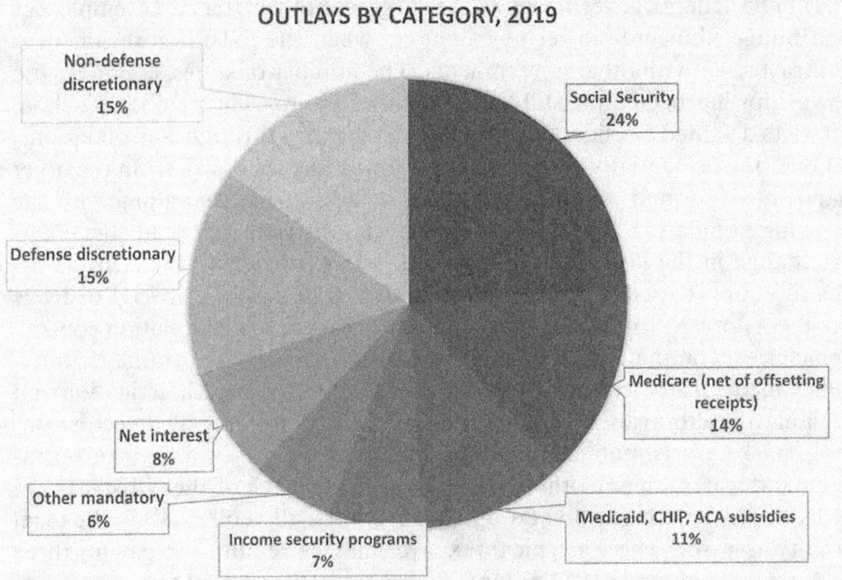

Source: House Committee on the Budget, Chairman John Yarmuth (2019). https://budget.house.gov/publications/fact-sheet/frequently-asked-questions-about-federal-budget.

Approximately 56 percent of the federal government budget goes to individual entitlements including Medicare, Medicaid, and Social Security as well as other income security programs (see Exhibit 1.12). Net interest is currently at eight percent. Another six percent are mandatory expenses to international organizations, federal pensions, and a variety of other governmental functions. Defense spending, considered discretionary is 15 percent of the budget. All other agencies such as Health and Human Services, Department of Education, Veterans Affairs, Homeland Security, the State Department, etc. are the final 15 percent. An interesting side note about the size of programs versus the size of administrative costs is the Social Security administration budget which includes the expensive-to-administer Supplemental and Disability programs, issued $768 billion in benefits. The agency only cost $12 billion to administer, representing about 1.5 percent in overhead, which contrasts with health insurance overhead estimated at over 20 percent.[27] Of course, not all agencies can point to such high levels of efficiency.

State government spending priorities are similar in some ways (see Exhibit 1.13 for an example). If health care and welfare are likened to Medicare, Medicaid, and Social Security, they take up about 49 percent of the budget example. In other ways, the federal and state budgets are quite different. Public safety (protection) typically represents only about 4 percent of state budgets, which is far less than the national defense. Because state government is more labor intensive, pension costs are typically higher than

Exhibit 1.13

Example of state spending: California—fiscal year 2021

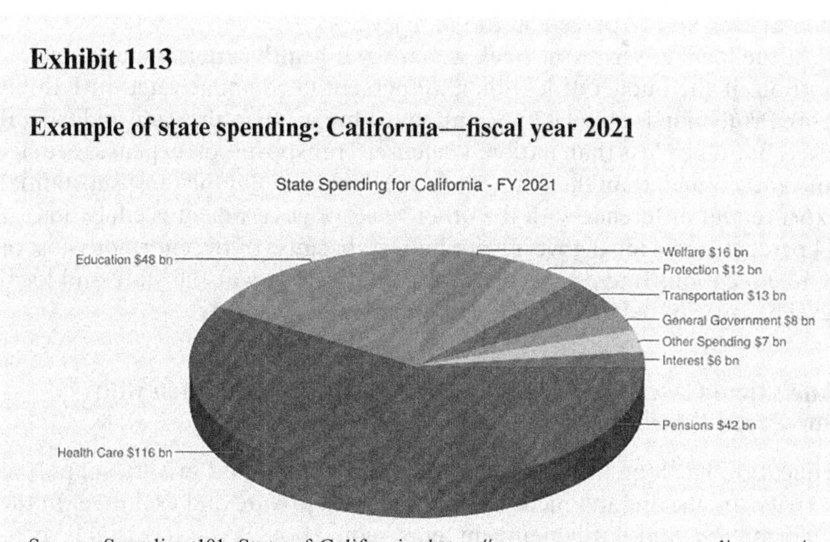

Source: Spending 101: State of California. https://www.usgovernmentspending.com/california_state_spending_pie_chart.

Exhibit 1.14

Example of local government spending: cities, counties, and special districts in California—fiscal year 2021

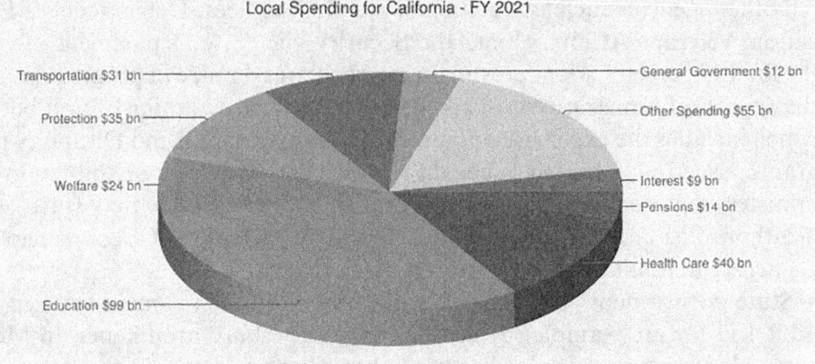

Source: USSpending-101.com. https://www.usgovernmentspending.com/local_spending_2022CAbn.

the federal budget (16 percent). The most dramatic difference is in the cost of education, which consumes less than one-half percent of the budget at the federal level and 18 percent at the state level.

At the local government level, welfare and health care is a much smaller portion of the budget at less than 20 percent (as demonstrated in Exhibit 1.14). Protection is about 12 percent, much higher than the state and federal levels but much less than national defense. Transportation expenses are significantly higher than the other levels at 11 percent. But the most substantial expense and difference with the other levels of government is education, at 34 percent of the local government budget, because of the enormous cost of K-12 education. Interest payments are relatively low at the state and local level because of balanced budget requirements.

Analytical Case: The Changing Face of Higher Education with For-Profit Education

Education has long been considered both a public- and private-supported activity. In ancient and medieval times, it was private and exclusive. In the Reformation and Enlightenment eras, education was increasingly considered necessary to a good society, and thus more of a public necessity.

Uneducated masses could not adequately govern themselves and were often denied the vote in the US well into the twentieth century. Thus, while soldiers of the Continental Army all fought against the tyranny of British taxation without representation, since three-quarters of them signed their name with an "X" indicating illiteracy, they still could not vote after the American Revolution. Colonies, and then states such as Massachusetts, were more aggressive in setting up public education schemes, but many Southern and Western states had illiteracy rates encompassing one-quarter to one-third of their adult males as late as the 1870s.

From 1850 to the 1970s, private education became more limited to (a) religious-based education (especially Catholic and Quaker grade and high schools), and (b) exclusive higher education such as Harvard and localized liberal arts colleges. However, it is important to note that this was invariably a nonprofit model. In the 1970s, this nonprofit model of higher education began to change when a variety of for-profit institutions expanded greatly with more flexible approaches and the maturation of online education. Examples are the Apollo Group (which includes the University of Phoenix), American Public Education, Education Management Corporation, Kaplan Higher Education, Capella Education, and Walden University.

To their credit, these universities as a group helped expand educational opportunities by lowering standards and giving students a second or third chance. They expanded flexible arrangements for working students by providing an anywhere-anytime philosophy to the degree possible. They also used programmed education techniques for maximum efficiency where possible, encouraging students to engage in activity- and group-based education more than was common in traditional higher education institutions. Such methods reduce the amount of instructor time and energy, but when well planned on a mass basis, can still provide a good technical education. Of course, this prodded many traditional institutions to become more flexible and innovative, especially in online education.

The success and massive growth of for-profit institutions from primarily technical and certificate institutions has also fueled their problems related to low standards, fraudulent recruitment practices, and profiteering. Investigated by the US Senate in 2012, the industry had turned from a specialized, vibrant, flexible alternative, to one that utilized armies of recruiters (i.e., over 35,000 for 30 for-profit institutions in 2010) and depended on federal loan guarantees and other types of federal financing for over 80 percent of their funding. Sadly, the dropout and default rates have been very high at for-profit institutions, and nearly half the students annually leave with large loans but without a degree. Ultimately Corinthian Colleges closed in 2015 and ITT Educational Services closed in 2016 because of accumulated bad public relations and legal disputes.

Questions for Discussion and Analysis

1 Should for-profit universities be more highly regulated? If so, should the regulation be based on more protection for students or less waste of federal funds? If not, why?

2 States and communities have provided subsidized higher education to ensure quality mass education. Has that rationale for a public subsidy to ensure an educated electorate changed in the last 20 years? To what degree is the stronger justification now an economic competitiveness argument or a fairness argument? Should subsidies to community colleges be decreased?

Source: Committee on Health, Education, Labor, Pensions, United States Senate (2012). For Profit Higher Education: The Failure to Safeguard the Federal Investment and Ensure Student Success

Practical Skill

Researching Government Jobs

Government is a wonderful source of jobs, benefits, and services. We will focus on jobs for this skill tip. Jobs are located at the federal, state, county, and special district levels. Some common examples of some of the best job sites are:

- USAJobs (federal)
- jobs.ca.gov
- caljobsource.com/cagov
- cityjobinfo.com

Skills Exercise: Research Government Jobs

Look at jobs at the local government, state government, and federal government levels, and report on one at each level that you would find interesting to consider.

Summary and Conclusion

1 Business–government relations vary widely from country to country and are defined by how the private and public sectors interact in their numerous complementary, cooperative, and conflicting roles. They also vary by the differences in strategies used to implement public policy, monetary policy, fiscal policy, the amount of government protection for society's most vulnerable, the

amount of promotion of the business sector domestically and internationally, the amount of prohibition of government competition, and the influence of the private sector on government policy-making.

2. Business–government relations constitute a necessary skillset for modern business people because government in modern society is large and thoroughly integrated into our lives. Further, our contract-based government contributes enormously to the highest quality of life that the world has ever experienced, but it is by knowledgeable and thoughtful citizens who understand the strengths and weaknesses of government that we can make it perform at its best, rather than at its worst.
3. The debates about the scope and robustness of government have been extensive since the beginning of the country. How active a role should government play in shaping the economy? How large should government become in terms of employees and budget? Has the growth of government been an appropriate function of a complex society and a contributor to a higher quality of life and/or has the growth become excessive? And what exact roles should government play? Eight roles it currently plays were identified.
4. Some of the examples widely thought to be good included providing a system of money, regulating banking and trading, insuring deposits, and providing protection from international market manipulation; providing our social contract through a system of authorized laws; providing public welfare for the most vulnerable in society; providing roads, bridges, lighting, and sewers for common usage; ensuring the protection of the country; reducing risk with regulation of water systems, airline safety, and food and drug safety; and providing shared social infrastructure efficiently, such as education.
5. Areas where government is not working well include when governments take over completely; when there is the collusion of powerful interests, such as when big business and big government become too enmeshed and self-dealing; when corruption becomes common; when policy-makers push governments to take on issues that they are not as well suited for; when the public sector runs into the limits of its efficiency/value and effectiveness over the long term because of escalating complexity or when agencies become inefficient over time or their mandates become outdated; and when special interests take advantage of a system that is not aware of the real costs and benefits accruing to the few.
6. An increasing problem for the public sector in the last 50 years is that it is often given tasks that are nearly impossible to accomplish, or it is the target of attacks that are not based on the facts, such as accurate perceptions on taxation levels, foreign aid, and prison responsibilities.
7. Both the private and public sectors need to find internal ways to reform, and must be prepared to be externally reformed from time to time. Paul Light categorizes four types of government reform. Reforms can focus on greater efficiency, less waste, ensuring fairness, and encouraging high performance.
8. There are over 89,000 governments. Different levels of government focus on different functions. The federal government has a special focus on national security, and now individual security, through insurance and entitlements. State and local governments have a focus on domestic safety, education, transportation and infrastructure, and civil regulation.

Key Terms

- Active government
  Central planning
- Business–government relations
- Special interests
- Supply side
- Fiscal policy
- Keynesian economics
- Economics
- Free market philosophy (laissez-faire)
- Monetary policy
  National defense
- Types of government reform
- Glass–Steagall Banking Act
- Public safety
  Savings and loan debacle
- US debt versus US deficit
- Government roles

Study Questions

1. How are business–government relations defined? Is this similar in most countries?
2. What forces have caused the growth of government in modern times? What forces have constrained even more growth?
3. What are the eight contemporary roles of American government?
4. What are examples of good government? What are examples of when government functions poorly? When does government commonly get blamed, either inaccurately or unfairly?
5. What are commonly thought of as sectoral strengths for the public and private sectors?
6. What are the types of reform that are made in the public sector?
7. What are the major foci of each level of American government?

Notes

1. Valerie Marcel (2009). National Oil Companies Control 80% of the World's Oil. *Foreign Policy*. September/October.
2. The famous OMB Circular 76 reads:

   > The longstanding policy of the federal government has been to rely on the private sector for needed commercial services. The competitive enterprise system, characterized by individual freedom and initiative, is the primary source of national economic growth. The federal government has grown to perform a myriad of commercial activities, in addition to providing citizens with a range of programs from law enforcement to stewardship of federal lands. Services in these and other areas are provided by a blend of federal government and private sector sources. For the American people to receive maximum value for their tax dollars, all commercial activities performed by government personnel should be subject to the forces of competition, as provided by this Circular.

3. Robert, Pear (2007). Bill to Let Medicare Negotiate Drug Prices Is Blocked. *New York Times*, April 18.
4. Brinkley, D. (1997). Democratic Enlargement: The Clinton Doctrine. *Foreign Policy, 106*: 111–127. doi:10.2307/1149177.
5. See, for example, Paul Krugman (2012). *End This Depression Now!* New York: W. W. Norton.

6 End-of-Term Report: The Economy Is Better than the Woes of America's Economy Suggests. *The Economist*, September 1, 2012.
7 The statistics come from the US Census.
8 Messaoud Hammouya (1999). Statistics on Public Sector Employment: Methodology, Structures and Trends (SAP 2.85/WP.144). Geneva: Bureau of Statistics, International Labour Office.
9 This data comes from the White House historical tables. http://www.whitehouse.gov/omb/budget/historicals.
10 The Committee of Seventy, Philadelphia Police Department Governance Study, June 1998.
11 See also the many articles at: www.governmentisgood.com.
12 Steven Greenhouse (2013). Share of the Work Force in a Union Falls to a 97-Year Low, 11.3%. *New York Times*, January 29.
13 Samuel Goldman (2013). Big Government, Complex Government, and the Future of Conservatism. *The American Conservative*, January 4.
14 Robert McIntyre, Matthew Gardner, Rebecca Wilkins, and Richard Phillips (2011). *Corporate Taxpayers & Corporate Tax Dodgers 2008–2010*. Washington, DC: Citizens for Tax Justice. Matthew Gardner, Lorena Roque, and Steve Wamhoff. (2019). Corporate tax avoidance in the first year of the Trump tax law. Institute of Taxation and Economic Policy. December 16. https://itep.org/corporate-tax-avoidance-in-the-first-year-of-the-trump-tax-law/.
15 Conor Clarke (2009). Why Buffett Pays Less than his Secretary. *The Atlantic*, March 18.
16 See Alan L. Moss (2008). *Selling Out America's Democracy: How Lobbyists, Special Interests, and Campaign Financing Undermine the Will of the People*. Westport, CT: Praeger. For a recent example, see Monique Morrissey. (2020). The war against the Postal Service. December 16. Economic Policy Institute. https://www.epi.org/publication/the-war-against-the-postal-service/.
17 John Fritze (2009). Average Family Health Insurance Policy: $23,375 up 5%. *USA Today*, September 16.
18 Chuck Marr and Nathaniel Frentz (2013). Federal Income Taxes on Middle-Income Families Remain Near Historic Lows. Center on Budget and Policy Priorities, April 11.
19 The IRS reports (according to the *Tampa Bay News*, Barack Obama Says that Some Billionaires Have a Tax Rate as Low as 1 Percent, December 6, 2011).

The IRS offers a breakdown of what the 400 top earners paid in effective tax rates:

0 percent to 10 percent: 30 filers
10 percent to 15 percent: 101 filers
15 percent to 20 percent: 112 filers
20 percent to 25 percent: 52 filers
25 percent to 30 percent: 46 filers
30 percent to 35 percent: 59 filers

20 John Norris (2011). Five Myths about Foreign Aid. *New York Times*, April 28.
21 See the Borgen Project. http://borgenproject.org/.
22 US Incarceration Rates. Wikipedia.
23 Catherine Rampell (2012). Record Corporate Profits. *New York Times*, November 29. Erik Sherman (2020). Corporate Profits Skyrocket as Post-Holidays Look Grim for Millions. *Forbes*, November 25. https://www.forbes.com/sites/eriksherman/2020/11/25/corporate-profits-skyrocket-as-post-holidays-look-grim-for-millions/?sh=20b8e48a58bc.
24 Bank Failures. Wessels Living History Farm. http://www.livinghistoryfarm.org/.

25 Jason DeParle (1990). "Robin HUD" Given a Stiff Sentence. *New York Times*, June 23; Housing and Reform Act of 1989.
26 The Housing Opportunity Program Extension Act of 1996 gave public housing authorities the tools to screen out and evict residents who might endanger other existing residents due to substance abuse and criminal behavior. In 1998, Congress allowed local housing authorities to open up more public housing to the middle class.
27 Policy Basics: Top Ten Facts about Social Security (2020). Center on Budget and Policy Priorities, August 13. https://www.cbpp.org/research/social-security/top-ten-facts-about-social-security.

References

Black, B. (2005). *The Best Way to Rob a Bank Is to Own One: How Corporate Executives and Politicians Looted the S&L Industry*. Austin: University of Texas at Austin Press.

Blinder, A. S. (2008). Keynesian Economics, in D. R. Henderson (ed.) *Concise Encyclopedia of Economics*, 2nd edn. Indianapolis: Library of Economics and Liberty.

Clark, C. (1977). The Scope for, and Limits of, Taxation, in Barry Bracewell-Milnes, Colin Clark, Walter Elkan, Ivor F. Pearce, A. R. Prest and Charles K. Rowley (eds.) *The State of Taxation* (pp. 19–28). London: Institute of Economic Affairs.

Friedman, M. (1962). *Capitalism and Freedom*. Chicago, IL: University of Chicago Press.

Giles, C., Atkins, R., and Guha, K. (2008). The Undeniable Shift to Keynes. *Financial Times*, December 30, 2008.

Goodsell, C. (2004). *The Case for Bureaucracy*, 4th edn. Washington, DC: CQ Press.

Gorges, M. J. (1996). *Euro-Corporatism: Interest Intermediation in the European Community*. Lanham, MD: University of America Press.

Hau, J., and Hasmuth, R. (2013). *The Chinese Corporatist State: Adaptation, Survival and Resistance*. New York and Oxford: Routledge.

Hayek, F. (1989). *The Collected Works of F.A. Hayek*. Chicago: University of Chicago Press.

House Committee on the Budget, Chairman John Yarmuth (2019). https://budget.house.gov/publications/fact-sheet/frequently-asked-questions-about-federal-budget.

Keynes, J. M. (1936). *The General Theory of Employment, Interest and Money*. Basingstoke: Palgrave Macmillan.

Lehne, R. (2006). *Government and Business*, 2nd edn. Washington, DC: CQ Press.

Light, P. C. (1997). *The Tides of Reform: Making Government Work 1945–1995*. New Haven, CT: Yale University Press.

Markham, J. W. (2006). *A Financial History of Modern US Corporate Scandals*. New York: M.E. Sharpe.

Montross, C. (2020). *Waiting for an Echo: The Madness of American Incarceration*. New York: Penguin.

Moynihan, D. P. (2020) *Populism and the Deep State: The Attack on Public Service under Trump*. SRRN: https://ssrn.com/abstract=3607309.

Peacock, A. T., and Wiseman, J. (1961). *The Growth of Public Expenditure in the United Kingdom*. London: Oxford University Press.

Perry, J., and Rainey, H. (1988). The Public–Private Distinction in Organization Theory: A Critique and Research Strategy. *Academy of Management Review, 13(2)*:182–201.

Porter, Roger B. (2002). Government–Business Relations in the United States. Paper for the Transatlantic Perspective on US–EU Economic Relations: Convergence, Conflict and Cooperation. April 8.

Rainey, H. G. (2009). *Understanding and Managing Public Organizations*, 4th edn. San Francisco, CA: Wiley/Jossey-Bass.

Siaroff, A. (1999). Corporatism in 24 Industrial Democracies: Meaning and Measurement. *European Journal of Political Research, 36*:175–205.

Smith, A. (1937). *The Wealth of Nations.* New York: The Modern Library.

Spending 101: State of California. https://www.usgovernmentspending.com/california_state_spending_pie_chart.

Stanford Encyclopedia of Philosophy (2002). Hobbes's Moral and Political Philosophy. http://plato.stanford.edu/entries/hobbes-moral/.

US Spending-101.com. https://www.usgovernmentspending.com/local_spending_2022CAbn.

US Census Bureau, Department of Commerce (2012). https://www.census.gov/

Yergin, D., and Stanislaw, J. (1998). *The Commanding Heights: The Battle for the World Economy.* New York: Simon & Schuster.

2 Perspectives about Business—Government Relations in Society

Thomas McWeeney

Chapter Contents

Case 2 Scenario

ABC's Relocation

Zach's father, Zeddic, was recently promoted to interim CEO of Acme Bottling Company (ABC), a hi-tech manufacturing plant in Anyplace, about 15 minutes from the City of Somewhere. ABC has a large presence in Anyplace, and packages natural liquid and solid products in eco-friendly containers. In fact, ABC is how Zach and Zoey met. Zoey's friend Tyler had been working there part time, earning money for college. Tyler introduced Zach and Zoey.

Zach's dad had been the Chief Finance Officer at Acme Bottling for the past five years and understood the operation of the company well. Zeddic had been excited about becoming interim CEO and hoped to work it into a permanent position. Yet his first month was unexpectedly challenging and overwhelming, especially regarding the company's decision to relocate.

ABC has operated for over 20 years in Anyplace. The company signed a long-term lease for the land with the city. During the past two decades, because of the rising real estate market, Anyplace has doubled the land rent, which increased production costs for ABC. Two

DOI: 10.4324/9781003178620-3

years ago, a neighboring state established an industrial park less than 100 miles away. To attract new businesses, especially hi-tech ones like ABC, they were providing very favorable tax incentive packages, and extremely low rent leases. The industrial park was also closer to two major customers and one major supplier for ABC.

When the idea of relocation was proposed, Zeddic led a comprehensive cost–benefit analysis as CFO that included all critical production factors—capital, labor, land, utilities, taxes, logistics, etc. Knowing relocation could potentially reduce production costs by 20 percent or more, ABC's shareholder board was in favor of the relocation and unanimously appointed Zeddic the interim CEO.

The rumor of relocation quickly spread and Zeddic suddenly found himself in a lion's den. He was confronted by concerned employees everywhere he went. They felt the 100-mile drive to the industrial park was not a desirable commute; the majority would have to move their families or resign. And even though the industrial park had finished basic infrastructure construction, it was still not in a great residential area. In a management meeting, the union leader spoke out about the possibility of a strike in protest.

The Anyplace city government was deeply concerned about the idea as well. As the city's largest employer, ABC had over 800 employees; relocation of the company could be devastating. For the past few years, Anyplace had worked closely with the company and had accommodated many of ABC's needs for land, infrastructure, tax breaks, and so on. Several government officials and local politicians attempted to persuade Zeddic to abandon the idea. The city manager was a personal friend of Zeddic and he was growing increasingly annoyed. He even considered this a betrayal of their friendship.

Neighboring community owners and land developers wanted to talk with Zeddic. They were afraid the vacancy would affect the environment, security, and land value of the neighborhood. Two local suppliers constantly called him for meetings. They were concerned that relocation would add to their transportation costs. The owner of a restaurant where Zeddic often had lunch expressed regret that he would lose him, and his employees, as major customers. Several local and national reporters wanted to interview him about the relocation and employee compensation.

Even Zach's mother, Zelda, would not give her husband a break. Several things bothered her. A college professor working toward her tenure, the next few years would be critical for her career. Her two youngest, Zach's little brother and sister, were now in schools that were located in a very good district; starting over again in a new district would be difficult. Plus, Zach's relationship with Zoey was going very well and Zelda could see that her son was beginning to think seriously about a future with her. Zelda had been very supportive of Zeddic in the past, but this time ...

Zach's father must make a decision that affects short-term profitability, long-term strategy, and many stakeholders. While Zeddic thought at the time that the cost–benefit analysis he conducted was thorough, he now realizes that many other factors affect both the long-term strategy and the integrity of ABC. This chapter explores a variety of perspectives of which managers must be aware if they are not to be surprised and overwhelmed, as Zach's father now is.

This chapter discusses three viewpoints about business–government societal relations in the United States (US), namely, the shareholder perspective, strategic perspective, and stakeholder perspective with examples. The shareholder perspective tends to look at business in isolation and to emphasize economic analysis and profit-making for individuals, proprietors, and in the case of larger companies, shareholders. The strategic business perspective tends to look at what it takes to have a successful company. The stakeholder perspective sees itself as subordinate to society. When any of these idealized perspectives are corrupted by excessive influence of special interests or an economic elite, it creates a problem called crony capitalism.

Introduction: The Theories of Business–Government Relations

There are many perspectives on business–government societal relations. For simplicity, here we look at three views that capture some of the most important differences. If we decide to narrowly look at the institution of business itself, largely from an economic point of view, then we might assume a business-centric or relatively "pure" shareholder perspective. If we decide to look at business in relationship to other institutions with which it is in competition but with which it also shares medium-term synergies, we might adopt a strategic perspective. If we decide to look at business as a long-term means to a better society and quality of life over many generations, rather than as simply a means of individual wealth, then we may use a more socially or ethically based viewpoint or a stakeholder perspective.

A general point should be made about these three perspectives: they are not a comprehensive list. When looking at business as institutions in society, for example, we have focused primarily on the central role in Western business, which emphasizes economic means of organizing society over religious or ideological means. In theocratic states, religion may be viewed as more central to society than business, and ideological states may focus more on the importance of social harmony and equity than wealth creation.

So while we will choose examples that highlight these specific perspectives, the reality is that the mix is generally more subtle and complex.

Perspectives of Business and Society

The Shareholder Perspective

The *shareholder perspective* tends to look at business in isolation and to emphasize economic analysis and profit-making for individuals, proprietors, and in the case of larger companies, shareholders. It tends to exclude other values and institutions from consideration. Thus, internal efficiency and external market analysis leading to dynamic competition and innovation are emphasized. Non-intervention by government and other institutions in the affairs of business are valued so that there can be a sharp focus on the business at hand. Implicitly, it advocates small government in terms of ownership, taxes, regulation, and subsidies, and a relatively unrestrained market. The principal duty of government is to ensure that markets function properly, and to correct market failures if there are any, but to do so with the least possible intrusiveness. See Exhibit 2.2 for a discussion of the causes of market failures. Corporations should only respond to legal requirements and government policies that affect their business.

The theoretical roots of this mindset can be traced to Adam Smith and his book *The Wealth of Nations* (1776), wherein Smith shifted the focus in economics from being state-centric under the formerly dominant mercantilist

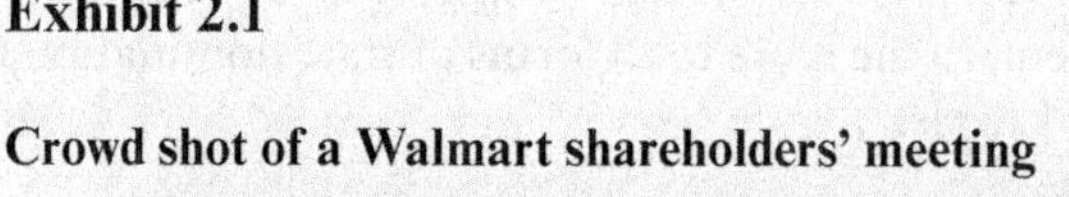

Exhibit 2.1

Crowd shot of a Walmart shareholders' meeting

Source: Wikimedia Commons. (Flickr). The 2010 Walmart Shareholders' Meeting at Bud Walton Arena in Fayetteville, Ark, on Friday, June 4, 2010.

approach to his market-based approach. He asserted that the greatest good for society comes when businesses compete freely. In a perfectly competitive market, no single participant is powerful enough to affect the prices or other terms of sale. Producers sell goods to consumers who are attracted by products of the best quality and the lowest price.

To do so, producers devote their energies to technological and management innovations to improve productivity and to create values. Since consumers are determined to maximize their benefit with the lowest cost, the choices of individual consumers lead to the greatest benefit of the society. The market produces an efficient economy that optimally allocates resources and spontaneously coordinates activities among competitive producers.

Smith's "invisible hand" of the market was not only important for domestic exchange, but for international exchange as well. His intellectual successor, David Ricardo, systematized this capitalist approach at the global level. His theory of comparative advantage argued not only for specialization among individuals but also for free trade among countries. He asserted that there is always benefit from free trade, even if one party (e.g., a resource-rich country with highly skilled workforce) is more productive in every possible area than its trading counterpart (e.g., a resource-poor country with unskilled laborers). The key to realizing the mutual benefits of trade is that each concentrates on the activities where it has a relative productivity advantage.

The negative effects of wealth concentration following the industrial revolution led to theories for more state-centric, or socialistic approaches, from milder forms advocated by Saint-Simon and John Stuart Mill using government as a force for poverty reduction and progressive improvement of society in a capitalist system, to the more total forms of state domination for public good of Marx and Engels.

Exhibit 2.2

Market failure

Market failure is used to describe the problem when the allocation of goods and services by a free market is not efficient. In theory, an economic situation is efficient when no one can be made better off without making someone else worse off.

Many reasons contribute to market failure:

- *Public good.* In economics, a public good, as compared to commercial good, is one that is both non-excludable (impossible to prevent people who have not paid for the good from using it) and non-rivalrous (one consumer does not reduce its availability to others). Examples of public goods include fresh air, national defense, knowledge, lighthouses, etc. Because of the nature of public goods, even though they are in demand, the market does not create incentives for their production.

- *Information asymmetry.* In transactions where one party has more or better information than the other, it creates an imbalance of power and causes the transaction to go awry. The problem of information asymmetry happens in business transactions such as used-car sales, buying insurance, purchasing real estate, etc.
- *Non-competitive market.* This includes monopoly, in that there is only one provider of a produce of service; monopsony, in that there is only one buyer in a market; and other defections in market structure.
- *Principal–agent problem.* In principal–agent relations, instead of being motivated to act in the best interest of the principal, the agent may pursue his or her own interests. For example, a patient (the principal) is not sure whether her doctor (the agent) is recommending expensive treatment because it is truly necessary for the patient's health, or because it can bring income for the doctor.
- *Externalities.* In economic theories, an externality is a cost (negative externality) or benefit (positive externality) that is incurred by a party who was not involved in the transaction of the goods or services that caused that cost or benefit. Toxic air emitted by a manufacturing plant that pollutes and affects the health of residents in a community is an example of negative externality. An example of positive externality is the Research and Development (R&D) by a company that discovered a new production technique that can be adopted by other firms in the industry.

Market failure often leads to government intervention in a particular market. For example, monopolies that emerged in the oil industry during the late nineteenth century in the US led to a series of government antitrust regulations.

These late nineteenth-century theories affected all governments in the early twentieth century, until the excessive role of the state in economics was challenged by Friedrich Hayek and the Austrian School in Europe, and later the University of Chicago School of Economics in the US (founded by John D. Rockefeller), as discussed in Chapter 1. With the conversion of the former Soviet Union and its client states in the 1990s, as well as China and Vietnam adopting relatively capitalist economies, the "age of the market" now dominates the world economic stage. Its virtues include macro-level system efficiency, self-organization, consumer focus, and robust innovation, among others.

Nonetheless, there are weaknesses in this purist approach to market capitalism. One of them targets the imperfections of market. The perfectly competitive market is rare. In reality, individuals' pursuit of maximizing self-interest often leads to various types of systemic fraud and corporate monopolies that are not efficient. For critics, the prospect of market failure demands government vigilance and intervention, such as regulations, wage and price controls, bailouts, and social and corporate insurance programs as well as welfare stabilization programs. Throughout the history of the US, the government's role has expanded as a result of correcting market failure (see Chapter 3).

Second, it is argued that although business often states that it wants small government, in reality business is as demanding as any other special interest group, and often more successful in reaping benefits (Carney 2011). For example, small-government advocates in Congress are often vociferous about maintaining a large defense establishment, and keeping military bases and weapons producers in their districts open.

Finally, it is often argued that markets place too much emphasis on monetary and material gains and, as a result, erode humanity. Society, they argue, does not exist to promote business, but rather business is an avenue to promote a good society. An excessive emphasis on the profit motive can lead individuals and corporations to abuse legal loopholes, to exploit the disadvantaged, to pollute the environment, and to eliminate opportunities for future generations by fiscal mismanagement or ecological destruction.

An example of the relatively purist perspective can be observed by the Heritage Foundation Economic Freedom Index (2021). It ranks countries based on ten indicators in four major areas:

- Rule of Law (property rights, freedom from corruption).
- Limited Government (fiscal freedom, government spending).
- Regulatory Efficiency (business freedom, labor freedom, monetary freedom).
- Open Markets (trade freedom, investment freedom, financial freedom).

According to its 2021 ranking, the top countries are (in order): Singapore, New Zealand, Australia, Switzerland, Ireland, Taiwan, the UK, Estonia, Canada, and Denmark. The US, ranked 20, was brought down by the government spending and rule of law categories. Note that over half of the countries with a higher Heritage Foundation ranking have a lower per capita than the US. This indicates that it is the capitalist principles, more than the effects of the system, that are paramount in this mindset. While 20th place is still honorable (out of a list of 177 countries), the gap between it and the two countries at the top is substantial. The following critique accompanied the ranking: "It's overall score has decreased because of a decline in fiscal health."

An almost perfect example of the shareholder perspective in the US corporate arena is investment banks. Examples of investment banks include JPMorgan Chase, Goldman Sachs, Morgan Stanley, and investment arms of various mixed mega-banks such as Bank of America and Citi. Investment banks underwrite securities, assist in mergers and acquisitions, trade derivatives and equities, and provide other financial services. They also advise others how to invest. Investment banks must be careful to keep their privileged information confidential and not to use such information to their own advantage (insider trading). Such institutions tend to be very averse to any government intervention in their affairs, and welcome a volatile market place where money can be made more quickly. In those rare instances in which government stabilization or support may be considered by most as necessary, this industry is still generally not inclined to agree or be appreciative of it. While these banks certainly take advantage of strategic government interactions, such as the sale of government securities or the acquisition of troubled competitors through governmental receivership, they do so on the best terms they possibly can in order to make money, not to do good or improve their reputation (other than being brutally competitive).

The Strategic Business Perspective

If the shareholder perspective reveres the market and the ideal of the owner and stockholder, the strategic perspective admires individual companies and the teams of people who make them work successfully. Put differently, the shareholder perspective tends to look at what it takes to have a successful world market using classical economics as a matter of principle, and *the strategic business perspective tends to look at what it takes to have a successful company*. Thus, one looks more at the theory of capitalism, the other looks at the practice of it.

This pragmatic approach to business shifts the focus in two ways, which are ultimately in some tension with each other. First, the strategic business perspective is competitive in highly pragmatic and concrete terms. What do companies have to do to be competitive against specific rivals and to make as large a profit for owners as possible? Of course, basic competitive strategy looks at the most efficient and effective use of capital, labor, technology, and innovation. In this aspect, business is fighting for survival and there is a Darwinian sense of drama in businesses being created, competing, succeeding, or vanishing as young companies thrive and adapt if factors are right, or fail. It emphasizes "playing the game" well, coming in first, and/or eliminating dangerous rivals to "corner the market" when possible. The business world is tough, and tough companies must be competent and sophisticated in marketing, sales, recruiting talent, international business, and other management areas and must be disciplined at practicing these skills. Not surprisingly, the competitive company wants low taxes and few regulations from government to maximize profits and compete internationally. It wants a stable economic policy and strong national performance indicators to facilitate growth. Market size is important, so it wants government protection where it is vulnerable to international competition, and trade barrier reductions for foreign markets.

Yet a strategic approach is not just about competition, but also about collaboration (Porter 1998). Good strategy will include networking, occasionally positioning oneself to be a part of a winning team rather than a sole winner, and finding win-win solutions. Networking provides market intelligence and goodwill. Being a corporate team player allows better supply chain management, cooperative and profitable ventures with other companies, and economies of scale, size, and comparative strengths. In many cases, it is not winning that is most important, but rather it is *not* losing. A negotiated settlement may be more sensible than a long, drawn-out legal or labor fight in which even the winning side is much weaker. Internally, collaboration leads to better coordination, teamwork, and talent development. Externally, companies explicitly or implicitly depend on a collaborative environment with government in numerous areas.

Governments purchase billions of dollars' worth of goods and services, so many businesses find it important to be savvy about government procurement and contracts. The Department of Defense, the largest purchaser, spends about $300 billion in goods and services annually. Lockheed Martin and Boeing Corporation are examples of companies that live and die by government contracts despite its private sector business (CRS 2021).

Governments play a key role in establishing an environment of high-quality human resource availability through public education, job training programs, and educational support via loans and subsidies. Governments play important roles in creating a healthy environment via health care systems and in providing good infrastructure for goods movement. Governments are also a critical part of powerful market clusters (see Chapter 9), most noticeable for technology hubs today. Likewise, governments help or hinder new business development, from programs that assist business incubation and expansion to regulations that make launching business start-ups daunting. Since government's roles in this regard take resources, business's interest in low taxes is somewhat transfigured to an interest in good value for taxes. Further, the interest in small government is converted into one of wanting government to be large enough to be effective or supportive.

The dynamic tension of the competitive and collaborative roles that strategic companies want is demonstrated in business groups such as Chambers of Commerce, where goals for low taxes may contrast with the price of substantial services useful for business. See the business-led Council on Competitiveness goals in Exhibit 2.3.

A strength of the strategic approach to business–government relations is that it is more balanced and realistic than the shareholder perspective. It embeds business in the dynamics of society, while still giving business the central role. On the negative side, the strategic perspective is so inclusive and relativistic that it is difficult to know what it stands for because circumstances change so frequently and dramatically. If the shareholder approach can be rigid in its principle-based orientation, the strategic perspective can be unclear, inconsistent, and ethically dubious.

Exhibit 2.3

US Chamber of Commerce policy recommendations

The US Chamber of Commerce sponsors business forums. Below are some of the recommendations that they made for national policy leaders in 2020 which call for a robust partnership of business and government.

- Establish the White House National Competitiveness and Innovation Council (NCIC)—and parallel State Competitiveness and Innovation Councils—to create a national vision for US competitiveness and innovation in the 21st-century global economy.
- Build a whole-of-nation strategy for developing and deploying critical dual-use technologies that will shape the industries of the future, national security and global grand challenges.
- Establish a new Technology Statecraft Initiative and International Innovation Corps.
- Establish regulations, government procurement policies, and reforms in antitrust and competition policy to support the industries of the future.
- Restore federal R&D investment to 1960 levels of two percent of GDP.
- Establish a new, nonprofit American Innovation Investment Fund with initial public-private capitalization of $100 billion.
- Establish the US Digital Infrastructure Access and Inclusion Initiative.
- Extend the mission of national labs to encompass economic competitiveness and permit co-funding with private sector partners.
- Redesign federal economic development programs by adopting innovation metrics and performance standards for new block grant programs.
- Realign federal, state and local workforce development programs and training to enable a highly skilled, digitally competent, innovation workforce beginning at the junior and high school levels.

Source: Council on Competitiveness (2020)

An example of the strategic approach at the international level is the World Economic Forum's Global Competitiveness Index, rating competitiveness in 141 countries (Global 2019). Its 12 "pillars" include both the role of government and the state of business development in countries: quality of government institutions (e.g., low corruption and reasonable taxes), infrastructure (e.g., roads and ports), macroeconomic environment (e.g., low government debt), health and primary education, goods-market efficiency, higher education and training, labor-market efficiency, financial market development, technological readiness, market size, business sophistication, and innovation. Singapore ranked as the most competitive in 2019, with the US second. Russia and China are prominent examples of the differences in the shareholder and strategic perspectives. While both do well in competitiveness—with China at 28 and Russia at 43—these relatively authoritarian states drop—to 107 and 92, respectively—in the Economic Freedom Index, a hallmark of the shareholder perspective.

At the state level, a similar index is the Beacon Hill Institute Competitiveness Report (Competitiveness 2018). In 2018, it gave the top ten rankings to: Massachusetts, Iowa, Texas, South Dakota, Idaho, Nebraska, Minnesota, Utah, Virginia, and Colorado. Note that while low tax rate is a sub factor in the scale, a high-tax state ultimately got the top spot. California was in the middle at 20th. While there are various company competitiveness surveys, it is hard to surpass the stock market, which keeps the pulse on the overall track record of companies in milliseconds. Not only do increased profits drive up stock prices, so, too, do announcements of new products, cooperative agreements with other companies, government contracts, and inexpensive out-of-court settlements; similarly, it is not only low profits or losses that signal lower comparative prices but also corporate scandals, increased tax liabilities, onerous regulations (but note: not all regulations are onerous and some actually stabilize markets and drive long-term profits up), and corporate feuds that result in loss of energy rather than productivity gains through innovation.

An example of companies that practice a highly strategic approach are various types of community and regional banks. Community banks are depository institutions that are generally owned and operated locally. They have strong roots in the community with local businesses and families, capitalizing on their understanding of local needs and conditions. Although they represent the bulk of all banks by number, they are a relatively small part of the depository banking industry (less than 15 percent), with mega-banks like Bank of America and Citi capitalizing on their ubiquity and marketing prowess. Therefore, community banks are careful to use their local connections strategically by having senior employees join local professional organizations, sponsoring local events, and participating in local nonpartisan policy-making. They often benefit by getting the business of the largest local companies and agencies in the region because of perceptions by local businesses of the importance to invest locally when possible.

The Stakeholder Perspective

While the shareholder perspective sees itself as separate from society and the strategic perspective sees itself as a part, and at the center of, society, *the stakeholder perspective sees itself as subordinate to society* (Freeman 1984). While profits are important and one of the mainstays of business, they do not crowd out other business and social values in the stakeholder view. Profit maximization, the driving force in other business perspectives, is by nature a short-term view, and does not fully take into account either long-term equity interests or the value of reputation. Furthermore, the stakeholder view *consistently* looks at community and environment as necessary factors to consider, not just when legally required or advantageous to do so. A collaborative style that emphasizes a win-win approach is not case specific, as in the strategic perspective, but adopted as a preferred mode of operation. Competition is not eliminated, but success is comprehended as a product of quality and hard work rather than cleverness or market manipulation.

Exhibit 2.4

The Boeing Company

A replica of the original "Red Barn" where the Boeing Company started.
Source: Wikimedia Commons. (n.d.) https://www.boeing.com/history.

Founded in 1916 by William Boeing, the Boeing Company is an American multinational aerospace and defense corporation. Today, Boeing is not only the second largest government contractor (second to Lockheed Martin) based on defense-related revenue, but also the largest exporter by value in the US.

Ever since the company's existence, the business of Boeing has been strongly connected to and influenced by government activities and policies. In 1917, when the US entered World War I, Boeing started to build seaplanes for the Navy. When the war ended in 1918, Boeing was incapable of selling new airplanes because a large surplus of cheap, used military planes flooded the market. Instead of going out of business, Boeing started selling other products, such as dressers, counters, furniture, and Sea Sleds, a kind of flat-bottom boat.

In the 1920s, Boeing won government contracts for mail planes, and consequently created an airline. However, the Air Mail Act passed by Congress in 1934 prohibited manufacturers and airlines from being under the same corporate umbrella, so the company had to split into three smaller companies—Boeing Airplane Company, United Airlines, and United Aircraft Corporation.

During World War II, Boeing built a large number of bombers for the Army and its production was largely scaled up. After the war, as orders for bombers were discontinued, around 70,000 employees of Boeing lost their jobs. In the 1950s, with government support in R&D, Boeing diversified its products and became a leader in commercial jet manufacture.

In the 1970s, Boeing survived a series of strikes, including the decline in military spending after the Vietnam war, the revamping of the space programs, the economic recession, and the shrinking of government financial support for the development of new aircraft.

In the 1980s as passenger air traffic increased, Boeing was facing intensified competition, mainly from Airbus, a European commercial airline manufacturer established in 1969. As both parties became concerned about the subsidies paid by government to the large civil aircraft manufacturers, the European Community and the US started bilateral negotiations for the limitation of government subsidies to the industry. Negotiations led to the EC–US Agreement on Trade in Large Civil Aircraft in 1992, which imposed stricter rules than the World Trade Organization (WTO) on government support.

After several decades of success, Boeing started to lose ground to Airbus and its lead in the airline industry in the 2000s. The two competitors also entered into a series of disputes related to government subsidies. On September 15, 2010, WTO ruled that Boeing had received illegal subsidies, such as R&D aid from the National Aeronautics and Space Administration (NASA) and the Defense Department as well as tax-related export subsidies and tax incentives from the states of Illinois, Kansas, and Washington.

Given the fact that the company's business largely depends on government contracts and policies, Boeing has been consistently building political connections and contributing to political campaigns. For example, in the 2008 presidential campaign, candidate Obama received

$197,000 in contributions from the company, by far the largest campaign contribution from Boeing employees and executives (Carney 2011). The investment pays off well for Boeing. For example, US diplomats are notorious marketing agents of Boeing. They often help push sales of jetliners to other countries. As a result, Boeing sells about 70 percent of its commercial planes to foreign buyers and is the single largest exporter of manufactured goods in the US (Lipton, Clark, and Lehren 2011).

Source: Based on the history of Boeing at https://www.boeing.com/history/

A long-term mindset encourages an attitude of sportsmanship in competition, with the accent being on getting better rather than simply winning in the short-term. Thus the semi- and intangible benefits of customer confidence, employee loyalty, and civic trust are valued more highly as genuine practice rather than merely as sales pitches. Civic and government organizations are more likely to be perceived as partners in social productivity rather than impediments to business success. While this view is sometimes considered the ethical view, it is also a more holistic view that enhances accountability and avoids cost-shifting onto others in society or into the future.

The pursuit of a good reputation for pragmatic purposes and the importance of business ethics are ancient concepts. At the beginning of the twentieth century, notable attempts were made to encourage self-regulation. The Better Business Bureau was founded in 1912 to advance reputation certification and self-enforcement, and to discourage scams and wrongdoing. Other early efforts to provide voluntary industry standards were the Good Housekeeping Seal of Approval (launched in 1909) and Consumer Reports (started in 1936). A new renaissance of business ethics began in the 1970s with the expanded use of the concept of corporate social responsibility (Carroll 1979), which looks at social accountability as a necessary component of corporate behavior. This topic is dealt with in detail in Chapter 6.

When examined from a corporate point of view, a wide variety of indicators can be used, depending on the breadth and emphasis of the perspective. Businesses can be more mindful of employee relations, often providing more services and stability for employees than is required by the market. Businesses can improve their reputations based on environmental practices that limit habitat destruction, reduce waste, encourage recycling, diminish one's carbon footprint, and so forth (Birchall 2006). They can also try to ensure that lower-cost foreign labor is not exploited in the drive for profit maximization. They can provide good corporate governance and openness when publicly traded, and direct philanthropy or indirect service to the community via employees or the company itself.

There are numerous rankings that look at these various factors, but one that focuses on social responsibility is the journal *3BL Media*, which provides an annual list of the 100 Best Corporate Citizens based on impact on the environment, climate change behaviors, avoidance of human rights abuse, quality employee relations, open corporate governance, community-based philanthropy, and financial integrity. The top three major corporations in the 2021 report were (in order): Owens Corning, General Mills, and HP Inc. On the other hand, various media also track and publicize bad behavior such as the Public Eye Awards (aka The Most Despicable Corporation Awards) and ad hoc lists. Goldman Sachs has ranked well in various types of award programs such as a best place to work; it also has also been frequently slammed despite being the most powerful investment house in the world. It recently paid a staggering $2.9 billion fine for bribery and fraud related to the national wealth fund for the county of Malaysia (DOJ 2021). This type of financial success without scruples has long since been noted:

> Goldman Sachs is the vampire of finance capital. Never one to waste a crisis—whether a subprime mortgage bubble, a bank collapse or a Euro-failure—Goldman Sachs makes good money from most of them. And the company does not shy away from deals that might ruin entire countries. Between 1998 and 2009 Goldman Sachs pocketed horrendous fees to hide half of Greece's public deficit by means of accounting tricks. These financial constructions eventually ruined Greece and plunged the EU into a financial crisis with no end in sight even now—another crisis from which Goldman Sachs has already profited handsomely and will continue to do so: so far Goldman's profit is at least 600 million dollars and Greece owes the bank 400 million per year until 2037, for a total of more than 10 billion dollars at the expense of European taxpayers. Goldman Sachs is the epitome of a money machine with an opaque and matchless network of allies in top positions such as ECB-chief Mario Draghi. Governments come and go. Goldman Sachs stays.
>
> (Public Eye 2013)

The stakeholder perspective is sometimes used to rate and rank countries as well, but with some adaptation of the focus. The "employee loyalty" aspect becomes "quality-of-life" measures, such as with the UN Human Development Index that looks at life span, per capita income, and years of schooling. The wealthier countries of Europe and the Anglophone world (e.g., the US, Australia, Canada, New Zealand, but not South Africa) do well in this measure, Russia is in the upper middle ranks and China is in the lower middle ranks, while African countries tend to dominate the bottom.

A wide variety of environmental issues are ranked by the Environmental Performance Index (2021). Richer countries tend to do better in environmental rankings, and the US has risen in recent years to 24th as a

Exhibit 2.5

Protestors holding a banner: "US Treasury Under New Management" (Washington, DC)

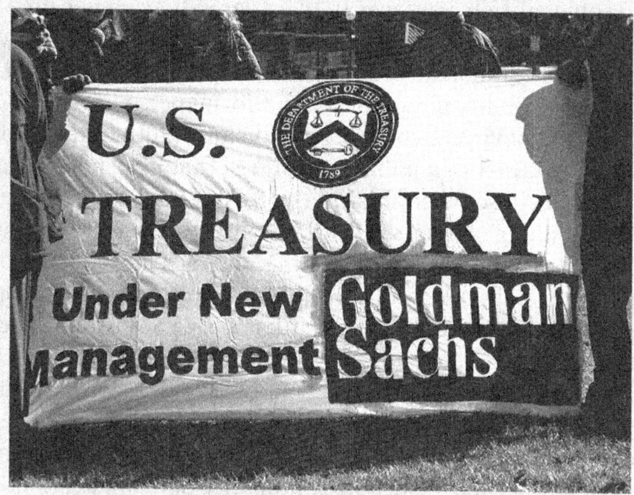

Source: Wikimedia Commons (2011). Takomabibelot.

"good performer." Doing much more poorly are the transitioning states of Russia (58) and China (120), whose focus on growth has overwhelmed environmental consciousness.

"Public reputation" becomes configured as "domestic freedoms" or assistance to the most vulnerable. Examples of rankings of the democratic rights are Freedom House and the Index of Freedom. Again, the European and Anglophone countries tend to do very well here, with the US normally near the top. On the other hand, Russia, China, and the oil-rich states of the Middle East (e.g., Qatar, United Arab Emirates, Saudi Arabia) do very poorly as authoritarian regimes.

Vulnerability is measured by income disparity, known as the Gini coefficient, in which the lower the fraction of 1, the more equally national income is distributed. For example, most European countries range between .25 and .32 (high equality), the US, Russia, and China are in the moderately high inequality range (.38 – .41) ranking from 94th to 120th in comparative terms, and Singapore has a rank of 147th with a .46 Gini coefficient. Only a handful of Latin American and African countries have Gini coefficients above .50, such as South Africa, Haiti, and Brazil. Another index of national philanthropy, foreign aid, is the annual OECD survey of aid donors. While the US gives the most because of the size of its economy, as a percentage of gross national income, it ranked 19th out of 24 in 2013.

Exhibit 2.6 gives some examples of how different countries are ranked in the three perspectives that we have examined. The US is often at or close to the top in terms of shareholder and strategic business approaches. It is given stiff competition by northern European countries, Singapore, Hong Kong, Korea, and some oil-rich countries in these capitalistic dimensions. The US also does well in most civic surveys that emphasize national income and political freedoms, as do northern European countries. However, in terms of other social responsibility indicators, its performance is lower, falling to the middle in terms of environmental protection and 120th in terms of income distribution, in contrast to a public perception that it is either a classless or middle-class society. Some countries like Russia have improved economic competitiveness (after its financial collapse in 1985) despite poor rankings in economic and political freedoms. China, too, has moved from one of the least competitive countries in the world after World War II to one of the most competitive. On the other hand, it has only modestly provided more freedom, the benefits of its financial expansion have been largely limited to the top third of its population, and its environmental record is poor.

In terms of highly stakeholder-oriented industries, development banks are a pure example of the perspective. Development banks can be international, such as the World Bank, or local, such as community development banks, which will be our focus here. Community development banks are still commercial banks in the US, but their mission is to generate economic development for moderate- and low-income individuals and regions. They generally target financially underserved individuals and businesses, consciously try to do good, and not only involve stakeholders, but try to improve the lives of the most vulnerable ones. Such banks are certified by the US Treasury as meeting appropriate guidelines. Examples of such banks in the US include Carver Federal Savings Bank in New York, ShoreBank in Chicago, Hope Community Credit Union in Jackson, MS, and Neighborhood National Bank in San Diego. Internationally, the most famous example of a massively successful community bank is Grameen Bank of Bangladesh, which made microfinance to the very poor a perspective of success and earned the founder a Nobel Peace Prize.

In summary, a comparison of the three perspectives indicates that they fall along a spectrum. In its purist form, the shareholder perspective emphasizes the complete-as-possible separation of business and government,

Exhibit 2.6

A comparison of four countries and their economic, competitiveness, and civic responsibility rankings shareholder perspective: EPI/Human Development Index

Country	*Heritage Economic Freedom (2021; 160 countries)*	*Global Competitive ness Index (2019; 141 countries)*	*Human Development Index (2021; 189 countries)*	*EPI (2020; 132 countries)*	*Gini Coefficient of Income Distribution (World Factbook; 174 countries)*
Singapore	1	1	11	39	147
US	20	2	17	54	120
Russia	92	43	58	58	94
China	107	28	85	120	100

would even shun assistance from government, and implicitly wants as small a government as possible, with nearly all services being provided by the private sector and an absolute focus on wealth creation. At the other end of the spectrum, the stakeholder perspective asserts that business interests should never be at the expense of society's long-term interests, cooperation for social benefit is for everyone's benefit, and that when business self-regulates there can be less government. Somewhere in the middle is a more strategic approach, which is probably the most common because of its pragmatic implications. The strategic approach accepts the role of government as a given and as generally useful, utilizes the many opportunities to prosper from the sale of products, services, and various types of cooperation with government, uses its influence to ensure that government policies are as favorable as possible, and ultimately appreciates government for doing those things that are not very profitable. These roles are summarized in Exhibit 2.7.

When the Ideal Perspectives Become Corrupted: Crony Capitalism

Each of the perspectives already identified is ideologically distinct, and, for discussion purposes, assumes that business–government relations are transparent, fair to all groups in society, and relatively free of corruption. However, these "ideal" perspectives are often degraded to varying degrees, and when this is so, the type of perspective reported to be important by the regime may be less important than the level and types of business influence functioning at the expense of the public good. We identify this general problem as crony capitalism. *Crony capitalism* refers to an economy, or parts of an economy, in which there are close relationships between business and government that lead to favored treatment of individuals, companies, or even entire industries at the expense of the public good. For this discussion we include crony socialism (e.g., in contemporary China) and related terms that are sometimes used to identify power collusion by elites such as

Exhibit 2.7

Comparison of three perspectives of business–government relations

Perspectives	*Shareholder*	*Strategic*	*Stakeholder*
Role of Societal Interests	Complete separation of financial and societal interests	Mix of financial interests of which some social interests are a strategic part	Financial interests should never override social good
Integration of Private and Public Sectors	Sectors should be as separate as possible; there should be as little regulation or financial incentives for business (as distorting the market) as possible	The sectors do work together and business should benefit from the advantages and support of government; lobbying and taking advantage of incentives is a fact of life	The business sector should not manipulate the public sector for its selfish ends, because in the long term, there are social costs to pay; furthermore, it is unethical
Size of Government	Government should be as small as possible; private sector perspectives are generally preferred in all arenas	Government needs to be large enough to ensure basic services that provide a minimum quality of life in which an advanced economy thrives	Government does not need to be as regulatory and intrusive if business has some degree of self-regulation and strong professional norms
Key Values	Short-term wealth creation, self-reliance, dynamic destruction by market; win–lose philosophy	Long-term wealth creation, synergy of sectors and selective partnerships, pragmatic use of and even exploitation of government, do good when it is profitable and sound to do so; change is both strategic/rational and a result of legal forces as society dictates; game theory (remember that others remember bad behavior)	Wealth creation never at expense of some stakeholders; inclusion of stakeholders or stakeholder interests whenever possible and useful; win-win strategies almost always possible and make everyone feel good; concern for the world we live in is integrated into business principles

decadent capitalism, no matter whether the country has leanings toward being a plutocracy (ruled by wealth) or kleptocracy (ruled by theft). The effect of crony capitalism is to stifle competition and distort the market using government power for the few.

Crony capitalism can be thought of as a spectrum, from blatant biases toward business and/or family elites who forcefully dominate both government and the economy, to subtle biases that simply give elites a substantial but long-term edge over start-up innovators, poorly financed companies, or localized businesses wanting to break into national markets. The most blatant version is the *strongman model* in which a domineering leader and his/her allied group occupy the government by force or rigged elections. This model is common in dictatorships and quasi-dictatorships common to South America, Africa, the Middle East, and central Asia. Such countries witness occasional criminal charges against successful business people to eliminate competition, and the jailing of political competitors who want a more fair political and legal system. While such countries are a part of the capitalistic system generally, a key feature is the erratic enforcement of vague laws, giving government officials opportunities for bribes. Russia is an example of such a country.

A second version that is only somewhat subtler is the *fused political-bureaucratic elite model*. This is an aristocratic model where family or in-group asset owners tend to dominate both business and politics. Generally bribery and corruption are rampant. Examples of this model include Indonesia, China, Mexico, Brazil, India, and many other developing countries.

The subtlest version is the *economic elite dominance model* where economic elites do not have full control but do have outsized influence because of the power of money. Those with a lot of money will always have some additional power, but unchecked, that power can become overwhelming and thereby distort the market and create unhealthy imbalances in civil society. Five of the means by which powerful financial interests in society can corrupt the economic-political system are identified below.

1 Powerful economic elites can have the ability to change critical administrative rule-making because of the long-term resources they wield, leading to a condition called regulatory capture. At its most complete, regulatory capture means that the primary function of regulatory bodies is to keep newcomers out, rather than monitor established industries or license holders. This is most prone to happen in licensing and in heavy state involvement of "rent-seeking" sectors such as large-scale transportation, energy production, commercial real estate, and defense (via government contracts) at the corporate level, or high-end professions at the individual level. For example, when licensing becomes more about ultra-high standards, it may actually be more beneficial to the members of the profession to reduce competition rather than for the good of the public. Another example is where economically advantaged

groups have the ability to exert excessively expansive patent rights, holding competitors up in the courts for years as JPMorgan did in the budding electric industry with Westinghouse in 1895.

2 Powerful economic interests can exert immense influence via outright control of media or through paid political and policy messaging. Such messaging sometimes bombards the public with direct arguments for policy issues or political stances. However, it is also often to disseminate information that is purposely confusing or highly distorted, or to make complaints about largely fictitious challenges being faced by industries that are actually financially very well off.
3 Powerful economic interests have increased opportunity to be members of the political establishment (rather than just influence it) when the cost and challenge of running for major offices is more difficult. For example, while the poor can run for the US Senate, the average Senator was worth about $2.4 million in 2021, excluding private residences and pensions.
4 Powerful economic interests can buy access based on economic support of candidates as well. This can lead to not-so-subtle government intervention. A famous example was exposed in the Charles Keating scandal that erupted in 1989. Keating amassed a fortune in the poorly regulated savings and loan industry, but went on to make enormously risky business decisions with depositors' savings and bondholder investments. As he saw his decisions leading to greater and greater losses unknown to the public, his contributions to five US congressmen grew. When regulators began to look at taking the bank over, he asked the congressmen to intervene in his behalf in 1987, and all of them did to varying degrees, which resulted in the initial investigation being halted. By the time Keating's savings and loan finally failed, it cost taxpayers $3 billion to support depositor savings and left an additional 23,000 bondholders without recourse. Subsequently, three of the congressmen were formally reprimanded and two received informal reprimands because of the extraordinary damage caused by their unwise intervention. While this case became public, American history is also famous for cases in which big money has been quietly successful, such as the presidential election victory of McKinley who was heavily financed by tycoons like Andrew Carnegie and John D. Rockefeller.
5 Powerful economic interests can sometimes have the ability to "buy off" portions of the electorate with threats (e.g., loss of employment) or by making unwise concessions to the public that will return to haunt the country later. Greek tycoons, in league with Wall Street and the government of the day, kept the Greek economy floating with usurious loans despite unsustainable public expenditures. When the financial downturn occurred in 2008, the public received a rude awakening when it learned that it had a heavy price to pay in terms of reduced services, pensions, and public sector workforce.

Exhibit 2.8

Selective examples from Corruption Perceptions Index published by Transparency International for 2020. Singapore, the US, Russia, and China are highlighted

Country	*CPI Score*	*CPI Rank*
Denmark	**88**	1
New Zealand	**88**	1
Singapore	**85**	3
Canada	**77**	11
US	**67**	25
Taiwan	**65**	28
Israel	**60**	35
Italy	**53**	52
China	**42**	78
Mexico	**31**	124
Russia	**30**	129
Bangladesh	**26**	146
Nigeria	**25**	149
Iraq	**21**	160
Haiti	**18**	170
North Korea	**18**	170
Libya	**17**	173
Venezuela	**15**	176
Somalia	**12**	179

Source: Author-constructed table based on Transparency International data. https://www.transparency.org/.

It is important to remember that none of our ideological perspectives of business–government relations is exempt from crony capitalism. Strongly shareholder-oriented countries such as Hong Kong and Singapore have still allowed virtual monopolies of government controlled areas to flourish, driving up the cost of living. Strongly strategic-oriented countries such as Russia and Mexico have been unable to find a moral balance as the economic drivers favor crony businesses while government corruption flourishes. Even countries that utter a strongly shareholder-oriented philosophy, such as China and Greece, have evolved agendas that seem to have less to do with helping the poorest in the long term than aimed primarily at aiding the richest third in society.

Where does the US stand on various rankings of its level of crony capitalism? If one looks at outright government corruption, the US stands as the 29th *least* corrupt out of 180 countries; that is a relatively low level and is primarily aimed at political corruption rather than administrative bribery. However, the US corruption ranking has fallen recently due to attacks on whistle-blowers and inspectors general responsible for reporting corruption. See Exhibit 2.8 for an example of a prominent overall corruption index of countries.

Another vantage point is to look at the level of wealth in sectors in which government regulation gives insiders (those with established wealth) an edge; in a ranking by *The Economist*, the US was the 17th *most* prone to crony capitalism based on rent-seeking industries rather than entrepreneurial industries. For this survey, this means that the US still has more of its super-wealth in entrepreneurial industries such as the booming technology sector. Some other examples of countries high in both types of crony capitalism include Russia, Ukraine, Indonesia, Mexico, and the Philippines. Hong Kong is an unusual case in which outright corruption is very low, but the lack of an anti-competition law until very recently has resulted in numerous, well-entrenched oligopolies; despite its tiny size, the special administrative region is home to 70 billionaires as of 2020 (Forbes 2021). Japan and South Korea are examples of where neither of these surveys fully picks up the governmental influence of Japanese or South Korean informal conglomerates (called *keiretsu* and *chaebol*, respectively) because despite their anti-competitive power domestically, they remain highly competitive industries on the global stage.

A final frame of reference is the relative spread of income distribution across the population as a proxy for the product of crony capitalism. In other words, from this viewpoint, when the distribution of wealth in a country is moderate and there is a strong middle class, crony capitalism is in check; when there is a large lower class, a small middle class, and a super-rich upper class, crony capitalism is likely operating. The data here shows that the gap between rich and poor has been increasing around the world since the 1980s, including the US where policies have encouraged what some have labeled winner-take-all philosophies (Piketty 2014).

Analytical Case: The Lewis Group of Companies

The Lewis Group of Companies (LGC) (http://www.lewisop.com) is a privately held real estate development corporation which focuses on mixed-use planned communities and residential subdivisions in California and other states, as well as building and owning rental communities, shopping centers, office parks, and industrial buildings. Founded in Claremont, California in 1955, LGC has developed thousands of homes, apartments, retail, office, and industrial space for the city and its surrounding areas, as well as elsewhere in California and other states. Real estate development is a multifaceted business. It typically involves a process where a developer purchases a parcel of land, determines the marketing of the property, develops the design and building programs, obtains financing, builds the structures, and leases, manages, or sells it. The company tries to make relationships with local officials prior to committing to projects to ensure support (or steer clear of the project early on) with the officials who will inspect plans and buildings countless times, the transportation department with regard to infrastructure, the zoning department with regard to use permission, and the state environmental protection agency with regard to an environmental impact assessment. Should Native American remains be discovered or water run-off adversely affect other properties, additional government officials will be on site quite quickly!

Real estate development is critical to a community, because it affects the appearance, the mix of land uses, the infrastructure (such as roads, water, sewerage, drainage systems, and utilities), and ultimately the economic condition of the community. It is one of the riskiest yet most profitable businesses because there is a long investment period without positive cash flow, and economic downturns or unexpected problems can scuttle projects with enormous loss of sunk costs.

The Lewis company currently hires over 400 employees in a variety of areas. The development process requires skills of many professionals, such as architects and civil engineers to address project design; market consultants to determine demand and a project's economics; attorneys to handle agreements and government approvals; environmental consultants to analyze a site's physical limitations and environmental impacts; inspectors and title companies to provide legal descriptions of a property; lenders to provide financing; and public relation experts to deal with issues related to media and the communities. The top management of the company is also heavily involved with strategic planning in all the jurisdictions in which the company operates.

Questions for Discussion and Analysis

1 With what issues does LGC have to deal with government? How important are good relations with government officials in LGC's industry?
2 If you were the CEO of LGC, which perspective would you adopt to develop BGR strategies? Why? Visit the company's website. Based on information from the company's website, what BGR perspective do you think the company has used? What is the evidence?
3 Who are the stakeholders of LGC? What are the "stakes" they have with LGC, and vice versa?

Practical Skill

Stakeholder Analysis

Stakeholder analysis refers to the process of identifying the individuals and groups that are likely to affect, or be affected by, a proposed course of action and analyzing their impact on the action, as well as the impact the action will have on them. It is a technique that is widely used in decision-making, project management, and conflict resolution.

Stakeholder analysis is used when there is a need to clarify the consequences of the envisioned change to ensure the successful outcomes of the action. There are a variety ways of conducting stakeholder analysis. Generally speaking, all of them include two components:

1 *Identifying stakeholders.* Any proposed course of action may involve a multitude of stakeholders that can be impacted or cause an impact on the action. In a given situation, the primary stakeholders are those who are ultimately affected, either positively or negatively, by the action. Secondary stakeholders are those who are indirectly affected by the action. It is critical to identify all stakeholders, to comprehensively understand the implications of a proposed action.
2 *Mapping stakeholders.* The potential list of stakeholders for any proposed action may exceed the capacity of analysis; therefore, it is more feasible to focus on the important stakeholders. To map stake holders is to develop a table or picture by categorizing the members and assigning priorities in certain ways. Some commonly used dimensions for categorizing (and degrees to prioritizing stakeholders) include power/influence (high, medium, low), attitude/support (positive, neutral, negative), and need/interest (strong, medium, weak) (Mitchell, Agle, and Wood 1997).

The map is often presented in a matrix format with two dimensions of interest. A third dimension can be added by integrating color scheme, font size, or symbols.

For example, a stakeholder map may look like:

	Positive Attitude	*Neutral Attitude*	*Negative Attitude*
High Power	Stakeholder A	Stakeholder B	Stakeholder C
Medium Power	Stakeholder D	Stakeholder E	Stakeholder F
Low Power	Stakeholder G	Stakeholder H	Stakeholder I

The table will help decision-makers better understand the impact of the action, set up priorities, balance the cost and benefits, and ultimately make a wise decision.

Skill Exercise: Stakeholder Analysis of ABC's Relocation

Read the opening case scenario: ABC's relocation. Create a list of stakeholders for ABC's relocation, identifying who are the primary, secondary, and key stakeholders (if there are any). Using the power–attitude matrix above, map the stakeholders.

Discuss how the analysis may inform you and how you would resolve the issue, if you were Zach's father, Zeddic.

Summary and Conclusion

1 Theories about business, government, and society are numerous. We examined three common business-centered approaches that often underlie public discussions of what proper business–government relations should be. We also examined a business–government perspective in which relations have been corrupted.

2 The first of two business-centric stances was the shareholder perspective. It considers only business interests, and asserts that the two sectors should be as separate as possible, with the implicit assumption that government should also be as small as possible. Its strength is its focus on economic principles of a pure market and the dynamism and innovation that such a focus can ideally lead to. Its weaknesses are that, pragmatically, business only wants government to step aside in terms of short-term gains, and rarely accounts for external effects and long-term effects, even negative ones for the market itself.

3 The second market-based stance was the strategic perspective. It assumes that business is but one of many players, and looks at maximizing business's success in a competitive and political world. From a long-term vantage point, it also includes a subordinate consideration of collaboration for both profit maximization from joining core competencies, as well as for public trust-building and public relations. Its weakness is that there is no ethical framework, and so ethical lapses may become common unless clear rules are spelled out in law (which limits flexibility).

4 The third market-based approach was the stakeholder perspective. It assumes that business is a fully integrated element of society, and must give as much attention to the interests of internal and external stakeholders as it does to owners or shareholders. It emphasizes the idea that society must balance both democratic as well as economic principles to be just and ensure social cohesion. Its strengths are that it reintegrates the social values that we were brought up to cherish and takes a long-term perspective toward business interests. Its weakness is that it is often argued that it, too, frequently goes beyond the appropriate realm of business, which is simply to make a profit and create jobs.

5 Understanding these different perspectives of business and society is useful to sort out complex debates and conflicting assertions. Often those involved in debates are essentially talking past one another because they have fundamentally different assumptions. However, even more importantly, those making arguments often change their assumptions to suit the specific argument, thereby having an eclectic and incoherent approach. Since government is not a monolith, but rather an enormous set of complex operations, it is also important to be able to understand the three major ways that it attempts to fulfill the American public's expectations. For example, the US Security and Exchange Commission is committed to the shareholder perspective by guaranteeing a fair playing field, the US Trade Representative's office fights for

the strategic position of American products, and the US Department of Health and Human Services is an advocate for the various constituents that make up society as represented in the stakeholder approach. A more sophisticated understanding of government, and the multiple approaches it is expected to embrace, allows business people to interact with government with both more comfort and effectiveness.

6 Finally, it is also important not to confuse the three different approaches listed above with crony capitalism, which is when any of these perspectives becomes distorted and corrupted to provide unfair advantages to small elite groups in society, using government as a primary tool. Crony capitalism ranges from the flagrant variety exhibited in dictatorships to the subtler varieties found in all democracies. While crony capitalist tendencies can never be eradicated, they can be enormously reduced, which ultimately is both critical for maintaining the trust of society in its business and government institutions, as well as for the long-term good of a healthy market economy.

Key Terms

- Competitiveness index
- Regulation
- Strategic business perspective
- Economic freedom index
- Shareholder perspective
- Stakeholder
- Subsidies
- Gini coefficient
- Stakeholder analysis
- Tax breaks
- Government "ownership"
- Stakeholder perspective

Study Questions

1 What are the issues that cause market failure? How can/does government deal with each of the issues?
2 What are the government policies that have affected the business of Boeing?
3 What are the advantages and disadvantages of using each of the three business-oriented approaches (the shareholder, strategic, and stakeholder perspectives)?
4 What do you think the balance of the three government-oriented perspectives (ownership, regulation, financial leverage) should be? What do you think the balance actually is? What direction do you think it is going? Discuss with examples.

References

Annual State Competitiveness Index: 18th (2020). Beacon Hill Institute. https://beaconhill.org/economic-competitiveness

Birchall, J. (2006). Wal-Mart Picks a Shade of Green. *Financial Times*, February 7. http://www.ft.com/cms/s/0/ba5fd83a-977d-11da-82b7-0000779e2340.html#axzz2-MRLDEOZu.

Boeing history. (n.d.) https://www.boeing.com/history.

Carroll, A. B. (1979). A Three-Dimensional Conceptual Model of Corporate Social Performance. *Academy of Management Review*, *4*:497–505.

Council on Competitiveness (2012). A Clarion Call for Competitiveness. http://www.compete.org/images/uploads/File/PDF%20Files/Clarion_Call.pdf.

Council on Competitiveness (2020). Competing in the Next Economy. https://compete.org/2020/12/14/competing-in-the-next-economy/

CRS (Congressional Research Service) (2021). Defense Primer: Department of Defense Contractors. https://crsreports.congress.gov/product/pdf/IF/IF10600.

DOJ (2021). Goldman Sachs Charged in Foreign Bribery Case and Agrees to Pay Over $2.9 Billion. https://www.justice.gov/opa/pr/goldman-sachs-charged-foreign-bribery-case-and-agrees-pay-over-29-billion.

Forbes (2021). The World's Billionaires. http://www.forbes.com.

Freeman, E. (1984). *Strategic Management: A Stakeholder Approach*. Boston: Pitman.

Heritage Foundation Website (2021). 2021 Index of Economic Freedom. http://www.heritage.org/index/ranking.

Lipton, E., Clark, N., and Lehren, A. (2011). Diplomats Help Push Sales of Jetliners on the Global Market. *The New York Times*, January 2. http://www.nytimes.com/2011/01/03/business/03wikileaks-boeing.html?pagewanted=all&_r=0.

Mitchell, R., Agle, B., and Wood, D. (1997). Toward a Theory of Stakeholder Identification and Salience: Defining the Principle of Who and What Really Counts. *Academy of Management Review*, *22(4)*:853–886.

Piketty, T. (2014). *Capital in the Twenty-First Century*. Cambridge, MA: Belknap Press of Harvard University Press.

Porter, M. E. (1998). Clusters and the New Economics of Competition. *Harvard Business Review*, *76(6)*:77–90.

Public Eye (2013). Hall of Shame. http://www.publiceye.ch/en/hall-of-shame/shamegoldmansachs/.

Transparency International (2021). *Corruption Perception Index*. https://www.transparency.org/en/cpi/2020/index/nzl.

3 Historical Development of Government's Roles with Business

Chapter Contents

This chapter identifies eight fundamental roles of government that have evolved over five very different phases of historical government throughout US history. Beginning with the first Anti-Central Government Era and the development of the first US Constitution in 1781 (the Articles of Confederation), the chapter examines four additional historical periods, including the Small Government Era, the Moderate-Sized Government Era, the Big Government Era, and the Rightsizing Government Era.

The eight roles of government that most affect business are as (1) a provider of monetary and fiscal structure, (2) a provider of infrastructure, (3) a purchaser, (4) a regulator of business, (5) a social architect, (6) a service provider, (7) a safeguarder against risk, and (8) a promoter of business. These eight different roles of government are presented in the discussion of the five phases of US historical development.

DOI: 10.4324/9781003178620-4

Case 3 Scenario

Zoey's Pet Store

Zoey has always been a pet lover, as we have learned from her commitment to her horse, Happy. She has dreamed of owning a pet store ever since she was child, but could never really quite figure out how to make that work. Zoey has now graduated from business college with a bachelor's degree in entrepreneurial management. She learned a substantive entrepreneurial skillset, including entrepreneurial opportunity analysis, business development, finance, marketing, small business management, and so on. Knowing about her long-time dream, Zoey's grandma recently gave Zoey her old house near Main Street in the City of Somewhere as a graduation gift. Zoey had been living in the house while going to school and was thrilled that she wouldn't have to move. In fact, Zoey always thought the house could be turned into an interesting business of sorts. And now it would be—her very own pet store!

Having lived in the house, Zoey knew that there was a lot of adult foot traffic from the veterinarian on the corner and from Splurge, the jewelry store next to it. The U Scream Ice Cream shop next to the jeweler guaranteed a lot of kids coming by. There was ample parking in front of her house, too; the only thing that seemed a little off-putting was the condition of the sidewalk out front and the faded look of the Victorian-style house. But overall, Zoey was thrilled.

Zoey feels that she is ready for her new venture; she wants to name her pet store "Happy Paws," so she needs to register the business name with the county clerk's office. As she gathers ideas together for her business, she finds that she has to deal with many more government issues. Zoey wants to run the business legally, so she must obtain all necessary federal and state licenses and permits. She was also told when she first inquired about her business that she cannot use her grandmother's house as it is right now. Zoey has to contact the municipal planning department to make sure the property and its improvements are compliant with zoning ordinances and regulations. Since Zoey wants her business to be a Limited Liability Company (LLC) as well, she needs to contact the Internal Revenue Service (IRS) about business taxes and obtain an Employer Identification Number (EIN). In addition to the federal government, she also has to contact the state agency for state and local tax registration.

Even though Zoey does not have plans to immediately hire any employees, she still needs to contact government agencies for worker's compensation insurance, unemployment insurance, disability insurance, and the like. Thank goodness her boyfriend Zach has offered to help out for free after work as much as he can! And she can count on her best friend Tyler to assist a bit after hours as well, especially creating product displays and a website.

Zoey's list is daunting and continues to grow, and it's only just after noon today! This makes her idea about the business seem like an extensive undertaking and causes her frustrations. It's a good thing that U Scream Ice Cream is just a few yards down the street. Zoey grabs her purse and calls Zach to see if he can meet her there.

Zoey is facing issues that are common to business owners today. A good understanding about the government's roles with business and knowledge about adequate resources will help her achieve her business goals. This chapter introduces the theoretical underpinnings of government institutions and public policies that are relevant to businesses. The development of government's various roles with business in their historical contexts will be reviewed. The text also teaches fledgling business owners how to access resources and gain the skills needed for successful government interactions.

Introduction: Growth of Government with Democratization of Quality of Life

The benefits of modern life spring from many sources. Science has brought us cures and preventions for innumerable diseases, thousands of new products—from stainless steel to plastic, the ability to predict the weather with satellites, and improved agricultural products, among many other advances and innovations. Technologies have brought us mass production, progressive modes of transportation, myriad types of communication, and so on. Yet our improved life is also the result of higher standards imposed upon the quality of life, and these standards are chiefly provided by our social expectations as expressed through government. We want our money system to be secure, our roads to be smooth and free, our food and drugs to be safe, our products to be sound, our basic opportunities for education to be available to all, and our businesses and jobs to be protected from unfair competition. And we expect that all these benefits, and countless others, will be identified, delineated, and adequately regulated by government today. As discussed in Chapter 1, using the example of disaster assistance, government is much larger today because the roles we expect it to perform are vastly more substantial and demanding than even a century ago.

This chapter provides the background of that growth in government, beginning with the American Revolution, which itself was a consequence of government—Great Britain's, that is—imposing oppressive rules on the new American colonies to benefit the powerful and rich back home. Using the eight roles of government that most affect business, we examine five historical periods: the *Anti-Central Government Era*, the *Small Government Era*, the *Moderate-Sized Government Era*, the *Big Government Era*, and the *Rightsizing Government Era*. These different roles of government were introduced over time and expanded at different rates, and today some of the roles that government plays are under more pressure to be reduced or changed (or rightsized) than others.

For example, the federal regulation of business was virtually non-existent for the first century that the country was in existence. This was largely due to the fact that businesses tended to be much smaller and more locally focused, and because of that were far less able to have any noticeable or negative widespread environmental impact, and were also less able to monopolize whole markets. Business had almost total freedom, except for breach of contract. Local regulation of business was largely limited to the tasks of licensing and taxing. When these conditions changed dramatically after the Civil War, eventually government regulation was used to recalibrate an economic system that had fallen victim to unfairly distorting what was once a fair market.

The *Anti-Central Government Era* coincided with the Articles of Confederation and was relatively short-lived, stretching from 1781 to 1787. States were sovereign and virtually no federal involvement with business was contemplated.

The *Small Government Era* lasted from 1787 to 1887, during which time the country grew from 13 small colonies to 38 states spanning the continent. During the Small Government Era, the population grew to be 15 times the size it had been; the percentage that was urban versus rural grew from just 3.35 percent to 30 percent in that century. The US government accepted the role of facilitating growth in select sectors (railroads, colleges) in order to advance continental development.

The *Moderate-Sized Government Era* is defined as the period from 1887 to 1933, a time during which the economic GDP expanded greatly and which included the "age of invention." As the introduction of technology began to change urban life, leading to great industrial success but also producing significant challenges to the quality of life for many Americans—governments at all levels began to explore minimal interventions that provided some restraint on business practices.

The *Big Government Era*, from 1933 to the 1970s, was ushered in by the Great Depression (1929–1939), followed closely by the vast and expensive World War II, but also included a quarter-century post-war boom. With the collapse of the national economy, the federal government assumed an expanded role in regulating business to maintain a stable economy and address serious social needs.

The *Rightsizing Government Era* began in the 1970s and presently continues, as the limits of government began to exceed the expectations that had accumulated and the resources it was likely to get. During this period, GDP growth has slowed, real wages are often stagnant, and tough choices have to be made about addressing old problems, all while envisioning and implementing an ideal for the largely post-industrial society we are becoming. As a reaction to government becoming too large and inefficient, governments at all levels began a sustained period of adjusting the policies and practices of business to respond to the dominant political beliefs of the time.

The Anti-Central Government Era (1781–1787): Very Limited Roles

The origin of the US began with the rebellion against the British government. On July 2, 1776, the Second Continental Congress, composed of members from the 13 colonies, adopted a Resolution of Independence in a move for separation:

> Resolved, That these United Colonies are, and of right ought to be, free and independent States, that they are absolved from allegiance to the British Crown, and that all political connection between them and the state of Great Britain is, and ought to be, totally dissolved.

In the Declaration of Independence, the founding fathers of the nation stated their fundamental reasons for creating a new government:

> We hold these truths to be self-evident, that all men are created equal, that they are endowed by their Creator with certain unalienable Rights, that among these are Life, Liberty and the pursuit of Happiness.—That to secure these rights, Governments are instituted among Men, deriving their just powers from the consent of the governed,—That whenever any Form of Government becomes destructive of these ends, it is the Right of the People to alter or to abolish it, and to institute new Government ....

To the founding fathers, the powers of governments should be derived from the consent of the people governed, and, it follows, the right to change or to abolish those powers of governments should also be in the hands of the people.

During the founding era of the nation, the prevailing sentiment was the strong fear of a forceful central government. This led to the drafting and passage of the Articles of Confederation. The *Confederation* was a voluntary association, or league, of independent member states who agreed to only a limited number of restrictions on their freedom. Under the Articles, the Congress of the Confederation—a government of the 13 colonial states—was established on March 1, 1781.

Under Article II of the Articles of Confederation, each state still retained its sovereignty, minus several agreed-upon functions that were relinquished to the fledgling central government. All state and municipal governments functioned relatively as they had in the past, in some cases for 150 years. Taxes were collected by the state, justice and laws were handled separately by each and, as a local example, municipalities typically required citizens to maintain their adjacent sidewalks and streets. The Articles allowed the single-bodied central government, Congress, to print money, maintain an army for the common defense, appoint ambassadors, and pay off the national debt of the war, but not much more.

Most critically, Congress did not have the authority to levy taxes; rather, they could only request proportional levies from the states, which could be, and were commonly, ignored. Debts from the American Revolution often languished, putting the credibility of the nation's government at risk. The inability to raise money also meant that most of the army was dissolved, allowing incursions from the British in Canada and the Spanish in Florida to jeopardize the mutual welfare of the states. An inability to put down a small rebellion in Massachusetts in a timely fashion when assistance was requested was the last straw as the vulnerability and fragmentation of the new country became obvious.

The country had a plan for the development of the West, but lacked the wherewithal to physically carry out the concomitant transportation, communication, and military needs. A special session of Congress was called in 1786 to consider a new national charter for government, one that would provide a central government with enough power to provide core functions such as defense and foreign relations, and some basic internal government roles. The idea was for a federal system in which the bulk of governance was to be administered by the states.

The Small Government Era (1787–1887): More Limited Roles

On September 17, 1787, the Constitution was approved by delegates from the 13 states. The Constitution addressed the major concerns of the colonists—(1) the fear of government power, but a recognition that the new country needed a stronger government; (2) the challenge of finding a governing principle that would be supported by both the four states with the largest population and the seven smaller states; and (3) a strong desire to protect minority rights (the fear of the "tyranny of the majority"). In so doing, the new Constitution established several fundamental principles, such as popular sovereignty under the control of the people, and limited central government, in direct contrast to the powerful British government against which the colonial states had rebelled. It also provided separation of powers—with checks and balances among three branches of government—in order to prevent any one of them from gaining too much power (Bardes et al. 2012).

The Constitution granted the national government a number of powers, including the ability to tax foreign goods, to print money, to establish a system of federal courts, to set up agencies for national issues such as foreign affairs and treasury, and to regulate commerce among the states. Each state still retained the right to control commerce within its borders. Another important enumerated power was the ability to create a postal system and accompanying roads, a function that would become a hallmark responsibility for a country that was growing ever Westward and constantly evolving in its modes of transportation.

The most significant growth of government roles in this era was in those associated with substantial infrastructure support (primarily transportation) and the promotion of business through foreign policy. Although the monetary and fiscal structure role was modest, it was still important and is reviewed first below for context. Much more modest roles existed in public purchasing, social architecture, and direct social service provision.

Provider of Monetary and Fiscal Structure

What we often take for granted today as a central role of government started with Alexander Hamilton, who served as Secretary of the Treasury in the George Washington Administration (1789–1797). With support from President Washington, Hamilton convinced Congress to pass a financial program that funded the debts of the American Revolution, established a national bank, set up a system of tariffs and taxes, and built up friendly trade relations with Britain. See Exhibit 3.1 for a brief history of banking in the US.

Hamilton's efforts in building a strong national government with a broad financial base faced resistance from the Republican Party (which differs from the present-day Republican Party), led by Thomas Jefferson (1743–1826) and James Madison (1751–1836). Jefferson argued for strong state and local governments and a weak federal government. To Jefferson, nothing that could possibly be done by individuals at the local level should be undertaken by the federal government. When Jefferson won the election of 1800, in his inaugural speech, he promised a limited government that would preserve the order among the inhabitants but "leave them otherwise free to regulate their own pursuits of industry, and improvement" (Jefferson 1975). By the end of his second term, Jefferson had significantly reduced national debt, the number of executive department employees, and military spending. He set a Conservative fiscal path that was generally followed by the federal government in the Small Government Era.

Promoter of Business

Despite President Jefferson's anti-central government views, he went to war with the Barbary pirates in the northern Mediterranean, and he bought the Louisiana Purchase through executive order, doubling the size of the US. These measures protected American shipping on one hand, and opened up a vast commercial opportunity on the other.

Also during Jefferson's tenure, the American Industrial Revolution was indirectly stimulated by the *Chesapeake–Leopard* Affair, a naval incident between the British warship *Leopard* and American frigate *Chesapeake*. In short, the crew of the *Leopard* attacked the *Chesapeake*. The *Chesapeake* was caught off guard and quickly surrendered to the British after firing only one shot. The British boarded the American frigate looking for deserters. They seized four men and hanged one for desertion. The affair aroused outrage among Americans and harsh calls for war with Great Britain. As a result, Congress passed the Embargo Act, which stopped the export of American goods, and thus hurt commerce. However, it also stopped the import of goods from other countries, which encouraged American industrialization. Eventually, it was also one of a number of aggravations that led to the War of 1812 against Great Britain.

Another important political event was the Monroe Doctrine in 1823. President Monroe declared that foreign powers could not become involved in the affairs of independent countries in the Western Hemisphere, with the implied threat of military intervention by the US. This doctrine was put forth because of the fact that most of the Spanish New World colonies had declared independence between 1817 and 1823, and the US did not want Spain or any other world powers to take advantage of these new weak states. It also made the entire North and South American continents part of the special US sphere of influence. This was tested in Mexico during the American Civil War, when French Emperor Napoleon Bonaparte III invaded Mexico for unpaid loans, and persuaded Austrian Hapsburg Duke Maximilian to become its Emperor. After the US Civil War was over, the US created a blockade of Mexico and massed 50,000 soldiers at the US border. Because of an internal rebellion and the prospect of a war with the US, the French withdrew their forces and the Emperor was deposed without an American incursion.

Exhibit 3.1

First Bank of the United States

Source: Wikimedia Commons (2012). Kanan H. Jani.

First Bank of the United States (1797–1811): 116 South 3rd Street, Philadelphia, PA.

The First Bank of the United States was established by the US Congress on February 25, 1791. It was championed by Alexander Hamilton, first Secretary of the Treasury, with the belief that the bank was necessary to stabilize the economy, improve the nation's credit, and facilitate the operations of financial business. Hamilton's idea encountered severe opposition led by Secretary of State Thomas Jefferson, who charged that the bank would benefit merchants and investors at the cost of the general mass.

Unlike commercial banks, the First Bank was a central bank, which is a public institution that assumes the authority to oversee a country's fiscal and monetary issues, such as national currency, money supply, interest rates, as well as the operation of the commercial banking system.

The First Bank was chartered for 20 years. After its expiration, the bank was succeeded by the Bank of North America, and later the Second Bank of the United States. When the charter for the Second Bank of the United States ended in 1836, the country did without a central bank for over 75 years. In 1913, under the Federal Reserve Act, the Congress created the Federal Reserve System (also known as the Federal Reserve or the Fed) to be the central bank of the US, which is still in operation today. Over time, the role of the Federal Reserve has expanded.

The US expansionist policies during the nineteenth century were a great boon to American business and not merely limited to the Louisiana Purchase and the Monroe Doctrine. Some other prominent actions of the US government included the purchase of Florida (1819), the annexation of Texas (1845)—which led to the Mexican–American War (1846–1848) and opened the way to the annexation of California (1850) and other western areas north of the Rio Grande—the Gadsden Purchase (1853), and the purchase of Alaska (1867). All in all, albeit indirectly, the US was a substantial and self-conscious promoter of business interests in the Small Government Era, which is ultimately not surprising given the strong commercial heritage of the former colonies.

After the Civil War, a period called the Gilded Age began. The Gilded Age was a reference to the immense fortunes that were being created. Numerous super-rich industrialists, business people, and financiers emerged, such as John D. Rockefeller, J. P. Morgan, Andrew W. Mellon, Andrew Carnegie, Henry Flagler, Cornelius Vanderbilt, and the Astors. The positive aspects of this period included the facts that the economy was booming, real wages were increasing, and the US was preparing to emerge as a world power. Negative aspects of this period could be seen in the rampant industrialization that brought poor and sometimes horrific working conditions for many, and the fact that the South did not participate in the boom. There was also a growing resentment toward the fabulously wealthy, who were thought to have gotten much of their wealth in underhand ways, such as the extensive use of child labor, policies used to keep immigrant labor wages low, substandard products, and cozy deals with the government. All of these factors assisted in giving rise to a negative term for this elite class—Robber Barons. See Exhibit 3.3 for a profile of John D. Rockefeller, an example of a prototypical Gilded Age Robber Baron.

Exhibit 3.2

Crewmen of the *Chesapeake* prepare one cannon shot during the *Chesapeake–Leopard* affair

Source: Wikimedia Commons (1896). Willis J. Abbot.

Exhibit 3.3

Profile of a Robber Baron: John D. Rockefeller

Profile of a Robber Baron: John D. Rockefeller (18 years old).
Source: Wikimedia Commons (1991). Project Gutenberg. Yergin. https://commons.wikimedia.org/wiki/File:John_D._Rockefeller_aged_18_-_Project_Gutenberg_eText-t_17090-crop.jpg.

John D. Rockefeller lived from 1839 to 1937, a period of great commercial change. He received a better-than-average middle-class education, readily absorbed the skills of mathematics and debate, and learned to appreciate music and discipline. Early jobs as a bookkeeper, operations manager, and distributor set him up well for his entry into the kerosene business. When he entered the business, kerosene was just becoming a substitute for the expensive and diminishing lighting fuel, whale oil. By the time he was 24, he and his partners had built their first kerosene refinery. He expanded the refinery business in his late

20s, and proceeded to corner the market in his early 30s. In 1872, his company, Standard Oil, absorbed 22 of 26 local competitors. Thereafter, he used his power with railroads to get exceptional deals, and Standard occasionally dropped pricing below market costs to crush all significant competition. Standard owned its own pipelines, tank cars, and home delivery network. To increase the use of his commodity and often to turn waste by-products to productive use, Rockefeller encouraged Standard Oil to develop (or acquire the license for) dozens of oil-based products including paint, tar, Vaseline jelly, and chewing gum. Standard was refining over 90 percent of the oil in the US by the end of the decade. In 1882, he melded his many companies in the modern diversified corporation, Standard Oil Trust, and invented the futures market by selling rights to stored oil. In the 1880s, Standard Oil was producing 85 percent of world production at its peak, which dropped thereafter; nonetheless, it still maintained nearly 70 percent of overall world refining by the time it was broken up in 1911 into 34 different companies. By 1902, an audit showed Rockefeller's wealth at $200 million; it rapidly increased to $900 million by the time he retired. Because his oil stock continued to increase in value in retirement, his fortune was valued at approximately $1.4 billion at his death. Not only was he the richest man in the world—estimated by the *New York Times* as $192 billion in 2007 dollar value—it ranks him as the wealthiest man in modern times. Despite his merciless and sometimes unscrupulous business practices, Rockefeller was a devout Baptist, and gave approximately one half of his fortune to philanthropy.

Government as Infrastructure Provider

During the war with Great Britain in 1812, America realized the importance of an effective transportation system. As early as 1806, President Thomas Jefferson authorized the construction of the first national road—Cumberland Road (part of today's US Route 40), which connects the Potomac and Ohio Rivers.

With the notable exception of the transcontinental railroads, state and local governments were the primary supporters of this role. Most state and local infrastructure projects were small but important in terms of building up municipal transportation systems. However, a significant number of them changed the nation's economy. The construction of the Erie Canal in 1817 was a state government transportation project that brought an enormous impact to commerce in New York and Lake Erie. The 363-mile water route now extended from the Atlantic Ocean all the way to the tip of the

Great Lakes. The canal project was championed by Jesse Hawley, a flour merchant in Geneva, New York, who envisioned selling large quantities of grain grown on the western New York plains to the eastern seaboard. New York Governor DeWitt Clinton received approval from the legislature for $7 million to be used in its construction. Construction started in 1817 and the canal was officially opened on October 26, 1825. The Erie Canal reduced transportation costs immensely, fostered a population surge in western New York State, and made New York City the chief US port and trade center.

A second state and local government infrastructure example was the rise of American bridge building. A classic illustration would be the succession of the world's longest suspension bridges completed during the Small Government Era. Starting with the Wheeling Bridge in 1849, connecting Wheeling, West Virginia and Ohio, this long suspension construction spanned the Ohio River. The Roebling Suspension Bridge in Cincinnati took the honor of longest bridge in 1867. The Brooklyn Bridge, connecting the two New York City boroughs of Manhattan and Brooklyn in 1883, was the next to be the world's longest, and held the title for decades. All are still in active use today, and in fact, regionally funded bridges kept the record in the US until 1981.

Perhaps the most significant role government played with business during this era was in the active development of the railroad system. State governments usually granted charters to create the railroad corporations, which were given a limited right of eminent domain to buy needed land for a railroad project. In assisting business corporations in building the railroads, government also provided crucial technical support, especially through detailing officers from the Army Corps of Engineers, the nation's only repository of civil-engineering expertise. Railroads in the US started with a 13-mile section of the Baltimore and Ohio Railroad in 1830. The second railroad corridor to open in the nation ran 136 miles from Charleston to Hamburg in South Carolina. Though initially slow to begin, starting from 1850, the US railroad system experienced phenomenal growth (see Exhibit 3.4).

Exhibit 3.4

Railroad mileage increase by groups of states

	1850	*1860*	*1870*	*1880*	*1890*
New England	2,507	3,660	4,494	5,982	6,831
Middle States	3,202	6,705	10,964	15,872	21,536
Southern States	2,036	8,838	11,192	14,778	29,209
Western States and Territories	1,276	11,400	24,587	52,589	62,394
Pacific States and Territories		23	1,677	4,080	9,804
Totals	9,021	30,626	52,914	93,301	129,774

By the start of the Civil War, railroads linked the most important Midwest cities with the Atlantic coast. However, it was the massive support from the US federal government in terms of land grants and loans that led to the first transcontinental railroad, which started construction at the end of the Civil War and finally completed work at Promontory Point, Utah in 1869. It connected two railway lines—the Union Pacific's rail line that originated in Omaha, Nebraska and ran toward the West, and the Central Pacific rail that began in Sacramento, California and ran toward the east. With two additional transcontinental lines being completed in 1883, federal support was no longer needed. In fact, the wealth and power of the railroads would become an issue in the next era.

The expanded transportation system and abundant natural resources of the country, as well as the great acceleration of technological innovations, largely fueled the industrial revolution in the US. Starting in 1820, the US rapidly evolved from an agrarian state to an industrial power. By 1860, 16 percent of Americans lived in cities with populations of 2,500 or more people, and one third of the nation's income now came from manufacturing. During the 1870s and 1890s, the US experienced the fastest economic growth in its history to date.

Modest Roles: Government as Purchaser, Service Provider, and Social Architect

The development of the transportation infrastructure also largely expanded government's role as purchaser with business. Transportation projects often involved large public funds paid to private corporations for design, construction, operation, and maintenance. In addition to the infrastructure development, government's role as purchaser was also largely enhanced through military contracts in this time period.

As early as the Revolutionary War, colonial rebels came to know the advantages of purchasing military supplies from business (Weitzel 2011). Robert Morris (1734–1806), whom Congress appointed to be the first Superintendent of Finance in 1871, installed the first sealed-bid system for military contracts. Morris' system was constantly adapted and modified over the course of the next several decades. By the Mexican–American War of 1846–1848, Army quartermasters became the official contracting agents for the Army, taking on the responsibilities of sustaining remote combat-ready forts across the vast American frontier. In the early years of the Civil War, quartermaster officers used a variety of ways to obtain necessary military supplies, from advertising for large-quantity contracts, to making small direct purchases, to even using the authority to build their own factories for military goods (Weitzel 2011). Military contracts became a critical vehicle for sustaining and supplying US Army forces. Of course, the purchase of supplies escalated dramatically during wars, which included the war of 1812, the Mexican–American War, and the Civil War.

The government's original role as service provider began with the Post Office, which was an early federal department and the nation's first communication system. Otherwise, the service provider function was negligible at the beginning of this long period, but later became a modest role as the country grew wealthier. Counties and other local governments sometimes created "poor farms" and/or county hospitals. Poor farms provided a means for orphaned children and the destitute to receive shelter, support, and work at public expense. County hospitals after the Civil War began providing medical care for the indigent or rural care for fees in areas where doctors would otherwise be lacking. Wealthier municipalities started supplying some other services such as public libraries, although all social services were supported more by means of charity than by government in this era.

The government's role as social architect also started out as virtually nonexistent, with no compulsory education, no public education infrastructure, and relatively high illiteracy, as was common at that time in the world. Much elementary education was supported by religious institutions, in particular the Catholic Church. While there were some very early examples of public education being supported by local governments, the practice did not start to become commonplace until mid-century. One of the provisions of the vast government land grants to the railroads was that they set aside land to be used for schools.

In the first half of the nineteenth century, higher education was primarily a privilege for men belonging to the upper class. That started to change with the Morrill Land Grant College Act of 1862. That Act sold off federal lands and gave one-time federal endowments to propel at least one state-level university to accept students of merit with more affordable fees in every state in the union. Dozens of these universities rank among the top 100 universities in both the US and world today. The system produced a large number of agricultural scientists and industrial engineers who constituted the crucial human resources of the managerial revolution in government and business. The system also laid the foundation for the educational infrastructure that supported the nation's technology-based economy.

The Moderate-Sized Government Era (1887–1933): Somewhat Expanded Roles

The political landscape for the US tended to have an internal focus during this time frame, as the economy bustled with Western expansion and settlement, and the incorporation of new inventions such as light bulbs, telephones, automobiles, and airplanes kept business and government busy. Nonetheless, it was an imperialist age, and while the US acquisition of land outside the continental US was more modest than some of its European counterparts, it was generally more strategic in the long-term. The last significant war of land expansion occurred with Spain in 1898; the US was drawn into World War I late and US business did extremely well.

The Modern-Sized Government Era inherited the problems of the Gilded Age (1877–1893), which was replaced by the Progressive Era (roughly 1890–1920), a period which focused on both reforming and expanding government.

The most prominent Progressive of the period was President Theodore Roosevelt, who had a longer-term perspective and affected the course of government in many areas by using popular opinion, or what he called his "bully pulpit" (bully at the time meant "superb" and pulpit referred to the White House) to implement earlier legislation, as well as to protect the environment. The era saw widespread expansion of government's role in the economy and society. The most dramatic increases were in federal government regulation, going from virtually none to substantial regulation of the behemoth organizations that had sprung up since the Civil War. Yet government also grew in financial infrastructure, transportation infrastructure, social architecture, service provision, and risk protection.

Regulator

The expansion of the railroad system also created a handful of large railroad companies that wielded vast power, such as the New York Central, Union Pacific Railroad, Central Pacific Railroad, and the Southern Pacific Railroad. In response to monopolistic practices (such as price fixing, rate discrimination, etc.), under the Interstate Commerce Act of 1887, Congress created the Interstate Commerce Commission (ICC) to regulate the business activities of railroads. This defining piece of legislation started to shift the power of regulating big business from the states to the federal government and became the first in a string of important legislative initiatives to curb the power of monopolies and trading cartels.

During the 1880s and 1890s, a new corporate conglomerate, the so-called "trust" such as Standard Oil (refer back to Exhibit 3.3) emerged in great numbers, some of which engaged in business practices that imperiled free competition. To deal with the monopolies emerging in oil, commodities, and horizontal business cartels, anti-trust laws were passed, the most important of which was the Sherman Anti-trust Act of 1890. Famous monopolies that were broken up by this type of legislation included Standard Oil (1911), American Tobacco (1911), Alcoa (1945), and AT&T (1984).

The Clayton Anti-trust Act and companion Federal Trade Commission Act of 1914 not only strengthened the Sherman Anti-trust Act, but also supported the criminalization of unfair trade practices such as price fixing, which had sent many business executives to jail, as exemplified in the famous General Electric and Westinghouse price-rigging scandal that saw seven executives go to prison in 1961. But not all anti-trust and non-competitive prosecution activities moved to the federal level; state attorneys-general have continued to pursue corporate and individual cases. In particular, New York, California, and Virginia have been active.

Other types of business regulation emerged in this era. The Food and Drug Act was initiated in 1906, in part due to the public outrage over unsanitary meatpacking conditions revealed by Progressives such as Sinclair Lewis. To enforce the policy to its fullest, the government later created the Food and Drug Administration (FDA) in 1927.

Not all increases in regulation were at the federal level. A massive new type of regulation, local zoning, had its genesis in this era. While local zoning had long been a prerogative of state and local governments, the need for comprehensive planning and more technically sophisticated zoning regulations became apparent as the country's population doubled during this period. Cities had to deal with great fires, sanitation, transportation needs, compatible usage, and aesthetics, and they had to channel economic development more rationally.

In 1916, building on a half century of rather disjointed efforts, New York City adopted a modern and comprehensive set of zoning regulations that set the pattern for zoning in the rest of the country. Eventually the constitutionality of zoning ordinances was challenged, but it was upheld by the US Supreme Court in the 1926 case entitled the *Village of Euclid, Ohio v. Ambler Realty Co.* The government's right to specify how land could be used, and to require conformance through authorized planning processes, including initial public input, were firmly established in this seminal decision.

Other Areas of Governmental Role Growth

In terms of fiscal and monetary structure, this period included two major events, both occurring in 1913. The first was the re-creation of a central bank, to be known as the Federal Reserve. This was partially a reaction to the fact that the great Panic of 1907 had been personally stabilized by the financier J. P. Morgan, in an age growing more leery of Wall Street bankers and manipulation by the super-wealthy. The second event was the Sixteenth Amendment to the Constitution, which allowed for federal income taxes that were not temporary (as was done during the Civil War), nor that imposed undue implementation issues on the federal government (as intervening Supreme Court decisions indicated would otherwise be necessary for constitutionality).

The effect of this amendment empowering Congress to levy federal taxes was threefold. First, it shifted substantial taxing authority to the federal government. Up until then, the bulk of taxing authority was reserved for state and local governments, with the exception of during the Civil War. Second, it meant that as tax burdens became heavier with much expanded services in the twentieth century, most of the tax growth was preempted by the federal government. This would eventually provide federal leverage over states in the 1960s through the 1980s, but is a position from which the government has generally been retreating in recent decades. Third, it provided the federal government with a way to indirectly distribute wealth when it chose to do so. For example, the federal government had high tax rates for the rich during and immediately following World War I, and from the Great Depression through the 1960s. In fact, during much of these periods the super-rich had special tax categories, which were done away with at the end of the Great Depression, when the rich and super-rich alike were taxed heavily for nearly 30 years. Thus, wealth distribution in the US narrowed considerably from 1940 to 1980, but has been allowed to expand ever since.

Transportation and other infrastructure demands continued to escalate during this period as cities paved more streets and sidewalks, provided electric lighting, built airports, constructed better sewage and sanitation systems, and created other improvements. Counties and state governments followed suit, to a more limited degree, in rural areas and in connecting cities.

In terms of social architecture, public schools at all levels expanded during the moderate-sized government period as an increasing number of states implemented compulsory education laws that forced attendance. Though public schools appeared as early as 1635 in the US, it was during the Progressive Era that the nation started to dramatically expand the public education system. By 1918, every state had enacted compulsory laws requiring students to complete elementary school (Graham 1974). The demand for high schools also proliferated. This, in turn, accelerated teacher colleges, often called normal schools, which initially were two-year, post-secondary institutions of higher education. Relatedly, service provision beyond physical infrastructure expanded to such things as more public libraries, drinking water for cities, and irrigation water for rural areas. Assistance to the poor during this era started to shift from poor farms to small, temporary welfare subsidies.

Safeguarding against risk was largely limited to attacks by Native Americans, invading forces, or the provision of justice systems. When it came to disasters, local governments were on their own. Sometimes a state legislature might pass special legislation for one-time assistance, but that was a rare occurrence, and even rarer was federal assistance with its tiny tax base. The Army Corps of Engineers would occasionally assist in rebuilding infrastructure, as it did with an extensive levee system after the Great Mississippi Flood of 1927. An example of the minimal government assistance provided in the nineteenth century was the great Johnstown Flood of 1889. Johnstown was a community that was essentially wiped out when a dam broke, but other than the Army Corps rebuilding a bridge and one small state government allocation of funds, the town depended almost entirely on charity. Because the event was so large, dramatic, and sad, relief did come in from around the world, although in smaller crises, local residents would find themselves completely on their own.

US government domestic and foreign policies continued to promote business by protecting growing corporate interests around the world. Domestic policy pursued the settlement of the West and the US Army fought a series of wars with Native Americans, who were required to live in increasingly restricted areas. The appropriation of large tracts of land in the American West opened up incredible development opportunities for business.

The US also acquired a series of strategic footholds around the world during this time period. In the Pacific, in addition to the Philippines and Guam, which were acquired from the Spanish, it annexed Hawaii, Midway Island, Samoa, and Johnston Island. Any residual foreign influence in the Caribbean was largely eliminated by annexing Puerto Rico and making Cuba a US protectorate. Assistance was provided to the break-away Colombia province of Panama, resulting in a 1904 treaty with the new country allowing the US to build, operate, and own the Panama Canal, which it did from 1914 to 1999. When business interests were perceived to be jeopardized, US military forces interceded in a number of Central American and Caribbean countries from the 1890s to 1920, and occasionally did so in other places around the world such as China and Korea.

While the country started the Moderate-Sized Government Era with internal frontiers, it ended it as a fully consolidated continental power, with some trappings of empire. The wilder expansion of the business that had begun in the Gilded Age was somewhat tamed by anti-trust legislation, but the Progressives focused on prohibition (against the use of alcohol) and on implementing the franchise of women (their new right to vote). Thus, the mood of the country relaxed again in regard to business during the heyday of the "roaring twenties."

The period ended with three Presidents in a row who largely advocated laissez-faire market practices and the reliance on philanthropy and volunteerism for social problems—Harding (a publisher), Coolidge (a lawyer), and Hoover (a veteran politician). These pro-business Presidents gave the business community a much freer hand; so free, in fact, that the over-speculation of stocks, land, and commodities resulted in the perceived need for greater government involvement in the next period.

The Big Government Era (1933–1970s): The Peak of Government

The Wall Street Crash of 1929 triggered a worldwide depression. In the US, the Great Depression ushered in a period of government intervention in business affairs through President Franklin D. Roosevelt's New Deal policies, with an expansion in financial infrastructure, and a new and greater emphasis in government as regulator, social architect, and purchaser, effectively enlarging government's role in safeguarding against risks. The period also experienced World War II, which the US entered more quickly than the previous world war and which was waged on two fronts. The war was not especially profitable for business because of high tax rates, but it did further enhance business capacity vis-à-vis the rest of the world from which it profited greatly after the war ended. The war was very expensive for government, which paid for it by maintaining high individual tax rates for several decades, but nonetheless the post-war economy boomed.

The government also maintained its other roles as infrastructure provider, service provider, and promoter of business. The success of government in this period was also partially its downfall, as expectations for greater and sustained intervention, and for the continuous improvement of the quality of life, continued to rise. At the same time, however, both personal and government resources began to reach their limits in an avidly capitalist society.

Fiscal Infrastructure and the New Philosophy Government–Business Relations

As the longest and deepest economic crisis in US history, the Great Depression lasted over a decade and at its height had an unemployment rate of over 25 percent. President Hoover, a moderate Republican, was nonetheless a well-documented humanitarian and likely would have assisted sooner if not for his highly Conservative Secretary of the Treasury, Andrew Mellon. The multimillionaire Secretary held his position from 1921 to 1932 until Congress started to consider his impeachment. In 1921, he had successfully advocated that the high federal tax rates from World War I were excessive, and that more moderate rates would lead to less tax evasion. In boom times, and when the needs for services were at historic lows, he had been effective at slowly but steadily decreasing the national debt by approximately half, despite the low tax rates.

When the Great Depression hit, and perhaps because he was never really aware of its full magnitude, Mellon thought the economic event was just a large market correction that would "purge the system" and provide new motivation to work harder after the fiscal and moral dissipation of the 1920s. At the beginning of the depression, Mellon was able to keep tax rates for the wealthy extremely low and, most importantly, cut government expenses, which only increased the pressure on the economy. By the end of his presidential term, Hoover had overridden him, increased taxes for the well-off, and expanded services for the unemployed, but it was too late to make a difference in the economy and salvage any chance for his re-election. Further, the tariff war that had been initiated during Hoover's presidency added to the collapse of international trade, which decreased more than two thirds in the midst of the depression.

Franklin Roosevelt, who overwhelmingly won his campaign against Hoover, did not have a clear idea of his "new deal" when elected President; however, he soon realized in office that the Depression was still getting worse and, as bad as the economy was in 1932 when he was elected, it had not yet hit bottom. He quickly came to believe that the once-in-a-century event needed government to play the financial role normally reserved for all-out war. He ultimately introduced long-term counter-cyclical measures in the economic war, believing that government must spend and go into debt in times of economic downturn and subsequently pay off that debt when the economy was once again good. As discussed in Chapter 1, this belief came to be called Keynesian economics.

Exhibit 3.5

Unemployed men queuing during the Depression outside a soup kitchen opened in Chicago by Al Capone

Source: Wikimedia Commons (1953). U.S. Information Agency.

Exhibit 3.6 shows the change in federal government spending as a percentage of the Gross Domestic Product. In 1929 at the start of the Great Depression, federal government spending was only 2.9 percent as it successfully paid off the enormous World War I debts from a decade earlier. By 1932, federal spending was at 7.8 percent of the economy when social net programs such as social security were established. With World War II and a total war economy, federal spending represented an astounding 40.6 percent of the economy in 1945. For several years after World War II, it shrank to the low to mid teems. The Korean War increased the federal budget into the 20 percent range (16–24 percent) where it remained for 66 years (1952–2018) even through the Great Recession of 2008–2010. Spending on the COVID-19 pandemic created a spike in spending to 31.4 percent. This heightened spending is expected through at least 2022 when spending is expected to decline into the mid-20 percent range which is a level that will still contribute to a rapidly escalating debt.

Government as Regulator

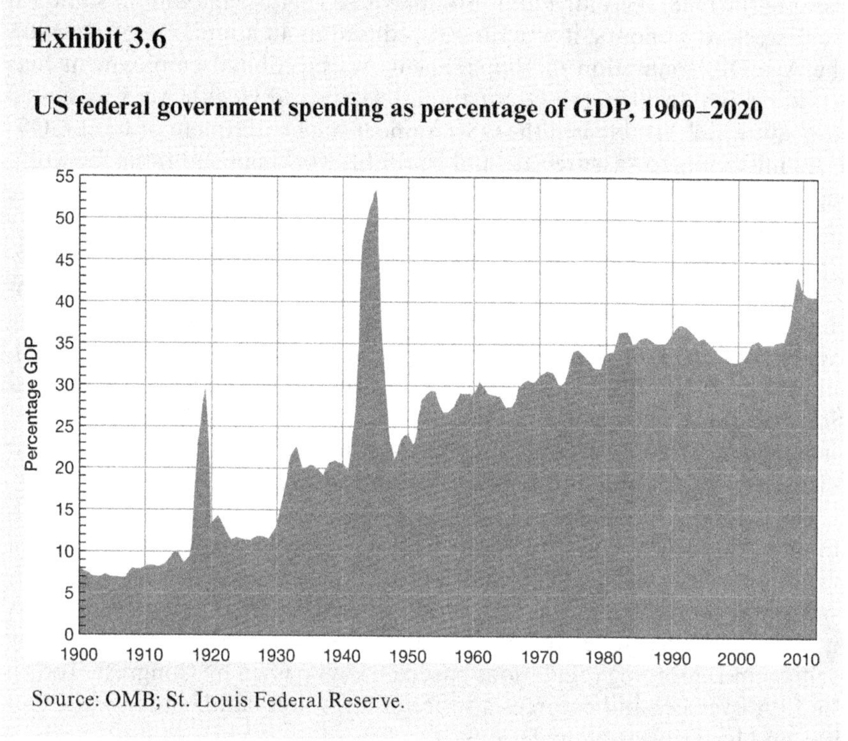

Exhibit 3.6

US federal government spending as percentage of GDP, 1900–2020

Source: OMB; St. Louis Federal Reserve.

Responding to the Crash of 1929, President Franklin D. Roosevelt established the US Securities and Exchange Commission (SEC) in 1934. This independent, quasi-judicial regulatory agency was given the power to regulate the stock market and prevent corporate abuses in security offerings, sales, and financial reporting. It holds the primary responsibility to this day for enforcing federal securities laws and regulating the securities industry. In addition to the Securities Exchange Act of 1934 that created the regulatory agency, the Commission also enforced other tools to protect investors, including the Securities Act of 1933, the Trust Indenture Act of 1939, the Investment Company Act of 1940, and the Investment Advisers Act of 1940.

The American Industrial Revolution also produced a massive number of working laborers; however, there was virtually no labor legislation in the country. In 1874, Massachusetts passed the nation's first law to limit the working time of women and children employed in factories to a maximum of ten hours a day. By the 1930s, child labor was much reduced, as compulsory education laws tended to keep children in school most of the year.

As part of the New Deal legislation, the National Labor Relations Act of 1935 granted workers the right to form unions and engage in collective bargaining. In 1938, the Fair Labor Standards Act set the maximum standard work week to 44 hours; it was further reduced to 40 hours in 1950. In 1967, the Age Discrimination in Employment Act prohibited employment bias based on age. In 1970, the Occupational Safety and Health Act was signed into law, which established the OSHA under the Department of Labor. OSHA's mission is to "assure safe and healthful working conditions for working men and women by setting and enforcing standards and by providing training, outreach, education and assistance."[1]

A variety of laws at both the federal and state levels were passed to regulate consumer affairs. At the federal level, consumer protection laws included the Fair Debt Collection Practices Act of 1968, the Truth in Lending Act of 1968, the Fair Credit Reporting Act of 1970, and the Fair Credit Billing Act of 1975, all of which are enforced by the Federal Trade Commission and the Department of Justice. At the state level, many states adopted the Uniform Deceptive Trade Practices Act to prevent unfair or fraudulent business practices and untrue or misleading advertising.

The federal government started to regulate water- and land-related pollution in the 1940s. The regulation effort was extended to air pollution and hazardous waste in the 1950s and 1960s. Citing rising concerns over environmental protection and conservation, President Nixon created the EPA in 1970. The EPA serves to protect human health and the environment by writing and enforcing regulations based on laws passed by Congress. Today, the EPA oversees and enforces a series of air, water, land, endangered species, and hazard waste regulations.

Government as Safeguard against Risk

The Great Depression had a devastating effect on people both rich and poor. In the US, unemployment rose to 25 percent. The poverty rate of senior citizens exceeded 50 percent in the early 1930s (Garraty and Foner 1991). In 1935, President Roosevelt introduced his "second new deal," especially through the Social Security Act. Social Security, referring to benefits based on old-age, widowed survivors, and disability insurance (OASDI), is an insurance program that attempts to limit the impact of old age on the elderly. This Act was complemented by the Medicare Act of 1965, which addressed one of the largest expenditures of the elderly—health care. Today, the combined spending for all social insurance programs, including Social Security, Medicare, Medicaid, unemployment, and other welfare programs, constitutes over half of federal government expenditure.

In addition to social insurance programs, the Glass–Steagall Act of 1933 created the FDIC to provide deposit insurance, which guarantees the safety of deposits in member banks. As of 2012, the FDIC warrants up to $250,000 per depositor per bank.

Disaster assistance became a function of the President's office after World War II, and special appropriations became a yearly function. This function was formalized into an agency in 1978 when the Federal Emergency Management Agency (FEMA) was created and became a more formalized part of the annualized budget process. Unlike the Johnstown Flood a century earlier, when survivors hoped for charity and assistance from the Red Cross, the first thing victims in later-day major disasters had come to ask was, "Where's the [federal] government?"

Government as Social Architect

Public parks were largely created in the Progressive Era, but were greatly expanded in the era of Big Government. In 1916, the National Park Service (NPS) was created by Congress through the National Park Service Organization Act. The agency is responsible for the management of all national parks, many national monuments, and other conservation and historical properties with various title designations. Though state park systems dated back to 1885, when New York designated Niagara Falls as a state park, a massive expansion of the system started in the 1930s, when around 800 state parks across the country were developed with assistance from federal job-creation programs.

Many of the unemployed were put to work in building these parks by virtue of the Works Progress Administration (WPA), which also provided massive aid to other infrastructure projects across the county. At its height, the WPA provided employment for over three million workers; it was abolished when its job was done in 1943, and the country experienced a severe worker shortage due to the military enlistment of over nine million citizens.

The Federal National Mortgage Association, commonly known as Fannie Mae, was founded in 1938 during the Great Depression—as yet another part of the New Deal—to expand home ownership by increasing the secondary mortgage market. This allowed lenders to reinvest their assets into more lending, in effect increasing the number of lenders in the mortgage market by reducing the reliance on thrifts.

Government as Purchaser

State and local governments are primarily employers because of the services they render, and they do a minimal amount of purchasing relative to the GDP. Historically, the federal government was only a *major* purchaser during times of war, as Exhibit 3.6 indicates. However, after World War II, despite the initial reduction of the military and its budget, the expenses of the military became proportionately greater than they ever had been before. This occurred for two reasons. First, there was a new sense that the US was the primary bulwark of democracy in the world, since World War II had ravaged Europe. Its standing army requirements were many times greater than in the past, especially after the Korean War (1950–1953). Second, the technology of war became increasingly expensive as ships, airplanes, missile systems, and even soldier gear escalated in price. For example, the famous World War II B-29 cost approximately $750,000, or $10 million in current dollar value, while the cost of the equally famous "stealth bomber" (the B-2) ran to approximately $750 million each, an increase of 1000 times in nominal dollars, or 100-fold in inflation-adjusted dollars. This lucrative industry not only provides a huge internal market for American business, but also adds to the private defense industry's ability to be the leading arms exporter in the world.

Government's Other Roles in the Big Government Era

Government continued its huge role in infrastructure. Two examples are particularly important because they meld together the roles of transportation and national security. The first is the Federal Highways Act of 1959, which created the modern freeway system in the US. Although this was not the first Federal Highways Act, its massive scope and active federal planning transcended previous legislation. The second example was in 1970, when the Nixon Administration and the Federal Reserve provided financial assistance to Penn Central Railroad on the basis that the company provided crucial national defense transportation services. The argument to bail out Penn Central would be used again in future economic crises.

Government's role as basic services provider was further advanced during the Big Government Era, increasing in rural services, such as rural electrification in 1936 to provide better urban–rural equity. Federal support of state and local welfare assistance programs became a larger part of state budgets. Welfare became more robust, leading to some complaints by the end of this period that it had, in fact, become too institutionalized and was creating a "welfare culture" for a segment of the poor. Corporate "welfare" also grew through a variety of tax incentive programs, sometimes referred to as tax loopholes.

Government's role as promoter of export business was less obvious, but probably not diminished after World War II, when it became a superpower. A particular area of support was the oil industry, where the bulk of US-owned oil and gas production was on foreign soil after World War II. Domestically, after World War II, state and local government began creating economic development agencies (EDAs) to fight urban blight and decay. These agencies grew in size and scope, and eventually expanded to include rural blight, employment support in specialized "empowerment" zones, and even infrastructure.

Even as government still increased in size and scope in the 1970s, there were signs that the world was changing, and the roles of government would need to be shifted, and in some cases reduced, and occasionally even eliminated.

The Rightsizing Government Era (1970s–Present): Resurgence of the Market and Efforts in Shrinking Government

From the end of World War II through the 1960s, the US was an economic powerhouse, with only the Soviet Union as its political and economic match in the Cold War era (1947–1991), a period of time when capitalist and communist ideologies were in a highly confrontational mode. By the 1970s, the hegemonic economic position (i.e., overwhelming dominance) of the US had eroded for a number of reasons.

First, the unique US economic position immediately after World War II could not be sustained. Because of the massive destruction of the advanced economies in Europe and Asia, the US inherited a manufacturing vacuum that was easy to fill. As world production capacities resumed in the decades after the war, US production returned to more realistic, although still very high, levels.

Next, the second age of colonialism ended (approximately 1860–1960). Eventually this meant that a number of commodity industries were nationalized by former colonies and poorer independent countries asserting their economic independence from European and American hegemony. In the oil industry, this was particularly dramatic. International oil cartels, that came into existence as newly independent countries bound together, started demanding substantially higher prices, wreaking havoc in the US and other oil-dependent countries and affecting prices starting in 1973. As a result, government leaders attempted to control inflation by limiting spending, resisting tax cuts, and reining in growth in the money supply.

Additionally, during this era, a series of government policies was enacted in an attempt to disinvest government responsibilities through *deregulation*, *privatization*, and devolution to the state (by the federal government) and to local governments (by the states), thereby reducing its roles as regulator and service provider. However, because of the popularity of government services, benefits and the stability it provides, the era of downsizing has neither been easy to accomplish nor consistent. Sometimes outright downsizing and deregulation has occurred. As frequently, however, government roles have adopted new programs as obsolete ones have been abolished, or it has had to reinstate some programs because of extraordinary needs.

Regulation and Deregulation

Influenced by the changes in the world economy and research at the University of Chicago—led by Milton Friedman (1912–2006), Friedrich Hayek, and others—governments started to deregulate some policy areas in the 1970s. Deregulation refers to the act or process of removing or reducing government regulations of business or industry. Transportation was the first major industry to be deregulated. It was initiated in the Nixon Administration and pursued by several administrations thereafter. It led to the passage of several deregulation Acts by Congress, such as the Railroad Revitalization and Regulatory Reform Act of 1976 during the Ford Administration, and the Airline Deregulation Act of 1978, Staggers Rail Act of 1980, and the Motor Carrier Act of 1980 during the Carter Administration. The movement gained much more momentum during the Reagan Administration. In 1980, Reagan promised an economic revival that would be achieved by cutting taxes and reducing the size and scope of federal programs. Simultaneously, Reagan introduced expansionary fiscal policies aimed at stimulating the American economy after a recession; thus, federal control was reduced in many areas, but its overall budget was not. He also extensively deregulated banking, finance, and corporate reporting requirements.

Even though the goal of deregulation was to encourage economic growth by greater reliance on market forces, the results of deregulation were full of controversy. Some studies found that transportation deregulation did, in fact, lead to increased competition, communication choices, and creation of new firms and jobs. It was estimated that trucking deregulation alone produced a gain to US industries in shipping, merchandising, and inventories of between $38 and $56 billion per year (Moore 2007).

However, sometimes deregulation led to very poor results as well. In the financial sector, extensive deregulation policies were blamed for several economic crises (Cali, Ellis, and te Velde 2008). The savings and loan crisis of the late 1980s and early 1990s was caused by improperly guaranteeing deposits at savings and loan banks without regulatory controls, which encouraged them to make risky investments. By the time the federal government stepped in, the bank insurance of most states had been wiped out and the number of savings and loans that collapsed skyrocketed to hundreds per year. A special federal agency, the Resolution Trust Corporation (in existence from 1989 to 1995) was set up with the mission of closing down and selling off the assets of approximately one quarter of all the S&Ls in the US—at a final cost of about $90 billion. The industry was re-regulated.

This was followed by an extensive series of private sector accounting scandals in the early 2000s, which led the Sarbanes–Oxley Act of 2002 to re-regulate fiduciary responsibilities. The Great Recession of 2008, partially exacerbated by unwise banking practices and widespread fraud in the subprime mortgage industry, ultimately led to some re-regulation of the investment and commercial banking industry. On July 21, 2010, the Wall Street Reform and Consumer Protection Act was signed into law by President Barack Obama to strengthen the regulation of the financial market. An example of poor implementation of deregulation in the energy sector at the state level occurred in California in 2000. The energy deregulation policies in California led to an artificial spike in consumer costs by Enron that was estimated at between $40 and $45 billion (Weare 2003). The scandal sent over a dozen employees to prison for extended sentences, caused the demise of the company, and also the collapse of the powerhouse accounting firm Arthur Anderson who was found guilty of abetting Enron crimes.

President Trump campaigned on deregulation and quickly issued an executive order (13771) that required the elimination of two regulations every time one new regulation was promulgated. While modest regulation in many areas occurred, a prime target was environmental regulation, an area that his predecessor (Obama) had been active in regulating. The Trump administration replaced the Clean Power Plan, weakened the Endangered Species Act, terminated oil and natural gas extraction bans, reduced the Coal Ash Rule disposal requirements, and downgraded the Mercury and Air Toxic Standards. President Biden is slowly reversing the Trump era environmental deregulation. Within six months of taking office, about half of the Trump policies were overturned, stopped when they were last within a 180 window of implementation, by the Biden administration (Eilperin, Dennis, and Muyskens 2021). While executive orders can be issued immediately, and noncontroversial and minor regulations can be promulgated in less than a year, controversial and high stakes regulation changes—which are an extension of authorized law—normally take two to four years.

Service Provision

Besides deregulation, privatization was another policy largely pursued by governments in this era. Privatization is the process of transferring government services, functions, and public properties to private sector organizations, which include both for-profit and nonprofit businesses. Under Reagan's Administration, privatization gained its momentum. In 1987, a President's Commission on Privatization was established to increase private participation across a broad range of policy areas, including low-income housing, air-traffic control, the postal service, prisons, and schools (Linowes 1988). The policy was also pursued by President George Bush, who carried on the privatization initiatives, especially in support of market mechanisms as the vehicle for school reform. Under the banner of "reinventing government," the Clinton Administration drove the movement to its peak. With the mantra of "running government like a business," governments at all levels introduced the private sector into publicly paid-for services. Government services ranging from trash collection to prison management have been increasingly contracted out to business firms, with a relatively high level of success.

Also notable was the 1996 welfare reform, which reversed the trend to increase support to the poor. Many states also reformed their welfare systems, and reduced benefits and services, although some of these services have been restored since the Great Recession in 2008. Unemployment benefits have historically received long "extensions," both to prevent workers from descending into poverty and homelessness, as well as to help stabilize the economy.

The COVID-19 pandemic starting in 2020 recorded an historic effort by government to counterbalance the shutting down of part of the economy for over a year and causing severe dislocations in much of the rest of the economy. This leads some to consider the management of government as entering a new age (Economist 2021). Some of the many enormous programs included:

- Two rounds of stimulus checks to individuals.
- Grants to small businesses.
- Mortgage eviction regulations.
- Food stamp expansion.
- Mortgage relief.
- Emergency grants to students.
- Lowered interest rate (Fed rate).
- Lowered interest rates for student loans.
- Unemployment extensions and temporary "bonus" payments.

The effectiveness of restoring the economy in record time—market and employment—was remarkable. However, these programs both added to an already alarming debt and debt trajectory, and has nearly exhausted government's capacity to respond to future crises until a period of fiscal constraint restores financial balance to the federal government and Federal Reserve (Duguid 2021).

Providing Monetary and Fiscal Control: Mixed Signals

The rightsizing government sentiment in finance accelerated in the last years of the Clinton Administration and during the bulk of the George W. Bush Administration. In 1999, President Clinton signed the Graham–Rudman–Hollings Act, which repealed the Glass–Steagall Act of 1933, separating investment banking from depository commercial banks. George W. Bush's Administration implemented the new Act forcefully by downsizing the remaining oversight function. However, the 2008 financial crisis halted this "hands-off" trend.

Recent government policies, especially those related to business affairs passed during and after the crisis, demonstrated once again the rationale of Keynesian economics. During the 2008 financial "meltdown," in order to bail out the failing financial industry, the federal government had to nationalize Fannie Mae and Freddie Mac, the two largest mortgage insurance companies that were created and privatized by Congress. The Federal Reserve System injected $85 billion to take the world's largest insurance company, American International Group (AIG), under its control. It also injected over a trillion dollars of liquidity into the financial system to keep it from collapsing. In addition, Congress passed a $700 billion bailout bill to stabilize the whole financial system. This was subsequently dwarfed by the trillion-dollar packages passed by Congress to stabilize the economy as reported above, as well as the $3 trillion equity buying implemented by the Federal Reserve to prop up the market.

Meanwhile, the automobile industry, most notably the "Big Three"—General Motors, Chrysler, and Ford—also received a bailout of $35 billion to allow them to restructure and jettison their legacy debts. Following the crisis, Congress passed the Housing and Economic Recovery Act of 2008 to restore confidence in the domestic mortgage industry. Under the Act, the Federal Housing Finance Agency was established as a new regulator and endowed with expanded powers and authority. The emphasis was to be on small business, but critics asserted that a large portion of the trillion-dollar aid in the Payroll Protection Act went to the better connected (Medici 2021). Later programs were more tightly designed to go to small business continuing to struggle.

Safeguard Against Risk

Contrary to the rightsizing trend, government expanded its role in healthcare reform with the passage of the Patient Protection and Affordable Care Act (PPACA) on March 23, 2010. With the intent to decrease the number of uninsured Americans, PPACA requires insurance companies to cover all applicants and offer everyone the same rates, regardless of pre-existing conditions or gender. Although sometimes criticized as a government takeover of the healthcare industry, it is more accurate to characterize it as an increase in the regulation of the industry, whose proportional costs exceed those of other advanced democracies.

Other Roles

While the government's role as social architect/service provider increased with healthcare reform, it has decreased dramatically in education. States have tended to put less money into K-12 education as prison costs have continued to rise, and have been steadily defunding their universities and community colleges for the last quarter century, a trend that accelerated after 2008. As a consequence, tuition at many public institutions has been rising rapidly to make up for the shortfall.

The role of promoter of business has been more mixed. On one hand, governments at all levels have been keenly aware of increased global competition and have opened trade offices and sharpened their export skills. Domestically, however, the growth of economic development agencies has been questioned. Although California was the first state to create economic development agencies in 1945, it was also the first to withdraw all state support in 2012 in an effort to localize redevelopment and to reduce the diversion of tax monies from education to economic vitality. It remains to be seen whether this becomes a national trend. See Exhibit 3.8 for a synopsis of the eight roles of government (excluding defense and justice).

Exhibit 3.7

The Colonial Revival headquarters of Fannie Mae, located at 3900 Wisconsin Avenue, N.W., Washington, DC

Source: Wikimedia Commons (2008). Fannie Mae staff photo.

Fannie Mae and Freddie Mac are known as government-sponsored enterprises, which refer to legal entities created by Congress to undertake commercial activities on behalf of government.

In 1938, President Roosevelt created the Federal National Mortgage Association (FNMA or "Fannie Mae") to facilitate home sales and reduce bank failures during the Great Depression. Fannie Mae purchased, held, and insured mortgages from banks. This allowed lenders to create more mortgages at lower prices because the risks associated with mortgage defaults were shifted to Fannie Mae. The creation of Fannie Mae largely contributed to the home-ownership increase after World War II.

In 1968, the federal government privatized Fannie Mae, which became a publicly traded company. Two years later, Congress established the Federal Home Loan Mortgage Corporation (FHLMC or "Freddie Mac") to provide loans and loan guarantees, which facilitated the emergence of a market for mortgage-based securities (MBS). Freddie Mac purchased a large quantity of mortgages, pooled them together, and sold mortgage-backed securities to investors. The guarantees of mortgages, as well as the pooling of mortgages, reduced the risk and encouraged more investment into the mortgage-backed securities and, subsequently, more bank lending. To compete with Freddie Mac, Fannie Mae adopted the same business strategy. Following the track of these two corporations, more and more private financial institutions entered the MBS market.

The 2008 subprime mortgage crisis hit Fannie Mae and Freddie Mac most severely, as they had been the major players in the mortgage market. As the two companies' bonds were massively distributed among the public, including the retirement funds of hundreds of millions of people, general money market funds, domestic bonds owners, as well as foreign governments, their bankruptcy could lead to a global upheaval.

On September 7, 2008, the federal government took Fannie Mae and Freddie Mac under the control of the Federal Housing Finance Agency (FHFA). To advance funds for stabilizing the two corporations, the federal government had to increase the national debt ceiling by $800 billion, to $10.7 trillion, in order to accommodate the regulatory authority of the Treasury over the two firms. In September 2019, the Treasury and FHFA announced that Fannie Mae and Freddie Mac would retain their earning in order to increase capital reserves. This was done as a step toward eventually transitioning the two organizations out of conservatorship.

Ongoing Debate

The debate about the proper roles for government often gets heated, and sadly is often driven more by ideology than by facts and clear logic. As reviewed in Chapter 1, government and the private sector do have some overlap, but they have two different rationales. Each sector tends to have areas in which it is inherently stronger, but exceptions are not difficult to point out.

Overgeneralizing for clarity, *government* tends to be better at functions that call for democratic input, due process, a long-term perspective, equity, justice, and protection of the less fortunate. *Business* tends to be better at paying attention to market signals, creative destruction, a short-term perspective, customized opportunities, wealth creation, and incentivizing individuals.

Of course, government should be business-like and business should be ethical. Yet government will never fully act as a business, because it is not a business and is expected to act like a government, with transparency, accountability, wisdom, fairness, and other democratic virtues. Nor should business be expected to act like a government, because that is not its function.

Exhibit 3.8

Eight important but variable roles of government[2]

	Anti-Central Government, 1781–1787	*Small Government, 1787–1887*	*Moderate-Sized Government, 1887–1933*	*Big Government, 1933–1970s*	*Rightsizing Government, 1970s-Present*
Provider of monetary and fiscal structure	Minimal	Modest ↑	Substantial ↑	Great ↑	Great but shifting ↔
Provider of infrastructure	Modest	Substantial ↑	Great ↑	Great ↔	Reduced ↓
Purchaser	Modest	Modest ↔	Modest ↔	Substantial ↑	Substantial ↔
Regulator of business	Virtually none	Virtually none ↔	Substantial ↑	Substantial ↔	Reduced and shifting ↓
Social architect	Virtually none	Modest ↑	Substantial ↑	Great ↑	Reduced and shifting ↓
Service provider	Virtually none	Modest ↑	Substantial ↑	Substantial ↔	Shifting ↔
Safeguard against risk	Virtually none	Virtually none ↔	Minimal ↑	Substantial ↑	Substantial ↔
Promoter of business	Virtually none	Substantial ↑	Substantial ↔	Substantial ↔	Substantial but shifting ↔

When the argument gets too heated, with one side asserting that government can do no wrong and the other asserting it can do no right, the argument becomes unsophisticated and misses the point. The important questions we want to ask are: given our democratic and economic system, what do we want government to do? Given what we want it to do, how, then, can we ensure that it does as good a job as possible?

The first question is the scope-of-government question, which is primarily policy focused. We do not, for instance, have to have a city-run trash pick-up system, nor do we have to have a standing army. The issue is how well we understand the consequences so that we may plan accordingly. It is easy to privatize the city-run trash collection, and the consequences of poor implementation are relatively modest: increased costs and more littered streets. The consequences of privatizing the military, however, may result in not only increased costs, but national security concerns.

Rightsizing the scope of government is an appropriate cycle if the policy areas are considered carefully. Timing is also important in this question. Special support for the Post Office for 180 years made sense because of the vital need of the country to have a secure communication system. It made little sense in an age of multiple communication systems including the Internet, and when there were now other mail services such as Federal Express and UPS. Thus, it was privatized, albeit with strong Congressional strings and oversight attached.

Providing financial regulations makes little sense unless, without those regulations, cheating and fraud become easy, common, and detrimental to the survival of the financial system itself. This came to pass after the collapse of Wall Street in 2008, and in a responsive measure, the securities market has now been somewhat re-regulated. Because of the complexity of financial regulation, it is difficult to see if the scope has been too much, too little, or just enough in the short-term. Perhaps more important currently is role of government in managing and regulating the centralization and corporatism of the American economy in which banking, and e-commerce have joined other sectors in being controlled by fewer companies than in the past. In turn, this has helped fuel the greatest wealth gap since the Gilded Age (approximately 1870–1910) in which a handful of individuals have more assets than the entire lower half of the US population (Horowitz, Igielnik, and Kochhar 2020).

Yet, as important as the scope is the question about the quality of government. Like business, sometimes it does a better job and sometimes it does not. Just as business is constantly evolving and reinventing itself, government needs to constantly change, too. However, generally we call business change "innovation," and government change "reform." So it is important not only to ensure that government's roles fit the current times and needs, but is essential to assist it to do well in those roles. This book will enable you to look at both these complex issues more analytically, and give you the skills to critique both government and business, as well as arrive at your own more sophisticated ideas about the matters that surround the basis of our society.

Analytical Case: Should Government Bail Out the Big Financial Companies?

The 2008 financial crisis[3] is thought by many to be the worst financial crisis since the Great Depression. The crisis was triggered by the burst of the housing bubble, a result of a complex interplay of government policies that encouraged home ownership and borrowing. Such government policies, in the absence of regulatory framework keeping up with new financial practices, led to irresponsible underwriting practices of both lenders and borrowers. These actions provided easier access to mortgages for subprime borrowers and contributed to the expansion of subprime lending.

The crisis started on March 10, 2008 when the Dow Jones Industrial Average plunged to its lowest level since October 2006, falling 20 percent from its peak just five months before. The downturn swept the whole of Wall Street. Bear Stearns, a global investment bank and securities trading and brokerage business, was among the worst affected. The company was interconnected with other banks up and down Wall Street. Fearing systemic risks that may affect the financial system as a whole, should Bear Stearns go bankrupt, Ben Bernanke, the Chairman of the Federal Reserve, determined the risks were too great to allow a Bear Stearns bankruptcy. The worry was also shared by Henry Paulson, the Secretary of the Treasury Department. In pondering whether to bail out Bear Stearns, Paulson posed the question of *moral hazard*: if you bail someone out of a problem caused by themselves, what incentive will they have to avoid making the same mistake in the future?

Anticipating the *system risk*, the Federal Reserve Bank of New York provided an emergency loan to Bear Stearns; however, it still could not avert the collapse of the company. Finally, the company was forced to be sold to JPMorgan Chase for a price far below its pre-crisis market value.

This was just the prelude of the crisis. Within six months of the federal takeover of Fannie Mae and Freddie Mac, as well as the selling of Merrill Lynch to Bank of America, Lehman Brothers started to collapse. This time, moral hazard trumped system risk. Bernanke and Paulson, under the pressure of exhausting bailout funds, decided not to intervene, in the hope that the risk of Lehman Brothers' bankruptcy could be contained. Lehman Brothers' bankruptcy, however, triggered a market avalanche. The stock market dropped by hundreds of points right after the opening bell. The company was far more interconnected than Bernanke and Paulson had thought. Systemic risk became a reality. Banks stopped lending in the fear that other banks would not be able to pay them back. The credit markets became frozen and commerce ground to a halt.

Meanwhile, the world's largest insurance company, American International Group (AIG) was plunging to the rim of bankruptcy. AIG had invested tens of billions in risky investments that were tied to the housing market. The precipitous failure of such a big organization can be extremely disruptive. Fully aware of the potential risk, the Fed decided to lend AIG $85 billion and took the world's largest insurance company under government control.

As one firm after another crumbled, systemic risk kicked in and a fear of losing control swept over Wall Street. Bernanke was afraid that the meltdown could no longer be handled on a case-by-case basis and the Fed reached its limit. They had to get government involved in a broader rescue.

On September 18, Paulson and Bernanke met with key legislators to propose a $700 billion emergency bailout through the purchase of toxic assets. On October 3, 2008, President George W. Bush signed the Emergency Economic Stabilization Act and approved the $700 billion bailout bill.

Questions for Discussion and Analysis

1 Should government rescue these big financial companies? What are the implications of the bailout?
2 How would Adam Smith and Alexander Hamilton view the bailout?
3 How could we effectively prevent such a crisis from happening in the future?

Practical Skill

Accessing Resources for Starting a Business

If you want to start a business legally and smoothly, like Zoey is trying to do, you need to deal with many issues. Many people who start a business may not be as lucky as Zoey, who earned an entrepreneurial management degree. The good news is that government provides abundant resources to help small businesses to start and to grow.

A very useful resource for business starters is the Small Business Administration (SBA). The agency's official website (www.sba.gov) offers comprehensive guidelines for starting a business. The agency also runs over 300 district offices across the country, providing professional counseling, training, and business development services. Special assistance is also offered to women, veterans, and export-oriented business owners. Most small businesses rely on lenders to provide the capital they need to either open a business or to finance capital improvements. Even though the SBA does not loan money directly to small business owners, it offers extensive loan assistance and loan programs to help them finance or grow their business. Information about its loan programs and services is available at the website.

Skill Exercise: Government's Roles in Starting a Business

Study the guidelines for starting a business on the SBA website. Create a list of things you need to deal with when starting a business, highlight the issues that concern government, and link the issues to the various government roles introduced in the chapter.

Find the SBA district office in your community. Search for programs the office offers to businesses.

Summary and Conclusion

1 Government plays many roles with business.
2 Under the prevailing anti-central government sentiment, the powers of government were initially extremely limited at the founding of the republic under the Articles of Confederation.
3 The government was reformulated under the Constitution to allow a greater, but still balanced, role for a central government whose powers were shared with states and citizens, as well as its own branches. For one hundred years, the Small Government Era demonstrated a substantial role in transportation infrastructure and the promotion of business, but less in fiscal and monetary infrastructure, purchasing, and social architecture, and virtually none in business regulation and risk protection.
4 The Moderate-Sized Government Era developed the role of regulator most forcefully to deal with the growth of the modern monopoly. Almost all other roles expanded as well.
5 The Big Government Era was shaped by the Great Depression and World War II. Financial infrastructure, purchasing, social architecture, and risk protection all reached very high levels by the end of the period.
6 Starting from the late 1970s, the resurgence of the market model pressed government into considering rightsizing through deregulation and privatization. Government generally reduced its roles as regulator and service provider and was considered successful and moderately popular. However, some deregulation had dire consequences and had to be reinstituted.
7 The 2008 economic crisis brought the nation into a heated debate about the many roles of government and exactly which ones should be reduced, shifted, or even increased. Sometimes lost in this discussion is the importance of the quality of those policies. If well done, an appropriate assortment of regulation and deregulation policies can lead to balance, stability, and a healthy market, or, if not done well, can lead to a bloated governmental structure or encourage private sector corruption.

Key Terms

- The Confederation Deregulation Moral hazard
- Privatization System risk

Study Questions

1. What do you think is the proper role of government in business affairs? What role(s) of government should be enhanced or reduced?
2. According to the theories of Smith, Hamilton, Keynes, and Hayek, what are the proper roles of government in the economy? What were the historical conditions that led to the popularity of their theories, respectively?
3. Consider what might have happened if there had been no anti-trust regulations in the US. What would subsequent American history have been like? Would the eventual popular sovereignty have been destroyed or advanced?
4. Despite the historical preference for small government, American governments' roles and responsibilities are constantly expanding. Why did this happen? What are the factors that lead to government expansion? What do you think are the effective ways of rightsizing or shrinking government?

Notes

1. See the OHSA website: http://www.osha.gov/about.html.
2. Categories used for global description: virtually none, minimal, modest, substantial, great, shifting, reduced. *Virtually none* means government activity was insignificant. *Minimal* means that it was significant but highly limited or circumscribed. *Modest* means it was significant but not a dominant factor in government functions. *Substantial* means that it was important to both government and business but did not have dominant influence. *Great* indicates a dominant influence. *Shifting* indicates that the various subfactors were moving in different directions in terms of government influence. *Reduced* means that government was reducing its influence somewhat by reducing funding, privatizing, contracting out, deregulating or simply abolishing select functions.
3. The case is developed largely based on the PBS Frontline documentary *Inside the Meltdown* at http://www.pbs.org/wgbh/pages/frontline/meltdown/.

References

Bardes, B., Shelley, M. C., and Schmidt, S. W. (2012). *American Government and Politics Today: The Essentials*, 2011–2012 edn. Boston, MA: Wadsworth Cengage Learning.

Cali, M., Ellis, K., and te Velde, D. W. (2008). The Contribution of Services to Development: The Role of Regulation and Trade Liberalization. Overseas Development Institute, Project Briefing, No. 17, December 2008. http://www.odi.org.uk/resources/docs/2382.pdf.

Depew, C. (ed.) (1895). *One Hundred Years of American Commerce 1795–1895* (p. 111). New York: D.O. Haynes & Co.

Duguid, K. (2020). Federal Reserve's $3 Trillion Virus Rescue Inflates Market Bubbles. Reuters: July 13.

Economist (2021). The World Is Entering a New Era of Big Government. *The Economist*. November 20. https://www.economist.com/leaders/2021/11/20/the-world-is-entering-a-new-era-of-big-government.

Eilperin, J., Dennis, B., and Muyskens, J. (2021). Tracking Biden's Environmental Actions. *The Washington Post*, August 5.

Graham, P. A. (1974). *Community and Class in American Education, 1865–1918*. New York: Wiley.

Garraty, J. A. and Foner, E. (1991). *The Reader's Companion to American History*. New York: Houghton Mifflin.

Horowitz, J., Igielnik, R., and Kochhar, R. (2020). Trends in Income and Wealth Inequality. *Pew Research Center*, January 9.

Jefferson, T. (1975). First Inaugural, in M. D. Peterson (ed.) *The Portable Thomas Jefferson* (p. 290). New York: Penguin Books.

Linowes, D. F. (1988). *Privatization: Toward More Effective Government*. Report of the President's Commission on Privatization. Urbana: University of Illinois Press.

Moore, T. G. (2007). Trucking Deregulation, in D. R. Henderson (ed.) *The Concise Encyclopedia of Economics*. The Library of Economics and Liberty. http://www.Econlib.org/library/Encl/TruckingDeregulation.html.

U.S. Office of Management and Budget and Federal Reserve Bank of St. Louis. (2021). Federal Net Outlays as Percent of Gross Domestic Product [FYONGDA188S], retrieved from FRED, Federal Reserve Bank of St. Louis. https://fred.stlouisfed.org/series/FYONGDA188S.

Weare, C. (2003). *The California Electricity Crisis: Causes and Policy Options*. San Francisco, CA: Public Policy Institute of California. http://www.ppic.org/content/pubs/report/r_103cwr.pdf.

Weitzel, M. (2011). *History of Army Contracting*. US Army. http://www.army.mil/article/54337/History_of_Army_Contracting/. April 4, 2011.

Wikimedia Commons (1991). *Project Gutenberg*. Yergin. https://commons.wikimedia.org/wiki/File:John_D._Rockefeller_aged_18_-_Project_Gutenberg_eText-t_17090-crop.jpg.

Yergin, D. (1991). *The Prize: The Epic Quest for Oil, Money, and Power*. New York: Simon and Schuster.

4 Economic Policies

Jonathan Anderson

Chapter Contents

Case 4 Scenario

Policies and Peppermint

Zach and Zoey are at U Scream Ice Cream, just down the street from Happy Paws, Zoey's store that will open soon. Zach comments that Zoey was right about foot traffic from the veterinarian's office on the corner—people have been stopping in front of Zoey's shop daily to watch the progress! They both order a single scoop of peppermint ice cream.

Zoey has learned there are many government economic policies that can affect her business, directly or indirectly. In a market-based system, she can start such a business as long as she meets various regulations about incorporation and licensing and the care of animals. Zoey knows that most of the products she intends to sell must disclose the ingredients they use or the materials from which they are manufactured. She eventually wants to find a line of organic products for her customers, as many people who have stopped have expressed an interest in them.

DOI: 10.4324/9781003178620-5

Zoey also just learned the Somewhere City Council is toying with downtown revitalization and a possible ordinance mandating retailers to beautify the area between their storefront and the street. The ordinance may not pass since many retailers oppose the increased costs, which could be a significant burden for her as she opens. However, the city's economic development initiative might pay for 50 percent of the expense, and the spruce-up sure would make her place look better.

Zoey was able to get a couple loans because interest rates have been kept low by national government policy to stave off the worst effects of a recession. Zach even took out a small loan to help, and Zach and his father pitched in with all of the paperwork, too. However, this same government policy means the economy will be slower to rebound. Although Zoey's personal and business taxes will be modest because they are progressive, and she will have virtually no profit after she pays herself, they still affect her bottom line and her ability to survive as a business. Zach and Zoey walk out of the ice cream shop and stroll past Splurge jewelry store.

Government policy has also allowed online businesses to thrive without taxes for a number of years, which puts pressure on brick-and-mortar businesses such as Zoey's. Fortunately, her state has recently imposed an online sales tax when companies have a large online presence (over a million dollars of sales) or a physical presence in the state. That means big companies like Overstock and Petco must collect sales taxes and remit them to state government, as must her local competitors. Of course, Zoey would have to collect sales taxes if she opts to have an online presence, too, something that she is considering. So much to juggle! Zach and Zoey pause for a moment in front of the Splurge window display and Zoey admires an unusual pink diamond ring. "Someday," she says to Zach, "when my business is successful, I'm going to be able to afford something as beautiful as that."

So even in this small business example, we see numerous examples of many of the policies that are discussed in this chapter regarding market freedom, regulations, information disclosure, tax liabilities, economic subsidies, interest rates, recessionary smoothing, and trade policies.

Introduction

The US is a democratic society. Through our governance process citizens decide what they want, including functional roles and economic policies. In the last chapter, we looked at the evolution of this process through an examination of government roles. In this chapter, we take a different vantage point by looking at current government policies through the lens of microeconomic and macroeconomic theories.

Microeconomics looks at how human incentives (e.g., profits from hard work) and disincentives (e.g., laws criminalizing certain behaviors) work in an economic setting. We look at five economic policy areas from a microeconomic perspective and assess where the US tends to focus on balance.

Macroeconomics is the science that looks at how whole national economies work. Areas of interest in macroeconomics include fiscal policies (i.e., tax levels, how taxes are spent, and levels of public debt), money supply, interest rates, antirecessionary actions, trade, and capital flows. Every person should have a keen instinct with which s/he reacts to what is going on in the economy. Further, each business person should understand how pertinent government policies will affect them and their operations—from regulatory to monetary to fiscal policies—no matter whether it is a small business or corporation, serves an exclusively domestic clientele, or has an international customer base. Fortunes are frequently made (and sometimes lost) by understanding and working within the parameters of government policies, and little but wasted time is to be had by complaining about policies that have already been publicly approved. For example, while breaking up monopolistic companies is much feared, historically it has proven extraordinarily profitable for those owning the companies, as well as providing a well of opportunities in opened-up industries. On the other hand, businesses that do not pay attention to monetary policy may find that they are critically overextended just when the Federal Reserve tightens credit.

Microeconomic Policies

Microeconomics[1] assumes that individuals will make rational choices in their best interests when provided with the opportunity. These choices spur competition, which, in turn, spurs hard work and innovation. Because of the massive number of decision points occurring in the market, allowing prices to float (Adam Smith's invisible hand) is strongly preferred over government-controlled pricing. As a capitalist economic system, these principles are often infused in US economic policies. However, microeconomics does not cover all areas of economic activity, and the assumptions of perfect and high-performing markets must often be enhanced with government intervention. For example, armies lie outside of microeconomics because they are not paid for by individuals. Society has the right to regulate businesses to ensure that they do not excessively corrupt the environment. Consumers need accurate or relatively full information to make good decisions. Monopolies, price fixing, bid rigging, and so on sabotage the invisible hand. And without a reliable legal system to protect contracts of not only the wealthy but the poor, transactions will slow and the market will shrink. US economic policies in microeconomic policy areas, then, must decide what the right balance is, and exactly how to ensure that the market functions well, without being overly regulated. We look at five areas.

Size-of-Sectors Policy: Division of Responsibilities

It is possible to have entirely state-run or command economies without a private sector. Even production of consumer products can be run by the government, and the labor market and all production quotas can be planned. Such comprehensive planned or "command" economies were tried in Russia, eastern Europe, China, North Korea, and Cuba, among others in the twentieth century, but only a few remain. Experts generally agree that only China made lasting economic and social strides under their command economy (see Lawrance 1998 and Chapter 12 for a discussion of this "mixed" case), and even that country has elected to migrate to a capitalist system.

Socialist systems (within the capitalist sphere) have a substantial private sector, but still rely heavily on the government. While consumer and industrial goods are under the control of the private sector, the public sphere is more likely to operate the health system as a fully run government enterprise (called the "single payer" policy option in the US), comprehensive retirement plans, extensive public transportation systems, and power industries. For countries with oil and gas, retaining these rights often produces an enormous profit center that may be used to defray higher taxes, as discussed below. Historically, socialist systems have a mixed record of success, ranging from some of the most successful economies in the world—such as in Scandinavia—that have virtually eliminated poverty (Campbell and Pedersen 2007), to less successful ones—such as in South America, Africa, and Asia—in which the opportunities of state control are squandered by poor management by government or outright corruption.

In capitalist economies, the bulk of the economy is run by individuals, private companies, and nonprofit organizations. Governments still provide national defense, public safety, and economic and market stability, but tend to have more modest levels of social welfare programs such as education and default health care, and strongly resist intervening in consumer and industrial markets. Capitalist economies have been the mainstay of the modern world since the emergence of Europe from feudalism in the 1300s. Capitalist economies have a wide range of effectiveness as well, depending on the quality of implementation and the fortunes, or misfortunes, of history. Today, capitalism is enjoying the largest resurgence it has seen since the "roaring twenties." While the US capitalist system is not as unfettered as it was in the 1920s, government policies since put in place make the severity of an event like the Great Depression less likely, but not impossible if poor fiscal and debt mismanagement occurs in the long-term.

Sector policy in the US provides that all consumer and industrial goods are privately provided, the oil and gas industry is entirely private (Makhijani 2013), the healthcare industry is shared but highly lucrative for the private sector, education is largely public or publicly subsidized, transportation is largely shared (e.g., public roads and private vehicles), and retirement via Social Security is shared, since it is only a safety net rather than a full pension system. While approximately 38 percent of the economy in the US is controlled by the public sector, much of that directly funds private sector activities. For example, government purchases by the military branches run into hundreds of billions of dollars. Nonprofit organizations may be contracted to provide public social services. And government runs many risk pools such as flood insurance, bank insurance, and Social Security that, if run properly, pay for themselves over time. Let's look at two types of government control.

Most functions of government act as an expense for government, either through taxes or user fees, but on occasion they can provide revenue similar to profit for cross subsidization. When government has full authority, it can be established with three different financial goals. First, government can run functions with its own personnel and accountability largely through political, executive, and legal parameters. This ownership is wholly or largely subsidized by taxes, but the expense in many areas is lessened by user fees. Most core government agencies, including defense, public safety, corrections, K-12 education, basic infrastructure, public heritage resources such as parks and public lands, space exploration, justice, etc., operate primarily on tax receipts. Such agencies are set up in law, strictly regulated, and controlled by the annual legislative appropriation process. To provide more flexibility or cost savings, frequently governments subcontract some of their responsibilities. For example, various US governments "own" 100 percent of the prison population by responsibility, but subcontract out approximately 8 percent of the prison population to for-profit corporations (Wikipedia 2021). The private prison population in the UK, Australia, and Canada is an even larger percentage than in the US.

Second, government can run self-funded operations with the explicit intent that they are not profit-making and have a degree of independence from central government functions. The conversion of the Post Office to the Postal Service, for instance, was to force government postal services to be efficient on one hand, but to ensure the public interest in universal rural delivery and modest cost on the other. In the US, federal examples include Fannie Mae, Freddie Mac, the Export–Import Bank, the Federal Deposit Insurance Corporation, the Federal Crop Insurance Corporation, the Corporation for Public Broadcasting, and the Tennessee Valley Authority. State governments often set up universities as public corporations but nonetheless subsidize them heavily.

Finally, in less common instances, government can own profitable production or resources as a proprietor, stockholder, or investor where profitability is expected. Local governments often have utilities that subsidize the general fund, state governments have lotteries that pay for education or other social goods, and national governments may own and operate oil and other mineral operations. For example, most of the oil companies in the world are operated or largely controlled by their respective governments, with primary exceptions being the US, the UK, the Netherlands, and Canada. See Exhibit 4.1 regarding sovereign wealth funds for more information about this profit-making model and the long-term investment that it can lead to.

Exhibit 4.1

Sovereign wealth funds

Sovereign wealth funds are created by governments for long-term investment (Jen 2007). The purpose of the investments varies from specifics such as pensions, education, and social welfare to general fund stabilization. In the latter case, the idea is that should resources run out, there will continue to be a stream of income for the long-term. Investments can also function as "rainy day" funds when there is a short-term but severe economic downturn. Funds can be created by general tax revenue, but are more often generated by one-time resource development opportunities related to the sale of oil and gas, minerals, and land. The countries with the largest amount of sovereign wealth funds include (in order) China, the UAE, Norway, Saudi Arabia, Singapore, Kuwait, Hong Kong, Russia, Qatar, and the US.

The US example is interesting in that the federal government has no sovereign wealth funds; they are all instruments of state governments. The State of Texas has two funds, which were created shortly after statehood (1854 and 1876) for regular and university education, and combined are the largest. Alaska's permanent fund results in extremely low state tax rates and an annual refund to citizens between $500 and $2500 most years. Other states that have sovereign wealth funds are listed below.

Texas (2)	*55 billion*
Alaska	52
New Mexico	20
Wyoming	13
North Dakota	4
Alabama	2.5

An interesting comparative case is the UK and Norway. When North Sea oil reserves opened up, they were divided among four countries, the bulk going to the UK and Norway because of their long coastlines. Prime Minister Margaret Thatcher was just coming to power, and she pledged to downsize government, including privatizing coal and other commodities, and did not elect to create a state-owned oil company, or create a sovereign fund. The revenues amounted to nearly 10 percent of the national budget, and helped fund a small economic boom. Today, the reserves are less productive and the lease revenues quite small. Norway took a different path, creating a private corporation (Statoil) but retaining 60 percent ownership. Like the UK, its leases provided annual income, but it invested a portion of the income in a sovereign fund. That fund is now worth over a trillion dollars, over three times the size of the government budget, and is required to be invested in the Oslo Stock Exchange, supporting Norwegian industry. Furthermore, Norway has kept taxes high (so it has not squandered its wealth), but its per capita income is one of the highest of any substantially sized country. The economic status of the inhabitants and country is perhaps the soundest in the world.

Regulatory Policy

Although governments in capitalist economies do not run large portions of the economy, governments are charged with regulating all sectors (including the government sector itself) by establishing prohibitions, requirements, and legal standards such as laws against fraud, zoning ordinances, requirements for employee safety, and environmental regulation. Yet outright regulation is not the only tool governments use to incentivize behavior (Lunn 2014). Governments can also use financial leverage to encourage certain behaviors, no matter whether it is tax deductions for charitable contributions or mortgage deductions, or subsidizing companies to hire difficult-to-employ individuals, to reduce the unemployed population. Finally, governments can choose not to regulate or incentivize, but can still encourage self-regulation by industry, consumer, and citizen conscientiousness, and encourage ethical and model practices. Let's look at each of these options.

Government Influence by Regulation

Governments, through their elected representatives, get to tell people what to do. Many laws and regulations are common sense or common decency, such as those concerning assault, battery, bribery, burglary, child abuse, domestic violence, drug trafficking, embezzlement, extortion, forgery, fraud, identity theft, kidnapping, money laundering, murder, perjury, rape, robbery, tax evasion, theft, treason, and vandalism. And, of course, this is just a sampling of laws that are widely supported, although people may disagree about definitions and respective punishments.

In terms of the business–government paradigms that we have already examined (Chapter 2), regulation of business is in lieu of control by government ownership. The "ideal" use of a regulatory framework in capitalist theory is when there is the least possible regulation in order to have an orderly and fair business environment. Generally, the cost of implementation of regulations is borne by business in terms of opportunity costs and compliance with restrictions on business practices. The smaller, but still significant, cost of enforcement is generally borne by government.

There are five generic areas of regulatory oversight of business. These are only mentioned here since they will be discussed in depth later in this, or other, chapters (primarily Chapter 3, government roles, and Chapter 5, social regulations). The first is related to the safeguard of patents, debts, and contracts. For example, the Constitution provides for orderly management of bankruptcy by the courts. Second, the protection of the market is critical in terms of ensuring a fair playing field and a stable source of money and credit. Government intervention in this area has increased since the Great Recession of 2008. The proper treatment of employees includes rights regarding working conditions, collective bargaining, wages, unemployment, employer invasiveness, and discrimination, among others. This area has seen the withdrawal of government support. Another area is the welfare of customers. Some important areas include fitness of products or goods, scams, product safety, and consumer credit. In general, although the theory of *caveat emptor* (i.e., let the buyer beware) prevails in the US, it is overridden by a number of risk-reduction considerations commonly accepted today. Finally, there is the protection of the environment. With the creation of the federal Environmental Protection Agency in 1970, efforts to protect air, water, land quality, and endangered species, and efforts to prevent excessive pollution and manage disposal of hazardous waste increased. While the EPA was created under a California Republican President, in recent decades Democrats have been the strong supporters of environmental regulations (e.g., Presidents Obama and Biden) and Republicans have sought to limit and reduce environmental regulation (e.g., Trump).

Dozens of federal laws cover each of these domains. Each state also has its equivalent regulation, with supplementary or higher standards. In addition to the five generic areas of regulatory oversight, there is the specific regulatory oversight for every industry. In some US industries, regulation is extensive, such as in banking, oil and mineral refinement, nuclear energy, transportation related to safety, and health care. In others, such as the regulation of sales and ownership, it is relatively lax or nonintrusive. An important recent example of regulation is the Dodd–Frank Wall Street Reform and Consumer Protection Act of 2010, which re-regulated the financial market to some degree in the wake of the Great Recession and the financial excesses that caused it.

Government Influence by Financial Methods

A second means of the government influencing business is by using a variety of financial methods. Such methods may either increase government expenditures or decrease its revenues. With the rise of market mentality throughout the world, governments have been encouraged to use financial incentives over regulation when possible. They are also increasingly expected to use their financial leverage for the direct benefit of business when it does not harm the public good. This has been especially true in the Anglophone countries, where financial methods have long been closer to the *raison d'être* of society. There are six different methods of using financial methods to influence business: tax breaks, subsidies, infrastructure development, services to support business, service and product procurement, and below-market value use of government resources. A mixture of a regulatory and financial method is when government requires behaviors, but sets low fines more as an encouragement to do good, rather than as a substantial deterrent against violations (see Chapters 8–10). The strength of this perspective is that it can provide a less intrusive and disliked method for government's arsenal in trying to achieve a balanced social agenda. The challenge is that government has limited resources, and issues of equity quickly get raised when there is a perception of abuse or misuse of government support.

Use of the "Bully Pulpit" of Government

The term "bully pulpit" was coined by President Teddy Roosevelt in referring to his ability to use his office to advocate for the public good—in his case, promoting the expansion of the federal park system (Goodwin 2013). Even though governments may not require or financially subsidize behaviors, like parents, governments may still encourage socially conscious and ethical behaviors. They may encourage civic behavior in public service announcements, websites, and public statements. They can support the use of watchdog groups that self-regulate businesses, such as the Better Business Bureau or numerous environmental and health-rating systems.

It can foster neighborhood associations and do-good professional associations such as the National Academy of Public Administration (as opposed to member advocacy organizations). Perhaps one of the most important areas is in encouraging philanthropy, which it does by both financial incentives (substantial tax deductions) and public acknowledgment and praise.

Over the years, the federal and state governments have passed many reforms to reduce the number of regulations and streamline regulatory processes. For example, the Paperwork Reduction Acts of 1980, 1995, and 2010 seek to limit the paperwork burden that can be required of citizens and businesses, as well as to streamline collection. While nearly every President has voiced interest in reducing red tape, the Clinton Administration made it a major policy initiative with then Vice President Al Gore as the leader.

Information Symmetry Policy: Regulation of the Market to Make It More "Perfect"

A system based on markets, competition, and rational behavior has a number of assumptions. One of the important assumptions is access to valid information to make good comparisons, and thus encourage efficiency and innovation on the producer's side, and economy and value on the consumer's side. Information asymmetry is when one side of the buyer–seller equation has inadequate information and can take advantage of the other side. While this is more frequently the case for buyers who are consumers, it is sometimes also true for sellers who are the producers.

It is possible to adopt a "buyer beware" philosophy that lets the market deal with the issue. This philosophy can work well in simple markets, such as used household goods, where expectations are low and liabilities are small. However, this solution has two major problems. First, many of today's products and transactions are highly complex and far beyond the normal consumer to master. Buying a complex product like a car is challenging. Even when used cars are sold in an "as is" category, which is equivalent to "buyer beware," the seller normally must significantly discount the price. Or imagine buying a house without recourse, in which there was an undisclosed cracked foundation, only obvious during the rainy season. Second, when the entire market is unregulated, then everyone must assume the worst, transactions are far slower and more cautious, and prices are substantially higher. Appropriate regulation actually lowers prices in consumer-oriented societies.

There are many ways in which products and services are regulated to protect consumers from fraud, willful concealment, or deceptive practices. Consumers can read product labeling. Contracts for services must disclose various conditions. Contracts for properties must disclose different types of exceptional liabilities. Companies must provide fair statements of their worth and financial practices for potential and current stockholders. Guarantees must be honored. Harmful materials or dangerous features are prohibited. Ratings of health or quality may be required. Consumers can use civil litigation, with or without lawyers, as one source of recourse. Alternatively, consumers may turn to divisions of consumer protection that are found as separate agencies or in state-attorney offices as well as many larger counties and cities. Rampant or egregious disregard of regulations frequently involves the US Department of Justice, and other federal agencies such as the Comptroller. Some examples of Major Fines are listed below for 2020.

Not only do regulations serve to protect consumers in promoting a more perfect market, they can also protect sellers from fraudulent or deceptive

Organization Fined in 2020	*US Agency Issuing the Fine*	*Amount*	*Issue*
Wells Fargo	Department of Justice	$3 billion	Account fraud
JP Morgan	Department of Justice and the Commodities and Futures Trading Commission	$920 million	Illicit trading
Citi	Office of the Comptroller of the Currency	$400 million	Risk management failures
Western Union	Federal Trade Commission	$154 million	Compensation for scam victims
Deutsche Bank	New York state regulators	$150 million	Lax regulation of criminal Jeffrey Epstein
USAA Federal Savings Bank	Office of the Comptroller of the Currency	$85 million	Risk management failures
Capital One	Office of the Comptroller of the Currency	$80 million	Data breach

practices by buyers. By far the most important tools for business are the rules upholding contracts. Because of the legal enforcement provisions in contracts, for example, lack of payment for cars and other products can result in repossession, and lack of payment for a house or apartment in foreclosure or eviction. Use of a false credit card is illegal. Disruptive consumers can be expelled or prohibited. Again, regulations increase the ease and speed of negotiations; countries that do not have strong contract laws or have poor enforcement tend to be cash economies with much lower per capita volume of transactions.

Monopoly Restrictions: Regulation of the Market to Make It More "Perfect"

A second major assumption of capitalist economies is that there are both choices for consumers and competition among companies (Samuelson and Nordhaus 2009). A lack of choice has two negative consequences for consumers. First, when there is a lack of choice due to monopoly, consumers are constrained into what are often less-than-ideal products or services. For example, for decades before the breakup of the largest US telephone company (AT&T, at that time known as "Ma Bell") in 1982–1984, it only offered a single plan of service based on a standard system of local and long-distance charges. Although it was a very well-managed company, provided a stream of technical improvements, and was required to keep most rates reasonable due to heavy regulation, it was only innovative in a technical sense and did not provide significant variety for consumers. Incredible as it seems today, the widespread use of color and the compact phone did not occur until the "princess phone" series debuted in 1959, touchtone dialing was only widely introduced in 1963, and modular jacks were not available until the 1970s. After divesture, companies provided more payment plans and features such as caller ID, and promoted cell phones and eventually Internet access, making telephones practical, handheld computers.

The other major problem with monopolies is the opportunity to charge high prices for poor service or quality. (Government monopolies can produce high taxes or fees for poor service as well.) Regulating monopolies only works relatively well when there is a public right to do so (e.g., public communication needs), the service is relatively straightforward, and the cost of enforcement is not too onerous.

The need to break up monopolies and limit cartels involved in price fixing has been recognized and addressed by government for over 100 years through anti-trust laws. The Interstate Commerce Act of 1887, which focused on the railroad industry, was the first law to provide consumers some protection from the effects of railroads acting as monopolies in some areas and cartels in others. That Act has been broadened today to include other forms of transportation. The Sherman Anti-Trust law was passed in 1890 to address the issue of monopolies and cartels in all industries; this legislation was expanded and strengthened by the Clayton and Federal Trade Commission Acts in 1914.

Collectively, these Acts prohibited the creation of monopolies (via mergers and acquisitions), the functioning of monopolies (e.g., when a company can unilaterally use predatory pricing to quash competition), restricted collaboration among businesses (e.g., price fixing), and prohibited corporate cooperation to restrict free trade (cartels). Famous historical examples of anti-monopoly company break-ups (beyond AT&T mentioned above) include Standard Oil, American Tobacco Company, and the Aluminum Company of America (later called Alcoa). A famous example of price fixing is provided in Exhibit 4.2. A more recent case found Microsoft guilty of anti-competitive bundling; the company was not broken up since there were other consumer options, but the remedy cost Microsoft nearly $70 billion in a suit and a series of consent decrees lasting 21 years (Chan 2011).

While the goals of anti-competition laws are admirable, the practice is highly political and subject to many influences, differing corporate philosophies, and subjective judgments. For example, US Steel was exceedingly big in 1920 and used its monopoly to charge higher prices, but still won its anti-trust suit; in the mid-1920s Ford had over 50 percent of world automotive production and yet it actually drove prices down dramatically, and thus was never the target of an anti-trust lawsuit.

The last 20 years has seen an age of mergers and acquisitions in airlines, banks, and the entertainment/communication industries, and, on balance, an age of corporate concentration, despite robust litigation by DOJ and the Federal Trade Commission. A related, but nonetheless separate, issue is economic leverage over the economy, rather than just on street-level prices. For example, banking continues to be a relatively competitive industry; however, the largest banks are generally considered "too big to fail" because their collapse could have a negative domino effect on the economy. This has become a rallying cry for many corporate critics who see the necessity of government bailouts as providing a kind of expensive insurance exclusively for the largest banks (because small banks are allowed to fail, which they do in considerable numbers) and as encouraging the largest banks to engage in riskier behavior. President Biden issued Executive Order 14036 on July 9, 2021, "promoting competition in the American economy," but it remains how this policy statement gets translated into concrete actions against the corporate juggernauts that have come to dominate US business.

Comparatively, the US, European Union, and other Anglophone countries (e.g., Canada) have the most robust anti-competition laws (Hylton and Deng 2006). Such laws are weaker or lacking in South America, India, and Japan, in which monopolies have existed for a long time, or in China and Russia, in which the conversion to capitalism has been accompanied by the rapid ascendance of corporate empires pieced together and re-created from former state industries.

Exhibit 4.2

Price fixing in the US

Archer Daniels Midland corporation is an American food company that has a dominant global position in the food processing industry (and bioenergy), with an annual revenue of approximately $90 billion a year.

In the 1990s, company executives routinely managed market prices around the world in cooperation with colleagues in other industries, or what is more commonly known as price fixing and cartel collusion. Despite the fact that the practice had been relatively blatant and long-standing, it was largely unnoticed because of the modest effect on world food prices, until a senior executive named Mark Whitacre tried to extricate himself from embezzling charges by informing about price fixing in Archer Daniels Midland (ADM) related to the animal food additive, lysine.

Because of the anti-competition laws that were broken, three top executives went to prison, the company was fined $100 million, and the corporate reputation was tarnished. Whitacre also ended up in prison for 8.5 years on tax and wire fraud, as well as money laundering (Lieber 2000). This story was captured in the 2009 movie *The Informant*, starring Matt Damon as Whitacre.

Property Rights Policy: Property and Contracts

Private property is held in low regard in communal societies and communist states, moderate regard in socialist states, and high regard in capitalist states. The Native Americans have always held land communally as bands or tribes rather than as individuals, even after they were transferred to reservations in the 1800s. Traditional communist states essentially outlawed private property ownership; current communist states such as China have kept communist parties but largely abandoned the economic principle of communal ownership of property. Many former communist countries now practice high levels of "crony capitalism," in which public officials and the courts strongly favor the rights of the well connected, often blatantly using condemnation proceedings to forcibly evict people. Countries with a more socialist leaning, as in Europe, strongly support private ownership, but bend it to public needs more sharply, such as in public planning to ensure the protection of agricultural lands and public spaces.

On the other hand, capitalist states such as the UK, the US, Canada, and Australia give the highest regard to private ownership. The idea is that individuals will best develop the land if it is privately held. In the US, the right to take private land is possible under a process known as eminent domain, but the US Constitution requires appropriate compensation under the Fifth Amendment "takings" clause. Generally, eminent domain is limited to public needs for transportation such as roads, expansion of public facilities such as schools, military needs (rarely used today because of the massive build-up of military facilities in the twentieth century), and to restore public blight to better conditions. While it is allowable to use eminent domain for economic development purposes, such as parcel consolidation by cities for economic development (Kelo v. City of New London, 2005), it is highly unpopular and frequently receives a lot of adverse media attention; therefore, the practice of using condemnation for economic development is relatively limited.

While all modern societies use contracts of some type, they vary by extent and detail. At their most informal, agreements can be confirmed by interfamily marriage, smoking a peace pipe, or simply shaking hands, a custom still occasionally upheld as binding in the US when witnesses are present and in special circumstances. The use of written contracts is the common practice around the world, and the use of extensive details has been taken to its logical extreme in the US, in which consumers must hire specialists such as lawyers or real estate agents, and companies routinely have large legal departments or divisions to manage contracts. This is in part because the US legal system honors contracts robustly, only allowing their abrogation under extraordinary conditions. This is understandable, since the US was founded by a series of social–legal contracts including the Mayflower Compact of 1620 (see Exhibit 4.3), various state charters granted by the kings of England, the Declaration of Independence, the

Articles of Confederation, and, ultimately, the US Constitution itself. While one can bemoan the state of contracts—the fine print, the esoteric language, and their enormity nowadays—nonetheless the ability to rationalize and regularize agreements and ownership provides a bedrock economic base of predictability that fosters transactions and investment so pivotal to the workings of a capitalist system.

Macroeconomic Policies

Beyond keeping the market in balance, countries must consider the roles that they will play in establishing the economic structures within which the market will operate, and manage their own role in the economy. Some macroeconomic policies are essentially the other side of the coin from microeconomics; the size of the public sector (large or small) is certainly related to fiscal policies regarding government revenues and expenditures. Some macroeconomic policies are looked at on a national level; trade policy, for instance, is a discussion of competition on a global, rather than merely domestic, scale. Other policies are clearly outside the direct focus of microeconomics, such as recessionary policy and monetary policy. Here we consider seven macroeconomic areas.

Fiscal Policy

Revenue Policy

Until the Civil War, tariff revenues (i.e., taxes on goods coming into the country) generally constituted 90 percent or more of federal revenues, declined to 50 percent or so until the federal income tax was enacted in 1913, and today are only a bit more than 1 percent of federal revenue.[2] Today, tariffs, fees, fines, and miscellaneous income account for less than 5 percent of the total revenue collection. Over 95 percent of revenue is via taxes on citizens—income, payroll (e.g., Social Security and Medicare), corporate, and excise taxes (generally sin taxes). Thus, revenue policy today is really tax policy. Tax policy includes decisions about the types of taxes collected, tax exemptions, tax progressivity, tax enforcement, and overall rates of public taxes.

Taxes can be either broad based or specific. Broad-based taxes are assessed on everyone (e.g., income tax or sales tax), while other taxes focus on specific things (investing, buying certain products, owning certain things). The US uses a wide mix of tax strategies, with the federal government relying most heavily on income taxes (business taxes provide about 10 percent of tax receipts), state governments relying on smaller income and/or sales taxes, and local governments relying most heavily on property taxes. The federal and state marginal tax rates for business have been dropping over recent years.

Exhibit 4.3

***Mayflower* passengers signing the Mayflower Compact**

Source: Wikimedia Commons (1932). Jean Leon Gerome Ferris.

In 2021, the federal rate was 21 percent and state rates ranged from zero to 11 percent. However, tax dodging and the increasing use of tax havens (e.g., Anguilla, the Bahamas, Bahrain, the Cayman Islands, the Isle of Man, and Vanuatu) by corporations has further decreased minimized business taxes to effective aggregate rates below 20 percent. Examples of companies with effective tax rates (including in other countries) below 15 percent in 2020 include Hewlett Packard, Netflix, Amazon, Microsoft, and Apple.

Tax deductions, credits, and exemptions are called tax expenditures. They decrease the taxes required of individuals or corporations if they spend their money in a certain way—say investing in business expansion or spending on alternative energy or contributing to charities. Through tax expenditures, government strives to stimulate certain parts of the economy or certain kinds of spending.

Taxes can be regressive, flat, or progressive. Regressive taxes charge everyone the same amount for a product or service, but a larger percentage are those with lower incomes. Taxes on food are a prime example of a regressive tax. Flat taxes charge the same amount of tax to everyone. A 10 percent across-the-board income tax is flat because the "pain" of taxes is relatively equal. A progressive tax makes those with more disposable income pay a greater portion of it in taxes. The US Federal income tax is progressive because the official marginal rate ranges from 10 to 39.6 percent.

Tax enforcement can be made easy or difficult by policy, and enforcement can be lax or aggressive. Because of underpayment and non-payment problems, policy-makers can always increase revenues by increasing staffing levels in revenue agencies. However, that means tax agencies have more ability to conduct tax audits, which is frequently strongly opposed by the business community. Similarly, tax enforcement can be more aggressive in going after tax fraud, corporate cheats, and deadbeat individuals, depending on the policies set up by legislators and elected executives. In 1984, a new federal statute created a Sentencing Commission, which, among other areas, raised the sentences in tax evasion considerably. Yet after a 2005 Supreme Court decision, federal judges have much more flexibility, which they have increasingly been using to downgrade sentences. For example, despite sentencing guidelines, billionaire Ty Warner got off with probation for evading taxes on over $100 million in income in 2014 while actor Wesley Snipes got a 2.5-year sentence for tax fraud several years before. On the other hand, in order to stem the rise in identity theft refund fraud, long prison terms have been going to violators (Novack 2014). Still another example is when the Trump organization CFO was prosecuted for tax fraud in 2021, but in that case the primary reason was to create legal leverage to get him to turn on his employer.

The debate about the appropriate level of taxes has always been strident, because nobody likes to pay them and everyone would like them to be lower. One problem is that most people underestimate the benefits that they receive from government, and overestimate what they actually pay (e.g., most people pay an effective rate far lower than the "official" marginal rate). Another problem is perception—any tax at all seems high. For example, tax rates for the wealthy are a fraction of what they were from the 1930s to the early 1980s (e.g., the marginal rate in 1944 was 94 percent!), but there continues to be strong pressure to reduce them further. Despite the near-unanimous disapproval of taxes, Oliver Wendell Holmes was quoted as saying, "I like to pay taxes. With them I buy civilization." He was referring not only to the basic security, enormous infrastructure, and manifold services that government provides, but the Enlightenment and quality of life that it creates through education, legal due process, and democratic processes that are costly but transformative.

On a global comparison, the US's level of taxation is approximately in the middle. More socialized countries have significantly higher tax rates, but more aggressively neoliberal countries tend to be better than the US when all levels of taxation are taken into account.

Expenditure Policy

Although there are many ways to look at how governments spend the money they collect (or borrow), we will look at only two here. First, we will look at expenditure via the size of its employee workforce. Then we will briefly discuss the challenges of different types of spending emphases.

In the earliest days of the country, the federal, state, and local governments were all relatively small. For example, less than one tenth of one percent (.007 percent) of the population was employed by the federal government (civilian) in 1800, and the bulk of those were employed by the Post

Office; state and local governments were also very small.[3] Federal civilian employment grew to .7 percent of the population in 1940, to 1.4 percent by 1970 when it reached its peak, and in 2010 had shrunk to .7 percent of the population. The peacetime average employment for all governments (local, state, and federal) grew from 4.2 percent of the population immediately after World War II to 6.4 percent in 1970, 7.4 percent in 2000, and declined to 6.4 percent by 2012. After the initial boost to government employment at the beginning of the 2008 fiscal crisis, which was intended to prevent employment in both sectors from collapsing simultaneously, government was cut in proportional and absolute numbers. By 2013, total government employment was the smallest percent of population since the 1960s. While the current level of 14 percent of the entire workforce working for government may seem high in comparison to before World War I (when roads were largely unpaved, street lighting was minimal, public education was rudimentary, and public health coverage was primitive), the US remains at the bottom of the list of developed countries, with only a handful having smaller public sector workforces such as the Netherlands, Germany, Australia, New Zealand, Japan, and South Korea.

Absolute government employment has grown since World War II (see Exhibit 4.6), but it has grown very differently among the various levels of government. Federal employment has been relatively flat in absolute numbers, while state government has grown moderately. Outpacing federal and state levels, local government growth has been very substantial with its focus on service provision.

A second way to look at expenditure is by policy areas. Which areas will get how much of a specific pie? In Chapter 1, we discussed spending levels in specific policy areas related to federal, state, and local governments, so here we will only examine a "big picture" perspective—security versus welfare. On the one hand, how much should be spent on police, prisons, parole systems, prosecutorial agencies and departments, the court system, the military, national security agencies, spy agencies, and other domestic and foreign security issues? On the other hand, how much should be spent on education, transportation, disaster assistance, emergency services, public health and support of the healthcare system, social welfare, corporate support (via economic development, bailouts, or subsidies), environmental protection, and other issues related to the well-being of the country's citizens?

As a wealthy country, the US is able to focus on both in economic terms, but on the whole, more attention is paid to security than welfare. For example, the US has the highest incarceration rate in the world—639 per 100,000 people, or five to ten times greater than the rate of most other developed countries, for example, the UK at 130 per 100,000. It also has the largest number of people behind bars of any country in the world, at 2.19 million prisoners. To get a visual sense of the number of facilities needed to maintain the prison population, see the location of jails and prisons in California in Exhibit 4.4.

Exhibit 4.4

Prisons and jails in California

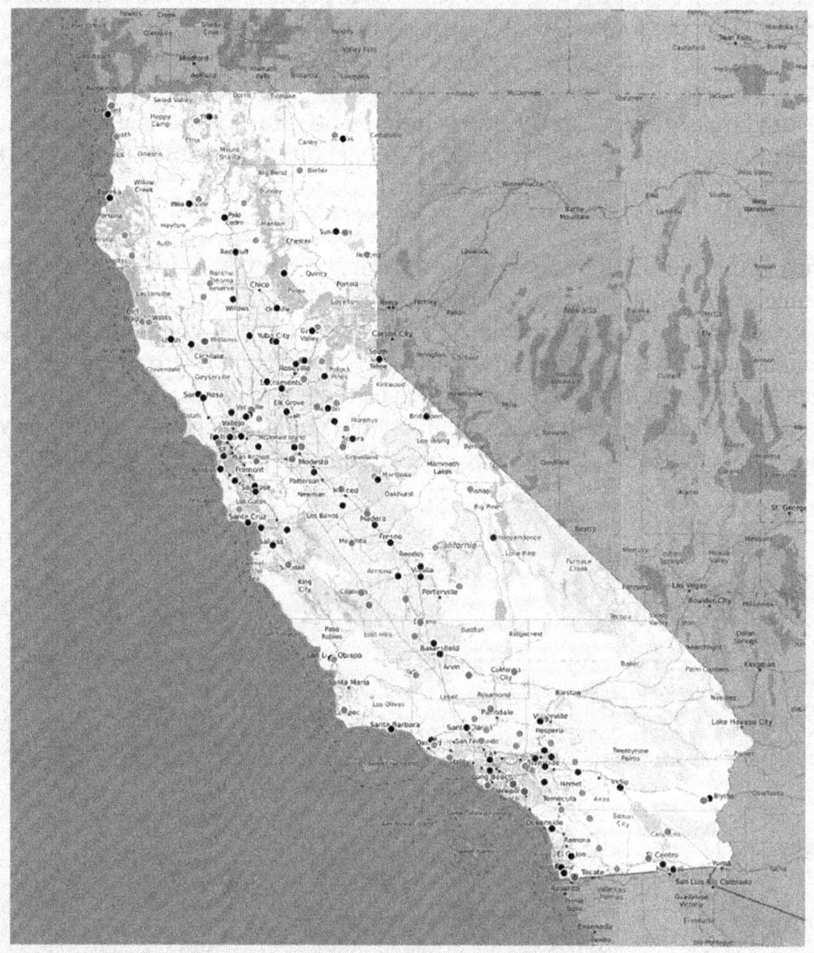

Source: Wikimedia Commons (2020).

Location of jails and prisons in California.

The state prison system has 35 facilities, and the counties and cities have over 100 long-term facilities. The federal government has 13 long-term facilities and eight prison camps in California.

The US military is able to carry on several small wars simultaneously (e.g., the Iraq War was 8.8 years and the war in Afghanistan has lasted over 20 years). Not surprisingly, recent military expenditures have been high (see Exhibit 4.5) and match the total expenses of the next 11 countries combined (SIPRI 2021). Despite its wealth, the US does perform acceptably in welfare, but ranks at the lower end of advanced democracies in areas such as education (25th in education overall but first in higher education, World Population Review, 2020), public health outcomes (37th according to the World Health Organization, 2021), and environmental protection where it has been improving (24th according to the Environmental Performance Index, 2021).

Debt Policy

During the 2007–2010 recession, the federal government relied on extra government spending (or equity and bond purchases) to attempt to stimulate the economy. Economists debate the actual impact, but there is no question that aggregate demand increases when government borrows money and then spends it in the current economy. The theory is that this provides a catalyst that will stimulate underlying actual demand, such that government spending will be replaced by private spending as the economy recovers.

Exhibit 4.5

Military spending

2020 Rank	*Country*	*Spending (Billions)*	*Percent of Global Spending*
	World Total	*1,981*	*100*
1	US	778.0	39
2	China[a]	252.0	13
3	India	72.9	3.7
4	Russian Federation	61.7	3.1
5	UK	59.2	3.0
6	Saudi Arabia[a, b]	57.5	2.9
7	Germany	52.8	2.7
8	France	52.7	2.7
9	Japan	49.1	2.5
10	South Korea	45.7	2.3
11	Italy	28.9	1.5
12	Australia	27.5	1.4
2–12		760.0	38.8

Source: Author and Stockholm International Peace Institute
a SIPRI estimate.
b The figures for Saudi Arabia include expenditure for public order and safety and might be slightly overestimated.

There is a great deal of debate, but little consensus about the impact of the government deficit on the economy. First of all, let's be clear on some terminology. Debt is something that is a collective ongoing measure of how much is owed, whether that is personal or governmental. The national debt is the total of what the US government owes to lenders. The deficit is an annual budgeting concept. At the end of any year a budget is in surplus or deficit. It has either spent more or less than it has received from revenue. If the federal government ends the year in deficit, that must be covered through borrowing, which increases the cumulative national debt.

The US government borrows money through the mechanism of selling Treasury Notes (T-bills) or savings bonds. The Treasury Department offers bonds at a certain rate of interest and purchasers fund the governmental debt. The government also funds the deficit by borrowing from other governmental accounts, like Social Security or Medicare. In the 2021 fiscal year, the national debt was approximately $28 trillion, of which almost a third was held by other government funds, and half of that was from Social Security. The amount of debt held by the Federal Reserve skyrocketed during the COVID pandemic. It had nearly doubled to 25 percent in just a few years in 2021 as the Fed tried to support the market.

Debt is generally not allowed by state constitutions as a part of the annual budget process. However, state and local governments nonetheless borrow money for long-term obligations primarily through bond measures, which are considered separate from the general fund. At one time, these bond measures were used largely for expensive infrastructure improvements in which the expense was essentially being amortized (e.g., spreading out the cost of a sewer system or bridge over a number of years). Today, local government bond issues are more frequently used for services and, occasionally, for general fund support. State and local combined debt stood at about $3.4 trillion in 2021, with Illinois having the worst debt ratio and Alaska having the least proportional debt.

As with the workforce and budget, however, it is important to evaluate the size of the debt in relation to the economy as a whole. The US national debt is a function of many factors, but the two most dramatic factors are war and recession. The great wars—the American Revolution, the Civil War, and World Wars I and II—caused huge national expenditures that took decades to pay off. In the case of World War I, for example, there was not enough time to pay down the debt completely before the country was mired in depression, so it was rolled into the costs of new national calamities.

There are two ways to bring down the size of debt. One way is to pay it off as one would do in a household or business. Thus, after World War I, subsequent Presidents and Congresses ensured that every year from 1920 through 1930, the national debt was being paid down with small but steady surpluses, to approximately 35 percent of the absolute amount borrowed. Yet almost as important as decreasing the size of the debt was renewed expansion of the economy. Between payments for debt reduction and increased growth in the economy, the overall debt was reduced from a 1919 high of 32 percent to less than 15 percent in 1929.

Beginning in the 1980s, different economic philosophies have affected the debt cycle. Tax rates were perceived to be too high in the 1970s, which led to tax reductions at all levels of government. Services were not reduced at the same time, however, so revenue and expenditure patterns rarely matched, pushing up annual deficits and overall debt in the same way that a war normally would. A reverse of this pattern occurred in the latter part of the Clinton Administration when a Conservative Congress and a "new Democrat" President vied with one another in an effort to reform government. One positive example was the Welfare Reform Act of 1996, which kept in place programs that ensured the very poorest children and their mothers would continue to get assistance, but that reduced excessive use and abuse of the program in order to cut costs. The pattern was again reversed under a Republican presidency in the early 2000s, with new tax cuts and increased defense spending, raising the debt modestly (about $1.5 trillion), even though the economy was expanding rapidly. The collapse of the economy in 2008 triggered substantial new deficit spending, as was seen during the Great Depression in the 1930s to prevent excessive retraction of the economy. It was further exacerbated by the COVID-19 pandemic starting in 2020 when government spending surged and revenues were stagnant.

Monetary Policy: Money Supply and Interest Rates

Monetary policy concerns control of the money supply or how much money is in circulation. The money supply consists of how much money people and companies have, plus what they have borrowed. The assumption is that the more money that is available, the more will be spent, and that will grow the economy. The money supply is controlled primarily by increasing or decreasing the cost of money, which means the interest rates of borrowing. By the law of supply and demand, the lower the interest rate, the cheaper it is to borrow money and the more spending will happen. The higher the interest rates, the less money is borrowed and spent, reducing demand and depressing economic activity.

In the US, monetary policy is controlled by the Federal Reserve System. The Federal Reserve (or Fed) is a quasi-governmental independent entity governed by seven members who are nominated by the President of the US and confirmed by the Senate for 14-year terms. The long terms are meant to insulate the governors from political pressure. (For more information, see www.federalreserve.gov and also Chapter 2.)

Two main areas where the Fed influences the money supply are in setting interest rates and regulating bank activity. The Fed loans money to the Federal Reserve banks and sets interest rates for those loans. The rest of the banks in the country tend to follow the ups and downs of the interest rates set by the Fed. So when the Fed raises its interest rates, the whole system raises its rates and the cost of borrowing money goes up, reducing the number of loans and thus the money supply available to be spent. The Fed will do this when it perceives the economy to be strong and it wishes to slow economic growth. Conversely, when the economy is not doing well and the Fed wants to increase the money supply available to be spent, it lowers its interest rates. The Fed rate has been low or zero since 2009. See Exhibit 4.6.

Exhibit 4.6

Effective federal funds rate showing a trend of very low rates recently

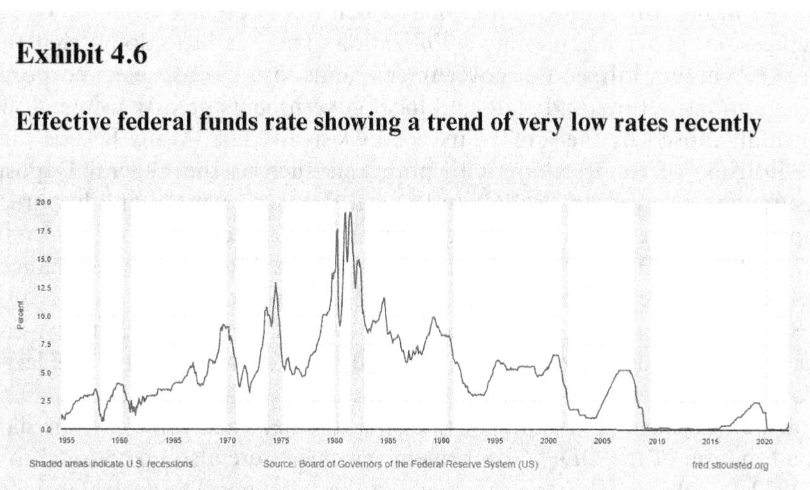

Source: St. Louis Federal Reserve

Another other way the Federal Reserve influences the money supply is by the rules it imposes on banks, particularly the amount of cash reserves (Reserve Rate) a bank must have on hand. The higher the percentage of a bank's assets that must be kept on hand, the less it is able to lend. Reducing the Reserve Rate increases the money available to be lent and spent. While the Fed may want to stimulate lending, it must also be careful to make sure banks retain enough cash to stay solvent. The Federal Reserve may also attempt to influence the economy through buying or selling Treasury bill investments; however, the impact is debated since money is essentially just moving from one account to another. There are other regulations on banks imposed by the US Treasury Department and the Security and Exchange Commission, but monetary supply is essentially a Federal Reserve domain.

Recessionary Policy

Recessionary policy has already been extensively discussed in Chapter 1 in terms of comparing the competing visions of what is known as demand-side economics (e.g., Keynesian) versus supply side (e.g., the Chicago School of economics philosophy). In the ideal, Keynesian economics promotes a strong and large capitalist private sector with a moderately sized government to provide a variety of ongoing national, local, and individual functions such as defense, education, and transportation. Because of the normal ups and downs of the business cycle, it also advocates strong government spending when the business cycle is down, especially in infrastructure and employment. It also advocates programs that tend to collect money over the long-term, such as unemployment insurance, and that will be drawn upon more heavily in bad times. Such programs, which were absent during the Great Depression, provide economic stabilization. There is little doubt that the large Keynesian infusion of government funds into banks, select corporations, infrastructure, and state and local governments greatly softened the downfall caused by the Great Financial Crisis of 2008. Many believe that the infusion of funds, along with programs such as the Federal Deposit Insurance Corporation (FDIC) and Social Security, averted another great depression. Government spending again averted an economic meltdown in 2020 with the COVID-19 shutdowns; no counterbalancing revenue enhancements were made so national debt increased sharply.

Supply-side economics points out the power of a growing economy. For example, the federal government dutifully made payments on the large World War I debt and brought it down one third in absolute terms by 1929. However, because of economic expansion, the debt had fallen by one half as a function of the GDP. Government revenues were also up considerably in 1929, largely owing to the expansion of the economy. The central insights of supply-side economics are that, in the long-term, a stable absolute debt becomes less significant as the economy grows, and a vital private sector economy becomes more important in order to maintain that growth.

A big challenge for Keynesian economics is one of being virtuous in good times. It is easy to spend money when it is flowing into the Treasury, rather than save it for a rainy day. While economic discipline at the federal level was good through the 1970s, it collapsed in the 1980s. Conservatives wanted to cut government heavily except for a build-up in defense, and Liberals refused to eliminate programs. In the end, Conservatives were able to cut taxes and ratchet up defense spending, Liberals got to keep their programs, and so the deficit began to grow. While there was a round of sensible deficit reduction during the Clinton presidency, when fiscal Conservatives pressured Clinton and the Democrats into paying down the debt during the economic boom, this resolve vanished thereafter, with neither Conservatives nor Liberals willing to make the necessary sacrifices. Thus, when the recession hit in 2008 and the business lockdowns occurred in 2020, the debt was already skyrocketing, and Keynesian spending patterns took the US back to World War II highs. On the other hand, the challenge of supply-side economics at the macro-level is one of remembering that it only works on an economic upswing, and that downturns are inevitable. Indeed, the excessive enthusiasm of supply-side economics can lead to a short-term policy-making perspective, unrealistic assumptions for the long-term, and excessive austerity when the economy is most fragile.

Trade Policy

One of the big changes to the economy has been the extent to which it has become globalized. This is such an important issue that Chapter 11 is entirely devoted to it. In this chapter we will outline some definitions and some government business interactions. See Exhibit 4.7 for the trade symbol of our era, shipping containers!

Exhibit 4.7

Trade policy and the enormous historic impact of tariff policy on the US economy and politics

By Pat Whelan,
Published on June 23, 2020 Free to use under the Unsplash License

Tariff policy has affected the economy and politics in fundamental ways but is not generally recognized today. Four important effects are described below.

Wars. It is not an understatement to say that tariff and tax issues were the most important cause of the American Revolution as represented by the Boston Tea Party of 1773. Americans wanted more control over their economic destiny. Tariffs nearly caused a civil war in 1832 when South Carolina adopted the Ordinance of Nullification, declaring the tariffs null, void, and nonbinding in the state. If not for the strong action of President Andrew Jackson, the South would probably have seceded because of the very high tariff rates in the Tariff Act of 1828, also known as the Tariff of Abominations. Finally, while tariffs were not the major cause of the Civil War for Southerners who wanted low tariffs, the election of a Republican president (Abraham Lincoln) whose party's platform was higher tariffs made the political divide significantly more difficult to overcome.

Protectionism. Most Americans think that the US has always been a free trade country. This is not true. From the American Revolution until World War II, the US has been among the most protectionist countries in the world and for over 50 years (1863–1913) was the most protectionist country the world with minor exceptions. The major exceptions were the mid-1830s through the beginning of the Civil War, and from 1913 to 1922. The moderate to very high protectionist policies until the 1940s ensured that American industries had become mature and efficient in the large US market. With extraordinary dominance of the US economy after World War II, it only made sense to change its stance and to build a trade regime that encouraged all countries to lower tariffs.

Revenue policy. Up until the introduction of the income tax in 1913, tariffs and excise taxes were the primary source of revenue for the federal government. Today, tariff revenues are only about five percent. It should also be noted that higher tariffs have not always meant higher revenue. The lower but moderate tariff rates in the 1830s through 1863 actually increased revenue enormously because of much greater import volume.

Trade Balances. Until the 1970s, the US on average had trade surpluses. Since the 1970s trade deficits have dominated. Being a leader in free trade, but in a country with high labor costs with a well-off consumer-oriented public, has made trade deficits inevitable. However, the appetite for less free trade and more protectionism was demonstrated in the election of President Donald Trump and his dramatic realignment of Republican economic values.

Trade policy refers to rules about transactions involving money crossing national borders. Since each country tends to have its own currency, to buy and sell across borders usually requires an exchange of those currencies. Usually this is just an electronic transaction. If the US buys more from foreign markets than it sells to them, the economy is said to be in a trade deficit. The US last ran a trade surplus in 1975. The economic impact of this deficit is another one of those debated issues. Essentially, as long as other countries accept dollars, it is unlikely to have any great impact.

Despite the general economic debate, to the extent that US consumers buy more products from outside the country, we reduce demand for US products and thus reduce US employment. If this is not balanced by products that we sell overseas, it can have an ongoing effect on national employment. Most of the jobs that have been lost overseas have been low-skilled jobs in labor-intensive industries. Labor intensive means more of the cost of a product is taken up by personnel costs. Capital intensive means more of the cost is taken up by technological (machine) costs.

As long as labor costs in some countries continue to be significantly lower than the US, industries that use a lot of unskilled labor will tend to establish themselves in those countries. This is seen as part of normal market forces, which are assumed to balance out in the long run. The government may decide to intervene in trade for several overlapping reasons: because of unfair market practices, to protect US jobs, or for national security reasons.

Unfair labor practices occur when governments protect their local industries vis-à-vis similar industries in other countries. This can happen in a variety of ways. The most typical and easiest to see are tariffs. A government can protect an industry through tariffs on competing imports, and so these practices are called "protectionist" policies. Government may also help a local industry through tax breaks, through government-sponsored research or subsidized transaction costs. Or a country may not impose a tariff but instead limit the number of such products allowed to be imported and sold locally (quotas). A government may simply have a local mandate to protect jobs, regardless of whether the competitive practices are unfair or not. There may be a government-sponsored campaign to "buy local" and requirements that imported products be labeled with their country of origin—which can be challenging in a globalized production process. Finally, there may be a self-defined national security reason to protect industries (e.g., a fear that if we depend on another country for all production of product X, they might at some point withhold it from us). So we must preserve our ability to produce our own, even at a higher cost. For example, because of past oil embargoes from Middle Eastern countries, the US established a National Petroleum Reserve where oil is stockpiled in the event of an interruption.

The concept of market efficiency has been promoted worldwide, and since the end of World War II in the late 1940s there have been international agreements and organizations that have striven to reduce tariffs, and promote a free market globalized economy. Since US economy dominated the world economy, it has been a leader in this effort to provide a more capitalist-oriented, global, economic system. Nonetheless, the US often violates its own precepts or has internal disagreements about the ideal parameters of trade in a complex world. For example, like many countries, the US continues to be mildly protectionist toward its weaker agricultural products, some goods such as footwear, and is highly protectionist toward its vast military-industrial complex. See Chapter 13 for an in-depth treatment of these various organizations.

Capital Flow Policy

Capital flow policy refers to the ability of capital to move from one national economy to another without excessive regulations and restrictions. It generally does not refer to equity ownership in stock markets (i.e., passive portfolio ownership). Measures that impede capital flows include investment outflow restraints, foreign direct investment (FDI) caps, land ownership embargoes, and currency exchange restrictions.

Restricting citizens from investing in foreign companies or select foreign countries is diametrically against capitalist principles. With the dominance of the market orientation in the world today, few major economies, other than some such as China, Iran, and Nigeria, still restrict outflows substantially. However, developing countries have a special problem in this regard because the richest people in the country may prefer to invest abroad rather than in their own country where it may be desperately needed, or they may simply be highly protective of their money. This syndrome is called capital flight.

Investment inflows provide capital for businesses to expand. Investment caps limit the amount of money that can be invested by foreign individuals and corporations in companies in certain industries. Industries that are commonly capped at 49 percent or below around the world, and include domestic transportation (especially airlines), energy companies, and banks. For example, the US caps foreign direct investment in airlines and media. In absolute terms, the US has the greatest amount of FDI; other major FDI hosts are China, the UK, Germany, Belgium, France, Canada, Switzerland, and Singapore. As a percentage of their economies, numerous countries outstrip the US, with Singapore and Switzerland leading the way.

While land ownership embargoes and challenging regulatory processes on foreign ownership are technically a small part of financial flows, they do tend to greatly enhance or discourage the open market climate for business and investment.

Currency exchange restrictions are also a small part of the global economic system, but like land ownership restrictions, tend to encourage or discourage the open market climate of a country. Most countries have eased currency exchange restrictions, except for declaration purposes to reduce international money laundering.

Overall, US policies related to capital flows are quite open, resulting in a moderately high rating in relation to other countries. (See the US International Trade Commission for more information on US FDI data.)

For an overview of all the policies discussed in the chapter, see Exhibit 4.8 regarding traditional US economic policy areas and trends.

Economic Policies at Different Levels of Government

Most of the issues that have been addressed in this chapter have related to the federal government. The federal government has the largest tax and spending impact. The federal government has the Constitutional role of printing money and controlling its supply. The federal government has sole control of interactions with other countries and with interstate commerce. In addition, the Constitution, with its "Supremacy Clause," states that federal policy takes precedence over state and local policies.

However, state and local governments still have large impacts on both business and local economies. State and municipal governments spend money and can stimulate economic activity through tax incentives or subsidies. They can further impact business through regulations, planning, and permitting. These topics are explored in depth in Chapters 8–10.

Analytical Case: Policies

The President is up for re-election. Both the President and the opposing party candidate are asked to present their "jobs policy." The President presents a plan that includes raising the minimum wage, creating a job training program to help workers transition to new skills, increasing student aid, and increased spending on state infrastructure.

The opposing candidate presents a plan for deregulation, including dismantling the EPA and the Consumer Product Safety Commission and drastically cutting governmental spending. Both policies have pros and cons.

They will both affect the economy in different ways. Predict some of the intended and unintended consequences of these proposed policies (assuming they actually become law as intended). Create a 2 × 4 table that lists the pros and cons of the two candidates' "jobs Bills."

Questions for Discussion and Analysis

1 How will the two policy approaches affect supply and demand?
2 How will they differently affect the money supply, and what impact will that have?
3 What intended and unintended consequences may result from the different policies?

Exhibit 4.8

Traditional US economic policy areas, possible choices, and recent trends

Traditional Micro- or Macroeconomics	*Economic Policies Related to Business and Public Sector*	*Possible Extremes in Economic Principles (e.g., Free Market versus State Control)*	*US Economic Policies in Recent Decades in Terms of Pure Free Market Principles in Global Comparison*
Microeconomics	1 *Size-of-sectors policy:* division of responsibilities between public and private sectors, e.g., consumer goods to public transportation to public safety	No private sector No public sector except defense	Moderately large private sector: 40/60 split, with private sector having all high-profit areas (e.g., oil and gas) and public having defense and welfare
	2 *Regulatory policy:* voluntary, incentive based, or rule based	Most rules are voluntary or incentive based Most regulations are rule based	Moderate use of regulation: use of all types of regulations; increasing regulation of environment and decreasing regulation of labor market
	3 Regulation of the market to make it more "perfect": *information symmetry policy*	High level of consumer information Low level of consumer information	Relatively high level of consumer information
	4 Regulation of the market to make it more "perfect": *monopoly policy*	No monopolies Many monopolies (private and public)	Moderate: a number of oligopolies in oil, technology, etc., and few government monopolies outside core functions
	5 *Private rights policy:* contracts and property	Great protection of contracts and property rights Little protection of contracts and property rights	Very high level of contract and property rights
Macroeconomics	6 Fiscal policy: *revenue policy*	Low taxation or some rebates High levels of taxation	At the global average level of taxation as a percentage of income

7 Fiscal policy: *expenditure policy*	Only public safety and defense Additional areas include infrastructure, public welfare, risk, business promotion and economic development, etc.	Moderate balance between safety and defense and welfare/economic development with an increasing emphasis on safety and defense
8 Fiscal policy: *debt policy*	No debt allowed Maintenance of debt OK	High debt level policy currently
9 *Monetary policy:* money supply and interest rates	No central bank, no national currency, unregulated interest rates Central bank, national currency, and management of moderate interest rates	Strong use of monetary structures and tools
10 *Recessionary policy:* cyclical or counter-cyclical	Cut public spending in recessions and depressions to keep budget in balance Use of counter-cyclical fiscal and monetary policy to prevent and mitigate recessions and depressions	Moderate to strong use of counter-cyclical measures in 2008 recession, but none in the decade before
11 *Trade policy:* level of protection for internal markets	No tariffs, subsidies, restrictions to protect domestic industries Use of tariffs, subsidies, restrictions to protect domestic industries	Low-moderate use of open trade policies: low use of tariffs, moderate use of subsidies, relatively low level of technical restrictions
12 *Capital flow policy:* free or restricted	No restrictions on capital flows-out or in—across national borders Severe restrictions on capital flows—out or in—across national borders	No restrictions on outflow; low restrictions on inflow (except for national security interests)

Practical Skill

Finding Economic Data

An important element of planning your business is understanding market conditions. Some data is particular to the product, but other data is about the economy in general. The federal Bureau of Labor Statistics is a key source for data. State offices may also collect statistics. The BLS breaks down employment and unemployment rates by state and local area, computes the consumer price index, and includes economic data.

Skill Exercise

Select a city or county. From BLS databases http://www.bls.gov, report the five-year trend of:

1 The unemployment rate
2 Inflation
3 Local wages
4 Average education of workers.

Summary and Conclusion

An overall, detailed table summarizing the five microeconomic and seven macroeconomic government policy trends we have discussed in this chapter is provided in Exhibit 4.8.

Key Terms

- Capital flight syndrome
- Information symmetry
- Public corporations
- Capital flow policy
- Interstate Commerce Act
- Recessionary policy
- Cartel
- Regulatory policy
- Caveat emptor
- Macroeconomics
- Revenue policy
- Command economy
- Microeconomics
- Sherman Anti-Trust Act
- Crony capitalism
- Monetary policy
- Size-of-sectors policy
- Debt policy
- Monopoly policy
- Sovereign wealth fund
- Expenditure policy
- Price fixing
- Too big to fail
- Fiscal policy
- Property rights policy
- Use of the bully pulpit

Notes

1 Here we are interpreting microeconomics as classical economics.
2 See the Harmonized Tariff Schedule (HTS) administered by the US International Trade Commission (USITC): http://usitc.gov/tata/hts/bychapter/index.htm.
3 The statistics come from the US Census.

References

Campbell, J. L., and Pedersen, O. K. (2007). The Varieties of Capitalism and Hybrid Success: Denmark in the Global Economy. *Comparative Political Studies, 40(3)*:307–332.

Chan, S. P. (2011). Long Antitrust Saga Ends for Microsoft. *Seattle Times*, May 12.

Goodwin, D. K. (2013). *The Bully Pulpit: Theodore Roosevelt, William Howard Taft, and the Golden Age of Journalism*. New York: Simon & Schuster.

Hammouya, M. (1999). *Statistics on Public Sector Employment: Methodology, Structures and Trends*. (SAP 2.85/WP.144). Geneva: Bureau of Statistics, International Labour Office.

Hylton, K. N., and Deng, F. (2006). *Antitrust Around the World: An Empirical Analysis of the Scope of Competition and their Effects*. Boston University School of Law: Working Paper Series, Law and Economics.

Jen, S. (2007). Sovereign Wealth Funds: What They Are and What's Happening. *World Economics, 8(4)*, October–December.

Lawrance, A. (1998). *China under Communism*. London: Routledge.

Lieber, J. B. (2000). *Rats in the Grain*. New York: Four Walls Eight Windows.

Lunn, P. (2014). *Regulatory Policy and Behavioral Economics*. OECD Publishing. doi: 10.1787/9789264207851.

Makhijani, S. (2013). Profits for Oil, Gas & Coal Companies Operating in the U.S. and Canada. *Oil Change International*, September 26.

Novack, J. (2014). Federal Judges Are Cutting Rich Tax Cheats Big Sentencing Breads. *Forbes*, May 14.

Samuelson, P., and Nordhaus, W. (2009). *Macroeconomics*. New York: McGraw-Hill.

Scott, D. (2011). Combined State Debt: More than $4 Trillion of FY 2011. *Governing*, October 25.

SIPRA (Stockholm International Peace Research Institute) (2021). http://portal.sipri.org/publications/pages/expenditures/splash-expenditures.

Wald, M. L., and Ivory, D. (2014). G.M. Is Fined over Safety and Called a Lawbreaker. *New York Times*, May 16.

Wikimedia Commons (2020). https://www.openstreetmap.org/. https://commons.wikimedia.org/wiki/File:Map_of_all_federal,_state,_and_county_incarceration_facilities_in_California.png.

Wikipedia (2021). Private prisons at https://en.wikipedia.org/wiki/Private_prison.

Part II

Business–Nonprofit–Government Relations in the Sociopolitical Arena

5 Protection of Consumer, Employee, and the Environment

Ann Johnson

Chapter Contents

Case 5 Scenario

A Polluter's Quagmire

Tyler's father, Tomas, is the owner of Trujillo Landscaping, Inc., a sod and landscape company started by Tyler's grandfather Teodoro, located at the edge of the City of Somewhere. The company is dedicated to the production, sale, and installation of lawn grasses and other landscaping products, so it is important for his business that he keep weeds controlled and make his sod grow lush and green. For that purpose, Tomas uses both pesticides and a chemical fertilizer to ensure he produces the best products.

DOI: 10.4324/9781003178620-7

Recently, a grassroots citizen group—the Friends of Somewhere—expressed concerns about the contents of a nearby water table to the local newspaper. Last week, a representative from the group visited Trujillo's and talked with Tomas about the issue. The representative warned him that his products might have a direct impact on neighborhood water quality and urged him to switch to organic pesticides and fertilizer.

Tomas was deeply concerned. He looked into manufacturing his own products with organic substances and found it to be prohibitively expensive. Tomas learned that the pesticides he used would really only penetrate about a foot into the soil, so something else must be contaminating the water table. He also learned that some amount of pollution would be an unavoidable byproduct of the chemical compositions of most pesticides and fertilizers and each state has its own regulations about the distribution and disposal of toxic substances. Tomas is unsure of where to turn to find information regarding how to more safely apply a product and dispose of residual toxic substances. He is also eager to know how to comply with any regulations concerning groundwater.

At dinner that evening, Tyler suggested to his father that perhaps he could ask the Friends of Somewhere for a little guidance. Or maybe pay Zoey a visit. After all, she had just gone through much of the regulatory setup for her own business and helpful websites and contacts may be fresh in her mind. Tyler's father thought that was a good idea. Besides, he needed to deliver a couple corkscrew junipers for the entrance of Happy Paws anyway, a grand-opening gift from one business owner to another.

Later, while doing historical research, Tomas discovered that there had once been a well on his land. When the EPA investigated, they indeed discovered the old well, which was allowing runoff to penetrate the water table. It was almost completely obscured at the edge of the Trujillo Landscaping property. But now, with the discovery, Tomas was able to take the appropriate steps to remedy the problem and preserve the good name his family worked so hard to create.

Government as Regulator of Business

Regulation is a type of government intervention in economic activity through commands and controls enforced with coercive power. Government as a regulator of business has evolved over three major periods in the United States (see Chapter 3). The first occurred in the Moderate-Sized

Government Era (1887–1933) with the passage of the Interstate Commerce Act in 1887, which established the Interstate Commerce Commission (ICC) to regulate railroad rates. Following the same tradition, legislation was enacted to shore up anti-trust powers as well as consumer rights in the early twentieth century. During the Moderate-Sized Government Era (1933–1970s), regulation was extended to industries as well as to labor markets. The trend was accelerated in the 1960s and 1970s when many social regulations addressing externalities and hazards were introduced. Regulation was expanded to consumer products, the workplace, and the environment. The third period, the Rightsizing Government Era, introduced economic deregulation to several industries such as transportation, telecommunications, electric power, and natural gas transmission.

Regulation at any level of government balances the needs of public and private interests (Lehne 2006). These needs can be societal as well as economic (see Chapter 4). This chapter focuses on social regulation and the interplay between government, the private sector and citizen groups. Three areas of social regulation will be covered, starting with consumer protection, then moving to employee protection and, finally, to environmental regulation. The summary of these areas is intended to provide an overview of the evolution and current status of how businesses have adapted their practices to comply with government mandates and will illustrate approaches taken by the public and private sectors to accomplish these measures.

Theories of Regulation

Philosophically, Emile Durkheim stated that people will be destroyed and societies will disintegrate without some sort of social regulation, particularly when there is rapid economic progress. Of all organizations, the state is most equipped to provide for the welfare of the system and protect labor. Thus, the government has the moral obligation to fulfill these purposes (Jones 1986). Because people will not naturally check their own wants, regulations are a check on greed (Jones 1986).

In the modern US system of government regulations, two dominant theoretical frameworks emerge when social regulation is discussed. *Public interest theory* contends that regulations benefit the public in areas where market competition does not necessarily help the public. One example where the market would not benefit the public is "natural monopolies," areas where the circumstances make it unlikely for competition to exist, such as utility companies or, in the non-economic context, employment discrimination (Lehne 2006). Another area that would not be regulated without government intervention is the environment.

Competing ideas exist as to why we regulate. *Public choice theory* of governmental regulations promotes the view that interest groups and politics are mainly driven by monetary interests, and that the ends are more important than the means. Sometimes it is argued that the private sector is able to act on behalf of the agency that is supposed to be practicing oversight. Thus, regulations benefit the private sector and not the public. Public choice theory has been criticized as an over simplification of human behavior (Lehne 2006). Critics of public choice theory point out that some behavior is altruistic and is clearly not motivated by individuals gaining money. For example, people may vote for social programs that benefit others but not themselves. Thus, values and ideology may matter more than what interest groups can offer to voters from those elected (Lehne 2006). *Self-regulation theory* suggests that socially conscious consumers can cause industry to self-regulate (Volden and Wiesman 2009). Regardless of which theoretical framework seems the most accurate, social regulations have become increasingly intricate, and it is crucial that firms are aware of when their business practices involve an area that is covered by these social regulations.

The US Regulatory Framework

The US Constitution provides the authority for regulation. Article 1, Section 1 of the Constitution grants Congress the sole power to enact laws. The power to regulate commerce among states is given to Congress by Section 8 of Article 1 of the Constitution. Meanwhile, the Constitution also places limits on regulation. The Fifth Amendment to the Constitution limits government regulatory power by stating that "No Person shall be deprived of life, liberty, or property, without due process of law; nor shall private property be taken for public use without just compensation." This due process protection is extended to actions taken by states via the Fourteenth Amendment.

Regulation, as both a political and economic instrument, takes place through an open public process, which allows interested parties to participate (see Chapter 7). Most regulations, except anti-trust laws, are implemented by independent commissions and executive branch agencies. The courts also play a critical role in interpreting regulatory statutes, assessing their constitutionality, and ensuring procedural due process. Many legal principles of regulation have come from court decisions that constitute the common law, which refers to a body of law developed by judges through court decisions as opposed to statutes passed by the legislative process or regulations promulgated by the executive agencies.

Although the Constitution does not explicitly authorize Congress to delegate policy-making to agencies, regulatory agencies assume the responsibility to promulgate rules, make policies, and resolve disputes. Laws written by Congress provide the authority for regulatory agencies to write regulations. Regulations explain the technical, operational, and legal details necessary to implement laws. Regulatory agencies take two basic forms—independent commissions and executive branch agencies. Independent commissions, such as the Federal Reserve System, Federal Trade Commission, International Trade Commission, Securities and Exchange Commission, National

Labor Relations Board, Consumer Products Safety Commission, and so on, make policies through majority-rule voting and formal rule-making procedures.

Most executive branch regulatory agencies are housed in a cabinet department, which has its administrator appointed by the President or a cabinet secretary. Examples include the OSHA in the Department of Labor (DOL), FDA in the Department of Health and Human Services (HHS), and National Highway Traffic Safety Administration (NHTSA) in the Department of Transportation (DOT). The EPA is an independent executive branch agency and does not belong to a cabinet department.

To implement statutes passed by Congress, regulatory agencies assume an important activity of rule-making, which refers to the process that executive and independent agencies use to create, or promulgate, regulations. Typically, Congress first sets broad policy mandates by passing statutes, then agencies create more detailed regulations through rule-making. In addressing the concern about agencies in exercising their powers, Congress enacted the Administrative Procedure Act (APA) of 1946, providing that agencies' rule-making procedures should be consistent with the APA. The APA also grants parties the right to sue for judicial review of an agency action under the framework of procedural due process; that is, if an agency fails to follow APA procedures, or procedures it has established, the courts can overturn the agency's decision. In addition to *procedural due process*, the courts review regulatory actions for whether they are *arbitrary or capricious*, which addresses the issue if an action by the agency exceeds the scope of the mandate and if it has a basis in the record of evidence that agency keeps. The courts also review regulatory actions for *substantive due process* to ensure they conform to the Constitutional requirements.

The implementation and enforcement of laws involves regulatory agencies that assist or force regulated entities to meet legal requirements, as well as hold entities legally accountable for any violations.

Government as a Protective Regulator

Government's regulation to business generally falls into two categories—economic (or industrial) regulation and social regulation. *Economic regulation* sets prices or conditions on entry of firms into an industry. It also includes the regulation of financial firms. *Social regulation*, otherwise, involves the correction of externalities (see Chapter 2) and is largely protective in nature. It is concerned with the qualities of the goods and services produced, the conditions under which production occurs, as well as the impact of production on society. *Social regulation* is applicable to many or all industries and affects a broad spectrum of social groups. It involves government dictating the details of production, such as the design of products, the conditions of employment, and the nature of the production process. One factor to distinguish economic regulation from social regulation is that the two have followed very different paths in recent decades. Whereas there has been a decline in economic regulation, a rapid expansion of social regulation has been observed, as described earlier. When the deregulation movement started in the 1970s, more social regulatory agencies—including the EPA and OSHA—were created. There appears to have been a great public demand for government to take a more active role in social regulation. US social protective regulation generally covers three areas, namely consumer protection, employee protection, and environmental protection, which are mainly governed by the federal regulatory framework. Exhibit 5.1 summarizes the federal regulatory framework of the three areas.

Consumer Protection

Consumer protection refers to the regulatory framework designed to ensure the rights of consumers, as well as fair competition and accurate information in the marketplace. The underlying rationale of consumer protection is to correct market failure associated with asymmetric information (see Chapter 2). A market economy espouses consumer sovereignty, which refers to the paramount power of the consumer to affect the operation of a market. In a market economy, "consumption is the role end and purpose of all production" (Smith 1937, p. 38) and consumers have the freedom of choice—they are free to accept or reject any products in the marketplace; therefore, producers have to effectively respond to the needs of consumers in order to pursue profit. This assumes that consumers are capable of making rational decisions in a competitive market filled with a large number of buyers and sellers. Yet in reality, consumers are often in a disadvantaged situation where they don't have enough information to make rational choices.

In the past, the relationship between the buyer and seller was governed by the common-law concept of *caveat emptor* ("buyer beware"), which assumed that both buyer and seller were equally knowledgeable about the merchandise and, in the case of a dispute between the buyer and seller, the buyer had to undertake the burden to convince the judge or jury that the seller deliberately misrepresented the condition of the merchandise before it was sold. The Industrial Revolution fundamentally changed the landscape when a wide range of manufactured goods was produced, and consequently, the average person could no longer fully understand the intricacies of the many products in the market.

The increased demands for protecting consumer rights have led to the passage of various laws and regulations. Roughly, these laws and regulations comprise three major areas—prevention of fraud and misrepresentation of food, drugs, and cosmetics; protection of consumers from unfair competition and deceptive practices; and consumer product safety (Langran and Schnitzer 2007).

Exhibit 5.1

US Federal Social Protective Regulatory framework

Social Regulation	*Regulatory Agencies*	*Major Laws*
Consumer Protection		
• Fraud and misrepresentation of food, drugs, and cosmetics	The Food and Drug Administration (1931) [HHS]	The Pure Food and Drug Act of 1906 The Meat Inspection Act of 1907 The Food, Drug, and Cosmetics Act of 1938 The Public Health and Service Act of 1944 Drug Amendments of 1951, 1958, and 1962 The Medical Device Amendment of 1976 The Nutrition, Labeling, and Education Act of 1990 The Generic Drug Enforcement Act of 1992 The Best Pharmaceuticals for Children Act of 2002 The Pediatric Research Equity Act of 2003
• Unfair competition and deception	The Federal Trade Commission (1914)	The Federal Trade Commission Act of 1914 The Wheeler–Lea Amendment to the Clayton Act of 1938 The Wool Products Labeling Act of 1939 The Fur Products Labeling Act of 1951 The Textile Fiber Products Identification Act of 1958 The Cigarette Labeling and Advertising Act of 1966 The Fair Packaging and Labeling Act of 1966 The Truth-in-Lending Act of 1968
	The Consumer Financial Protection Bureau (2011)	The Poison Prevention Packaging Act of 1970 The Fair Credit Reporting Act of 1970 The Consumer Product Warranty Act of 1975 The Fair Debt and Collection Practices Act of 1977 The Truth in Savings Act of 1991 The Credit Card Accountability Responsibility and Disclosure Act of 2009
• Product safety	The Consumer Product Safety Commission (1972)	The Flammable Fabrics Labeling Act of 1954 The Refrigerator Safety Act of 1956 The Federal Hazardous Substances Labeling Act of 1960
	The National Highway Traffic Safety Administration (1970) [DOT]	The Hazardous Substance Act of 1964 The Child Protection Act of 1966 The National Traffic and Motor Vehicle Safety Act of 1966 The Poison Prevention Packaging Act of 1970
	The Drug Safety Oversight Board [FDA]	The Public Health Smoking Act of 1970 The Consumer Product Safety Act of 1972 The Medicare Reform Act of 2003

Social Regulation	*Regulatory Agencies*	*Major Laws*
Employee Protection		
• Employee welfare	The Department of Labor The National Labor Relations Board (1935) The Occupational Safety and Health Administration (1973) [DOL]	The National Labor Relations Act of 1935 The Fair Labor Standards Act of 1938 The Labor Management Relations Act of 1947 The Labor Management Reporting and Disclosure Act of 1959 The Occupational Safety and Health Act of 1970 The Family and Medical Leave Act of 1993
• Anti-discrimination	The Equal Employment Opportunity Commission (1964)	The Equal Pay Act of 1963 The Civil Rights Act of 1964 and 1991 The Age Discrimination in Employment Act of 1967 The Vocational Rehabilitation Act of 1973 The Pregnancy Discrimination Act of 1978 The Americans with Disabilities Act of 1990 The Violence Against Women Act of 1994, 2013
Environmental Protection		
	The Environmental Protection Agency (1970)	The Refuse Act of 1899 The Oil Pollution Acts of 1924, 1961, 1973, and 1990 The Water Pollution Control Acts and Amendments of 1948, 1956, and 1972 The Clean Air Acts of 1963 and Amendments of 1970, 1977, and 1990 The Water Quality Acts of 1965 and 1970 The Endangered Species Preservation Acts of 1966 and 1969 The Air Quality Act of 1967 The National Environmental Policy Act of 1970 The Endangered Species Act of 1973 The Safe Drinking Water Act of 1974 and Amendments of 1992 and Renewal of 1996, 2011 The Resource Conservation and Recovery Act of 1976 The Environmental Response, Compensation, and Liability Act of 1980 The Hazardous and Solid Waste Amendments of 1984

Prevention of Fraud and Misrepresentation of Food, Drugs, and Cosmetics

Regulations to prevent fraud and misrepresentation of products are designed to protect consumers from the adulteration, misbranding, or mislabeling of food, drugs, and cosmetics. Regulations against product adulteration or fraud have a relatively long history. From colonial times to the late nineteenth century, most food and drug regulations were enacted at the state and local level. For example, the state of Massachusetts adopted a food adulteration law in 1641, requiring the official inspection of beef, pork, and other meat. In the mid-1800s, the states of Virginia and Ohio started to enact laws against the adulteration of food and drugs. During the remainder of the century, the scale and scope of state food and drug regulation expanded significantly. Yet with increased interstate competition, regulation at the federal level was deemed necessary.

In the late 1800s, pure-food bills were introduced in Congress, but failed to become law due to opposing business interests. Several events built up public sentiment for protection and eventually led to the passage of the Pure Food and Drug Act of 1906 and the Meat Inspection Act of 1907. One of those notable events was the publication of Upton Sinclair's bestseller, *The Jungle*, in 1906, which vividly described the filthy conditions of the meat-packing industry in Chicago. After reading the book, President Theodore Roosevelt ordered an immediate investigation of the industry. Public pressure eventually issued a new lease of life to the shelved bills and pushed them through Congress. The Pure Food and Drug Act of 1906 is the first significant piece of consumer protection legislation at the federal level. It outlawed interstate trade of "adulterated" or "misbranded" foods, and required producers to indicate the presence of mixtures and/or impurities on product labels.

The adulteration and misbranding provisions of this law also applied to drugs, which went beyond state legislations' protection at that time. Enforcement of the Act became the duty of the Bureau of Chemistry, a division under the US Department of Agriculture. The Bureau of Chemistry was renamed the Food and Drug Administration (FDA) in 1931. In 1940, the FDA was transferred from the USDA to the Federal Security Agency, which eventually became the Department of Health and Human Services in 1979.

During the Depression of the 1930s, there was a resurgence of public interest in consumer protection, due to exposure of various consumer abuses, including filthy, decayed, and insect-infested food, as well as the false or misleading advertisement of drugs. The FDA and its supporters started to lobby Congress in favor of stronger legislation that would give the agency greater authority to regulate the patent medicine industry. However, their efforts were seriously obstructed by the patent medicine industry itself and its congressional allies. In 1938, a tragedy finally broke the deadlock between the two parties, when over 100 people were killed as a result of consuming a liquid sulfa drug called "Elixir Sulfanilamide," which had been marketed without being tested for toxicity. Public outcry over the tragedy eventually led to the passage of the Food, Drug, and Cosmetics Act of 1938, which gave the FDA greater oversight over the food and drug industry. The agency's authority was extended to include cosmetics and therapeutic devices. The new law required that drugs be marketed with adequate directions for safe use and the FDA was granted the power to regulate the therapeutic claims drug manufacturers printed on their product labels. Most importantly, the Act introduced mandatory pre-market approval for new drugs, meaning that drug manufacturers had to demonstrate to the FDA that a new drug was safe before it could be released to the market.

The Food, Drug, and Cosmetics Act went through several amendments, among which were the 1962 Drug Amendments, passed in response to a therapeutic crisis, as the use of a suppressant for morning sickness (thalidomide) by pregnant woman caused the birth of deformed babies in Europe. Under the amendments, drug companies were required to prove that drugs were both safe and effective prior to market release and the FDA was granted the power to oversee clinical trials for new drugs. In addition, the responsibility for regulating prescription drug advertising, which originally was given to the Federal Trade Commission (FTC) under the Food, Drug, and Cosmetics Act of 1938, was transferred from the FTC to the FDA. After these series of amendments, the United States became one of the toughest drug-approval regimes in the world.

Since the 1960s, regulation has continuously strengthened the government's authority over various aspects of food and drug commerce. For example, the 1976 Medical Device Amendment required premarket safety testing of medical devices. Similarly, the 1990 Nutrition, Labeling, and Education Act required nutritional labeling for all packaged foods, and the 1992 Generic Drug Enforcement Act granted the FDA authority to oversee generic drugs. More recently, the 2002 Best Pharmaceuticals for Children Act allowed the FDA to request pediatric drug testing sponsored by National Institutes of Health (an agency of HHS), and the 2003 Pediatric Research Equity Act mandated manufacturer-sponsored pediatric drug trials for certain drugs as a "last resort." However, some legislation has also weakened government's regulatory power over the industry. For instance, the 1976 Vitamins and Minerals Amendments and the 1994 Dietary Supplements and Nutritional Labeling Act preclude the FDA from regulating dietary supplements, as a result of the advocacy and lobbying efforts of the consumers and producers of "natural" or "herbal" remedies.

Prevention of Unfair Competition and Deceptive Practices

The prevention of unfair competition and deceptive practices involves government regulations of various forms of disclosure, including advertising, labeling, and product warranties, as well as consumer credit (Langran and Schnitzer 2007). This is a relatively broad area that is generally under the regulatory supervision of the Federal Trade Commission (FTC). The FTC is an independent agency with a bipartisan body of five members appointed by the President. The agency's principal mission is the promotion of consumer protection and the elimination and prevention of anti-competitive business practices.

The FTC was established in 1914 by the Federal Trade Commission Act signed by President Woodrow Wilson against trusts, which had been a significant political issue during the Progressive Era (see Chapter 3). The Act was passed following two Supreme Court decisions against Standard Oil and American Tobacco, who had used their size and clout to undercut competitors in a number of ways. Under the Act, the commission was authorized to issue "cease and desist" orders to large corporations to curb unfair trade practices.

Section 5 of the Federal Trade Commission Act granted the FTC the right to prevent unfair competition practices. Although Section 5 outlawed unfair methods of competition in commerce, it did not address the issue of fraud and deceptive practices.

Advertising

In the case of advertising, for instance, in 1931, the Supreme Court overturned the ruling of the FTC that Raladam, the manufacturer of Marmola (a tablet containing thyroid substance), misrepresented its product as a remedy for obesity. Although the Court found evidence of misrepresentation common among vendors of such remedies, it concluded that since no conclusive proof of damage could be drawn to Raladam or its competitors, the FTC could not prosecute consumer fraud; therefore, the court vacated the judgment. In response to the court's decision, the Wheeler–Lea Act of 1938 was passed to amend Section 5 of the Federal Trade Commission Act, specifically proscribing "unfair or deceptive acts or practices" and "unfair methods of competition," as well as providing civil penalties for violations. It added a clause to Section 5, stating "unfair or deceptive acts or practices in commerce are hereby declared unlawful." The amendment created criteria in determining an illegal advertisement, as far as it deceives a significant number of consumers and therefore is a representation, omission, or practice that is likely to mislead the consumer in their purchasing decision.

Labeling

Another area of disclosure under the FTC oversight is the labeling of products. Labeling is any written, electronic, or graphic communication on the package or on a separate but associated label of a certain product. A series of laws have been passed to protect consumers from product misrepresentation. For instance, the Wool Products Labeling Act of 1939, the Fur Products Labeling Act of 1951, the Flammable Fabrics Act of 1954, and the Textile Fiber Products Identification Act of 1958 required manufacturers to attach labels that specify the nature and content of the materials. The Cigarette Labeling and Advertising Act of 1966 set national standards for cigarette packaging and required all cigarettes sold in interstate commerce to be labeled with a warning that smoking can be harmful to health. The Fair Packaging and Labeling Act of 1966 required labels on many consumer products to state the identity of the product, the name and place of business of the manufacturer, packer, or distributor, as well as the net quantity of contents. The Poison Prevention Packaging Act of 1970 required the use of child-resistant packaging for drugs, chemicals, and other hazardous materials that can be unsafe for children. In recent years, whether or not to require labeling of genetically engineered (GE) or genetically modified (GM) foods has become an ongoing debate. Those in favor of labeling emphasize consumers' right to know what's in their food. Opponents point to the fact that no significant differences have been found between GE or GM and conventional foods and emphasize the expense and logistical difficulties of labeling. Although mandatory labeling of GE and GM foods has been proposed, there has been no action by Congress to date.

Product Warranty

A warranty refers to a guarantee or promise that provides an assurance by the manufacturer to the consumer that affirms specific facts or conditions of the goods being sold. Commonly, new goods are sold with an implied warranty that the goods are indeed as advertised. Used products, however, may be sold "as is" with no warranties. In the United States, Article 2 of the Uniform Commercial Code (which has been adopted with variations in each state) provides implied warranties. The Consumer Product Warranty Act (also known as the Magnuson–Moss Warranty Act) of 1975 was designed to protect consumers from deceptive warranty practices. Consumer products are not required to have warranties, but if one is given, it must comply with the Act. The Act also required that any written warranty be readily understood by consumers. The FTC was granted the authority to prescribe rules and regulations for deceptive practices.

Consumer Credit

Although credit cards of various types had been used for a long time, it was not until the 1960s that the credit card became popular. Financial institutions also made credit easier to obtain by consumers about this time, yet incomplete consumer credit information often made it difficult to choose between various types of loans. For many years, consumer credit activities were regulated by state laws, which were inconsistent in various aspects. The demand for protecting consumers against fraudulent and unfair credit disclosure practices eventually drove the federal legislative process and led to the passage of the Truth in Lending Act (TILA) of 1968. The law was designed to promote the informed use of consumer credit by forcing creditors to notify consumers of the actual cost of that credit. It required uniform or standardized disclosure of costs and fees to encourage competition in financing, from which the consumer can benefit. It also prohibits the issuance of a credit card without the consumer's oral or written agreement. Later, a handful of consumer credit protection laws were enacted, among which were the Fair Credit Reporting Act of 1970—aimed at protecting the privacy of consumers against the issuance of erroneous credit reports—the Fair Debt Collection Practices Act of 1977—establishing legal protection from abusive debt collection practices—and the Truth in Savings Act of 1991—establishing uniformity in the disclosure of terms and conditions regarding interest and fees and forbidding any misleading or inaccurate advertising for opening bank accounts. During the Great Recession of 2008 (see Chapter 3), which was partially attributed to the fraudulent lending practices of the financial industry, the Credit Card Accountability Responsibility and Disclosure Act of 2009 was signed into law by President Barack Obama. The Act, also known as the Credit Cardholders' Bill of Rights, mainly aimed to establish fair and transparent practices by limiting how credit card companies can charge consumers.

In 2011, the Consumer Financial Protection Bureau (CFPB) was established as an independent agency of the US government, responsible for consumer protection in the financial industry. The CFPB was authorized by the Wall Street Reform and Consumer Protection Act of 2010, as a response to the financial crisis of 2007/08 and the subsequent Great Recession. The bureau is located inside and funded by the Federal Reserve and affiliated with the US Treasury Department. In addition to writing and enforcing rules for financial institutions, supervising their operations, and monitoring financial markets, it also collects and tracks consumer complaints. While the agency's purview over some banks was curtailed in 2018, and it was ruled an executive agency because of its structure in 2020 by the Supreme Court, it remains a robust constraint on fraud and abuse in the financial industry.

Consumer Product Safety

Product safety regulations were often established as responses to tragedies or consumer advocacies. One early example was the passage of the Flammable Fabrics Labeling Act of 1954 after serious injuries and deaths caused by the ignition of clothes made from synthetic fibers. The federal automobile safety standards were promulgated in the 1960s, mainly driven by the consumer movement advocated by Ralph Nader. In 1965, Nader published his book *Unsafe at Any Speed*, accusing car manufacturers (mainly the manufacturer of Corvair, General Motors) of resistance to the introduction of safety features. General Motors responded to Nadar's criticism by hiring an investigator to find evidence against him, which made Nader a national leader of a consumer movement for car safety. In 1972, the Consumer Product Safety Act was passed as a result of alarming findings regarding consumer product safety in a report presented at a congressional hearing. The report indicated that over 20 million people were injured by unsafe consumer products annually, among whom about 30,000 were killed and over 100,000 were permanently disabled (US Senate Committee on Commerce 1972).

The authorities that oversee product safety are relatively diffused. Generally speaking, most product safety issues are under the authority of the Consumer Product Safety Commission (CPSC), which is an independent agency of the US government established in 1972 under the Consumer Product Safety Act. The CPSC regulates the manufacture and sale of over 15,000 consumer products, ranging from clothes to vehicles. Products such as alcohol, tobacco, guns, and explosives, which involve high risks and are often associated with criminal behaviors, are regulated by the Bureau of Alcohol, Tobacco, Firearms, and Explosives in the US Department of Justice. Drug safety is supervised by the Drug Safety Oversight Board of the FDA. Automobiles are regulated by the National Highway Traffic Safety Administration, which is a branch of the US Department of Transportation. The agency was established in 1970 to enforce the Federal Motor Vehicle Safety Standards.

State Regulations of Consumer Protection

In addition to federal regulation, a number of states such as (but not limited to) Colorado, Delaware, Illinois, and Ohio, have adopted the Uniform Deceptive Trade Practices Act (UDTPA). The Act aims at preventing deceptive trade practices such as unfair or fraudulent business practices, as well as untrue or misleading advertising. States that have not adopted the UDTPA often have similar, other laws. States may choose to implement food safety standards, such as the Manufactured Food Regulatory Program Standards (MFRPS), developed by the FDA. Some states, including Florida, Delaware, and Minnesota, have legislated requirements that contracts be written at reasonable readability levels that common consumers can understand.

California has by far the strongest consumer protection laws as a result of rigorous advocacy and lobbying by many social interest groups such as the Consumer Federation of California, California Consumer Protection Foundation, Utility Consumers' Action Network, and Privacy Rights Clearinghouse. For example, the state's Unfair Competition Law broadly prohibits unlawful, unfair, and fraudulent business practices and deceptive advertising.

Most states have a Department of Consumer Affairs devoted to protecting consumers and providing legal services. For example, the California

Department of Consumer Affairs, with its 41 regulatory entities (25 boards, nine bureaus, four committees, two programs, and one commission), issues licenses in more than 100 business and 200 professional categories, including doctors, dentists, contractors, cosmetologists, and automotive repair facilities.

Employee Protection

Employee protection refers to the legal framework that protects the welfare of employees, including wages, working hours, health, safety, and working conditions, as well as the right for equal employment opportunities.

Employee Welfare

As a result of the industrial revolution, productivity increased exponentially, but the lives of workers worsened in many aspects. The demand for labor in heavy industry caused many employees to be drawn into a new working environment that prior generations had not experienced. Concerns about health, safety, and quality of life for workers began to take center stage as circumstances deteriorated.

There were a few early, scattered, regulatory attempts to address aspects of employee welfare at the workplace. For example, Massachusetts passed the nation's first law to limit the working hours of women and children employed in factories in 1874 (see Chapter 3). However, there was virtually no consistent labor legislation at the federal level.

Collective Bargaining and Unions

During the industrial revolution, as a result of frustration over wages, hours, and working conditions, workers began to organize into trade associations, called unions, to collectively bargain with employers (Dalton, Hoyle, and Watts 2006). The National Labor Relations Act (NLRA), also known as the Wagner Act, was passed in 1935 as a reaction to many of the employment practices of the industrial revolution (Dalton, Hoyle, and Watts 2006). NLRA is a foundational statute of US labor law, which granted private sector employees the right to organize into unions, engage in collective bargaining for better terms and conditions at work, and take collective action (e.g., strike) if necessary. The NLRA is enforced by the National Labor Relations Board (NLRB), an independent agency of the US government. It is charged with conducting elections for labor union representation, as well as investigating and correcting unfair labor practices.

In a unionized workplace, management will communicate about wages and other conditions of employment with the union representatives rather than with the employees themselves (Bernardin 2007). The union has a representative, who is voted in by union members. The employees are represented by the union during the bargaining process. If an employee believes they are being treated unfairly on the job, they will often file a grievance.

For employers with unions, collective bargaining specifically describes the process where management and unions negotiate terms of employment contracts specifying the wages and benefits for the contracted period of time (Bernardin 2007).

The NLRA largely drove the labor movement in the 1940s. About 25 percent of the workforce was unionized after World War II. During the war, unions agreed not to strike, in order not to destroy the war effort. When the war ended, the issue of falling wages across the board led to large strikes. From 1945 to 1946, there was a series of massive labor strikes affecting many industries and public utilities. Many policy-makers and businesses were threatened by the strikes, as well as labor unions' ideological affiliations to communism. As a response to the rising union movement, the Labor Management Relations Act (also known as the Taft–Hartley Act) was enacted in 1947 to restrict the activities and power of labor unions. The amendments added a list of prohibited actions (including many forms of strikes), or unfair labor practices, on the part of unions to the NLRA. It also required union officers to sign affidavits declaring that they were not supporters of the Communist Party or any organizations that might attempt to overthrow the US government. The Act still remains effective today.

After revealing the corruption and undemocratic practices of unions, in 1959 the Labor Management Reporting and Disclosure Act was passed to regulate unions' internal affairs as well as their officials' relationships with employers. The Act further restricts union activities in the United States.

In 2018 the Supreme Court disallowed the practice of "agency fees" common in 32 states including California in which nonmembers are required to pay fees to a union for representing all workers (but not for political activities). The ruling, called Janus v AFSCME, had a dramatic impact on the ability of unions to raise funds against members' consent.

Fair Labor Standards

In 1938, the Fair Labor Standards Act (FLSA) was signed into law by President Roosevelt as part of his New Deal legislation. The FLSA introduced a maximum 44-hour, seven-day work week and established a national minimum wage. Over 700,000 workers were affected by the Act, and over 130 million US workers are now covered by the FLSA.

The Wage and Hours Division of the US Department of Labor (DOL) governs minimum wage and overtime in accordance with the Fair Labor Standards Act (FLSA). Under the FLSA, when an employee works more than 40 hours a week, the employer is required to pay the employee time and a half normal wages. See Exhibit 5.2 for an example about Walmart, a frequent FLSA violator.

The Fair Labor Standards Act (FLSA) also governs the conditions of child labor. The FLSA requires children be 14 years old for most types of jobs, but must be 16 years old for mining, manufacturing, and transportation jobs (Bernardin 2007). State laws also may have a higher minimum for child labor laws. However, child labor laws are often violated, and it is difficult to monitor them in many workplaces.

The FLSA has been amended many times since its passage; the national minimum wage in 1938 was $0.25 per hour (25 cents), but it was $7.25 in 2021. States can, and many do, set a minimum wage above the national minimum. The State of Washington had a minimum wage of $13.69 in 2021. Some states allow their cities to have minimum wage rates higher than the state minimum; although not common, some city minimum wage rates are much higher than state rates such as the City of Seattle, which has a minimum wage rate of $16.69 per hour in 2021. The federal contractor minimum wage rate is $15.00.

Occupational Health and Safety

During the industrial revolution in the United States, the number of workers in factory jobs increased exponentially as people went from working in agriculture to working in more urban settings. Despite the sophistication of production methods, industry continued to focus on gaining wealth and not on workplace safety, which went largely unregulated. However, since the 1970s, cultural changes have caused less of a tolerance of risk (Bardach 2002). Decreased tolerance for possible injuries, combined with a greater concern for employee well-being, created a political environment where workplace safety could be more greatly regulated.

In 1970, Congress enacted the Occupational Safety and Health Act to ensure that employers provide their employees with a working environment free from recognized hazards such as toxic chemicals, unsanitary conditions, mechanical dangers, and excessive noise, heat, or cold. Under the Act, the Occupational Safety and Health Administration (OSHA) was established in the US Department of Labor and was charged with the authority to administer the Act.

Exhibit 5.2

Walmart FLSA litigations

The Fair Labor Standards Act of 1938 (as amended) provides standards for both minimum wages and overtime entitlement, and specifies administrative procedures by which covered work-time must be compensated. The Act also provides an exemption for individuals who are employed in executive, administrative, professional, and outside sales, as well as certain technical positions. To qualify for an exemption, employees need to meet certain tests regarding their job duties and be paid on a salary basis at not less than $455 per week; job titles alone cannot determine the exempt status.

Walmart has been a prime target for this type of violation in recent years and has suffered a number of adverse court decisions. For example, on December 23, 2008, the company announced that it settled 63 wage and hour lawsuits in 43 states, which cost the company between $352 and $640 million (Smith 2008).

In 2012, the DOL released another new violation that cost the company $4.83 million in back wages. The violations affected 4,500 Walmart workers. Walmart failed to compensate these employees with overtime pay, considering them to be exempt from the FLSA's overtime requirements. DOL investigation found that these employees were non-exempt and consequently due overtime pay for any hours worked beyond 40 in a week. In its settlement, Walmart agreed to pay back wages to its affected employees nationwide. Additionally, the company was subjected to $463,815 in penalties due to the repeat nature of the violation.

Source: Smith (2008)

OSHA is designed to prevent harm to the safety and health of workers. Safety regulations govern standard setting and industrial codes, whereas health issues address whether exposure to a particular chemical is a contributing factor for disease. Risk assessment of conditions that may cause injury or disease is particularly difficult. There is a balance in the burden between employers and employees (Eisner, Worsham, and Ringquist 2006). This balance can be a contested area and special interests and industry may lobby against certain regulations. Passing workplace safety standards is a politically salient practice. The government may announce mandates for a workplace safety practice. However, employers, industry, and other stakeholders may also lobby to advocate for their position.

Although the federal OSHA regulatory workplace safety framework provides a floor for minimum workplace safety standards, many states have agencies that actively monitor workplace safety. As with most federal relationships, federal law is a base, and state laws may provide for an additional level of oversight. The federal and state governments work in conjunction where the states may pass their own initiatives, but states must receive approval from OSHA (Bernardin 2007). Currently, 22 states have their own complete plans (US Department of Labor 2021). Other states have a partial framework, and OSHA may provide up to half the costs to assist these states.

Exhibit 5.3

The way we worked

Source: Lewis Hine (1909).

Although OSHA is an organization that ensures compliance with and enforcement of safety regulations, OSHA consults with and advises employers who need assistance This information and these resources may be particularly important for small businesses that may not have in house counsel or human resource specialists (US Department of Labor 2021).

Modern conditions have required increased technical understanding and guidance for employers regarding dangerous levels of exposure to hazardous materials and how to mitigate the effects. Businesses can take steps to ensure the safety of their employees and receive assistance with developing strategies to prevent harm. This is particularly true for small firms. For example, in 2011 and 2012, deaths occurred from methylene chloride used in refinishing bathtubs (US Department of Labor 2013). However, the health hazard may be reduced by using alternative chemicals or improving ventilation.

Family and Medical Leave

In 1993, the Family and Medical Leave Act was signed into law by President Bill Clinton. The law was intended to "balance the demands of the workplace with the needs of the families" (29 US C. § 2601). The US Department of Labor Wage and Hour Division was empowered to administer the Act.

The FMLA requires employers with 50 or more employees to allow leave for up to 12 weeks during a one-year period for an illness, to care for a child (after birth or adoption), or to care for a sick immediate family member (children, parents, or spouse) (US Department of Labor 2021). The definition of family members has been extended to include grandparents and other relatives where these relatives served the role of a parent. The FMLA applies to schools, public employers, and private schools with more than 50 students. Firms with fewer than 50 employees at a particular site must comply with the FMLA if the sites are less than 75 miles from each other and the number of employees totals 50 or greater. This provision is for businesses that can move employees around without any great inconvenience.

Employees must provide employers with 30 days' advance notice if the need for leave is foreseeable. If the need for leave is not foreseeable, then the employee must provide notice as soon as practicable. Although the same position may no longer be available at the end of the employee's leave, when employees return to work, the employer must allow them to return to a job that is substantially similar in terms of duties and salary (Klienman 2007).

In addition to providing for a more balanced lifestyle for workers, the FMLA has provisions to protect businesses as well. An employer may also have an affirmative defense if the employee was about to be terminated, regardless of the employee taking leave. Thus, if an employee is performing in an unsatisfactory manner, the FMLA does not require a position to be held at the end of the employee's leave. Employers may exempt employees who are in the highest ten percent of the income range or if the employee's absence will cause the firm to have a serious financial loss (Klienman 2007).

The FMLA provides flexibility for employers if their business would incur a serious financial hardship and the company may request that employees pay their own portion of the health insurance premium (Klienman 2007). Employees may be required to pay their own health insurance benefits, but must not be denied the same health insurance benefits as if they were not on leave. Employees may be required to reimburse the employer for insurance if the employee is able to return to work and does not do so.

Anti-Discrimination

Another area of government intervention in employee protection is through a series of anti-discrimination regulations. The rationale for those regulations is to create equal employment opportunity, which is considered a basic right of the US citizen (see Exhibit 5.4 for a brief discussion about Affirmative Action). Yet discrimination on the basis of gender, ethnicity, age, religion, disability, or any non-professional qualification criterion impedes the realization of true equality of employment opportunity.

Exhibit 5.4

Affirmative action

Affirmative Action refers to government policies that provide special opportunities for, or that are in favor of, disadvantaged groups who have suffered from discrimination.

In the United States, Affirmative Action was initially taken in the form of Executive Orders, which, having the full force of law, are government regulations issued by the President to help officers and agencies of the executive branch manage the operations within the federal government.

As early as 1961, President Kennedy issued Executive Order 10925, requiring government contractors to "take affirmative actions" to ensure equal employment. In 1965, President Lyndon B. Johnson signed Executive Order 11246, which banned employment discrimination based on race, color, religion, and national origin by organizations receiving federal contracts and sub contracts. In 1967, President Johnson issued Executive Order 11375, prohibiting hiring discrimination on the basis of gender in the federal workforce as well as among government contractors.

The Philadelphia Order (or the Philadelphia Plan) was the major Affirmative Action initiative under the Nixon Administration. The Order required government contractors in Philadelphia to hire minority workers under the powers of Executive Order 11246. The Order was extended to other cities. President Nixon also signed the Vocational Rehabilitation Act in 1973 to correct the problem of discrimination against people with disabilities. The Title 5 of the Act required private employers with federal contracts over $2,500 to take affirmative action to hire individuals with a mental or physical disability.

As a result of these efforts, in addition to federal agencies and government contractors, Affirmative Action was extended to universities and schools with federal contracts. They are all required to develop their own affirmative action plans and set up specific goals to increase the hiring of women and minorities.

In 1995 President Clinton, while reaffirming the need for affirmative action, issued a White House memorandum (Memorandum on Affirmative Action, July 19, 1995) calling for the elimination of any program that "(a) creates a quota; (b) creates preferences for unqualified individuals; (c) creates reverse discrimination; or (d) continues even after its equal opportunity purposes have been achieved."

US anti-discrimination regulations were largely driven by the nationwide civil rights movement. The first civil rights law, the Civil Rights Act of 1866, was signed by President Lincoln after the Civil War to protect blacks from employment discrimination. The law had very little impact on improving the employment conditions of black people, especially in the South.

Civil Rights Laws

In the late 1950s and 1960s, the African-American civil rights movement reached new heights that were characterized by major campaigns of civil resistance. Acts of non-violent protest and civil disobedience led to emergent situations between activists and governmental authorities, demanding policy-makers' immediate response to address the inequalities faced by black Americans. One of the most notable protests was the Birmingham campaign in 1963, in which students and children, when protesting against racial segregation, were attacked by high-pressure fire hoses and police dogs. On June 11, 1963, President John F. Kennedy delivered his civil rights speech, urging legislative action to end racial segregation.

The Civil Rights Act was signed into law in 1964, and outlawed discrimination based on race, color, religion, sex, or national origin. Title 7 of the Act deals with discrimination in employment. It prohibits discrimination with respect to privileges of employment, compensation, contract terms, and conditions of employment. The Act also created the Equal Employment Opportunity Commission (EEOC), an independent agency, to enforce laws against workplace discrimination. In 2011 and 2012, the EEOC extended discrimination to include sex-stereotyping (of lesbian, gay, and bisexual individuals) as well as protection to transgender status and gender identity, respectively.

The Act was amended in 1991 to strengthen some provisions as well as broaden the scope of protection. The amendment was in response to a series of ambiguous Supreme Court rulings that limited the rights of employees who had sued their employers. In addition to modifying some procedural requirements, the amendment authorizes jury trials on discrimination claims and allows plaintiffs to recover emotional distress and punitive damages.

Other Anti-Discrimination Regulations

There are several other anti-discrimination laws that fall under the authority of the EEOC. The Equal Pay Act of 1963, amending the FLSA, requires equal pay for men and women doing the same job. The Pregnancy Discrimination Act of 1978 bans employment discrimination against pregnant women. The Americans with Disabilities Act (ADA) enacted in 1990 prohibited employers (with more than 15 employees) from discriminating against disabled employees in hiring practices, promotions, and benefits, and must provide reasonable accommodations in the workplace for employees who are able to perform the essential functions of the job, where these accommodations do not create an undue burden on the employer, and where the modification may not create a significant expense. Some accommodations may include modifying a work schedule, obtaining modified work equipment and training materials, or increasing accessibility (Dalton, Hoyle, and Watts 2006). The Job Accommodation Network offers a good resource to clarify information regarding the complex issues of ADA (see Job Accommodation Network website's ADA library).

Employee Protection in States

State regulations vary greatly regarding employee protection. Some states have higher and some have lower minimum wage requirements than the federal government. If the state and federal laws regarding minimum wage differ, the higher of the two applies. Five states including Louisiana, Mississippi, Alabama, South Carolina, and Tennessee currently have no minimum wage laws (US Department of Labor 2021). Georgia has a minimum wage exception below the federal standard that applies to some agricultural workers ($5.15).

Many states passed right-to-work laws (Dalton, Hoyle, and Watts 2006), which prohibit union security agreements, or agreements between labor unions and employers that govern the extent to which an established union can require employees' membership, payment of union dues, or fees as a condition of employment, either before or after hiring. Unions may operate in these states, but employees cannot be compelled to be part of the bargaining unit. Currently, according to National Conference of State Legislatures' Right-to-Work Resources, there are 24 right-to-work states, but with the 2018 Janus v AFSME ruling, the difference between right-to-work states and those that are not is significantly less.

Some states, such as California, have passed their own Family Medical Leave Acts. The California Department of Fair Employment and Housing (DFEH) is responsible for administering these laws.

States generally prohibit discrimination, unless it involves a necessary occupational or professional requirement. For example, California enacted Proposition 209 to bar public institutions from discrimination on the basis of race, sex, color, ethnicity, or national origin in 1997. The state of Michigan enacted a similar law in 2006.

Environmental Protection

Rationale for Environmental Protection

Climate change has recently been a point of major concern and discussion in media outlets (Davenport 2014). Although natural causes may contribute to climate change, industrial and population growth have been cited as major contributors (EPA). Wealthy countries consume and are responsible for more than their share of pollution. Wealthy countries also have more resources for change.

Pollution will be, and has historically been, a byproduct of development (Baron 2013). The goal is not to rid the earth of pollution entirely, but to abate or lessen the problems of pollution where possible (Scheingold 2011). The question is to what degree development need occur in a sustainable manner. Environmental sustainability requires looking at the future. The positive effects of a clean environment on human health and the need for sustainability are not usually in dispute. The more contested questions include how to mitigate any negative effects on the environment, how to assess the cost of that mitigation, and how firms can still be economically viable while maintaining environmentally sustainable practices. Thus, creating business practices in the most cost-effective and sustainable manner is the critical challenge for the private sector. Consequently, firms need to be concerned about efficiency. Although the use of certain products may save energy or generally reduce the amount of pollutants released into the air or water, firms may need to determine whether selling a certain product or providing a service is cost-effective (Baron 2013).

Cap and Trade versus Command and Control

Government can use different methods to ensure that the private sector follows environmentally friendly practices, depending on the industry and the danger of the pollutant. Some of the ways that the government uses to regulate firms in an effort to reduce pollution include taxes on certain types of emissions, "command and control" of the design of manufacturing equipment to create fewer pollutants, and the "cap and trade system" where the government places an overall limit on a particular pollutant and businesses decide how to reduce emissions in a way that is most cost effective (Baron 2013).

The practice of cap and trade falls under the incentives method of compliance with government mandates for sustainable practices. The cap and trade approach assumes that the amount of pollution created from the process of producing a particular product or service can be known or determined before it occurs. Thus the government sets an overall limit or "cap" on a pollutant (Baron 2013). How to accomplish abatement of these substances is delegated to the individual firms. Cap and trade compels businesses to use the most efficient means possible to reduce pollution. A certain number of "permits" to emit a certain amount of a pollutant are issued in an industry, so the amount of overall pollution is controlled. Cap and trade can also be less burdensome on the government because it does not have to formulate and monitor engineering designs for each firm. These permits to emit a particular pollutant are distributed and can also be bought, sold, or traded among firms. The permits can also be used immediately or at a later time. Thus, the amount of emissions for a particular industry is capped and limited overall under this system. Firms find the most efficient engineering design for what they are producing and determine the best methods for limiting pollutants (Baron 2013). See Exhibit 5.5 for examples of cap and trade practices.

Role of Government and Legal Uncertainties

Technological change and the increased knowledge of health and ecological damage of pollutants requires a larger role in environmental protection. These changes require a more developed system of regulation. Until relatively recently, environmental law did not exist in the form we currently know, but was instead guided by advocacy groups and enforced by government regulators. Actions involving pollution were often brought into court as nuisance cases. The legal theory was that because landowners experienced harm to their property due to the actions of another property owner, as private citizens they could bring a civil case to court. Thus, the lawsuits were based on reduction of specific land values (Scheingold 2011).

Environmental law is a relatively new area and has some unique challenges beyond those of other administrative areas. First, the US Constitution is based on the rights of the individual, and not the rights of the collective or the greater good of society. Thus, concepts like "standing" (proving that the law will have an effect on the party bringing suit) can be problematic for environmental advocacy groups, whereas the rights to real property (land) and personal property are well defined in the US Constitution (Scheingold 2011). Other areas of ambiguity in the law that have increasingly been settled by litigation include "jurisdiction" (which court legally has control over the case), "standing" (discussed below), and "ripeness" (if the case is ready to be heard) (Scheingold 2011). Thus, in the environmental arena, the judges have interpreted the law to make it more predictable for the parties bringing and defending lawsuits.

For example, the US Constitution requires a "case or controversy" (Article 3, Section 2) exist, to establish that a plaintiff has standing to bring a grievance to the court system. An actual injury shown to the person or entity bringing forth the lawsuit must be demonstrated. In the case of *Massachusetts v. EPA* (2007, p. 533), the issue of which situations qualify as a "case or controversy" to establish standing was clarified. In this case, several parties jointly brought an action against the government to enforce environmental regulations. However, although several parties brought suit, the US Supreme Court found that only one plaintiff, the state of Massachusetts, needed to show standing. In this case, the court determined that the state of Massachusetts had standing because the state would be subjected to harm if sea levels rose as a result of greenhouse gases.

Although many legal issues remain unclear, advocacy groups have been successful in establishing legal precedents that can help their cause. The

Exhibit 5.5

Examples of cap and trade

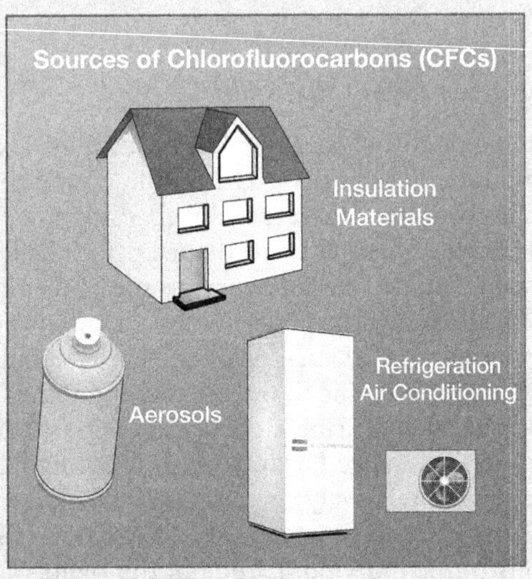

Chlorofluorocarbons (CFCs) were invented in 1928 by a scientist working at General Motors. It was a breakthrough for everyday life because CFCs allowed for effective refrigeration. This technology made foods become more transportable and have a longer shelf life. Air-conditioning made housing possible in previously uninhabitable locations. CFCs were widely used through the 1950s (Dray and Cagan 1993). In the 1970s, researchers began to question whether the particular composition of CFCs was connected to depletion of the ozone layer. The "Ozone Depletion Theory" proposed that the use of CFCs created a hole in the ozone layer, causing a loss of protection from the sunlight, damaging food, and increasing the risk of skin cancer (Dray and Cagan 1993).

Industry questioned the validity of the science. The first debate argued the validity of this theory itself. The second was concerned, assuming the theory was valid, with what should be done about it. The idea of building similar products using other materials that did not hurt the ozone layer was thought to be inefficient for manufacturing and prompted concerns about the market (Dray and Cagan 1993). Eventually, the government used cap and trade to restrict the level of

CFCs, with a goal of eventually eliminating the cap and trade system (Dray and Cagan 1993).

Another example of how cap and trade has been used as a tool to reduce toxic emissions involves the acid rain issue. Acid rain occurs when emissions such as sulfur dioxide (SO_2) and nitrogen oxides (NOx), often the result of coal-fired electric power plants, are released into the atmosphere and mix with water. States in the Eastern United States and the Great Lakes Region including Illinois, Pennsylvania, Ohio, and New York were major producers of these emissions. These practices effected nearby states where emissions from power plants would get into the air, travel with the wind, and cause damage in other states. This mixture is called acid rain, and it damages and kills off vegetation when it lands on the ground. As a result of the 1989 amendments to the Clean Air Act, the amount of SO_2 is limited to 8.95 million tons annually.

The mitigation of pollution in the atmosphere falls under the Federal Clean Air Act (CAA). Because there is a general cap, businesses working to comply with the CAA have options for how to reduce pollutants causing acid rain, while still maintaining production of energy. Some of these options include using coal with less sulfur, a process called "washing the coal" or "using devices called 'scrubbers' to chemically remove the SO_2 from the gases leaving the smokestack" (US Environmental Protection Agency 2021).

National Resources Defense Council (NRDC) brought litigation against the EPA to get the agency to enforce the Delaney Amendment, a law banning certain pesticides in food (Baron 2013). The courts found in favor of the NRDC (Baron 2013). (This principle is also demonstrated in the case of the Endangered Species Act.)

In some cases, the courts will push the agency to act. In 1998, the Kyoto Protocol required nations to reduce carbon emissions. Although a signatory to the Kyoto Protocol (without ratifying), the United States volunteered to reduce carbon emissions. In *Mass. v. EPA* (2007), the Supreme Court ruled that under the Clean Air Act, the EPA had to list whether CO_2 (carbon dioxide) was a pollutant (Baron 2013). Under the Obama Administration, CO_2 is indeed listed as a pollutant (Baron 2013). Although the Trump Administration diluted CO_2 regulations by extending timelines and levels, it did not eliminate them. The Biden Administration reversed this trend and immediately began increasing CO_2 regulatory requirements in a variety of areas.

Environment Protection Regulatory Framework

Widespread government regulation of the effects of pollution on the environment is a relatively recent development. In the early 1900s, President Theodore Roosevelt established the National Park System and relied heavily on the power given to him under the Antiquities Act allowing the executive to preserve land and sites of historical or scientific value. As an avid outdoorsman, Teddy Roosevelt also created the US Forest Service. In this tradition, Franklin D. Roosevelt expanded the national parks with his Great Depression era program, the Civilian Conservation Corporation (CCC). This program flourished until the United States' entry into World War II after the attack on Pearl Harbor (Franklin D. Roosevelt Library and Museum). However, in the first part of the twentieth century, land was still viewed as for the enjoyment of people rather than in terms of overall sustainability.

In the post-World War II era, ecology became a larger part of the public discourse as the population grew with the baby boomer generation and new housing was built for veterans returning home. Some began looking at the environment as a "public good" rather than just an economic resource. Most importantly, in the 1970s, public concern for the environment was running particularly high, affecting the political climate and making change possible that may not otherwise have happened. Some major events occurred during this era, altering public consciousness and leading up to the changes of the 1970s. In 1962, Rachael Carson wrote *Silent Spring* (Carson 1990), a book that raised public awareness of the dangers of DDT pesticides (a chemical pest control used as an insecticide from the 1940s and eventually banned from the United States in 1972) (US Environmental Protection Agency 2021). The Cuyahoga River near Cleveland, Ohio caught fire in 1969 from a spark from a rail car, igniting flammable materials floating on the river. This event was well covered by the media locally and nationally, causing a discussion regarding the value of natural resources and modern industrial developments. Although the river had caught fire several times before, this fire sparked the interest of the nation. These issues stirred the public's interest and illustrated the fact that environmental resources are not unlimited. Conservation advocacy for protection of federally owned lands became an issue in the forefront during this time (Bates and MacDonnell 2010). As a result, in 1969 Congress passed the National Environmental Protection Act (NEPA), mandating that negative environmental impacts of potential federal agency actions needed to be listed on environmental impact statements (EIS) (US Environmental Protection Agency 2021).

Formation of the EPA

Although environmental matters were addressed by different entities in the federal government in 1970, some thought that these older agencies were acting in the interest of those they were intended to regulate (Lehne 2006).

Ultimately, these functions were to be gathered under a single umbrella, the US Environmental Protection Agency. President Nixon issued an executive order, Reorganization Plan No. 3 of 1970 (an order codified as 5 US C. App. at 1132–1137, 1982) causing structural reform, and the creation of the EPA. The agency was to be a single, independent, executive agency not at the cabinet level, and unique inasmuch as it was not created by Congress. Born in the wake of elevated concern about environmental pollution, the agency was established on December 2, 1970 to consolidate a variety of federal research, monitoring, standard-setting, and enforcement activities to ensure environmental protection (Connelly et al. 2003).

However, this formation structure created unusual regulatory challenges. Since agencies had their "own traditions and styles" (Connelly et al. 2003, p. 307), after the EPA was formed from different area agencies, legislation in single issue areas occurred (Connelly et al. 2003). "The fragmented structure of the EPA was reinforced by legislation, such as the Clean Air and Water Acts, which tended to focus on specific media" (Connelly et al. 2003, p. 307). This piecemeal policy-making occurred in part because of the political importance of environmental issues being dealt with individually as they appeared on the public's radar screen, rather than reconstructing a framework altogether; for example, having separate departments take on different tasks. Instead of monitoring enforcement and research, Congress set out legal areas separately, like air, water, and pesticides (Marcus 1991).

Legislation

The US Code lays down different government subjects of authority by title. Most environmental statutes are under Title 42 of the US Code, which covers "public health." Numerous environmental laws cover a broad range of relatively diverse environmental issues. A complete list of environmental laws and executive orders can be found in Laws and Regulations at the EPA official website (www.epa.gov). In the following, we introduce a few important pieces with regard to water pollution, air quality, endangered species, and oil pollution.

WATER POLLUTION

The Refuse Act of 1899 is considered the first environmental law passed by Congress. The Act prohibited "dumping of refuse" into navigable waters. In the absence of the EPA, the Act was administered by the Army Corps of Engineers, focusing on controlling debris that obstructed navigation.

Subsequently in 1948, 1956, and 1972, the Federal Water Pollution Control Act, commonly referred to as the Clean Water Act (CWA), and a number of other amendments were enacted to regulate the various aspects of water pollution. The principal body of the CWA in effect is based on the Federal Water Pollution Control Act Amendments of 1972. The CWA's primary goal is to prevent water pollution and maintain the integrity of the nation's waters and wetlands, as well as to provide public assistance for the improvement of wastewater treatment. The CWA established the structure for regulating pollutants discharged into waters. It also gave the EPA the authority to implement pollution control programs, such as setting wastewater standards for industry.

Exhibit 5.6

EPA's Superfund

In the 1980s, the EPA developed the Superfund program to clean up sites where toxic dumping had already occurred. The Superfund project includes 2,000 sites and has cost $600 billion. So that taxpayers are not overly burdened, parties that are responsible for the pollution are liable for paying for the clean-up (Baron 2013). More than 60 percent of toxic clean-up has been paid for by polluters (Baron 2013). If the party does not agree to finance clean-up of the pollution it has created, the EPA can pursue action in federal court to compel the companies to pay (US Environmental Protection Agency 2021).

The Superfund has lost popularity over time. Firms argued that at the time they dumped the waste it may have been legal. Also, all sites have to be cleaned to the same standards, when the levels of pollution dumped may differ. Initially, there was a tax on firms in general to pay for the Superfund clean-up projects (Baron 2013). Congress removed the tax on firms charged with site clean-up. This money now comes from the federal government and those firms that have caused the toxic dumping are responsible to pay for the clean-up from their own pollution (Baron 2013).

The CWA does not directly address groundwater contamination, which is covered by the Safe Drinking Water Act, Resource Conservation and Recovery Act, and the Superfund program. The Safe Drinking Water Act of 1974 gave the EPA the authority to set standards for drinking water quality and oversee the implementation of standards by state and local water suppliers. The Act was amended in 1992 and 2011 to regulate more contaminants. The renewed Act requires all community water systems to provide consumer information (i.e., consumer confidence reports) about any significant contaminants in their water supply. The Resource Conservation and Recovery Act of 1976, which amended the Solid Waste Disposal Act of 1965, regulates the disposal of solid waste and hazardous waste and sets standards for groundwater monitoring. Exhibit 5.6 discusses one way the EPA has tried to address the problem of toxic clean-up of pollution.

OIL POLLUTION

The Oil Pollution Act of 1924, under the authority of the Public Health Service, prohibited the discharge of oil into coastal waters. In later decades, a number of oil pollution Acts were enacted. The Oil Pollution Act of 1961, mirroring the International Convention for the Prevention of the Pollution of the Sea by Oil (OILPOL) of 1954, prohibited the discharge of fossil fuel pollutants from nautical vessels along the US coastline. The OILPOL was an international environmental protocol evoked to restrict the disposal of hazardous waste that could potentially contaminate marine ecosystems. The 1973 Amendments of the Oil Pollution Act accentuated the OILPOL and acknowledged the embargo of coastal zones in trans-boundary waters. In 1990, as a response to the *Exxon Valdez* oil spill (see Exhibit 5.7), Congress enacted the Oil Pollution Act to mitigate and prevent civil liability from future oil spills off the US coast. The Act requires oil firms to have a plan to prevent potential future spills as well as a detailed containment and cleanup plan. The Act significantly improved oil spill governance in the United States.

Exhibit 5.7

***Exxon Valdez*, deepwater oil spill**

Source: Wikimedia Commons (2016).

Although environmental harm may not be a result of intentional decisions made by a corporation, firms are financially responsible for employee negligence or human error and mechanical malfunctions. The 1989 *Exxon Valdez* oil spill along the coast of Alaska and the more recent BP oil spill in the Gulf of Mexico are major examples of environmental disasters for which companies were held financially responsible for the error as well as the clean-up. In the case of the *Exxon Valdez* oil spill, the oil tanker ran aground, and although all of the circumstances were not clear, it was known that the ship's captain had been consuming alcohol and that another ship member made a navigation mistake (State of Alaska 1990). The *Exxon Valdez* disaster is particularly well known for the amount of wildlife harmed in Prince William Sound.

As a result of a guilty plea to criminal charges, the oil company agreed to pay a fine of $150 million. However, due to the company's compliance with clean-up efforts, the fine was reduced to $25 million. Exxon agreed to pay $100 million in restitution and a settlement of $900 million over a period of ten years (US Environmental Protection Agency 2013). The EPA coordinated clean-up efforts between Exxon and the state and federal governments (Memorandum of Agreement and Consent Degree 1991). These agreements fell under the Environmental Response, Compensation, and Liability Act of 1980, 42 US C. S 9601 et seq. and the Clean Water Act or Federal Water Pollution Control Act, 33 US C. SS 1251–1376, as amended. As a result of the *Exxon Valdez* oil spill, Congress passed the Oil Pollution Act of 1990, increasing the safety measures for oil tankers (US Environmental Protection Agency 2021).

The Deepwater oil spill in the Gulf of Mexico by British Petroleum in 2010 was the largest oil spill in US history. On April 20, 2010, the Deepwater Horizon rig exploded, killing 11 people. Much of the reason that the oil spill was so damaging was because BP was unable to close the Macondo well at the bottom of the ocean for 87 days. The spill was devastating to marine wildlife and to the tourist industry in the states bordering the Gulf. BP paid $25 billion to clean up the damage (Barrett 2013).

AIR QUALITY

In 1963, the United States enacted its first law, the Clean Air Act, addressing the issue of air pollution. The Act designated the EPA as the authority to develop and enforce regulations to protect the public from airborne contaminants. Later, the 1967 Air Quality Act mandated enforcement of interstate air pollution standards. A series of amendments to the Clean Air Act were passed in 1970, 1977, and 1990, enhancing and expanding the regulatory controls for air pollution. The 1970 amendments largely expanded the regulatory power to require comprehensive federal, as well as state, regulations for both stationary and mobile pollution sources. The 1990 amendments extended the coverage to acid rain, ozone depletion, and toxic air pollution. Most noticeably, the amendments mandated new auto gasoline reformulation, established standards for Reid vapor pressure (a measure of the volatility of gasoline) and leveled controls on evaporative emissions from gasoline. These standards have been extended to, and implemented by, many states.

ENDANGERED SPECIES

The Endangered Species Act of 1973 addresses how to protect species from extinction as a consequence of economic growth and development. The predecessor of the Act was the Endangered Species Preservation Act of 1966, which authorized the Secretary of the Interior to list and protect endangered native fish and wildlife species. The Endangered Species Conservation Act of 1969 amended the 1966 law to prohibit the importation and subsequent sale of species in danger of worldwide extinction in the United States. See Exhibit 5.8 for an example of the Endangered Species Act in action.

Exhibit 5.8

The Spotted Owl issue

The purpose of the 1973 Endangered Species Act became controversial with the Spotted Owl issue. Old growth forests in the Pacific Northwest were being logged in a clear-cutting style, where trees are not selectively cut to avoid soil run off and not otherwise protected by legislation, state, or federal laws. Particular wildlife species, whose numbers were low, lived in these old growth forests. One of the species for which the forests serve as a habitat is the Northern Spotted Owl. In the case of the Spotted Owl, the Sierra Club Legal Defense Fund (SCLDF) became involved and strove to use laws as tools in the hope that federal courts would interpret those laws in a positive way to accomplish their objective of environmental protection. The timber companies strove to achieve the results they wanted through Congress.

The Northern Spotted Owl was not listed as an endangered or threatened species in 1989. When the case initially was brought to federal district court by the SCLDF, the court ordered the US Fish and Wildlife Service to list the Spotted Owl as threatened or endangered. Although the USFWS listed the Spotted Owl as endangered in 1990, it did not designate a critical habitat to protect the owl from losing its home and avoid endangerment. The US Federal District Court for the District of Oregon ordered the agency to do this also (Kagan 2004).

Source: Wikimedia Commons (n.d.).

The SCLDF also sued the National Forest Service. The court held that there was a need to preserve the entire biological community. US District Court for the District of Oregon found that the Northern Spotted Owl was "now threatened with extinction." This ruling was appealed to the Ninth Circuit Court of Appeals and upheld. Part of the significance of this ruling is that it was "rejecting the agency's scientific and legal counterarguments" (Barnes 2004, p. 16).

Implementation and Enforcement at Federal and State Level

As opposed to many other federal agencies that operate out of Washington, DC, where the vast majority of decisions are made at headquarters, the EPA has ten regional districts dividing up the states and territories. Regional offices are largely responsible for compliance with, and as with many regulatory agencies, settling with industry actors. Like many regulatory agencies, legal settlements are far more common than litigation, which tends to be used in only cases of clear criminality or significant corporate–government disputes (Eisner, Worsham, and Ringquist 2006).

Some states choose to depart from the federal government by increasing protection due to physical, political, and economic environments in varying regions. These differences from federal practices occurred in the two most populous states of the US, California and New York, with two major pieces of federal legislation—the Clean Air Act and the Clean Water Act.

Although the CAA mandates minimum standards for air quality, California has determined that due to the smog level and particular circumstances of the state, it needed more stringent standards for automobiles. The California Air Resources Board passed "clean car" rules regulating the production, transportation, and emission of fossil fuels from cars creating greenhouse gases (Rogers 2013). These rules will require the auto industry selling new cars in the state to have almost no emissions by 2025, forcing the automakers that market in the state of California to adapt (Rogers 2013).

Similarly, certain states question whether the CWA is adequate to protect water quality. As natural gas is more relied on as an energy source, the effects of the hydrofracking style of drilling become a greater concern. Hydrofracking, or more commonly "fracking," is the practice of drilling through bedrock using water pressure, to reach any underlying fossil fuels. Afterward, the water needs to be disposed of in such a way as to not pollute the drinking water supply. Although many states, including Wyoming and Pennsylvania, have allowed fracking, the issue has been particularly contentious in New York. Upstate New York has suffered from the post-industrial economy (DeWitt 2013). The Marcellus Shale deposit is located below the surface of many northeastern states, including New York, and covers a large deposit of natural gas (Hobson 2013). However, the New York legislature is unconvinced that the practice of fracking is safe for groundwater, and, for now, the practice is prohibited (DeWitt 2013).

Further, the state of California has numerous types of ecosystems. Therefore, as a state with a population over 38 million that is continuing to grow, California has specific guidance for what types of chemicals can be used in various landscaping practices (University of California Agricultural and Natural Resources 2006). There has been encouragement by groups to add more natively grown plants to the landscape (Matzge 2013). A list of approved chemicals that are less likely to hurt the water table is available at the California Cal/Ecotox website (www.oehha.ca.gov/cal_ecotox/).

The Debate about Social Regulation

Social regulation, like any other government intervention, is not free from political controversy. Whereas most people admit the need for social regulation, the degree to which government regulates a particular industry for a specific protective purpose tends to be a target of debate. Those in support of social regulation point out that it can enhance economic efficiency and improve people's well-being by eliminating unsafe and unhealthy products, by improving working conditions, and by reducing pollution. Consumer groups, civil rights groups, unions, and environmentalists are general advocates of social regulation.

Critics of social regulation are often represented by business interest groups as well as neoliberal economists. As the cost of social regulation is high, critics of social regulation often argue that many standards are not economically sound, in that costs may exceed benefits, leading to overregulation. Many regulations are rather rigid and ineffective, often stifling or reducing competition. They also point out that many rules and standards have unintended consequences, such as over burdening, market distortion, and tradeoff. For example, energy conservation and emission control regulations (e.g., the Energy Policy and Conservation Act of 1975) led to the production of lighter and more fuel-efficient cars, which may be less safe and contribute to higher fatality rates. In addition, many standards and regulations are considerably vague or poorly written, causing significant implementation obstacles and resulting in regulation apart from the original purpose and scope.

Although most policy-makers and economists agree that cost–benefit analysis helps in determining the optimal level of social regulation, there is disagreement on how to measure the cost and benefit of a particular regulation. The benefits of social regulation are difficult to measure and often realized only after the regulation has been passed and implemented. Some social values, such as equity, fairness, and humanity, are hard to quantify in economic terms. Although some studies have been conducted in this area, data on the impact of regulations was weak, sparse, and incomplete (Boyne 2003).

Despite these arguments, there are continuing problems in demanding additional social regulation. In reviewing US regulatory history, it is evident that most social regulations were enacted as a response to tragedies or crises resulting from irresponsible business practices. One cannot help but think that if corporations were more socially responsible, many social problems could be avoided and the need for government intervention would diminish.

Analytical Case: Employees with Disabilities

James Carson is the owner of Kaber Corporation (KC), which manufactures garments for weddings and other unique occasions. Because of increased demand, Carson has realized that KC can hire two new employees in addition to the 48 employees who currently work for KC. Twenty people applied, with varying levels of experience in the garment industry. These new employees must be able to sew detailing into the garments. Although KC has continued accepting and filling small regular orders, weekend events are where it makes the majority of its revenue. Among the pool of applicants are Mike Harvey and Jennifer Johnson. Both job candidates passed a basic sewing skills test in the management office prior to their interviews.

Harvey is in a wheelchair and unable to stand. Generally, employees need to stand when putting the details on garments because the garments are so long.

Jennifer Johnson has a documented panic disorder. Johnson is a competent seamstress but becomes agitated when put in stressful situations. Carson is concerned about Jennifer because they often do not have much time to fill work orders.

Questions for Discussion and Analysis

1 How are the job obligations similar and different for Harvey and Johnson? Can the employees fulfill the "essential functions" of the job?
2 What reasonable accommodations could be made?
3 Does it matter that the applicant passes the sewing test?
4 Do the large-scale orders that are the basis for the firm's income matter in this question?

Practical Skill

Complying with Government Regulation

It is critical for business to comply with government regulations, as violations always incur not only damages to society, but also costs to firms, such as the Walmart case indicates. Compliance with various laws can be onerous and complicated without effective planning and management. Here we use Trujillo Landscaping, Inc. as an example in our case scenario at the beginning of the chapter and offer a few tips about how to comply with environmental regulations.

Tip 1

Determine whether the legislation applies to your business. If you are not an independent business owner, ensure the competencies of other companies with whom you are contracting to do business. Have several checks on management and on design. Environmental legislation applies to businesses of all sizes and many sectors, such as food, agriculture, and construction, which is subject to specific laws and regulations.

Tip 2

Find out which laws are likely to affect your business and who enforce the laws. Know which level of government regulates your business or if it is regulated at more than one level.

Tip 3

Know where to find the relevant information. A good starting point will be the regulatory agency's official website. For example, the EPA website offers complete compliance guidance as well as compliance assistance training. In addition, the Small Business Administration also offers assistance for legal compliance for a variety of legislation. For example, the EPA Office of the Small Business Program offers information on how businesses may comply with environmental standards at the state and federal levels.

Tip 4

Develop a corporate compliance policy. If resources allow, it is best to develop a written compliance policy in consultation with relevant legal experts. The policy should be regularly reviewed and updated, routinely communicated to relevant staff, and supported by records of review and implementation.

Skills Exercise

Please brief Tomas Trujillo on the regulatory framework of the United States and advise Tomas where and how to find relevant groundwater regulations for the Trujillo Landscaping business.

Summary and Conclusion

1 The historical evolution of government indicates that social regulation was largely expanded during the Big Government Era. This chapter introduces government's regulatory role in terms of protecting the consumer, employee, and environment.
2 Public interest theory, public choice theory, and self-regulation theory offer different lenses through which to see the rationale for regulation. Regardless of which theoretical framework seems the most accurate, social regulations have become increasingly intricate, and it is crucial that firms are aware of when their business practices involve an area that is covered by these social regulations.
3 The US Constitution provides the authority for regulation. Regulatory agencies assume the responsibility to promulgate rules, make policies, and resolve disputes.
4 US social protective regulation generally covers three areas, namely consumer protection, employee protection, and environmental protection.
5 Consumer protection laws and regulations are comprised of three major areas—prevention of fraud and misrepresentation of food, drugs, and cosmetics, protection of consumers from unfair competition and deceptive practices, and consumer product safety.

6 Employee protection regulations protect the welfare of employee, including wages, working hours, health, safety, and working conditions, as well as rights to equal employment opportunities.
7 Environment protection is enabled through both cap and trade and command and control. The EPA assumes the authority to regulate a variety of environmental issues, such as air quality, water quality, oil pollution, and endangered species.
8 Despite various arguments against social regulation, such as high cost, unintended effects, market distortion, and ineffective regulation, social regulation is deemed necessary and will continuously correct irresponsible business practices.

Key Terms

- Affirmative Action
- Fair Labor Standards
- Right-to-work law
- Cap and trade
- Labeling
- Rule-making
- Collective bargaining
- Product warranty
- Self-regulation theory
- Consumer protection
- Public choice theory
- Social regulation
- Consumer sovereignty
- Public interest theory

Study Questions

1 Discuss the US regulatory framework. In your discussion, highlight the roles of the Constitution, federal regulatory agencies, the court, and state governments.
2 What are the three areas of consumer protection? Discuss fully and offer legislation examples.
3 Why is consumer protection necessary? What are the costs and benefits of consumer protection?
4 What are the two major aspects of employee protection? Discuss fully and offer legislation examples.
5 Why is employee protection necessary? What are the costs and benefits of employee protection?
6 Why is environmental protection necessary? What are the costs and benefits of environmental protection?
7 What are the arguments for and against social regulation?

References

Bardach, E. (2002). *Going by the Book: The Problem of Regulatory Unreasonableness.* New Brunswick, NJ: Transaction Publishers.

Baron, D. P. (2013). *Business and Its Environment.* Boston: Pearson.

Barrett, P. M. (2013). BP's Oil Spill Settlement Is Engulfed in Fraud. *Business Week*, August 6. http://www.businessweek.com/articles/2013-08-06/bps-oil-spill-settlement-is-engulfed-in-fraud.

Bernardin, J. H. (2007). *Human Resource Management: An Experiential Approach*. Boston: McGraw Hill-Irwin.

Boyne, G. A. (2003). Sources of Public Service Improvement: A Critical Review and Research Agenda. *Journal of Public Administration Research and Theory, 13(3)*:367–394.

Carson, R. (1990). "Silent Spring," in Diane Ravitch (ed.) *The American Reader: Words that Moved a Nation* (pp. 323–325). New York: HarperCollins.

Connelly, J., Smith, G., Benson, D., and Saunders C. (2003). *Politics and the Environment: From Theory to Practice*. London: Routledge.

Dalton, M., Hoyle, D., and Watts, M. (2006). *Human Relations*, 3rd edn. Mason, OH: Thomson South Western.

Davenport, C. (2014) Governments Await Obama's Move on Carbon to Gage U.S. Climate Efforts. *New York Times*, May 26. http://www.nytimes.com/2014/05/27/us/politics/governments-await-obamas-move-on-carbon-to-gauge-us-climate-efforts.html.

Department of Labor (2012). US Department of Labor Recovers $4.83 Million in Back Wages, Damages for More than 4,500 Wal-Mart Workers. News release, May 1. http://www.dol.gov/opa/media/press/whd/WHD20120801.htm.

DeWitt, K. (2013). Upstate Businesses Push for Tax Cuts, Hydrofracking. *North Country Public Radio*, September 4. http://www.northcountrypublicradio.org/news/story/22667/20130904/upstate-business-group-pushes-for-tax-cuts-fracking.

Dray, P., and Cagan, S. (1993). *Between Earth and Sky: How CFCs Changed Our World and Endangered the Ozone Layer*. New York: Pantheon Books.

Eisner, M. A., Worsham, J., and Ringquist, E. (2006). *Contemporary Regulatory Policy*, 2nd edn. London: Lynne Rienner.

Exxon Valdez Oil Spill Trustee Council (1991). Settlement. http://www.evostc.state.ak.us/facts/settlement.cfm.

Hobson, K. (2013). Health Questions Key to New York Fracking Decision, But Answers Scarce. *National Geographic Daily News*, April 30. http://news.nationalgeographic.com/news/energy/2013/04/130401-new-york-fracking-health-questions/.

Jones, R. A. (1986) *Emile Durkheim: An Introduction to Four Major Works*. Beverly Hills, CA: Sage Publications.

Kagan, R. (2004). American Courts and the Policy Dialogue: The Role of Adversarial Legalism, in Mark C. Miller and Jeb Barnes (eds.) *Making Policy, Making Law: An Interbranch Perspec tive* (pp. 13–34). Washington, DC: Georgetown University Press.

Klienman, L.S. (2007). *Human Resource Management: A Managerial Tool for Competitive Advantage*. Mason, OH: Thomson.

Langran, R., and Schnitzer, M. (2007). *Government, Business, and the American Economy*. Lanham, MD: Rowman & Littlefield Publishers, Inc.

Lehne, Ri (2006). *Government and Business: American Political Economy in Comparative Perspective*. Washington, DC: CQ Press.

Lewis Hine (1909). National Archives, Records of the Children's Bureau. www.archives.gov.

Marcus, A. A. (1991). EPA's Organizational Structure. *Law and Contemporary Problems, 54(4)*:5–40.

Matzge, S. (2013). University of California Sonoma Master Gardeners, Water-Wise Lawn Alternatives: When to say No to Lawn. http://ucanr.edu/sites/scmg/Lawn_Replacement/Water-Wise_Lawn_Alternatives/.

Memorandum of Agreement and Consent Degree (1991). State of Alaska Civil Action No. A91-081 CV., August 29. http://www.evostc.state.ak.us/pdf/settlement/MOA_consent_decree082991.PDF.

Nader, R. (1965). *Unsafe at Any Speed: The Designed-In Dangers of the American Automobile*. New York: Grossman Publishers.

Rogers, P. (2013). California's "Clean Car" Rules, February 18. Retrieved from Yale Environment 360: http://e360.yale.edu/feature/californias_clean_car_rules_help_remake_us_auto_industry/2492/.

Scheingold, S. (2011). *The Politics of Rights: Lawyers, Public Policy and Political Change*, 2nd edn. Ann Arbor: The University of Michigan Press.

Smith, Adam (1937). *The Wealth of Nations*. New York: The Modern Library.

Smith, Allen (2008). Wal-Mart Wage and Hour Settlement May Cost More than Half a Billion. *Society for Human Resource Workplace Law Library-Compensation*. http://www.shrm.org/legalissues/federalresources/pages/wal-martwageandhour-settlement.aspx.

State of Alaska (1990). Exxon Valdez Oil Spill Trustee Council: Details about the Accident Final Report. http://www.evostc.state.ak.us/index.cfm?FA=facts.details.

University of California Agricultural and Natural Resources (2006). Pesticides: Safe and Effective Use in the Home and Landscape. http://www.ipm.ucdavis.edu/PMG/PESTNOTES/pn74126.html.

US Department of Labor (2013). Methylene Chloride Hazards for Bathtub Refinishers. https://www.osha.gov/dts/hazardalerts/methylene_chloride_hazard_alert.html.

US Department of Labor (2021). https://www.osha.gov/dcsp/osp/index.html.

US Environmental Protection Agency (2021). https://www.epa.gov/.

US Senate Committee on Commerce (1972). Hearing of National Commission on Product Safety, 91st Cong., 2nd Sess., p. 37.

Volden, C., and Wiseman, A. E. (2009). A Theory of Government Regulation and Self-Regulation with the Spector of Non-Market Threats. *American Political Science Association*. http://politics.as.nyu.edu/docs/IO/10410/volden_paper.pdf.

Wikimedia Commons (2016). Office of Response and Restoration. https://response.restoration.noaa.gov/about/media/10-photos-tell-story-exxon-valdez-oil-spill-and-its-impacts.html.

Wikimedia Commons (n.d.). Dominic Sherony. https://www.google.com/search?q=spotted+owls+wikimedia&source=lnms&tbm=isch&sa=X&ved=2ahUKEwjM8cnUjtv5AhVBLEQIHQyECFYQ_AUoAXoECAEQAw&biw=1315&bih=589&dpr=1#imgrc=gEgKio2kIdgnvM.

6 Corporate Social Responsibility

Doing Well *and* Doing Good

Kimberly Collins

Chapter Contents

Case 6 Scenario

Zoey's Dilemma at Happy Paws

When Zoey had initially planned her pet store, it was going to sell pet products, but not include live pets. However, Zoey soon realized she would be hard pressed to compete with the major pet store chains if she did not have some live animals for variety and interest. Live animals tend to draw people into pet stores if they are cute or unusual and Zoey had those large picture windows in the front of her grandmother's old house that were perfect for showing off little puppies or turtles to passersby.

DOI: 10.4324/9781003178620-8

But Zoey couldn't afford a complex array of animals, and the pets must be alone in the store overnight. Even though she'd be right upstairs, she was still concerned over a large live inventory. She decided on just a handful of puppies at a time, a couple kittens, some tiny turtles, goldfish and one other simple variety of fish, and gerbils. The animals increase traffic and sales but they are a challenge. What do you do when the puppies are split up and one must stay alone in the store overnight? What if a puppy doesn't sell? The tiny turtles are big sellers but Zoey has learned the Food and Drug Administration (FDA) has banned them because they tend to spread salmonella, a special genus that causes human infection; ironically, the FDA is generally ignored by pet stores on this regulation. Should she be concerned? The turtles in her shop window practically drag people in. The gerbils are cute, but the children that they are given to lose many of them within a day or two and sometimes within the first hour, with parents often coming back for another to calm an upset child. Should she be happy for the extra income or should she be concerned about this?

Introduction

After the environmental scandals of the 1980s and 1990s (e.g., the Bhopal accident and the *Exxon Valdez* oil spill), a barrage of accounting scandals from 2000 to 2002 (e.g., Enron), the mortgage and insurance scandals associated with the economic downturn of 2008 (e.g., widespread deceptive mortgage lending and the highly risky securitized insurance schemes of companies like AIG), and the out-and-out scams of financial moguls such as Bernie Madoff and Allen Stanford (Markham 2015), there have been a number of consequences. First, the morality of business has been questioned by the public and business itself (Kurlantzick 2003; Pearce and Doh 2005). This has led to new regulation (in some cases simply re-regulation) of industries that were not capable of policing themselves and where both the public and investors were held liable for the financial misdeeds of individuals or companies. Second, there has been a tremendous interest in fostering individual morality across sectors, tightening legal accountability, and promoting corporate social responsibility. Businesses across the spectrum have found that it is not only the right thing to do, but the wise thing to do as well (e.g., Seto-Pamies and Papaoikonomou 2020; Gong et al. 2021); business schools have followed business's lead as well as their urgings for a more robust ethics curriculum (Medeiros et al. 2017; Wymer and Rundle-Thiele 2017).

Ethics is a system of beliefs about how to behave. When one complies with society's system of beliefs, one is moral; when one does not, one is either amoral at best (acting in a fashion that is neither good nor bad), or immoral (in contravention of proper behavior) at worst. Societies dictate general systems of ethics through their culture, and their stated convictions about bad, good, and exceptionally good action. Behavioral minimums are expressed as laws and "hard" rules (where some sort of sanctions may be levied), which may be broad and sweeping, or detailed and narrow. Broad behavioral expectations that exceed bare minimums and are strongly encouraged are expressed as professional and organizational norms, which may have sanctions if flagrantly violated. The highest ethical behavior is considered exemplary. The ethics of societies is quite stable, but does evolve over time as the contingencies and the long-term needs and preferences of society change (Rokeach 1973; Van Wart and Denhardt 2001).

Social Expectations

General Social Expectations

Because systems of ethics are never exact, individuals can have a substantial range of acceptable beliefs and actions within societies. Nonetheless, certain strong beliefs will permeate all of society (Van Wart 1998). In the case of American society, some of the most fundamental values are honesty, fairness, and legality. Honesty is prized as a means to build trust and long-term relationships. It means no lying, no shading the truth, and no hiding information from those with a right to know. Fairness is valued in a democratic society built on equality of opportunity and mutual respect over birth or station in life. It means no cheating or self-dealing, and following organizational and professional rules. Legality, or being law abiding, is critical in a nation built on the rule of law and founded on a Constitutional compact. Although these are always at the top of American values lists, there are many others as well, such as consistency (a reasoned attempt to act from principle rather than from whim), coherence (a reasoned attempt to connect principles and to make them as harmonious as possible), and reciprocity (a reasoned attempt to act toward others as you would have them act toward you). While honesty, fairness, and legality generally constitute the basics of ethical behavior, high ethical standards require people to act out their principles with consistency and coherence, and to express compassionate reciprocity in their daily actions. Ethical exemplars in society are those who are willing to put others before themselves in order that substantial good will thereby be achieved, or those who show courage in the face of adversity or personal loss in doing what is moral for the sake of principles or compassion (Comer and Schwartz 2017).

Specific Social Expectations

Groups and individuals in society often have specific ethical expectations within the general context that will emphasize certain values more than others. Particularly important for our discussion are the ethical expectations of different professional groups. Consider judges, spies, nurses, and soldiers. Do they all have the same specific ethical expectations? We expect judges to be very high in honesty, fairness, legality, consistency, and coherence. Judges must be truth-tellers, scrupulously even handed, masters of the law, and great followers of precedent and the philosophy of law. Yet we do not expect judges to be judged, or to be exceptional in selflessness or courage. On the other extreme, CIA spies are expected to put aside their honesty, fairness, and legality in their formal roles when they may be required to assume alien identities that are maintained by lies, deceit, or even breaking foreign laws. However, CIA spies are expected, as a matter of course, to be selfless in risking their freedom and courageous in risking their lives. Another simple comparison is between soldiers and the nurses who serve with them. While soldiers have the responsibility to harm enemy combatants in the fray of war, nurses have an opposite responsibility to help all combatants equally as they are called upon to treat them. This is not to say that values are entirely relativistic or that anything goes, but rather to say that values are contextual and that one's occupational function features strongly in this specification of values.

What Is Business Ethics at the Individual Level?

In seeking a definition of ethics for a particular profession, then, we realize that it is a combination of both the general requirements of society (laws) and expectations (norms), that were discussed above, but also the specific values emphasized by a sector or industry, in this case business. What are the specific values of American business (de George 1999)? American business is founded on capitalistic beliefs, which are, in turn, founded on competition and the promotion of personal gain (and company profits). When exercised fairly, competition provides merit because those who work hard and have talent are rewarded. It also encourages personal responsibility and enhances the general good by vetting the best ideas, goods, and services in an ongoing dynamic selection process. Personal gain provides the incentive for people to do their best and work their hardest within a personally chosen context in which other important values in life, such as family, religion, and relaxation, are balanced.

It should be noted that public sector organizations are not exempt from market-like concerns, indirectly expressed through the allocation of scarce resources and market pressures to both increase and manage costs. Thus, a prime organizational value of public sector agencies is efficiency, but unlike the private sector, much higher standards of transparency, participation, appeal, and review are required, which both diminish efficiency and increase costs. Efficiency concerns surfaced as a primary factor in the 1990s through increased performance measurement, oversight, and outright competition (Berman and Van Wart 1999) and continue to be a part of the public debate.

Because individuals do not give up their general role in society, business people cannot abnegate (disregard) their other basic responsibilities. Honesty, fairness, and legality are still full expectations as they would be from teachers, mayors, nonprofit managers, or assembly-line workers. Exemplary behavior is when those in business do the right thing while not required to do so, even though it will be a short-term expense (e.g., voluntarily recalling a hazardous product or installing higher safety standards), or giving back to the community from which they got their success and wealth.

Exhibit 6.1 examines the levels of business morality from a progressive perspective, from immoral behavior to amoral to (basic) morality to exemplary behavior. It uses the two major values discussed here: competition and personal gain.

Because ethical behavior is often more complex than commonly supposed, it is useful to think of it as a four-part process (Brown and Trevino 2006)—awareness, judgment, motivation/intention, and behavior. One needs to be aware of who is involved in decisions and what the issues are. For example, if one is unaware of ethics, accounting, or environmental laws, one is likely to violate them. One has to have the analytic ability to see the connections and ramifications of different types of decisions. For example, if one is not well versed in good management practices, one may ascribe an ethical breach to the poor virtue of an individual employee when in fact it may be a systemic training and culture issue. One has to have the motivation to act on one's (hopefully good) judgment (De Tienne 2021). For example, one may perceive one's own "small" moral lapse but ignore it because "everyone does it" or "you are really owed more than you get anyway." And one has to know how to act and successfully implement judgments. Just because you know wrong-doing has occurred and want to take action, it does not mean that you will have the understanding of corrective processes or the courage to do the appropriate thing.

With this background, we can proceed to a definition of business ethics from an individual's perspective: *One is ethical in business to the degree that one complies with the laws of the land and obeys appropriate organizational rules, seeks to meet professional norms such as providing quality goods and services, as well as social norms such as exercising honesty and fairness, and strives to achieve the highest standards of morality such as prevention of harm and donating back to society part of the proceeds of one's success.*

Business Ethics at the Organizational Level: Corporate Social Responsibility

The same logic of ethics applies to private companies and publicly held corporations as it does to individuals. Although there are many models of corporate social responsibility that are relatively complementary (Redman 2005), the one by A. B. Carroll (1979) will be used here. He suggested a progressive model, with levels of responsibility. At the base or *economic* level,

Exhibit 6.1

Business-specific individual ethics: a progressive moral perspective

	Immoral	*Amoral*	*Moral*	*Highly Moral (Exemplary)*
Competition	• Winning is all that matters • Lying, cheating, and even law-breaking is OK if undetected	• Winning is by far the most important value, but danger of being detected is not worth the risk • Shading truth and hiding information is OK; always go to the edge of the rules (dog-eat-dog); minimum legality is acceptable (loopholes should be utilized; let the buyer beware; manipulation of the system is OK if legal)	• Winning is important but there are other important values • Honesty, fairness, and legality are substantive; for example, honesty means sharing unpleasant information, fairness means not manipulating the rules, and legality means following the spirit of the law	• Winning is a byproduct of competence, excellence, diligence, and positive psychological traits (optimism, compassion, resilience, etc.) • Being a good team player is as important as being a good competitor • Sportsmanship is more important than winning • While winning provides benefits, losing also provides lessons from which to learn
Personal Gain	• Personal gain above all • Lying, cheating, and even law-breaking is OK if undetected	• Personal gain is only important value; other than value of avoiding punishment • Legal mandates must be complied with (but); concealing truth is generally OK; legal profiteering (manipulation of rules) is OK; minor infractions are OK if one is willing to pay the price (fine)	• Personal gain motivation is important but greed (excessive self-interest) is a vice • Honesty, fairness, and legality are substantive; for example, honesty means sharing unpleasant information, fairness means not manipulating the rules, and legality means following the spirit of the law	• Personal gains that are sustained (even if modest) or large morally require a contribution back to the community that supported the wealth generation • Contribution of time to the community • Contribution of money for community or to charities

the business must provide quality goods and services that are valued by consumers. These goods and/or services, in turn, provide jobs to employees, a source of revenue for suppliers, profits to shareholders, and wealth to owners and senior managers. The other fundamental base value is abiding by its *legal* responsibilities, because if a company is not law abiding, it risks social opprobrium (harsh criticism) at a minimum, and scandal that can bring down a company at its worst. After these absolute foundational responsibilities come *ethical* responsibilities, which are those that may not be required by law, but are socially accepted norms of honesty, decency, and fair play. Companies may not be required to give ample notice when a layoff is to occur but to the degree they can forewarn employees, they are more ethical and trustworthy. Finally, there are *discretionary* responsibilities, which are those that include voluntary efforts to be environmentally friendly, enhance human rights, be an employer of choice, provide philanthropy, and so on.

In sum, *Corporate Social Responsibility is meeting basic economic needs through diligence and innovation, exceeding legal requirement by fulfilling the spirit of the law, while simultaneously finding ways to enhance the community and planet with mutually beneficial actions, and when possible, provide outright acts of charity.*

Exhibit 6.2 provides a graphic presentation of the levels of responsibility in Carroll's perspective on corporate social responsibility. The last bullet in each category identifies the problems with limiting corporate social responsibility too narrowly. For example, the company that pursues only profits is likely to see laws as obstacles to be circumvented when possible, or ignored if detection can be escaped.

Arguments for Building an Ethical Corporate Culture

No one argues against corporate responsibility (i.e., economic and legal aspects). However, some people do argue against corporate *social* responsibility. Milton Friedman (1970) is famously known for his argument that corporations should focus on profit-making in a fair legal context (i.e., legal framework providing as "perfect" an economic market as possible). However, in general, the public and most corporations do not contest the importance of including social responsibility, but rather how much social responsibility and under what conditions.

Starting with the absolute base of business ethics, corporate responsibility is providing profits and conforming to legal mandates. The importance of profit-making is incontestable in a capitalist system. Generally speaking, profits—even high ones—are not contested as long as they are the result of innovation, quality products and services, and value added to customers and society, but not the result of fraud or market manipulation. Even using Friedman's very narrow definition, market manipulation is a distortion of competition and the principles of capitalism and calls for government regulation to correct the "playing field."

Exhibit 6.2

Corporate Social Responsibility (CSR): a successive level approach

Economic Responsibility	*Legal Responsibility*	*Professional Responsibility*	*Civic Responsibility*
Corporate Responsibilities		*Social Responsibilities*	
• Responsibility to provide goods and services that are desired • Responsibility to provide wages, pay bills, and provide wealth (e.g., dividends) • Those stuck at this level think: if winning competitive battles and profit-making are the only values, then evading the law is good, the appearance of honesty is more important than the reality, and assistance to the community is a distraction to business	• Responsibility to comply with the laws of the land regarding employment practices (e.g., discrimination), work practices (e.g., labor laws), and environment (e.g., pollution) • Those stuck at this level think: if successes at competition, profits, and *strict* legality are *all* that matters, then professional norms are a luxury that should only be used when advantageous and giving back to the community is not a business function	• Responsibility to strive for social and professional norms regarding employment practices (diversity), long-term employee needs (health care, retirement, development), and environment (e.g., recycling) • Those stuck at this level think: if ethical organizations do their fair share in terms of treating employees well, customers fairly, and respecting the community, why should they do more?	• Responsibility to strive for the highest social and professional standards, share wealth more equitably with those responsible for its generation, give back to the community (e.g., charity, community programs), and actively prevent harm (e.g., voluntarily complying with international bans) • Often these organizations are known as industry leaders, originators of best practices, employers of choice, and social exemplars (e.g., "green" or socially conscious organizations)

Source: Adapted from Carroll (1979).

A breach of practical responsibility is the case of excessive pay to employees. In one variation, older companies might have provided wages and benefits to line workers that were out of line with global competition (aka the company having excessive "legacy" costs). Such "legacy" costs can push a company into bankruptcy. Of course in the long term, capitalist theory does not assert that bankruptcy is wrong, in the sense that different industries move around the globe according to wage structures. Another variation is that of executive pay that is either disproportionate or not linked to long-term performance. It is a company responsibility to ensure that executive pay is fair and not set by executives themselves. For example, in 1993, Disney CEO Michael Eisner earned $203 million (primarily exercising stock options), 68 percent of the profit that year for Disney, which experienced a major downturn in revenue as his salary escalated (*New York Times* 1994). Further, it is a responsibility to ensure that boards of directors earn their salaries and exercise their oversight. In general, the wise management of a company is a part of its bedrock responsibility.

Law-abiding behavior is also a foundational responsibility. Violations of the law bring ruin to individuals, bankruptcy to companies, and increased regulation to industries, including governments themselves. Even when companies are not ruined by legal breaches, empirical evidence suggests that they are damaged (Baucus and Baucus 1997). Not just individual cases, but whole classes of cases, are not hard to find, given the enormous increase in exposure of wrong-doing since 2000. The exposure of wrong-doing is increased when markets burst, such as the dot.com bust in the early 2000s, and when the entire market collapses, as it did in 2008 with the excessive market leverage (and profit taking) in the mortgage, stock market, commodity, and insurance industries. See the international list of corporate accounting scandals starting in 2010 (Exhibit 6.3) and note how few US companies are on the list. This is largely a result of the Sarbanes–Oxley Act, which reined in the reckless and lawless activities which had proliferated profusely just a decade earlier.

Although there are many types of legal breaches, the example we will use here is accounting fraud. Large numbers of companies "cooked" the books to increase profits realized for the short-term, inflate market activity, and keep losses off the books, etc. In the worst cases, companies and individuals perpetrated fraud to steal billions of dollars from investors, employees, and taxpayers in brazen, illegal schemes. Additionally, external auditors either did not catch or note these financial breaches, or in some egregious cases, actually aided companies in nefarious activity. Further adding to this problem, the bond-rating agencies were lax in their oversight, giving high ratings to agencies that were in reality on the verge of bankruptcy (Lowenstein 2008). The worst string of accounting scandals occurred from 2000 to 2002, and culminated in the far-reaching Sarbanes–Oxley Act of 2002, which only had three opposing votes in all of Congress. Without trust in the market, investors abandon it as they have done in many markets around the world

Exhibit 6.3

Recent corporate accounting scandals with US companies

Company	*Year*	*Country*	*Accounting Issue*
Kinross Gold	2010	Canada	Overstated asset values
Lehman Brothers	2010	US	Failure to disclose Repo 105 misclassified transactions to investors
Amir-Mansour Aria	2011	Iran	Business loans without putting any collateral and financial system
Bank Saderat Iran	2011	Iran	Financial transactions among banks and getting a lot of business loans without putting any collateral
Sino-Forest Corporation	2011	Canada-China	Ponzi scheme, falsifying assets
Olympus Corporation	2011	Japan	*Tobashi* using acquisitions
Autonomy Corporation	2012	US	Subsidiary of HP
Penn West Exploration	2012 to 2014	Canada	Overstated profits
Pescanova	2013	Spain	Understated debt, Fraudulent invoices, Falsified accounts
Petrobras	2014	Brazil	Government bribes, Misappropriation, Money laundering
Tesco	2014	UK	Revenue recognition
Toshiba	2015	Japan	Overstated profits
Valeant Pharmaceuticals	2015	Canada	Overstated revenues
Alberta Motor Association	2016	Canada	Fraudulent invoices
Odebrecht	2016	Brazil	Government bribes
Wells Fargo	2017	US	False accounting
1Malaysia Development Berhad	2018	Malaysia	Fraud, money laundering, abuse of political power, government bribes
Wirecard AG	2020	Germany	Allegations of fraud
Luckin Coffee	2020	China	Inflated its 2019 sales revenue by up to US$310 million

Source: Wikipedia, Accounting Scandals. https://en.wikipedia.org/wiki/Accounting_scandals.

Note that there are many other types of scandals other than accounting scandals, involving corporate lying/cover-up, product liability, corporate disasters (such as the Exxon Valdez spill or the Union Carbide Bhopal explosion), spying, etc. Historically the newest scandals include security breaches of customer personal data which included Alibaba in 2019 and LinkedIn with 700 users affected in 2021.

when governments either fail to provide the conditions of a fair market, or intervene in the market in order to reduce competition for the benefit of elite interests (e.g., Blush 2008). See Exhibit 6.4 for a listing of the most prominent securities laws.

Exhibit 6.4

Laws that govern the securities industry

There are many laws that cover corporate responsibilities. The major ones covering securities are listed below. The latest, Sarbanes–Oxley, was far reaching after the enormous number of scandals occurring in 2002.

Securities Act of 1933
Securities Exchange Act of 1934
Trust Indenture Act of 1939
Investment Company Act of 1940
Investment Advisers Act of 1940
Sarbanes–Oxley Act of 2002

Arguments for Social Responsibility

Self-interest is a powerful incentive, sometimes leading to incentive and even illegal activities by companies as illustrated in Exhibit 6.5 by Tesla CEO Elon Musk. However, proponents of social responsibility and most in the corporate community themselves suggest there is not only an ethical responsibility to moderate self-interest, but a bottom line value in exceeding simple legal requirements to investors, employees, the environment, and consumers. Although empirical evidence was initially weak (Aupperle et al. 1985; Rechner and Roth 1990), more recent research has consistently found a modest to strong relationship (Goekeke and Fogliasso 2020; Bian et al. 2021). First, investors, consumers, and employees are far more aware of corporate social responsibility records (Margolis and Walsh 2003). As Exhibit 6.6 indicates, all major corporations are annually rated on their corporate citizenship. Perhaps the most well-known ranking, started by business ethics and now conducted by CRO, rates companies on environment, climate change, human rights, philanthropy, employee relations, financial, and governance. The top 100 companies get wide coverage and bragging rights, as do those who are at the top in specific categories. Nearly all corporations report on their corporate social responsibility in their annual reports, and external validation is now the expectation of those claiming to be robust in this category.

Exhibit 6.5

Insensitive CEO at Tesla

Tesla CEO Elon Musk was insensitive during the 2020 pandemic endangering the lives of his employees. Because of a rapidly increasing infection rate, California enacted health measures that restricted many businesses' operations, including Tesla.

Most non-essential businesses were ordered to stop operating. Nonetheless, the company called its workers back to its Fremont factory while the government order was still in effect. However, this first attempt of defiance was forestalled when Alameda County officials intervened, only to be met with fierce verbal attacks from CEO Musk.

Unabashed, a month later, Tesla called back its workers and started manufacturing vehicles, which was still in defiance of the legal mandate. However, after the company was back in operation, county officials decided to allow Tesla to reopen as an "essential business."

The reopening was met with controversy, and many workers contracted the coronavirus soon after opening. Musk later attempted to be sympathetic about the situation and said employees could stay at home if they felt unsafe. However, some of those that did were subsequently terminated.

Source: Wikipedia. Elon Musk. https://en.wikipedia.org/wiki/Elon_Musk

Exhibit 6.6

10 Best corporate citizens of 2021 (administered by 3BL Media)

Overall Rank	*Company*	*Score*
1	Owens Corning	91.66
2	General Mills, Inc.	86.31
3	HP, Inc.	85.67
4	Cisco Systems, Inc.	84.48
5	Intel Corporation	83.89
6	Newmont Corporation	83.03
7	Accenture plc	82.92
8	Ecolab, Inc.	82.88
9	AT&T, Inc.	82.87
10	Citigroup, Inc.	82.47

Source: 3BL Media, LLC.

Note: 3BL Media is the current "owner" of the "100 Best Corporate Citizens rankings." Evaluations based on transparency and performance factors across eight pillars: climate change; employee relations; the environment; ESG performance; finance; corporate governance; human rights; and stakeholders and society. 3BL collects data and information from only public sources.

While investors and employees may not make strength in corporate social responsibility the priority factor in decision-making, it frequently is a determining factor once economic factors are accounted for, and it is an all-things-being-equal calculus (Orlitzky, Schmidt, and Rynes 2003; Assaf et al. 2017; Wang et al. 2021). Since numerous "cause" organizations work hard to target companies they consider offenders of various social responsibilities, bad publicity is a very powerful disincentive. Further, social responsibility in general, but especially social initiatives such as adopting a problematic community or policy issue, can lead to enormous good (if "soft") publicity (Porter and Kramer 2002; Lenz et al. 2017).

Finally, there is the moral argument, which is quite popular in the general public, but which is far from universally accepted by all business theorists or business people. The range of opinion is neatly captured by two of the examples already cited. Milton Friedman (1970) said that there

> is one and only one social responsibility of business—to use its resources and engage its activities designated to increase profits so long as it stays within the rules of the game, which is to say engages in free and fair competition, without deception or fraud.

On the other hand, Bill Ford said: "A good company delivers excellent products and services, and a great company does all that and strives to make the world a better place." The moral argument is that companies are not just legal entities, but are legal "persons," and as such, they share the same responsibilities to society that individuals do.

Harking back to the founding of the country, when capitalist economic principles were laid down as one pillar of society, the idea was that capitalism's emphasis on the market as a means to harness the best of competition, merit, innovation, and efficiency would lead to the ultimate betterment of all. However, capitalism was not the only pillar of society. The democratic pillar asserted equality under the law and promised that the affluent would not be able to excessively dominate the public agenda. The third pillar was a religious or moral one, in which citizens would contribute to the "common weal" by serving in the military and on juries, paying taxes, voting, and contributing to social projects and charity as their means allowed.

Principles and Values in the Public Sector with Its Demands for Constraint and Accountability

As discussed earlier in the chapter, while there are society-wide ethics and norms, at the sector and occupational levels there is a good of variation. Competition, loyalty to the company, profits and other capitalistic values tend to be substituted with public service motivation, strict merit, due process, equity, transparency and other civic and egalitarian values. Public sector organizations are created to be more long-term oriented, cautious, deliberative, and open to public inspection. Exhibit 6.7 identifies four major principles that have to do with the career civil service, strict legal compliance, robust rights of the public, and the need for strong leadership despite the much heightened constraints that exist in the public sector.

Exhibit 6.7

Public sector principles and values

Principles	*Positive Public Sector Values*
Understand the values in the career civil service	Treat employees fairly and equally, respecting their privacy and Constitutional rights
	Expect employees to maintain high standards of integrity and concern for the public interest
	Require efficiency and effectiveness of operations
	Safeguard civil servants from political intrusion
Foster legal compliance and integrate non-civil service systems as appropriate	Give deference to political leadersç
	Work with and support non-civil servants in the private and nonprofit sectors to achieve efficiency and economy when they are working on behalf of the public good
Understand that the public has rights beyond merit principles	Ensure transparency of public information
	Protect the privacy of citizen's personal information
	Supply citizens with easy access to information and greatest degree of voice in public affairs as possible
	Ensure citizen due process rights
Provide leadership for public sector organizations	Provide well-designed innovation
	Foster appropriate risk-taking but ensure that it is minimized, reasonable, and authorized
	Provide vision and inspiration for public sector work
	Strive for excellence
	Nurture professionalism that leads to the need for less supervision

Source: Montgomery Van Wart, Author (2016).

Striking the Right Balance of Responsibilities

While few would take as narrow a stand as Friedman on corporate social responsibility today, if only because the market itself now exposes and punishes those who are especially recalcitrant in the long term so much more effectively, the issue of the proper balance of responsibilities is very much with us. Some common, but not universally, held beliefs about corporate social responsibility are:

- The dual responsibilities of economic viability and legal compliance are essential. Only nonprofits and government organizations do not have a responsibility to produce profits.
- All companies and corporations have a responsibility to act ethically as well—to exceed legal minimums by actively seeking to mitigate environmental impact, to treat employees well, to contribute to the community as resources will allow, etc. Indeed, it is pragmatic to act ethically if medium- and long-term corporate interests are being protected even in such areas as environmental impact (Thomas 2001).
- It makes economic and moral sense for successful companies, which have profited from a stable and healthy society, to adopt discretionary responsibilities such as corporate social initiatives (Goekeke and Fogliasso 2020). The wealth of major corporations can be used to do good, provide a business perspective on social problems, and provide another example of leadership.

An underlying theme is that of balance (Bian et al. 2021). A financially strapped company may need to focus nearly exclusively on economic survival, but cannot focus on economic profits by violating the law. Better to go out of business with integrity than to violate its compact with society. A productive company should expand its responsibilities, but do so in a pragmatic way that will not overwhelm its financial standing. Successful companies can afford to divert substantial resources without distracting from the financial leadership that they have attained.

Encouraging Ethical Behavior

Organizational Level

What can organizations do to encourage ethical behavior at both the company and individual levels? A variety of methods are suggested.

1 Once it is acknowledged that profits and strict legality are not the only values to be pursued, a broader analysis of the various stakeholders of a company is required. Just as *stakeholder analysis* is one of the most fundamental tools of strategic planning, performance measurement, and

public relations, so too is it the foundation of making ethical decisions (Freeman and Gilbert 1988). Stake holders can largely be divided into those inside the company and those outside.

Inside stakeholders (potentially) include private owners, stockholders, executive officers, boards of directors, and employees. Inside stakeholders are concerned about the short-term profit-making, long-term viability of the company, and its reputation to varying degrees. It is an ethical truism that a dominant focus on the short-term perspective will ultimately give way not only to ethical breaches, but ultimately to pragmatic problems as well, as companies squander their financial edge for profit taking. The longer the time frame, the more the stakeholder analysis will be diversified.

There are many *potential* external stakeholders—creditors, suppliers, customers, governments, local communities, the general public, unions, and competitors. *Creditors* want to know that the company's debts will be paid just as *suppliers* want to know that their goods and services will be ordered and paid for in a timely and reasonable fashion. *Customers* want a fair mix of value and quality. *Governments* at various levels are concerned with regulating the legal aspects of companies—such as environmental protection standards and product safety, to providing a supportive base for operations in terms of infrastructure, workforce education, etc. Governments also have to manage the negative externalities of companies such as employee layoffs and closed facilities. *Local communities* (similar but not identical to governments) want companies to be good corporate citizens in terms of paying employees well, and providing local charity. Variously, the *general public* can be thought of as having a primary concern for the larger social issues such as environmental protection, international ramifications of good work and trade practices, and the systemic issues of good corporate governance. *Unions* are concerned with employee rights, pay, and working conditions. Even *competitors* are a part of a good stakeholder analysis because they are key to setting industry standards and occasionally function as corporate partners.

In some instances the number of significant stakeholders is quite large and in other cases it is quite small, depending on the scope of the issue or issues involved.

2 A thorough stakeholder analysis and a corporate commitment to balancing social responsibilities with economic and legal ones should be reflected in *mission and values statements*.
3 *Guidelines and codes of conduct* can provide concrete language about minimalist expectations as a bulwark against wrong-doing. They can be of great assistance in delineating what is inappropriate as well as specific steps to take in case of ethical breaches. *Codes of ethics* can provide tangible language about what individuals and groups should strive for and identify exemplary behavior (Van Wart 1996, 2003).

4 *Ethics training* ensures knowledge of rules and encourages inspirational convictions toward being a moral exemplar.
5 Many larger companies have an *ethics officer* and or an *ethics hotline*.
6 An emphasis can be placed on executives and managers being *role models* of fairness, commitment, and charity.
7 An *ethics award* can be added to a company's recognition program.
8 A *social responsibility audit* can be conducted to see if the balance of social responsibilities is appropriate for the company in its current status, as well as to ensure that the company is meeting its stated convictions and goals. Can social responsibilities be added that both save the environment and save costs, provide employee enrichment and increase efficiency, provide increased transparency while enhancing public image, etc.?
9 More successful corporations can consider adopting a social initiative. Social initiatives can be modest, such as an ongoing program to keep a highway clean, to contribute food and manpower to a local nonprofit like Second Harvest, or to encourage a big brother/sister program. Larger social initiatives by wealthy companies can include the adoption of a community or by taking a stand on a national social problem such as worldwide water conservation.
10 Successful companies can strive for ethics awards, either at the national level (such as becoming a top 100 corporate citizen), or locally.

Individual Level Ethical Analysis

What basic skills do *you* need to conduct an ethical analysis? First, one has to be sensitive to the fact that significant decisions have consequences beyond the individual and usually beyond the company. Several pragmatic questions will generally identify whether more ethical analysis is necessary.

First, am I OK with this decision being publicized and will it stand up to public scrutiny?

Second, what if everyone did what I am doing? Would the community or society be better or worse off? In this context, a company that is facing bankruptcy may be more ethically justified in cutting pay temporarily, than a company making record profits would be in freezing pay in a period of high unemployment.

Third, who are the stakeholders involved? If you do not know who will be affected by decisions, you cannot consider their interests.

Fourth, what are the *concrete* ethical issues involved? Do they involve economic, legal, and/or social responsibilities?

Finally, what alternatives exist that maximize as many of these competing values as possible? This means that the importance of various values must be weighed, because they will not necessarily be equal. Considering all values—and the weights of those values—when considering alternatives means that relatively optimal solutions will be selected. In fact, often with

Exhibit 6.8

Beyond The Green Corporation: imagine a world in which eco-friendly and socially responsible practices actually help a company's bottom line: it's closer than you think

Under conventional notions of how to run a conglomerate like Unilever, CEO Patrick Cescau should wake up each morning with a laser-like focus: how to sell more soap and shampoo than Procter & Gamble Co. (PG). But ask Cescau about the $52 billion Dutch–British giant's biggest strategic challenges for the twenty-first century, and the conversation roams from water-deprived villages in Africa to the planet's warming climate.

The world is Unilever's laboratory. In Brazil, the company operates a free community laundry in a São Paolo slum, provides financing to help tomato growers convert to eco-friendly "drip" irrigation, and recycles 17 tons of waste annually at a toothpaste factory. Unilever funds a floating hospital that offers free medical care in Bangladesh, a nation with just 20 doctors for every 10,000 people. In Ghana, it teaches palm oil producers to reuse plant waste while providing potable water to deprived communities. In India, Unilever staff helps thousands of women in remote villages start micro-enterprises. And responding to green activists, the company discloses how much carbon dioxide and hazardous waste its factories spew out around the world.

As Cescau sees it, helping such nations wrestle with poverty, water scarcity, and the effects of climate change is vital to staying competitive in coming decades. Some 40 percent of the company's sales and most of its growth now take place in developing nations. Unilever food products account for roughly ten percent of the world's crops of tea and 30 percent of all spinach. It is also one of the world's biggest buyers of fish. As environmental regulations grow tighter around the world, Unilever must invest in green technologies or its leadership in packaged foods, soaps, and other goods could be imperiled. "You can't ignore the impact your company has on the community and environment," Cescau says. CEOs used to frame thoughts like these in the context of moral responsibility, he adds. But now, "it's also about growth and innovation. In the future, it will be the only way to do business."

A remarkable number of CEOs have begun to commit themselves to the same kind of sustainability goals Cescau has pinpointed, even in profit-obsessed America. For years, the term "sustainability" has carried a lot of baggage. Put simply, it's about meeting humanity's needs without harming future generations. It was a favorite cause among economic development experts, human rights activists, and conservationists. But to many US business leaders, sustainability just meant higher costs and smacked of earnest UN corporate responsibility conferences and the utopian idealism of Western Europe. Now, sustainability is "right at the top of the agendas" of more US CEOs, especially young ones, says McKinsey Global Institute Chairman Lenny Mendonca.

Source: Engardino et al. (2007)

good ethical reasoning the final outcome can become a win-win solution, and sometimes problems can be married together to create new opportunities! Even when ethical dilemmas simply mean making tough choices, however, the decisions will be better and easier to justify. Below is a case regarding the ethics involved in modern-day retail.

Analytical Case: The Ethics Involved in the Modern Retail Store

Big Box Corporation is a modern low-cost department store. To keep its costs down, it has a number of standard practices that ensure profitability.

First, it aggressively keeps costs low and does not rely extensively on sales to build long-term rather than temporary customer loyalty. Therefore, it is a global buyer with no "buy-American" policy. In fact, while it does ensure that its products are legally made, it does not concern itself with non-governmental protocols on recommendations about working conditions or child labor.

Second, it keeps its market prices extremely low by ensuring that the jobs of line workers are as simple and repetitive as possible, so that workers can easily be trained and replaced. Big Box Corporation has been largely successful at keeping unions out of its stores in all but a few instances. This means that many of the workers are the second or third wage earners in homes and that many of its employees are part-time retired workers or young workers seeking their first jobs. As importantly, these wage earners, who earn just above minimum wage, do not normally have significant benefits such as health care and retirement. Many of the workers do not need them because they are covered by a first wage earner or do not care about them because retirement has occurred or is a distant concern. A small, but not tiny, percentage of the line workers qualify for government benefits such as child health care. Middle managers are recruited from "the floor" and get improved wages and modest benefits, but are still paid very modestly by management standards. Store managers are generally professionally trained and analysis driven to examine profitability trends, cost–benefit ratios, contingency analysis, etc., and thus rarely come from the floor. They are largely recruited from corporate manager-training programs populated by college business majors and MBA graduates. After serving as an assistant store manager with modest pay (each store has three to five assistant store managers) for a period of three to seven years, opportunities to become a store manager often open up. Store managers are well paid for retail.

Third, Big Box Corporation prefers to locate its stores just outside of cities, when they are not land-locked by other cities, in order to avoid city taxes. This has the side advantage of cheaper land for large parking areas. Alternatively, when locating in an urbanized area with adjacent cities, as is common today, Big Box always considers two or three options in adjacent jurisdictions that will be desirous of having the store. By doing so, the store can make the jurisdictions compete aggressively, and can get excellent multi-year tax concessions (sometimes up to a decade) as well as infrastructure improvements such as road widening on the arterial to the store, traffic lights, and sewer and utility extensions.

Fourth, Big Box Corporation is large enough that it can force suppliers to maintain ownership of products until point of customer sale. In other words, unlike smaller retailers that must buy goods to stock shelves and then discount unsold goods, thereby competing with their own goods not on sale, Big Box does not pay suppliers until goods are registered as sold. In experimenting with new products, it risks the loss of shelf space but has no inventory cost liability. Unsold goods are simply returned, although the supplier must pick them up or abandon them.

Fifth, because of its size, Big Box is able to stay abreast of current trends and appeal to all but the smallest niche markets. This means that it is able to push old-fashioned stores with less efficient practices out of business, absorb their market share, and maintain a lock on the market environment for the cost-conscious buyer who is impervious to all stores except other corporations with a similar style, or stores that carry only discontinued products that they have purchased for pennies on the dollar but whose product lines vary enormously month by month.

Sixth, while not immune to "green" initiatives, Big Box knows that most of its customers place a much larger premium on value than on environmental concerns and thus it caters to that preference. When enough customers are perceived to be interested and the cost differential is modest, Big Box occasionally offers a product that can be marketed as "environmentally friendly."

Seventh, Big Box is careful not to dilute its efficiency and profits thrust with local charity issues. Charity is done, but almost exclusively at the corporate level, so that it can easily be "counted" for accounting purposes, and easily be identified for corporate public relations.

Questions for Discussion and Analysis

1 What are the *possible* ethical questions that are involved? (At least seven are implicitly identified in the case.) This question is often asked at the same time as the following question.
2 Who are the stakeholders who are/will be affected in this scenario and what are their interests? (This is covered in the previous chapter.)
3 What are the *concrete* ethical issues that you feel need to be considered? (This requires narrowing down the list of possible ethical issues, which should be done after identifying stakeholders and their interests.) What alternatives exist? How do these alternatives maximize various values, given the weight of those values?
4 What recommendations do you have in how the situations you chose to address could be/should have been resolved or improved? *Or*, state if no changes are necessary, and the reasons why the status quo is acceptable.

Practical Skill

Ethical Reasoning

Ethical reasoning is the logic about right and wrong personal and business conduct. It requires a person to understand their professional ethical roles, recognize ethical issues in a business scenario, assess their own ethical values and the social context of problems, think about how different ethical perspectives might be applied to the ethical dilemmas, and consider the ramifications of alternative actions.

If you find yourself in situations where your ethics are challenged, what should you do? Try this simple ethical reasoning framework:

- Get a clear understanding of the situation, differentiating facts from your assumption.
- Conduct a stakeholder analysis, determining who's really involved and the degree to which their interest is affected. (You have learned this in Chapter 2.)
- Define the conflicting interests and values and identify the higher-order values involved. Ethical conflict or dilemma always involves conflict of interests and values. Sometimes it is not to make right or wrong decision, it is to make right versus right decision based on your personal and professional judgment.
- Identify the options that you can reasonably take. You need to know that although none of the options satisfies all the interests involved, some options do a better job.
- Identify the potential consequences of your options. Some options may be correct but disastrous; other options may work at one time but not others; still other options may reap gains in the short run but losses in the long run.

Skill Exercise: Stakeholder Analysis of ABC's Relocation

Read the opening case scenario: Zoey's dilemma at Happy Paws. Apply the above framework to analyze the issues that Zoey is facing. Discuss how the analysis may inform you and how you would resolve the issue, if you were Zoey.

Summary and Conclusion

1 When corporations and the private sector engage in corruption and excessively self-serving behavior, the legal system is frequently changed to regulate areas of societal concern more tightly.
2 Ethics is a system of beliefs about how to behave, and morals reflect one's actual behaviors.
3 General social expectations permeate all of society and include such values as honesty, fairness, and legality. There are also specific social expectations, so that we have different standards for judges, business people, soldiers, and spies. Even so, it is not difficult to discern the difference among business people who are immoral, amoral, moral, and exemplary.

4 Corporate social responsibility is meeting basic economic needs through diligence and innovation, exceeding legal requirements by fulfilling the spirit of the law, while simultaneously finding ways to enhance the community and planet with mutually beneficial actions, and when possible, provide outright acts of charity. This can be thought of as the basic corporate responsibilities of economic success and legality and the social responsibilities of professionalism and civic responsibility.
5 Today, the stakes for being known as a good and honorable organization are being made more critical by "cause" organizations that attack corporations they perceive as lacking basic corporate social responsibility.
6 The basis of ethical analysis is sensitivity to ethical issues, stakeholder analysis, thinking long and hard about the tough ethical issues, and making sure that alternatives are examined and the values underlying those decisions are well understood.

Key Terms

- Amoral
- Ethical exemplars
- Social responsibility
- "Cause" organizations
- Ethics
- Audit
- Corporate responsibility
- Moral
- Stakeholder analysis
- Corporate social responsibility
- Professional norms
- Social norms

Study Questions

1 To what degree do you think your system of ethics comes from your religion, your parents, your peers, and your education? Place an approximate percent on each and provide an example.
2 What drives people and companies to be of low morality, even while they are asserting ethical principles? Provide some examples of both ideal and wicked business leaders.
3 To what degree do you think it is the government's responsibility to ensure a relatively fair playing field? Give an example of when the government has done a good job in ensuring a fair playing field, done too little, or done too much.
4 Do you think that American business ethics are improving, deteriorating, or staying about the same over the last 50 years?

References

Assaf. A. G., Josiassen, A., Ahn, J. S., and Mattila, A. S. (2017). Advertising Spending, Firm Performance, and the Moderating Impact of CSR. *Tourism Economics, 23*(7), 1484–1495.

Aupperle, K. E., Carroll, A. B., and Hatfield, D. J. (1985). An Empirical Examination of the Relationship between Corporate Social Responsibility and Profitability. *Academy of Management Journal, 28*(June):446–463.

Baucus, M. S., and Baucus, D. A. (1997). Paying the Piper: An Empirical Examination of Longer-Term Financial Consequences of Illegal Corporate Behavior. *Academy of Management Journal*, i40(February):129–151.

Berman, E., and Van Wart, M. (1999). The Ethics of Productivity: Toward Increased Dialogue and Customer-Based Accountability. *International Journal of Organizational Theory and Behavior, 2*(3–4):413–430.

Bian, J., Liao, Y., Wang, Y. Y., and Tao, F. (2021). Analysis of Firm CSR Strategies. *European Journal of Operational Research, 290(3)*:914–926.

Bisoux, T. (2008). The Socially Responsible Curriculum. *BizEd*. July/August:22–30.

Blush, J. (2008). Behind the Russian Stock Market Meltdown. *Business Week*, September 17. businessweek.com/globalbiz/content/sep2008/gb20080917_169033.htm.

Brown, M., and Trevino, L. (2006). Ethical Leadership: A Review and Future Directions. *Leadership Quarterly, 17*:595–616.

Carroll, A. B. (1979). A Three Dimensional Conceptual Model of Corporate Performance. *Academy of Management Review*, October:497–505.

Comer, D.R., and Schwartz, M. (2020). Farewell to the Boasting of Posting: Encouraging Modesty on Social Media, in Schwartz, M., Harris, H., Highfield, C. and Breakey, H. (eds.) *Educating for Ethical Survival* (Research in Ethical Issues in Organizations, Vol. 24, pp. 63–75). Bingley: Emerald Publishing Limited. https://doi.org/10.1108/S1529-209620200000024004

De George, R. (1999). *Business Ethics*. New York: Prentice-Hall.

DeTienne, K. B., Ellertson, C. F., Ingerson, M. C., and Dudley, W. R. (2021). Moral Development in Business Ethics: An Examination and Critique. *Journal of Business Ethics, 170(3)*:429–448.

Engardino, P. with Capell, K., Carey, J., and Hall, K. (2007). *Business Week*, January 29.

Freeman, R. E., and Gilbert, D. R. (1988). *Corporate Strategy and the Search for Ethics*. Upper Saddle River, NJ: Prentice Hall.

Friedman, M. (1970). The Social Responsibility of Business Is to Increase Its Profits. *New York Times Magazine*, September 13, *30*:126–127.

Goedeke, M. J., and Fogliasso, C. (2020). Is CSR Becoming a Corporate Requirement? *Journal of Managerial Issues, 32*(2):162–175.

Gong, G., Huang, X., Wu, S., Tian, H., and Li, W. (2021). Punishment by Securities Regulators, Corporate Social Responsibility and the Cost of Debt. *Journal of Business Ethics*, 171(2), 337–356.

Heijltjes, M. (2007). Learning to Lead—Responsibly. *BizEd*. November/December: 32–37.

Kurlantzick, J. (2003). Liar, Liar: In the Race to Make Money, Some American Businesses Have Been Lying their Pants off—But Is Success at Any Cost Really Worth the Price? *Entrepreneur, 4*:69–74.

Lenz, I., Wetzel, H. A., and Hammerschmidt, M. (2017). Can Doing Good Lead to Doing Poorly? Firm Value Implications of CSR in the Face of CSI. *Journal of the Academy of Marketing Science, 45*(5):677–697.

Lowenstein, R. (2008). Triple-A Failure. *New York Times*, April 27. http://www.nytimes.com/2008/04/27/magazine/27Credit-t.html.

Margolis, J. D., and Walsh, J. P. (2003). Misery Loves Companies: Rethinking Social Initiatives by Business. *Administrative Science Quarterly*, *48*:268–305.

Markham, J. W. (2015). *A financial history of modern US corporate scandals: From Enron to reform*. New York: Routledge.

Medeiros, K.E, Watts, L. L., Mulhearn, T. J., Steele L. M., Mumford, M. D., and Connelly, S. (2017). What Is Working, What Is Not, and What We Need to Know: A Meta-Analytic Review of Business Ethics Instruction. *Journal of Academic Ethics*, 1–31:245–275.

New York Times (1994). Eisner Pay Is 68% of Profit. Section 1, p. 48.

Orlitzky, M., Schmidt, F. L., and Rynes, S. L. (2003). Corporate Social and Financial Performance: A Meta-analysis. *Organization Studies*, *24(3)*:403–441.

Pearce, J. A., and Doh, J. (2005). Enhancing Corporate Responsibility through Skillful Collaboration. *Sloan Management Review*, *46(3)*:30–39.

Porter, M., and Kramer, M. R. (2002). The Competitive Advantage of Corporate Philanthropy. *Harvard Business Review*, December:57–68.

Rechner, P., and Roth, K. (1990). Social Responsibility and Financial Performance: A Structural Equation Methodology. *International Journal of Management*, December:382–391.

Redman, E. (2005). Three Models of Corporate Social Responsibility: Implications for Public Policy. *Roosevelt Review*, *1*(1):95–108.

Rokeach, M. (1973). *The Nature of Human Values*. New York: Free Press.

Samuelson, J. (2009). Toward Sustainable Change. *BizEd*, July/August:30–35.

Seto-Pamies, D., and Papaoikonomou, E. (2020). Sustainable Development Goals: A Powerful Framework for Embedding Ethics, CSR, and Sustainability in Management Education. *Sustainability*, *12(5)*:1762.

Thomas, A. (2001). Corporate Environmental Policy and Abnormal Price Returns: An Empirical Investigation. *Business Strategy and the Environment*, *10*:125–134.

Van Wart, M. (1996). The Sources of Ethical Decisionmaking for Individuals in the Public Sector. *Public Administration Review*, *56(6)*:525–533.

Van Wart, M. (1998). *Changing Public Sector Values*. New York: Garland Publishing.

Van Wart, M. (2003). Codes of Ethics as Living Documents: The Case of the American Society for Public Administration. *Public Integrity*, *5(4)*:331–346.

Van Wart, M., and Denhardt, K. (2001). Organizational Structures as a Context for Organizational Ethics, in Terry Cooper (ed.) *Handbook of Administrative Ethics*, 2nd edn (pp. 227–241). New York: Marcel Dekker.

Wang, Y., Su, M., Shen, L., and Tang, R. (2021). Decision-making of Closed-loop Supply Chain Under Corporate Social Responsibility and Fairness Concerns. *Journal of Cleaner Production*, *284*:125373.

Wikipedia, Accounting Scandals. https://en.wikipedia.org/wiki/Accounting_scandals.

Wikipedia. Elon Musk. https://en.wikipedia.org/wiki/Elon_Musk

Wymer, W., and Rundle-Thiele, S. (2017). Inclusion of Ethics, Social Responsibility, and Sustainability in Business School Curricula; A Benchmark Study. *International Review on Public and Nonprofit Marketing*, *14*:19–34.

7 Business's Involvement in Government

Alexandru Roman and Joshua Steinfeld

Chapter Contents

Case 7 Scenario

Zach's Original Business Idea

Zach graduated several years ago with a double degree in physics and engineering. Last summer, while helping Zoey with Happy Paws, Zach came up with a business idea of his own. If successful, the business will introduce a product and a service highly demanded on the market—an all organic pet product line, from foods and treats, to shampoos and medicines. The business concept is novel, with good potential for success. Zach was already thinking he could use all the blemished goods from his grandparents' produce farm that weren't suitable for grocers.

Unfortunately for Zach, the pressure of student loans, which he is now repaying, looms large over his finances. He doesn't possess the funds or the credit history necessary to borrow money to start his business. He'd taken out that loan to help Zoey last year, too. Zach's business idea is a long-term endeavor with a low initial return on

DOI: 10.4324/9781003178620-9

investment; as such, most funding opportunities, such as raising capital from investors, currently seem unrealistic.

Zach's idea doesn't need much to become operational. The business would probably give him enough income to make his student loan payments. There must be something out there that could help. But what? For the first few years, until it develops into a full-fledged, self-sustaining enterprise, Zach could work part time and dedicate the rest of his time to expanding his product line.

Thinking about his options, Zach remembered the concept of lobbying, to which he was introduced in his government–business relations class. Lobbying could be the solution to his situation. Zach had a hard time imagining he was the only graduate facing a similar dilemma; surely there were more like him. In addition, he remembered hearing that his city, Anyplace, had unveiled a new strategic plan that focused on business development. It dawned on Zach that the municipality's interests and his needs (and the needs of many other recent grads) would align perfectly. The municipality could help local graduates with their student loans; in return, the grads would develop businesses that would help the local economy, attract investors, and could eventually evolve into large local employers.

With this in mind, Zach decided to bone up on the intricacies of local lobbying. He wondered if he could lobby himself or if he would have to hire someone. He was also unsure how long it would take to get a response. He did not even know whom he should lobby, or from what angle to approach the question. So many things needed to be answered. Zach was, however, excited for the first time in months that he may have come across a viable solution. His first step was to visit the municipality's website and identify how to proceed with his plan in an ethical manner. He couldn't wait to tell Zoey.

After scanning the website for Anyplace, Zach decided to visit the municipal Small Business Administration Office. Once there, he was introduced to the idea of small business incubators. Zach learned that Anyplace was among the cities that had small business incubators managed through its Department of Economic Development. Good news!

There were, however, several challenges. Although he met the basic qualification for an incubator award, it was highly competitive, and unlikely, as a first-time entrant, that he would receive it. Historically, the reviewers also favored graduates from the local college, and Zach had gone to Somewhere State. Finally, the decisions made by the community advisory board are rather political in character. All things being equal, those with political or social connections get the nod. Quality is necessary, as the saying goes, but not sufficient.

Still, not all was lost. In doing his homework, Zach found he indirectly knew someone on the committee, whom he could ask for "advice." That would increase his visibility in the actual award meeting. There was another thing working in his favor. His father Zeddic was good friends with an Anyplace council member. He decided to find out if the council member would allow him to use his name as a referee. While Zach did not go to the local university, he did have a high-level contact at the local college where he had taken a summer course—another reference? Luckily, that college representative was the chair of the committee. Finally, Zach's mother's best friend was a freelance writer for the paper. He could write into the proposal his intent to get some free press for his business and the incubator program; his mother's friend could also "conveniently" advertise the merits of incubators through other related articles.

Zach now had a plan. He knew his goal, developed a strategy, and identified individuals who would help him get there. Everything seemed set for success. With all these things in his favor, one of the incubator awards was all but his. Yet something made Zach feel uneasy. Although everything he was doing was entirely legal and would be normal practice for anyone lobbying a certain issue, something still bothered him. Should he engage in advocacy to compete for the incubator award or should he leave the proposal to compete on technical merit alone? On the other hand, would the council appreciate the true merits of his proposal if they were not properly explained and pointed out?

It is within this context that Zach came face to face with an important lesson about the realities of the social matrix—science and business can rarely be separated from politics and there is a thin line between appropriate advocacy and unwarranted bias. Zach had had enough stress for today. It was time to meet Zoey and Tyler at Happy Paws.

Introduction

Regardless of what our personal perspectives or preferences might otherwise be, the role played by government in the economy is far reaching and highly unlikely to significantly diminish at any point in the near future. Government constructs and manages the legislative and regulatory environment within which business operates. One would be hard pressed to identify a legal economic activity that is not tied directly or indirectly to a specific governmental activity. Indeed, any business process is bound to the laws that regulate its field of operation. When considered in aggregate, governmental actions become a critical variable in the equation of business and economic success. A timely and orderly intervention by government can make a difference in avoiding an economic crisis. At the same time, however, unwarranted and misplaced governmental interference can also misalign the fragile economic equilibrium.

Most of the popular debates regarding the interaction between government and business could lead one to believe that the relationship between them falls in either one of two extremes. Some might assert that business is meticulously controlled by government through heavy regulation, while others might argue that business routinely imposes its will on government. Although the former might be the case within heavily centralized economies and the latter might occur on separate occasions, most of the time, business–government relations are sure to be much more complex than that. Extremes do exist, but so do golden middles. Government gets heavily involved in business operations; nevertheless, business does also command a great deal of influence in matters of governance.

The interaction between government and business is not a one-way street. Influences, ideas, finances, and human resources travel with regularity in both directions. In many ways, the business–government relationship can be described as a dense network of interdependencies built on trust. Historically, the involvement of government in business has received the bulk of public and academic attention, leaving the other direction significantly underexplored. Yet, this does not mean that the involvement of business in government is negligible or that it is somehow inconsequential. Quite the opposite: business actively—and at times even aggressively—gets involved in matters of government. In fact, within certain contexts, especially in cases when government does not hold the necessary expertise in certain matters, business becomes a de facto agent of governance.

Cornelius Kerwin and Scott Furlong, two scholars who are renowned for their studies on rule-making, have suggested that the participation of private enterprises in the design of rules, by which they will eventually be regulated, is often overlooked and underestimated in terms of its impacts (Kerwin and Furlong 2010). According to these scholars, many private sector companies, contrary to popular narratives, are highly interested in regulation and often volunteer to assist governmental agencies in their design. In some instances, since regulation can serve as entry barriers, there is more push for regulation from business than from the government itself. It is common, for example, that within an emerging industry government might not have any expertise on the matter and might have to rely entirely on private sector players to provide the knowledge and structure for designing a specific regulation, or perhaps even allow the players to self-regulate. Currently, there is a strong relationship between government, regulatory agencies, and the industries that are being regulated. The strength of this relationship can be attributed in part to the large involvement that business has in questions of governance.

Taken together, it would be a mistake to think that the involvement of business in government is trivial. Even if this aspect of the relationship does not receive nearly as much attention as the other side of the relationship, it is equally important. Furthermore, its dynamics are sometimes difficult to trace and are fraught with complexities. As a result, when analyzing the involvement of business in matters of government and governance, one should be rather careful when jumping to conclusions or making sweeping generalizations. Although the popular press might periodically suggest there are many questions and concerns that could be raised about the democratic nature of business involvement in government, there are also many benefits that come with the existence of these relationships and interdependencies. As such, there is much to be gained from a detailed and systematic exploration of business's involvement in government. When it comes to these sorts of discussions, it pays to take a broad perspective and to consider the influences of all the variables that come into play.

Government's attention is, like the attention of international non-governmental organizations (NGOs) for that matter, or any other valuable resource, limited. Although by its very nature government has to attend to any issue that is of importance to its citizens and business, there are many instances when government simply does not have the resources or knowledge base to address all ardent issues at once. In developed democracies, it is expected that all interests have the right to have their concerns voiced. Within this context of limited attention and resources, ideas and goals—regardless of whether they originated from the citizens or business—have to compete in order to make it onto the governmental or inter-governmental agenda. While an issue might be important, government or NGOs might not address it until it is made known that a specific problem is of great importance and needs to be addressed. The communication between government and non-governmental actors, then, becomes critical in the larger scheme of things. In order to estimate the needs of business and develop practical regulatory environments, government needs both citizens and business to actively participate in the decision-making process.

Neither citizens nor business interests hold a monopoly over government's agenda. John Kingdon, a renowned public policy scholar, has suggested that the manner in which a governmental agenda changes, commonly known as the Multiple Streams Theory (see Exhibit 7.1), is an extremely complex process that encompasses both rational and incremental aspects. One of the key roles in the entire process is played by those who advocate, for their own purposes or in the name of others, the merits of addressing a certain issue in a specific way. These policy entrepreneurs vie for attention from legislators (or international NGOs) and attempt to push an idea through whenever a window of opportunity is opened. The success of any policy being passed in a given form is in large part hedged on the ability of these entrepreneurs to effectively communicate and advocate the validity of their perspectives.

Exhibit 7.1

The multiple streams of public policy

Over a period of four years, John Kingdon studied multiple cases of how public policy was designed in the US, interviewing a total of 247 policy-makers. By the end of his research, Kingdon had developed a simple, yet powerful, perspective on the process by which the governmental agenda changes and public policy is formulated. His primary purpose was to understand how social issues make their way into government's agenda and how that agenda is modified.

According to Kingdon, the policy arena—particularly the federal one—can be envisioned as a space filled with a "soup" of ideas through which three important and independent "streams" of policy activity flow: the problem stream, the policy stream, and the politics stream. The problem stream consists of those social questions that are believed by the public and policy legislators to be problems that should be addressed by government. The policy stream entails all possible "solutions," developed and advocated by professionals, policy communities, or interest groups, which are available for legislators to pick from when addressing a specific policy issue. Finally, the politics stream is made up of macro-political factors such as public mood, elections, or national and international events that create the environment for a specific legislative action. Each stream flows independently of the others and is guided by its own rules. Change can happen at any point in time within any one of the three streams without affecting the flow of the other two. For policy change to occur, however, all three streams have to join when a window of opportunity opens. Only then can government's agenda change and policy be formulated. At the heart of the dynamics behind all this lie the policy entrepreneurs. These policy actors, such as lobbyists, scholars, and policy communities, follow each stream closely and try to influence the flow. When a "window of opportunity" opens up, they move fast to push the social issues they are representing on the agenda or to make the case for their preferred solution to be adopted. The process is not always rational. Sometimes policy entrepreneurs have an existing solution and they search for a problem to which they could attach the solution; at other times, problems and solutions might be created for the sole purpose of advancing one's career.

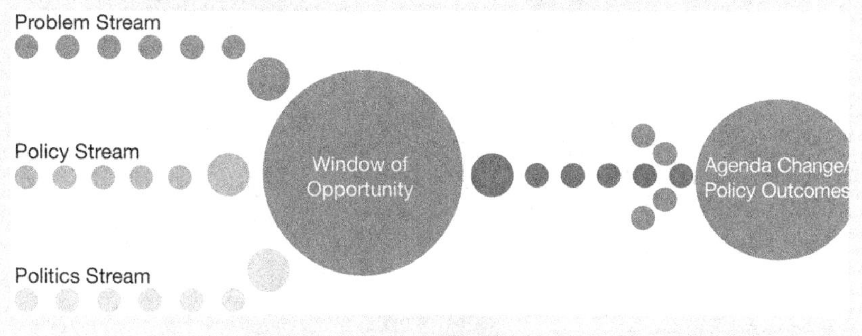

Lobbying: Local, National, International

Communication between business and government takes on many distinct forms. Some means are more effective than others, but collectively they all have a place within the realm of governance. Lobbying, controversial in nature and often the attention of media and Internet scrutiny, is perhaps the most widely known and easily recognizable form of interaction, primarily due to its history. Currently in the US, lobbying is perhaps one of the most direct, fundamental, and salient means by which interest groups pursue their political agendas. Lobbying has been a staple of the American political landscape for a very long time, but it is now also becoming an important part of the political makeup of other democracies such as France and the UK (Rival 2012).

In general, lobbying can be defined as the process by which representatives of certain groups are attempting to influence—directly or indirectly—public officials in favor of or against a particular cause. Lobbyists represent a professional group that specializes in legislative or administrative advocacy. Their services can be purchased, like those of lawyers or contractors, by any individual, organized interest, organization, or government. The purchasers of lobbying services are typically referred to as lobbying clients. Assuming that there is a paying client, almost anybody, given the right set of circumstances and experience, would be able to legally engage in lobbying. Exhibit 7.3 provides a glimpse at the general profile of a successful, if sometimes controversial, lobbyist.

Exhibit 7.2

The lobby of the House of Commons

Source: Wikimedia Commons (1886). Liborio Prosperi.

Lobbyists can affect legislative actions in a number of ways—by promoting candidates, policies, raising money, engaging in strategic advertising, building advocacy coalitions, polling, developing get-out-to-vote (GOTV) strategies, or recruiting volunteers (Thurber and Nelson 2000). One should be careful, however, not to assume that lobbying always targets legislative action. For some interest groups, no action—that is, no new legislation or reform—can be viewed as positive, hence a desired outcome. For those parties that enjoy an economic advantage, it might be convenient to maintain the status quo; as a result, such entities will invest heavily in opposing any sort of change that might jeopardize their current standings and ways of doing business. This type of lobbying is often called defensive lobbying.

At first glance, the nature of lobbying and the manner in which it works might appear misleadingly simple; this is far from being the case. One should not think of lobbying as mere expenditure intended to support a certain position. Simply put, lobbying is not a simple exchange of funds for the passage (or filibuster) of a given legislation (although, often that might appear to be the case). It is also to a certain degree wrong to think of lobbying as being nothing else but an exchange of money for influence. The dynamics involved are somewhat more complex than typical descriptions would lead us to believe. To some extent, it is perhaps best to think of lobbying as a process of negotiation within a certain domain among a number of interested parties, with lobbyists acting as the representatives of some of the groups involved. Each party has its own interests that it wants to protect, since it most likely stands to lose if matters are not resolved in a favorable way.

Exhibit 7.3

Profile of a lobbyist

Name:

Tony Podesta, Founder and Chairman of Podesta Group

Hometown:

Chicago, Illinois

Education:

BA, University of Illinois at Chicago
MA, Massachusetts Institute of Technology (MIT)
JD, Georgetown University Law Center

According to a number of accounts, Tony Podesta has been among the most influential Democratic lobbyists in Washington, DC (Bedard 2009; Eisler 2007; Lichtblau 2010). He is highly connected with Washington's elite; in particular, he has had close ties with Democratic administrations (Bedard 2009).

Podesta started his career in Washington in 1970 when he came to work for Common Cause. From 1981 to 1987, he served as the founding president of People for the American Way. In 1988, together with his brother John, he founded the Podesta Group. The firm went on to become one of DC's top lobbying and public affairs firms. Among others, Tony Podesta has served on the transition teams of Presidents Bill Clinton and Barack Obama. In the early part of his career he was most often associated with media clients and issues of public relations (Eisler 2007). With time, however, his client list became highly diversified. Some of the high-profile names for whom he has lobbied include British Petroleum, Lockheed Martin, General Dynamics, and Bank of America.

His career stumbled after he was investigated for violating the Foreign Agents Registration Act but the case was ultimately closed without charges in 2019. Before the scandal and divorce ripped his career from 2014 to 2018, the Podesta Group had revenues of about $40 million.

As a rule, none of the funds spent by business on lobbying go directly to public officials; all the funds go to lobbying firms. The lobbyists use these funds to develop a case and a strategy on how to influence legislators on making a decision that would be favorable for their client firm. In order to do so, lobbyists engage in research, reach out to political constituencies, and meet with administrative and legislative agencies. In this sense, lobbyists engage in a very important function; they supply public agencies, politicians, and their aides with a large amount of data that is used by legislators to reach more informed and educated decisions. By providing information to politicians and public agencies, lobbyists might indirectly save time and financial resources, which otherwise might have to be spent by public agencies to collect such data. Within the context of the overall process, given the fact that usually every organized interest will make use of lobbying services or will engage in lobbying on its own, the process develops into a negotiation rather than a money-for-legislation exchange. From this perspective, then, lobbying and lobbyists are an essential part of a healthy and effective legislative mechanism.

It would seem that there is not too much difference among lobbyists at first glance, but this is not necessarily true. Although lobbyists generally use a common set of tactics and have rather similar job descriptions, there are also many important differences among various types of lobbyists. Like many other professionals, lobbyists become specialized within a certain area. Some lobbyists engage in defensive lobbying, while others search for opportunities within incoming legislation. Furthermore, lobbying firms don't always have the expertise to address every single issue in-house, so for certain issues, firms might have to go outside and hire someone else. As is the case with most endeavors, a lobbying firm's previous successes nurture future business. If a lobbying firm has proven to be effective in negotiating for their clients within a given policy domain, it is highly likely that it will continue to attract business from other interested parties for those types of policy questions. Once a certain level of trust and communication channels on a specific issue have been developed between parties, it is highly probable that these arrangements will be resilient, in particular if a firm has shown to generate satisfactory results for both business and legislators.

There also are important differences between lobbying at the local, national, and international levels. At the local level, the questions addressed are often more limited in scope and more specific in terms of their outcomes. Local-level lobbying usually targets—again, directly or indirectly—procurement practices and ordinances. Lobbyists typically attempt to influence council members, city administrators, or public opinion through media campaigns or by attending public meetings.

The stakes at the national level are obviously much higher than those at the local level. At the national level, the number of competing interests is much greater than at the local level, which dramatically increases the level of complexity and ambiguity. As a result, lobbying is undertaken in a more systematic fashion—it is long-term oriented and takes on a more professionalized and specialized character.

Matters get even more complicated when it comes to international-level lobbying. National differences and the lack of one undisputed decision-making body add an additional layer of complexity to international lobbying that is not present at the national level. Those who lobby at the international level can approach a number of parties such as non-governmental organizations like the International Monetary Fund or World Bank, or can lobby foreign governments in part. Reaching consensus or change at the international level is much more difficult and expensive than doing so either nationally or locally. Lobbying at the international level seldom yields immediate results and at times might take a decade for a desired change to take place.

Business has several decisions to make before engaging in lobbying (Rival 2012). First, it has to determine what kind of lobbying strategy is preferred—active, anticipatory, or passive. It then needs to decide on the number of issues to lobby and the desired outcomes. Usually firms either attempt to maximize gains or minimize losses. A third important decision that has to be made regards the entity engaged in the lobbying activity. For instance, businesses can choose between having internal lobbyists and hiring someone from outside. Firms also have the choice to lobby separately or collectively. In addition to determining who is going to lobby for the firm, the business has to also consider the target of the lobbying. Two particularly important questions are who (politicians, public agencies) or what level (local, national, international) the lobbying campaign will target. A final—and major—decision is the manner in which the lobbying will be done. There are several options available to business: they can use direct or indirect pressure, interact with legislators, or employ a combination of both.

One lesser-known fact about lobbying is that lobbyists' work does not stop with the passage of a legislative package. Every piece of legislation that is ever created, even if it is hundreds of pages long, almost never goes into enough detail to account for all possible scenarios during its implementation. It is an accepted fact of public administration that public agencies have to interpret the ambiguity of legislative mandates, hence becoming active shapers of public policy. Legislators, for political reasons, habitually use vague terms and conditions; such tactics ensure that there will likely be fewer reasons to motivate a political impasse. Yet public agencies cannot rely on ambiguous language during implementation. They have to clarify what politicians were undecided about, couldn't agree upon, or did not know how to resolve and therefore passed on to public agencies.

It is within this context that lobbyists often continue their work. In the same manner that they were involved in the design of a piece of legislation, they can actively participate in shaping its interpretations. The larger the room for discretionary interpretation, the more there is to gain from influencing public agencies' perspectives. It is not uncommon with certain legislation, especially on highly technical topics, to let the public agencies decide on the majority of details. As a result, in their struggle to find the best way to implement a certain policy, public agencies regularly find themselves having to rely on lobbyists, among others, to provide them with additional information about the possible impacts of various scenarios. Yet one should remember that with the power to inform also comes the power to misinform. The same mechanisms that are brought into play by lobbyists to support a much needed policy can just as easily be triggered to kill an incoming reform or to mislead an agency in regard to any possible impacts.

In a very real sense, almost all major federal legislation in the US has been influenced—with significant parts even being written—by lobbyists. Lobbying is by any measure a big industry. According to OpenSecrets in 2020, total lobbying spending by clients added up to \$3.5 billion (see Exhibit 7.4).

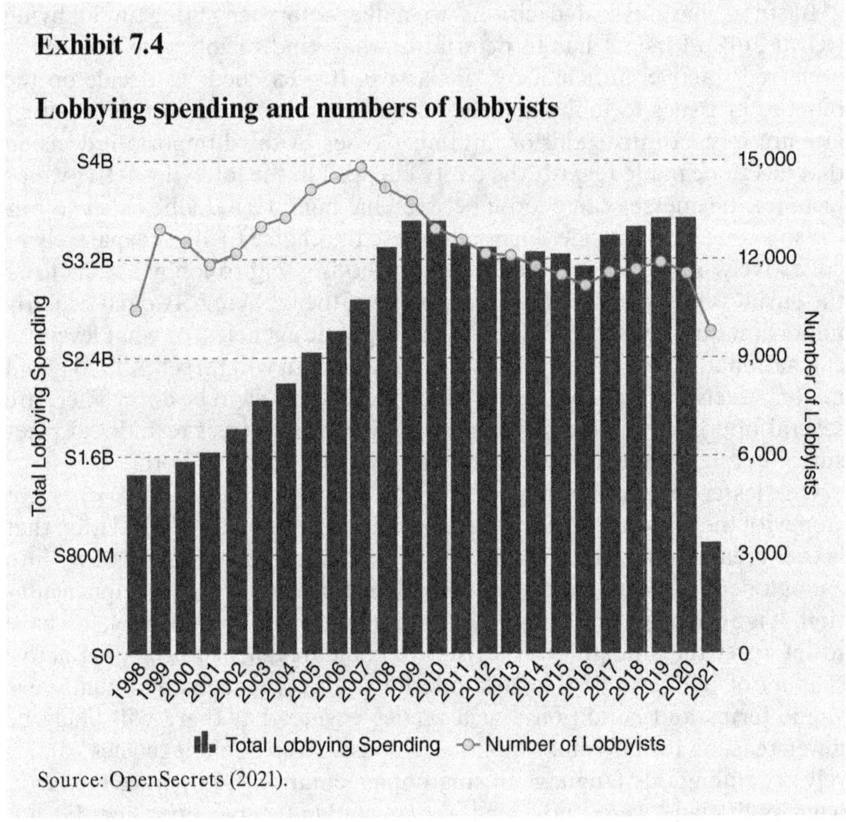

Exhibit 7.4

Lobbying spending and numbers of lobbyists

Source: OpenSecrets (2021).

This is still quite a sizeable amount, representing spending of just over \$21 million for every day that Congress was in session. The amount spent on lobbying in 2012 was larger than the Gross Domestic Product (GDP) of 43 countries in the world (The World Bank 2021). Yet, despite the fact that \$3.5 billion is an imposing amount on its own, it still may represent only a very small portion of what is actually spent on lobbying activities. This number does not include funds spent on coalition building, advertising and media campaigns, grassroots or grasstops advocacy, research funding, or any other form of advocacy that is in essence lobbying, but is not necessarily reported as such. The \$3.5 billion represents the amount disclosed by lobbying firms and clients due to extant regulation; there are many other types of lobbying spending that neither firms nor clients are required to disclose or that simply cannot be tracked accurately.

Along similar lines, although decreasing in recent years, the number of registered and active lobbyists in Washington is still relatively large at well above 10,000 individuals (see Exhibit 7.4). According to OpenSecrets, the premier site for tracking lobbying and which incorporated The Center for Responsive Politics, there were a total of 11.544 registered and active federal lobbyists in 2020; decrease from the 14,845 lobbyists that were active in 2007 (OpenSecrets 2021). Again, just as for spending, this total does not include every individual who engages in lobbying activities. Many professionals regularly involved in what can be considered lobbying might not have to register as such. Hence, even if 11,544 sounds like a large number, in reality it may be only a fraction of the actual number of individuals engaged in some form of lobbying.

The US Chamber of Commerce is by far the leader in terms of spending among lobbying clients. The US Chamber of Commerce represents the interests of over 3 million businesses of different sizes, from many regions and from a variety of sectors (US Chambers of Commerce 2021). It is estimated that for the 2018–2021 period, it has spent $1.7 billion on lobbying (Exhibit 7.5) (OpenSecrets 2021). This is more than the next three lobbying clients have spent on aggregate for the same period. In terms of traditional lobbying firms, the numbers are somewhat more evenly distributed, Akin, Gump ($50 million), Brownstein, Hyatt ($48 million), and the BGR Group ($32 million).

Exhibit 7.5

The biggest spenders on lobbying in the US

Lobbying Client	*Total Spent*
US Chamber of Commerce	$1,682,870,680
National Assn of Realtors	$679,455,978
American Medical Assn	$449,189,500
American Hospital Assn	$429,369,624
Pharmaceutical Research & Manufacturers of America	$428,285,550
Blue Cross/Blue Shield	$402,678,101
General Electric	$371,932,000
Business Roundtable	$324,900,000
Boeing Co	$304,088,310
Northrop Grumman	$302,492,213
AARP	$301,741,064
Lockheed Martin	$285,099,238
AT&T Inc	$275,414,644
Exxon Mobil	$275,082,742
Verizon Communications	$267,855,359
National Assn of Broadcasters	$253,148,000
Southern Co	$246,320,694
Edison Electric Institute	$244,411,416
Comcast Corp	$227,939,323
Altria Group	$221,285,200

Source: OpenSecrets (2021).

Lobbying, Politics, and Influence

Common wisdom would suggest that money buys attention and influence, which eventually leads to desired outcomes (Green 2004). Although this seems relatively plausible, there is only scarce empirical evidence that this is indeed the case. For the most part, scholars tend to think that in a developed democracy the link between the two exists, but it is generally quite weak. For example, it has been suggested that the idea that campaign contributions by business lead to direct beneficial legislative outcomes is mostly a myth (Sorauf 1992). Quantifiable evidence that traces spending on lobbying to concrete benefits for the firms that have spent the funds is difficult to verify. Overall, there are many reasons why there is not more research on the topic; the most important, however, might be the fact that many of the variables are difficult to trace and objectively quantify. In fact, lobbying data was not readily available until the Lobbying Disclosure Act of 1995. The Act forced firms to declare their spending on lobbying services, which, for the first time, provided researchers with a systematic set of relatively reliable data.

Some of the more recent academic accounts do, nevertheless, find that there might be a strong link between what business spends on strategic lobbying, and eventual positive legislative outcomes. By some accounts, it was estimated that firms in the US that increase their lobbying expenditures by 1 percent in a given year might be able to reduce their effective tax rates, which is the actual rate paid once all deductions have been factored in. In other words, for each extra $1 spent on lobbying, firms might receive anywhere from $6 to $20 in tax breaks (Richter, Samphantharak, and Timmons 2009). These reductions in effective tax rates come through such means as research credits or modified tax depreciation schedules for certain types of equipment and they are advantageous only for particular industries or just for a small number of firms (McIntyre and Nguyen 2004). Political connections are often, if not always, quite valuable for American business (Vidal, Draca, and Fons-Rosen 2012). The link between economic benefits and political connections appears to be even clearer in other countries. Studies have shown that in the EU (Chalmers and Macado 2020), France (Bertrand et al. 2007), Indonesia (Fisman 2001), Malaysia (Johnson and Mitton 2003), Germany, Russia, and many others (Faccio 2006), companies that have direct connections with political appointees stand to gain financially from such associations. See Exhibit 7.6 for an example of a lobbying firm's claims.

Lobbying, both domestically and internationally, has been receiving increased levels of criticism and scrutiny in recent years. Part of the criticism might be unwarranted, as lobbyists do make for a convenient target when things go wrong.

When blame needs to be assessed, individuals who are engaged in advocacy are labeled "lobbyists," yet when lobbyists' support and expertise

Exhibit 7.6

An example of lobbying specialization and claims

Patton Boggs describes itself as follows on its website.

Game-Changing Advocacy and Legal Services

At Patton Boggs, we go beyond the obvious. By combining legal expertise with lobbying know-how and business savvy, we offer insights and perspectives that others can't. Over the past fifty years, we have established ourselves as a trusted partner and have formed strategic alliances with government and industry leaders within the US and abroad. This collaborative approach means that we can represent our clients' best interests through legal, legislative, and executive action. As a result, we are consistently ranked among the top law and advocacy firms.

A History of Innovation

Founded in 1962, we were the first major law firm to recognize that all three branches of government offered avenues to achieve our clients' goals. What started as an international law firm specializing in global business and trade has since evolved into a full-service firm covering all areas of legal practice.

The Strength of Diversity

The Patton Boggs team comprises more than 500 lawyers and professionals in offices around the world. Supported by a firm culture that encourages collaboration across political, geographical, and practice-area boundaries, our clients benefit from a dynamic group of problem solvers with access to cutting-edge resources and ideas.

Patton Boggs. Your partner in all matters where law, government, and business intersect.

Source: Patton Boggs website (2014)
https://www.squirepattonboggs.com/en

are needed, they are conveniently called "stakeholders." Part of the blame is, nevertheless, well deserved and has been raised due to valid and serious concerns. The events associated with Jack Allan Abramoff are a case in point. Abramoff, once a lobbyist for Preston Gates & Ellis and Greenberg Trauring, was the driving force behind one of the biggest lobbying scandals in US history. Due to the role he played in the infamous casino lobbying scandal, he received a six-year sentence in a federal prison in 2006 (Smith 2011). Abramoff was convicted on charges of mail fraud, tax evasion, and conspiracy to bribe public officials. He was released in December, 2010, after serving 43 months behind bars (Smith 2011; The Federal Bureau of Prisons 2013).

A number of other lobbyists, aides, and political actors who were implicated in the scandal, including US House of Representatives member Robert William "Bob" Ney (R-Ohio), were also found or pleaded guilty to various charges of unethical behavior as a result of their direct involvement with Abramoff. Even for those who do not follow American politics closely, the story and some of the names might be familiar, since it was the subject of the popular 2010 film *Casino Jack*, with Kevin Spacey playing Jack Abramoff.

Many members of the political elite, while diverging on other issues, are making a habit of agreeing when it comes to lobbying. Former President Barack Obama and former Alaska Governor Sarah Palin, for instance, have very little in common it terms of their individual and political profiles, yet they seem to agree when it comes to the role of lobbyists in Washington. At one point in time, President Obama was quoted stating that if "you don't think lobbyists have too much influence in Washington, then I believe you've probably been in Washington too long" (Bacon 2007). In light of his beliefs, Barack Obama went as far as refusing, at least directly, to accept any campaign contributions from federally registered lobbyists.[1] One of the primary points of the President's dissatisfaction was associated with the "army of lobbyists" attempting to sabotage the passage of a bill that changed the practices in the student loan industry. Palin, too, has been very vocal in criticizing lobbying practices.

According to her, among other things, lobbyists played an important role in the lax regulatory oversight which eventually led to the failures of Fannie Mae and Freddie Mac (Powers 2008).

Lobbying is an effective means of channeling governmental attention, but it is also an extremely expensive one (see Exhibit 7.7). Only those who can effectively organize or afford it can call on it. Moreover, on occasions lobbying has been used to support actions that are not generally considered to be in the best interest of the public. If one's voice being heard becomes a direct function of the financial clout one can command, this raises a serious problem. What happens to the interests and needs of those who are not able to properly organize or lobby? Should they be deemed as unimportant? Recently, a large number of political figures and scholars have become very concerned about the nature of lobbying and about some of its direct and indirect effects. Some have even gone as far as to equate with corruption the growing power and resources being poured into lobbying in recent decades (Harstad and Svensson 2011). Their main concern rests primarily with the fact that linking governmental attention to lobbying expenditure can lead to significant challenges and dangers to the overall workings of a democracy. Perhaps more challenging is the growth of political nonprofits that can keep donors secret. Such contributors are known as "dark money donors" and have been protected by the landmark Citizens United v FEC US Supreme Court case in 2010. OpenSecrets.org estimated that dark money exceeded $1 billion in 2020.

Exhibit 7.7

Lobbying by business example: Whirlpool Corporation

Whirlpool Corporation is an American manufacturer of home appliances. Its headquarters are located in Benton Harbor, Michigan. According to the company's website, "Whirlpool Corporation is a leader of the $120 billion global home appliance industry" with its appliances being marketed "in nearly every country around the world" (Whirlpool Corporation 2013). Whirlpool markets such brands as Maytag, KitchenAid, Jenn-Air, Amana, Bauknecht, Brastemp, and Consul.

Whirlpool Corporation usually lobbies along a number of issues. A multinational manufacturer, the company is interested and generally lobbies for such matters as trade, finance, taxes, and manufacturing. In 2009, 2010, 2011, and 2012, tax lobbying represented one of the top foci for the corporation. Taken together, during this period the company spent approximately $3.2 million on lobbying (OpenSecrets 2021). The company, with the support of a strong Michigan political representation, lobbied for favorable tax treatment, in particular for tax credits. The company's main argument revolved around the fact that it provided Americans with jobs. As a direct result of the lobbying efforts, Whirlpool managed to secure the renewal of energy tax credits for producing high-efficiency appliances for 2012 and 2013, with an estimated worth of $120 million (Rowland 2013).

However, the moral dilemmas that are associated with lobbying are by no means recent occurrences. Concerns about the voices of the majority and the "haves" being heard over those of the minority and the "have-nots" are present in all democracies and have troubled many great Americans. James

Madison, the fourth US President and the "Father of the Constitution," asserted that there is a degree of truth in the fact

> that our governments are too unstable, that the public good is disregarded in the conflicts of rival parties, and that measures are too often decided, not according to the rules of justice and the rights of the minor party, but by the superior force of an interested and overbearing majority.
>
> (Madison 1787/2011)

These powerful words remind us that for a democracy to be successful, there is a need to strike a delicate balance between all interests involved. It is not an easy balance to achieve or maintain, and yet, it is an indispensable one.

Sector Exchanges

In typical discussions of business–government interdependence, the two sectors are often depicted as clearly separable. Indeed, it is much easier to think of the public sector standing on one side of the aisle and the private sector on the other. For simplification purposes this dichotomy is very practical and useful, but it also introduces a lot of ambiguity. It is not always clear or easy to determine where government ends and private sector begins. Similarly, it is difficult to decisively delineate the difference between what makes something of public interest or of private interest alone. Philosophers and public administration scholars have struggled with these types of questions for centuries and it is highly unlikely that they will provide a completely satisfactory answer any time soon. What is important to remember here is that the relationship between business and government is much more fluid than is typically portrayed by general accounts.

Hiring Former Officials from and into Businesses (The "Revolving Door")

Many individuals who are currently employed in high-ranking positions by governments have at one point in time worked in the private sector. Many of them, once they leave their public positions, will return to jobs in the private sector. Most of the time these individuals will return to positions with the same companies that employed them before they assumed office. This practice of hiring former officials into and from businesses is known as the "revolving door." It is a legal and accepted practice for a number of governments around the globe.[2] The cartoon in Exhibit 7.8 nicely captures this rather blatant phenomenon.

There are several important rationales for the continued existence of such practice. First, business lies at the foundation of any economy. The livelihood of any country is highly dependent on how well its economy performs.

In order for the economy to perform as desired, it is critical that government is able to understand the needs of business and communicate effectively with the private sector. Hiring public officials who have long tenures in a given sector or industry allows government to tap into their experience and networks when attempting to fulfill its role. Having former business leaders on board maximizes the chances that government and business can communicate effectively.

Second, it is often believed that officials with extensive private sector backgrounds can bring expertise that otherwise might not have been available to government. These officials can provide guidance and insights into how to develop legislation that would better serve the needs of the overall economy.

Exhibit 7.8

A lobbying cartoon

"Our industry is committed to the environment. All of our lobbyists are 100% recycled congressmen."

Source: Cartoon Stock.

Third, it is expected that public officials hired from business would bring with them not only new perspectives, but also new practices that would allow them to reshape—and perhaps even reform—some administrative processes. Incoming Presidents regularly use the political appointee positions available to them as mechanisms to redesign, reshape, or refocus certain public agencies.

Finally, public officials are hired from business in order to serve as checks for the agencies or administrative processes of which they are put in charge. The new officials who come in with a business background have no alliances to the public agency or institution they are supposed to oversee. In this sense, they are not obligated to be loyal to any outdated practices or personnel who might not be performing up to par. As a result, the new officials will not abide by existing unwritten rules, since it is highly unlikely that they will be aware of them. By not being in touch with their agencies' informal cultures, they can check and restrain their actions when agencies might act outside of the parameters that were envisioned by their mandates.

The motives for the private sector hiring public officials, regardless of whether they have a previous business background or not, are in many ways similar to those behind hiring business people into government. Throughout their government employment, individuals learn a great deal about how government works. When they are brought on board by businesses, they can use their knowledge about the dynamics of government to help their new companies in dealing with government in a more effective way. Among other things, they can ensure that businesses remain compliant with the regulations that govern them. In addition, bringing on board former high-ranking public officials can lend important levels of reputation and legitimacy to companies hiring them. By employing such officials, companies are perhaps also increasing their chances of obtaining positive results in their future contacts with government. Taken together, there are a great number of benefits that government and business can receive from exchanging expertise by means of employing experts from one another and by maintaining open channels of communication.

The cumulative effect of the revolving door is rather impressive (Exhibit 7.9). For example, according to the Center of Responsive Politics, President Barack Obama's Administration employed at least 390 individuals who have "passed" at one point in their careers through the "revolving door" (OpenSecrets 2021). George W. Bush's Administration employed 665 such individuals.

Along similar lines, over half of the members of Congress who lose their bids for re-election have found employment elsewhere (OpenSecrets 2021). Most of the time, their new positions were in the private sector, either with lobbying firms or a lobbying client. In 2007, the *Washingtonian* magazine comprised a list of the top 50 lobbyists operating in Washington (Eisler 2007). Out of the top 50 lobbyists, 13 were previous congressmen, three were family members of congressmen, 21 were former staffers, and only 13 had no explicit government affiliation.

The hiring of former officials into and from businesses is not without negative aspects. Questions are often raised about the conflicts of interests that arise in such cases. For instance, it is hard to believe that a political appointee could indeed remain unbiased and objective if assuming a position with an agency that regulates his or her former employer. On one hand, the public agency might be in dire need of the expertise that the appointee brings; on the other hand, there are many ways in which former loyalties can affect one's decision-making. Political appointees with a business background

Exhibit 7.9

The number of "revolving door" professionals by agency from the 1990s to 2020 according to OpenSecrets.org database

Agency	*Number of Revolving Professionals*
White House	769
US House of Representatives	662
Dept of State	335
Dept of Defense	321
Dept of Commerce	315
Dept of the Treasury	297
Presidential Transition Team	263
Dept of Health & Human Services	251
Dept of Justice	235
Dept of Energy	232
Environmental Protection Agency	208
Dept of Army	203
Federal Communications Commission	203
US Senate	196
Executive Office of the President	191
Office of US Trade Representative	190
Dept of Transportation	190
Office of Management & Budget	187
Dept of Agriculture	187
US Diplomatic Missions	149

Source: OpenSecrets.org (2021).

might have the incentive and the opportunities to influence procurement practices, regulation, oversight, and governmental strategic planning in ways that would favor, directly or indirectly, their former industries or companies (Leaver 2009).

By many accounts, "schmoozing" government officials in order to obtain procurement contracts is a common occurrence in Washington (Palmer 2005), and appointing former business leaders to political positions might only further facilitate the process. Moreover, at some point, many business professionals will most likely return to working for the private sector. Given that their former employers may well become their first choice once they leave government, it is only rational for them not to burn the bridges connecting them to the companies that employed them before assuming their official position. In order to maintain the possibility of a swift return into business in the future, these public officials might be inclined toward providing favors for their former companies.

Another, less often discussed, point of concern with the revolving door phenomenon is that the time that individuals from business spend in a government position gives them the opportunity to gain intimate knowledge about how government works. These experiences allow them to understand better how to maneuver the administrative and political environments, hence increasing the probability of successfully obtaining a desired decision for their companies once they return (Merle 2004). In addition, serving as political appointee provides the fertile ground for developing working and personal networks. These new relationships can be exploited at any point in the future should the need for a favor arise. During their government employment they can learn specific details about the competitors of their previous employers. They can also acquire subtle details about how decisions are swayed one way or another; for instance, what criteria are used by government to award a certain type of contract or to allocate a certain type of spending.

Once they return to the private sector, these former public officials can use the information and knowledge they have collected during their tenures to help their new employers land lucrative contracts. The information, especially when it deals with competitors or future governmental actions, can be very valuable for any company in terms of its strategic placement. For instance, if government is expected to invest heavily in a certain type of equipment or service at some point in the future, but only a few individuals are aware of this, then the companies that have access to this insider information will be in a greater position to profit by supplying the new demand. Given that private sector salaries are much higher when compared to public sector service, many public officials might decide "to cash in" their government experience and connections (Public Citizen 2005). Many scholars are extremely concerned that the prospect of a huge payoff post-public-employment might distort the motivational frameworks for those who aspire to work for government, which in the long run could change the type of individuals attracted to public service (Besley 2005; Kaiser 2009; Mattozzi and Merlo 2008).

Regardless of its wide existence in practice, one should not underestimate the level of disapproval that "revolving door" practices can sometimes motivate. In fact, President Barack Obama's 2008 election campaign was in large part hinged on fighting extant lobbying and "revolving door" dynamics. On his first day in office, on January 21, 2009, the President signed Executive Order No. 13490—Ethics Commitments by Executive Branch Personnel (Obama 2009). The order imposed a ban on gifts from lobbyists. It also, among other moves, extended the "revolving door" ban to two years. This meant that all new employees, who were not lobbyists before their appointments, would not be able to participate for two years in matters that were substantially related to their former employer or client. The ban was also valid for a two-year post-employment period. The restrictions imposed by Executive Order on former lobbyists entering new positions with government were even stricter. Judging by the White House's visitor access records, however, it seems the order has had little effect in terms of significantly diminishing the communication and meetings between public officials and their private counterparts (Sunlight Foundation 2013; The White House 2013). Pledging to "drain the swamp," President Trumps ethics rules followed President Obama's fairly closely. However, in a highly controversial action, President Trump rescinded his ethics order on his last day in office, allowing members of his administration to take up lobbying positions and lobby their former agencies immediately. President Biden's ethics pledge (Executive Order 13,989) was far more extensive than any of his predecessors.

Public Procurement

Another way in which the private sector is involved with government is when it sells goods and services to public agencies. For example, the USS Gerald R. Ford is a $13.3 billion aircraft carrier purchased from Newport News Shipbuilding (Correll 2022). The governmental purchase process is called public procurement. It includes military armaments, temporary professional services, road and building construction, furniture, spaceships, clothing, social services such as meals on wheels, pure and applied research (currently about $140 billion for the US federal government!), uniforms and clothing, a vast array of equipment and supplies, and so on.

Public procurement engages in an acquisition function and a provision function: (1) The acquisition function involves acquiring goods and services from businesses; (2) The provision function involves providing goods and services for government and public use. In this way, the government and business sector are reliant upon each other. As was seen during the COVID-19 pandemic, the public sector relied on the public sector to create vaccines (with and without subsidies) so it could purchase and distribute them to the US and the world through the Defense Production Act—over one billion vaccines!

Public procurement takes place at the federal, state, and local levels of government across a host of departments, agencies, and branches, for which the rules, regulations, policies, procedures, tools, and techniques vary in details but not in principles. At the federal level of government procurement, the federal acquisition regulations (FAR) dictate the procurement requirements. Procurement policies set out the rules for the solicitation method (competitive or sole source), proposal evaluation (best value or lowest price), contract type (firm-fixed or cost-reimbursable), and contracting method (performance or incentive-based).

Prospective contractors are presumed to know the law, including the limits of the authority of government personnel. If a mandatory requirement is missing which is authorized in procurement law, the law takes precedent over any contract, and the requirement is assumed. More importantly, omissions or violations of procurement requirements allow for contract award challenges. Since competitors have an incentive to challenge awards, great care must be exercised to ensure that the contracts are well executed. In fact, about 2,500 protests are made each year, but most of which are dismissed. However large this number may seem, the federal government issues about 11 million contracts a year so the percentage is actually smaller than private sector procurement contract disputes (GAO 2022).

In local and state government procurement, city or county procurement policy manuals or state procurement codes guide decision-making in a similar fashion.

Curry (2017) identifies six phases of contract management that are used to procure public goods and services: Pre-solicitation, Solicitation, Proposal Evaluation, Contract Award, Contract Administration, and Contract Close-out. A contracting action must take place for the appropriate identification, location, development, production, distribution, and delivery of these goods and services. The public sector contracting process is, in all-but-rare cases, a competitive one (see Atkinson 2019; Brunjes 2020), but the award of contracts is based on price, quality, and fulfillment capability, so the lowest bid is not always the awardee.

In pre-solicitation, representatives of the procuring entity may attend trade shows, conferences, or exhibits, including individual outreach, to better understand the marketplace and availability of goods and services. However, it is important to note that those involved in the pre-solicitation research phase are generally excluded from the rest of the process to reduce likelihood of favoritism and enhancing the likelihood of a protest.

The solicitation phase involves the procuring entity's construction of a solicitation document that lays out the requirements and specifications of the products or services needed. There are typically two mechanisms for doing this. First, an invitation to bid (ITB) can be floated to the private sector in cases where the government is very clear about the exact requirements and specifications. On the other hand, a request for proposal (RFP) requires a detailed bidder response to solicitation where the government puts the onus on the private sector to offer an organizationally specific approach to providing the service needed.

There are two common methods for proposal evaluation: lowest-price, technically acceptable (LPTA) and best-value source selection (BVSS). With LPTA, the procuring entity is seeking to choose the bidder with least expensive solution that meets the strict requirements of the government. According to BVSS, the procuring entity is allowed to consider non-price factors in selecting the winning bid. The non-price factors can include everything from suitability, quality, speed, dependability, environmental impacts, and social impacts. It should also be noted that substantial amounts of federal, state, and local procurement may have set-asides for businesses based on company size and gender. For example, the US Small Business Administration awarded contracts for $146 billion in fiscal 2020, a portion of which was set aside for companies primarily owned by women (SBA 2021).

The contract award phase is where the bids are evaluated according to various scoring schemas laid out in the RFPs devised by a procuring entity. Some scoring protocols are relatively formulaic because of the nature of the product or service being solicited, but some involve more qualitative factors and more procurement specialist discretion.

Contract administration ensures that the contractor performance is up to the contract specifications. Monitoring activities may include requirements for company and/or government quality control, testing, evaluation, and surveillance through metrics, performance measures, benchmarks, and milestones. Change orders occur when the procuring entity wants to modify the work it initially requested, generally resulting in additional costs to the government.

The contract close-out phase occurs when all milestones have been met and the work is completed. Contract close-out is especially important in finalizing and maintaining positive relationships between the public and private sector entities, as these relationships should be built and nurtured for long-term sustainability for all parties involved.

Finally, it is important to note that public procurement specialists, no matter whether they are working for or with the government, are invariably in high demand. Public procurement is a sizable field with good-paying jobs.

Promoting Your Agenda Ethically

Any pluralistic democracy is paradoxical in nature. On the one hand, its structures allow for many voices to be heard; on the other hand, the more voices there are, the easier it is for them to drown in their own collective buzzing. As the number of voices increases, it becomes critical that there is a certain harmony in their timing and resonance. The latter cannot be achieved without trust. It is important that citizens trust their government to make wise decisions about what, when, how, and to whom to listen. Trust lies at the foundation of the smooth and effective operation of any country, its business, and its government.

In the last few decades, public trust in government has unfortunately been steadily declining. One of the primary reasons behind this decline can be traced back to the way in which the lobbying industry, including the "revolving door," works (Maskell 2007; Lessing 2010; Jacobson 2011). In the US, the system of checks and balances, the presence of independent watchdogs, and the free press are highly likely to prevent major fraud and corruption from occurring. Still, sometimes they might not be enough. Recent times have seen several important steps being taken in order to improve political conditions and alleviate public concerns. These actions were designed to ameliorate some of the negative aspects of lobbying and the "revolving door" practice by imposing additional constraints and requirements through new regulation.

The 1995 Lobbying Disclosure Act (LDA) represents one of the more notable efforts to instill structure to lobbying in Washington. LDA defined a federal lobbyist as someone who is employed or retained by a client for compensation, has made more than one lobbying contact for his or her client, and spends at least 20 percent of his or her time working on lobbying activities for a client during a three-month period (United States Senate 2013). The LDA also defines the term "lobbying activities" as

> lobbying contacts and efforts in support of such contacts, including preparation and planning activities, research and other background work that is intended, at the time it is performed, for use in contacts, and coordination with the lobbying activities of others.
>
> (United States Senate 2013)

The LDA was followed by the Lobbying Transparency and Accountability Act (LTAA) of 2006 (The Library of Congress 2013a). Among other things, the Act amended some of LDA's language and requirements and added further restrictions and disclosure obligations on lobbyists and their lobbying activities.

In 2007, an additional effort to improve some of the conditions associated with lobbying and the revolving door phenomenon was made by passing the Honest Leadership and Open Government Act (HLOGA) (The Library of Congress 2013b). The Act attempted to limit or even exclude revolving door practices, to increase transparency, and to minimize the use of privately funded gifts and travel (The Library of Congress 2013b). All three legislative acts, LDA, LTAA, and HLOGA, require lobbyists to register and to disclose the identities of those whom they are working with or attempting to influence. Furthermore, lobbyists are also expected to disclose the subject matter of their efforts and the amount of money spent for such purposes. It is important to note, however, that the current definition of a "lobbyist" under LDA, LTAA, and HLOGA is rather narrow and does not account for every individual who might otherwise engage in lobbying.

Although not lobbyists by definition, there are many other individuals who interact with legislators, through testimonials, participation in rule-making, or via personal contacts, and attempt to influence their decisions in terms of public policy. Given that there are so many different means by which business can make its interests heard, the reported dollar amount spent by business on lobbying might only be the tip of the iceberg in terms of business's involvement in government. Further, the actual number of individuals engaged in lobbying activities, between registered and unregistered advocacy activists, might well be over 100,000. It is simply too difficult to come up with an exact estimate, since the line between lobbyist and policy advocate is blurred. In addition, it is not totally clear how strictly the three legislative acts discussed above are enforced in reality; enforcement appears to be particularly lax when it comes to post-employment restrictions (Rasor and Baumann 2007). On many occasions, newly elected officials who would otherwise have to obey the restrictions imposed by extant regulation, can obtain waivers that would allow them to directly deal with their former employers as soon as they assume office.

The most important thing to remember here is the fact that business, through its lobbying activities, remains an indispensable part of the legislative process. The nature of the political system and political decision-making in a pluralistic democracy is such that even with all its associated negative aspects, business expertise and involvement in government is needed. It is needed to get issues on the agenda, to shape the eventual policy and solution, and to pass the corresponding legislation. As such, it is difficult to envision that even the most earnest of future reform efforts could ever remove inter-sector placement, lobbying, or lobbyists from the policy scene. It is always difficult, if not simply impossible, to get rid of something or someone that you need.

However, it is critical when promoting a given agenda that one does so in an ethical manner. In the long run, everyone—including the system as a whole—stands to lose more than they gain if those who advocate for a living are not guided by an ethos of ethics. Without lobbying, certain issues may never reach the governmental agenda and hence remain unaddressed. It is within this context that lobbying becomes a vital dimension of governance. Lobbyists also facilitate communication between the legislative bodies, public agencies, and policy communities, increasing the probability of a policy being successfully passed. Similarly, without lobbying and the "revolving door," government would have less access to expertise, which would mean that the resulting policy might not be as effective as it could otherwise have been. Serious problems arise, however, when individuals engage in lobbying activities with a total disregard for the needs of others, without fully considering the impacts of their advocated position, and without following basic ethical principles. The more frequently that unethical behavior on the part of advocacy activists is observed, the less trust citizens will have in democratic institutions. Trust in government is an extremely valuable, but fragile, resource for any democracy; it cannot be nurtured, nor can it grow, if citizens believe that government is responsive only to a handful of elite interests.

Unethical promotion of an agenda might be effective in the short run, but over time the negative consequences of unethical behavior will take a toll on an individual's standing. Any small gains that might have been made initially can be quickly erased by the negative attention that unethical advocacy can bring to an issue. As lobbying can be characterized as a negotiation, it cannot produce the expected results without all those involved respecting the fundamental tenets of the democratic process.

Analytical Case: Ethics Involved in Lobbying

A large parcel of land in the city of Ethicsland has become available for development. The property is conveniently located near the business and shopping center of the city. Many of the city residents believe that the downtown lacks enough green space, and the large parcel provides the perfect opportunity to address this public need. Previous city councils had attempted to correct the situation, but this is the first time that a real opportunity has presented itself. The Mayor of Ethicsland, Ann Principle, knows that most of Ethicsland's residents would be in favor of the parcel being developed into green space; however, she is also aware of the city's financial needs, and knows the city council would be open to listening to other proposals, particularly those with revenue-generating potential.

Given its central and possibly lucrative location, the parcel's availability has attracted a lot of attention, especially from local businesses and developers. Although the issue has yet to reach the council's agenda, the matter has motivated a lot of behind-the-scenes interaction. The Mayor, as an important decision-maker, has become the target of a number of advocacy efforts. Ann has been contacted by city residents, environmental activists, business lobbyists, and even state officials. A decision that appeared so clear in the beginning, has become increasingly ambiguous and contentious.

In all her years of public service, Ann has never before felt this overwhelmed and in need of advice. When she received an invitation for lunch from Elizabeth Craft, her best friend whom she hasn't seen in a long time, she was very pleased. Elizabeth, besides being an old friend, was also a former public official with extensive experience on complex public matters such as the one Ann was facing. Given their common past and the trust that she had in her friend, Ann is sure that this lunch will be beneficial in terms of helping her make a final decision on the parcel. There is, however, one thing that makes Ann uneasy. After her last stint in public office, Elizabeth occasionally engaged in lobbying efforts for local construction firms. Ann isn't sure whether the timing of Elizabeth's call was purely coincidental or related to her lobbying activities. Still, Elizabeth is her best friend—can Ann really doubt her?

There are several ethical questions that enter the equation in this case:

1 Should Ann accept the lunch invitation from Elizabeth?
2 Should the Mayor consult with her best friend on a matter of public interest?

3 Should the lunch and the conversation during lunch be made public?
4 Is it morally acceptable for Ann to accept a lunch invitation from an individual whose most recent professional involvement was in lobbying?
5 Should Ann allow Elizabeth to pay for lunch?
6 What if during lunch Elizabeth does not bring up the matter, but when Ann asks her opinion on it she offers advice that would be favorable to developers for whom Elizabeth has lobbied in the past?
7 What if Ann ends up following Elizabeth's advice—would that be morally acceptable?

Practical Skill

Lobbying Government Effectively

Given the limited resources at the disposal of government, it simply might not be able to address all the complex issues that it is facing at one particular point. At times, even some of the most deserving and publicly critical issues might receive little attention from government. In addition, the nature of a democracy is such that major decisions take time, significant political regard, and concerted effort. Within this context, lobbying becomes an important mechanism that can be employed to correct the situation.

The number of issues that concomitantly vie for government's attention—the decision of which issue warrants immediate attention and which should be left for later—is not easy and can quickly become a highly con tested political process. Although each case is different, many of the dynamics and strategies are common for lobbying activities at all levels. In order to effectively lobby, there are several general steps that should be followed:

- Become familiar with all local, state, and federal legislation guiding lobbying practices
- Develop an extensive body of expertise on the subject
- Decide on the general lobbying policy and strategy
- Bring together and align all the policy communities interested in the matter

- Identify who will engage in lobbying and who will be targeted by the lobbying efforts
- Develop policy networks, communication channels, and working relationships with legislators and public agencies
- Be patient and attentive for windows of opportunity to open up
- Don't expect quick resolutions. One has to engage in lobbying ethically and one has to realize that lobbying is a negotiation rather than a "winner-take-all"-type game. Effective lobbying is a process that requires long-term and persistent commitment.

Summary and Conclusion

1 Business–government interaction is extremely complex. It is by no means a one-way endeavor. Similar to how government is routinely involved in private sector matters, business is often involved in governance. The involvement of business in government takes on numerous forms. Lobbying and inter-sector hiring are the two most common and well-known approaches by which business gets directly involved in policy decision-making.

2 Lobbying can be understood as the process by which a given interest group or policy community tries to influence the perspectives and eventual decisions of legislators and administrative regulators. In many ways, lobbying is a negotiation process among a number of distinct groups of interested parties. Lobbying serves a number of positive functions. It provides legislators with research, it develops and maintains communication channels, and it raises awareness and support for a specific issue. There are, however, many serious concerns regarding lobbying. In particular, it is believed that lobbying leads to biased decisions favoring those who have the most financial clout. Another concern is that the dynamics behind lobbying can endanger the basic and fundamental principles of democratic deliberation.

3 It is common for public officials to be hired from and into business, a practice often referred to as the "revolving door." Currently, a high number of high-ranking federal officials have at one point in time been employed by the industries that they help regulate. Upon completion of their work for government, a significant percentage of these officials will return to their previous employers. Similar to lobbying, the "revolving door" is often criticized for the fact that it could serve as the basis for biased and preferential treatment.

4 There have been a number of recent efforts to instill order and structure in terms of lobbying and "revolving door" practices. Among them,

the most important are the 1995 Lobbying Disclosure Act (LDA), the Lobbying Transparency and Accountability Act (LTAA) of 2006, the Honest Leadership and Open Government Act of 2007, and Presidential Executive Orders. All these pieces of legislation define accepted practices and impose restrictions on lobbying and "revolving door" practices. Although some enforcement is rather lax, the progress made in the past two decades has been significant.

5 Trust in government is an important ingredient of economic success. This is especially true in the case of democracies. Trust is, however, a very fragile asset; it can be easily damaged. For democracies to operate effectively and as envisioned by design, it is necessary that all those involved in the legislative process—including business—pursue their interests in an ethical manner and with a deep regard and respect for the public interest. Any unethical lobbying or "revolving door" practices will only decrease trust in government and will result in losses for the entire society in the long run.

Key Terms

- Appointed official
- Policy stream
- The Lobbying
- Disclosure Act of 1995
- Conflict of interest
- Politics stream
- Effective tax rate
- Presidential Executive Order No. 13490
- Lobbying
- The Lobbying
- Transparency and Accountability Act (LTAA) of 2006
- Lobbying activity
- Problem stream
- Lobbying client
- Revolving door
- Lobbyist Tax rate
- Multiple Streams Theory
- The Honest Leadership and Open Government Act of 2007
- Policy entrepreneur

Study Questions

1 What is the role of business in designing regulation?

2 According to Multiple Streams Theory, what are the three streams that flow through the federal policy space?

3 What is the role of policy entrepreneurs, such as lobbyists, in changing the agenda of government?

4 What are the main justifications for having "revolving door" practices? What are the main criticisms associated with such practices?

5 Why is conflict of interest on the part of legislators such an important issue?

6 Why might the numbers of officially registered lobbyists not be representative of the actual numbers of individuals engaged in lobbying or advocacy?

7 What is the length of the "revolving door" ban imposed by Presidential Executive Order No. 13490?
8 Which are the three major Acts that have targeted lobbying activities and "revolving door" practices since 1990?
9 Why is it important to advocate your interests ethically?
10 What are some of the steps that can be taken in order to ensure that you pursue your cause in an ethical manner?

Notes

1 Barack Obama did accept contributions from state lobbyists and from law firms associated with lobbyists. See Morain, D. (2007). An Asterisk to Obama's Policy on Donations: A Presidential Hopeful's Refusal of Lobbyist Money Has Its Limits. *LA Times*. http://articles.latimes.com/2007/apr/22/nation/na-obama22.
2 Each country, however, might have different types of legislation governing the practice. Some countries might have no rules at all, while other rules might be much stricter than those imposed in the US. Regulation usually deals with the length of the "cooling-off" period; that is, the amount of time that a public official has to wait before assuming a position in the private sector after leaving government.

References

Atkinson, C. (2019). Full and Open Competition in Public Procurement: Values and Ethics in Contracting. *International Journal of Public Administration*, *43*(13):1169–1182.

Bacon, P., Jr. (2007). Edwards, Obama Press Lobby Issue. *Washington Post*, August 6. 44. http://voices.washingtonpost.com/44/2007/08/edwards-obama-keep-pressing-lo.html.

Bedard, P. (2009). Podestas Rule Washington and Obama Guest List. *US News*, November 2. http://www.usnews.com/news/washington-whispers/articles/2009/11/02/podestas-rule-washington-and-obama-guest-list.

Bertrand, M., Kramarz, F., Schoar, A., and Thesmar, D. (2007). Politically Connected CEOs and Corporate Outcomes: Evidence from France. *Crest*. http://www.crest.fr/ckfinder/userfiles/files/Pageperso/kramarz/politics_060207_v4.pdf.

Besley, T. (2005). Political Selection. *The Journal of Economic Perspectives*, *19*(*3*):43–60.

Brunjes, Benjamin. (2020). Competition and Federal Contractor Performance. *Journal of Public Administration Research and Theory*, *30*(*2*):202–219.

Cartoon Stock. https://www.cartoonstock.com/directory/i/influence_peddling.asp

Chalmers, A. W., and Macedo, F. S. (2020). Does It Pay to Lobby? Examining the Link between Firm Lobbying and Firm Profitability in the European Union. *Journal of European Public Policy*. doi: 10.1080/13501763.2020.1824012.

Correll, D. S. (2022). New in 2022: USS Gerald R. Ford expected to deploy for the first time this year. *Navy Times*. January 4. https://www.navytimes.com/news/your-navy/2022/01/04/new-in-2022-uss-gerald-r-ford-expected-to-deploy-for-the-first-time-this-year/

Curry, W. S. (2017). *Government Contracting: Promises and Perils* (2nd Ed.). New York: Routledge.

Denhardt, J. V., and Denhardt, R. B. (2007). *The New Public Service: Serving, Not Steering*. Armonk, NY: M. E. Sharpe.

Eisler, K. (2007). Hired Guns: The City's 50 Top Lobbyists. *Washingtonian*, June 1. http://www.washingtonian.com/articles/people/hired-guns-the-citys-50-top-lobbyists.

Faccio, M. (2006). Politically Connected Firms. *American Economic Review, 96(1)*:369–386.

Fisman, R. (2001). Estimating the Value of Political Connections. *American Economic Review, 91(4)*:1095–1102.

GAO website (2022). https://www.gao.gov/legal/bid-protests/search?processed=1&page=0

Goodsell, C. T. (2004). *The Case for Bureaucracy: A Public Administration Polemic*, 4th edn., Washington, DC: CQ Press.

Green, M. (2004). *Selling Out: How Big Corporate Money Buys Elections, Rams through Legislation, and Betrays our Democracy*. New York: HarperCollins.

Harstad, B., and Svensson, J. (2011). Bribes, Lobbying, and Development. *American Political Science Review, 105(5)*:46–63.

Jacobson, G. C. (2011). Obama and the Polarized Public, in J. A. Thurber (ed.) *Obama: The First Two Years* (pp. 19–40). Boulder, CO: Paradigm Publishers.

Johnson, S., and Mitton, T. (2003). Cronyism and Capital Controls: Evidence from Malaysia. *Journal of Financial Economics, 67(2)*:351–382.

Kaiser, R. G. (2009). *So Damn Much Money: The Triumph of Lobbying and the Corrosion of American Government*. New York: Random House Digital, Inc.

Kerwin, C. M., and Furlong, S. R. (2010). *Rulemaking: How Government Agencies Write Law and Make Policy*, 4th edn. Washington, DC: CQ Press.

Leaver, C. (2009). Bureaucratic Minimal Squawk Behavior: Theory and Evidence Form Regulatory Agencies. *American Economic Review, 99(3)*:572–607.

Lessing, L. (2010). How to Get Our Democracy Back. *The Nation*, February 22. http://www.thenation.com/article/how-get-our-democracy-back#axzz2ZbR8n7Dp.

Lichtblau, E. (2010). Lobbyist Says It's not about Influence. *New York Times*, July 1. http://www.nytimes.com/2010/07/02/us/02podesta.html?_r=2&.

Madison, J. (1787/2011). Federalist No. 10: The Same Subject Continued (The Union as a Safeguard against Domestic Faction and Insurrection). Project Gutenberg.

Maskell, J. (2007). *Lobbying Law and Ethics Rules Changes in the 110th Congress*. Congressional Research Service.

Mattozzi, A., and Merlo, A. (2008). Political Careers or Career Politicians? *Journal of Public Economics, 92(3)*:597–608.

McIntyre, R. S., and Nguyen, C. T. D. (2004). *Corporate Income Taxes in the Bush Years*. Washington, DC: Citizens for Tax Justice and the Institute on Taxation and Economic Policy.

Merle, R. (2004). Recruiting Uncle Sam: The Military Uses a Revolving Door to Defense Jobs. *Washington Post*. http://www.highbeam.com/doc/1P2-146514.html.

OpenSecrets (2021). https://www.opensecrets.org/.

Osborne, D., and Gaebler, T. (1992). *Reinventing Government: How the Entrepreneurial Spirit Is Transforming the Public Sector*. New York: Plume.

Palmer, K. (2005). Schmooze or Lose: Contractors Rely on Personal Connections and Insider Information to Win Contracts. *Government Executive*. http://www.govexec.com/magazine/features/2005/12/schmooze-or-lose/20778/.

Patton Boggs website (2014). https://www.squirepattonboggs.com/en.

Powers, R. (2008). Palin Blames Lobbyists Like Her Campaign Manager for the Failure of Fannie Mae and Freddie Mac. *ThinkProgress*, September 17. http://thinkprogress.org/politics/2008/09/17/29350/palin-blames-davis/?mobile=nc.

Public Citizen (2005). "Revolving Door" Restrictions on Federal Employees Becoming Lobbyists. http://www.cleanupwashington.org/lobbying/page.cfm?pageid=40.

Rasor, D., and Bauman, R. (2007). *Betraying Our Troops*. New York: Palgrave Macmillan.

Richter, B. K., Samphantharak, K., and Timmons, J. F. (2009). Lobbying and Taxes. *American Journal of Political Science, 53(4)*:893–909.

Rival, M. (2012). Are Firms' Lobbying Strategies Universal? Comparison of Lobbying by French and UK Firms. *Journal of Strategy and Management, 5(2)*:211–230.

Rowland, C. (2013). Tax Lobbyists Help Businesses Reap Windfalls. *Boston Globe*, March 17. http://www.bostonglobe.com/news/politics/2013/03/16/corporations-record-huge-returns-from-tax-lobbying-gridlock-congress-stalls-reform/omgZ-vDPa37DNlSqi0G95YK/story.html.

Smith, J. R. (2011). In Jack Abramoff's Memoir, "Capitol Punishment," an Unrepentant Reformer? *Washington Post*, December 9. http://www.washingtonpost.com/entertainment/books/in-jack-abramoffs-memoir-capitol-punishment-an-unrepentant-reformer/2011/11/30/gIQAxZIpiO_story.html.

Sorauf, F. J. (1992). *Inside Campaign Finances: Myths and Realities*. New Haven, CT: Yale University Press.

Sunlight Foundation (2013). http://sunlightfoundation.com/.

The Federal Bureau of Prisons (2013). Inmate Locator. http://www.bop.gov/iloc2/InmateFinderServlet?Transaction=NameSearch&needingMoreList=false&FirstName=jack&Middle=&LastName=abramoff&Race=U&Sex=U&Age=&x=0&y=0.

The Library of Congress (2013a). Lobbying Transparency and Accountability Act of 2006. http://thomas.loc.gov/cgi-bin/bdquery/z?d109:s2128.

The Library of Congress (2013b). Honest Leadership and Open Government Act of 2007. http://thomas.loc.gov/cgi-bin/bdquery/z?d110:s1.

The White House (2013). Visitor Access Records. http://www.whitehouse.gov/briefing-room/disclosures/visitor-records.

The World Bank (2021). GDP. http://data.worldbank.org/indicator/NY.GDP.MKTP.CD.

Thurber, J. A., and Nelson, C. J. (eds.) (2000). *Campaign Warriors: Campaign Consultants in Elections*. Washington, DC: Brookings Press.

United States Senate (2013). Lobbying Disclosure Act of 1995. http://www.senate.gov/legislative/Lobbying/Lobby_Disclosure_Act/TOC.htm.

US Chambers of Commerce (2021). About the US Chambers of Commerce. http://www.uschamber.com/about.

Vidal, J. B. I., Draca, M., and Fons-Rosen, C. (2012). Revolving Door Lobbyists. *American Economic Review, 102(7)*:3731–3748.

Whirlpool Corporation (2013). About Whirlpool Corporation. http://www.whirlpoolcorp.com/about/overview.aspx.

8 The Third Sector—Nonprofit Organizations

Sharon Velarde Pierce

Introduction to the Public, Private, and Nonprofit Sectors

Our society and economy are often divided into three sectors: the public sector (government), the private sector (business), and the nonprofit sector (a variety of civic, labor, nonprofit business, social, and advocacy organizations). The public sector consists of government-controlled services that provide for both basic and essential needs of the general community. The private sector is populated by organizations run by individuals, partners, or shareholders. These organizations are run for profit and regulated through local, state, and federal governments. While a distinct sector, the nonprofit sector frequently collaborates with the other two. The main purpose of a nonprofit organization is to help the public—as communities or members—in some way. Each of the sectors has their own mission and issues to address (Phillips and Levasseur 2004; Piscitelli and Geobey 2020).

Briefly, the private sector focuses on making money for private good through a market-based system of exchange. It inherently values competition, innovation, shareholder values, maximum efficiency, and, above all else, profit. The public sector largely raises money through taxes and, to a lesser degree, fees for services, for functions deemed to be of public merit and related to protection, regulation, public services, etc. It inherently values regulatory compliance, safety, national security, and a competent, politically neutral bureaucracy. The nonprofit sector largely raises money from the public (donations), business philanthropy, and government contracts for services. It tends to inherently value services that promote the community or some part of it, the well-being of its cause or constituents, and awareness of various societal needs or member contributions to society. While international non-governmental organizations (INGOs) are not a focus of this chapter, it should be noted that they play the additional role of being international "watchdogs" related to international agreements on human and environmental standards (Silverman 2015).

DOI: 10.4324/9781003178620-10

Exhibit 8.1

Focus of the three sectors

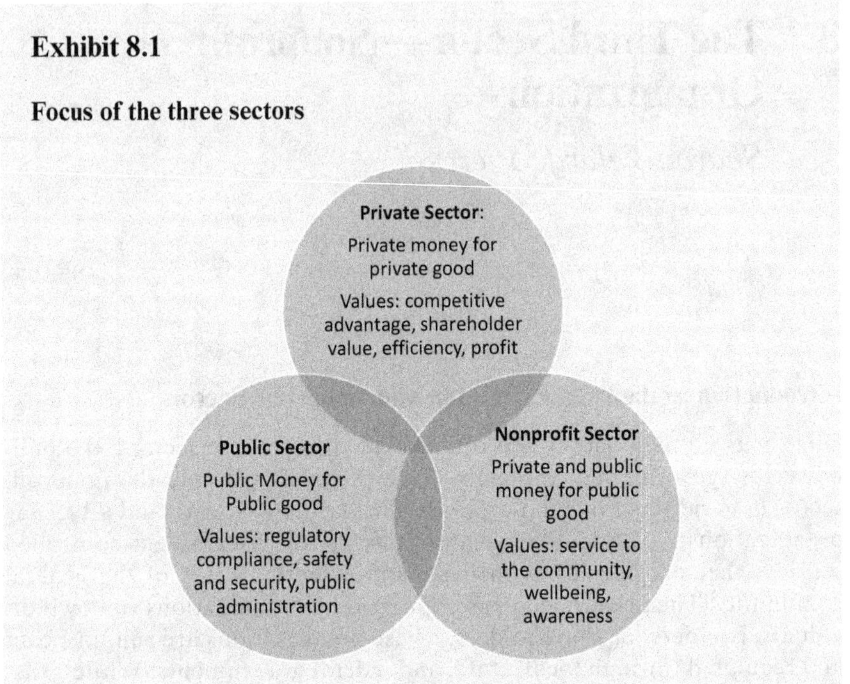

Historical Context of the Third Sector

Formed for the purpose of serving a public good rather than the pursuit and accumulation of wealth or investor profit, currently over 1.4 million nonprofit organizations are registered with the IRS of the United States (US). No one person or group of people can "own" a nonprofit organization, nor may nonprofits issue stock or pay dividends. Nonprofits must have bylaws approved by the IRS that make clear that a Board of Directions makes the policies for the organization, and they hire the CEO/President who, in turn, is responsible for all operations of the organization. *Ownership* is the major difference between a for-profit private business and a nonprofit organization.

Charities and civic groups have been part of the American fabric since colonial times. The St. George's Society of New York, founded in 1770, is considered the oldest nonreligious charity in the US. For over 250 years, it has provided care and comfort when and where it is needed most, in New York. The first private family foundation in the US was the Russell Sage Foundation which was founded in 1907 for "the improvement of social and living conditions in the United States" by a gift of $10 million from Margaret Olivia Slocum Sage (1828–1918), widow of railroad magnate and financier Russell Sage. Today, the Russell Sage Foundation continues to study and disseminate knowledge about social problems.

Society's charitable needs were first addressed through the actions of local individuals and groups that took on the responsibility of helping economically, physically, or socially dependent citizens. The general sentiment of "social responsibility" led to the establishment of a private, voluntary sector. Organizations such as churches, mutual benefit societies, and private philanthropy provided funding and services to various types of dependent citizens in need of this assistance (Gibelman and Demone 1989). Even though public-nonprofit partnerships were sometimes formed centering on assistance, the services being offered were scarce and limited in scope, only impacting small groups of people or small areas and did not assist large portions of the needy population (Kettner and Martin 1987). This minimalist approach reflected a philosophical belief that citizens were responsible for providing for themselves, or in dire circumstances on local public sector relief (such as public almshouses or quarantine hospitals), rather than relying on government intervention on a broad scale (Smith and Lipsky 1993).

Voluntary organizations that focused on people creating organized assistance to those in need locally really began to emerge in the early 1800s and expand thereafter by wealthy individuals, religious groups, and groups of civic-minded citizens. Common charitable organizations during the nineteenth century were elementary and secondary schools, universities, orphanages, community hospitals, museums, symphony and operas, and libraries. Local and regionally focused nonprofits remain the largest in number to this day, but have been overtaken in volume of spending by national charities.

While some charities with a national scope were transplanted from Great Britain such as the Young Men's Christian Society (1861), Society for the Prevention of Cruelty to Animals (1866) and the Salvation Army (1880), these were exceptions until the after the Industrial Revolution had created social challenges on a society-level scale, which led to the Progressive movement. The Progressive Era (approximately from the 1890s through the 1920s) experienced a political movement centralized on furthering social and political reform, curbing political corruption endemic to "political machines," and restricting the political influence of large corporations. The model for the home-grown national charity was Clarissa Harlowe Barton, known as Clara. During the Civil War Barton risked her life to bring medical supplies and support to soldiers in the field. Afterward in 1881, she founded the American Red Cross, and it quickly became a large, bureaucratic, nonprofit organization to meet the needs of society in disasters and wars. Innumerable philanthropic organizations of all types sprang up through the 1920s, from those stemming from local communities such as the Rotary Foundation (1917) and Shriners Hospitals for Children (1922), to charity foundations created by "captains of industry" such as the Carnegie Foundation (1905) and the Rockefeller Foundation (1913).

The Great Depression of the 1930s, however, challenged the belief that the nonprofit sector had the capacity to independently remedy the many hardships resulting from the long and severe recession, even with its enhanced capacity (Salamon 1993). A philosophical and political shift toward enlarging public sector's responsibilities grew stronger and led to integrating the efforts of the public sector and nonprofit agencies to address the widespread, acute, human needs that accompanied the Depression. Due to this great economic strife, federal, state, and local governments began to subsidize nonprofit organizations, and this became an independent method for delivering social services. The public sector stepped in and focused on creating government agencies to assist and financially support private, voluntary agencies as they dealt with the societal needs of the time (Gronbjerg 2001).

To implement this new strategy, the federal government passed the Social Security Act of 1935, providing economic security to citizens over the age of 65. This legislation created a social insurance fund that workers paid into during their working years and then upon retirement at 65 provided them with a guaranteed income until their death (Kramer 1981). This New Deal legislation changed the face of welfare as it shifted much of the responsibility for the senior population from local communities and nonprofits to the federal Social Security Administration (Netting et al. 1990). For two decades, there was a steady increase in government funding for many welfare services through funding to state and local welfare organizations that implemented new, badly needed social programs (Smith and Lipsky 1993).

While nonprofit exemptions emerged as early as 1894 in the US tax code, the current structure was codified into law by the Revenue Act of 1954. Because the law stipulated that individuals' and corporations' contributions to nonprofits were deemed nontaxable by federal and state governments, they had to be included in the tax code. Today, Sections 501(a), (b), and (c) of the tax code stipulate that individuals and corporations do not have to pay taxes on the income they contribute to most nonprofits and, likewise, nonprofits do not pay taxes on these contributions that they received as income. Exceptions include nonprofits formed as civic leagues, labor organizations, and social clubs.

By the late 1970s, "purchase of service" contracting between nonprofits, for-profit corporations, and government agencies was the primary vehicle through which the government delivered social services (Wedel 1979). Salamon described this shift as an elaborate system of third-party government. This third-party government was the creation of the federal government overlapping with the nonprofit sector we see today (Salamon 1995, p. 41). Under this arrangement, the federal government acts as a provider of funds and direction while the actual delivery of services is carried out by third parties under federal or state contracts to address governmental priorities. The nature and extent of this partnership led to the development of a mutually dependent relationship between the public and nonprofit sectors, giving rise to the unique characteristic of the nonprofit sector and its interdependence with the public sector.

Throughout the decades, governmental social policy can be described as a pendulum, swinging from right to left and back to right. In the 1960s and 1970s, the focus was on social programs and a movement away from military expenditures. In the 1980s, the pendulum swung to the right with the election of Republican Ronald Reagan. Consequently, there was a shift away from the progressive trends of the 1960s and 1970s. The priorities of the government became shrinking the size of government and reducing the federal budget, but increasing expenditures for national defense. This Conservative change in direction led to federal policies reducing governments' social responsibilities and led to a rebirth of reliance on voluntarism that echoes earlier forms of private, voluntary agencies (aka nonprofits) before the Great Depression. President H. W. Bush's slogan, "a thousand points of light," captured the importance of a return to local responsibility for the social needs of communities (Danziger and Haveman 1981).

Types of Nonprofits

It is estimated that there may be a million nonprofits incorporated in the US, but many are nonfunctioning or so small that they don't file with the IRS. The IRS has 29 categories of nonprofits. However, only a handful are numerous and important for our current examination of the topic.

Charitable Organizations 501(c)(3)

Three-quarters of all nonprofit organizations fall under 501(c)(3), or charitable organizations that do not operate for the benefit of private interests. Instead, these organizations focus on humanitarian assistance including religious, educational, charity, scientific, and literary organizations. Exhibit 2 displays the 2016 distribution of public charities by type of organization. Human services groups—such as food banks, homeless shelters, youth services, sports organizations, and family or legal services—composed over one-third of all public charities (35.2 percent). They were more than twice as numerous as education organizations, the next-most prolific type of organization, which accounted for 17.2 percent of all public charities. Education organizations include booster clubs, parent-teacher associations, and financial aid groups, as well as academic institutions, schools, and universities. Health care organizations, though accounting for only 12.2 percent of reporting public charities, accounted for nearly three-fifths of public charity revenues and expenses in 2016. Education organizations accounted for 17.3 percent of revenues and 16.9 percent of expenses; human services, despite being more numerous, accounted for comparatively less revenue (11.9 percent of the total) and expenses (12.1 percent of the total). Hospitals, despite representing only 2.2 percent of total public charities (7,054 organizations), accounted for about half of all public charity revenues and expenses (49.8 and 50.6 percent, respectively). Charities in other categories, including social benefit, arts, churches, and the environment, are numerically one-third of all 501(c)(3)'s, but represent only 11.6 percent of the revenues in this type of nonprofit.

Exhibit 8.2

Number and revenues of reporting public charities by subsector reporting revenues

	Number	*Percent of Number*	*Revenues*	*Percent of Revenues*
Human services	111,797	35.2	243.0	11.9
Education	54,632	17.2	353.8	17.3
Other education	52,471	16.5	127.4	6.2
Higher education	2,161	0.7	226.4	11.1
Health	38,853	12.2	1,208.5	59.2
Other health care	31,799	10.0	192.5	9.4
Hospitals and primary care facilities	7,054	2.2	1,016.0	49.8
Other public and social benefit	38,071	12.0	117.1	5.7
Arts	31,894	10.0	40.2	2.0
Religion related[a]	20,880	6.6	19.4	1.0
Environment and animals	14,932	4.7	19.8	1.0
International	6,956	2.1	39.7	1.9
All public charities	318,015	100	2,041.5	100.0

[a] Not all churches report income to the IRS.
Source: National Center for Charitable Statistics, 2017, adapted by author.

Nonprofits classified as "charitable" are prohibited from political action that attempts to impact legislation and participating in campaign activities for or against candidates (*Exemption Requirements—501(c)(3) Organizations|Internal Revenue Service*, n.d.). Donations, whether in cash or noncash form (i.e., donated property, clothing, resources), made to 501(c)(3) groups are tax deductible (*Tax Information on Donated Property|Internal Revenue Service*, n.d.). In addition, religious organizations are automatically provided tax exemption by reason of Code § 501(c)(3).

Charities are typically funded through donations from individuals and foundations, government grants, and membership dues. All income for 501(c)(3) groups is tax exempt (*Are Nonprofits Tax Exempt|UpCounsel 2021*, n.d.). 501(c)(3) organizations are subject to some restrictions. Restrictions include self-dealing (transactions with organization insiders), excessive compensation, and limited lobbying and political activities, requiring minimum distributions for activities, and restricting certain kinds of commercial or investment activities. In addition, there are state level restrictions that might apply. For instance, state laws may impose restrictions such as a minimum number of governing board members, or limits on the number of governing body members that may be compensated ("Non-Governmental

Organizations (NGOs) in the United States," n.d.). Faith-based organizations face the same regulations as other charity organizations, with the exception that they are not required to file annual updates notifying the IRS of changes in the composition of the group (*IRS Tax Exempt and Government Entities- Group Exemptions*, n.d.).

Civic League, Social Welfare Organization or Local Employee Association 501(c)(4)

501(c)(4) is another category with approximately 120,000 nonprofits. Civic leagues, social welfare organizations, and local employee associations have fewer restrictions when it comes to political activity such as lobbying while in the pursuit of their social welfare mission. The purpose of these organizations is to support individuals within the group who may have fallen on hard times, the general welfare of the organization's members, and are usually considered to be community organizations. Nonprofits can apply for this designation with Form 1024 and file annual returns with Form 990 or 990 EZ.

Social Advocacy Groups—501(c)(4)

Some social welfare organizations are disqualified from obtaining 501(c)(3) status because they fail to serve a wide enough "charitable class," but they can become a 501(c)(4) (Galle 2020). The main category of organizations within the 501(c)(4) tend to be categorized as social advocacy groups that lobby or promote some sort of social or political effort. Funding support for these organizations typically come from donations or membership dues. They also engage in fundraising, lobbying, and efforts to educate the public about their cause. A majority of the 120,000 social advocacy groups are for education and other noncontroversial causes, but some advocacy groups have causes that are or have become controversial because of splits in American Society including Greenpeace, the National Association for the Advancement of Colored People (NAACP), the NRA (National Rifle Association), the ACLU, the National Organization for Women (NOW) and the Oath Keepers Education Foundation.

Other 501(c) Types

Only four of the other categories have tax contribution deduction status like 501(c)(3) status. Those categories are corporations organized by an act of Congress (category 1) such as the Smithsonian Museum, fraternal societies (category 8 and 10) such as the Elks Association and Freemasons, and cemetery companies (category 13).

Other categories of 501(c) that have tax exempt status but to whom contributions are not tax deductible—similar to 501(c)(4)s—include labor and agricultural organizations (category 5), business leagues, chambers of commerce and sports leagues (category 6), social and recreational clubs (category 7), teachers' retirement fund associations (category 11), state chartered credit unions (category 14), mutual insurance companies that are owned by the policyholders (category 15), veterans' organizations created before 1880 (category 23), and state-sponsored organizations providing health coverage for high-risk individuals (category 27).

How Nonprofits Are Created

The creation of an NGO usually happens when a group of individuals (citizens or noncitizens alike) comes together in an informal organization to discuss common interests, issues, or concerns. These informal organizations do not need government involvement or approval. However, when the informal groups start to seek certain legal benefits such as tax exemptions, they must formally incorporate and register as a nonprofit/NGO under the laws and regulations of the federal government as well as the various 50 US states.

To incorporate an informal group under federal law, the group must have a constituted board of directors, a mission statement that makes clear its contribution to the public good, bylaws, and a required set of policies such as those covering conflict of interest and non-discrimination. The group must also have fiscal policies that describe how the organization will manage its funds as well as the annual report due to the federal government. When these pieces are in place to the satisfaction of the IRS, it will issue what is called an EIN number, which identifies an authorized nonprofit for its transactions.

The next step is to seek formal status with the state in which the main office of the organization is located. This process involves submitting a brief description, mission, name, address, and the payment of a fee. These processes are embedded in government agencies so as to ensure that politicians and their political parties do not bias the determination of which organizations are allowed to become nonprofits ("Non-Governmental Organizations (NGOs) in the United States," n.d.).

Structures of Nonprofits/NGOs

Governing Boards

Governance refers to how an organization is governed, how it is controlled and managed, and by whom. Generally, the body of laws applicable to the governance of tax-exempt organizations is federal, not state law. As noted above, the legislation governing the creation and operation of nonprofit organizations address matters relating to the organization's governance. Tax-exempt organizations that are corporations are governed by either a board of directors or a board of trustees; both have the same powers.

Usually when the exempt organization is a trust, it may have a board of trustees or be governed by a single, sometimes corporate, trustee. How the nonprofit organization is structured determines how its directors are selected. A nonprofit organization's officers are usually elected by the governing body or by the organization's members, with the election process outlined in the organization's bylaws.

Again, as noted above, nonprofit organizations are required to have a set of bylaws that provides for its internal operating rules and regulations. Although federal law does not require specific language in the bylaws, many states have individual requirements for the content of bylaws for nonprofit organizations. Beyond legal requirements, bylaws are a necessary part of a nonprofit organization, and it is wise to have the assistance of an attorney who specializes in nonprofits when drafting them. Bylaws are a legally binding document that nonprofit organizations must submit to the Internal Revenue Service and state agencies.

Types of Governing Boards

To carry out their mission and ensure compliance with the mission as approved (which is called misrepresentation when non-mission related activities occur), nonprofits have structures that are different than those of for-profit companies. The governance is usually structured in three ways.

- Management by board of directors with executive director/CEO (operating board model) is also known as a functional structure with a CEO. This governance structure is found most commonly with those having a small workforce and where one person does most of the daily decision-making. However, it is the board that makes large-scale decisions and monitors the executive director through frequent meetings. The downside of this governance structure is that if a disagreement emerges about management, it can get out of hand rapidly and a board may not be able to reverse decisions until a new executive director is in place. Positions in this model may be full time, part time, or even volunteer-based.

Management by CEO with an advisory board is a program-based model with a CEO. This is a governance structure where the CEO supervises a larger staff and has more authoritative control over the majority of the operations. The board acts as advisor to the CEO and contributes guidance on specific issues such as financial choices and policies about human resources. The board has less power than the CEO and tends not to influence operational choices, which might be positive or negative depending upon the ability of the CEO. This governance structure works best in large bureaucratic nonprofits with many departments and employees, each with different responsibilities.

Exhibit 8.3

Organizational chart with an operating board

Stakeholders (public citizens, funders, volunteers, staff, other organizations, etc.)
Board of Directors
Chief Executive Officer
Employee / Employee / Employee / Volunteer

Non-management structure is a functional model with no CEO and where, more than likely, the board and the staff are all volunteers. One person, or maybe two people, on the board serve as chairperson or co-chair to manage the organization's operations. Since everyone has an equal voice in how the decisions are made, this governance structure is the most democratic. However, because by necessity the focus tends to be a day-to-day operation, this can lead to a lack of vision, direction, and growth, as well as a tendency to be less funded. These often tend to be new start-up nonprofits (Lucas, n.d.; McNamara, n.d.).

The Governing Board Responsibilities

Within most governance structures for nonprofit organizations, there is usually a board of directors. The board is usually composed of volunteers or even a few staff members who are working together to carry out the distinct goal(s) of the organization. According to governance theory and best practices, the board's role and responsibility is to cooperatively set the strategic direction and provide oversight, but leave the day-to-day operations to the staff (Lucas, n.d.; Piscitelli and Geobey 2020).

Exhibit 8.4

Management with CEO and advisory board

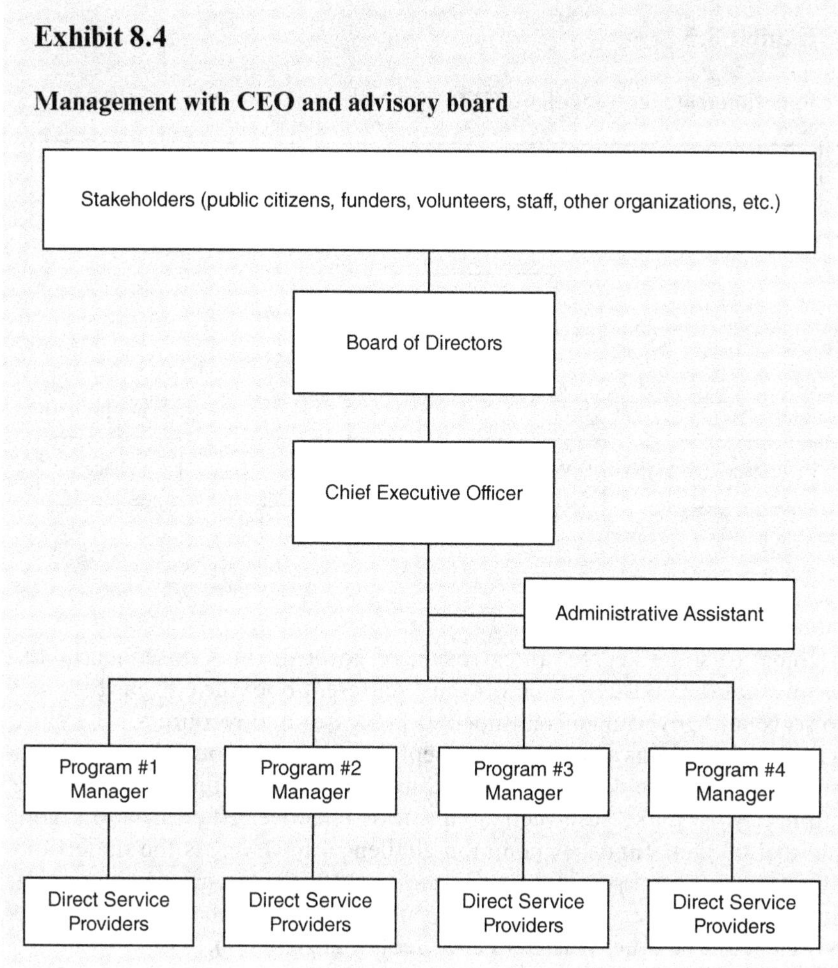

Why would an individual join a board of directors? It comes down to sense of civic motivation and impact. Individuals join a board of directors to make an impact, to contribute to its effectiveness, or to represent a stakeholder group. Therefore, board members come from various walks of life, with different goals and concerns, and represent various groups. While this diversity ensures a broader, more democratic perspective, it can also cause tension and cause boards to experience dysfunctional dynamics (Lucas, n.d.; Piscitelli and Geobey 2020).

There is also the question about whom the nonprofit boards represent. Because the government frequently contracts for the delivery of services through grants and contracts with nonprofits, some nonprofit organizations

Exhibit 8.5

Functional structure with no CEO

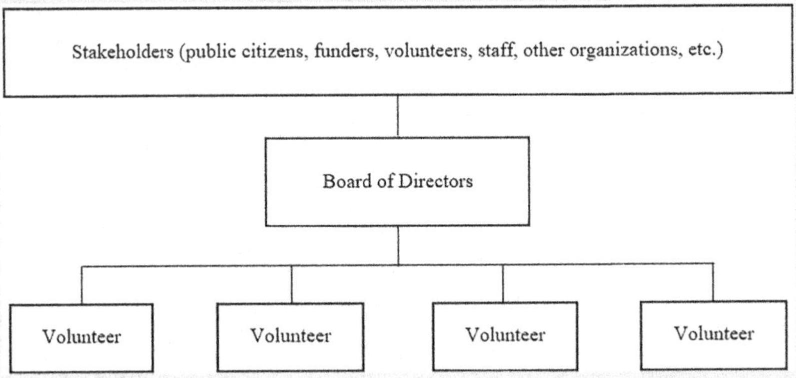

become, to some degree, an extension of government. Consequently, this means that the board of directors must represent both the citizens they seek to serve and government's authorized processes and resources. Therefore, when someone joins a board to represent a "particular group of constituents-[it is] an exercise in democratic voice." Board members' responsibilities are, ultimately, to make sure their nonprofit is effective, efficient, and a good steward of their funds. A common challenge, however, is the underfunding of many social services which lead to difficult decisions by nonprofits about balancing service quality and sufficiency on one hand, and scope of outreach on the other (Piscitelli and Geobey 2020, p. 77).

Managing Staff and Service Volunteers

The human resources of nonprofits are a delicate balance between and integration of paid staff and volunteers (Fang et al. 2021). A good integration of these two types of resources can lead to an effective and efficient NPO, while poor integration will frequently lead to a shortage of volunteers and inefficiency. The National Center on Charitable Statistics reports that approximately 30 percent of nonprofits fail to exist after ten years. Generally, human resources and how they are managed determine failure and survival (Ebarb 2019). How much of each type of staff really depends on the level of productivity required, the capital they have to work with, and the ability to recruit and motivate volunteers (Handy et al. 2008).

Staff

Unique among NGOs is that they have a higher satisfaction level when compared to other sectors. Further, NGO employees have more trust in management than those in other sectors. On the other hand, NGO staff make less when compared to their for-profit competitors. So, what is drawing staff to this sector compared to the others? The answer is that the nonprofit section provides various incentives like job satisfaction, opportunities for promotion, job clarity, and services in certain areas that focus on the betterment of humankind. These incentives are somewhat like the public sector when compared with the choice of working for the private sector. Yet there are some important differences between public and nonprofit sectors that may draw individuals to one sector over the other such as job security as opposed to "doing good" (LeRoux and Feeney 2013).

Once individuals are drawn into the nonprofit sector, they will need focus on their ability to build relationships with, and manage, volunteers. Paid staff in nonprofit organizations can be replaced by volunteers if they are at the same skill level and experience, and vice versa. This interchangeability between paid staff and volunteers shows that tasks in NPOs are fluid within the organizations and that tasks fluctuate. However, volunteers are not a substitute for paid staff, but rather enhance the capabilities of the organization. Though there is a valid fear of paid staff being replaced by volunteers, this problem can be solved by labor unions. It is not unusual, for example, for labor unions in Canada to write provisions into collective agreements that attempt to defend paid staff against substitution by volunteers (Handy et al. 2008).

Volunteers

Individuals that give time, money, experience, and specialized skill or knowledge often seek emotional or social compensation when being a volunteer. See Exhibit 8.6 for a charming example of some young volunteers. Volunteers are central to the survival of many NGOs as they provide free labor and expand the range of skills available. They also allow the organization to use paid resources more strategically. However, if volunteers are dissatisfied, they reduce their participation or stop volunteering altogether. On the other hand, if volunteers feel they are stakeholders in the organizations for which they are working, they are likely to be engaged, fulfilled, and a valuable resource (Maes 2012). Not infrequently, volunteers put pressure on the NGO to become more effective and efficient (Hustinx 2005; Lorente-Ayala et al. 2019; Zollo et al. 2019).

The economic choice to successfully engage volunteers comes with the responsibility of the NGO to know their volunteers and maintain high retention rates. High turnover rates can lead to loss of morale, know-how,

Exhibit 8.6

Training children to be volunteers

Source: Photographer, Chuck Lafferty. (Wikimedia Commons).

quality reductions, loss of resources to retrain new recruits, and other operational issues. To help prevent this, volunteers need to be managed effectively through constant training and improved connections between the volunteer and organization in order to enhance loyalty (Hustinx 2005; Handy et al. 2008; Zollo et al. 2019). Because loyalty, motivation, and satisfaction are key to retaining volunteers, NGOs need to know how to hone in on the individual desires and wishes of their volunteers (Lorente-Ayala et al. 2019).

Building a Nonprofit

The process of creating a nonprofit in the US can easily be broken down into four steps, which reflect the steps of incorporating a business, plus the step of filing for tax exemption with the IRS and state.

1 Mission Statement. While there have been debates over the impact and importance of a mission statement, the reason why the mission statement is key is that it presents the overview of the work and the reasoning behind why the nonprofit is needed. It is likely the central aspect in making sure a nonprofit can succeed as it sets up the management of the organization and the activities upon which it will focus (Liu 2015; Pandey et al. 2017). A solid mission statement attracts potential staff who have the passion and skills to pursue and make a difference. Additionally,

mission statements can impress stakeholders and create a strong image of the organization and its activities for potential funders. Mission statements are usually added to various points of contact like Internet homepages, business cards, letter headers, and posters and are used to reinforce the goal and branding of the charitable organization (Pandey et al. 2017). In terms of the actual composition, mission statements should be succinct, well-crafted, and avoid the use of vague language or jargon in order to effectively communicate the charitable organization's brand and identity (Liu 2015; Pandey et al. 2017).

2 Business plan. A business plan is a document that details the various aspects of the business concept. There are three parts to a business plan: (1) the problem and/or need within society and economy that is called for, (2) the goal(s) of the organization as it relates to the problem/need, and (3) a description of how the organization will address those needs within the organization's actions. The "how" in a business plan is very important to be able to gain grants and individual donors. Moreover, the business plan discusses detailed way(s) in which the organization will use its various resources (including human capital), the basic structure of the organization achieved through methodical research and reflection (vs. trial and error) (Liu 2015; Clippinger and Moore 2019), and how it will evaluate the degree to which its actions have achieved its goal(s).

3 Incorporate in your state. To incorporate, you must start by (1) creating a nonprofit name and (2) registering it in your state. The National Council of Nonprofits website has resources for who to contact in order to start the registration process in each state: www.nasconet.org/resources/state-government/. (3) Lastly, one must file Articles of Incorporation within your state accompanied by a certificate of disclosure, proof of corporate name, and filing fees (Liu 2015).

4 Apply for Tax-exempt Status. This part of the process is often the most difficult step and must be done correctly to be successful. Paperwork for the state and local authorities must be filled out as well. It is strongly advised that, when getting ready to file paperwork to the IRS, state, and local authorities, you consult a local attorney who specializes in nonprofits to make sure you are in compliance with all regulations (Liu 2015).

Legal and Regulatory Frameworks

A fundamental precept in nonprofit law is the concept of the purpose of a nonprofit organization. Being a nonprofit does not mean an organization is prohibited by law from earning a profit. In fact, it is quite common for nonprofit organizations to generate a profit. Rather, the definition of nonprofit organization essentially relates to requirements which determine what must be done with the profit(s) earned or otherwise received.

This concept is best understood through a comparison with the concept of a for-profit organization. There is a fundamental distinction between the two types of entities. The for-profit organization has owners that hold the equity in the enterprise and directly retain earnings or indirectly receive earnings through dividends and stock splitting. Hence, that is what is meant by the term "for-profit" as it is designed to generate a profit for its owners.

By contrast, a nonprofit organization is not permitted to distribute its profits to those who control it, such as directors and officers. Instead, the income and profits must be used to achieve the goal(s) of the organization. To distribute income or profit to board members and staff would violate the prohibition of private gain to which nearly all tax-exempt organizations are subject. For example, Ivy League institutions typically have $20 billion in endowments which generate enormous earnings, but those earnings are either dispersed for student scholarships or authorized programmatic goals, or retained in order to build a greater capital base for the endowment itself.

Technically, there is no legal requirement that organizations incorporate to successfully fulfill their missions of serving the public. However, when receiving financial support from private and public sources, an organization must be incorporated, which includes filing Articles of Incorporation and all supporting documents with state and federal authorities. Incorporation provides many distinct advantages such as limited liability, authority to seek outside financial support, tax advantages, structure, and accountability. There are some disadvantages in incorporation for very small nonprofits such as loss of centralized control and the laboriousness of the process itself.

Tax Exemption

Organizations with civic and public-serving missions who do not distribute profits are not necessarily tax exempt, although most entities with nonprofit missions do qualify for classification as an exempt entity under the tax rules. Whether a nonprofit organization is entitled to tax exemption, initially or on a continuing basis, is a matter of law. If a nonprofit organization qualifies for a tax exemption, at the federal or state law levels, or both, then it is a formal, incorporated nonprofit organization. As previously discussed, there are 29 major categories of tax-exempt nonprofit organizations in the federal tax law. Not all of them have comparable exemption at the state level.

Tax Treatment of 501(c)(3)

Under Section 501(c)(3) of the Internal Revenue Code, an organization must be organized and operated exclusively for exempt purposes, and not for the benefit of private interests or to any private shareholder or individual (*IRS Tax Exempt and Government Entities- Group Exemptions*, n.d.). This means that individual and corporate donations are tax free to the donor and this provision is an incentive for donors to give. Tax exemption is provided for a variety of charitable organizations that are "organized and operated exclusively for religious, charitable, scientific, testing for public safety, literary, educational, or other specified purposes and that meet certain other requirements" (*Exempt Organization Types|Internal Revenue Service*, n.d.).

Donations to a 501(c)(4) (aka c(4)'s) are not deductible by donors. While some of these community organizations like youth recreation associations or volunteer fire departments might have failed to become a 501(c)(3) due to tax-law technicalities, others are focused on advocacy. These advocacy groups have become an important political spending apparatus and are rising in popularity because of their ability to lobby in pursuit of charitable, educational, or recreational ends.

The key factor accounting for the rise of the c(4) is due to the Supreme Court's case *Citizens United (2010). Citizens United* changed the precedent that there were limits for corporate donations under federal election-laws and, as a result, political action organizations were no longer prohibited from becoming tax exempt. Further, due to tax secrecy laws, donations to these political action organizations incentivize donors who prefer to make anonymous political donations. Citizens United has led to what is called "dark money" (Galle 2020).

Lastly, it is ambiguous whether the IRS can reliably identify donations to 501(c)(4) organizations that are carelessly (or deliberately) deducted from the donors' tax returns. Donors are supposed to keep records and report their donations annually, but the IRS does not have the staff and resources to routinely audit the millions of tax returns that it receives each year (*IRS Tax Exempt and Government Entities- Group Exemptions*, n.d.).

The Nonprofit and Government Relationship: Lobbying

Lobbying is a time-honored tradition of communicating with elected or appointed officials for the purpose of influencing legislation and other public policy. Lobbying by nonprofit organizations is legal and an effective way of communicating with legislators an organization's views on a pending issue, to promote a favorable climate for those served, and to directly influence the outcome of decision-making. In addition, lobbying is often referred to as advocacy and "government relations" and is permitted by the First Amendment to the US Constitution relating to freedom of speech and the right to petition to redress grievances. However, lobbying should not be confused with campaigning and publicly supporting candidates (or parties) for office. Campaigning activities are prohibited under US tax law for nonprofits.

Lobbying is regulated at both the state and federal levels. Although there may be similarities between state and federal requirements, lobbyists must register separately with federal and state regulatory agencies. The Lobbying Disclosure Act, PL 104–65, was enacted on December 19, 1995, and provides registration and reporting requirements for lobbying Congress and the Executive Branch. It also includes special restrictions on the lobbying of 501(c)(4) tax-exempt organizations which receive federal funds. The Lobbying Disclosure Act defines "lobbying contact" as:

any oral or written communication (including an electronic communication) to a covered executive branch official or a covered legislative branch official that is made on behalf of a client with regard to:

- i the formulation, modification, or adoption of Federal legislation (including legislative proposals);
- ii the formulation, modification, or adoption of a Federal rule, regulation, Executive order, or any other program, policy, or position of the United States Government;
- iii the administration or execution of a Federal program or policy (including the negotiation, award, or administration of a Federal contract, grant, loan, permit, or license); or
- iv the nomination or confirmation of a person for a position subject to confirmation by the Senate. (Levin 1995).

On September 14, 2007, President George W. Bush signed into law the Honest Leadership and Open Government Act, which made substantive reforms affecting lobbying in response to excessive use of revolving door relations, contribution lobbying, and outright fraud. It strengthened reporting requirements, gift disclosure, and travel financed by lobbyists (*Honest Leadership and Open Government Act of 2007*, n.d.).

Ethics

Nonprofit organizations rely on the public trust to carry out their missions. They have a special obligation, both legally and morally, to uphold the highest standards of ethical practice, to be accountable to their boards and to the public, to avoid conflicts of interest, and to treat employees with dignity (see Exhibit 7 for some prominent nonprofits).

The Internal Revenue Service regulations require that nonprofit organizations may not be "operated for the benefit of private interests." This prohibition is the foundation of the public benefit requirement, and the legal, as well as ethical, principle for all charitable nonprofit organizations. The Sarbanes–Oxley Act of 2002 includes two provisions that apply to nonprofit organizations. This includes the prohibition against destruction of documents that are tied to a criminal investigation and prohibition of retaliation against whistleblowers. This provided nonprofit organizations a guideline to have a board-approved whistleblower protection policy, as well as a policy on document retention and destruction. Furthermore, the IRS Form 990, Part VI, includes numerous questions focusing on governance practices that demonstrate accountability and transparency to focus policies associated with conflict of interest, managing conflict, and executive compensation. In addition, state laws may address accountability and transparency practices. For example, some states prohibit loans to board members.

Exhibit 8.7

Examples of Nonprofits focusing on emergency social services, religion, and health

Credit: Photos by Wikimedia Commons (various).

According to Doug Wallace (McNamara 2000), an organization that exhibits high integrity has the following characteristics:

1 A clear vision and picture of integrity exist throughout the organization.
2 Over time, the vision is owned and embodied by top management.
3 The reward system is aligned with the vision of integrity.
4 The policies and practices of the organization are aligned with the vision providing clarity.
5 There is an understanding that all significant management decisions have an ethical value to them.
6 Everyone is expected to work through conflicting-stakeholder value perspectives (McNamara 2000).

Ethical Lapses Related to Nonprofits

Wherever people are involved, there will be ethical lapses, and the nonprofit sector is no different. To reduce ethical lapses in the public sector, government employees and leaders are highly regulated, and transparency is a part of the rule of law. Businesses are less regulated than government itself but have a strong need to provide robust internal controls and ethics standards to maintain short-term profitability and long-term protection of the brand. Like business, nonprofits have incentives for strong internal control since regulation is relatively lax. However, unlike business which is normally monitoring funds and resources it has generated itself, nonprofits are generally managing other people's money. This makes the sector particularly vulnerable to manipulation and occasional abuse and scandals (ACFE 2020; McDonnell and Rutherford 2018, 2019).

Below we review some of the types of internal and donor scandals that occur with nonprofits.

Ethical Lapses Inside Nonprofits

Fraud and embezzlement. The IRS reported that there were over a third of a million reports of charity fraud by taxpayers in 2017 (Morgan 2021). One famous case involves the Baptist Foundation of Arizona. When the BFA filed for bankruptcy in 1999, it had $460 million more in liabilities than assets (Zikai 2018). Fraud in the world healthcare industry, in which nonprofits make up a substantial portion, is estimated to account for 7.3 percent of revenue or about $470 billion, resulting from billing schemes, kickbacks, and hospital fraud, among others (Stowell et al. 2018).

Self-dealing behaviors of organizational members. Some charities allow their organization leaders to make outsized and sometimes outrageous salaries, which are particularly inappropriate in a nonprofit setting. Tiffany Carr (Coalition Against Domestic Violence) represents an egregious example who schemed to be paid $7.5 million over three years (Klas 2021). Another egregious case is Jack A Brown III, the Chief Executive Officer of CORE Services Group, which provide homeless facilities for the City of New York, who made over $1 million a year and employed numerous relatives (Thaler 2021). Wayne Lapierre and the NRA is still another (Hrywna 2020). While most executives escape criminal charges (but many get money clawed back), the damage to their organizations can damage contributions or bring down the nonprofit (Yin et al. 2021). A notable exception are nonprofit CEOs in industries competing directly against for-profit organizations. It is not uncommon, and not generally questioned, when hospital CEOs make salaries and benefits above a million dollars a year.

Exaggeration related to inefficiency. Because of less control not only on finances, but on productivity measures as well, nonprofits are sometimes culpable of exaggerating their productivity, especially when their efficiency is poor. For example, a client contact is counted as a successfully completed case. In some cases such reporting represents legal fraud, as it did with the Feed the Children Foundation in which the amount used for charity hovered around 20 percent when it was investigated by Charity Watch (2009). The names for such organizations is "badge charity" because an inordinate percentage of the funds donated go to professional fundraisers and operating expenses of the charity rather than the cause. Even the American Red Cross has been found guilty of gross exaggeration on occasion (Elliott and Sullivan 2015).

Pseudo-nonprofits. There are several types of pseudo-nonprofits. Some get IRS authorization despite their support of lucrative enterprises such as the National Hockey League, PGA Tour, the National Football League, NY Stock Exchange, etc., but some eventually become private corporations. Some allow others to think that their organizations are nonprofits, when they are fully owned by the founders such as the Chan-Zuckerberg Initiative. Finally, some misrepresent themselves entirely, raising money for the poor while using their funds to assist the wealthy and powerful (Medina et al. 2019).

Sexual abuse related to nonprofits. Because nonprofits frequently work with children and the vulnerable, they are relatively susceptible to child and sex abuse. A report on the Catholic Church estimates the number of abused children in France over a 70-year period was 330,000 (Associated Press 2021). Similarly, a legal team asserted that there were some 92,000 reported cases of sexual abuse in the Boy Scouts of America (McLaughlin and Vera 2020).

Ethical Lapses Related to Donors

Tax avoidance and wealth shielding. The wealthy have an array of strategies to reduce their tax liabilities, and charity deductions are a valuable tool in their arsenal. According to the IRS, charitable deductions are "typically limited to 20–60 percent of their adjusted gross income and varies depending on the type of contribution and the type of charity. [But] The law now allows taxpayers to apply up to 100 percent of their AGI" (IRS 2021). In fact, it is estimated that billionaires pay just 8.2 percent of their yearly income in taxes, considerably lower than the average American (White House 2021).

False assertions related to donating. Former President Donald Trump enjoys boasting, and his charity giving is no exception. While one analysis found that he made donations of $130 million, all but $10 million were donations of land he was unable to develop and therefore relatively useless (Solender 2020). In 2019, he was fined $2 million for charity abuse.

Reputation grandstanding and moral "washing." Being philanthropic is nearly required for well-off celebrities in the public eye, so it is not surprising that their gift-giving is news; it's almost a part of their job. It is quite different for wealthy people who want to distract from concurrent misdeeds or the unpleasant way in which they attained some or most of their wealth. Well-known examples include the Sacklers (the opioid crisis), sex offenders Harvey Weinstein, Jerry Epstein, and Roger Ailes, and Bernie Madoff (Ponzi scheme promoter) (e.g., Lins et al. 2020).

Donor self-dealing. Sometimes the intentions of donors are not for giving, but rather for receiving side benefits. A prime mechanism is donor-advised funds in which oversight is light and temptation is high to direct funds to one's own businesses or friends. It is so prevalent that the IRS goes out of its way to warn against abuse:

> The IRS is aware of a number of organizations that appeared to have abused the basic concepts underlying donor-advised funds. These organizations, promoted as donor-advised funds, appear to be established for the purpose of generating questionable charitable deductions, and providing impermissible economic benefits to donors and their families (including tax-sheltered investment income for the donors) and management fees for promoters.

Summary and Conclusion

This chapter has discussed the history and growth of the nonprofit or third sector, compared its organizational nature with those of the other two sectors, and examined US laws that govern how nonprofits may receive and spend nontaxable contribution. It has also examined how the US government has increased its engagement with the third sector as a means to outsource services and goods in efficient and effective ways while engaging citizens in the process of providing public good. Governments need partnerships to solve the most complex problems facing society (Phillips and Levasseur 2004) and business needs the support of nonprofits to temper the short-term and self-interested focus of capitalism. The nonprofit sector is essential for the US and its citizens in order to preserve the importance of community, engagement, beneficence, and the long-term sustainability of people and the planet.

References

ACFE (Association of Certified Fraud Examiners) (2020). *Report to the Nations: 2020 Global Study on Occupational Fraud and Abuse.* https://legacy.acfe.com/report-to-the-nations/2020/

Associated Press (2021). About 333,000 Children Were Abused Within France's Catholic Church, a Report Finds. *NPR.* October 5. https://www.npr.org/2021/10/05/1043302348/france-catholic-church-sexual-abuse-report-children

Are Nonprofits Tax Exempt|UpCounsel 2021 (n.d.). UpCounsel. Retrieved September 5, 2021, from https://www.upcounsel.com/are-nonprofits-tax-exempt.

Charity Watch (2021). Charity Watch Hall of Shame. https://www.charitywatch.org/charity-donating-articles/charitywatch-hall-of-shame.

Clippinger, D., and Moore, D. (2019). *Business Report Guides: Research Reports and Business Plans.* Business Expert Press. http://ebookcentral.proquest.com/lib/csusb/detail.action?docID=5638719

Danziger, S., and Haveman, R. (1981). The Reagan Budget: A sharp break with the past. *Challenge, 24(2)*:5–13. https://doi.org/10.1080/05775132.1981.11470682

Difference Between NGO and Non-Profit Organizations|Difference Between (n.d.). Retrieved September 5, 2021, from http://www.differencebetween.net/business/difference-between-ngo-and-non-profit-organizations/.

Ebarb, T. (2019, September 7). Nonprofits Fail—Here's Seven Reasons Why. *NANOE|Charity's Official Website.* https://nanoe.org/nonprofits-fail/.

Elliott, J., and Laura Sullivan, L. (2015). How the Red Cross Raised Half a Billion Dollars for Haiti and Built Six Homes Even as the Group Has Publicly Celebrated Its Work, *ProPublica* and *NPR*, June 3. http://muckrakerfarm.com/2015/06/how-the-red-cross-raised-half-a-billion-dollars-for-haiti-and-built-six-homes/

Exempt Organization Types|Internal Revenue Service (n.d.). Retrieved September 9, 2021, from https://www.irs.gov/charities-non-profits/exempt-organization-types.

Exemption Requirements—501(c)(3) Organizations|Internal Revenue Service (n.d.). Retrieved September 5, 2021, from https://www.irs.gov/charities-non-profits/charitable-organizations/exemption-requirements-501c3-organizations.

Fang, D., Fombelle, P., and Bolton, R. (2021). Member Retention and Donations in Nonprofit Service Organizations: The Balance Between Peer and Organizational Identification. *Journal of Service Research*, *24(2)*:187–205. https://doi.org/10.1177/1094670520933676.

Galle, B. (2020). The Dark Money Subsidy? Tax Policy and Donations to Section 501(c)(4) Organizations. *American Law and Economics Review*, *22(2)*:339–376. https://doi.org/10.1093/aler/ahaa009.

Gibelman, M., and Demone, H. W. (1989). The evolving contract state. In Demone, H. W., and Gibelman, M. (eds.) *Services for Sale: Purchasing Health and Human Services* (pp. 17–57). New Brunswick, NJ: Rutgers University Press.

Gronbjerg, K. A. (2001). The U.S. Nonprofit Human Service Sector: A Creeping Revolution. *Nonprofit and Voluntary Sector Quarterly*, *30(2)*:276–297.

Handy, F., Mook, L., and Quarter, J. (2008). The Interchangeability of Paid Staff and Volunteers in Nonprofit Organizations. *Nonprofit and Voluntary Sector Quarterly*, *37(1)*, 76–92. https://doi.org/10.1177/0899764007303528.

Haveman, H. A., Rao, H., and Paruchuri, S. (2007). The Winds of Change: The Progressive Movement and the Bureaucratization of Thrift. *American Sociological Review*, *72*(1), 117–142.

Honest Leadership and Open Government Act of 2007 (n.d.). FEC.Gov. Retrieved September 8, 2021, from https://www.fec.gov/updates/honest-leadership-and-open-government-act-of-2007/.

Hrywna, M. (2020). NRA in Crosshairs of Two AGs. *NonProfit Times*, October 6. https://www.thenonprofittimes.com/legal/nra-in-crosshairs-of-two-ags/

Hustinx, L. (2005). Weakening Organizational Ties? A Classification of Styles of Volunteering in the Flemish Red Cross. *Social Service Review, 79(4)*:624–652. https://doi.org/10.1086/454388.

Hustinx, L., Cnaan, R. A., and Handy, F. (2010). Navigating Theories of Volunteering: A Hybrid Map for a Complex Phenomenon. *Journal for the Theory of Social Behaviour, 40(4)*:410–434. https://doi.org/10.1111/j.1468-5914.2010.00439.x.

IRS (2021). https://www.irs.gov/.

IRS Tax Exempt and Government Entities- Group Exemptions (n.d.). Retrieved September 5, 2021, from https://www.irs.gov/pub/irs-pdf/p4573.pdf.

Kettner, P. M., and Martin, L. L. (1987). *Purchase of Service Contracting.* Newbury Park, CA: Sage Publications.

Klas, M. E. (2021). Florida Claws Back $5 Million from Nonprofit after Spending Scandal, *Tampa Bay Times.* August 26. https://www.tampabay.com/news/florida-politics/2021/08/26/florida-claws-back-5-million-from-nonprofit-after-spending-scandal/

Kramer, R. M. (1981). *Voluntary Agencies in the Welfare State.* Berkeley: University of California Press.

LeRoux, K., and Feeney, M. K. (2013). Factors Attracting Individuals to Nonprofit Management over Public and Private Sector Management. *Nonprofit Management and Leadership, 24(1)*:43–62. https://doi.org/10.1002/nml.21079.

Levin, C. (1995, December 19). *S.1060-104th Congress (1995-1996): Lobbying Disclosure Act of 1995* (1995/1996) [Legislation]. https://www.congress.gov/bill/104th-congress/senate-bill/1060.

Lins, K. V., Roth, L., Servaes, H., and Tamayo, A. (2020). Gender, Culture, and Firm Value: Evidence from the Harvey Weinstein Scandal and the #Me-Too Movement. May. Ssrn.com/abstract=3594338.

Liu, A. (2015, September 24). How to Start a Nonprofit In the U.S. *UpCounsel Blog.* https://www.upcounsel.com/blog/how-to-start-a-nonprofit-in-the-u-s.

Lorente-Ayala, J. M., Vila-Lopez, N., and Kuster-Boluda, I. (2019). How can NGOs Prevent Volunteers from Quitting? The Moderating Role of the NGO Type. *Management Decision, 58(2)*:201–220. https://doi.org/10.1108/MD-04-2019-0531.

Lucas, T. (n.d.). *How Nonprofits Work: Structure, Functions, and Typical Roles.* NPCrowd. Retrieved September 7, 2021, from https://npcrowd.com/how-nonprofits-work/.

Maes, K. (2012). Volunteerism or Labor Exploitation? Harnessing the Volunteer Spirit to Sustain AIDS Treatment Programs in Urban Ethiopia. *Human Organization, 71(1)*:54–64. http://dx.doi.org.libproxy.lib.csusb.edu/10.17730/humo.71.1.axm39467485m22w4.

McNamara, C. (n.d.). *Traditional Organizational Structures in Nonprofits.* 4.

McDonnell, D., and Rutherford, A. C. (2018). The Determinants of Charity Misconduct. *Nonprofit and Voluntary Sector Quarterly, 47(1)*:107–125.

McDonnell, D., and Rutherford, A. C. (2019). Promoting Charity Accountability: Understanding Disclosure of Serious Incidents. *Accounting Forum, 43(1)*:42–61.

McLaughlin, E. C., and Vera, A. (2020). At Least 92,000 Have Filed Sex Abuse Claims against the Boy Scouts, Legal Team Says. *CNN*, November 16. https://

www.cnn.com/2020/11/16/us/boy-scouts-sex-abuse-deadline-bankruptcy/index.html

Medina, J., Benner, K., and Taylor, K. (2019). Actresses, Business Leaders and Other Wealthy Parents Charged in U.S. College Entry Fraud. *The New York Times*. March 12. https://www.nytimes.com/2019/03/12/us/college-admissions-cheating-scandal.html

Morgan, R. E. (2021). *Financial Fraud in the United States, 2017.* US Department of Justice, Office of Justice Programs, Bureau of Justice Statistics.

National Center for Charitable Statistics. (2017). Donations Insights December 2017 Data. Urban Institute. https://nccs.urban.org/data/donations-insights-december-2017-data.

Netting, F. E., McMurtry, S. L., Kettner, P. M., and Jones-McClintic, S. (1990). Privatization and Its Impact on Nonprofit Service Providers. *Nonprofit and Voluntary Sector Quarterly, 19(1)*:33–46.

Non-Governmental Organizations (NGOs) in the United States (n.d.). *United States Department of State*. Retrieved September 4, 2021, from https://www.state.gov/non-governmental-organizations-ngos-in-the-united-states/

Pandey, S., Kim, M., and Pandey, S. K. (2017). Do Mission Statements Matter for Nonprofit Performance? *Nonprofit Management and Leadership, 27(3)*:389–410. https://doi.org/10.1002/nml.21257.

Phillips, S., and Levasseur, K. (2004). The Snakes and Ladders of Accountability: Contradictions between Contracting and Collaboration for Canada's Voluntary Sector. *Canadian Public Administration, 47(4)*:451–474. https://doi.org/10.1111/j.1754-7121.2004.tb01188.x

Piscitelli, A., and Geobey, S. (2020). Representative Board Governance: What Role Do Board Directors Have in Representing the Interest of Their Constituents? *Canadian Journal of Nonprofit and Social Economy Research, 11(1)*:12–12. https://doi.org/10.29173/cjnser.2020v11n1a323.

Salamon, L. M. (1993). The Marketization of Welfare: Changing Nonprofit and For-profit Roles in the American Welfare State. *Social Service Review, 67(1)*:17–39.

Silverman, B. (2015). The Role of Civil Society Organizations in the United States. *Yale Journal of International Law, 40(1)*:199–202.

Smith, S. R., and Lipsky, M. (1993). *Nonprofits for Hire: The Welfare State in the Age of Contracting.* Cambridge, MA: Harvard University Press.

Solender, A. (2020). Vast Majority of Trump's Charitable Giving Reportedly Came From Land Deals, *Forbes*, October 23. https://www.forbes.com/sites/andrewsolender/2020/10/23/vast-majority-of-trumps-charitable-giving-reportedly-came-from-land-deals/?sh=76d12401610d

Stowell, N. F., Schmidt, M., and Wadlinger, N. (2018). Healthcare Fraud Under the Microscope: Improving Its Prevention. *Journal of Financial Crime, 25(4)*:1039–1061. DOI: 10.1108/JFC-05-2017-0041.

Tax Information on Donated Property|Internal Revenue Service (n.d.). Retrieved September 5, 2021, from https://www.irs.gov/charities-non-profits/contributors/tax-information-on-donated-property.

Thaler, S. (2021). NYC Cuts Ties with One of the Biggest Homeless Shelters in the City after It Was Revealed CEO Collected more than $1 Million a Year in Salary and Steered Millions of Dollars in Business to other Companies He Controlled. *Daily Mail*, November 23. https://www.dailymail.co.uk/news/article-10235463/NYC-cuts-ties-one-biggest-homeless-shelters-CEO-got-1M-salary-year.html*US*

Human Rights Network: Why Do "Shadow Reporting?" (n.d.). Retrieved September 4, 2021, from https://www.njjn.org/uploads/digital-library/resource_492.pdf

Wedel, K. R. (1979). Purchase of Service Contracting: A State of the Art Review, in Wedel, K. R., Katz, A. J., and Weick, A. (eds.), *Social Services by Government Contract: A Policy Analysis* (pp. 327–341). New York: Praeger Publishers.

White House (2021). New OMB-CEA Report: Billionaires Pay an Average Federal Individual Income Tax Rate of Just 8.2%, Author. September 23. https://www.whitehouse.gov/omb/briefing-room/2021/09/23/new-omb-cea-report-billionaires-pay-an-average-federal-individual-income-tax-rate-of-just-8-2/

Wikimedia Commons (various). FEMA: Red Cross: https://commons.wikimedia.org/wiki/File:FEMA_-_28112_-_Photograph_by_Mark_Wolfe_taken_on_02-06-2007_in_Florida.jpg; Church: Filetime (Angell St). 2020. https://commons.wikimedia.org/wiki/File:First_Baptist_Church_in_America_from_Angell_St_2.jpg; Kaiser Permanente Building: Coolcaesar, 2006, https://commons.wikimedia.org/wiki/File:Kaiser_Permanente_Building.jpg

Yin, L., Mao, R., and Ke, Z. (2021). Charity Misconduct on Public Health Issues Impairs Willingness to Offer Help. *International Journal of Environmental Research and Public Health, 18*(*24*):130–139.

Zikai, T. (2018). An Overview of Economical Corruption in USA and Analysis of Its Future. *Journal of Humanities Insights, 2*(*1*):43–50.

Zollo, L., Laudano, M. C., Boccardi, A., and Ciappei, C. (2019). From Governance to Organizational Effectiveness: The Role of Organizational Identity and Volunteers' Commitment. *Journal of Management & Governance, 23*(*1*):111–137. http://dx.doi.org.libproxy.lib.csusb.edu/10.1007/s10997-018-9439-3.

Part III

Business–Government Relations in Economic Development

9 Economic Development

Chapter Contents

Case 9 Scenario

Renovating Happy Paws

Zoey was very grateful for her grandma's old house to start Happy Paws pet store. She knew that it gave her a boost many others never get. The house is located right off Main Street, where most of the city's commercial activities take place; more importantly, there is the veterinarian's office on the corner, Splurge Jewelry, and the U Scream Ice Cream shop nearby, which seem to keep customers walking by. Recently, the city invested substantial funds to pave the streets, renovate the buildings, and install the landscaping, attempting to develop the neighborhood into a pedestrian-friendly epicenter, with the ultimate goal of attracting more tourists and businesses to the city.

DOI: 10.4324/9781003178620-12

Zoey can see how desirable the location is for her business. However, Zoey is not very happy with the current look of the exterior of the house. Zoey's grandma had inherited the house decades ago and kept the inside meticulous. Despite the impressive Victorian style and the wonderful big windows for display, the exterior is not in the best shape and doesn't fit in well with all the sprucing-up the city itself has done in the neighborhood. The roof has some curled shingles and it leaks in Zoey's upstairs bedroom when it rains. A few pieces of the wood siding are warped. The front porch is sagging a bit and the whole exterior is in need of a paint job. And the list goes on … All these items add to her renovation costs, which she cannot afford.

Zoey brought up the renovation issue last evening when Zach and Tyler were helping restock Happy Paws. When Tyler mentioned that his uncle, who had an old restaurant on Main Street, had gotten some government money to renovate his business, Zoey was intrigued. Tyler said that as a historic building, the restaurant had qualified for some historic preservation tax incentives and energy efficiency and conservation grants, which ended up largely covering his renovation costs. Zoey was amazed and eager to know if she and her grandma's century-old building were eligible for those government programs and where and how she could get such information. She could hardly keep her mind focused and almost forgot to feed the fish before she closed!

Introduction

Both business and government have a shared interest in economic development, which aims at promoting the economic health and standard of living for a designated area. A robust, growing economy not only creates more demand for business products and services and enhances firms' confidence in their investment, but also provides opportunities to establish new customers, new products, and new markets. For government, economic development can lead to higher incomes, lower unemployment, and increased tax revenues, all of which will better enable government to deal with many of its daily challenges, such as eliminating poverty, protecting the environment, enhancing public services, and improving the welfare of people in their jurisdiction. Despite their different emphases, government and business often act in concert when it comes to economic development, an area that often involves intensive business–government interaction.

This chapter introduces many growth and development concepts, theories, and practices in relation to local economic development. Specifically, a variety of financial and non-financial tools that government utilizes to induce economic development are discussed. The chapter will help students obtain a basic understanding of the rationale behind each of the tools, as well as hone the skills needed to explore government financial resources for business purposes.

Economic Growth and Development

Economic growth is the increase in the amount of goods and services produced by an economy over time. Economic growth is concerned with wealth enhancement—that is, the increase (or loss) in financial value. It is conventionally measured as the percent rate of increase in real gross domestic product (GDP) or gross national product (GNP). Growth is usually calculated in real terms (i.e., inflation-adjusted terms) in order to "net out" the effect of inflation on the price of goods and services produced. The overall world GDP rate has been slowing down since the 1950s and 1960s when it averaged 5 percent per year with ample room for growth after World War II to more recent years when it has averaged approximately 3 percent (World Factbook 2021).

The annual percent change of GDP is often used to compare the magnitude of economic growth among countries and regions. For example, with an average 9.0 percent growth rate from 1992 to 2021, China has long been the fastest-growing large economy in the world (World Factbook 2021). In comparison, the US economy has slowed down from 3.5 percent in the 1990s to 2 percent in recent years. See Exhibit 9.2 for a view of US economic growth over the last few decades.

The measurement of economic growth as a change of GDP or GNP emphasizes financial values (and neglects all other non-financial values) but has its intrinsic drawbacks. It will be elaborated upon in the following chapter on industrial recruitment.

When economic growth is expressed on a per capita basis, it is normally used to measure the overall economic well-being of a population (i.e., the standard of living of people in a given region), which has been a central focus of economic development. *Economic development* generally refers to the concerted efforts of government, business, and communities to promote economic growth, as well as the overall economic and social well-being of people in a specific area.

The idea of economic development was conceived during the period of post-WWII reconstruction worldwide. The central focus of development at the time was to enhance economic growth. For example, in his 1949 inaugural speech, President Harry Truman stated that "[g]reater production is the key to prosperity and peace." Since then, economic development strategies have been focused on achieving growth through industrialization, especially planned alteration of production and employment structures, often at the cost of agriculture and rural development worldwide. This narrowly defined development focus led to the economic growth of many development countries in the 1950s and 1960s, but unfortunately did not bring about the

Exhibit 9.1

Latest World Economic Outlook Growth Projections

(real GDP, annual percent change)	2021	PROJECTIONS 2022	2023
World Output	6.1	3.6	3.6
Advanced Economies	5.2	3.3	2.4
United States	5.7	3.7	2.3
Euro Area	5.3	2.8	2.3
Germany	2.8	2.1	2.7
France	7.0	2.9	1.4
Italy	6.6	2.3	1.7
Spain	5.1	4.8	3.3
Japan	1.6	2.4	2.3
United Kingdom	7.4	3.7	1.2
Canada	4.6	3.9	2.8
Other Advanced Economies	5.0	3.1	3.0
Emerging Market and Developing Economies	6.8	3.8	4.4
Emerging and Developing Asia	7.3	5.4	5.6
China	8.1	4.4	5.1
India	8.9	8.2	6.9
ASEAN-5	3.4	5.3	5.9
Emerging and Developing Europe	6.7	-2.9	1.3
Russia	4.7	-8.5	-2.3
Latin America and the Caribbean	6.8	2.5	2.5
Brazil	4.6	0.8	1.4
Mexico	4.8	2.0	2.5
Middle East and Central Asia	5.7	4.6	3.7
Saudi Arabia	3.2	7.6	3.6
Sub-Saharan Africa	4.5	3.8	4.0
Nigeria	3.6	3.4	3.1
South Africa	4.9	1.9	1.4
Memorandum			
Emerging Market and Middle-Income Economies	7.0	3.8	4.3
Low-Income Developing Countries	4.0	4.6	5.4

Source: IMF, *World Economic Outlook*, April 2022

Note: For India, data and forecasts are presented on a fiscal year basis, with FY 2021/2022 starting in April 2021. For the April 2022 WEO, India's growth projections are 8.9 percent in 2022 and 5.2 percent in 2023 based on calendar year.

INTERNATIONAL MONETARY FUND IMF.org

Source: IMF, World Economic Outlook Database. https://www.imf.org/en/Publications/SPROLLs/world-economic-outlook-databases#sort=%40imfdate%20descending.

Exhibit 9.2

US GDP growth

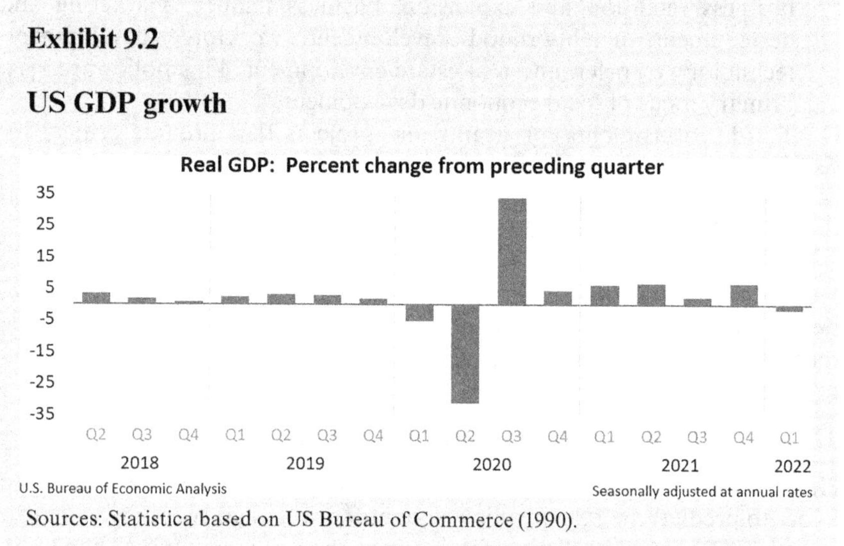

Sources: Statistica based on US Bureau of Commerce (1990).

expected improvement in the level of living for large groups of people. In the 1970s, many economists and policy-makers launched attacks on the rising gap of income distribution and widespread poverty around the world. This led to an expanded focus of economic development that included the elimination of unemployment, poverty, and inequality in addition to the acceleration of economic growth. For example, Nobel laureate Amartya Sen (1983) points out that "economic growth is one aspect of the process of economic development." Development should be viewed as a multidimensional process which involves the policies and actions by which a nation or a region improves the economic, political, and social well-being of its people. Such policies and actions can involve multiple areas, including development of human capital, public infrastructure, regional competitiveness, environmental sustainability, social inclusion, health, safety, literacy, and other initiatives.

Whereas economic growth is an indicator of market productivity, economic development is a policy intervention endeavor aimed at improving the economic and social well-being of people. Policies and actions of economic development generally encompass three areas:

- First, governments' overall policy framework to enhance market stability and sustainable growth, including monetary and fiscal policies, tax policies, currency value and exchange rates, regulation of financial institutions, domestic trade policies, and trade agreements with other countries. This is often the focus of development at the national and international levels.
- Second, governments' policies and practices to enhance employment, increase the tax base, and improve people's level of living through

business retention and expansion, business finance, marketing and development, neighborhood development, workforce development, technology transfer, and real estate development. This policy area is a primary focus of local economic development.

- Third, governments' programs and projects that provide critical infrastructure and services such as the transportation system, utilities, parks, affordable housing, public safety, disaster protection, and education. This can be the focus of governments at all levels.

Part III of this book will focus on economic development policies and practices at the local (or domestic) level, whereas Part IV will discuss many of the theories and polices at the international level.

Theories of Growth and Economic Development

Growth theory is the part of economic theory that seeks to explain (and hopes to predict) the rate at which a country or regional economy will grow over time. Economists distinguish between short-run economic changes in production and long-run economic growth. A short-run variation in economic growth is called the business cycle, which is made up of increases and drops in production that occur over a period of months or years. Generally, economists attribute the ups and downs in the business cycle to expected fluctuations in aggregate demand. In contrast, the topic of economic growth is concerned with the long-run trends in production. Due to the prevailing assumption that GDP per capita is directly correlated to standard of living, it is generally taken for granted that growth in economic production is desirable. Research into the causes of growth has been motivated by the interest in maintaining long-term growth in production, and of moderating the effects of recessions.

Classic Growth Theory

The modern concept of economic growth began with the critique of mercantilism (see Chapter 1), led by the Scottish philosopher and economist, Adam Smith. Mercantilism, which was based on trade, suggests a nation can gain wealth by maintaining a positive balance of trade with other nations. Governments would attempt to foster growth by discouraging imports (money leaving the country) and encouraging exports (goods leaving the country). Imports were discouraged by imposing tariffs. Exports were encouraged by granting monopolies intended to make favored merchants more competitive in foreign markets. This enabled monopoly-holders like the Dutch East India Company and the Hudson's Bay Company to manipulate prices in hopes of eliminating competition from other countries. Once a company's monopoly became international, it could raise prices and reap profits from its original investment.

Given its emphasis on production of goods for export and on price manipulation, the mercantilist system did not favor the working population. Local consumption was not a factor in economic prosperity, with the consequence that laborers and farmers generally lived on a level of bare subsistence. The people primarily responsible for economic growth received few of its benefits. The main beneficiaries of mercantilism were the trading companies and the governments that supported their operations.

In critiquing mercantilism, Smith recognized that three factors contribute to production: land, labor, and capital. Considering these three factors, his production function may be expressed as:

$$Y = f\left(K, L, T\right)$$

where

Y is the output of an economy,
K represents the capital,
L denotes labor force, and
T stands for land.

In Smith's theory, the combination of the inputs is expected to increase returns to scale through the production process. In the production function, output increases proportionally more than the simple increase in all inputs. This is because increased output expands the market and leads to both internal and external economies of scale, which will eventually lower the cost of production. This process is made possible by improvement in production techniques and a greater degree of division of labor. Division of labor increases labor productivity and increased productivity leads to higher wages, which enables more people to enjoy the products instead of just small elites. Higher labor income promotes the consumer market and creates more demand for products. This demand is then met with further increases in productivity as a result of a more efficient division of labor, and so forth. Working together, this set of dynamics constitutes a positive growth loop. For Adam Smith, economic growth contributes to an increase in consumption which benefits all sectors of the economic community.

However, it should be noted that despite the dynamic in the growth loop, Smith's theory never suggests that economic growth can be indefinite. Given the fact that land is a major production factor and that land is limited, Smith's growth model is ultimately constrained by environmental factors.

Economic Development Theories

Eighteenth- and nineteenth-century classic growth theory provided the base for further development and expansion of theories on economic development. Among them, *neoclassical economic theory* is the most widely practiced.

Neoclassical economic theory focuses on development and expansion of an economy. In alignment with Smith's free market ideal, it asserts that an economy will reach a natural equilibrium if capital can flow without restriction. The mobility of capital in a free market implies that capital will naturally flow from high labor and production cost areas to low labor and production cost areas, as the latter provide a higher return on investment. Therefore, poor regions would attract capital as prices for labor and property are lower in the overall market, and all areas would eventually reach a state of equal status if the market worked perfectly. Neoclassical economic theorists, as led by Milton Friedman, emphasize the negative role of government in development and oppose government regulations on the movement of firms from one area to another, as well as any restrictions that could make such movement undesirable to firms.

Several useful ideas have been derived from neoclassical theorists. Following the free market principles, communities should attract capital with their resources, such as land, labor, infrastructure, financial incentives, etc. Disadvantaged communities should strive to gain the necessary resources to compete against other areas in their market environment. Furthermore, government "red tape" (or excessive regulations) or other barriers are undesirable to economic development. Overall, government's role in economic development should be very limited, intervening as little as possible. It should also be relatively passive, and not aggressively seek economic development, but rather strategically use available resources to attract business for development purposes. The rationale has also underscored the recent upsurge in privatization, especially regarding the deregulation of transportation, energy, banking, and other industries in the United States and abroad (see Chapter 11).

Neoclassical economic theory, along with the policies and practices it can spawn, has been criticized by many local economic development advocates. Whereas neoclassical theorists claim that, in theory, the market will eventually reach a natural equilibrium and that all areas will have an equal economic status, their opponents point out that in reality, market imperfections, many of which are structural, always lead to unbalanced growth and development among regions, as well as unequal distribution of benefits from growth among groups. The interplay of market forces as a result enlarges the gap between areas and diverges the regional income (Myrdal 1957). The model is also blamed for its tolerance of excessive social inequality and its tendency to overshadow communities for the sake of corporate interest. Furthermore, the theory shines little insight on why some areas remain competitive despite relatively high production costs.

Location theory, on the other hand, seeks to explain an area's competitiveness in terms of firms' locational orientation—what factors of an area contribute to a firm's location choice. Location theorists assume that firms, in order to maximize their profits, choose locations that minimize the cost of transporting goods to the market place. The costs of transportation, and subsequently the logistics and activities for storing and distributing goods and services, affect a firm's location. Other factors such as the costs of labor and energy, the accessibility to suppliers, the availability of infrastructure, and the climate, culture, education, and training programs, and government performance also affect the quality of a location. Therefore, communities should manipulate these factors to their best possible advantage in order to attract businesses. Unlike the neoclassical school, location theorists generally assert that government should play a critical role in enhancing the location. A capable, cooperative, and responsive government can potentially better meet business's needs for land, infrastructure such as transportation and roads, education, and other public services. Various government policies, micro or macro, economic or non-economic, potentially affect many of the critical factors that deter mine the desirability of a location. For example, government public safety policies affect the crime rate of an area, which has an enormous effect on its economic viability and its overall success.

Several variants of location theory provide insights into economic development from different perspectives. *Economic base theory* analyzes growth from the demand side rather than the supply side. It differentiates the economic activities of an area into two components—those which meet the local demands and those which satisfy the demands outside the community. The former is non-basic, which does not lead to growth, while the latter is basic, which will generate local wealth and jobs. The theory asserts that the means of strengthening and growing the local economy is to develop and enhance the basic sector, which is the "engine" of the local economy. Communities should recruit businesses that have a market beyond the local area, devote their local labor and material resources to the success of those businesses, and strive to reduce any barriers that may hinder the development of those export-oriented industries.

Growth pole theory rejects neoclassical theorists' claim that growth "should" flow to less costly regions and argues that indeed the opposite happens *unless* there is a dynamic industry with a competitive edge in capital, technology, and political influence (Perroux 1983). Such industries are propelled by poles of growth. A pole or hub is characterized by core industries around which linked industries develop because of the core industries' demand (from suppliers), as well as its provision of goods and services (to customers). The expansion of a core industry leads to the expansion of investment, output, employment, and new technologies, as well as the emergence of secondary growth poles.

Central place theory focuses on the critical role of urban centers in regional economic development. According to this theory, urban centers contain specialized industries (especially retail stores) that serve a broad area. They are surrounded and supported by a number of small jurisdictions that provide resources and markets for the urban centers. Residents of a small jurisdiction have to go to these central, urban areas for specialized products and services that are not provided in their own communities. Therefore, economic development efforts should direct resources to the development of a designated central place that will improve the economic well-being of the whole region (Bradshaw and Blakely 1979).

In analyzing the competitive advantage of places, Michael Porter (1990) integrates these concepts into his *cluster theory*. Clusters are geographic concentrations of interconnected firms in related industries, specialized suppliers, and associated institutions, such as government, universities, and trade associations, in a particular field. Since most cluster participants are not direct competitors but rather serve different segments of industries, they not only compete but also cooperate, which make them better. The synergy among them produces growth. According to Porter, a major role of government is to facilitate or upgrade cluster development.

Economic Development Strategies

Economic development theories have influenced practices, especially government's strategies to enhance development. Generally speaking, government, and in particular states and localities, use three strategies to stimulate economic development:

- *Industrial recruitment* is primarily a locational approach by which governments subsidize businesses to lure more investment into their jurisdictions or to prevent indigenous firms from leaving. Despite the political controversies about—and the legal challenges to—the use of government incentives, industrial recruitment still plays a significant role in local economic development. Chapter 9 will elaborate upon recruitment practices and their implications in the United States.
- *Entrepreneurial strategies for economic development* refers to the approach that governments use when adopting policies that promise to increase public revenue by focusing primarily on the creation of new firms and technology development. In recent years, entrepreneurial strategy has frequently emphasized engaging local governments, private business and development firms, and local nonprofit organizations to create new opportunities for investment in declining or stagnant communities. The discussion of entrepreneurial strategy will be included in Chapter 10. Thus, the neoclassical concept of innovation is harnessed in the context of location theory in this strategy.
- *Privatization* is the delegation of public duties to the private sector. It is deeply rooted in the market-oriented economic ideal, and thus neoclassical economic theory. Privatization, unlike the other two strategies, seeks to reduce government intervention in an economy. For example, deregulation, a strategy wherein government removes, reduces, or simplifies restrictions on business to encourage (in theory) the efficient

operation of markets, has been pursued in the past to encourage the development of market-oriented economy. In recent years, privatization, in the form of public–private partnerships, has been increasingly used for local economic development due to practical reasons. Chapter 10 introduces other forms of privatization, which are pursued by government because of either practical or ideological reasons beyond economic development, and which, as a side effect, create opportunities for the private sector to do business with government.

Financial Tools for Economic Development

To pursue the different strategies for economic development, state and local governments in the US have created and implemented a variety of instruments and techniques for raising or allocating funds. This section introduces the most common financial tools used by states and local jurisdictions to fund their economic development purposes.

Tax Reductions (Aka Tax Breaks)

Tax reductions, or tax breaks, that are provided by states and local governments to assist economic development include various kinds of abatements, credits, and exemptions.

Tax abatement is a full or partial reduction of the tax liability of a given piece of real estate for a specified number of years. It is often granted to new or rehabilitated industrial or commercial property in blighted conditions or areas. The use of commercial property tax abatement in the United States can be traced back to 1640 when the state of Connecticut granted tax reductions for the production of manufacturing items, such as flax seed oil, iron and steel, and malt liquor (Alyea 1967). In 2004, 35 of the 50 states offered stand-alone property tax abatements, which constitute an integral component of their economic development programs (Dalehite, Mikesell, and Zorn 2005). Some states also allow localities to offer tax reductions on their property taxes in conjunction with their economic development programs (Wassmer 2007). For example, in the State of New Jersey, municipalities grant tax abatements to businesses and developers to enhance employment opportunities, attract residents, and lure commercial establishments, while developing vacant or underutilized properties. In view of the comparatively high property tax rates in New Jersey, abatement can be a valuable incentive for developers and investors; yet a recent study found that such tax abatements also resulted in significant foregone revenue and introduced tax inequalities (State of New Jersey 2010).

Tax exemption is the freedom from an obligation to pay a particular tax. It generally refers to a statutory exception to a general rule rather than the mere absence of taxation or a deduction of taxable items. Many states offer tax exemptions to business for purchases, investments, and activities other than real estate development. Such exemptions are commonly granted for the purchase of raw materials, machinery, and equipment. In the US, most states and localities exempt any goods from sales or use taxes that are used directly in the production of other goods (i.e., raw materials) as well as the purchase of new equipment (e.g., equipment for research and development); also generally exempt from inventory taxes are goods in transit, to promote employment in warehousing, shipping, and transportation. For example, California Revenue and Taxation Code Section 129 specifies that "business inventories" that are eligible for exemption include "all tangible personal property, whether raw materials, work in process or finished goods, which will become a part of or are themselves items of personally held for sale or lease in the ordinary course of business."[1]

Tax credit is a reduction in the tax bill, commonly used to encourage job creation, investment, and research and development activities. Credits may be offered to individuals as well as entities against income or property taxes, and are generally non-refundable to the extent they exceed taxes otherwise due. Most state enterprise zone programs offer employers a tax credit for each new job or each new employee who lives in the zone. Some states offer

Exhibit 9.3

Possible sources of potential small business deductions

- Advertising
- Phones (landline, fax or cell phones related to business)
- Computer & internet expenses
- Transportation and travel expenses
- Commissions and fees
- Interest expense
- Professional fees
- Office supplies
- Rent expense
- Office-in-home
- Wages paid to employees
- Employee benefit expenses
- Contract labor expenses paid to subcontractors and independent contractors
- Depreciation
- Amortization of intangible assets (e.g., patents or copyrights held)
- Business insurance
- Repairs, maintenance of office facility, etc.
- Estimated tax payments made (including property taxes and sales taxes if applicable)
- Health insurance

Source: IRS (2021).

credits for investment in depreciable capital stock. Approximately 43 states provide various tax credit programs, such as brownfield credits, pollution control credits, renewable energy credits, and historical preservation credits, among others. See Exhibit 9.3 for an example of a typical checklist of small business deduction possibilities.

Public Borrowing

State and local governments may also borrow from the public through issuing bonds to fund economic development. This function is often assumed by special authorities, such as an industrial development authority, economic development authority, redevelopment authority, and so on, rather than being assumed by municipalities themselves. Those financial authorities lend money to private businesses, often at a below-market rate in an effort to induce investment. The *industrial revenue bond* (IRB) and *tax increment financing* (TIF) are two commonly used methods of public borrowing.

IRBs, industrial development revenue bonds (also sometimes called IDRs or IDBs), are often issued by state and local government public authorities. Subsequent loans are either at favorable rates (partially by means of federal tax exemption) and/or guaranteed. Rather than from a tax, a revenue bond guarantees repayment, and that guarantee is solely based from monies generated by a specified revenue-generating entity associated with the purpose of the bond (i.e., economic development). Such a bond is not backed by the full faith and credit of the issuing government; nor does it require voter approval. Taxpayers are not implicated in the bond issuing. While enjoying the low interest rate, the private beneficiary bears full liability for repayment or default. The proceeds of the bond issue are often used to finance private industrial facilities or equipment. For example, ColorGraphics, one of the largest printers in the western United States, used an IRB issued by the Industrial Development Authority of the City of Los Angeles to purchase a new $8.6 million printer, which helped create new jobs and retain employees, because the advanced printing technology better met customer demand.[2]

The use of IRBs began during the Great Depression and became universal in the 1970s. As foregone federal revenues increased (because of tax-exempted government bonds), Congress became concerned about the costs of such practices. A series of Acts were passed to limit the use of IRBs, such as the Revenue Adjustment Act of 1968. Since 1988, the federal government has authorized what is referred to as a Volume Cap, which is the maximum annual amount of tax-exempt private activity bonds that can be issued in each state. Annually, each state receives an allocation of Volume Cap, or the so-called "state ceiling," based upon an IRS Inflation Adjustment (which was $95 per capita for 2013) and IRS Calendar Year Resident Population Estimates.

With the decline of IRB use, another public borrowing mechanism—TIF, or tax increment financing—has become a more important development tool at the disposal of local governments. TIF is a municipal bond issue based on the expected increase in property taxes that are collected by an economic development agency. It is often used for redevelopment, which is a special type of economic development that focuses on attacking problems in blighted areas (Chapter 10 will discuss this topic in detail). TIF is a financial mechanism to leverage anticipated future gains in taxes to subsidize current improvements, which are themselves projected to create the conditions for the expected gains. The completion of a redevelopment project often results in an increase in the value of the surrounding real estate, which leads to additional tax revenue. Such a "tax increment" within a specifically defined development area is dedicated to finance the debt that is issued to pay for the project.

Due to widespread abuse of TIF funding by local economic development agencies, TIF was discontinued in California, a state which began their use in 1952. Every other state except Arizona and Wyoming use TIF for economic development purposes.

Special Taxes (Earmarked for Development)

Local governments and special authorities are increasingly using specifically established taxes, often as surcharges designed to shift the burden of development from residents to visitors, for a particular economic development purpose. Such financial tools range from sales and hotel taxes, to sin or nuisance taxes.

Special sales taxes, often levied as a specifically designated percentage on top of the state sales tax, have been increasingly used for funding economic development. For example, all cities in Texas can impose a local economic development sales tax rate of not more than 2 percent through a development corporation. The State of Missouri allows citizens to authorize a supplemental sales tax of not more than 0.5 percent dedicated exclusively for certain economic development initiatives in their home municipality.

Given that tourism is a driving factor in economic development, a local Hotel Occupancy Tax (HOT) or Transient Occupancy Tax (TOT) is considered a legitimate way to fund programs that encourage tourism or economic development. A city or a county can impose a HOT by passage of an ordinance or by adopting an order or resolution, but they are subject to legislative caps. For example, cities in Texas with populations of less than 35,000 can impose a HOT in their extraterritorial jurisdiction, but the combined city, county, and state hotel tax rate cannot exceed 15 percent. In California, HOTs generally range from 7 to 14 percent, and are largely used to advance tourism and economic development.

To finance public or quasi-public works such as sports stadiums, art museums, or municipal auditoriums, which often are taken as anchor projects to stimulate consumption and employment, local governments may impose sin or nuisance taxes in various forms. For example, the City of Cleveland in Ohio used sin taxes on alcohol and tobacco to fund the construction and renovation of three sports venues, which have generated both substantial revenues and jobs.

Other Financial Devices

In addition to all other financial resources, the local government *general fund* (other than tax breaks, which are reductions from the general fund) can be an important funding source for economic development. General funds provide the resources necessary to sustain day-to-day activities and thus pay for all administrative and operating expenses of government. The general funds of local governments are similar to a firm's general ledger account, which records all assets and liabilities of the entity that are not assigned to a special purpose.

Besides funding the administrative and operating costs of local economic development agencies, a general fund may serve as the ultimate guarantor of investments to reduce the risk of, and therefore get better rates for, municipal bonds. It may also provide insurance programs, such as flood insurance in coastal areas. A general fund can also provide improvements and services that promote development, such as new roads and other infrastructure, or special programs such as training and education, which can assist business. Seed money, one-time grants for development, revolving funds, or the loan of property for charitable purposes can all be financial devices accessed by means of a general fund. However, in recent decades, as entrenched fiscal stress became epidemic, governments have become more reluctant to use monies in their general fund for economic development.

Global and national economic development trends have created challenges for both governments and businesses. In recognition of the limitations of traditional economic development efforts, governments have been aggressively and innovatively seeking new mechanisms. Since the 1980s, governments at all levels have increased their usage of *public–private partnerships* (PPP or P3) to introduce private investment to economic development, especially in public infrastructure and facility projects. PPPs, sometimes referred to as public–private venture, are contractual arrangements between public- and private-sector entities, typically involving a government agency contracting with a business or nonprofit entity to renovate, construct, operate, maintain, and/or manage a facility or system, in whole or in part, that provides a public service. In such a contractual arrangement, the private-sector partner usually makes a substantial cash, at-risk, equity investment in the project, while the public-sector partner gains access to a new revenue stream or service delivery capacity without having to make substantial capital investment. The private partner obtains a steady return on investment from tolls, user charges, performance-based fees, related real estate development, or other revenues. It is typical under such an arrangement for the government agency to retain ownership of the public facility or system while each party shares in income resulting from the partnership. PPPs have increasingly been used in both developed and developing countries worldwide to encourage economic development, especially to build and manage critical public transportation projects, ports, railways, airports, utility infrastructures, schools, hospitals, and other facilities and services. Chapter 10 will offer more discussion about this financial tool.

In addition to seeking private investment, other new mechanisms have also been explored. For example, beginning in the 1980s, the State of Oregon has earmarked lottery revenues for economic development. As of today, 25 percent of Oregon's lottery funds are allocated for job creation and economic development, providing assistance for a variety of Oregon's industries such as manufacturing, high-tech, agriculture, fisheries, solar, medical, tourism, and small businesses. Other states have tapped their public employee pension funds to offer small public venture capital programs, either with private venture capital firms or through direct venture investments. For example, the State of Massachusetts allows public pension funds to be invested in any opportunities that will benefit the economic climate of the Commonwealth as a whole. In 2013, the State of Wisconsin had a heated debate about whether or not to use the state pension fund to pay for economic development initiatives.

Federal Resources

Despite the fact that federal funding for economic development has declined from its peak in the late 1970s, a broad range of federal agencies operate grant programs in support of local development. These agencies include the Department of Commerce, the Small Business Administration (SBA), the Department of the Treasury, the Department of Labor (DOL), the Department of Agriculture (USDA), the Department of Health and Human Services, and the Internal Revenue Service (IRS). The agencies typically operate economic development programs indirectly via the provision of grants and other funding to state and local governments and nonprofit entities, which, in turn, provide economic development for businesses through direct financial and advisory support, or through the improvement of infrastructure. This section discusses several current major funding sources for states and localities.

One of the oldest federal economic development programs, the *Community Development Block Grant* (CDBG), passed in 1974 and designated to the Department of Housing and Urban Development (HUD), has long been a major federal source of economic development funds. In 2020, the funding allocation was $3.4 billion. It provides annual grants to states and local governments (usually economic development agencies) to develop decent housing and suitable living environments, and to expand economic opportunities, primarily for low- or moderate-income families. Local communities can borrow against future CDBG grants through Section 108 (a loan guarantee program from HUD) for economic development, housing rehabilitation, public facilities, and large-scale development projects.

Established in 1994, the *Community Development Financial Institutions Fund* (the CDFI Fund) is a program within the Department of the Treasury. The CDFI Fund seeks to channel investment dollars into distressed communities by providing federal funds in the form of equity, loans, grants, and deposits to community development corporations, banks, and credit unions. These organizations, known as CDFIs, all have a common mission of both working toward revitalizing economically depressed communities or communities underserved by mainstream financial institutions, and of improving the quality of life for those who live and work in these communities.

Under the Department of Commerce's National Institute for Standards and Technology, the *Technology Innovation Program* (TIP) is a grant program that encourages government and business partners to cost share the early-stage development of innovative but high-risk technologies. The *Manufacturing Extension Partnership* (MEP) program was established to meet a critical national need, namely, to assist small and mid-sized manufacturers create and retain jobs, and enhance productivity and competitiveness through process improvements and innovation.

To improve the social and economic well-being of people, the Department of Health & Human Services (HHS) offers a number of programs. The *Compassion Capital Fund* (CCF), provided by the Administration for Children and Families, is designed to support charitable organizations who serve disadvantaged social groups such as the homeless, elders in need, at-risk youth, previous addicts or prisoners, families in transition from welfare to work, and those in need of skills and knowledge to form and sustain healthy marriages. Designed to introduce faith-based initiatives to the federal funding process, CCF also extends its services to include job training, counseling, economic development, and entrepreneurialism. The *Job Opportunities for Low-Income Individuals* (JOLI) by the Office of Community Services provides grants to nonprofit organizations that address the economic needs of low-income individuals and families through the creation of sustainable business development and employment opportunities.

Non-Financial Tools for Economic Development

In addition to financial tools, local governments also use a variety of non-financial mechanisms for economic development.

Planning

Planning is the management process of thinking about and organizing resources and activities in order to achieve a desired outcome. Many of the desired outcomes for local economic development include more and better jobs, increased investment and income, increased social welfare, and so on.

The planning process attempts to involve the critical stakeholders of the local community to establish the vision for development, to engage in public discussions, and to reach consensus on goals to be achieved as well as plans in general.

The process often affects the entire environment of the community and involves a multitude of actors. Local governments, commonly represented by the economic development planning committee, may charge an economic development corporation or a similar organization with the job of helping develop city, county, or regional plans. Local economic development agencies also frequently play a critical role in organizing the process. Other institutions such as chambers of commerce, business associations, citizen or community groups, workforce development agencies, and labor organizations often participate in the process.

The planning process may start with targeting the program's geographic scope and gathering relevant information about the area, such as its economic base, current employment structure, existing problems, and so on. With comprehensive analysis, planning organizations may select a broad strategy to resolve the issues as well as specific projects that implement the strategy. Once the projects are determined, planners start to build action plans to implement the projects, specify project details, establish monitoring or evaluation mechanisms, and eventually launch the project. The planning for economic development in local communities can be carried out independently, yet more often than not it is integrated with other public planning, such as environmental, land use, transportation, regional, or urban and spatial planning.

Zoning

Zoning refers to the system of land-use regulation (see Chapter 3), which involves the practice of designating permitted use of land based on mapped zones separating one set of land uses from another. See Exhibit 9.4 for a simple example of city zoning. Zoning may include regulation of the kinds of activities acceptable on particular lots (such as open space, residential, agricultural, commercial, or industrial), the densities at which those activities can be performed (from low-density housing such as single-family homes to high-density such as high-rise apartment buildings), the height of buildings, the amount of space structures may occupy, the location of a building on the lot (setbacks), the proportions of the types of space on a lot (e.g., how much landscaped space and how much paved space), and how much parking must be provided.

Zoning policy is often implemented to promote economic development. Through zoning, government can set aside a sufficient amount of land for industrial or commercial use. Government can also promote development by allowing flexible zones and rules in the zoning code. For example, incentive zoning is often used to circumvent strict site regulations to provide a reward-based system to encourage development that leads to desirable outcomes. Typically, the method establishes a base level of limitations and a reward scale to obtain public benefits in exchange for certain land uses and project features.

Eminent Domain

Eminent domain refers to the inherent power of government to seize a private property or an individual's rights to property with due monetary compensation, but without the owner's consent. In the United States, the Fifth Amendment of the Constitution provides that "private property shall not be taken for public use without just compensation." This power was given to the states through the 14th Amendment, and in turn, the states, through their own constitutions and legislation may delegate this privilege to local governments. Therefore, governments at all levels have the right to seize private property without the owner's consent, but they must justify that their taking is for public use as required by the Fifth Amendment.

The private property is taken either for government use or by delegation to third parties who will devote it to public use or, in many cases, economic development.

Exhibit 9.4

A zoning map, City of Inkster, Michigan

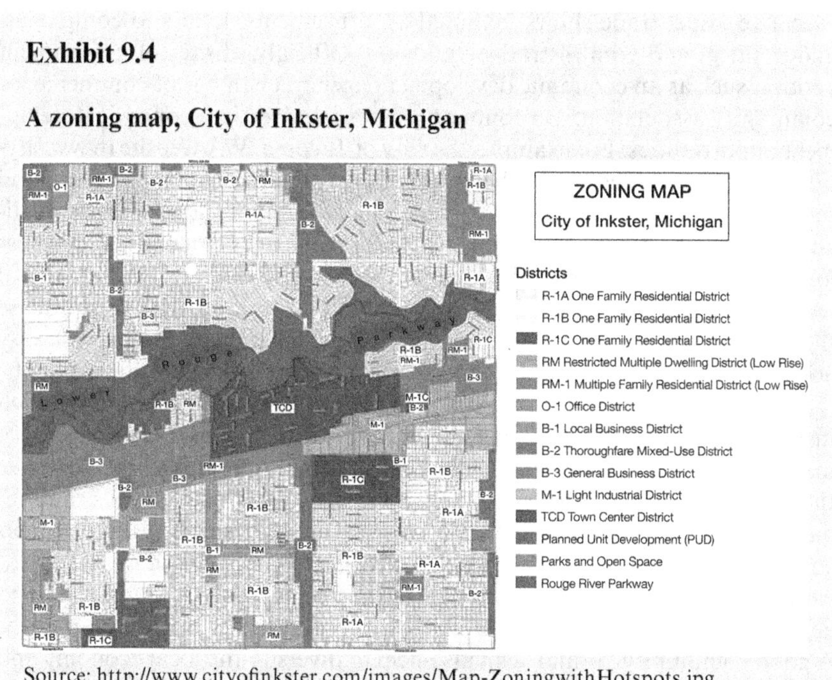

Source: http://www.cityofinkster.com/images/Map-ZoningwithHotspots.jpg.

Governments often need to assemble land in their jurisdictions for economic development purposes. For assembling large, contiguous lots of land for large-scale economic development projects, governments have to rely to a large degree on the power of eminent domain to acquire the necessary properties, which can be then redeveloped in a way consistent with the project requirements.

Eminent domain can be a controversial tool for economic development, and sometimes homeowners are able to hold out, as is visually illustrated in Exhibit 9.5. Another example of the challenges is provided in the case of the Disney theme park development at Anaheim (see Exhibit 9.6).

As local governments aggressively compete against each other to attract new businesses, the use of eminent domain to assemble land for development purposes is becoming more prevalent. Local governments often view those public takings as an opportunity to attract new businesses, create jobs, eliminate blight, and increase the tax base and renown of their jurisdiction. However, many citizens view eminent domain as state infringement of private rights. It is especially contested when property is taken from one private owner and transferred to another for private gain.

Marketing

Marketing is not just for businesses selling their products and services, but also for government to promote their jurisdictions as prime locations for business. Government marketing includes websites, special events, corporate executive visits, trade shows, national advertisements, letters to companies, and political and administrative "junkets." Official websites of government entities, such as an economic development agency, chamber of commerce, or community association, are common venues to advertise economic development opportunities. For example, the City of Tacoma, WA website (www.cityoftacoma.org/business) publishes a wide range of development programs and services information for business, which include choosing a location, available properties, starting a business in Tacoma, business incentives, business loan program, neighborhood business district program, etc. At the federal level, SelectUSA (http://selectusa.commerce.gov/) was created to showcase the United States as the world's premier business location and to provide easy access to federal-level programs and services related to business investment.

Many communities also engage in strategic marketing planning, which involves systematically assessing the opportunities and barriers and setting marketing goals and priorities for local economic development. To make them the top of the list for visitors, new residents, and new business and industry, local communities realize that they need to stand out from their competition. When a locality is able to differentiate itself, showcase its local assets and strengths, and present unique opportunities, businesses and consumers are more likely to be attracted to and invest in the community. A good community "brand" can also help to diversify the local economy and enhance the quality of day-to-day life for the entire region. For instance, in recognition of the city's large concentration of pure, fresh water, the City of Milwaukee, WI aggressively marketed itself as the "Freshwater Hub of the World" to attract freshwater research and water-technology companies that focus on water energy, agriculture, and other technologies.

Exhibit 9.5

Eminent domain: a holdout

Source: en.wikipedia.org.

Exhibit 9.6

Disney Theme Park in Anaheim

Source: Wikimedia Commons. Disney Annaheim.

In January 1990, the Disney Company announced its plan to build a new theme park in either the City of Anaheim or the City of Long Beach. In the late 1980s, the US—and especially the State of California—was experiencing a big drop in employment. At the beginning of the 1990s, the economy started to pick up. However, Orange County, among other counties, was lagging behind. Given the economic climate, the local government could not afford to lose any opportunities for development. This project would bring both jobs and income into a county that was desperately in need of an economic upswing.

On December 12, 1991, Disney declared that as a result of environmental legal challenges to their proposed park in Long Beach, they would not pursue the Long Beach project, and would instead concentrate on the Anaheim project.

Anaheim and Disney sealed a deal for "Westcot," a theme park projected to cost $3 billion. Westcot was projected to include a 5,000-seat amphitheater, shopping district, hotels inside and outside the park, and two of the nation's largest parking garages. Additionally, the theme park was expected to have an international theme wherein visitors would travel through miniature versions of the Americas, Europe, Africa, and Asia. The park would also implant a vision of the future to explore the marvels of science and nature.

A year after Disney's formal announcement that it intended to pursue the Anaheim Westcot project, the city released its Environmental Impact Report (EIR) of the project. The intended project area would affect several school districts and many privately owned properties. The EIR projected increases in traffic, pollution, noise, and classroom crowding. After six months of considering the EIR, the Anaheim City Council announced it would nonetheless approve the new Disney resort and would implement eminent domain despite potential objections.

Following the city's approval of the Westcot project, five school districts and two groups of private individuals filed suits against the City of Anaheim. The suits alleged that the city did not adequately consider the EIR and that the city's proposed use of its eminent domain power to obtain property for Disney was improper. By September 15, 1993, Disney had settled with the five school districts with tutoring programs, a junior press corporation, a junior orchestra, medical vans for immunizations and health screenings, and a scholastic honors society. Disney also settled with both of the private groups so that it could proceed with park development. However, by that time it had been decided to change the theme of the new resort from an international one (and thus the cancellation of Westcot) to a California-based theme, eventually called Disney's California Adventure.

Source: The case was revised based on Baker, T. D. (1994)

Ombudsman

A business ombudsman is another service, often provided by government agencies, for helping firms to navigate the various government regulations, programs, and services. The ombudsman's services may also include resolving problems and complaints for businesses, investigating commercial opportunities, helping to identify and evaluate options, and recommending changes in policies or procedures for a positive effect. The Department of Commerce provides ombudsman services to firms or economic development organizations on a case-by-case basis to address issues or questions involving federal regulations, programs, or activities related to existing, pending, and potential investments. Many localities offer their economic development staff to assist new businesses and developers by serving as a project partner during all phases of due diligence and development.

The scope of economic development encompasses a wide spectrum of government policies and actions including the overall national policy framework to enhance market stability and suitable growth, the provision of infrastructure and services, and policies and practices to enhance employment, increase tax base, and improve people's level of living. Local economic development practices have been influenced by a variety of growth and development theories upon which government has developed and utilized a wide range of strategies and techniques to attract business investment and encourage and sustain economic growth. These strategies and tools well illustrate government's influence on business. Smart business practitioners should be well informed about these tactics and tools and strategically explore them to achieve a solid business purpose. Yet, ethical and responsible business persons should also be aware of the economic and political implications embedded in each of the tools, as well as their potential impact to stakeholders.

Analytical Case: California's Enterprise Zone Program

Enterprise zones are areas established by government in which special policies are implemented to encourage economic growth and development. Enterprise zone policies generally offer tax concessions, infrastructure incentives, and reduced regulations to attract investments and private companies into the zones. The philosophy of the enterprise zone is associated with the theory of supply-side economics and the assumption that investors and employers will respond positively to tax incentives and reduced government regulation.

In the United States, enterprise zones are often proposed to stimulate economic activity in distressed areas. As compared to other places, these areas have higher unemployment rates, lower income levels, lower employment opportunities, vacant land, and decayed buildings and infrastructure. Enterprise zone programs provide the incentives to businesses to overcome economic obstacles that hinder economic growth.

Until recently, the State of California had four types of Geographically Targeted Economic Development Areas. These areas were:

- *Enterprise Zone (EZ).* Forty-two EZs had been authorized by the state legislature, targeting economically distressed areas throughout California since the 1980s.
- *Local Agency Military Base Recovery Area (Lambra).* Lambras were developed to attract reinvestment and create re-employment opportunities on certain former military bases in California.
- *Manufacturing Enhancement Area (MEA).* The program focused on stimulating job creation in the border region.
- *Targeted Tax Area (TTA).* TTA offered incentives that were only available to companies located in the area and engaged in a

special trade or business, such as food processing, trucking and warehousing, air transportation, etc.

Each of these areas had related tax incentive benefits as well as a variety of locally provided incentives and benefits. The purpose of these tax incentives was to stimulate business investment and job creation for qualified disadvantaged individuals in state-designated economically distressed areas. The enterprise zone areas in California were generally fast-growing areas with foreign-born populations and high rates of unemployment. Zone residents had lower incomes and more welfare dependency.

Despite the incentives and benefits, the existing zone programs were found to have produced very modest economic benefits in California. Zone and program area incentives and resources provided little job creation and business investment. Part of the problem was the severe lack of resources to support enterprise zone and program activities. The net effect of various credits was modest and did not overcome myriad other more important influences on business investment and location decisions, including the advantages of location, the costs of land and appropriately skilled labor, the costs and availability of financing, and the costs of compliance with federal, state, and local permitting and regulatory requirements. California's zone programs simply did not offset the many negative economic factors (real and perceived), affecting zone and program area businesses. In addition to the modest benefits, zone programs were also found to have grown over time to include some of the state's wealthiest places, with much of the tax benefit going to firms in San Francisco.

To correct the issue, the state legislature approved Governor Brown's proposal to end the state's tax breaks in zone areas, which cost California nearly $700 million in 2010 (Vara 2013). The Governor instead proposed a new statewide business incentive program designed to benefit those businesses in depressed areas that pay workers relatively high wages (Sola and Ha 2013). Program credits were also proposed to focus more on neighborhoods and cities with especially high unemployment and poverty rates, though businesses in the current enterprise zones could still benefit from them. Businesses in manufacturing, biotech, and some other industries would qualify for tax breaks for buying machinery.

Questions for Discussion and Analysis

1 What are the factors that led to the modest economic impact of California's former enterprise zone programs?

2 Do you agree with Governor Brown's reform of the program? Why or why not?

Practical Skill

Leveraging Government Resources

Governments, including federal, state, and local governments, are major grantors to business. Each year, billions of dollars in grant funds are distributed to those who know how to find them and submit well-written grant proposals. Your road map to creating your own success story starts with learning the facts about government grants. Government grants are neither personal/business loans, nor are they financial aid of any kind. They are not intended for personal benefit, nor are they required to be paid back. Most grants are awarded to universities, researchers, cities, states, counties, and nonprofit organizations, but many businesses (especially small businesses with certain industry standards) may also qualify. Such grants give small business owners the opportunity to start and expand a business and create new technologies and services that help them compete in the global market.

Find a Grant

To receive a government grant, you must apply as an individual or organization with the intent of generating benefit to the public.

A useful website is www.grants.gov, which is managed by the Department of Health and Human Services. The website posts most government grant opportunities and provides access to grants from other endowments and foundations. You can search for grants by keyword, category, or agency.

The All American Grant Guide (www.allamericangrantguide.com) is another very useful website for learning about and finding a grant. The website also offers a step-by-step guided process for grant application.

State and municipal grant applications are available by going to your state website and searching under grants. For example, the State of California lists various grant opportunities at www.ca.gov/grants.html. Similarly, you can also search for local government resources. As an example, the City of Los Angeles creates an incentive finder for local businesses (www.losangelesworks.org/businessServices/incentive-finder.cfm), as well as a website for seeking government loan assistance (http://ida.lacity.org/).

Meet the Criteria

In order to win the grant, your business or project needs to adhere to the grant's specific requirements. Eligibility will differ based on the type of grant you pursue. Read the specific requirements insisted on by the grant provider, who needs to know that you can deliver on your commitment as the grant's recipient.

Apply

The application process can be complex and lengthy. Thanks to the WWW, nowadays most government grants can be applied for at their funder's website. Each funder has its own requirements and criteria that should be followed carefully. Be sure to complete the entire grant application and attach supporting documentation requested by the funder. Most grant applications can be submitted electronically. Some funders require both an electronic copy and a hard copy be mailed to them. It is a good idea to apply for multiple grant opportunities. Since there is no guarantee that you are going to get a grant—and no limit to the number for which you can apply—the more you apply for, the better your chances of getting funding for your small business.

Skill Exercise: Apply for incentive programs

Suppose Happy Paws is located in your area and Zoey is asking for your help. Based on what you have learned in this class, try to search various federal, state, and local government sources for potential grant, loan, or tax incentives that Zoey's business may be qualified to receive. Develop a list of such opportunities and their requirements and advise Zoey how to proceed.

Summary and Conclusion

1 Both government and business are interested in economic growth and development. While economic growth is the increase in the amount of the goods and services produced by an economy over time, economic development refers to the concerted efforts of government, business,

and communities to promote economic growth, as well as the overall economic and social well-being of people in a specific area.

2 Classic economic growth theory provided the basis for the development of many theories on economic development. In alignment with free market economics, neoclassical economic theory opposes government intervention and views development as a natural expansion of an economy. A variety of location-based theories seek to explain an area's competitiveness in terms of a firm's locational orientation as well as factors that produce local economic growth.
3 Theories provide guidance to practice. Government generally uses three strategies, namely industrial recruitment, entrepreneurial strategy, and privatization, to encourage economic development.
4 To pursue their economic development strategies, governments have implemented a variety of financial methods which include tax reduction, public borrowing, special taxes, and resources from the federal government, general funds, and public–private partnerships.
5 Non-financial tools for economic development include planning, zoning, eminent domain, marketing, and ombudsman services. Each of these tools and methods has its own economic and political implications that demand ethical and responsible consideration.
6 Business students should learn to explore government resources to advance their business goals.

Key Terms

- Central place theory
- Growth pole theory
- Tax abatement
- Cluster theory
- Industrial recruitment
- Tax credit
- Economic base theory
- Industrial revenue
- Tax exemption
- Economic development
- Bond
- Tax increment
- Economic growth
- Location theory
- Financing
- Eminent domain
- Neoclassical economic
- Zoning
- Entrepreneurial strategies
- Privatization

Study Questions

1 What are the differences between economic growth and economic development? How are these two concepts connected?
2 What are the major economic development theories? What insights does each of them offer to the practices of economic development?
3 If you are a retail business owner, what are the factors that will affect your business location choice?
4 What are the different financial and non-financial methods government uses for economic development?

5 What is eminent domain? What are the implications of using eminent domain for economic development?

Notes

1 State of California Board of Equalization, Property Tax Rules, Rule 133. Business Inventory Exemption, p. 1. http://www.boe.ca.gov/proptaxes/pdf/rule133.pdf, accessed August 21, 2013.

2 More information about the IDA bond for ColorGraphics can be found at http://ida.lacity.org/.

References

Alyea, P. E. (1967). Property Tax Inducements to Attract Industry, in R.W. Lindholm (ed.), *Property Taxation USA* (pp. 139–158). Madison: The University of Wisconsin Press.

Baker, T. D. (1994). Public Use, Private Taking and Economic Growth or Disney's Latest E(minent Domain)-Ticket. *Western State University Law Review*, 21: 547–561.

Bradshaw, T. K., and Blakely, E. J. (1979). *Rural Communities in Advanced Industrial Society*. New York: Praeger.

Dalehite, E. G., Mikesell, J. L., and Zorn, C. K. (2005). Variations in Property Tax Abatement Programs among States. *Economic Development Quarterly*, *19*:157–173.

IMF, World Economic Outlook Database. https://www.imf.org/en/Publications/SPROLLs/world-economic-outlook-databases#sort=%40imfdate%20descending.

IRS. https://www.irs.gov/publications/p334#en_US_2021_publink1000313491.

Myrdal, G. (1957). *Economic Theory and Underdeveloped Regions*. London: Duckworth.

Perroux, F. (1983). *A New Concept of Development*. Paris: UNESCO/Université du Paris IX.

Porter, M. E. (1990). *The Competitive Advantage of Nations*. New York: The Free Press.

Sen, A. (1983). Development: Which Way Now? *Economic Journal*, *93*(*372*):745–762.

Sola, M., and Ha, Y. (2013). California Eliminating "Wasteful" Enterprise Zones. *San Francisco Public Press*, July 1. http://sfpublicpress.org/news/2013-07/california-eliminating-wasteful-enterprise-zones, accessed July 5, 2013.

State of New Jersey (2010). *A Programmatic Examination of Municipal Tax Abatements*. Office of the State Comptroller. http://www.nj.gov/comptroller/news/docs/tax_abatement_report.pdf, accessed August 21, 2013.

Statistica based on US Bureau of Commerce. https://www.statista.com/statistics/188165/annual-gdp-growth-of-the-united-states-since-1990/.

Vara, V. (2013). Governor Rethinks Enterprise Zones. *Wall Street Journal*, June 30. http://online.wsj.com/article/SB10001424127887323998604578565673282015746.html, accessed July 5, 2013.

Wassmer, R. W. (2007). The Increasing Use of Property Tax Abatement as a Means of Promoting Sub-national Economic Activity in the United States. *Social Science Research Network*. http://papers.ssrn.com/sol3/papers.cfm?abstract_id=1088482, accessed August 21, 2013.

World Factbook (2021). https://www.cia.gov/the-world-factbook/.

Wikimedia Commons. Disney Annaheim. Horst Frank. https://commons.wikimedia.org/wiki/User:Horst_Frank~commonswiki/Gallery.

10 Industrial Recruitment

Chapter Contents

Case 10 Scenario

ABC's Bargaining

Previously we learned that Zach's father Zeddic, CEO of Acme Bottling (Chapter 2), was considering moving the company, a large operation of 800 employees. His profit margin was becoming too squeezed for things to remain as they were, and any technical improvements, including shedding some employees, would not be sufficient for the profitability he wanted to achieve. When he approached the city administration about getting a rent reduction, he was graciously brushed aside with the argument that his rent was already low, given the prime

DOI: 10.4324/9781003178620-13

location and the upgrades the city had provided in the past. By negotiating with a city that was trying to lure his company, his financial analysis discovered that he could reduce production costs by an enormous amount—a figure approaching 20 percent. Zeddic knew the first logical step was to discuss the decision to move with the board, which was keen on increasing profitability.

Still, Zeddic had not anticipated the torrent of reactions that he had gotten in the press, ranging from anger in the community, to a sense of betrayal from his family, whom he had not yet consulted and who would also need to relocate. In hindsight, Zeddic now realizes his focus on financial matters had led him to ignore political and community realities. However, he is now trying to rectify the situation. Initially, everyone in Somewhere blamed Zeddic for threatening to abandon the city that they felt had nurtured and helped launch his successful company. Zeddic has his work cut out for him. He needs to change that perception to one in which Somewhere has, over time, come to neglect his company. And he needs to show that the neglect will have to change—and quickly—if the company is not to move.

Using talking points from a report he prepared, he points out the following issues:

- The rent the company pays in the city-owned industrial park has doubled. The company is now too large to be in that industrial park, and cannot afford to make changes to infrastructure on a property it does not own.
- The city has given three- to five-year tax abatements to most substantial startups. ABC has never gotten a tax abatement.
- Several new companies were sold city land at a price far below market value. The appearance is that his industry is no longer a priority for the city, and relocating the company to a more hospitable town only makes sense, as matters currently stand.

The Mayor set up a special meeting with Zeddic. His team suggests the rent can be reduced by 50 percent. Zeddic thanks the Mayor and his team, but points out that the company really needs the security of owning its land and that the other city's offer is still financially more attractive. Meanwhile, Zeddic also meets with the people trying to recruit his company, and explains why there must be a delay in the negotiations. He is surprised when they offer to provide a ten-year lease-to-own contract at the same cost.

Going back to the City of Somewhere, Zeddic tells them he will only stay if the contract is converted to a lease-to-own. His city is initially shocked at the demand; however, the Mayor and all but one member of the council agree to change the contract to a five-year lease-to-own at the same lower rate. Knowing that Zeddic is serious, they also offer to provide a five-year tax abatement on the land after transfer, an extremely low tax rate after expiration of the tax abatement, and to make appropriate changes in the industrial park to make it self-sufficient. The city, it appears, does indeed want to keep the company right where it is, and understands the ramifications of losing a large employer.

Zeddic and his board agree to remain in the City of Somewhere. Zeddic calls his wife Zelda to tell her that she doesn't have to worry about leaving her teaching job, or moving the kids to a new school district. Zelda is thrilled and calls Zach on his lunch break. Zach thinks about calling Zoey, but he has a better idea. He jumps in his car and drives over to Splurge Jewelry.

Introduction

Macroeconomic theories such as classical economics (Smith 1776; Ricardo 1817) and neoclassical economics (Veblen 1900; Friedman 1953) describe and prescribe how overall *global* economies work. They do not describe how countries or regions should be successful, other than to be efficient in production and strategic about comparative advantage. Early mercantile economics in sixteenth- and seventeenth-century Europe, neo-mercantile economics (state corporatist economics particularly prominent in rapidly expanding Asian countries), and demand-side economics (Keynes 1936) describe how *countries* can try to foster better conditions for their competitive advantage. Strategies here usually involve national-level tariff policy, tax policies favoring specific industries, government acting as a countercyclical economic stabilizer, governments insuring that the elements for comparative and strategic advantage like transportation, infrastructure, and education are present, and so on. Theory at this level provides insight into the pros and cons of using broad, and rather blunt, instruments to reduce the radical spikes in the economic cycle or to modestly adjust the competitive playing field while trying not to excessively warp free market conditions to appease local special interests or cause international retaliation.

Location theory, what is now commonly called *cluster theory* (Porter 1990), and municipal-level entrepreneurialism move that discussion of competitiveness to the *regional and local level*. Cluster theory is the focus of this chapter; municipal entrepreneurialism is the focus of the next. See Exhibit 10.1 for an illustration of the differing economic theoretical thrusts.

Exhibit 10.1

The focus of various economic theories

Level of Focus	*Economic Theories that Address the Focus*
Global	• Classical economics
• Neoclassical economics (supply side)	
• Marxist economics	
Country	• Mercantile economics
• Neo-mercantile economics (state corporatism)	
• Demand-side economics (Keynesian)	
• Dependency theory economics	
Regional	• Cluster (location) economics
• Municipal entrepreneurism	

Cluster Theory

As stated earlier, clusters are geographic concentrations of interconnected companies, specialized suppliers, firms in related industries, and associated institutions in a particular field that compete but also cooperate. *Geographic concentration* means that these clusters have physical proximity. *Interconnected* means that there is an important synergy among groups such that the whole is more than the parts. In clusters everyone cooperates, even those competing for the same customer base, because of the incentive to entice a greater market share for the region or area, and because resources are better when shared. Porter's theory (1998) represented a new way of thinking about location, basing linkages and complementarities across industries and institutions, and escaping more rigid industrial or political classification systems.

Clusters affect competition in three broad ways. First, *clusters increase the productivity* of companies in the area. They draw more customers to the area. People know that a street, neighborhood, city, or region has a concentration of good products at competitive prices. Four or five locally owned restaurants in a tourist town may do better than isolated restaurants because of the street's reputation for food and choice. Clusters force companies to offer either high-quality, low-cost, or specialized products/services because of the compactness of competition. They must know their comparative advantage to other nearby companies or go out of business. Think of how new- and used-car dealers frequently co-locate, so that many people simply go the area, and visit two or more dealerships simultaneously.

Second, *clusters drive the direction and pace of innovation*, which underpins future productive growth. In clusters, competitors are always looking for an edge that leads to innovation. Because of proximity in clusters, new ideas are quickly transferred (copied) and refined or reinvented, leading to further innovation. The fashion industry (e.g., Milan, New York, Paris, Rome, London, and Los Angeles) is known and notorious for this process, as witnessed by the "creative theft" from high-end couture to rack designers, and the evolving decision of a "season color" by the fashion elite.

Third, *clusters stimulate the formation of new business*, which expands and strengthens the cluster itself. Because of the reputation and vitality of clusters, they tend to draw in not only more customers, but also new businesses. Of course occasionally companies go out of business for various reasons (often including higher rents), but this merely opens up opportunities for new businesses. Some new businesses may not even be in competition with others in the current cluster because they bring new supplies into the area, or will bring a related but different product to the array than is currently offered.

Let's use a wine-growing region as a specific example. Wineries tend to co-locate. Suppliers become local to provide equipment such as bottles, barrels, corks, labels, grape stock, and technology. Local governments and educational institutions tend to find ways to support the success of the cluster. Tourists flock to the area for wine tastings in relatively close proximity, bulk purchasers come to find vintages suitable to their needs, and local restaurants flourish, specializing in wine selections.

Exhibit 10.2

Wine clusters in California

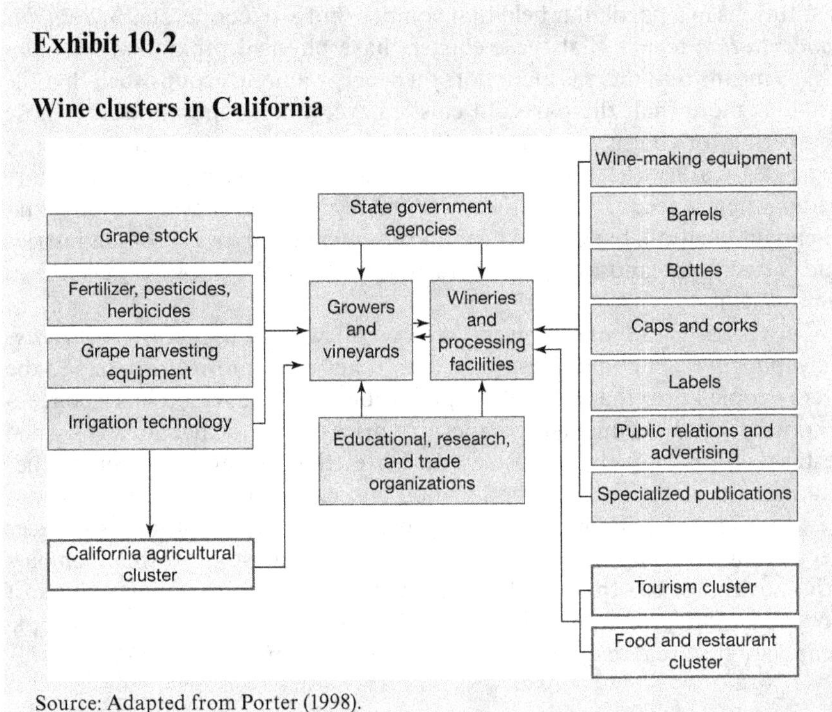

Source: Adapted from Porter (1998).

In California, there are five major regions, but the wine growers inevitably tend to co-locate their official wineries in specific cities or towns. Wine sales from California were $40 billion in 2020, down 3.5 billion due to the pandemic and extensive fires (Wine Institute 2021). The state accounts for about 10 percent of world production. Exhibit 10.2 shows us where these clusters generally occur.

So why do clusters work? There are a number of reasons, including:

- Clusters bring together a pool of resources—workers, suppliers, related services—that provide depth, security, and choices/diversity.
- Locality enhances cooperation, since most cluster participants are not direct competitors but rather serve different segments of industries.
- They provide local competition that gives fast feedback on innovations, trends, price, and quality.
- Ironically, entry into a cluster is initially easier because there is great demand for new workers and new ideas.
- Clusters facilitate niche specialization that cannot normally be sustained outside of clusters.
- Clusters bring together sophisticated local customers who know the state of the art and give tough feedback that provides the opportunity to become best-in-class.

This means that clusters tend to be very valuable to the areas that have them. They stimulate the economy with natural diversification. Clusters are not a single company or industry but a group of organizations that have a synergy and a related set of products. They provide renown. Clusters are very good at what they do and get positive reputations. They provide local wealth, and with more local ownership, more money stays in the community. Generally, clusters provide more high-paying jobs. Because they tend to be at the productivity frontier and doing large volume, clusters customarily can afford to pay for the best workers.

Based on these factors, economists have been able to determine clusters mathematically (Mayer 2005), with average wages 10 percent higher than the national average and a higher growth rate as well. The formation is:

- Location quotient > 1.25
  where
  ei = local employment in industry
  ie = total local employment
  Ei = national employment in industry i
  E = total national employment (if the *LQ* > 1, the local share of employment in a particular industry exceeds the national share of employment in the same industry → locally the industry is more concentrated).
- Average wages at least 10 percent above national average.
- Growth rate > national growth rate.

What is the role of the government in cluster development? A major role is "facilitating cluster development and upgrading" because of the increases in productivity and salary (Porter 1990). "Governments should reinforce and build on established and emerging clusters rather than attempt to create entirely new ones." Government should help all firms, generally. However, government must not attempt to set policies that help individual firms, distorting the market (in line with macroeconomic principles). Therefore, government should promote competition and invite distant/foreign partners. To do its part, government can:

- Remove obstacles, relax constraints.
- Support resources such as necessary infrastructure.
- Support human capital development such as education and training programs.
- Assist export promotion.
- Encourage local R&D efforts.
- Sponsor forums to bring cluster participants together.
- Encourage industrial parks.
- Sponsor independent testing or certification if it is useful.

So from a practical perspective, location does matter, to both external investors and local stakeholders. From the external perspective, investors want to consider the mix of factors as they consider the comparative advantages of different areas. From a local perspective, areas must ensure that they have enhanced local or regional factors if they want to be competitive. These factors include many in which government plays a huge role, from general and specialized educational programs, to infrastructure, quality of life, and so on. Those areas that are particularly successful will have one or more major regional cluster of industries that will provide a competitive advantage leading to a good reputation, higher salaries, and economic dynamism. Our final example in this respect is Silicon Valley in Exhibit 10.3.

Exhibit 10.3

Silicon Valley and its roots in community and the government

The original Silicon Valley area is just south of San Francisco, encompassing the Santa Clara Valley and cities such as San Jose, Cupertino, Los Altos, Palo Alto, Santa Clara, and Sunnyvale. Today, Silicon Valley is considered to encompass San Francisco, Santa Cruz, and parts of Alameda, and it includes the highest concentration of billionaires in the world. The list of tech companies that have primary and secondary offices in this cluster reads like a who's who: Adobe Systems, Apple, Cisco, eBay, Facebook, Google, Hewlett-Packard, Intel, National Semiconductor, NetApp, Netflix, Oracle, and Yahoo! Over 4,000 IT-related firms are found along Highway 101 from San Jose to San Francisco, and this number jumps considerably when neighboring counties are included. It accounts for one third of all the venture capital in the US. The cluster includes both hardware and software invention, Internet utilization research, semiconductors, high-end IT manufacturing, and military research. A quarter million well-paid IT workers support this cluster. Innumerable specialized industries also support this area, such as legal firms, which are the best in the world at IT copyright, infringement, and licensing. This cluster has been so successful that its name—Silicon Valley—has become synonymous with the concept of a high-tech area.

How did this cluster evolve, in an area that was agricultural at the end of World War II? The single most important factor was the massive role played by Stanford University. First, Stanford's leadership was aggressive in fostering its students to found companies such as Hewlett-Packard and Litton Industries in the 1940s and 1950s. The second step was Stanford's industrial park, created in 1951, which housed the likes of Eastman Kodak, General Electric, Lockheed, Hewlett-Packard, and Varian Associates. Stanford University supplied world-class engineers as well as helped to solicit enormous amounts of venture capital as the area was beginning to take off. Government funding was tremendously important in the early years for the basic research that it subsidized. Government also promoted innovation by creating an almost complete ban on non-compete clauses in employment agreements, which helped foster startups.

Next, we need to consider two important aspects that business people must be knowledgeable about when considering investing and expansion decisions. First, what is the political context of local economic development, and second, what are the concrete bargaining positions that are likely to have the most leverage?

Political Context of Local Economic Development

While growth is largely popular in the US, it is a mistake to think that types of growth or interest in growth is unchanging; quite the contrary is true.

Neighborhoods, cities, and entire regions take on very different macro-level perceptions about the nature of growth that is good. Local preferences can range from "any growth at any cost," all the way to "fighting all growth at any cost." Even when growth is considered desirable, the reasons may lead to very different variations. This section looks at three models of growth. The first is the *pro-growth model*, which *is strongly in favor of economic development*. The second is the *slow- and no-growth model*. It *emphasizes the problems associated with growth*. The final model is the *smart growth*, which *seeks to find a sensible balance* between the pro- and anti-growth adherents *through good planning, and awareness of community interests and environmental interests*. While individuals within an area may have differing views, here we focus on the community consensus, which becomes embedded in local codes, ordinances, economic development strategies, and public relations.

Pro-Growth Model

Local economic development through growth (here thought of as land improvements) has many benefits. It potentially brings an inflow of capital and resources, job growth, quality-of-life improvements, and opportunities to build community infrastructure. It can also be used to fight urban and rural decay or simply to bring back areas to their former glory, aka gentrification.

A pro-growth model is a coalition interested in the development and re development of land. Undeveloped (unused or raw) land in the pro-growth model should be developed for highest present value, and land for redevelopment is often brought together with government financial subsidies and, if necessary, power (i.e., eminent domain). Pro-growth, therefore, is interested in raising the aggregate value of land by increasing the overall development of land or the intensification of its use. Land intensification means converting farm and open space to residential and commercial, or lower-class-housing high rises or "high-class" commercial. Growth can occur in many ways. In cities and towns it may be by in-fill projects that have not previously been improved, adding suburban or exurban housing/commercial areas at the edge of cities, or redeveloping land already in use for residential, commercial, or manufacturing purposes. In rural areas, growth may be new tracts of housing, industrial complexes or parks, building up commerce along major roads (arterials), or redeveloping rundown areas for new use.

A special but important class of cases related to pro-growth as redevelopment is to reduce "blight." There are many aspects to blight including:

- A concentration of buildings that are in serious decay or unsafe and that often have serious building code violations.
- Poor real estate values, high vacancy rates, and numerous abandoned buildings and lots.
- Land-use patterns that reduce incentives for renovations or new development because of an excess of bars, liquor stores, or other businesses

that cater exclusively to adults, and that tend to encourage public safety problems.

- Absence of neighborhood grocery stores and businesses that support residents.
- High crime rates.
- Residential overcrowding.

While the role of government is relatively important in economic development, in the case of blighted areas, it is essential because of the need for community support, land acquisition, subsidies, and zoning changes.

The composition of pro-growth adherents is usually made up of land developers, investors, residents interested in increased land values for their homes or with public flagship projects nearby, and local governments interested in greater property and sales taxes. The underlying philosophy, therefore, is very much in line with commercial capitalism. The power base of the growth model tends to be wealthy developers and those with community connections, those underwriting political candidates, and those with public visibility who speak of the future as growth oriented.

When there is a powerful and successful pro-growth group that dominates the policy, administrative, and business agendas, it is often called a "growth machine." A true growth machine includes:

- Large public entrepreneurs connected to the community.
- A generally supportive public.
- A strong support base in government (especially the city council or board of supervisors).

For example, in a city, the growth machine may be a coalition of local businesses wanting expanded population, land developers seeking business opportunities, and a majority of the city council. Those players come together to pursue an agenda of urban growth and intensification of land use. When cities are experiencing rapid growth over a sustained period of time, especially during economic expansions, it is inevitably because of the presence of a growth machine. In fact, as we shall discuss in the next model, it is concern that the growth machine is focusing on short-term profits and tax revenues, rather than sustainability or adequate planning for economic slowdowns or recessions, that leads to substantial critique. Rapid and relatively unrestrained growth is called the "boom model." A balanced economic development model focuses on following comprehensive plans, restraining zoning ordinances for all but the most well-considered cases, and ensuring that infrastructure and other costs are fully included in the planning approval process. Indeed, in an ideal world, cities and counties would be countercyclical in their restrictions and fees, increasing them in the good times to restrain growth and relaxing them in bad times to encourage it. However, political and economic realities make this nearly impossible to achieve.

A Slow- and No-Growth Model

The *slow-growth model* is supported by coalitions of groups interested in slowing or stopping various types of development because the effects of fast growth are considered too negative. Negative effects of growth can include sprawl, traffic congestion, environmental degradation, insufficient infrastructure, excessive cost shifting to current taxpayers for development projects, and degradation of existing communities by downgrading current use, among others. The boom model of growth is particularly worrying to slow-growth advocates, who often believe in a "small is beautiful" philosophy and question unrestrained growth on ideological as well as pragmatic grounds (Schumacher 1973). At a local level, they are concerned that the growth frenzy of boom development will overwhelm government's capacity to regulate and monitor bad effects, ruin quality of life because of loss of open space, and that local business will be squeezed out by corporate interests in the rush to develop. At a grander level, they argue that the limits of healthy growth in the world and the US have already been exceeded (e.g., today in the US, there are about 335 million people, which is expected to increase to 440 million by 2050).

Sprawl, broadly defined, refers to the lax use of land. In this sense it is "the process in which the spread of development across the landscape far outpaces population growth" (Ewing, Pendall, and Chen 2002). The National Trust for Historic Preservation calls sprawl "poorly planned, low-density, auto-oriented development that spreads out from the center communities." A more technical and operationalized definition is that sprawl creates a pattern of land use in an urban area that exhibits low levels of some combination of eight distinct dimensions of land use—density, continuity, concentration, clustering, centrality, nuclearity, mixed use, and proximity (Cutsinger and Galster 2006). Traditional urban sprawl, which spreads out from the city center, is one of the most common, but it is not the only type; there is also low-density sprawl, commercial strip sprawl, and scatter (aka leapfrog) sprawl, seen in Exhibit 10.4.

Sprawl is also used as the umbrella term for a wide number of negative effects related to poor planning and careless regulation. Some of those side effects are more cars, less public transit, more traffic fatalities, poor air quality, aesthetic ugliness and strip malls, duplication of infrastructure which leads to lack of sustainability, environmental degradation, and cost shifting of development to current taxpayers. In the US, the search for the "American Dream" came to be defined in the 1950s as living in the suburbs. People would commute to the city for work, and drive to the grocery store, cleaners, department store, dentist, and schools in separate trips by car. However, soon the commute times became very long, pollution caused by cars became an enormous health and aesthetic problem, and the many inner suburbs deteriorated. Of course, today, sprawl is a world-wide problem, even in countries that have been more proactive in limiting it historically (Wang, Shi, and Zhou 2020). Exhibit 10.4 illustrates some of the negative results of sprawl.

Exhibit 10.4

Types of sprawl

Traditional urban sprawl: LA

(a)

Source: Wikimedia Commons (2014).

Commercial strip sprawl

(c)

Source: Wikimedia Commons (2021).

Scattered sprawl

(b)

Wikimedia Commons (2013a).

Low-density sprawl

(d)

Source: Wikimedia Commons. U.S. Fish and Wildlife (2013).

Sprawling development is extremely costly to maintain from a public sector perspective because of the extensive per person upkeep of roads, water, sewers, other utilities, and services requiring rapid response times (police, medical). Additionally, small and less affluent families may find the upkeep of sprawling suburban homes costly, beyond their means and energy.

The *no-growth model* is a specialized case which is created by a coalition interested in stopping all growth to the degree possible. No-growth models tend to be promulgated in fully built-out areas, especially when they are historical districts and areas undergoing gentrification, in which modern and mass structures are not wanted. Although not common in the US, there is also tremendous interest in preserving agricultural and open space in Europe and Japan where there is a greater sense of the community's right to preserve land use for future generations. While fertile agricultural land in the US has

Exhibit 10.5

Negative effects of sprawl

Smog problem in Beijing

(a)

Source: Wikimedia Commons (2013b).

Example of modern traffic congestion

(b)

Source: Wikimedia Commons (2012).

Ghettoization of inner suburbs

(c)

Source: Wikimedia Commons (2020).

suffered enormous losses, the preservation of land for uniqueness and open space through federal, state, and municipal parks, monuments, forests, and wetlands has been extensive since started by President Grant (with Yellowstone) and popularized by President Teddy Roosevelt. The preservation has been far more extensive in the Midwest and Western US.

Example of Extensive Open Space Preservation in the Western US

California's National and State Parks

- 118 state parks.
- 8 state forests.

- 9 state recreation areas.
- 11 state wildlife areas.
- 5 state historic sites.
- 1 state nature preserve.
- 11 state reserves.
- 9 state fish hatcheries.
- 9 national parks.
- 19 national forests.
- 3 national historic sites.
- 1 national seashore.
- 31 national wildlife refuges.

The composition of slow-growth coalitions is made up of:

- Residents who fear that their area will be neglected, degraded, or are offended by the "ugliness factor" or excessive arterial commercial strip development.
- Commercial interest groups who feel that the new growth will unfairly compete with local businesses, especially those worried about the vitality of town and small city centers.
- Environmentalists who fear the loss of farmland, open spaces, wildlife preserves, natural ecosystems, and land-air-water degradation by profligate land use.
- Taxpayers who feel that excessive or inefficient subsidies are being used to support development, or that public entities will bear excessive costs over time.
- Local governments whose land is all largely in use and whose values are already relatively high.

The base for slow growth, then, becomes concerned voters/taxpayers, passionate rather than commercial leaders, and activist community associations (e.g., neighborhood associations). Zoning becomes highly restricted, building and renovation guidelines are detailed and demanding, community input into new development is upheld, and development fees are high. While this applies to a lot of upper-middle-class communities that are largely built out, it is nearly ubiquitous in exclusive cities like Beverly Hills, CA, Lake Forest, IL, Darien, CT, Saratoga, CA, Mercer Island, WA, Naples, FL, and Brookline, MA.

It should also be noted that the lines of pro-growth, slow growth, and no growth are not always clear. For example, hypothetically, we can imagine an urban advocate who represents a poor neighborhood that needs jobs and wants to encourage businesses to relocate downtown and who generally takes a pro-growth position. However, when the advocate learns of a stadium project that would demolish part of the neighborhood, sporadically increase congestion, and bring few jobs, he might become vehemently slow growth. Or coming from the other end of the financial spectrum, a wealthy developer may spend an enormous amount of money and time getting land rezoned from open space to residential, and getting zoning variances to allow high rises and commercial exemptions downtown. However, when a high-rise condominium complex is proposed in his extremely affluent residential community, the developer may become outraged and personally appear at the planning board meeting (where he is well known) to oppose the development project.

Smart Growth: A Rational Compromise?

Smart growth is a public–private approach to managing growth, which emphasizes growth through careful planning. It promotes a balance among the profit of individuals, community goals, and social equity such as environmental concerns—as well as long-term sustainability. It emphasizes special growth patterns, including substantial amounts of high-density, mixed/integrated use, and transportation fluidity. A definition of smart growth is "an urban planning and transportation theory that concentrates growth in the center of a city to avoid urban sprawl; and advocates compact, transit-oriented, walkable, bicycle-friendly land use, including mixed-use development with a range of housing choices" (Daniels 2001) (Exhibit 10.6). It has been followed in Europe for many decades and is considered to have been largely, and often spectacularly, successful in that context (EU Commission 2010).

Exhibit 10.6

Typical bike garage in a downtown European City

Source: Wikimedia Commons (2008).

The record for smart growth in the US has been more mixed with the challenges of getting Americans to adopt smaller cars, adopt urban centers with greater density to support better public transit utilization, and use more bikes, among other measures.

The recommended practices of smart growth include:

- High-density, mixed land use.
- Strong use of planning with clustered development and protection of agricultural and open space (such as the use of "urban growth boundaries").
- Full costing and implementation of infrastructure at beginning of construction.
- Integration of affordable housing and social equity concerns.
- Traffic grids allowing for alternative routes.
- More emphasis on non-automotive means including pedestrian walkways and bike paths.
- Narrower streets.

About two thirds of the states either have legislation in place or have a strong coalition that encourages municipalities to adopt smart growth at their level. An example is California, which has sought to strengthen planning. First, in 1963, it created the Local Agency Formation Commission (LAFCO) to oversee city incorporations, annexations, and creation of special districts. A part of this was the requirement for comprehensive planning by established cities. The Cortese–Knox Local Government Reorganization Act of 1985 consolidated three separate local government statutes governing growth issues to rationalize and coordinate them. This was strengthened in 2000 by the Cortese–Knox–Hertzberg Local Government Reorganization Act which required counties to consult with affected cities prior to approving any development or land-use change within a sphere of influence. Currently, the State's Commission for Local Governance for the twenty-first century sets out five principles for California's growth, including:

- The requirement for regional perspectives.
- The requirement for greater efficiency of land use.
- Greater public investment.
- Fiscal reform.
- Adherence to equity considerations.

An example of an Eastern state that encourages smart growth is Maryland, which in 1997 passed the Neighborhood Conservation and Smart Growth Act. The principles of that Act were:

- To limit low-density development and strip malls.
- To encourage pedestrian and bike paths as well as transit ridership.
- Stronger regional planning with state review.
- A job creation tax credit for priority areas.
- Subsidies for workers in older neighborhoods.

Smart growth is not without its critics. Smart growth as a strategy urges a compact city and reduction of dependency on the automobile. Since Americans love their space and cars, the immediate reaction has often been negative. At the extremes, between large cities with massive sprawl and more compact cities, the more compact cities have largely been proven to reduce travel distances, commute times, pollution, and other negative effects, as well as provide more alternatives (Newman and Kenworthy 1989). However, in the middle and smaller range, the data have been less conclusive because public transit may be less practical and intensive. Critics also argue that where space is available, as it is on a relative basis in the US compared to Europe and eastern Asia, why not use it? Further, critics argue that the market is a better regulator than planning experts. They also assert that the argument that sprawl creates greater public expense in the long-term for municipalities is largely a myth (Cox and Utt 2004). Thus, while poor or absence of planning certainly leads to problems within several decades, the formula for what is good planning is far from exact. Smart growth has worked well in some American settings, but not in all. However, it has provided a useful alternative to the "big is beautiful" perspective, which has allowed for a more careful analysis of options, rather than just building more freeways and noise walls.

Industrial Recruitment

Industrial recruitment is a locational approach by which governments subsidize businesses to lure more investment into their jurisdictions or to prevent indigenous firms from leaving. This approach focuses on creating locational incentives for both existing and enteral enterprises by lowering their production factor costs. Under this approach, government uses various economic development tools, including tax and financial incentives as well as land use and public infrastructure improvement, to encourage private investment, expecting that public subsidies on the capital and operating costs of private firms will produce sufficient economic growth to offset the expenditures.

The strategy is often understood as a product of competitive federalism, which assumes that the diversity of services offered by state and local governments creates a market for public goods. The use of industrial recruitment always results in competition among state and local governments.

Industrial recruitment is generally a case-by-case approach, by which government negotiates with individual firms about the incentive programs in order to attract them from outside or to prevent them from leaving their jurisdictions. The programs offered by government may vary case by case, based on a series of economic, political, and institutional conditions. Both government and business can leverage their resources to enhance their bargaining position in a recruitment negotiation.

The Factors Determining the Bargaining Positions of Business

Government sets up standard business conditions through laws and ordinances and by implementing up taxing, zoning, and service provision procedures that apply across the board to all businesses. But what if business wants "special" conditions and has a lot to offer a governmental area? For example, what does a state, city, and/or county do if the issue is the location of a new headquarters (high-paying jobs), factory (jobs, taxes in future), stores (especially Big Box stores for sales tax revenue), or sports stadium (providing national recognition, tourism)? For prized commercial enterprises, business frequently sets up competition among state and/or local governments who, in turn, offer special packages. Let's look at reasons why government may be interested in such opportunities.

Although government tries to deal with all business in the same general way, when larger commercial ventures arise, there are strong reasons to adjust local requirements. The standard reasons include new jobs (of any kind), high-quality jobs, a broader tax base, a particular profile of business that fits into the community's current or desired profile, and/or positive public relations.

For its part, what business hopes to achieve are one or more of the following goals:

- Free land or cheap land.
- Multi-year tax breaks.
- Various types of direct and indirect cash outlays, including governmental investments, loan guarantees, subsidized loans, etc.
- Zoning variances (e.g., from height and architectural requirements).
- Assistance with land assembly.
- Costly infrastructure improvements such as sewer and lighting to the curb or building, road alterations (installation of stop lights, sidewalks, lighting, landscaping), and special services provided, such as education.

Ultimately, there are three major factors that affect the bargaining relationship and the amount of leverage that a business has: the *market conditions*, the *political conditions*, and the *planning system* (Kantor and Savitch 1993). Market conditions involve the circumstances or forces that make cities more or less appealing to private investors in terms of demand for land, location, amenities, etc. The political conditions are the party and citizen activism through which public sector decisions affect development; that is, what is the ability of business to influence government policy through political rather than economic means? Finally, there is the planning system that determines the degree to which various governments work in concert with one another when bargaining with business.

Market Conditions

A variety of factors give business a stronger hand in bargaining when market conditions are right. One of the most important is the level of need, and sometimes desperation, of the local government for the jobs and tax revenues of a potential business enterprise. This may be because the area is attractive to the enterprise but the jurisdiction is not economically diversified or that the area has liabilities due to its location, workforce, or infrastructure. A second favorable factor for business is when its capital and/or resources are moveable and flexible, and not tied to a particular location. Finally, business also has an advantage when there are other highly attractive locations for the business to consider. For example, a company with a lot of jobs that is struggling in the market may have leverage because of the fear of job loss to a city or location if the company has the profile that another jurisdiction is looking for.

The contrary conditions are poor for business. When a jurisdiction is well off, it has far less incentive to accommodate business. For example, communities that are considered to be fashionable addresses are less likely to bargain. When companies already have sunk costs into the area, they are less likely to be given new advantages, unless the case for expansion or relocation is extremely strong. The threat to move a manufacturing plant that is doing well is difficult to sustain. Finally, when a business needs to be located in a certain jurisdiction to get to its customers, business has considerably less latitude to negotiate or expect special considerations.

Political Conditions

Political conditions can have a large impact on the willingness of government to bargain and the leverage of business to take advantage of such opportunities. When voters are not paying attention, business has more opportunity to strike deals with politicians and administrators. This may lead to a healthy opportunity for entrepreneurialism, or it may lead to reduced thoroughness or even graft, but the result nonetheless gives business a smaller group to satisfy. Thus, low party competition is good for business, no matter the party in power. Also, outright citizen apathy leaves business freer to strike favorable deals. Sometimes voters are more aware, but public opinion is strongly in favor of business inducements to particular industries such as a sports stadium, or voters simply perceive the need for jobs as paramount because of recessionary conditions.

Political conditions become negative when there is an active citizen base that scrutinizes all government deals, even those deals that may seem advantageous at first glance. Also, when there is a lot of political competition between parties, or among local candidates, bargains with business may be heavily scrutinized for competitive political advantage. Being on record as supporting a set of business accommodations may come back to haunt a politician when the project stalls, goes over budget, a scandal emerges, or the company fails. In other cases, politicians and administrators may be hungry for the tax revenues that a business would bring in, but may also be wary because the business is considered a low-wage provider that sends its profits outside the community, ultimately hurting locally owned businesses.

Planning System

A business's leverage is much enhanced when government is not tightly organized. In the US, which has a federal system, local governments have a good deal of autonomy, and that creates considerable zoning variation as well as a lot of competition among jurisdictions. In many cases, businesses can play local governments off one another to increase their advantage. For example, if a developer has two good locations for a new shopping center that are close to the border of two adjacent cities, the developer will have enormous leverage in procuring tax abatements, zoning variances, and the like. In Europe, where unitary states predominate, such leverage is minimal because laws and rules are national or regional. Another important factor is the strength of the planning culture. Densely populated and relatively affluent areas tend to have far more comprehensive and strict zoning ordinances (strong planning cultures) than do loosely populated and less affluent areas.

Under certain conditions, the planning system can be made more robust and less advantageous to business for bargaining. When states pass statewide planning regulations, it reduces the maneuverability of business somewhat. When cities incorporate adjacent land and expand their borders, they have less likelihood of small-scale competitive bidding. When responses to major site locations are handled by a central body such as a regional council of government, the likelihood of a reasoned bid is stronger. States can also pass anti-poaching laws, making it more difficult for companies to locate close by primarily to gain governmental concessions.

Example of Bargaining Success

Riverside, CA, is a city by the Santa Ana River that realized its initial fortune with the creation of the orange industry in the 1870s. During that time, a fine hotel was built and eventually renamed the Mission Inn in 1903, the same year President Theodore Roosevelt stayed there. Over the years, ten presidents have stayed at the hotel, which was under nearly constant expansion from the turn of the century until the death of the original owner, Frank Miller, in 1935. The eccentric hotelier embedded a 500-year-old church into the building, vast thematic courtyards, one of the best bell collections in the world, and other world-class features including turrets, flying buttresses, Tiffany stained-glass windows, and catacombs. However, by the time of Miller's death, the facility was already starting to see some decline as the Great Depression settled in. It was sold by the family in 1956.

To prevent its further decline, the hotel was purchased by the Riverside Redevelopment Agency in 1976, a time at which there was even talk of tearing down the building. It was converted to apartments and eventually student housing for a while. In 1985, the city worked with a developer to renovate-to-own the National Historic Property. The $30 million project bankrupted the developer when the bank refused to extend the loan, so the property stayed with the city and the bank. After a series of attempts, and additional renovations, the city sold the property to Duane Roberts in 1990 for little more than the cost of completing the renovations, already three quarters done. Although not a hotelier by training, Roberts was a wealthy local businessman who had a personal passion for saving the landmark that he had revered since his childhood.

On December 30, 1992, the Mission Inn reopened to the public. It became an immediate success, and helped revive the downtown area, which was ailing, as so many downtowns were at that time. Today, the hotel is booming and co-hosts with the city the Festival of Lights, seen in Exhibit 10.7, an annual holiday light display with over 4 million lights and 150,000 visitors during southern California's enviably warm winter season.

The case of the Mission Inn illustrates the mutual challenges in bargaining. The city had to take over the historic property so that it would not be torn down, but that meant that the city was in a poor bargaining position if it wanted to sell it, since the rise of Las Vegas and Palm Springs had decimated its high-end clientele. Politically, the city initially held out for a good deal, and got one, but the company that offered the bid did not go through the process. When the second interim owner failed to complete the renovations and the sunk costs of the project became enormous, political opposition to any reasonable offer evaporated. The local control over the planning system meant the city could make whatever variances the business owner needed, and could even get historical landmark waivers. Ultimately, the new owner got a terrific deal on a world-class property, which he successfully manages to this day. Although the city struggled through a series of deals and subsidized the project over several decades, Riverside has ultimately done extremely well with the income from hotel taxes, visitor traffic to local businesses, and the events and widespread recognition that the hotel has provided in becoming a point of destination.

Example of Bargaining Excess

A well-known case of successful bargaining by business occurred in 1989 when United Airlines announced that it was creating a new maintenance hub that would employ 7,000 people and would result in hundreds of millions in new investment. It was to be a 24-hour, state-of-the-art facility for complex "heavy" maintenance on single-aisle Boeing and Airbus jets (Kantor and Savitch 1993). Ninety localities investigated the option, with Denver offering $115 million in cash and incentives and Oklahoma City offering $120 million relatively early

Exhibit 10.7

Festival of lights in Riverside, CA

Source: Wikimedia Commons (2000).

in the process. The competition was so fierce that United Airlines then made the bids secret and delayed the decision so the competition could play out. Ultimately, the lucky city was Indianapolis, a city eager to bring high-end mechanics jobs to the area. The full project finally cost $540 million, with the city and state putting up approximately $300 million, which was financed by bonds. In addition, United was never charged real estate taxes on the property, which is built on airport land (Adams 2003). The facility opened in 1994.

In this case, we see all the bargaining advantages being in the hands of the business, and we see business using them to its full advantage. The market conditions were such that Midwestern cities were extremely eager to get high-end blue-collar jobs to replace old manufacturing and agricultural jobs. The company had the advantage that it could place the facility anywhere in the country, where financial conditions were opportune. The political conditions were favorable because there was consent among all parties and individuals that this was a good project to seek; the only question was how much to put on the bargaining table in order to win the bid. The fragmented planning system in the US not only encouraged cities to try to undercut one another, but to get their respective states to add resources to their war chests in the battle to get the final contract. As can be seen here, the winning city had to pay the bulk of the project costs as well as provide a long-term subsidy in terms of full tax abatement and low rent.

Sadly, the plans did not work out as well for Indianapolis as it hoped. At its height, the facility employed fewer than 3,000, rather than the expected 7,500 employees. The rent of $700,000 was a fraction of the cost of the bond repayment at $14 million a year. When United Airlines declared Chapter 11 bankruptcy in 2002, it announced that it would be closing the facility of 1,400 in Indianapolis, and moving some maintenance to San Francisco and privatizing the rest. The facility officially closed in 2003, with United being able to renege on its bond obligations due to bankruptcy restructuring; the city, of course, could not. While the city and its airport now fully own the massive maintenance facility and they rent out parts of it, it will likely always be vastly underutilized, employing hundreds rather than thousands, and be a financial drain.

Although most cases of private–public bargaining result in win-win scenarios, as we saw in the Mission Inn case in Riverside, there are enough Indianapolis Maintenance Centers to make governments far more leery than they were in the heyday of big projects (from the 1970s to the early 2000s). The deals that many jurisdictions have made to get new manufacturing plants, sports stadiums, headquarters, and other flagship commercial projects have often left them sorry to have won. While the Boeing case is the epitome of business cleverly using its leverage, it is a profound cautionary tale for government and its bargaining agents.

How Government Should Protect the Public Interest

As the example of the Riverside Mission Inn illustrates, government can provide enormous support for the community. In this chapter, we focus on the role of government when it steps in to prevent economic decline and foster economic revitalization. The next chapter will look at when cities and counties take proactive stances to reshape their futures in ways that seem more like the corporate expansion associated with blue-chip companies. We have also seen how governmental economic development can go awry, sometimes dreadfully so, if policy-makers and planners do not follow rational planning principles appropriate for the public sector. Some of the principles include:

1 *Create a clear project plan.* This is common sense, but is often overlooked in the heat of a sudden opportunity. As importantly, make sure that the project plan fits in with the long-term comprehensive plan. The City of Indianapolis ran after the gigantic maintenance hub operation, offering double the resources of most other reasonable offers. Like a gambler without a limit, they got sucked into the bargaining process further and further, only to find that their fate was tied to a single business that continued to maintain an alternative location for flexibility. When the time came, the business exploited that flexibility, but the city was stuck without good contingency options. While retail location decisions are often little affected by the city incentives they secure (Lewis and Barbour 1999), the subsidies can become substantial and cumulative for the

cities that depend on them. Further, once tax breaks are made, other businesses apply pressure for the same treatment. What is a small gain for individual businesses can become a major "run on the bank" for local governments.

2 *Reduce incentives for dysfunctional competition among governments.* While the US federal system cannot reduce interstate competition, states can reduce local competition that provides unnecessary subsidies for highly profitable businesses that relocate in an effort to avoid basic taxes and to get government subsidies. Such tax manipulation requires residential taxes to be higher, and general government services—everything from street-sweeping to police protection to park maintenance—to be less financially supported (Williams 2007).
3 *Allow regional authorities a larger share in major initiatives.* When governments in a region cooperate on major business opportunities, such as sharing tax revenues from new business close to each other's borders, all can benefit. This takes a level of trust and cooperation that is difficult to achieve, but when successful, it means that businesses must provide their "fair share" of community support for the services they use and for the community from which they earn their profits.
4 *Depoliticize the process when contracts and bidding are in motion.* Political discussions and public debate are good during the comprehensive planning process, but can be dysfunctional during the bidding process, when focus and confidentiality are required.
5 *Ensure administrative competence.* First-class talent is necessary for success in any business venture, and the promotion and protection of civic economic development is no exception. A challenge is that for many large-scale projects, expertise is hard to come by without retaining external consultants. Poor administrators will either fail to attract business, or make poor deals that give away more than is necessary.
6 *Know who you are dealing with.* Companies and individuals have histories and reputations that provide less than a prediction but more than a hunch about what to expect. Do the people whom the government is dealing with have a reputation of high integrity or low trustworthiness, for being highly competent or sporadic, dependable or fair weather?
7 *Eliminate and revise an outdated economic development policy.* Economic conditions are dynamic, and so, too, should be one's economic development policy. States and localities that fail to keep their economic development policies up to date may find that decades later these policies create many unintended consequences, such as building up enormous coalitions because a dysfunctional policy has aggressive supporters who benefit from it. Proposition 13 in California is a case in point. It was designed to force local governments to become leaner and more accountable, which it did for a time. In the long term, it meant that long-time homeowners and most businesses paid a smaller and smaller portion of the tax base, starving local governments including schools, especially those located in older and poorer areas.

The Strategies that Business Can Use to Increase Its Success in Bargaining with Government

This chapter has highlighted the knowledge and skills that smart business people should be able to demonstrate:

- Know and appreciate the growth model of the targeted area. Has the area adopted policies that are pro-growth, slow growth, or smart growth? How can that be integrated into a business plan usefully? How can that awareness be highlighted for local decision-makers?
- Know the local factors affecting business advantages and disadvantages in bargaining. What are the favorable and unfavorable market conditions, political factors, and planning factors? Are any of these factors likely to shift in the near or middle term, and if so, what will the effect be? For example, where in the business cycle is the project now, and what effect will the inevitable expansion or contraction have?
- Related to both the community philosophy and status of bargaining leverage, determine strategic trade-offs and win-win prospects. Know what benefits are possible, most useful, and what can be offered to the city because it is easy to do so, or less important for success. This helps you craft a plan sensitive to local preferences, while protecting your own business interests.
- Spend the time necessary to meet and get to know the local players. Those players include political and administrative leaders, other business leaders, and even critics such as competitors, slow-growth cynics, or NIMBY (i.e., not-in-my-back-yard) activists. As was pointed out in Chapter 7, lobbying is to business–government relations what marketing is to the mass customer base. Yet in this chapter we also focus on the fact that many of these contracts rely on long-term cooperation, so that personal knowledge of local players and politics is also an advantage in business execution and operations later.
- Integrate a CRS perspective into the planning process as both an ethical necessity and pragmatic advantage. As stated in Chapter 6, corporate responsibility is the right thing to practice for not only ethical reasons, but for pragmatic ones as well. Identify the possible ethical issues and conundrums. Think through how to prevent appropriate cleverness and strong-willed negotiation from becoming deviousness, manipulation, or bullying that may later have negative consequences. Decide what possible community contributions might add to the business plan, while providing positive public relations.
- Be prepared to adapt the plan. Almost all projects, large and small, have numerous adjustments along the way. Good project managers will know this and be ready to adapt to changing conditions.

Analytical Case: Winter Park

In a quest for private capital, cities often compete with one another for sports franchises, tourism, transportation hubs, federal grants, and foreign trade. In order to realize mutual benefits, achieve common goals, and reach agreement, government must engage in exchange relationships—bargaining—with business. Three factors tend to make a difference:

1 Market conditions, which are the circumstances or forces that make the local jurisdiction more or less appealing to private investors. Such conditions include both the innate features of the locality and the position of the locality as reflected in larger economic fluctuations (e.g., housing market down-turns). Cities with strong market positions have more influence over the capital investment process.
2 Political context, which refers to the political process through which public sector decisions can affect economic development. It includes the scope of public participation, the extent to which participation is organized, and the ability of the system to ensure the accountability of the process.
3 The planning context, which refers to the relationships and methods used by government to regulate the marketplace. The two factors most critical here are the incentives that governments can offer and the coordinating powers that governments have to reduce interjurisdictional rivalry. A government with centralized power, non-particularistic policies, and financial support has more influence over investment and is better able to regulate economic development.

The Case of Winter Park, Florida

Winter Park is one of 17 cities in Orange County, Florida, and has a population of 28,000. It is a very well-off, land-locked city with extremely little available land. The city has to rely on the county to acquire and ensemble land for a large economic development project, if there is any. Land in the county is available but no longer abundant. Cities within or outside the county are competing for businesses and development.

Winter Park is an old and well-known resort town in Central Florida (along with Orlando), founded as a seasonal destination by wealthy New England industrialists before the turn of the twentieth century. Winter Park is considered both a historical and fashionable address, uncommon to many parts of Central Florida. The city draws thousands of visitors to annual festivals, including the Bach Festival, the nationally ranked Sidewalk Art Festival, and the Winter Park Concours d'Elegance. Due to its heavy emphasis on the arts and its scenic charm, Winter Park has traditionally attracted an eclectic mix of residents—wealthy Northerners, patrons of the arts, Old Florida families, artists, students, vacationers, and idealists. The citizens in Winter Park are extremely active in managing the activities of the city. For example, displeased with the local electric utility, in a referendum election of September 9, 2003, the citizens voted overwhelmingly to exercise the buy-out option in the city's franchise agreement with Progress Energy Florida (a private utility company) and to have the city own and operate its own utility.

Questions for Discussion and Analysis

Using the three factors identified in this chapter, analyze the case of Winter Park. Mark how the bargaining condition is favorable to business or government and discuss why.

Factors	*Favorable to Business*	*Favorable to Government*
Market conditions		
Political context		
Planning context		

Practical Skill

Investigate the Bargaining Used by your City or County

Bargaining positions of cities and counties vary greatly, as do the types of incentive that they offer when they do bargain. Investigate your city to find out:

- The amount of bargaining that occurs.
- Who is empowered to do the bargaining for the city.
- The types of situations that trigger bargaining.
- The types of incentives that tend to be offered.

Summary and Conclusion

1 Whereas macroeconomic theories describe and prescribe how overall global economies work, location theory (i.e., cluster theory) discusses competitions at the regional and local level.
2 Clusters affect competition in three broad ways: they increase the productivity of companies in the area, encourage drive and direction and pace of innovation, and stimulate the formation of new business. Government plays a critical role in facilitating cluster development and upgrading existing clusters.
3 Local preferences of economic development range from "any growth at any cost" to "fighting all growth at any cost." The pro-growth model is strongly in favor of economic development. The slow- and no-growth models emphasize the problems associated with growth. The smart-growth model seeks to find a sensible balance between the two through good planning, and awareness of community interests and environmental interests.
4 Industrial recruitment is a locational approach of economic development. The use of industrial recruitment always results in competition among state and local government.
5 Both government and business can leverage their resources to enhance their bargaining position in a recruitment negotiation. Three major factors affect the bargaining relationship and the amount of leverage that a business has: the market conditions, the political conditions, and the planning system.
6 Policy-makers and planners should follow rational planning principles, which include creating a clear project plan, reducing incentives for dysfunctional competition among governments, allowing regional authorities a larger share in major initiatives, depoliticizing the contracting process, ensuring administrative competence, knowing who you are dealing with, and eliminating and revising an outdated economic development policy.
7 Smart business people should know and appreciate the growth model of the targeted area, understand the local factors affecting business's bargaining position, be able to determine strategic trade-offs and win-win prospects, and be willing to spend the time necessary to meet and get to know the local players.

Key Terms

- Classical economics
- Cluster theory
- Demand-side economics
- Industrial recruitment
- Marketing conditions for bargaining
- Mercantile economics
- Neoclassical economics

- No-growth model of economic development
- Planning system conditions for bargaining
- Political conditions for bargaining
- Pro-growth model of economic development
- Slow-growth model of economic development
- Smart-growth model of economic development
- Sprawl

Study Questions

1. Different economic theories have different areas on which they focus. Explain how neoclassical economics, Keynesian economics, and cluster theory have different perspectives on what they seek to explain and the prescriptions that they tend to provide.
2. How do clusters work? Provide an example.
3. What are the typical models of growth that cities and other communities tend to adopt in their ordinances and zoning policies?
4. What are the factors that enhance or restrict the ability of business to bargain with cities, counties, and even state governments?
5. What are some of the things that a local government should do to protect the public interest?
6. What are some of the things that a business should do to enhance its bargaining position while retaining long-term options and reputation?

References

Adams, M. (2003). United Plan Could Leave City Holding $100M Bag. *USA Today*, April 15.

Cox, W., and Utt, J. (2004). *The Costs of Sprawl Reconsidered: What the Data Really Show*. Heritage Foundation Backgrounder, *1770*, June 25.

Cutsinger, J., and Galster, G. (2006). There Is No Sprawl Syndrome: A New Typology of Metropolitan Land Use Patterns. *Urban Geography*, *27*(*3*):228–252.

Daniels, T. (2001). Smart Growth: A New American Approach to Regional Planning. *Planning Practice & Research*, *16*(*3*/*4*):271–279.

EU Commission (2010). *Europe 2020: A Strategy for Smart, Sustainable and Inclusive Growth*. Brussels: EU Commission.

Ewing, R., Pendall, R., and Chen, D. (2002). *Measuring Sprawl and Its Impact*. Washington, DC: Smart Growth America.

Friedman, M. (1953). *Essays in Positive Economics*. Chicago: University of Chicago.

Kantor, P., and Savitch, H. V. (1993). Can Politicians Bargain with Business? A Theoretical and Comparative Perspective on Urban Development. *Urban Affairs Quarterly*, *29*(*2*):230–255.

Keynes, J. M. (1936). *The General Theory of Employment, Interest and Money*. London: Palgrave Macmillan.

Lewis, P. G., and Barbour, E. (1999). *California Cities and the Local Sales Tax*. San Francisco: Public Policy Institute of California.

Mayer, H. (2005). Taking Root in the Silicon Forest: The Role of High Technology Firms as Surrogate Universities in Portland, Oregon. *Journal of the American Planning Association*, *71*(*3*):318–333.

Newman, P., and Kenworthy, J. (1989). *Cities and Automobile Dependence: An International Sourcebook*. Aldershot: Gower.

O'Toole, R. (2001). The Folly of "Smart Growth." *Regulation*, Fall:20–25.

Porter, M. E. (1990). *The Competitive Advantage of Nations*. London: Macmillan.

Porter, M. E. (1998). *Competitive Strategy: Techniques for Analyzing Industries and Competitors*. New York: Free Press.

Ricardo, D. (1817). *Principles of Political Economy and Taxation*. Cambridge: Cambridge University Press.

Saiz, M. (2001). Politics and Economic Development: Why Governments Adopt Different Strategies to Induce Economic Development. *Policy Studies Journal*, *29*(*2*):203–214.

Schumacher, E. F. (1973). *Small Is Beautiful: A Study of Economics as if People Mattered*. London: Blond and Briggs.

Smith, A. (1776). *The Wealth of Nations: An Inquiry into the Nature and Causes of the Wealth of Nations*. Glasgow: University of Glasgow.

Veblen, T. (1900). The Preconditions of Economic Science. *The Quarterly Journal of Economics*, *14*(*2*):240–269.

Wang, X., Shi, R., and Zhou, Y. (2020). Dynamics of Urban Sprawl and Sustainable Development in China. *Socio-Economic Planning Sciences*, *70*:100736.

Williams, B. (2007). *Allocating Local Sales Taxes: Issues and Options*. Sacramento: California Legislative Analyst's Office, January 12.

Wine Institute (2021). https://wineinstitute.org/our-industry/statistics/california-us-wine-sales/.

Wikimedia Commons. Inkknife. 2000. https://commons.wikimedia.org/wiki/File:Mission_Inn_Lights_12-13-141_(15834781930).jpg.

Wikimedia Commons (2008). Ester Inbar. https://commons.wikimedia.org/wiki/File:BikesZurich_ST_08.jpg.

Wikimedia Commons (2012). B137. https://commons.wikimedia.org/wiki/File:Miami_traffic_jam,_I-95_North_rush_hour.jpg.

Wikimedia Commons (2013a). Joadl. https://commons.wikimedia.org/wiki/File:Feldkirchen_Nordwestansicht_Flugaufnahme_141226a.jpg.

Wikimedia Commons (2013b). 螺钉. https://commons.wikimedia.org/wiki/File:Smog_in_Beijing_CBD.JPG.

Wikimedia Commons. U.S. Fish and Wildlife (2013) Service. https://commons.wikimedia.org/wiki/File:A_shot_is_taken_on_a_hill_showcasing_urban_development.jpg.

Wikimedia Commons (2014). Alfred Twu. https://upload.wikimedia.org/wikipedia/commons/6/66/South-Los-Angeles-110-and-105-freeways-Aerial-view-from-north-August-2014.jpg.

Wikimedia Commons (2020). Andre Carrotflower. https://commons.wikimedia.org/wiki/File:Franklin_Street,_Rivertown,_Detroit_-_20201215.jpg.

Wikimedia Commons (2021). hyolee2. https://commons.wikimedia.org/wiki/File:Aeon_Yatsushiro_Shopping_Center_2021.JPG.

11 Public Entrepreneurs and Privatization

Chapter Contents

Case 11 Scenario

Good Buddy E-Solutions Doing Business with Government

Tyler and Zoey have been good friends ever since their college days at Somewhere State several years ago. Tyler majored in computer engineering and Zoey, as we learned, graduated with a degree in entrepreneurial management. After graduation, Zoey started Happy Paws Pet Store in the City of Somewhere, and Tyler found work with a large IT company in the same industrial park where he had his part-time job, at Acme Bottling Company, where Zach's father was the CEO.

Soon after Happy Paws opened, Zoey expressed an interest in expanding to online sales for her pet shop. Her boyfriend Zach was

DOI: 10.4324/9781003178620-14

developing a line of organic pet products, Acme Bottling Company was already lined up to do the packaging, and Zach and Zoey wanted to test market the products soon, and perhaps even allow people to start pre-ordering. Tyler set up a webpage and Zoey and Tyler ironed out the kinks. Having gone through the whole process of dealing with government rules and regulations, Zoey was rather adept at weaving her way through any red tape they encountered. She was even able to give Tyler's father a few pointers when Trujillo Landscaping ran into a problem with government.

That sparked an idea. Along the way, Zoey and Tyler decided to join forces and start another potential money-making business—Good Buddy E-Solutions—to provide e-commerce solutions for businesses. They were able to get Good Buddy up and running rather quickly since there was no brick and mortar involved. In the beginning, it was pretty quiet, but things changed dramatically when Good Buddy successfully won a contract from and developed the e-commerce platform for a leading e-commerce company. Because of that success, and great reviews, Good Buddy has been steadily growing and has gained a regional reputation for e-commerce website services. Tyler has taken over most of the day-to-day running of Good Buddy E-Solutions while Zoey runs Happy Paws and Zach develops his product line. But they are always looking for new business opportunities.

Last week, a friend of Zach's who works for the city government told them that the city was planning to outsource their e-government website and has published an RFP (request for proposals). Despite the numerous website service companies that may submit a bid for the contract, Zach's friend said that the City of Somewhere was impressed with Good Buddy and they had a decent chance. The city prefers to use local vendors whenever it can. Though Good Buddy has never dealt with government clients before, Tyler and Zoey were excited and confident about the opportunity, which may open the door for another market. Good Buddy has won a number of business contracts, but they know that contracting with government may be different from contracting with a private company, as government procurement is often regulated closely to prevent fraud, waste, corruption, and favoritism. Both Zoey and Tyler feel it is critical to understand the rules and processes of government contracting. They decide to attend a few seminars and do some research before they attend the contract bid meeting where they and other potential applicants can ask detailed questions prior to formal submission.

Introduction

Both business and government have a shared interest in economic development, in which they interact frequently, while each pursues their different goals. Governments often frame long-term strategy, which is a collection of actions and activities that help them to achieve their goals. In the previous chapter we introduced location-based industrial recruitment, which involves subsidizing existing firms in order to induce them to relocate or prevent them from relocating, as popular government economic development strategies. Unfortunately, such strategies often lead to a huge waste of resources as jurisdictions race to the bottom to claim credit for subsidizing high-profile firms. A growing number of governments instead have become "entrepreneurial"—in other words, they adopt policies that promise to increase public revenue and focus on nurturing new firms, high technologies, growing industrial sectors, and other high-growth businesses. Some governments are even more innovative in embracing characteristics previously restricted to the private sector, and in partnering with business for economic development. In addition, many policy-makers, especially free-market economists, believe that the less government involvement there is in the business realm, the more it will lead to a raised level of competitiveness, and therefore, higher productivity and more overall economic growth. Under such an ideology, privatization, especially deregulation, has been pursued as a way to induce economic development. Privatization goes beyond deregulation; in reality, other forms of privatization, though not necessarily targeting economic development directly, create opportunities for firms to conduct business with government.

Entrepreneurial Strategy

Entrepreneurial strategy refers to a collection of government economic development policies that focus on developing high-growth new firms and technologies. The emergence of this alternative to economic development can be traced back to the 1980s. Under the pressure of increased international competition, as well as federal stimulation of policy innovation at the state level, many states experimented with a wide range of programs such as support for research and development (R&D), technology transfer, workforce development, venture capital investment, and loan programs, among others. The trend was captured in Peter Eisinger's 1988 book *The Rise of the Entrepreneurial State*. Different from chasing firms outside the state, as is the emphasis of traditional locational strategy, these entrepreneurial programs aimed at enabling the integral growth of existing businesses already within the jurisdiction as well as nurturing new ones.

Unlike case-by-case industrial recruitment strategies, entrepreneurial strategies are generally policy driven. That is, government promotional programs are offered to all firms alike. States have historically been innovative at adopting policies to encourage the growth of business. For example, the state of Nevada legalized "wide-open" gambling in 1931. Under this liberalized regime, commercial gaming grew gradually. In the 1940s and 1950s, with the success of the Las Vegas Strip, the modern American gaming industry cluster emerged in the state. As of 2020, gambling and casino revenue constituted 34 percent of the state revenue. Because of this gambling revenue stream, Nevada does not levy a state income tax. Another example is the state of Delaware, which is famous for its friendly corporate and tax laws. Businesses from New York, New Jersey, and elsewhere are attracted to Delaware for purposes such as incorporation as they seek all legal means to reduce their tax bills. Nearly half of all public corporations in the US are incorporated in Delaware, and around 66 percent of the Fortune 500; it is no wonder that the state is often referred to as the State of Incorporation.

There are many other examples of states using special tax policies to lure businesses and commercial activities, such as no state corporate income tax in Nevada, South Dakota, and Wyoming; no state individual income tax in Alaska, Florida, Nevada, Texas, and Washington; and no sales tax in Alaska (may have city level sales tax only), Delaware, Montana, New Hampshire, and Oregon. For international examples, see Exhibit 11.1.

Exhibit 11.1

International examples of entrepreneurial strategies

Entrepreneurial strategy has been practiced worldwide. Here we offer a few examples:

Malta's Pharmaceutical Sector

Malta is a small island country in the Mediterranean, famous for its pharmaceutical industry. Pharmaceutical firms in Malta enjoy several advantages from various entrepreneurial policies offered by the country. Maltese companies are subject to 35 percent income tax on their chargeable income, but their shareholders are entitled to a refund of all or part of the tax paid upon receipt of a dividend, especially for trading income. It is critical for generic pharmaceutical manufacturers that Malta's legal framework provides effective patent protection and incorporates all obligations from international treaties. The protection of Maltese industrial property rights is not limited to the Maltese territorial boundaries, but also extends to other signatory countries of the international Patent Cooperation Treaty (PCT) and the European

Patent Convention. Malta offers various investment allowances, research and development incentives, and investment assistance, and most importantly, a supply of university-educated chemistry graduates and a highly trained workforce experienced in using the sophisticated and high-precision machinery of pharmaceutical companies.

Bahamas' Offshore Banking

In order to lessen the economy's dependence on tourism, the Bahamas government has followed a policy of diversification since the 1970s. The country focused on developing itself into an offshore banking center. Companies enjoy a variety of financial and legal advantages offered by the Bahamian government, such as low taxation, enhanced privacy, easy access to deposits, and protection against local political or financial instabilities. Policy incentives include freedom from taxation, democratic stability and investment incentives, preferential trade incentives, and an infrastructure that encourages, supports, and rewards international investment. Once a haven for pirates, drug dealers, and smugglers, the islands of the Bahamas are now not only a retreat of fine white sand and subtle coral-colored beaches, but also host to world-famous financial institutions. While it is no longer the world leader in offshore banking as it once was; financial services still constitute the second-most important sector of the Bahamian economy.

Dubai's Innovative Real Estate Development

Dubai City is the capital of Dubai, one of the seven emirates that constitute the United Arab Emirates (UAE) in the eastern Arabian Peninsula. To lessen its dependence on the oil industry, the emirate has adopted Western-style entrepreneurial business policies, which have diversified its economy, with the main revenues coming from tourism, aviation, real estate, and financial services. Dubai City is famous for its innovative large construction projects, such as skyscrapers and high-rise buildings, in particular the Burj Dubai ("Dubai Tower"), currently the tallest freestanding structure on earth. In addition, Dubai is home to other ambitious development projects including man-made islands, luxury hotels, and some of the largest shopping malls in the world. Dubai government's emphasis on real estate development resulted in the property boom of 2004–2006, which made Dubai one of the fastest-growing cities in the world. It has continued to grow rapidly, but has experienced enormous swings in its real estate market due to the Great Recession and COVID-19 pandemic.

Burj Khalifa Tower, Dubai
Source: Wikimedia Commons.

The more recent development of entrepreneurial strategy focuses on improving the capacity of local firms, enhancing growth-producing economic sectors, and developing "homegrown" projects (Eisinger 1988). Many states have utilized a variety of tools to achieve these purposes. In addition to the more traditional tools such as planning and development controls, financial support, economic and enterprise zones, and public infrastructure improvements, states are also experimenting with new tools such as business and innovation assistance centers, technology and business parks, venture financing companies, one-stop business information centers, micro-enterprise programs, technology transfer programs, workforce development programs, export promotion programs, and so on (Leicht and Jenkins 1994).

Unlike industrial recruitment strategy, which emphasizes reducing production factor costs, entrepreneurial strategy uses a "demand-side" approach, in which government takes an external market demand to spur new enterprise, production, and projects to meet that demand (Eisinger 1988). Government assumes the central role in launching new firms, creating new technology and products, developing new markets, and fostering the various growing economic sectors. For example, stemming from the concern that the economy was too dependent on the gambling industry, the state of

Nevada established the Industrial Development Revenue Bond program in 1981 to diversify the economy through attracting new business to the state. The program also won wide support from the existing business community.

Public Entrepreneurs

Another facet of entrepreneurial strategy captures the recent trend of government actively partnering with the private sector in launching "homegrown" economic development projects. Over the past three decades, many governments have experimented with more and more innovative policies and practices, and some now even embrace a number of characteristics indicative of the private sector in pursuing economic development. Typifying this entrepreneurial approach, government now regularly undertakes high-risk projects and utilizes innovative financing mechanisms such as speculative revenue bonds, tax increment financing, and public–private partnerships.

This trend is apparent in some American cities under the influence of globalization (Clarke and Gaile 1992; Hall and Hubbard 1998) but has clear parallels around the world (Aligica 2018; Melissanidou and Johnston 2019). These entrepreneurial cities differentiate themselves from other municipalities by pursuing innovative strategies to maintain or enhance their economic competitiveness in the global economy (Jessop and Sum 2000). They use specific, identifiable, and purposeful strategies to promote economic development and adopt a new discourse centered on innovation to establish an entrepreneurial business climate (Clarke and Gaile 1998). Specifically, they use market criteria rather than political criteria for public funds allocation. They may also involve themselves in complex financial arrangements via public–private partnerships. Some of them even take the role of an active capitalist, fully engaging in market activities with the expressed intent of seeking a return on investment (ROI) (Chapin 2002).

One of the hallmarks of these public entrepreneurs is the development of highly visible and expensive flagship projects, which are expected to be special activity generators. Such flagship projects include large sports facilities, convention centers, aquariums, shopping malls, and specialty museums. It is expected that such projects will have positive spillover effects to the local economy. Spillover effect refers to the externalities of economic activity or processes that affect those who are not directly involved. For example, the economic benefit of a large sports stadium is not only limited to within the facility itself, but also may extend to nearby restaurants, hotels, and retail stores.

This trend is apparent in redevelopment, especially in attacking the problems of urban decay or blight. See Exhibit 11.3 for an expanded definition of redevelopment and blight. For example, Chapin (2002) describes the City of San Diego: in pursuing its downtown redevelopment goals, San Diego partnered with private-sector entities in constructing the city's landmark BallPark District (see Exhibit 11.3), which contains not only the Padres BallPark, but also a pedestrian-oriented, urban neighborhood that includes a mix of retail, office, restaurant, hotel, and residential properties. Multiple players of both sectors entered into agreement, where each party financed and contributed to the overall project. Like their private-sector counterpart, the public-sector entity aggressively sought for a return on its investment in the form of a redeveloped city area, including new hotels, office buildings, retail space, and revenues generated by taxes on the new development and guests at the new hotels.

Despite the advantages offered by public entrepreneurship, such municipal capitalism also raises some concerns. First of all, the basic public–private partnership in economic development blurs the lines between public and private. Further, a partnership such as this does not come into being easily. For example, Peters (1998) opines that a relationship qualifies as a PPP only if:

1 It involves at least two actors, one of which is a public entity.
2 Each of the participating actors can bargain for themselves.
3 The relationship is long-term and enduring.
4 Each party contributes either material or symbolic goods to the relationship.
5 All participating actors share the responsibility for the outcome.

The partnership does not always bring together the best of both the public and private sectors and often leads to confusion regarding the roles of the actors. Despite the common goal of project success, public and private actors have significantly different objectives. There is an inherent conflict between the public sector's need for greater social good and the private sector's demand for profit (Ni 2012).

Second, there is the concern that if the public sector selects projects primarily based on profitability, then other worthy, yet unprofitable, projects may not be funded. Many public redevelopment projects, such as affordable housing, community centers, and public parks, are all socially beneficial and desirable projects, but fail as revenue generators. If a city has to choose between a public library and a potentially profitable aquarium, capitalistic public entrepreneurs may pursue the latter.

Exhibit 11.2

Redevelopment and blight

Redevelopment tends to refer to economic development for blighted areas, but occasionally also includes upscale redevelopment as well.

Blight is a two-faceted concept. *Physical blight* describes the deteriorated condition of housing, businesses, and industrial sites that have worsened over time due to human neglect and disinvestment. Physically blighted areas contain vacant or boarded-up buildings, weedy sidewalks, broken windows, and irregular or inadequate lots. Physical blight negatively impacts the visual aesthetics of the urban environment and creates safety concerns. Neighbor hoods exposed to blight are at an increased risk of various health, economic, and social problems. Historically, blighted neighborhoods also have higher rates of crime and illicit drug activity.

A blight area
Source: Wikimedia Commons (2007).

Failure to address physically blighted neighborhoods can lead to *economic blight*, when businesses leave an area of town, taking jobs and property tax dollars with them. The residents of those areas are more likely to be unemployed as a result. Economic blighted areas are characterized by decreased property values, discouraged business development, and high crime rates. Decreased property values mean less tax revenue to support issues relating to health care, public safety, and other public services. A compounding effect arises because people prefer to build new properties rather than reinvesting and rehabilitating existing properties whenever blight is present.

Federal and state redevelopment statutes give cities and counties the authority to establish redevelopment agencies (RDAs) and give the agencies the authority to attack problems of blight. The fundamental tools used for redevelopment by government include the authority to acquire real property, the power of eminent domain and land assembly, and the authority and obligation to relocate persons who reside in the property acquired by the RDA. The financial tools used for such operations include borrowing from federal or state governments, selling public bonds, and tax increment financing (see Chapter 8).

Exhibit 11.3

The San Diego Gaslamp District by Petco Park

San Diego Ballpark Village
Source: Wikimedia Commons (2013).

Thirdly, entrepreneurial economic development projects often entail high risks; a project failure can lead to huge public loss. Just as any private-sector innovation, public-sector entrepreneurial projects face no less a rate of failure (Lee 2018). Using the sports facility as an example, empirical studies found that such entrepreneurial projects often fail to produce the anticipated economic impacts, delivering very little in economic returns to a city (Baade 1996; Noll and Zimbalist 1997; Coates and Humphreys 1999; Hudson 1999). Sports facilities have failed as economic growth engines largely due to substitution effects. For instance, consumers who choose to spend money at the stadium may cut their spending in movie theaters, resulting in little increase in commercial activity. A second reason is leakage in the economy: sport team owners and players may take away the lion's share of the money earned at the stadium, but spend little of it in the local economy. In addition, since public-sector entrepreneurs are often less experienced in taking on risky projects and have less leverage in negotiations with the private sector when compared to their private-sector counterparts (e.g., major league sports are cartels), the failure rate is even higher.

In another example, in chasing sports teams, the City of San Bernardino, California, joined with the private sector via a baseball team and a real estate development firm in constructing a sport stadium with the hope of it becoming an activity generating center for the city. The project was funded by tax allocation bonds at a significantly higher than expected cost as projected private financial support fell short. Despite the attendance at the ball park being relatively promising, the city was charged with high management costs by the team management, leaving little "net profit" for the city. In addition, none of the originally projected economic spillover effects has materialized. The stadium stands alone, surrounded by empty lots, costing a large amount of money to simply maintain the facility. The stadium was eventually handed over by the city to a credit union.

Yet when these public–private partnerships work, they are the envy of their region and the pride of local citizens, as Exhibit 11.4 illustrates.

Exhibit 11.4

Victoria Gardens in Rancho Cucamonga

The Rancho Cucamonga Redevelopment Agency (RCRA) administers a variety of economic development, redevelopment, and housing-related programs that support businesses and residents in the City of Rancho Cucamonga. Established in 1981, the Agency has assisted in the elimination of blighted conditions, resulting in the development of new public facilities and affordable housing projects, improved infrastructure, and the creation of a strong local economy through business attraction/retention, workforce development, and tourism efforts. An entrepreneurial project, Victoria Gardens was developed by the RCRA through partnership with Forest City Development California, Inc., and the Lewis Investment Company of Upland, California.

Forest City and Lewis had exclusively negotiated with the RCRA since November 4, 1999. Working closely with the city, they conducted market studies and an economic feasibility analysis and prepared alternative site plans and physical design concepts for the proposed project. On July 19, 2000, the City of Rancho Cucamonga granted conceptual approval of the proposed preliminary project design. The approval by the City of Rancho Cucamonga of a Memorandum of Understanding (MOU) with Forest City symbolized a major milestone for the developers of the proposed project and allowed them to move forward with the development process. The plan underwent several refinements, as finally reflected in its current design. The project officially broke ground on September 16, 2003 and opened on October 28, 2004. The project encompasses a land area of 147 acres and an investment of $200 million.

Source: Wikimedia Commons (2009).

Located in the northwest quadrant of US Interstate Highway 15 and Foothill Boulevard/Route 66, in Rancho Cucamonga, California, the Victoria Gardens project includes approximately 1.3 million square feet of retail and office space, 14 acres of peripheral (out-lot) retail area, and 20 acres of multi-family housing. The venue includes over 150 retailers carrying fashions, shoes, and accessories for men, women, and children, in addition to restaurant choices and entertainment venues such as the Victoria Gardens Cultural Center, which features the Lewis Family Playhouse, Library, and Celebration Hall.

The project has been considered Rancho Cucamonga's new downtown. It represents the ideal setting for innovative retail shopping, working, and living opportunities combined with civic, cultural, and other amenities that complement the traditional family lifestyle. The blending of neighborhoods, commercial, civic, and cultural uses within the Victoria Gardens project promises to make it the center of activity for the Rancho Cucamonga community. In addition, because of its excellent location and accessibility from major freeways within San Bernardino County, it is also a destination location for over 3.6 million potential shoppers and families throughout the Inland Empire region.

Since being built, the project has generated significant economic, and other, benefits for the city. These include a combined total of over $5 million per year in new retail sales, property, and business license taxes. The project also has generated approximately 3,000 new permanent and part-time jobs. In addition, it has acted as a catalyst for additional economic development of a mixture of uses on surrounding land in the area.

Privatization and Deregulation

In addition to various entrepreneurial strategies, deregulation has been pursued by many governments for economic development purposes. Deregulation, the policy and practice of government reducing or removing regulations, is a special form of privatization. An introduction to privatization will help better explain the rationale behind deregulation.

Privatization

Privatization refers to both the policies and practices of delegating public duties and/or trusteeship to the private sector, either to a business that operates for a profit or to a nonprofit entity. Of course the extent of the governmental portfolio of ownership and trusteeship varies extensively around the world, with the most extensive public ownership being in communist states, moderate in socialist states, and least in capitalistic-oriented states. Thus, while privatization has been a topic of much discussion in the US, the level of privatization has always been very limited in comparison to many countries in the world. Privatization is based on the idea that government should shed parts of its portfolio of management responsibilities which it has held in trust for a variety of different theoretical reasons: efficiency and effectiveness of a single provider (e.g., postal service), national security (e.g., national mineral reserves and military bases), as a governmental profit center (e.g., energy), stimulating the market by providing or functioning as insurance (e.g., secondary mortgages and pension plans for citizens), and equity (e.g., public roads). The reasons for privatization are equally numerous and case specific but the three biggest include holding back innovation (e.g., communication), adding to government expense in some cases (e.g., public roads), and depriving the private sector of profit-making opportunities in some cases (e.g., the sale of public lands and the use of public lands for commercial purposes).

Privatization gained a new worldwide momentum in the 1970s and 1980s under the leaderships of Margaret Thatcher in the UK and Ronald Reagan in the US. This renewed interest in privatization was driven by the so-called New Public Management (NPM) movement, which aimed to modernize and render more efficient the public sector. The central tenet underpinning NPM holds that government should be run like business, and that the market-oriented management of the public sector will lead to greater cost-efficiency and resolve many contemporary social problems.

Driven by NPM under Thatcher, the UK privatized a large number of state-owned enterprises, such as British Airways, British Petroleum, British Aerospace, British Steel, British Telecom, and so on. In the US, privatization took a different track. Despite the lack of a Thatcher-like privatization agenda, the Reagan Administration created an interagency Privatization Working Group, which supported a whole series of federal privatization studies targeting candidates such as the Air Traffic Control System, Amtrak, Conrail (a freight railroad), etc. Reagan's privatization studies paved the way for subsequent real privatization during the Clinton Administration. Under Clinton, the federal government sold off the Elk Hills Naval Petroleum Reserves, the US Enrichment Corporation, many parts of the electromagnetic spectrum (selling the rights to transmit signals over specific bands of the spectrum to industry), as well as contracted out over 100 airport control towers and numerous military base functions (Poole 2004). More significantly, this trend has been extended to state and local governments—a multitude of government services such as utility, waste collection, human services, and prison and corrections which were traditionally kept in-house have been increasingly contracted out to the private sector.

Today in the US privatization and nationalization or state/local government assumption of new economic resource responsibilities are relatively counter-balanced. There continues to be a strong push for privatization of public lands, communication resources, transportation, and service intense functions of government (primarily at the state and local level). However, healthcare is a complicated and controversial area in which some nationalization has occurred via the Affordable Care Act and increased privatization of veterans' health. Such policies not only involve government's role as a direct conservator, but also government's more indirect role as a regulator, a discussion we turn to next.

Deregulation

Whereas privatization delegates public duties to the private sector, deregulation also delegates regulation of the private sector to itself, mainly through the invisible hand of the market. The underpinning rationale of deregulation is based on free-market economics, which in general says that government intervention in economic affairs is undesirable; and that fewer and simpler regulations would lead to a raised level of competitiveness, subsequent higher productivity and efficiency, and eventual economic growth.

Deregulation is similar to industrial recruitment in that both focus on reducing production factor costs. Instead of government investing through capital and tax subsidies, deregulation reduces governmental regulation of private economic activity. Proponents of deregulation generally view government forces as negative and feel they should be limited in order to maintain a legal and social environment for businesses to maximize shareholder profits.

Since the late nineteenth and early twentieth centuries, many industries in the US have been regulated by the federal government (see Chapters 1 and 2). One problem caused by regulation was that these industries often swayed the government regulatory agencies by lobbying through the legislative process, exploiting them to serve the industries' special interests; regulation by government sometimes became weak and ineffective, with the government hardly holding them responsible. Industries also thought they could be more profitable with less government intervention. In addition, many free-market economists believed that excessive regulations contributed to the economic stagnation of the 1960s and 1970s in the US.

As a special form of privatization, deregulation also gained much momentum in the 1970s, influenced by the theories of Friedrich Hayek, Milton Friedman, and other liberal economists, as well as research at the University of Chicago. Many economists, such as Alfred Kahn, played critical roles in participating in subsequent deregulation efforts by government. From the 1970s to the 1990s, the federal government significantly deregulated the industries of transportation, energy, communications, and finance. See Exhibit 11.5 for a list of the federal legislation deregulating various industries and Exhibit 11.6 for a successful example.

Exhibit 11.5

Federal deregulation Acts from the 1970s to the 1990s

Industries	*Deregulation Acts*
Transportation	The Railroad Revitalization and Regulatory Reform Act of 1976
	The Airline Deregulation Act of 1978The Staggers Rail Act of 1980
	The Motor Carrier Act of 1980
	The Bus Regulatory Reform Act of 1982
	The Surface Freight Forwarder Deregulation Act of 1986
	The Ocean Shipping Act of 1984 and 1988
	The Federal Aviation Administration Authorization Act of 1994
Energy	The Energy Policy Act of 1992
Communication	The Telecommunications Act of 1996
Finance	The Depository Institutions Deregulation and Monetary Control Act of 1980

Exhibit 11.6

The US Airline Industry: a positive deregulation example

In the early 1970s, the US economy experienced the worst downturn since the Great Depression, with stagnant economic growth, rising unemployment, and inflation. Economists from the University of Chicago attributed the inflation and rising fuel prices to rigid government regulations.

In the airline industry, the federal Civil Aeronautics Board (CAB) had regulated all domestic interstate air transport routes since 1938, leaving intrastate routes under the regulation of each state government. CAB's regulation covered almost every important area of airline operation including setting fares, routes, and schedules. Most of the major airlines, such as Pan Am, favored the rigid system because their profits were virtually guaranteed and they never had to compete with newcomers; but passengers who were forced to pay escalating fares disliked the system. In addition, the CAB was so notorious for its bureaucratic inefficiency that airlines were subject to lengthy delays when applying for new routes, fares, or schedule changes, which were not often approved.

In 1977, President Jimmy Carter appointed Alfred E. Kahn, a professor of economics at Cornell University, to be the chairperson for CAB. Under Kahn's leadership, a concerted push for deregulation developed and swiftly gained legislative results in 1978—the deregulation bill was passed and signed by Carter on October 24, 1978. The Act intended to remove various restrictions on airline operations over several years in the hope that competition would produce growth in the industry. The impact of deregulation was generally positive. A 1996 Government Accountability Office (GAO) study found that between 1979 and 1988, the average fare per passenger mile, adjusted for inflation, declined by nine percent at small airports, ten percent at medium-sized airports, and five percent at large airports (GAO 1996). Over the next 20 years, the airline industry employed twice as many people to fly almost three times as many passengers.

Jimmy Carter signs the Airline Deregulation Act of 1978
Source: Wikimedia Commons (1978).

Many state governments have also pursued deregulation for economic development. State deregulation policies mainly focus on reducing governmental regulation of employer/employee relations as well as relaxing environmental and other regulations that directly affect the production process. Early deregulation measures adopted by state governments were right-to-work laws that limited collective bargaining (see Chapter 4) during the 1940s, mainly in southern states. A right-to-work law does not aim to provide a general guarantee of employment to people seeking work, but rather is a government regulation that prohibits an established union requiring employees' membership, or payment of union dues or fees as a condition of employment, either before or after hiring.

In later decades, these laws have spread across central and western states, weakening unions and holding down labor costs. Several states also refused to adopt minimum wage laws and fair employment codes, strengthening the hand of employers in labor relations. Lower labor compensation costs led to favorable business climates. In the 1980s, states regained interest in deregulating these areas; policy advances included state right-to-work laws to hinder unionization, the absence of a state minimum wage law, and the absence of state fair employment legislation. As of 2021, 27 states, mostly in the South, upper Midwest and West, have adopted right-to-work laws (either by law or Constitutional provision). Five states (Alabama, Louisiana, Mississippi, Tennessee, and South Carolina) have no minimum wage law, and thus business must only respond to federal minimums.

Another area of state deregulation focus is environmental regulation, which has stirred much political controversy. The paradox of environmental laws is that overly strong regulations can lead to industrial flight, whereas lax regulations are feared to turn the country into a "pollution haven." The underlying rationale for deregulation here is that environmental regulations have a strong effect on industrial locations and that differential regulations between states will, at a minimum, induce specialization and perhaps significant capital movement to states with weaker regulations. In the US, environmental regulations vary from state to state. Although national environmental policies have certainly raised the minimum level of environmental standards, important differences in state environmental policies remain. Federal laws notwithstanding, regulations governing hazardous waste disposal, wetlands filling, air and water pollution, and wildlife protection vary considerably among different states.

Although the goal of deregulation is to encourage economic growth by greater reliance on market forces, not all deregulation policies have produced the desired outcome. Previous studies found that transportation deregulation generally led to increased competition, communication choices, and the creation of new firms and jobs. Similar to the airline industry's deregulation, trucking deregulation also produced a boost to US industries in shipping, merchandising, and inventories (Moore 1988). However, deregulation in the financial sector led to very poor results and the sector was re-regulated (as discussed in Chapter 3). There are also mixed findings about the economic impact of environmental regulation, as lax environment laws have not necessarily always led to economic growth (Meyer 1995).

Perhaps the most controversial deregulation has been in the energy industry, such as practiced in California. In 1996, California began to modify controls on its energy market and took measures ostensibly to increase competition. The policy largely contributed to the California electricity crisis of 2000 and 2001, in which the state suffered from multiple large-scale blackouts, illegal shutdowns of pipelines by Texas energy consortium Enron, and capped retail electricity prices. Yet as California significantly limited retail electric competition for most customers because of its poor implementation, other states across the country more successfully pursued deregulation for electricity, including Illinois, Maryland, Ohio, Pennsylvania, and Texas. Increased competition in these states has produced cost savings and innovative products and services, such as clean energy supplies and programs that give customers the flexibility to manage their energy use according to market prices.

Exhibit 11.7

The California electricity crisis: a negative example of deregulation

Deregulation of the electricity sector in the US began in 1992. The Energy Policy Act of 1992 eliminated obstacles for wholesale electricity competition, but the policy has not been adopted by all states. California passed the Electric Utility Industry Restructuring Act (Assembly Bill 1890) in 1996, allowing wholesale electric competition to begin in March 1998. Following the transition period, the three large investor-owned utilities, namely Pacific Gas and Electric (PG&E), Southern California Edison (SCE), and San Diego Gas and Electric (SDG&E), could purchase electricity from any independent trader or exchange.

The reform was a partial deregulation, where wholesale prices were deregulated, and retail prices were regulated for the incumbent utilities, based on the expectation that "frozen" retail rates would remain higher than wholesale prices. This expectation sounded reasonable, as in the 1990s the generating capacity in the western states usually exceeded the demand for electricity. But after the summer of 2000, the scenario changed—demand for electricity started to outpace the generating capacity, because of economic growth, weather patterns, some loss of hydropower capacity, and other conditions. Consequently, the deregulated wholesale market pushed electricity prices to unanticipated levels.

Because the state government had a cap on retail electricity charges, as rising wholesale prices for electricity consistently exceeded frozen retail prices, PG&E and SCE were forced to sell purchased power at a loss. Customers of SDG&E, by contrast, paid the market price, which was three times higher than it was the previous summer. On June 14, 2000, PG&E interrupted service for the first time in its history, affecting 100,000 customers in San Francisco. On December 7, 2000, suffering from low supply and idle power plants, the California Independent System Operator (Cal-ISO), which manages the California power grid, declared the first statewide Stage 3 power alert, meaning power reserves were below 3 percent.

Some speculative energy traders such as Enron also contributed to the crisis. As a leading player in the West Coast energy market, and supplying electricity for more than 2.6 million homes in the state, Enron was in a unique position both to control the power supply and lead the way in price gouging and market manipulation. For example, Enron discovered it could flood the state's transmission lines with more electricity than they could handle in order to collect "congestion payments." It could also shut down grids to create artificial shortages and charge higher prices, as Cal-ISO would pay traders a premium for providing more power than was required when energy supplies were tight. Enron's "gaming" actions assaulted the state's power supply for years and were largely concentrated at the height of the California energy crisis.

This crisis eventually led to the bankruptcy of PG&E and near bankruptcy for SCE in early 2001. On January 17, 2001, Governor Gray Davis had to declare a state of emergency and was forced to step in to buy power at highly unfavorable terms on the open market. The subsequent massive long-term debt obligations contributed enormously to the state budget crisis and resulted in widespread grumbling about Davis's administration.

Meanwhile, the City of Los Angeles was unaffected by the crisis because local public utilities in California, including the Los Angeles Department of Water and Power, were exempt from the deregulation legislation. The city sold its excess power to private utilities in the state, mostly to SCE, which prevented much of the greater Los Angeles area from suffering the long-term blackouts experienced in other parts of the state during the crisis.

Source: Congressional Budget Office (2001). Causes and Lessons from the California Electricity Crisis. September. http://www.cbo.gov/sites/default/files/cbofiles/ftpdocs/30xx/doc3062/californiaenergy.pdf

Contracting Out

Contracting out refers to the hiring of private-sector firms or nonprofit organizations to render goods or services for the government. In this method, the government agency retains ownership and overall control but employs the private vendor to actually provide the service. Contracting out has been traditionally practiced by government, especially in military and defense contracting. Government contracts have played a critical role and have largely encouraged the growth of the arms industry in the US. Today, government purchases from defense contractors cover a multitude of goods, including military aircraft, ships, vehicles, weaponry, and electronic systems, as well as services such as logistics, technical support, training, and security. Military contracts have made the nation by far the largest arms manufacturer and exporter.

Contracting out has gained popularity during the recent rising tide of privatization. As the dominant form of privatization in the US, contracting out encompasses a wide range of services, including administrative and general services in education, health, social services, and transportation. There is extensive use of contract workers in waste collection, street repair, street cleaning, building maintenance, and data processing.

The preference of contracting out reflects both practical and political considerations. Practically, contracting out allows government officials to retain substantial control over service production and delivery while seeking the cost-efficiency and improved quality promised by the private sector. Under contracts, government officials are largely involved in the design and oversight of production. In the case of poor performance by the private service provider, governments can either terminate the contract or shift to another vendor, or revert the service back to in-house provision, if the agency retains the equipment and expertise to do so. Politically, service features may be designed to give substantial benefits to select constituents in order to gain concessions from certain voters. Moreover, contractors are willing to influence decision-makers, such as elected officials, via campaign contributions or other political favoritism by sharing some of their contract benefits (Seidenstat 1999).

Other Forms of Privatization

Privatization can take many other forms, all aiming to shift functions and responsibilities, in whole or in part, from the government to the private sector.

Asset Sale

Asset sale refers to the transfer of ownership of government land, mineral, building, or other assets to the private sector. After the asset is sold, government will have no role in its financial support, management, or oversight. Asset sales have been practiced as a major form of privatization by many countries around the world, including in both the Western democracies such as the UK, New Zealand, and Australia, and transitional economies such as Russia, China, and many eastern European countries. In the latter countries, asset sales mainly involve the selling of state-owned enterprises. In the US, although the large-scale sale of state-owned enterprises is less common (because there was relatively little to sell off compared to more socialized countries), governments routinely auction off a variety of government-seized surplus and tax-foreclosed property and assets including land, houses, jewelry, cars, trucks, tools, computers, and so on.

Franchise

Franchise is a concession or privilege government grants to a firm to conduct business in a particular market or geographical area. For example, a city can grant a cable franchise to a private firm to operate cable television network in its jurisdiction. In facing increased financial challenges, many governments have extended franchise agreements into more traditionally monopolized government services. For example, in 1989, the State of California started to allow the private sector to enter into franchise agreements with the Department of Transportation for the development of new roads. Private firms, through franchise agreements, are enabled to finance, construct, and operate state highways with a concession of collecting tolls for a certain period of time.

Government Corporation

Government corporations are legal entities that are created by a government, generally with the intent of conducting revenue-producing, commercial-type activities on behalf of a government. They are normally free from certain government restrictions related to personnel and procurement. They include government-sponsored enterprises, a group of financial service corporations created by Congress and privately owned by stockholders. Fannie Mae and Freddie Mac, for instance, used to be government-sponsored enterprises but were nationalized during the 2008–2009 economic crisis and became government-owned corporations once again because of the cash subsidy they required to stay afloat. Government-owned or chartered corporations provide public services, but unlike government agencies, they have a separate legal personality from the government and maintain a high level of political independence. Some of them may receive government budgetary appropriations, but some also have independent revenue sources. This type of government corporation includes the Overseas Private Investment Corporation (OPIC), the Export–Import Bank of the US, the Federal Deposit Insurance Corporation (FDIC), the Tennessee Valley Authority, the US Postal Service, and Amtrak.

Grant

A grant (or subsidy) is a sum of money (or a privilege or rights) government gives to private companies to encourage their involvement in accomplishing public purposes. Grants and subsidies are commonly used to encourage economic development purposes, such as funding low-income housing and research and development (see Chapter 8).

Lease

Lease refers to the arrangement of government granting the temporary possession or use of government-owned properties and facilities to private organizations, usually for compensation at a fixed rate and with service and profit restrictions. For example, private airlines often sign an airport concession lease with government agencies and airport authorities for using terminal facilities. Although all commercial airports in the US are publicly owned, the private sector plays a significant role in their financing and operations. Airport rents and airport concession fees constitute the majority of airport revenue.

Public–Private Partnership

Public–private partnership (PPP or P3) is a contractual arrangement formed between public- and private-sector partners that can include a variety of activities involving the private sector in the development, financing, ownership, and operation of a public facility or service. Under widespread fiscal stress, this approach has been increasingly explored by all levels of government to introduce private investment into public infrastructure and services. For example, about half of the states around the country have enacted laws to allow private-sector entry into the development of transportation infrastructure via PPPs with government transportation agencies. The PPP has also become an important means of local economic development, especially for flagship projects as described earlier in this chapter. For a recent example of a highly successful PPP, see Exhibit 11.8 which describes the public–private partnership that rolled out the COVID-19 vaccines in record-shattering speed.

Exhibit 11.8

A successful public–private partnership example: the COVID-19 vaccines

Nearly all types of vaccine get some degree of US federal government support, but it is generally related to the perceived scope of the need and degree of health risk involved. So it is little wonder that the US government's role in rolling out the COVID-19 vaccine was enormous. At first glance, one may say that it was the ingenuity of the private sector pharmaceutical industry that created and manufactured the drug that led to the success. But closer examination of the financial and policy structures put in place make it clear that the government's numerous roles were massive.

The US government has invested well over $20 billion to the Biomedical Research and Development Authority for *basic research* for diseases that are difficult to inoculate since the year 2000. This has made the US the world leader in vaccine development.

The government spent approximately $1 billion in pre-clinical *trial support*. It spent another $2.7 billion on Phase III trial support. The trial support enabled many smaller pharmaceutical research agencies—some of whom worked with larger corporations—to join the search for a vaccine without significant investment loss. It also enabled diverse vaccines to be developed which allowed for comparative performance experience.

The government spent approximately $3 billion on *infrastructure support* to ensure rapid conversion and creation of facilities and manufacturing technologies.

Those American companies that were highly promising got advance contracts essentially eliminating market failure. Johnson and Johnson had a $1 billion contract for 100 million doses of their vaccine. Moderna contracts totaled $5 billion to produce 300 million doses. Pfizer, which had taken on all development and expansion costs on its own, had advance purchase contracts totaling $6 billion for 300 million doses. In addition, the government spent tens of billions on rapid implementation programs by supporting state, county, and municipal deployment.

While expensive for the government, in terms of the lives saved, the restoration of the economy, and world leadership in health promotion, all sides of the political spectrum have hailed the COVID-19 vaccine effort as government (and industry) at its best.

Source: Frank et al. (2021)

Voluntarism

Voluntarism refers to any public services conducted through either a formal agency volunteer program or a private nonprofit service organization. A service can be organized and funded by a government agency that enlists volunteers to provide all or part of the services offered. Such service may be directly supervised by the agency. For example, the National Park

Service recruits many youth, families, groups, and individual volunteers to help care for the national parks. A service can also be offered through a nonprofit service group. For example, the delivery of meals to homeless people is often funded by government assistance programs, but offered by nonprofit organizations such as the Salvation Army.

Voucher

Vouchers are government financial subsidies given to individuals for the purchase of specific goods or services from the private or public sector. Common examples include housing, school, and food vouchers. A school voucher, or an education voucher, can be used to fully or partially pay for the tuition at school, either public or private, that parents choose for their child. The voucher program enables parents the flexibility and control of selecting the preferred school for their child. In some states or local areas, the voucher can be used to cover or reimburse home-schooling expenses, while in other jurisdictions, vouchers only pay for tuition at private schools. Food stamps are another type of voucher provided to lower-income or poverty-stricken individuals by the federal Supplemental Nutrition Assistance Program. A housing voucher, also known as the Section 8 program, is a premium issued by the federal government to low-income tenants to pay for, usually part of, their rents to private landlords.

Limitations of Privatization

As governments at all levels face the challenges of growing public-service demands and stagnant fiscal capabilities, various forms of privatization have been increasingly explored, not only as a strategy to encourage economic development, but also as a viable way to cut costs and to introduce private-sector resources in providing public services. The scope and scale of public services and responsibilities have been continuously expanding into areas that were traditionally untouched by the private sector. For example, though national combat troops have never been privatized, the logistical services supporting military maneuvers are contracted out. In addition, whereas city, county, and state police forces are still kept in-house, jail, detention, and correction services are now provided by the private sector. These practices naturally raise some fundamental questions, including: what are the limits of privatization, can or should business undertake all public functions and services, and what are the implications of privatization?

The underlying assumption of privatization is that public and private sectors are alike and many government functions can be performed more efficiently and economically by the private sector. However, as introduced in Chapter 1, the political, historical, and cultural settings of the US have given rise to fundamentally different and characteristically distinct public and private sectors. Ultimately, the single most important characteristic—sovereignty—distinguishes the public sector from the private, especially at the federal level (Moe 1987). Sovereign power, which is only possessed by government, encompasses several attributes (Moe 1987), such as:

- *Coercive power*: The sovereign legitimately possesses the power to enforce its will, such as tax citizens and impose penalties on those who refuse to pay.
- *Power to go to war*: A sovereign can legitimately declare war against another.
- *Immunity from suit*: Except by their permission, a sovereign is not subject to legal constraints.
- *Indivisibility*: A sovereign is indivisible and cannot share its power with another entity claiming sovereignty.
- *Power to disavow debts*: A sovereign reserves the right to reject debts; the declaration of bankruptcy is not inhering to the sovereign.
- *Eminent domain*: A sovereign reserves the right to establish the rules for protection and transference of public and private property.

Privatization cannot go beyond the powers reserved by sovereignty. In addition, public policy-makers also attempt to differentiate what are the inherently government functions that should not be privatized. For example, the White House's Office of Management and Budget (OMB) Circular No. A-76 specifies that.

An inherently governmental activity is an activity that is so intimately related to the public interest as to mandate performance by government personnel. These activities require the exercise of substantial discretion in applying government authority and/or in making decisions for the government. Inherently governmental activities normally fall into two categories: the exercise of sovereign government authority or the establishment of procedures and processes related to the oversight of monetary transactions or entitlements. An inherently governmental activity involves:

1 Binding the US to take or not to take some action by contract, policy, regulation, authorization, order, or otherwise.
2 Determining, protecting, and advancing economic, political, territorial, property, or other interests by military or diplomatic action, civil or criminal judicial proceedings, contract management, or otherwise.
3 Significantly affecting the life, liberty, or property of private persons; or.
4 Exerting ultimate control over the acquisition, use, or disposition of US property (real or personal, tangible or intangible), including establishing policies or procedures for the collection, control, or disbursement of appropriated and other federal funds.

Whereas the inherently governmental functions shall not be privatized, OMB Circular No. A-76 also specifies that commercial activities, which are non-inherently governmental functions, can be contracted out to the private sector.

Although privatization provides practical solutions to many public-sector problems by introducing private-sector advantages such as financial resources, technical expertise, innovation, and quality goods and services, it also points to many political, economic, and management implications.

First and foremost, privatization weakens political accountability. A critical social value of American democracy is that public officials should be held accountable for their actions to the public through their elected officials. Whereas a government agency is directly accountable to elected officials, a private company has only an indirect and weak relation with elected officials and can only be held accountable by the contract. The public does not have any control or oversight of a private-service contractor. In addition, there is considerable diversion between the two parties' goals in service provision. While the private sector inevitably seeks profit, the public sector in general has much broader social objectives. For example, if a government-owned company providing an essential service is privatized, such as water supply to all citizens, its private owner could potentially abandon the social obligation to those who are less able to pay, or to regions where water service is unprofitable.

Second, privatization does not always lead to more efficiency or better service quality. Empirical studies have found mixed results concerning contracting out; private firms may not perform better than government in assuming public duties. As privatization involves significant administrative costs, including costs for facilitating the bidding process, selecting vendors, supervising contracts, and evaluating contractor performance, the efficiency gains of privatization may hardly justify the cost.

Third, the privatizing process could lack transparency, allowing the contractor and public employees controlling the contract to gain personally. The high stakes involved with winning contracts from government often push contracting firms to the edge of the law. There are substantive instances of corruption throughout US administrative history involving contracts with private contractors to perform a public service. Military contracting scandals have been continuous since the founding of the country because of the size, complexity, and often uniqueness of the requirements. Contracting under emergency conditions, even when that is the agency's mission as it is for FEMA, are also likely to lead to manipulation, false representation, and other types of abuse. For example, a recent example is Atlantic Diving Supply, a company that dominates the small business set-aside program but is itself enormous at the Department of Defense (Gregg 2021).

Lastly, the government may lose the capacity to perform or manage privatized duties. In the long run, government may lose its institutional memory for service provision, which will not only affect its ability to manage contracts, but also make it impossible to regain the capacity to perform those duties if necessary. In addition, as public employees may lose their jobs in the process, government is likely to encounter employee or union resistance.

Political Ideology and Economic Development Strategies

Three distinct strategies of economic development with their instances and implications are introduced. The industrial recruitment approach uses tax incentives, capital subsidies, land, public infrastructure improvements, and other public resources to lure external businesses and to retain and promote existing firms. The strategy, in which government indirectly, and even passively, contributes to economic growth, aims at reducing private-sector production factor costs.

Similarly, the deregulation approach, which seeks to reduce government's involvement (i.e., regulation) in economic affairs, also targets keeping production factor costs down by delegating private-sector autonomy in the market. These two approaches are in alignment with politically Conservative ideology, which believes that the free-market system, competitive capitalism, and private enterprise create the greatest opportunity and promote overall economic well-being.

In comparison, the entrepreneurial strategy takes on the idea that government is an active party in economic development. Public entrepreneurs seek to produce economic growth through establishing new firms, developing new technology and products, building new growth sectors, and launching growth-generating projects. This approach is in agreement with politically liberal ideology that emphasizes the need for government in economic affairs. Unlike the private sector, the government is motivated by public interest. Government's involvement in economic affairs retains the economic benefits in the hands of the state for greater social value.

In addition to the three strategies of economic development, the policy and practice of privatization in its various forms are discussed. Privatization shares with deregulation strategy the idea of limited government, which is a central belief of political Conservatives. They believe that large government presents a threat to individual freedom; whenever possible, the market provision of services is politically preferable over government's direct involvement.

Although the analysis of political ideology in relation to different economic development strategies provides business students with additional insights about the rationale behind each strategy and may help them better interpret specific government economic development policies in their political environment, generalizations about the relationship can be imprudent, as exceptions are both common and import ant. In many instances, economic development strategies are driven by practical needs instead of political beliefs.

Analytical Case: Private Corrections Services in the US

Due to the huge surge of incarcerations in the early 1980s with the "war on drugs," two private prison companies were established as the Corrections Corporation of America (now CoreCivic), and Wackenhut (now GEO Group). Both focused on medium detention facilities using a "cookie cutter" model. The government clients included the Federal Bureau of Prisons, US Marshalls, Immigration and Customs Enforcement, approximately 15 states (with Texas being the largest), and several dozen counties and cities. The business model was quite successful and had grown to 137,000 prisoners in 2012 when many years of scandals related to escapes, inmate abuse, poor inmate rehabilitation services, contract manipulation, and exorbitant fees charged to inmates started to overshadow savings to public budgets. The biggest blow was the decision by to Federal Bureau of Prisons to phase out private prisons in 2016. Private prison inmate populations shrank approximately eight percent from the peak over the next decade. However, after some service losses and enormous crash in stock prices, these corporations successfully ramped up their remote monitoring and residential facilities enormously during the Trump Administration where risks and opportunities for abuse were lower, and ultimately, profit margins were higher.

On one hand, there can be little doubt that most of the time private prisons can provide services more cheaply in the short-term, decrease long-term pension liabilities substantially, provide surge capacity, and provide some flexibility in prison and probation services. Yet study after study indicates higher recidivism rates with private prison populations, increased inmate protests and riots, management issues escalating due to high employee turnover and employee corruption (e.g., the selling of drugs), and a substantially higher level of negligence and abuse.

Questions for Discussion and Analysis

1 What are the benefits and challenges in privatizing prisons?
2 In what ways do you think privatizing prisons is different from privatizing roads or food services at national parks in terms of the government's responsibility to prisoners?
3 What differences, if any, do you think there are in a public sector entity relying on private prisons for 25 percent, 50 percent or 100 percent of the inmate capacity? For example, do you think it makes a difference if the government entity wants to change the contract when they have outsource 100 percent of the prison population?

Sources: The Sentencing Project, CoreCivic, GEO Group

Practical Skill

Doing Business with Government

Before Good Buddy E-Solutions (in our opening scenario) can pursue government contracts, it is critical for them to realize that contracting with government can be an onerous process, even though government business opportunities are abundant and sometimes favorable to small business, as governments often set aside a certain portion of contracts for them. This skill exercise will focus on small business, although the lesson may be applicable to large business. The exercise will mainly discuss state and local government contracts. For federal government contract, a good resource will be the Small Business Agency website: www.sba.gov/category/navigation-structure/contracting.

Register Your Business

To become a vendor for government, you are required to register with the procurement office. Some states offer an eProcurement database via their procurement agency's website. You may also inquire at the procurement agency for information regarding registration.

Qualify Your Business

To qualify as a government contractor, you need to be able to comply with government requirements. Each state or local government agency has specific requirements, ranging from a proven ability to complete a task, to tried-and-tested quality-control procedures. It is generally valuable if you could obtain small business certification, which will enhance your competitiveness. If your business is not qualified to hold a formal contract, you may team or subcontract with another company to improve your chance of winning a contract.

Understand the Market

Just like entering a new market, you need to do research. In this case, governments become your market. It is important to figure out where the best opportunities are by investigating their financial status, contracting history, budgetary cycle, and procurement code. Much of this information is available on government websites. Marketing to the government can be challenging. It is critical to build a good relation with government agencies. You need to engage in networking activities, such as attending government professional conferences or joining governmental associations to meet agency decision-makers.

Find Opportunities

Government contracting opportunities are general provided by state or local government procurement offices. There are also many commercial companies that provide their own database of government contracts. For example, www.findrfp.com offers an online database of active US and Canada government contracts. Contracting opportunities are often posted as a Request for Proposal (RFP) or Request for Tender (RFT), which asks for an offer to be submitted in response to a request. If a competitive bid is involved, it is posted as an Invitation for Bid (IFB), which asks for a bid, and the lowest bid will win. A Request for Quotation (RFQ) is normally for small contracts, often less than $25,000, which is kept simple so that the contract can be awarded quickly.

Bid for Contracts

When an opportunity is right for you, you need to write a proposal (or bid) and follow the rules and regulations. Make sure that you respond to each requirement outlined in the RFP and fill out any required forms and submit your proposal as stated. Government officials may contact you for the proposal.

Skill Exercise: Pursuing a Government RFP Opportunity

Target a state or local government entity and do a search for an RFP. Identify an RFP of your interest and specify what requirements are needed. Discuss your strategies to pursue the RFP.

Summary and Conclusion

1 In addition to industrial recruitment, government also uses entrepreneurial strategy and deregulation for economic development.
2 As a general policy approach, entrepreneurial strategy focuses on developing high-growth new firms and technologies. Recent developments in entrepreneurial strategy focus on improving the capacity of local firms,

enhancing growth-producing economic sectors, and developing "home-grown" projects.

3 Another facet of entrepreneurial strategy refers to government actively partnering with the private sector to launch flagship projects, especially for redevelopment purposes. Some public entrepreneurs pursue municipal capitalism to partner with firms aggressively seeking return on investment. There are significant risks and implications involved with this approach.
4 Deregulation, a special form of privatization, is another economic strategy that focuses on reducing or removing regulations to enhance market competitiveness, productivity and efficiency, and eventually economic growth.
5 Privatization goes beyond deregulation. Various forms of privatization, namely contracting, asset sales, franchises, government corporations, leases, grants, public–private partnerships, voluntarisms, and vouchers all offer the private sector opportunities to conduct business with government.
6 The policy and practice of privatization has significant social, economic, and political implications.
7 Industrial recruitment and deregulation are in agreement with politically Conservative ideology, while entrepreneurial strategy is better in alignment with politically liberal ideals.

Key Terms

- Asset sale
- Blight Contracting out
- Deregulation
- Franchise Government corporation
- Inherent governmental functions
- Lease
- Municipal capitalism
- Privatization
- Redevelopment
- Sovereign
- Voluntarism
- Voucher

Study Questions

1 Describe and compare the three strategies of economic development.
2 Look at the local municipal level. Do you see evidence of the three economic development strategies in local cities or counties?
3 What is municipal capitalism? Discuss the social, economic, and political implications of municipal capitalism.
4 What is privatization? What are the limits and implications of privatization?
5 Discuss the different forms of privatization. Provide examples.
6 Investigate a local economic development case. Discuss the economic impacts of and government roles in the case.
7 How extensive a role do you think government should play in economic development?

References

Aligica, P. D. (2018). *Public Entrepreneurship, Citizenship, and Self-governance*. Cambridge: Cambridge University Press.

Baade, R. (1996). Professional Sports as Catalysts for Metropolitan Economic Development. *Journal of Urban Affairs*, *24*(*5*):1–17.

Chapin, T. (2002). Beyond the Entrepreneurial City: Municipal Capitalism in San Diego. *Journal of Urban Affairs*, *24*(*5*):565–581.

Clarke, S., and Gaile, G. (1992). The Next Wave: Local Economic Development Strategies in the Post-Federal Era. *Economic Development Quarterly*, *6*:189–198.

Clarke, S., and Gaile, G. (1998). *The Work of Cities*. Minneapolis: University of Minnesota Press.

Coates, D., and Humphreys, B. (1999). The Growth Effects of Sports Franchises, Stadia, and Arenas. *Journal of Policy Analysis and Management*, *18*(*4*):601–624.

Eisinger, P. (1988). *The Rise of the Entrepreneurial State*. Madison: University of Wisconsin Press.

Frank, R. G., Dach, L. and Lurie, N. (2021). It Was the Government that Produced Covid-19 Vaccine Success. *Health Affairs*. May 14. https://www.healthaffairs.org/do/10.1377/forefront.20210512.191448/full/.

Government Accountability Office (GAO) (1996). Airline Deregulation: Changes in Airfares, Service, and Safety at Small, Medium-Sized, and Large Communities. GAO/RCED-96-79, April.

Gregg, A. (2021). Pentagon Awarded Massive Contract to Virginia Company a U.S. Senator Called 'Fraudulent': Defense Program Intended for Small Firms Has Been Dominated by a Single Company, Atlantic Diving Supply. *The Washington Post*, February 18.

Hall, T., and Hubbard, P. (1998). *The Entrepreneurial City: Geographies of Politics, Regime and Representation*. Chichester: John Wiley.

Hudson, I. (1999). Bright Lights, Big City: Do Professional Sports Teams Increase Employment? *Journal of Urban Affairs*, *21*(*4*):397–407.

Jessop, B., and Sum, N.-L. (2000). An Entrepreneurial City in Action. *Urban Studies*, *37*(*12*):2290–2315.

Lee, M., Han, X., Quising, P., and Villaruel, M. L. (2018). Hazard Analysis on Public–private Partnership Projects in Developing Asia. *Asian Development Bank Economics Working Paper Series*, No. 548 (pp. 1–24). https://www.adb.org/sites/default/files/publication/435871/ewp-548-hazard-analysis-ppp-projects.pdf

Leicht, K. T., and Jenkins, J. C. (1994). Three Strategies of State Economic Development: Entrepreneurial, Industrial Recruitment, and Deregulation Policies in the American States. *Economic Development Quarterly*, *8*(*3*):256–269.

Melissanidou, E., and Johnston, L. (2019). Contextualising Public Entrepreneurship in Greek Local Government Austerity. *International Journal of Entrepreneurial Behavior & Research*, *25*(*7*):1563–1579.

Meyer, S. M. (1995). The Economic Impact of Environmental Regulation. *Journal of Environmental Law and Practice*, *3*(*2*):4–15.

Moe, R. C. (1987). Exploring the Limits of Privatization. *Public Administration Review*, *47*(*6*):453–460.

Moore, T. G. (1988). Rail and Truck Reform: The Record So Far. *Regulation*, November/December:57–62.

Ni, A. Y. (2012). The Risk-Averting Game of Transport Public–Private Partnership. *Public Performance and Management Review*, *36*(*2*):253–274.

Noll, R., and Zimbalist, A. (eds.) (1997). *Sports, Jobs, and Taxes: The Economic Impact of Sports Teams and Stadiums.* Washington, DC: Brookings Institution Press.

Peters, B. G. (1998). With a Little Help from our Friends: Public–Private Partnerships as Institutions and Instruments, in J. Pierre (ed.) *Partnerships in Urban Governance* (pp. 1–10). New York: St. Martin's Press.

Poole, R. (2004). Ronald Reagan and the Privatization Revolution: Reviewing Reagan's Outsourcing Legacy. *Reason Foundation.* June 8. http://reason.org/news/show/ronald-reagan-and-the-privatiz.

Seidenstat, P. (ed.) (1999). *Contracting out Government Services.* Santa Barbara, CA: Greenwood Publishing Group.

Wikimedia Commons (1978). Jack E. Kightlinger. https://commons.wikimedia.org/wiki/File:AirlineDeregulationAct.png.

Wikimedia Commons (2007). millicent_bystander. https://commons.wikimedia.org/wiki/File:Urban_decay_Shreveport.jpg.

Wikimedia Commons (2009). JWut89LA. https://commons.wikimedia.org/wiki/File:Victoria_Gardens_American_Apparel.JPG.

Wikimedia Commons (2013). Rameez Raza. https://commons.wikimedia.org/wiki/File:The_bustling_Gaslamp_Quarter_of_San_Diego_at_night.jpg.

Part IV

Business–Government–Nonprofit Relations in the Global Market

12 Globalization and Free Trade

Chapter Contents

Case 12 Scenario

Expanding Double Z Beauty

Zach's grandparents had a 20-acre farm in a sunny southern canyon in a state where they could grow practically anything—avocados, oranges, tomatoes, you name it. Over the past several decades they developed a family business, Double Z Beauty, which produces and sells natural soaps and other organically grown skin- and hair-care products. Due to its natural ingredients and high-quality production, Double Z quickly gained a following and won several regional beauty product awards.

After graduating from college, Zach decided to join the family business. Recently, after talking with Zoey, he came up with ideas for a few organic pet products as well. Persuaded by Zach, the family made

DOI: 10.4324/9781003178620-16

a critical decision to hire Tyler to design and help launch a business website to start selling all Double Z Beauty products online. At first, the website did not generate significant sales for the business, but the scenario changed once the website was linked to Amazon.com and a few other commercial portals, a few tricks Tyler was getting good at applying. The excellent product reviews and customer service started to bring in a stream of retail and wholesale orders from all over the country. Last month, online sales even passed those of their family store and several local distributors and retailers combined. Zach's grandparents, eager to spend more time traveling, began to think of increasing Zach's company responsibilities.

In recent months, Zach has been receiving email inquiries from international customers and distributors interested in Double Z Beauty products. He took this as a very promising sign for expanding the business to a global market, but there is a long list of issues to overcome, such as shipping and distribution, payment and currency conversion, taxes and duties, advertising and marketing, products and packaging requirements, customer service, and so on. In addition, if the business sells to the international market, at some point Double Z will also need to consider expanding production. Currently the family farm produces just enough raw materials, now that there is also Zach's pet product line. But once they go global, the family will need to purchase some supplies elsewhere. Zach did market research and found that several farms across the border in Mexico could become potential suppliers.

In college, Zach took a couple classes related to international business. His initial impression was that international trade was the business of large corporations. Now, however, he knows that many small businesses have substantial international business transactions and Zach is wondering how a family business like Double Z Beauty could expand its business overseas. He decides to call Zoey and Tyler and meet for coffee before he talks further to his grandparents.

Introduction: Business and Government in an Era of Globalization

When we expand our focus beyond local economic development, it is easy to recognize that we live in a global economy today. Goods and services produced in one region are easily available in others. Information flows quickly around the world and international communication is commonplace. Capital and labor travel rapidly and frequently across borders. Both business and government now operate in a global environment and need to respond to various global imperatives. Whereas firms gain access to more investment opportunities, cheaper labors, more appropriate operation cites, better suppliers and distributors, advanced technologies and innovations, and larger markets, they are under more intense competition with not only domestic competitors, but also adversaries from other countries. In addition to domestic political and economic forces, firms also need to understand and respond to various political, economic, social, and cultural imperatives of the countries in which they invest, operate, sell, or buy.

Governments today often find that their autonomous power has been overshadowed by problems such as infectious diseases, terrorism, and climate change that can easily cross borders and demand international collaboration. They are facing increasingly difficult challenges, such as creating and retaining jobs, preventing tax evasion, and protecting the world's deteriorating environment, all of which are a result of global competition.

The global context also instills new meaning to the relationship between business and government. Governments often play a dual, yet paradoxical, role on behalf of business—on one hand, governments are requested to maintain a stable monetary and fiscal system, negotiate trade agreements, and set up foreign policies on behalf of the country to facilitate free trade as well as to enhance the competitive advantage of domestic firms in the global market place; on the other hand, governments are needed to protect domestic firms and disadvantaged groups from the sharp edges of a global economy. More importantly, governments act as representatives for national interests in global trade and financial institutions, such as the World Trade Organization, the International Monetary Fund, and the World Bank, the de facto governing powers in the global marketplace.

Today, businesses often find that execution of a domestically oriented strategy in this fast-changing global environment may be unwise. Students should learn how to take advantage of business opportunities overseas and how to interpret the global trends that directly affect business practices. It is critical for business to understand the trade regimes, foreign contexts, and global financial institutions in order to best capitalize on opportunities and avoid the problems related to lack of international business awareness.

Globalization and Neoliberalism

Globalization is an umbrella term for a complex series of economic, social, technological, cultural, and political changes that are seen as increasing interdependence, integration, and interaction between people and companies in disparate locations.

The process of globalization has been observed in different historical times. Some scholars trace its historical origin to the age of European discovery and voyages to the New World. Others observe its presence from the late nineteenth century to the early twentieth century as the world's economies became interconnected as a result of the industrial revolution.

The process has reached an unprecedented level since the 1980s, especially after the end of the Cold War. Distinguishing this current wave of globalization from earlier ones, Thomas Friedman, author of many thought-provoking books on globalization, says that today globalization enables "nation-states and corporations to reach farther, faster, cheaper, and deeper around the world than ever before" (Friedman 2005). For example, the top ten retailers have over 50 percent of the US market (RIS 2020).

In analyzing the causes of this new wave of globalization, technological advancement has commonly been recognized as one principal driver. Advances in transportation and telecommunications infrastructure have dramatically transformed economic life. The development of the automobile, aviation, and nautical technologies in the twentieth century has not only made international travel easy and affordable to individuals, but also enhanced corporations' capability to ship materials and products around the world. Information and telecommunication technologies, such as microchips, fiberoptics, satellites, and the Internet, have largely reduced the cost and time of long-distance communication and made it possible for companies to operate in multiple locations. The COVID-19 pandemic increased the information trajectory enormously, with videoconferencing around the world increasing from a minor aspect of the communication spectrum, to dominating communications and intra-organizational communications interactions (Chawla 2020).

Increased global awareness has also propelled the globalization process. In 1968, when NASA astronauts sent back the first picture of Earth from deep space (Exhibit 12.1), the Gaia sentiment was shared by many people and a new perspective toward our mother planet was adopted. Gaia was the Greek Goddess of the Earth. The word was borrowed to describe the view that our planet is an organism, an interconnected living system of soil, oceans, biosphere, and atmosphere, which is delicate, fragile, and yearning for protection. The sentiment has not only drawn a strong following from environmentalists, ecologists, New Agers, feminists, and other fringe social groups, but also largely driven the global environmental and humanity movements. People around the world are increasingly concerned about the welfare of all human and nonhuman life, preservation of Earth as our home, the balance between development and sustainability, as well as the growing confrontation between the zeal of nationalism, patriotism, and diversity and the yearning for peace, harmony, and unity.

Perhaps the most critical catalyst to the accelerated globalization process in the past three decades was the adoption of free market principles by a majority of the nation states around the world as a result of the triumph of capitalism over communism. This renewed interest toward free market economy has been referred to as *neoliberalism*, a term already much discussed in this text.

Exhibit 12.1

First picture of Earth from outer space

Source: NASA (1968).

To review the term, neoliberalism was originally thought of as the combination of the classical economic liberalism of Smith and Ricardo, combined with the social awareness of John Stuart Mill that the state must play a humanitarian role, and the awareness of Keynes that the large administrative state was also expected to play an important series of economic roles, from monetary and interest-rate stabilization to counter-cyclical economic fiscal policy in order to mitigate the ravages of the business cycle. Today neoliberalism almost always refers to the advocacy of a smaller government role and a more robust role for the market.

Neoliberalism Policies

Generally speaking, neoliberalism advocates transferring control of the economy from the public to the private sector with the belief that it will lead to improved economic health as well as a more efficient government. Policies advanced by neoliberalism are often referred to as the "Washington Consensus," a term coined to describe the policy package that gained consensus approval among the Washington, DC-based economic organizations, such as the International Monetary Fund (IMF), World Bank (see Chapter 13), and the US Treasury Department. The package includes a list of policies such as:

- *Free trade*: removal of trade barriers, like tariffs, subsidies, and regulatory restrictions.
- *Privatization*: transfer of previously public-owned enterprises, goods, and services to the private sector.
- *Competitive exchange rates*: accepting market-determined exchange rates, as opposed to government-fixed exchange rates.
- *Undistorted market prices*: refraining from policies that would alter market prices.
- *Limited intervention*: with exception only for promoting exports, education, or infrastructural development.
- *Fiscal rectitude*: cutting government expenditures and/or raising taxes to maintain a budget surplus.

Theories of International Trade

Free trade, advanced by neoliberalism, refers to a policy by which governments do not discriminate against imports or exports. It has long been a debatable topic. To its proponents, free trade maximizes the interest of consumers throughout the world by giving them a wider variety of goods from which to choose. Differences in the efficiency of land, labor, and capital make it profitable for nations to specialize in the production of goods and services in which their resource situation is the most advantageous, and exchange them for the goods and services of other nations with different resource advantages. If there were no restraints placed on the movement of goods and services from one region to another, or from one nation to another, then in theory the welfare of consumers would be maximized.

The benefits of free trade were theoretically explored by many economists, such as Adam Smith, David Ricardo, and others.

The theory of *absolute advantage* is generally attributed to Adam Smith. In his book *The Wealth of Nations* (1776/1937), Smith pointed out that countries could not all become rich simultaneously by following mercantilism, but they could gain together if they specialized in producing goods or services in which they had an absolute advantage and traded freely with each other.[1] Absolute advantage refers to the ability of a party (being an individual, firm, or nation) to produce a certain service or goods more efficiently than another one. The theory provides a basis for trade, in that if one party has absolute advantage over the other, the latter should buy from the former. Adam Smith described the theory by comparing labor productivity in the context of international trade. The simple comparison of labor productivity pointed to an intrinsic limitation of the theory—if a party has no absolute advantage in anything, then trade is not beneficial and would never occur.

The benefits of trade were further explored by David Ricardo (1772–1823), a British political economist. Ricardo's most important legacy was the theory of *comparative advantage*, a fundamental argument in favor of free trade among countries and of specialization among individuals. Ricardo argued that there is mutual benefit from trade (or exchange), even if one party (e.g., resource-rich country, highly skilled artisan) is more productive in every possible area than its trading counterpart (e.g., resource-poor country, unskilled laborer), as long as each concentrates on the activities in which it has relative productivity advantage (Hollander 1979).

Comparative advantage holds that if one country has an advantage over another country in the production of several goods, it should produce the good in which it has the greatest advantage and buy the good in which it has the least advantage from the other country. Gains can also arise from *specialization*—a concentration of labors and other resources for producing a single product, a practice which can lead to greater skill and productivity than would be achieved by the same number of workers and resources being devoted to the production of a variety of goods and services. Specialization due to trade based on comparative advantage provides mutual benefits to trading parties.

The theory can be better illustrated with the following example. Suppose that both the US and Mexico produce wheat and avocados. With one unit of input (i.e., labor, capital, land, etc.), the US can produce eight units of wheat and four units of avocados, respectively, whereas Mexico can only produce one unit of wheat and two units of avocados, as Mexico is less productive than the US in general due to a variety of factors such as land, climate, technology, skill, etc. Therefore, the US has absolute advantage over Mexico in producing

Exhibit 12.2

An example of comparative advantage

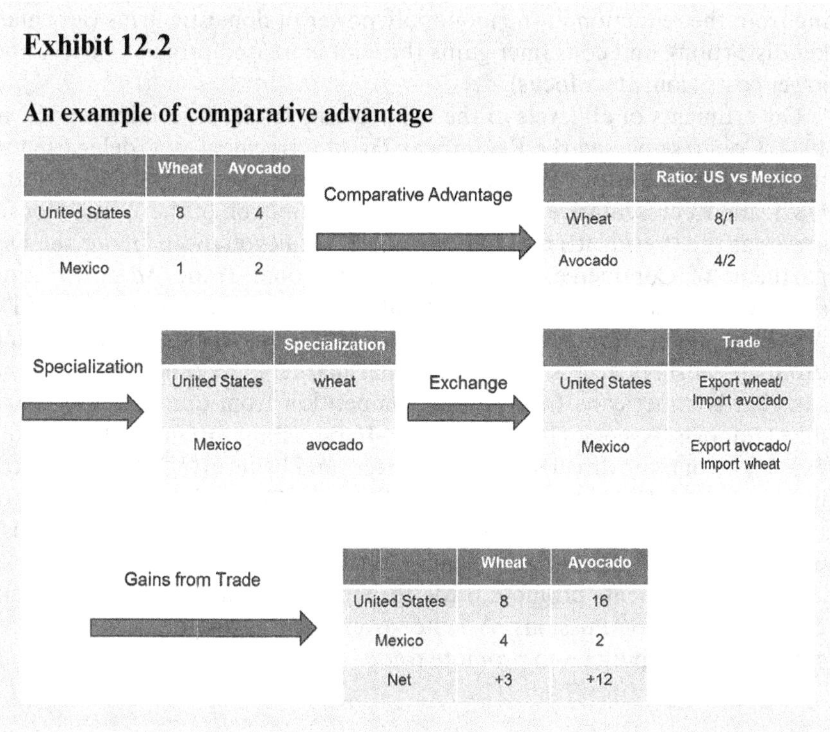

	Wheat	Avocado
United States	8	4
Mexico	1	2

	Ratio: US vs Mexico
Wheat	8/1
Avocado	4/2

	Specialization
United States	wheat
Mexico	avocado

	Trade
United States	Export wheat/ Import avocado
Mexico	Export avocado/ Import wheat

	Wheat	Avocado
United States	8	16
Mexico	4	2
Net	+3	+12

both products. Based on the theory of absolute advantage, trade between the two nations would never occur, as Mexico does not have any incentive.

However, comparing the advantages of the US over Mexico in the two products (Exhibit 12.2), the ratio of eight units of wheat over one is better than that of four units of avocados over two for the US; and vice versa, the comparison ratio of avocados is better for Mexico than that of wheat. Based on the theory of comparative advantage, the US in this example has a comparative advantage in producing wheat and should specialize in producing wheat, whereas Mexico has a comparative advantage in producing avocados and should therefore specialize in avocados. If the US devotes its one unit of resources that used to produce avocados to producing wheat, the US should gain eight units of wheat; and if the country trades the eight units of wheat with Mexico for avocados, it will gain 16 units of avocados, which is better than the original four units produced domestically. Similarly, if Mexico devotes the one unit of input for wheat to producing avocados, it will gain two units of avocados; if it trades with the US for wheat, it will gain four units of wheat, which is better than the original one unit of wheat produced with the same amount of resources. Through specialization and exchange, both parties gain.

Government Policies in Promoting Trade

Trade can contribute to economic growth in multiple ways. As the market potentially served expands from a national to world market, there are gains with declining per-unit production costs (greater efficiency), gains resulting from the reduction in the monopoly power of domestic firms (less market distortion), and consumer gains through increased product variety and lower costs (consumer focus).

Governments of all levels in the US promote trade, especially export. In 1934, Congress passed the Reciprocal Trade Agreement Act, delegating to the President the authority to negotiate trade agreements. The Office of the US Trade Representative (USTR), under the direction of the White House, serves as the President's representative in trade negotiation. Under the Department of Commerce (DoC), the International Trade Administration (ITA) promotes exports of non-agricultural US services and goods. ITA provides information assistance to Americans in selecting markets and products, ensures access to international markets by domestic firms, and safeguards Americans from unfair competition from dumped and subsidized imports. Agencies like the Export–Import Bank (EximBank) promote exports by making direct loans to exporters and by insuring and guaranteeing loans made by private lenders. The Overseas Private Investment Corporation (OPIC) provides insurance, such as loan guarantees and political risk insurance, for US direct investment in less-developed countries.

State governments promote trade through economic development agencies and trade commissions. A state government often offers a variety of subsidies or tax policies to promote trade.

Local government can create Free Trade Zones (FTZs) to attract companies. For example, Miami allows goods to be brought into the city FTZ tariff free. Firms will not pay a tariff until the product is assembled and leaves the zone. Such a policy will largely benefit firms that import and assemble goods with components from multiple foreign suppliers.

Trade Protectionism

Despite the potential gains backed by economic theories and government's efforts in promoting trade, free trade is not without opposition. Ironically, the biggest obstacle to free trade results from government's trade protection policies. Trade protection, or *protectionism*, refers to the economic policies that restrain trade between nations in an attempt to protect domestic industries from foreign takeover or competition.

The policy of trade protection takes its root from mercantilism (see Chapter 1). To mercantilists, in order to accumulate wealth, a nation should always maintain a positive trade balance by keeping the value of exports greater than that of imports. During colonial times, the British required that all colonial trade be conducted on British ships manned by British sailors (Sawers 1992). To protect British producers, the country also restricted the development of manufacturing industries. In doing so, the British maintained a positive trade balance with their colonies. However, it was during this period that the British followed the advice of Smith, Ricardo, and others to become fiscally liberal, which is to say advocates of low tariffs. Ironically, the US became very fiscally Conservative, frequently having the highest tariffs in the developed world in areas that it wanted to advance its "infant" industries or protect select agricultural interests. The US did not become the "neoliberal" leader until after World War two when its economic dominance made it favorable to do so (Irwin 2019).

Protectionism has been also practiced extensively by nation states in this era of globalization. Generally speaking, there are two types of protectionism—one set of policies seeks to protect domestic markets, such as tariffs, import quotas, and regulatory barriers; the other unfairly promotes domestic goods in foreign markets, such as export subsidies, exchange control, and dumping. See Exhibit 12.3 for protectionist arguments.

Tariffs

Tariffs are taxes imposed on incoming goods. It is the most common device used to restrict foreign trade. The rates of tariff may vary based on the type of goods imported. The Tariff Act of 1789 was the first trade protection Act passed in the US. The Act was intended to levy duties on incoming goods, wares, and merchandise in order to support government, and encourage and protect domestic manufacturers. For example, the Act established tonnage rates favorable to American vessels by charging them lower cargo fees than those imposed on foreign boats importing similar goods (Miller 1960).

Quota

Import *quotas* place limits on the amount of a product. The economic impact of an import quota is similar to that of a tariff, except that the tax revenue gain from a tariff will instead be distributed to those who receive import licenses. The US places strict tariffs on the import of sugar. The country is not only one of the largest sugar producers, but also one of the largest consumers of sugar in the world. The US sugar industry has enjoyed trade protection ever since 1789 when Congress enacted the first tariff against foreign-produced sugar. Today, the US government strictly controls sugar imports by means of Tariff-Rate Quotas (TRQs), which specify the amount of sugar that can enter the country from abroad at a low or zero duty. Additional sugar imports above TRQ levels will be imposed over-quota tariffs, which will be too high for firms to make a profit. For example, in 2012, the US allocated an import quota of 155,634 tons of raw cane sugar to Brazil, which had to pay an import duty not to exceed US$1.4606 cents per kilogram.

Regulatory Barriers

Regulatory barriers come in various forms. There are various administrative rules that may introduce barriers to imports. Such rules may concern food safety, environmental standards, intellectual property rights, employment-based immigration requirements, and so on. For example, after the Mattel toy scandal in 2007 (when toys manufactured in China used lead-based paint in excess of amounts allowable in the US), the US passed the Consumer Product Safe Improvement Act, imposing the toughest toy-making standards in the world. As a result of the regulations, the import of toys from China, Mattel's major manufacturer, was largely restricted, forcing the Chinese government to improve its product regulation. Some countries are accused of intentionally making trade-related regulations vague or undisclosed to hinder imports.

Export Subsidies

Government subsidies in the form of tax credits, lump-sum payments, loans, or free resources (such as water, public land, etc.) may be given to domestic firms to encourage exports. Agricultural subsidies are commonly paid by governments to farmers and agriculture businesses to influence the price and supply of agricultural products. Through various farm bills, the US pays over $20 billion in subsidies to farms and agribusiness. At their peak in

2000, subsidies made up 47 percent of total farm income in the US.[2] Agricultural subsidies often are a common stumbling block in trade negotiations. For example, the WTO trade negotiations were stalled in 2006, because the US refused to cut subsidies to a level where other countries' non-subsidized exports could be more competitive.

Exchange Control

Currency values can be manipulated to affect the trading relationship. Keeping the value of money low against other currencies can encourage lower imports and higher exports. Government, often through the national central bank, can practice exchange control by selling its currency in the foreign exchange market. Despite the benefit of improved trade balance, this policy can only be effective in the short run and it often leads to inflation in the country. China has been accused of manipulating exchange control over a long period of time (Kaushal 2018).

Dumping

Dumping refers to the selling of a product in another country at a cost lower than its production cost, which is often made up by government subsidy. Dumping may lead to conditions where one firm has a monopoly in a certain product or industry. For example, if a foreign firm wants to compete with a domestic firm that sells identical products, it prices its product far below the cost of producing it. To compete with the foreign firm, the domestic company has to lower its prices. Without equivalent protection from the foreign government, the domestic firm may lose money and exit the market. Thus, the foreign company gets the market share and may eventually monopolize the market. Dumping drives countries like the US to develop antidumping laws to forbid predatory dumping.

Economists generally agree that protectionism is harmful, primarily because its costs outweigh the benefits and it impedes economic growth. For example, one study found that consumers were paying an average of $139,000 for each job protected in 1990 in the apparel industry, while in that same period of time the average pay of a production worker was less than $15,000 (Hufbauer and Elliott 1994). Protection requires additional resources from other industries, and therefore it will reduce the output in other domestic industries. Protection often raises the prices of materials and goods and requires scarce government resources be diverted to them. In addition, consumers are harmed by reduced consumption of protected items, both because the protected item is more expensive and less will be bought, and because fewer are able to consume other items as well, owing to the greater price of protected goods.

Exhibit 12.3

Protectionist arguments

There are a variety of arguments for trade protection.

The national defense argument states that government should retain minimum production capacity and restrict trade, especially in key areas such as armaments. Free traders often argue that protection has been overused in such areas, and that there should be a very limited number of industries that qualify for protection.

The income distribution argument refers to the claim that government should help select disadvantaged groups, such as sugar farmers, in the trade games. Free traders warn that it tampers with the market and is unfair to other groups.

Protectionists claim that government policies should help improve the balance of trade, especially by reducing the trade deficit through limiting imports. Since government policies may distort the market, free traders think it should only be used sparingly and in the short-term.

Probably the most popular protection argument is associated with the protection of jobs. Many interest groups, especially those whose jobs are affected, care more than do general consumers, and advocate that government should protect select industries, such as agriculture, clothing, manufacturing, etc. Free traders would argue that even though there is pain for those involved, instead of protecting select industries, government should assist these workers in migrating to more efficient industries.

The infant industry argument states that government should help infant industry and give the industry time to mature, or build critical mass. Opponents of this claim point out that it is extremely difficult to wean industries off infant industry subsidies. They argue that the policy has been overused and it needs to be extremely limited.

There are also arguments associated with the spillover effects of certain industries, such as those engaging in research and development, and that those industries that provide social usefulness should be protected. The free traders debate that it is the market, and not the government, that will promote such industries.

Finally, the strategic trade policy argument states that we should design select trade policies by reason rather than the market, especially when the market is limited or imperfect. Those against trade protection argue that it too easily leads to market distortion and political manipulation.

Regional Economic Integration

There have been two evolving trends in the world economic environment. We have been observing the progress of globalization as largely driven by technology innovation, which has resulted in not only a globalized market for goods and services, but also a financial market in that the pool of savings is worldwide and financial intermediaries know no international boundaries. Meanwhile, it is also notable that countries around the world have been increasingly moving toward regional economic integration. *Regional economic integration* refers to agreements among countries, often in a geographically approximate region, to reduce, and ultimately remove, tariff as well as non-tariff barriers to the free flow of goods, services, and factors of production between each other.

The term integration in economics means the combination of business firms through contractual agreements, with the intention of reducing prices for distributors and consumers and increasing the combined economic productivity of the members. Economic integration aims to stimulate trade based on the economic theory of the second best, by which the best option is free trade and economic integration is treated as the second best for global trade where barriers to full free trade exist.[3]

The degree of economic integration can be categorized into several levels (Exhibit 12.4). From least integrated to most integrated, they are the preferential trade area, free trade area, customs union, common market, economic union, and finally, the political union.

Exhibit 12.4

Levels of economic integration

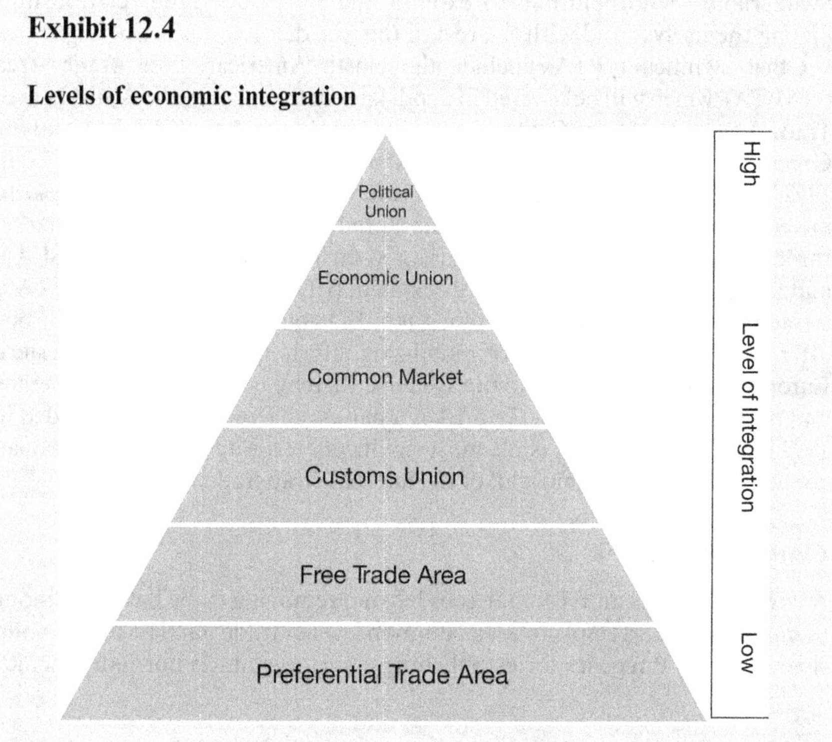

Preferential Trade Area (PTA)

A *preferential trade area* is a trading bloc that gives trade preferences for certain products to a set of trading partners covered in an agreement. A PTA attempts to reduce tariffs among participants, but does not completely abolish them. The line between a PTA and an FTA may be blurred, as almost any PTA has the main goal of eventually becoming an FTA.

Free Trade Area (FTA)

A *free trade area* is essentially a PTA with increased depth and scope of reduction in trade barriers. An FTA aims at the removal of tariffs and other trade barriers among members; however, each country may establish its own trade policies with nonmember countries. FTA is the most popular form of regional economic integration.

One of the longest lasting FTAs in the world is the European Free Trade Association (EFTA), which was established in 1960 by seven European countries—Austria, Denmark, Norway, Portugal, Sweden, Switzerland, and the UK—who were either unable or unwilling to join the European Community (the forerunner of the European Union; see Chapter 13). Those seven countries were often referred to as the Outer Seven as opposed to the Inner Six (Belgium, France, West Germany, Italy, Luxembourg, and Netherlands), which founded the European Community during that time. Today, EFTA has four members—Iceland, Liechtenstein, Norway, and Switzerland—who continue to expand and liberalize trade relationships among themselves and with the rest of the world.

Other significant FTAs include the North American Free Trade Area (NAFTA), which will be covered in depth later in the chapter, the ASEAN Free Trade Area (AFTA), the Central European Free Trade Area (CEFTA), and the Greater Arab Free Trade Area (GAFTA). AFTA is a trade bloc established in 1992 by the Association of Southeast Asian Nations (ASEAN). AFTA seeks to increase ASEAN's competitive edge as a production base in the world market through the elimination of tariffs and non-tariff barriers within the ASEAN and to attract more foreign direct investment (FDI) to the ASEAN. CEFTA is a trade agreement established among non-EU countries in southeast Europe after the Cold War in hopes of mobilizing efforts to integrate into Western European political and economic systems, thereby consolidating democracy and free market economics. GAFTA is a pan-Arab free trade zone founded in 1997 by Arabian states. It is the most significant trade agreement for Arabian countries, and covers almost all of the internal Arab trade.

Customs Union (CU)

A *customs union* is an FTA that goes beyond removing trade barriers among themselves, and attempts to set a common level of trade barriers against outsiders as well. Purposes for establishing a customs union normally include increasing economic efficiency and establishing closer political and social ties between the member states in order to move toward greater economic integration down the road. For example, the EU started as a customs union and has moved beyond this level. The oldest existing customs union is the Southern African Customs Union (SACU) established in 1910 among southern African countries. The union aims to maintain the free interchange of goods between member countries by levying a common external tariff and a common excise tariff to this common customs area. All customs and excise collected in the common customs area are paid into the National Revenue Fund run by South Africa, the custodian of the pool. The revenue, which constitutes a substantial share of the state revenue of the member countries, is shared among members according to a revenue-sharing formula as described in the agreement.

Common Market (CM)

At a higher level of integration, a common market removes trade barriers between members, sets up common external trade policy, and allows not only the free exchange of goods and services, but also the free movement of other factors of production (i.e., labor and capital) among members. *Common markets* facilitate the freedom of movement of all factors of production, which become more efficiently allocated, thereby further enhancing productivity. Transition from a national market to a common market can be very difficult, demanding a significant level of cooperation on not only trade policies, but also monetary, fiscal, and labor policies among member states. For years, the European Union had operated as a common market before it achieved a higher level of integration. In 2012, the Customs Union of Belarus, Kazakhstan, and Russia became a single market—the Common Economic Space. These countries continue to strive for a higher level of integration to create the Eurasian Economic Union.

Economic Union

An *economic union* requires even higher economic integration, which involves the creation of common national economic policies. An economic union not only facilitates a single market among members, but also requires a common currency, coordinated tax rates, and harmonized monetary and fiscal policies. Very few nation states have formed an economic union, as it demands a high level coordination of policy-making and bureaucracy among members and the sacrifice of sovereign power of nation states to that of a supranational governing system. Despite some members not adopting the common currency of the euro, the European Union is a highly integrated economic union. Other economic unions include the Caribbean Single Market and Economy (CSME), established in 1989, which strives to deepen economic integration beyond a common market, expand the economic mass of the Caribbean Community, and progressively integrate the region within the global trading and economic system.

Political Union

As economic integration drives beyond the economic union, it demands political integration to coordinate the governing system that ensures accountability to their constituencies. A *political union* facilitates a central governing system that coordinates the economic, social, political, and foreign policies of the member states. A political union can be viewed as a highly integrated quasi-autonomous nation state that operates with a confederated system of governance. The early 13 colonies of the US formed an example of a political union. In today's world, the European Union has achieved partial political integration as demonstrated in its governing structure. Chapter 13 will have an in-depth discussion of the political structure of the European Union.

The major regional trading blocs today are:

- European Union (EU)
- African Union (AU)
- Union of South American Nations (UNASUR)
- Caribbean Community (CARICOM)
- Central American Integration System (SICA)
- Arab League (AL)
- European Free Trade Association (EFTA)
- Eurasian Economic Community (EAEC)
- Association of Southeast Asian Nations (ASEAN)
- Central European Free Trade Agreement (CEFTA)
- North American Free Trade Agreement (NAFTA)
- South Asian Association for Regional Cooperation (SAARC)
- Pacific Islands Forum (PIF)

The trading world looks like the illustration in Exhibit 12.5.

Economic Integration among the Americas

Being one of the most important international traders, the US has progressively pursued trade agreements with other countries. As of 2021, the US has free trade agreements in effect with 20 countries.[4] These FTAs move beyond the foundation of the WTO Agreement, requiring more comprehensive and stronger disciplines. Many of the FTAs are bilateral agreements between two governments. But some, like the North American Free Trade Agreement and the Dominican Republic–Central America Free Trade Agreement, are multilateral agreements among several parties, which drive the regional economic integration among the Americas.

Exhibit 12.5

Major trading blocs

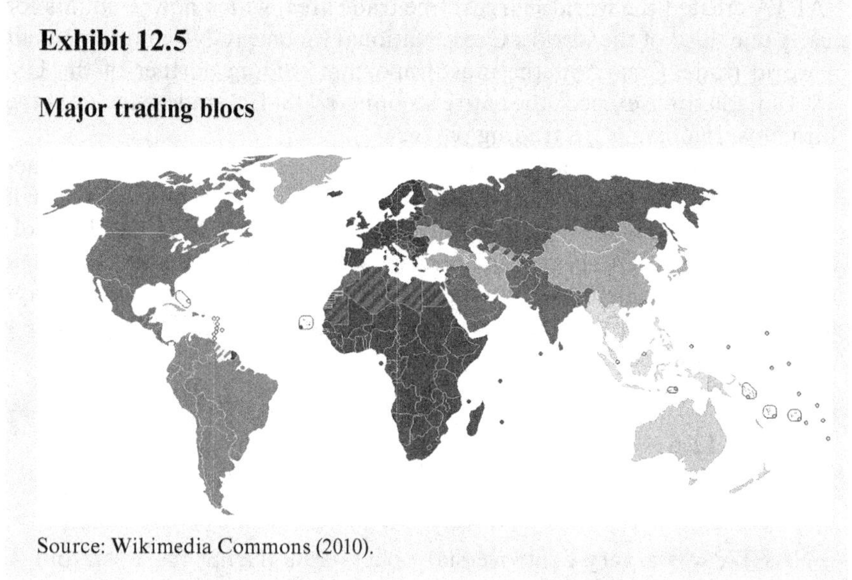

Source: Wikimedia Commons (2010).

North American Free Trade Area

The North American Free Trade Area is a trading bloc consisting of the US, Canada, and Mexico. It is an extension of the Canada–US Free Trade Agreement, which was signed in 1988 and entered into force in 1989. NAFTA was negotiated in 1992, ratified in 1993, and finally entered into force on January 1, 1994. It was revised and renamed the US–Mexico–Canada Agreement in 2020.

The objectives of NAFTA are to:

Eliminate barriers to trade in, and facilitate the cross-border movement of, goods and services between the territories of the Parties
Promote conditions of fair competition in the free trade area
Increase substantially investment opportunities in the territories of the Parties
Provide adequate and effective protection and enforcement of intellectual property rights in each Party's territory
Create effective procedures for the implementation and application of this Agreement, for its joint administration and for the resolution of disputes
Establish a framework for further trilateral, regional, and multilateral co-operation to expand and enhance the benefits of this Agreement.

Source: North American Free Trade Agreement, Chapter 1, Article 102 Objectives

NAFTA created the world's largest free trade area, which now accounts for nearly one third of the world's Gross National Income (GNI) and 18 percent of world trade. Canada is the most important trading partner of the US. US–Canada trade exceeds the entire amount of US–EU trade. Mexico is the third most important US trading partner.

NAFTA passed in Congress by a fairly small margin after weeks of acrimonious debate. Given that Mexico was a developing country, it was felt that America had little to gain by admitting Mexico into NAFTA. The policy debate of NAFTA became a notorious issue in the presidential campaign of 1992, when presidential candidate Ross Perot gained much political capital by saying that "the gigantic sucking sound you hear is the loss of American jobs to Mexico."

Exhibit 12.6

The NAFTA debate

NAFTA was a very controversial policy issue during the Bush and Clinton years. When the agreement was initially proposed in 1988, there was much debate as to whether the agreement should be ratified.

Proponents of NAFTA argued that NAFTA should be seen as an opportunity to create an enlarged and more efficient production base for the entire North American region, and that while some lower-income jobs would move from the US and Canada to Mexico, new jobs would be created in the US and Canada as economic growth occurred in Mexico as a result of the job transfers.

In addition, the international competitiveness of US and Canadian firms that moved production to Mexico to take advantage of lower labor costs would be enhanced, enabling them to better compete against Asian and European rivals.

Those who opposed NAFTA claimed that US and Canadian citizens would lose their jobs in alarming numbers as low-income positions were moved to Mexico to take advantage of lower wage rates.

Environmentalists also voiced concerns about NAFTA. Because Mexico has more lenient environmental protection laws than either the US or Canada, there was concern that US and Canadian firms would relocate to Mexico to avoid the cost of protecting the environment.

Finally, there was opposition in Mexico to NAFTA from those who feared a loss of national sovereignty. Mexican critics feared that NAFTA would allow their country to be dominated by US and Canadian multinationals, and Mexico would be used as a low-cost assembly site, while keeping their higher-paying jobs in their own countries.

The early years of NAFTA were affected by the Mexican currency crisis of December, 1994. Mexico's trade deficit increased in 1993 and 1994 to the point that it was losing its foreign financial reserves. The Clinton Administration provided a $40 billion assistance package to the Mexican government. The devaluation of the Mexican peso increased Mexican exports to the US and Canada and eventually led to the recovery of the Mexican economy.

Criticisms of NAFTA became rather subdued in the US, as later research indicates that NAFTA's overall impact has been generally positive. Trade between the US and its NAFTA partners has soared since the agreement entered into force, increasing at a more rapid rate than US trade with the EU. From 1993 to 2007, overall trade in goods among the three countries has grown from $297 billion to $930 billion, an increase of 213 percent, US exports to Canada and Mexico grew from $142 billion to $385.4 billion, an increase of 171 percent, and US imports from Canada and Mexico grew from $151 billion to $523.9 billion, an increase of 247 percent.[5] All countries experienced strong productivity growth. While some argue that the US has lost 110,000 jobs per year due to NAFTA, many economists dispute this figure because more than two million US jobs were created each year during the same time period. Perhaps the most significant impact of NAFTA has not been economic, but political. While the US entered into a war against terrorism in 2001, the increased political stability in Mexico as a result of NAFTA has helped create a safer backyard for US homeland security.

Dominican Republic–Central America Free Trade Area

On August 5, 2004, the US Senate approved the Dominican Republic–Central America–US Free Trade Agreement (CAFTA-DR) with five Central American countries—Costa Rica, El Salvador, Guatemala, Honduras, and Nicaragua—and the Dominican Republic. It is the first agreement between the US and a large number of developing countries. While the majority of the trade from Central America has enjoyed duty-free access to the US market, the agreement would benefit Central America through facilitating investment and intraregional trade and advancing regional integration. While these developing Central American countries often place high tariffs and other trade barriers on US exports, CAFTA-DR could not only reduce barriers to US goods and products, but also demand critical reform of their legal and business systems to promote transparency in rule-making, to improve and enforce the protection of intellectual property rights, and to provide clear guidance on customs issues.

Central America and the Dominican Republic represent the second largest US export market in Latin America, behind Mexico. US firms enjoy a 40 percent share of their import market. CAFTA-DR further enhances the trade relationship between the US and these countries. More than 80 percent of US exports of consumer and industrial goods became duty free in Central America and the Dominican Republic immediately upon implementation, with remaining tariffs phased out over ten years. The agreement establishes a secure, predictable legal framework for US investors in Central America and the Dominican Republic. In 2006, these six countries received $4.4 billion FDI from the US. Since the Dominican Republic, the largest economy of the six developing countries, implemented CAFTA-DR in March of 2007. The US has maintained a small trade surplus, and agreement has been considered a moderate success in promoting the benefits of a liberal trade agreement. However, the trade agreement has done little to assist improving work conditions as had originally been hoped (CRS 2019).

The unprecedented development of technology, the increased global awareness, and especially the adoption of neoliberalism worldwide have driven the process of globalization. Under the trend of globalization, regions have increasingly moved toward economic integration. These trends present both opportunities and challenges to business. This chapter has reviewed the historical evolution of and policies advanced by neoliberalism, examined the debates surrounding free trade, and introduced government policies in relation to promoting or protecting trade. Business students are expected to gain insights into building effective connections with government in the face of the challenges of a growing global market.

Analytical Case: Sugar Farmers and CAFTA-DR*

Mark Olson was a sugar producer who owned 500 acres of sugar beets in Willmar, Minnesota. In 2004, when the Dominican Republic–Central American Free Trade Agreement (CAFTA-DR) was proposed, sugar farmers like Olson were very vocal in opposition to the trade agreement. CAFTA-DR, with the intention to liberalize trade with five Central American nations and the Dominican Republic, became a divider in the agricultural industry. Most American agricultural groups, such as corn and dairy farmers, were in full support of the agreement, anticipating that the larger market would promise an additional 44 million consumers outside the US access to their products. Others, particularly sugar farmers like Olson, however, believed that CAFTA-DR would spell disaster for them.

Agriculture has been traditionally subsidized by government. Unlike most US farmers, sugar farmers were not directly subsidized by the government. Instead, the US sharply limited sugar imports, keeping sugar prices higher in the domestic market in the absence of overseas competition. Passing the CAFTA-DR agreement would result in falling trade barriers, and increased sugar imports from Central American countries.

According to Olson, other countries subsidized the production of their sugar. And under government subsidies, sugar farmers produced more than what their country needed and dumped their products onto the world market at a cost well below that of production. Olson claimed that the US sugar farmers were some of the most efficient sugar beet producers in the world, but they could not compete with other countries where farmers received government subsidies. Olson had invested half a million dollars in his business. In the US, 90 percent of the sugar was processed in farmer-owned co-ops like Olson's southern Minnesota beet sugar cooperative. The industry employed some 140,000 Americans. Leaders of the co-ops were afraid that if CAFTA-DR passed, foreign producers would dump sugar on the US market and eventually drive people in the sugar industry out of their jobs.

The Bush Administration argued that the sugar producers were overstating their case. It estimated that CAFTA would allow less than two percent more sugar from Central America into this country. Free trade advocates, who proposed to stop protecting the sugar industry, pointed out that the price of sugar in the US market was twice that of outside prices, which led to higher profits for sugar farmers, but higher prices for consumers.

Olson, on the other hand, argued that the price of sugar in the US was less than almost any other developed country in the world and consumers were not paying too much for sugar. He pointed out that the only people who complained about the price of sugar were the big candy companies, and that if they bought sugar more cheaply, consumers would not see a reduction in the cost of their products at all. Despite the debate, CAFTA-DR was narrowly passed by the US Congress (with a vote of 217 in favor and 215 against in the House of Representatives) in July 2005.

Questions for Discussion and Analysis

1 According to the theory of comparative advantage, should US farmers continue producing sugar?
2 According to Olson, other countries all subsidized sugar producers. In that case, should the US remove its import barriers to sugar or should the US subsidize American sugar producers?
3 What effect of CAFTA do you anticipate for American consumers?
4 If you were public policy-makers, how could government placate the different interests among citizen groups for CAFTA?

*The case was developed based on the PBS NEWSHOUR Video *Farmers Differ over CAFTA*, July 20, 2005 at 12:00 AM EST.

Practical Skill

Selling Overseas

Thanks to the Internet and globalization, small businesses like Double Z Beauty can easily tap into the international market for their goods or services. There are many government resources that you can explore. A convenient starting point can be www.export.gov. The website helps US companies that are interested in starting or expanding exports explore training and counseling programs, develop business plans, conduct market research, find foreign buyers, finance exports, and resolve trade problems.

Government agencies, such as the US Commerce Department (the International Trade Administration), the US Small Business Administration (US Export Assistance Centers), and the Export–Import Bank of the US all offer help. In addition, many states operate agencies aimed at helping small businesses export their products. For example, the California Governor's Office of Business and Economic Development (GO-Biz) (www.business.ca.gov) operates a California State Trade and Export Promotion (California STEP) project which leverages a statewide network of state, federal, private, and nonprofit trade promotion organizations to facilitate export promotion and activities in targeted industries and to drive exports for small businesses.

Skill Exercise: Critical Issues of International Trade

Create a list of critical issues that Zach needs to deal with if Double Z Beauty decides to sell overseas, and highlight the issues that deal with government. Browse related government websites and advise Zach on how to deal with those issues.

Summary and Conclusion

1 The world entered into a new era of globalization. Three driving forces contributed to the process: technological advancement, increased global awareness, and most importantly, the acceptance of neoliberalism globally.
2 Neoliberalism, as a renewed version of classic economic liberalism, promotes a free market economy in which free trade is a key policy.
3 Classic international trade theories, such as the absolute advantage and comparative advantage, provide the economic rationale for free trade.
4 Governments at all levels promote trade, especially export.

5 Government uses tariffs, quotas, and regulatory barriers to protect domestic firms. It also uses subsidies, exchange control, and dumping to create unfair competitive advantage.
6 There has been an accelerated trend of regional economic integration. A number of levels of economic integration include a preferential trade area, a free trade area, a customs union, a common market, an economic union, and a political union in the order of increased integration.
7 Despite controversy, the North American Free Trade Agreement and the Dominican Republic–Central American Free Trade Agreement, as well as the ongoing Free Trade Agreement of Americas, drive the regional economic integration among American countries.

Key Terms

- Absolute advantage
- Free trade
- Quota
- Common market
- Free trade area
- Regional economic
- Comparative advantage
- Globalization
- Integration
- Customs union
- Neoliberalism
- Specialization
- Dumping
- Political union
- Tariff
- Economic union
- Protectionism

Study Questions

1 What are the driving forces to globalization and regional economic integration? To what extent do these two trends converge and diverge?
2 Discuss the theory of absolute advantage and comparative advantage, with examples.
3 What are the government policies in promoting and protecting trade? Discuss and critique them with examples.
4 What are the different levels of economic integration? How are they differentiated?
5 What are the debating arguments associated with NAFTA? If you were Adam Smith or David Ricardo, how would you respond to the debate?
6 What are the opportunities and challenges that US firms may face if the FTAA is approved? How should they respond to the trade policy?

Notes

1 Adam Smith (1776). *An Inquiry into the Nature and Causes of the Wealth of Nations*, the Glasgow edition of the works and correspondence of Adam Smith, edited by R. H. Campbell and A. S. Skinner, 1981, Liberty Press.

2 Farm Subsidies over Time. *Washington Post*, 2 July 2006. http://www.washington post.com/wp-dyn/content/graphic/2006/07/02/GR2006070200024.html.
3 US Department of State. *Benefits of US Free Trade Agreements.* http://www.state.gov/e/eb/tpp/bta/fta/c26474.htm.
4 The United States has established free trade agreements with 20 countries: Australia, Bahrain, Canada, Chile, Colombia, Costa Rica, Dominican Republic, El Salvador, Guatemala, Honduras, Israel, Jordan, Korea, Mexico, Morocco, Nicaragua, Oman, Panama, Peru, and Singapore.
5 US Department of Commerce. *Top US Export Markets: Free Trade Agreement and Country Facts Sheets.* Summer 2008. http://trade.gov/media/publications/pdf/tm_091208.pdf/.

References

Chawla, A. (2020). Coronavirus (COVID-19) Zoom application boon or bane. Available at SSRN 3606716.

CRS (2019). Dominican Republic-Central America-United States Free Trade Agreement (CAFTA-DR).

Friedman, T. (2005). *The World Is Flat.* New York: Farrar, Straus and Giroux.

Hollander, S. (1979). *The Economics of David Ricardo.* Toronto: University of Toronto Press.

Hufbauer, G. C., and Elliott, K. A. (1994). *Measuring the Costs of Protection in the United States.* Washington, DC: Institute for International Economics.

Irwin, D. A. (2020). Trade Policy in American Economic History. *Annual Review of Economics*, *12*:23–44.

Kaushal, A. (2018). Politics in Global Currency Regulations: IMF & WTO Cooperation in the Light of Currency Dispute between USA and China. Gujarat National Law University, *JL Development & Policy*, *8*:17.

Miller, J. C. (1960). *The Federalists: 1789–1801.* New York: Harper & Row.

NASA (1968). http://www.nasa.gov/multimedia/imagegallery/image_feature_102.html.

RIS (2020). Top 100 Retailers. Retail Information Systems. https://risnews.com/top-100-retailers-2020.

Sawers, L. (1992). The Navigation Acts Revisited. *Economic History Review*, *45*(*2*):262–284.

Smith, A. (1937). *The Wealth of Nations.* New York: The Modern Library.

Wikimedia Commons (2010). Alinor. https://commons.wikimedia.org/wiki/File:Trade_blocs.png.

13 Examples of and Challenges for Trade Regimes in the World

Chapter Contents

Case 13 Scenario

Zoey's Sister Moves to China

Zoey's older sister, Zara, is a sales representative for MaxMachinery, a US-based supplier of heavy equipment for infrastructure construction. In the early 1990s, when China lifted many trade barriers, the company began exporting heavy machinery to China; over the past couple decades, the company has largely benefited from the trade, along with China's double-digit economic growth. In recent years, the Chinese central government has put more emphasis on economic development in the Western inland provinces. Following this policy lead, MaxMachinery targeted several provinces to expand its market. Among them, Sichuan province has been leading the economic growth and demonstrated a potential high demand for equipment.

DOI: 10.4324/9781003178620-17

To investigate the potential market, expand its sales, and better serve its customers in the region, the company decided to establish a resident office in Chengdu, the capital city of Sichuan, and dispatch Zara as the chief representative to the office.

As a sales rep, Zara has been doing business with the company's Chinese customers for several years. Zara even took Zoey over to China on spring break one year, and paid for her trip. In addition to traveling frequently between the continents, Zara learned to speak Chinese, understand the country's history and culture, and even use chopsticks. She has developed a good relationship with her Chinese customers, who often acknowledge her as a "Zhongguo Tong," an endearing nickname for China expert. Zara and her husband are excited about the new assignment. They have started to make plans for their long-distance relocation and Zara's husband has begun looking for opportunities to teach English at a university.

Despite the excitement, Zara also has some anxiety. Zara knows that many of her Chinese customers were former state-owned enterprises and that some of them, despite their private ownership, still have intrinsic connections with government. In the past, Zara mainly had to deal with the Chinese government indirectly through her customers, but now in order to set up the resident office and represent her company, she needs to deal with the Chinese government directly. Zara feels she must learn the political and administrative systems of the Chinese government and its economic and foreign trade policies, in addition to the policies and procedures for a foreign representative office.

As she is jotting down things she must do before departing, Zach calls with a special request.

Introduction

This chapter further examines neoliberalism and regional economic integration, which were introduced in Chapter 11, by introducing two in-depth cases—China and the European Union. As a driver to unprecedented globalization in the past three decades, neoliberalism (especially the free trade policies) has exerted enormous political, economic, and social impact on the world. This chapter offers a critique to neoliberalism policies and examines their impact by tracing the economic reform changes advanced in China since the late 1970s. In the light of regional economic integration, this chapter also offers a critique of regionalism and examines its impact on European countries. Given the fact that both the European Union and China are the two most important trading partners of the US outside the American continents, it is critical for business students to understand the political and economic institutions of these two large trading blocs, as well as their implications to US businesses.

Critique of Neoliberalism

Since the 1970s, neoliberal economic policies have been implemented to various extents across the globe as neoliberalism, a more modern version of capitalism (Exhibit 13.1), started to gain traction as a practical system of government. The impact of such policies on the world is enormous. While most countries that adopted a free market economy have experienced economic prosperity, they have also experienced an increasing gap between the rich and poor in addition to a large array of emergent social, economic, political, and environment problems.

Exhibit 13.1

Historical critiques of capitalism

There is considerable overlap between neoliberalism and capitalism. Neoliberalism is a special, newer version of capitalism, which itself is an economic system that revolves around commodity production controlled by owners for profit-making, and labor exploitation of the proletariat (working class) by the bourgeoisie (rich people). While still centered on commodity production and private ownership, neoliberalism also advocates for free, open markets, as well as deregulation as the solution to many of our problems. Historically, capitalism has been criticized through many theoretical lenses:

Critical Theory School

Critical theory is a social theory oriented toward critiquing and changing society as a whole. Taking its roots from Marxism, the critical theory school of thought opines that capitalism gives too much power to a few rich people and countries and that the power of the state should be used to equalize opportunity, wealth, and social structures.

Dependency Theory School

Because of trade, dependency theorists observe that resources flow from a periphery of poor and underdeveloped countries to a core of wealthy, developed states, enriching the latter at the expense of the former. They argue that capitalism is too tilted toward the historically advantaged countries who essentially "rig" the system in their favor.

Religious Teachings

Some religious teachings, from monasticism to theocracy, see that placing the pursuit of money first by capitalism tends to ignore our soul and potentially our humanity.

Exhibit 13.2

Gini index of wealth distribution

The more formal measurement of income inequality is known as the Gini coefficient or Gini index. An index of 100 percent means a single person grabs all the income; an index of zero means the country divides its income precisely equally among everyone.

Some cautions include: (1) the Gini index misses asset-based wealth such as land, and income not distributed in the form of money; (2) different surveys give slightly different results; (3) large diverse countries often look more unequal than small countries; and (4) rising inequality does not always mean worsening conditions. During the 1990s, for example, the American Gini index rose but the Gini index has continued to rise, but the poor are not that much poorer on average in a rich country. However, it remains to be seen what the long-term effects of the COVID-19 pandemic is on the poverty rate when government interventions cease and governments become squeezed by debt. For comparison, Gini indices in the world range from the Czech Republic's egalitarian 25 percent to South Africa's very unequal 63 percent. The US has the most uneven distribution of the advanced democracies.

The map below shows differences in national income equality around the world as measured by the national Gini coefficient 2021 (using the most recent data).

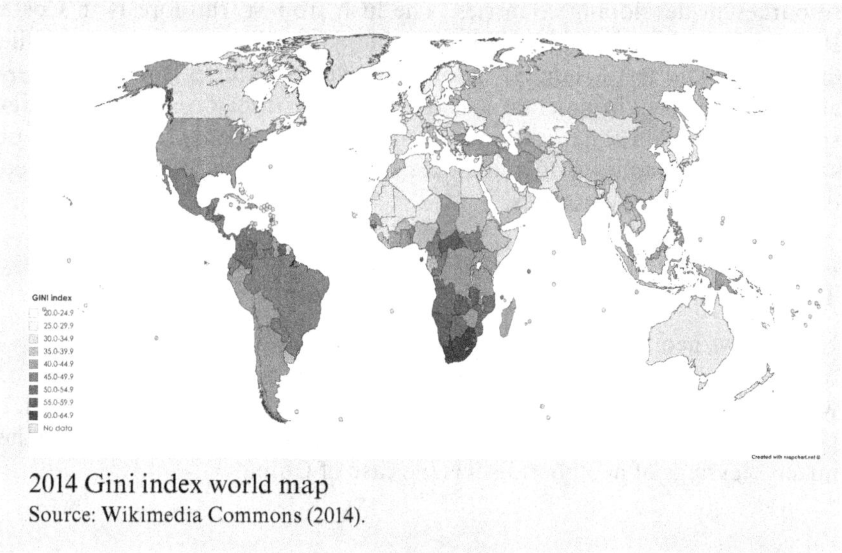

2014 Gini index world map
Source: Wikimedia Commons (2014).

The major group of neoliberalism critics comes from the opponents of the "Washington Consensus" (see Chapter 11). They argue that the Washington Consensus, consisting mainly of Western developed states, has used trade liberalization, investment liberalization, deregulation, and privatization to their own selfish ends: trade liberalization has a built-in advantage for the wealthy to exploit the labor and resources of poor countries or individuals; investment liberalization decreases a country's opportunity to provide its own economic and social path; deregulation reduces the state's role in trying to protect the disadvantaged, the less fortunate, the less powerful, and the future; and privatization reduces the state's role and puts everything in the orbit of capitalism; therefore, it puts everything up for sale (Broad and Cavanagh 1999).

Critics argue that neoliberalism is associated with the unfair distribution of wealth and power, which contributes to various forms of political, economic, and cultural exploitation and phenomena such as social alienation, economic inequality, unemployment, and economic instability. Despite neoliberal policies having produced economic growth in various regions around the world, income disparity, instead of shrinking, has been growing since the end of World War II. Ownership of the nation's wealth has been rising for the top 1 percent of America's richest people, with the top 1 percent owning 16 times more than the bottom 50 percent of the population (Fed 2021).

Environmental destruction around the globe is also occurring at an alarming rate. Export-led growth often depends on the plunder of natural resources in developing countries. The lush tropical rainforests in Costa Rica, rich fishing banks in Thailand, abundant mineral deposits in Chile and Brazil, and fertile land in Indonesia have all suffered from unrecoverable long-term environmental loss over the past three decades. The widespread destruction of natural resource systems has not only led to the loss of species and degradation of land, but has also threatened the very livelihood of the poor in these countries.

The Case of China

Ultimately, neoliberalism has its strengths and weaknesses, like any system. At the national and social level, neoliberalism creates some enormous winners, which point to the successes; and some enormous losers, which point to the structural disadvantages. A unique opportunity to examine the mixed blessings of neo liberalism is the case of China.

About China

The People's Republic of China (PRC) is located in the east of the Asian continent, on the western shore of the Pacific Ocean, and has a land mass of about 3.7 million square miles. It is the fourth largest country in size, next only to Russia, Canada, and the US.

China (Exhibit 13.3) is the most populous country in the world, with a population of 1.4 billion as of 2021; its population growth rate is somewhat lower than the US and far below India, which are the third and second most populous countries comparatively. When the PRC was founded in 1949, the country had 541.67 million inhabitants. In the following two peaceful decades after centuries of war, the population grew rapidly, reaching 806.71 million in 1969. Since the 1970s, China had implemented the policy of population increment control, which includes requirements of family planning, late marriages, late childbearing, and one child per couple. The policy has contributed to a decreased birth rate for the past several decades. China is a multi-ethnic nation of 56 ethnic groups. The majority of the population is of the Han ethnic group, accounting for 91.6 percent of the total, with the other 55 minority groups accounting for less than 9 percent. Population distribution is quite uneven across the country. The majority live along the east coast and central regions, which have an extremely high population density, whereas in Western inland areas, there are very few people.

China's administrative units are based on a four-level system. At the top level, is the central government. Directly under the central government is the provincial level, which consists of 23 provinces (including Taiwan) (see Exhibit 13.3), five autonomous regions (occupied mainly by minority groups other than Han), four municipalities (Beijing, Shanghai, Tianjin, and Chongqing, which are directly controlled by the central government), and two special administrative regions (Hong Kong and Macao). Hong Kong and Macao were occupied by Britain and Portugal after the Opium War of 1840. China resumed sovereignty over the two regions in 1997 and 1999, respectively. Under the provincial administrative units, there are numerous counties and townships. The Chinese government is a highly centralized administrative system (Exhibit 13.4), with each lower level of administrative units under the direct control of its upper level of administrative units.

China's government structure is similar to Western parliamentary systems (Exhibit 13.5), with both a president and a prime minister appointed by a parliament and a semi-independent judiciary branch. The National People's Congress (NPC), China's parliament, together with the Political Consultative Committee, a parliamentary advisory body, is the state's highest legislature. The NPC ratifies laws and has oversight and appointment responsibility for the State Council and courts. The nine-member Politburo Standing Committee of the NPC oversees the operation of the three branches of PRC government.

The presidency is a largely ceremonial office with limited powers. The State Council, namely, the Central People's Government, is the PRC cabinet and the highest administrative body. With its ministries, bureaus, commissions, and agencies, the State Council serves as the administrator and regulator of government functions and is headed by the Premier. The State

Exhibit 13.3

Map of China

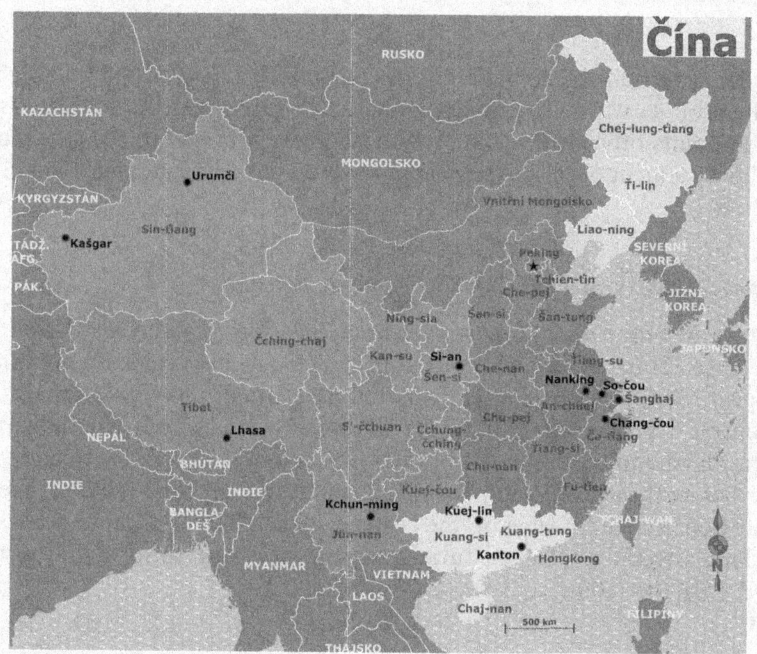

Source: Wikimedia Commons (2022).

Exhibit 13.4

Administrative regions of China

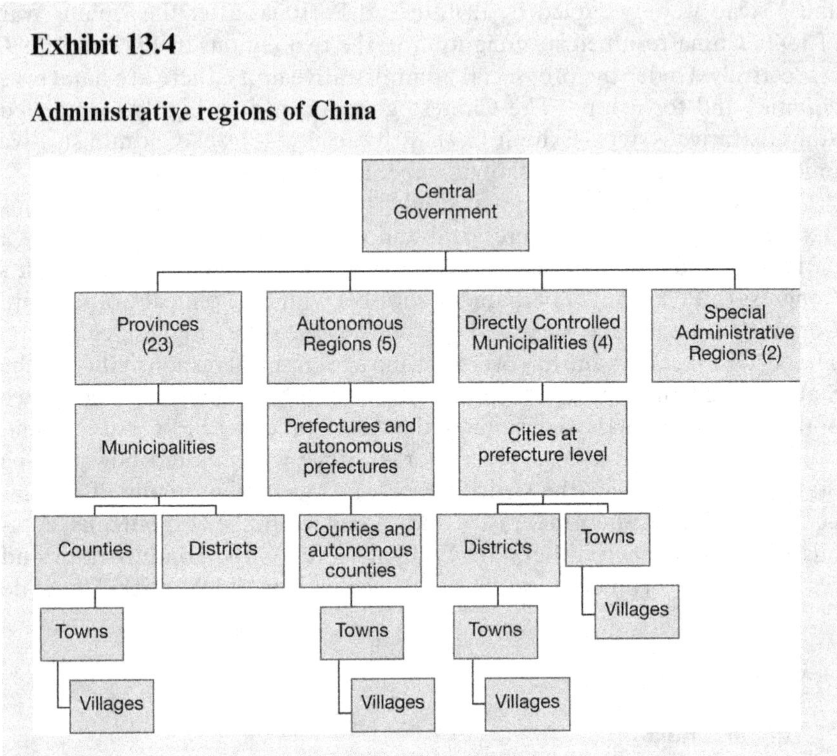

Council is responsible to the NPC and its Standing Committee, and reports to them on its work. The State Council also supervises the operations of, and appoints officials for, the provincial-level government; the provincial-level government oversees the next lower-level government, and so on down the line.

Historical Background of China's Economic Reform

China, one of the world's most ancient civilizations, had been a united empire since 221 BC. The country established far-reaching trade relations over the past 2,000 years, and as early as 100 BC, had set up international trade to central Asian countries along the Silk Road, a trade route extending from central China to the east coast of the Mediterranean. In the fourteenth century, before the age of Columbus, China made several large-scale voyages as far as Somalia and Kenya on the eastern coast of Africa. China possessed the largest economy for centuries, sharing over one third of the world's GDP, until the 1800s.

Exhibit 13.5

Chinese government structure

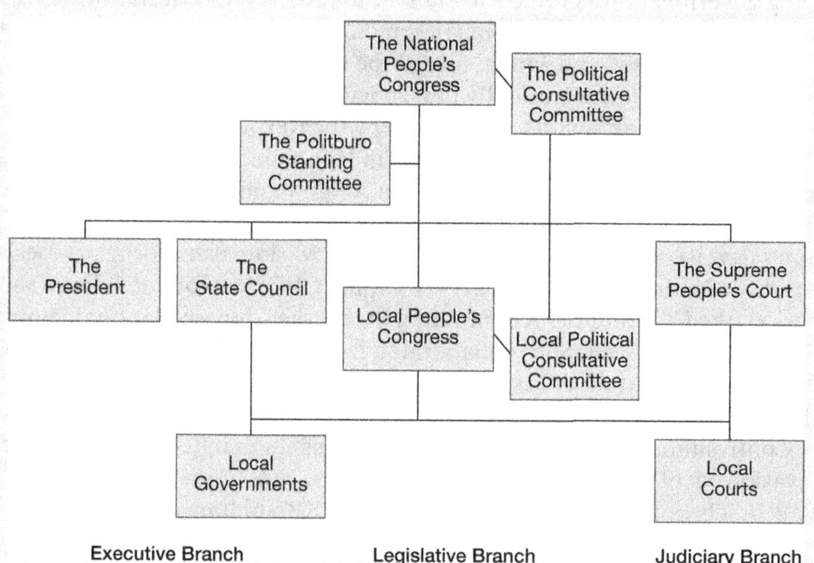

The Supreme People's Court and Supreme People's Procuratorate compose the top judicial branch. They report to the NPC and its Standing Committee and oversee the operation of the next lower level of courts and procuratorates, and so forth.

Unlike the US and other Western parliamentary systems, China operates with a one-party system. The Chinese Communist Party (CCP) is the overarching political authority in China and is headed by its general secretary, who also often assumes the role of President. The NPC's decisions largely reflect the party decisions. China's military, the People's Liberation Army (PLA), is also under the party. Although there are eight democratic parties other than the CCP, they are placed under the leadership of the CCP, mainly providing consultation and support to the CCP through ties with various social groups.

During the nineteenth century, the last imperial Dynasty of China, the Qing, declined rapidly. Britain smuggled large volumes of opium into China; subsequently, the Qing government imposed a ban on opium trade. To protect its profit, Britain launched a war and defeated China in 1840. The Qing government was forced to sign an unfair treaty with the British government. Since then, many countries, including Britain, France, Russia, the US, German, Italy, and Japan, forced the Qing government to sign various unfair treaties. China gradually descended to a semi-colonial country.

The Qing monarchy was overthrown by the Revolution of 1911, led by Dr. Sun Yat-sen. Dr. Sun, who had studied in Honolulu, Hawaii in his early life, envisioned a democratic republic for the country and established the Republic of China. However, the republic was torn by series of wars between Dr. Sun's new Republicans and various regional warlords and former imperialists. In 1921, the Communist Party of China (CPC) was founded. For a short period, the CCP and the Kuomintang (AKA the Chinese National People's Party, founded by Dr. Sun) collaborated in fighting other anti-revolutionary forces. When Sun died, his successor Chiang Kai-Shek began to suppress the CPC.

Confrontation between the two parties was interrupted by the Japanese invasion in 1937, which started the eight-year Sino–Japanese War, part of WWII. The joint resistance of the CPC and Kuomintang, along with assistance from the US, the Soviet Union, and other countries, finally defeated the Japanese in 1945. Shortly after, the Kuomintang launched a civil war against the CPC, led by Mao Zedong. By 1949, the Kuomintang government was finally overthrown and Mao chased Chiang Kai-Shek to Taiwan (officially the Republic of China), an island in the East China Sea.

Mainland China became the People's Republic of China in 1949. After over 100 years of continuous war and invasions, the new communist state was devastated and extremely poor. The Chinese government started to lead the country into recovery, building its agriculture and basic industries. During the First Five-Year Plan period (1953–1957), the average annual increase in the rate of national income reached over 8.9 percent. The following ten years (1957–1966) demonstrated significant economic growth under large-scale socialist construction.

Unfortunately, the Cultural Revolution (1966–1976) interrupted the growth and halted the economic engine. With its stated goal to enforce communism by removing capitalist, traditional, and cultural elements from Chinese society, the nationwide movement paralyzed China socially, politically, and economically. Historical and cultural sites, artifacts, and archives were largely eradicated and destroyed. A large portion of the population was forced to relocate, most notably the transfer of urban youth to rural regions. Millions of people were persecuted and suffered a wide range of abuses. Among the nation's top leadership, numerous senior officials, such as Deng Xiaoping (Exhibit 13.6) and others who were accused of taking a "capitalist road," were purged or persecuted.

Exhibit 13.6

Xiaoping, the Reformer

Xiaoping Deng and Jimmy Carter during the Sino–American signing ceremony in 1979.
Source: Wikimedia Commons (1979).

Xiaoping Deng (1904–1997) was the second paramount leader of China after Mao's death in 1976. Mao's designated successor, who insisted on continuing Mao's political ideologies and policies, was denounced by the Communist Party of China (CPC). The party restored Deng to power. From 1978 to 1992, Deng led the country through unprecedented reform toward a market economy.

During his early life, Deng studied and worked in France, where he was influenced by Marxism–Leninism and joined the CPC in the 1920s. After his return to China in 1927, Deng got involved in the communist revolutionary movement and gradually became a leader of the CPC during the Sino–Japanese War and Chinese Civil War. Following the establishment of the People's Republic of China in 1949, Deng assumed important roles in consolidating communist rule in southwestern regions of China.

During the Cultural Revolution, Deng was purged twice as a result of his economic policies, which were at odds with the political ideologies of Mao. Mao was afraid that Deng and others' economic policies could lead to restoration of capitalism and destruction of the communist revolution. As a result, Deng was forced to retire and was sent to a rural factory to labor as a regular worker.

In 1974, Deng came back to Beijing with the support of several senior CPC leaders. He gradually overcame his political opponents and consolidated control over the CPC. After prevailing amid the political turmoil, Deng began seeking a path for China, and in November 1978, Deng visited Singapore and other southeast Asian countries. In a meeting with Singapore Prime Minister Lee Kuan Yew, Deng was urged to open up and institute reforms, as well as to stop exporting communist ideologies. Consequently, Deng sent tens of thousands of Chinese to Singapore to learn from the experiences of the East Asian Tigers. In early 1979, Deng visited the US, meeting President Jimmy Carter and visiting companies such as Coca-Cola and Boeing, and government agencies such NASA. During that visit, Deng declared China's new policy priorities to be economic and technological development. In 1980, Deng led negotiations with the UK to return the territory of Hong Kong to China, meeting personally with British Prime Minister Margaret Thatcher. Deng pledged to respect the economic system and civil liberties of the then British colony and formulated the political principle of "one country, two systems," recognizing the coexistence of one political authority with two different economic systems, communism and capitalism.

China's economic system underwent significant changes through Deng's "socialism with Chinese characteristics" reform strategy. Despite the difference in terms, Deng's strategy largely reflected neoliberal ideals, which were popular at that time and had been practiced by many capitalist countries. In order to urge the CPC to abandon the ideological difference between communism and capitalism, Deng stated that "[i]t doesn't matter whether a cat is white or black, as long as it catches mice," implying that he did not care whether a policy was capitalist or socialist as long as it improved the economy. His pragmatic reform perspective has extensively influenced Chinese economic and social policies up to the present.

Source: Li, Cheng (2001). *China's Leaders: The New Generation*. Lanham, MD: Rowman & Littlefield Publishers, Inc.

Economic Reform of China

The passing of Mao in 1976 marked the end of the Cultural Revolution. The CPC reinstated Deng Xiaoping, previously general secretary of the CPC, who had been dismissed from the central leadership during the Cultural

Revolution. In 1979, China instituted a guiding policy of "reform and opening to the outside world" under Deng's leadership. Though framed as "socialist market economy" in his ideological concept of "socialism with Chinese characteristics," Deng's reforming strategies to a large extent reflect the concurrent neoliberal policies, especially in terms of privatization, free trade, and introducing foreign direct investment.

Privatization

Communist China completely eliminated private ownership of business in the 1950s and installed a highly regulated command economy with full public ownership. In 1978, China's economy consisted of 77.6 percent state-owned enterprises (SOEs) and 22.4 percent collectively owned enterprises. In an effort to resolve the problem of long term, extensive losses incurred by SOEs, the Chinese government experimented with a number of privatization policies, and eventually transformed a large portion of SOEs into a variety of economic entities suitable for market operation. By 2004, SOEs were reduced to less than 30 percent (OECD 2009); however, this trend has stopped under Xi Jinping. With his consolidation of power, and his drive to use the SOEs as a tool of market expansion in areas such as semiconductors and communication, there is renewed reliance on the SOEs. For example, during the COVID-19 pandemic, SOEs purposely expanded to counteract the temporary retreat of the private sector in order to stabilize the economy (Borst 2021).

Free Trade

From 1950 through 1978, China had largely closed its economy to the world. There was little trade with anyone, save the Soviet Union and a few other countries and regions. But Deng's open policy greatly promoted trade, foreign trade organizations were reorganized, and control of imports and exports was relaxed or strengthened depending on the balance of trade and the level of foreign exchange reserves. For example, between 1979 and 1999, China's foreign trade volume increased by 15.3 percent annually. While the growth rate of China's trade has continued and in 2021 China's share of world exports is approximately 15 percent, while the US is around 9 percent (Statistica 2021). China joined a number of international economic organizations, such as the World Bank, the International Monetary Fund, and the Asian Development Bank. China was one of the original signers of the General Agreement on Tariffs and Trade (GATT) in 1947. When founded in 1949, the PRC was not recognized as the legitimate government of China by the United Nations (UN). In 1971, the GATT revoked Taiwan's membership, pursuant to the UN's recognition of the PRC. At that time, however, China declined to join the GATT, regarding it as "a rich countries' club," mainly comprised of developed nations. After opening up, China became an observer of GATT in 1982 and applied to be a full member in 1986. After 15 years of arduous efforts, China formally became a member of the World Trade Organization (WTO) in 2001. Entering the WTO marked a new stage for China's foreign trade. China's imports and exports have experienced exponential growth since then. Today China is sometimes referred to informally as the "world's manufacturing superpower."

Foreign Direct Investment

In order to attract foreign direct investment (FDI), China has invested a large amount of human, material, and financial resources in developing infrastructure facilities, creating a favorable environment for foreign investors since the early 1980s. Meanwhile, the government has promulgated a series of economic laws and regulations to provide the legal basis and guarantee for foreign investors in China. While the US has traditionally been the world's leader in FDI, China took the lead position in 2021 during the COVID-19 pandemic (Statistica 2021).

The Effects of Economic Reform

Deng's reform policy has driven extensive development of various economic sectors. From 1979 to 2013, China experienced an average GDP increase rate of 9.85 percent and was the fastest-growing economy in the world. While China's expansion rate of increase has diminished, it continues to the lead the largest economies in sustained growth (Statistica 2021).

Due to a high economic growth rate, China has enjoyed an overall increase in standard of living. From 1978 to 2021, China experienced the world's highest rates of growth in both household consumption and total consumption, three times as fast as the US in the earlier years (Statistica).

Meanwhile, the country has also experienced a growing divide between rural, poor, and old people on one side, and urban citizens, young, and select officials on the other. The worsening of wealth distribution has increased faster in China than any other country in the world. Before the economic reform, the Gini coefficient for income inequality in China was low (0.200), among the lowest in the world; as of 2019, according to one source that tracks wealth indicators on an annual basis, China scored 46.5, having peaked at 0.491 in 2008 (Statistica 2021). Using the same source as a comparator, the US has hovered at 0.48 for a decade.

The export-oriented, high economic growth has created serious environmental problems in China, affecting its biosphere and human health. Lax environmental oversight has exacerbated the problems. Despite the central government issuing fairly strict regulations, local governments that undertake the actual monitoring and enforcement of those regulations are more interested in economic growth and are often willing to sacrifice the environment for it. For example, the capital city of China, Beijing, is notorious for poor air quality. The city, which lies in a topographic bowl, has significant industry, heats with coal, and is subject to air inversions that result in extremely high levels of pollution during winter months. Further, large construction projects, such as the Three Gorges Dam (see Analytical Case), often lead to irrevocable environment damages.

Corruption becomes entrenched and epidemic, as well as a top concern of the general public. Business deals often involve participation in corruption. Bribery, kickbacks, theft, and misspending of public funds cost a significant portion of the economy. In popular perception, there are more dishonest government officials than honest ones, a reversal of the views held in the first decade of reform in the 1980s (Yan 2004). According to a survey by Berlin-based organization Transparency International (2020), China was ranked 78th out of 179 countries in its Corruption Perceptions Index, more corrupt than most developed countries. The index defines corruption as the abuse of public office for private gain and measures the degree to which corruption is perceived to exist among a country's public officials and politicians.

Amid concerns about social equity, environmental issues, corruption, and other social, economic, and political challenges, China has been seen as a rising economic superpower in the world.

The US–China Relationship

Relations between the US and China, the world's two largest economies, have been generally stable, disregarding some periods of tension. In 1972, the two countries resumed trade relations and became one another's largest or second largest trade partner after 40 years of cooperation. China has maintained a net trade surplus with the US, especially in manufactured goods. The US trade deficit with China peaked in 2018, when President Trump began a trade war with China resulting in tit-for-tat retaliations. However, it has led to a modestly overall reduction in the trade imbalance and the Biden administration has maintained the same policy stance. Despite the net deficit, the US has a continuing advantage over China in commercial services such as banking, accounting, consulting, insurance, education, legal counsel, royalties and license fees, and travel. As the world's largest importer and exporter of commercial services, the US has constantly maintained a surplus in services (Statistica 2021), although this is being slowly eroded since the trade war.

US consumer goods companies were drawn to China following the economic reform. These firms entered the country by forming joint ventures with a Chinese company or government agency. Direct investment by the US in China ($124 billion in 2020) covers a wide range of manufacturing sectors, hotel projects, restaurant chains, petrochemicals, and so on. As the Chinese policy environment becomes more liberal, Chinese investors have been increasingly interested in the US market. China's foreign direct investment (FDI) in the US soared from less than $1 billion in 2007 to $38 billion in 2020 (Statistica 2021).

China is also a large foreign creditor for the US. As of 2021, China owned about $1 trillion of publicly held US debt (about $28 trillion), behind Japan by several hundred billion dollars. Far larger holders of US debt are Social Security Trust Fund and the Federal Reserve whose purchases of debt sky-rocketed starting in 2020 with the pandemic. China's much smaller ownership of US debt has largely mitigated most concerns of US debt being "weaponized" in a trade war of policy conflict between the two countries.

Despite increased trade and economic connections, there is also controversy in the relationship. The primary concern of the US is about China's trade protective policies. China has restrictive trade practices, which include exchange control, high tariffs, lack of transparency, requirements for firms to obtain special permission to import goods, and inconsistent application of laws and regulations. There are also concerns relating to human rights in China and the political status of Taiwan.

The US–China relationship has been interpreted by both politicians and economists as the world's most important bilateral relationship of the twenty-first century. Beginning in 2009, the two countries agreed to hold regular high-level talks about economic issues and other mutual concerns by establishing the biannual US–China strategic economic dialog. However, after unproductive talks with the Trump administration for a year, a series of major tariff increases was implemented by the US in January 2018, and increased in 2019. China retaliated, but at a much lower level. Discussions came to a halt and were only cautiously reinvigorated after the inauguration of President Biden who signaled he was open to talks, but not interested in making significant adjustments until trade balance improvements promised during the Trump administration were met.

Critique of Regional Economic Integration

In spite of China's rising economic power, countries around the world have also consolidated their political and economic influence through enhanced regional economic integration.

The movement toward regional economic integration has brought about both economic and political benefits to states. It is generally agreed that regional trading blocs stimulate economic growth in countries and lead to increased FDI and world production. Countries are becoming more specialized in those goods and services which they efficiently produce and are enjoying additional gains from free trade beyond international agreements such as GATT and WTO. Perhaps the more important benefits of regional trading blocs are political rather than economic. Economic interdependence among countries creates incentives for political cooperation, which reduces potential for violent confrontation. This partially explains the long-lasting peace around the world after the two world wars. When acting together, countries have more economic clout to enhance trade with other countries or trading blocs.

For example, a Trans-Pacific Partnership was created with members from around the Pacific in 2005 which included the US but not China. When an expansion of the TTP was planned, and signed by the US in 2011 under President Obama. However, the US public began to express interest in more protectionism (even the Democratic candidate for president signaled she would not endorse the deal put forward), and the US pulled out in 2017. It was revived in 2018, without either China or the US and became the third largest trading block in the world. It includes Australia, Brunei, Canada, Chile, Japan, Malaysia, Mexico, New Zealand, Peru, Singapore, and Vietnam.

Yet some observers are concerned about the distorted or limited free markets in regional trading blocs. By liberalizing trade only with neighbors, countries are discriminating against those not lucky enough to be asked to join the bloc. Some goods will be imported from other members of the free trade area at the expense of producers elsewhere. Members will begin to specialize in areas in which they lack a comparative advantage. In addition, integration is hard to achieve and sustain. Taxpayers have to undertake the burden of cost by adding another layer of governing structure over nation states. The governing institution of trading blocs leads to a potential loss of sovereignty and control over domestic issues. The nation state may benefit overall, but groups within certain countries may be hurt, especially those revolved around a comparatively disadvantaged trade in the bloc.

The Case of the European Union (EU): The World's Single Largest Economy

In light of the critique of trading blocs, we turn to examine the world's single largest economy—the European Union (Exhibit 13.7), which has achieved the highest economic integration. The European Union is (currently) a group of 27 countries that works cooperatively on many issues, including trade relations.

The economy and land mass of the EU is approximately same as the US. The EU population is larger at 447 million people, compared to the US at 335 million (2021), but per capita income in the US is somewhat higher. The EU accounts for about 19 percent of global trade (but only 6.9 percent of the world population), and the US is the EU's largest external trading partner. As a single economy, the EU and China are also the largest trading partners of the US.

The EU is the result of two major historical trends. The first force for European integration resulted from the devastation of Western Europe during two world wars, which caused a widespread desire for lasting peace. On the eve of World War I, Europe was still the economic powerhouse of world trade, roughly twice the size of the US. However, by the end of World War II, a shattered Europe was matched by the US in just 30 years. A pragmatic solution to repairing ties was to enhance trade relations among European countries themselves. Closer ties ensured not only peace but enhanced the likelihood of internal trade as well.

A second force behind the creation of the EU was fueled by European nations' desire to hold onto their critical mass as a player on the world's political and economic stage. As Europe's dominant position gave way to other major economies, initially the US but later others including Japan, South Korea, Latin America, and China, it needed to protect its economic standing by creating more integrated policies. Such policies (a) promoted efficiency by standardizing, (b) enhanced ease of trade for other countries, and (c) allowed for more effective trade bargaining as a group. Examples include the use of a common currency (the euro), measurement standardization (the metric system), and collective bargaining and sanctions by the EU at the World Trade Organization.

Exhibit 13.7

The European Union

Source: Wikipedia Commons (2020b).

Brief History of the Development of the European Union

The first forerunner of the EU was called the European Coal and Steel Community and was composed of Belgium, France, Italy, Luxembourg, the Netherlands, and West Germany. Coal and steel, as critical heavy industries, were the backbone of any economy at the time, so it created an environment for joint redevelopment in the postwar period. From the beginning, it was hoped that this would lead to further integration. In 1957, the six original members signed the Treaty of Rome, which created the European Community by establishing a customs union as well.

Despite French concerns about the supranational power of the EU in the 1960s under President de Gaulle, the Community continued to prosper, and in 1973 an important enlargement occurred with the additions of Great Britain, Ireland, and Demark. There were direct elections for the first European Parliament in 1979. Greece was brought into the European Community in 1981; it was struggling economically and hoped that ascension to the EU would modernize the country. Membership did help the economy, but the modernization of Greece was ultimately far less successful in bringing about financial accountability.

During the 1980s, the membership process became more rigorous, and application for inclusion, called ascension, would take several years and require a series of statutorily enacted monetary, fiscal, legal, and political adjustments prior to ratification of the process. Spain and Portugal were brought into the European Community in 1986, again requiring significant internal reforms, which was as much to help them modernize as expand the Community. In 1994, the Maastricht Treaty created the foundation of the current European Union (EU). This treaty added the possibility for members to join a common currency zone, strengthened sound fiscal policy requirements of all members, and added additional internal and external joint policy-making commissions. In 1996, Austria, Finland, and Sweden joined the EU. In 2004, the greatest enlargement occurred with the addition of ten countries: Cyprus, the Czech Republic, Estonia, Hungary, Latvia, Lithuania, Malta, Poland, Slovakia, and Slovenia. Soon thereafter, in 2007, Romania and Bulgaria, two countries with histories of authoritarian governments and weak economies, joined. In 2013, Croatia became the 28th member state. Current candidate states include Albania, the Republic of North Macedonia, Montenegro, Serbia and Turkey. Two important partners with the EU, affiliated through the European Free Trade Association, are Norway and Switzerland, both small but very wealthy countries. In 2021, Great Britain formally withdrew from the EU.

Today, the EU functions like a complex federal state, much the way the US does. The EU, functioning as central government, has an exclusive role vis-à-vis its members in customs (tariffs), competition rules, monetary policy for euro countries, fisheries, commercial policy, and some international agreements. It shares and coordinates policies and responsibilities with member countries in the internal market, social policies, the environment, transportation, energy, health, foreign policy, and defense policy.

Areas of Cooperation in Which Not All Members Participate

There are some areas in which joint participation is voluntary. Two prominent areas are monetary policy and currency and customs.

Eurozone: there is an overlapping monetary union that is made up of 19 of the 27 EU countries (Exhibit 13.8), with more becoming active members over time as they qualify. The currency of the system is called the euro, and helps build a single market under the control of the European Central Bank located in Frankfurt, Germany. The advantages of combining 19 currencies into one are obvious in terms of easing travel arrangements for citizens and tourists, eliminating exchange rate problems, providing price transparency,

Exhibit 13.8

Eurozone countries

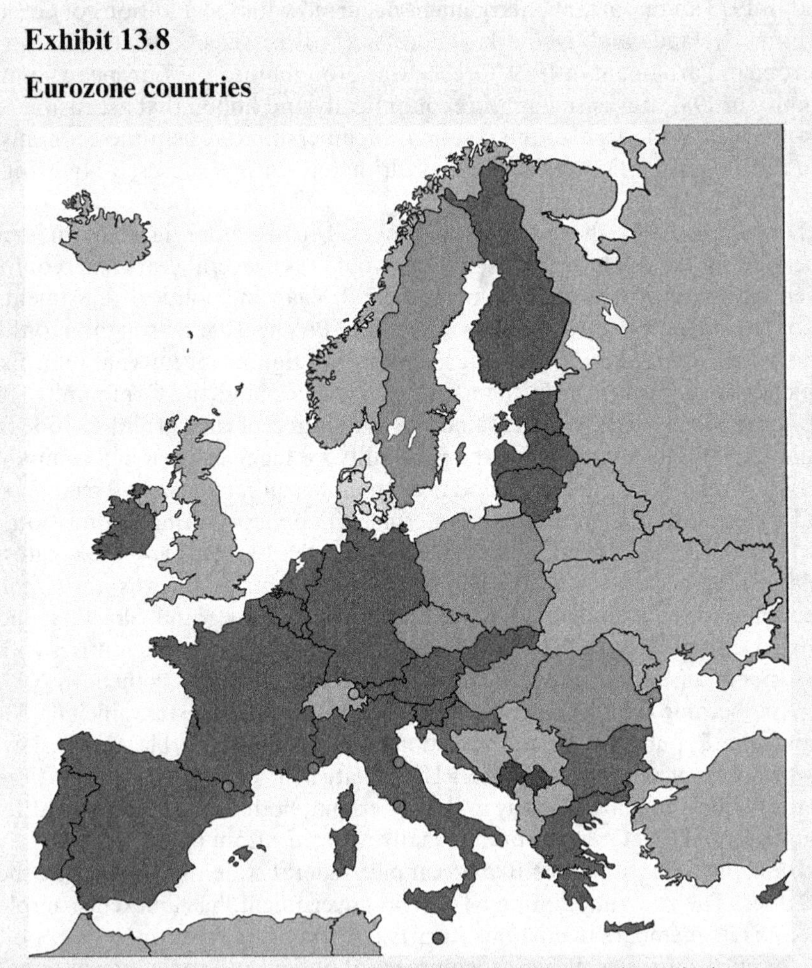

Darkest countries are in Eurozone presently, medium dark countries are in the process of joining. Lightest color countries not in Eurozone.
Source: Wikimedia Commons (2020a).

enhancing price stability, and providing the ability to cope with financial shocks. (It is not without its challenges too, as the European sovereign debt crisis has also indicated when countries with relatively large debt and/or weak banking systems could jeopardize the entire system.) Because the euro has become the second reserve currency in the world, it has become a political symbol as well.

Customs union: A second subgroup of nations in the EU belong to the Schengen Agreement. It provides for the abolition of border checks internal to the union and free access for all countries once inside its boundaries. Thus, it acts very much like a single state for international travel purposes. Today, the Schengen area encompasses most EU countries, except for Bulgaria, Croatia, Cyprus, Ireland and Romania. However, Bulgaria, Croatia, and Romania are currently in the process of joining the Schengen area alliance and already applying the Schengen to a large extent. Additionally, also the non-EU States Iceland, Norway, Switzerland, and Liechtenstein have joined the Schengen area. These two agreements mean that while international travelers in the past might have to carry four or five currencies and go through as many checkpoints, today travelers rarely need more than two currencies and may never go through more than the initial visa checkpoint.

The Economy of the EU

The economy of the EU is approximately $21 trillion in 2021 dollar value. Germany is the economic powerhouse of the EU with 25 percent of the GDP. France is next in size, followed by Italy and Spain.

The average per capita GDP income across the EU is approximately $44,000, relative to the US at approximately $63,000 according to the IMF for 2020. However, some of the top 25 wealthiest countries in the world in terms of per capita income such as Luxembourg, Austria, the Netherlands, Ireland, and Sweden are balanced out by many of the recent and much poorer members such as Bulgaria, Romania, and Croatia. The per capita income disparity between Romania at the bottom and Luxembourg at the top is six times. Exhibit 13.9 illustrates GDP per EU inhabitant.

Prior to the recession of 2008, the EU had been instituting fiscal constraint measures, but, unfortunately, not all members conformed. Greece has been the worst violator of fiscal restraint, followed closely by the Italian, Portuguese, and Irish central governments. Since the Great Recession only Ireland has seen a debt decrease (almost by 50 percent). Other EU countries with high proportional government debt levels (over 100 percent of debt to GDP include Spain, Cyprus, France, and Belgium). See Exhibit 13.10. The wealth distribution rate (Gini coefficient of.31) indicates that the EU has one of the most equitable distributions in the world, substantially better than the US (Gini: 45), and China (47.4) (US CIA 2021).

The Political Structure of the EU

Like any large federal state, the EU has a complex government that defies exact comparison with the US. However, rough similarities will be emphasized for ease of understanding. The capital of the EU is Brussels, Belgium, although some functions are situated in Luxembourg, Frankfurt, and elsewhere.

The legislative branch of government has two main elements—an "upper house" selected directly by countries (made up of two councils), and a "lower house" directly elected by citizens of the EU (in the form of a parliament). The upper house has a broad agenda-setting body called the *European Council*. It convenes at least four times a year with the heads of state or government in a formalized summit fashion. It has a president who serves a two-and-a-half-year term (renewable one time) and is not a head of state, but is chosen from former heads of state and selected by majority vote of the members to represent the EU externally and encourage consensus among members. The European Council does not have formal legislative authority, but it appoints members to the *Council of the European Union*, which does the actual voting on legislative issues and the budget. It is comprised of ministers selected by their home governments in different issue areas. Thus the voting body may vary, depending on what issue is at hand. For example, the Agriculture Council of the Council of the European Union is composed of the national ministers responsible for agriculture.

The second legislative body is the European Parliament, which functions as a "lower house." While the administrative headquarters is in Luxembourg and it occasionally meets in Strasbourg, France, it meets most commonly in Brussels, Belgium. After the exit of Great Britain it has 705 members directly elected every five years by their respective countries based on population size (e.g., Germany at 96, France at 79, and Italy at 76). However, members frequently vote along party lines (probably more similar to coalitions) that cross national borders; the two largest EU parties are the European People's Party (aka Christian Democrats) and the Progressive Alliance of Socialists and Democrats (aka S&D). The president of this body is elected by the membership of the European Parliament every two and a half years. In the past, it was primarily a consultative body in terms of debating legislation and proposing amendments. However, it has been acquiring more power as one of the two "houses" of the EU legislature.

The executive branch is constituted under the European Commission. It is headquartered in Brussels, Belgium. Commissioners are selected by each member country to serve for five years. The European Commission has approximately 10,000 employees. It proposes legislation, implements treaties (which are roughly equivalent to US federal laws), and other internal agreements. It, too, has a president who is appointed for a five-year term, and may

Exhibit 13.9

Comparative income of individuals in European countries

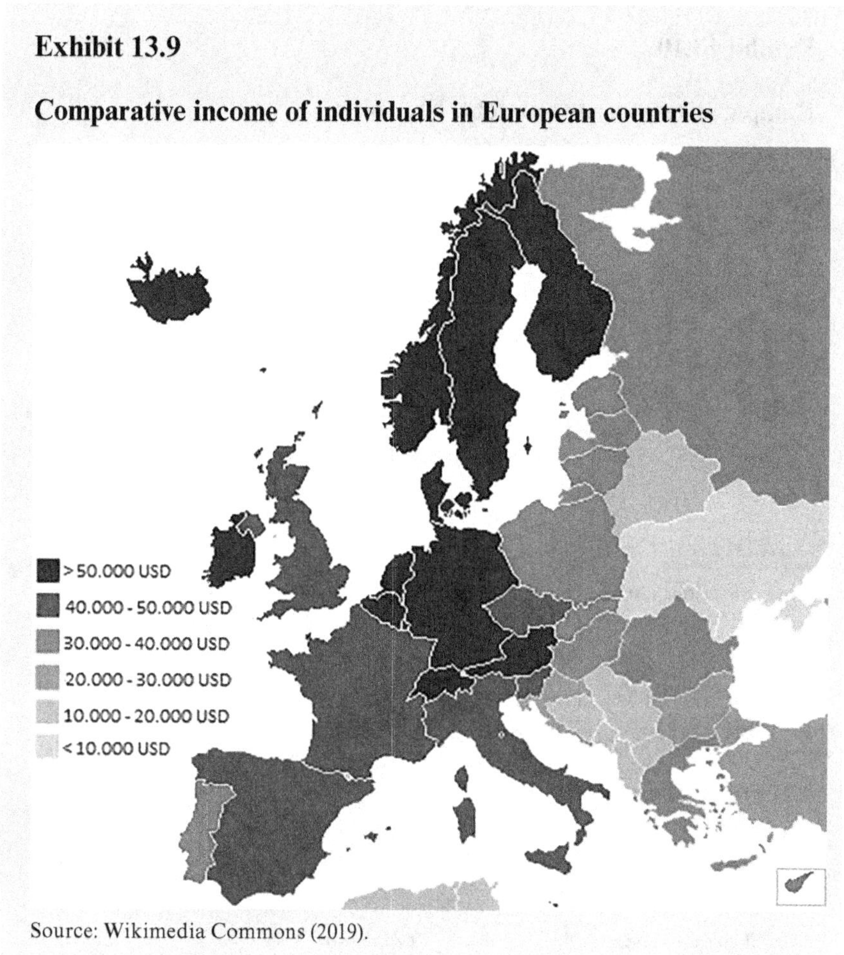

Source: Wikimedia Commons (2019).

be renewed. This is an important position in the EU federal system because of its continuity and ability to influence both legislation and execution of EU laws. The 2019–2024 president of the EU Commission is Ursula von der Leyen from Germany. The European Commission manages the EU budget, which was around €169 billion in 2020, only about 2–3 percent of the sum of the national budgets of all 27 EU member states.

Similar to the US, the EU has a strong judicial branch called the European Court of Justice. One judge comes from each country. It functions as the supreme appeals court for EU law for both internal and international issues. It has, for example, found the US to be in violation of European law or World Trade Organization treaties, and provided the legal basis for international legal dispute resolution. There is also an important financial body called the

Exhibit 13.10

Comparative government debt, EU countries

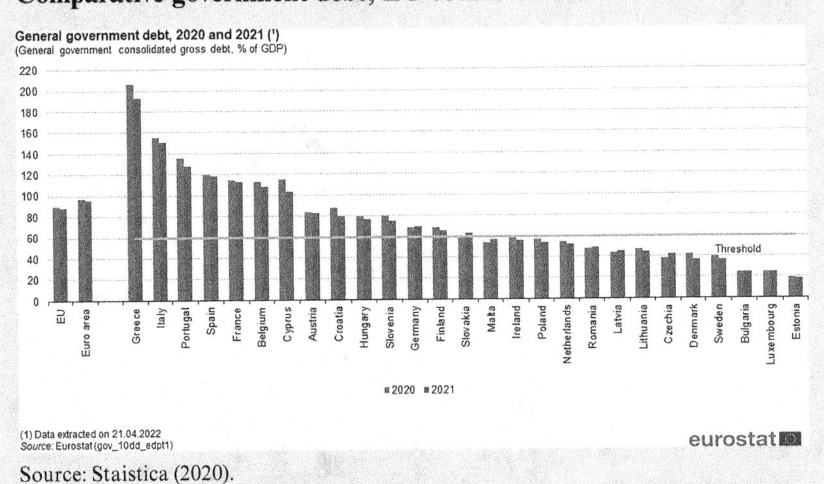

Source: Staistica (2020).

Exhibit 13.11

EU political structure

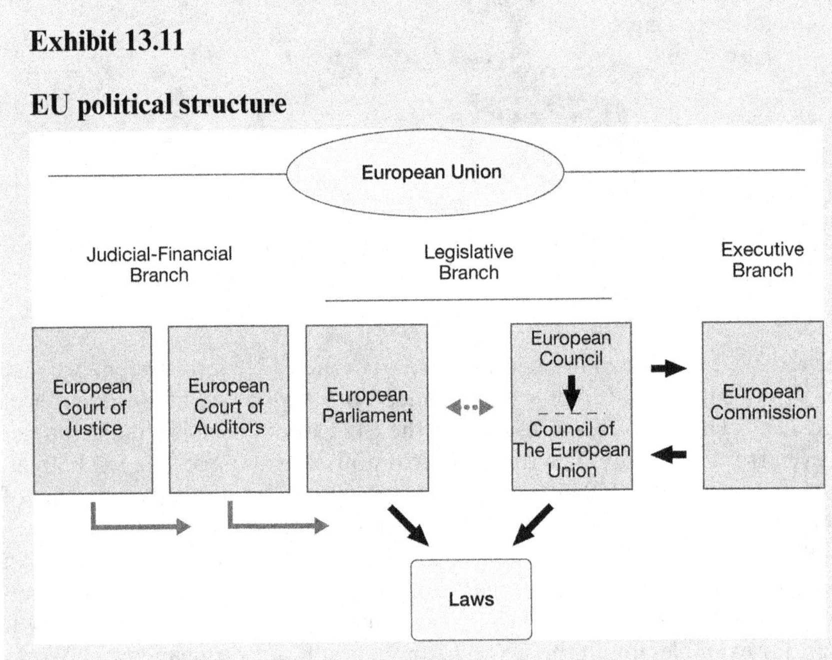

European Court of Auditors, which helps ensure the financial accountability of the EU budget. Both of these bodies are located in Luxembourg. A highly simplified formulation of the EU political structure is in Exhibit 13.11.

Challenges for the EU

Despite its obvious success, the EU has its substantial problems. For decades, the EU made fairly steady progress as countries clamored to join. Now, the momentum is gone, and additional progress is likely to be tempered by tougher realities. The referendum to pass an EU constitution was defeated almost before it started in 2005 and Great Britain pulled out of the EU in 2020. Concerns about border security among the Schengen countries and non-Schengen countries continue to simmer, with increasing concern about legal migration to northern Europe from southern and eastern Europe, and enormous concern about illegal migration from Muslim and African countries. Concerns about COVID have also increased tensions among member nations. Rising resistance to the new EU identity grows with the intensification of nationalism, heightened interest in more domestic labor protection, and increased ethnic tensions. There is also an increased, if quietly expressed, concern over the growing expense of EU bureaucracy in Brussels and Luxembourg, and the additional layer of administration. So while the EU has definitely been given a much more unified and powerful voice abroad and has reaped the benefits of a more rationalized and consistent business environment, its internal political consensus has weakened in the last decade.

Recapping, US business and consumers depend on international trade. Important categories of export are capital goods (e.g., machines, commercial aircraft, semiconductors, medical equipment, and computer equipment), industrial supplies and equipment (e.g., oil, chemicals, and plastics), automobiles, consumer goods, pharmaceuticals, agricultural products, and services (e.g., passenger and financial services). Exports create jobs. The US imports even more than it exports, keeping prices low for consumers, especially in consumer products and capital goods. Thus, it is critical for Americans to understand the basics of the other major trading entities in the world. With only 4.25 percent of the world population, the US remains an economic powerhouse. The economy of the EU in 2021 is as large as the US when using a PPP (purchasing power) basis, but slightly smaller than the US on a nominal GDP basis. They are growing at the same rate in the long term. In 2021, China's economy is now larger in terms of PPP, but still substantially smaller in terms of nominal GDP. China continues to grow faster than the US and EU and is projected to do so for decades. So knowing the basics of cultural and business expectations is increasingly important as the US continues to compete in an evolving world economy. Despite some doomsday predictions, the US has continued to hold its own since the major world economy shift in the 1970s, but it can only do so with savvy understanding about who it trades with and how international trade regimes operate.

Analytical Case: The Three Gorges Dam

Since market liberalization, as advanced by Deng's neoliberal policies in 1978, China's economy has grown at a breakneck pace. Accompanying this rapid industrialization has been a tremendous increase in demand for energy. To meet the nation's increasing need for electrical power, in 1992, and having managed to silence opposition, Chinese leaders officially approved long-conceived plans to harness the power of the country's largest river—the Yangtze—by constructing the world's largest hydroelectric dam (in terms of installed capacity), the Three Gorges Dam.

Exhibit 13.12

Three Gorges Dam

Source: Wikimedia Commons (2009).

The name refers to a 120-mile stretch of limestone cliffs along the upper reaches of the Yangtze River, where the water drops precipitously through Three Gorges—the Qutang, Wu, and Xiling. The region is a famous scenic and historical site, which is linked to many folklore and important historical events. Its natural beauty has inspired Chinese painters and classical poets for centuries.

Construction of the dam started in December, 1994 and the project was completed and fully functional in July, 2012. In full operation, the total electric-generating capacity of the dam is 22,500 megawatts, 20 times more than the Hoover Dam in America. The dam provides power to nine provinces and two cities. It also controls floods downstream on the Yangtze River and helps reduce flooding in important cities. By the end of 2008, the dam had cost the Chinese government over $23.5 billion in construction, relocating affected residents, and financing. It is estimated that full-cost recovery is expected to occur ten years after the dam starts full operation.

Despite the promises and benefits, the project encountered significant opposition, both domestically and internationally, as scientists, environmentalists, historians, and human rights groups criticized the extraordinary costs the dam has incurred.

The project fueled a heated debate over its feasibility. Many global scientists believed the dam could not control the river nor meet China's electricity demand. For example, after conducting several years' studies of the project's feasibility, the US Export Bank and the World Bank refused to finance the project because of its disastrous environmental and social consequences.

The project poses significant ecological dangers. It is reckoned as the most hazardous hydroelectric project ever attempted. The dam, which is 1.3 miles long and 610 feet high, created a 385-mile-long reservoir that totally engulfed the Three Gorges. Erosion in the reservoir, induced by rising water, causes frequent riverbank collapses and landslides. The dam prevents the dispersal of pollutants that enter the river, causing the quality of water in the upper banks of Yangtze to slowly fall. This drastic change and the destruction of natural habitat has also put endangered wildlife species, such as the Siberian crane and the Yangtze dolphin, at risk.

The dam also flooded 115,000 acres of farmland, 13 cities, hundreds of villages, and some 1,300 archeological sites. Cultural and historical relics were moved to higher ground, but the flooding inevitably covered undiscovered or irremovable relics. About 1.13 million people had to be resettled and about 140,000 residents were relocated to other provinces.

In recent years, Chinese engineers admitted there were many problems. The government is placing preventive measures to halt further deterioration and has also invested heavily in programs designed to restore and conserve the ecology of the area. Over 1,300 manufacturing ventures that constructed sewage disposal and waste treatment plants have been closed or relocated and thousands of people were resettled from disaster-prone areas.

Questions for Discussion and Analysis

1 Discuss the costs and benefits of the Three Gorges Dam to China.
2 How do you think the Chinese government can effectively address the issues of an increased demand for energy, protection of the environment, and human rights?
3 There are hundreds of construction, equipment, engineering, and financial firms all over the world that were involved in the Three Gorges Dam project (see Who's Behind China's Three Gorges Dam at www.threegorgesprobe.org/pi/documents/three_gorges/who.html). If you are representing one of them, what are your ethical considerations?

Sources: http://www.yangtzeriver.org/threegorges_dam/; http://en.wikipedia.org/wiki/Three_Gorges_Dam#Economics; Gleick, P. H. (2008–2009). Three Gorges Dam Project, Yangtze River,

China, URL: http://www2.worldwater.org/data20082009/WB03.pdf; International Rivers Network (2003). Human Rights Dammed off at the Three Gorges. URL: http://www.internationalrivers.org/files/attached-files/3gcolor.pdf.

Practical Skill

Dealing with Foreign Government

Globalization and free trade polices make conducting business abroad handy; however, it is not quite as easy as conducting business domestically. It is especially challenging to deal with government issues in a foreign country. Here are many useful informative resources for a US company to do business in a particular foreign country.

First, many US government departments provide useful information about foreign countries. The US Commercial Service's Market Research Library publishes The Country Commercial Guides (www.buyusainfo.net/adsearch.cfm?search_type=int&loadnav=no), to help US companies get started in exporting or increase sales to global markets. The State Department's US Bilateral Relations Fact Sheets (www.state.gov/r/pa/ei/bgn/) provide background information about foreign relations with a particular country. The State Department also provides information about travel in another country (www.state.gov/travel/). The CIA's World Factbook (www.cia.gov/library/publications/the-world-factbook/) provides general information on individual countries.

Additionally, some international organizations also offer insights on doing business in other countries from different perspectives. For example, the World Bank's Doing Business Project (www.doingbusiness.org/about-us) tells you how easy or difficult it is dealing with government issues, such as business registration, regulations, and their enforcement across countries. The International Monetary Fund publishes economic data for individual countries in its annual report (www.imf.org).

Thanks to technology advancements, as most countries around the world deploy e-government, relevant information about doing business in a specific country can be easily accessible via its official website. In addition, many commercial and nonprofit organizations also provide insights about specific government business regulations in a given country. For example, at www.guidemesingapore.com, you can find detailed information about setting up a representative office in Singapore. At www.wikihow.com, you can get insights about how to invest in India or other countries.

Generally speaking, there are three key issues wherein business needs to deal with government when conducting business abroad:

1 Gaining legal status of your business representative, which includes a visa for travel, resident registration, and other legal requirements for representing your business.
2 Gaining legal status for your business unit, which may be in the form of a representative office, an investment company, or a joint venture. This includes acquiring registrations and permits for conducting your business activities.
3 Abiding by the regulations of the country when conducting your business, which include a variety of economic, social, and environmental laws, rules, and regulations. The institutional environment of a foreign country may be similar or very different to that of the US. In dealing with such issues, it is wise for a business to build up connections through customers, to hire local companies or employees, and to seek assistance from their economic development or foreign trade agencies.

Skill Exercise: Critical Issues of Setting Up a Foreign Representative Office

A foreign representative office is an extension of the foreign company, and is often not allowed to conduct any business activities of a profit-yielding nature. It often only engages in activities such as conducting market research and feasibility studies.

Conduct web research and advise Zara about the government issues that she has to deal with when setting up a representative office in Chengdu, Sichuan, China. Such issues include:

1 How to gain legal status for traveling and residing in China.
2 How to gain approval for the representative office.
3 How to meet the relevant government regulations of a Foreign Representative Office.

Your web research should include at least the following Chinese government websites:

Ministry of Commerce: http://english.mofcom.gov.cn/

Sichuan Provincial Government: http://www.sc.gov.cn/10462/wza2012/english/english.shtml

Chengdu City Government: http://www.chengdu.gov.cn/echengdu

Summary and Conclusion

1. This chapter offers two in-depth cases—China and the EU—in the light of neoliberalism and regional economic integration. Because of the importance of international trade today, these two economies are important to understand.
2. Neoliberalism is subjected to criticisms from the historical intellectual critics of capitalism as well as opponents of the Washington Consensus.
3. With a highly centralized administrative system, China is an authoritarian state under the control of the Communist Party.
4. The economic reform led by Deng Xiaoping adopted the principles of neoliberalism, such as free trade, foreign direct investment, and privatization.
5. The impact of Deng's reform is mixed. Whereas China has experienced the world's fastest economic growth, neoliberalism has also led to problems of income disparity, corruption, and environment issues.
6. The EU emerged out of the World War II era, when there was a strong interest in unifying through trade and cooperative interests, rather than typical military competitiveness.
7. The EU as a collective entity is an economy and size relatively similar to the US. While the individual nation states continue to exercise some degree of autonomy, they increasingly work together with a common currency (the euro), common borders (Schengen area), central bank, and joint policy agreements in areas such as the environment.
8. More recently the EU's long-term success has been dramatically slowed as there are increasing concerns about the EU becoming too big, inclusive of too many weak economies, too ethnically diverse, and too inclined to ignore local culture.

Key Terms

- Critical theory
- Dependency theory
- Gini index

Study Questions

1. Integrating the case of China, offer a critique to neoliberalism.
2. Discuss and compare the administrative and political systems between China and the US.
3. Discuss the background and impact of China's economic reform, starting from the late 1970s.
4. Discuss the trade relationship between China and the US. Analyze the advantages and disadvantages to the US in this relationship.

5 Discuss why many individual countries of Europe, with their proud traditions, decided to band together. Provide at least two different rationales.
6 Because the EU often operates as a confederation, groups of countries within the EU may elect to set common policies that are not adopted (by treaty) by all countries. What are some examples?
7 How is the EU political structure similar and different to the US?
8 How did the 2008 economic recession illustrate and emphasize the rising challenges of the EU as it has expanded?

References

Borst, N. (2021). Has China Given Up on State-owned Enterprise Reform?: Rather than Allowing the Private Sector More Space, Beijing Wants a Tool for the Implementation of Government Policy. *The Interpreter.* April 21. https://www.lowyinstitute.org/the-interpreter/has-china-given-state-owned-enterprise-reform.

Broad, R., and Cavanagh, J. (1999). The Death of the Washington Consensus. *World Policy Journal*, Fall:80–88.

Fed (2021). Wealth by Wealth Percentile Group. Board of Governors of the Federal Reserve System. https://www.federalreserve.gov/releases/z1/dataviz/dfa/distribute/table/.

OECD (2009). State-Owned Enterprises in China: Reviewing the Evidence. *OECD Working Group on Privatization and Corporate Governance.* http://www.oecd.org/daf/ca/corporategovernanceofstate-ownedenterprises/42095493.pdf.

Staistica (2020). https://www.statista.com/statistics/269684/national-debt-in-eu-countries-in-relation-to-gross-domestic-product-gdp/.

Statistica (2021). https://www.statista.com/statistics/.

US Central Intelligence Agency (CIA) (2013, 2021). *The World Factbook.* https://www.cia.gov/library/publications/the-world-factbook/.

Wikimedia Commons (1979). Karl H. Schumacher. https://commons.wikimedia.org/wiki/File:Carter_DengXiaoping.jpg.

Wikimedia Commons (2009). La Grand Portage. https://commons.wikimedia.org/wiki/File:ThreeGorgesDam-China2009.jpg.

Wikimedia Commons (2014). M Tracy Hunter. https://commons.wikimedia.org/wiki/File:2014_Gini_Index_World_Map,_income_inequality_distribution_by_country_per_World_Bank_(monocolor_scale).svg.

Wikimedia Commons (2019). World Bank. https://commons.wikimedia.org/wiki/File:Europe-GDP-PPP-per-capita-map.png.

Wikimedia Commons (2020a). European Fiscal Compact ratification. https://commons.wikimedia.org/wiki/File:Eurozone_participation.svg.

Wikipedia Commons (2020b). Ssolbergj. https://commons.wikimedia.org/wiki/File:2020_EU_MAP.svg.

Wikimedia Commons (2022). Cacahuate. https://commons.wikimedia.org/wiki/File:China_regions_map_(cs).png.

Yan, S. (2004). *Corruption and Market in Contemporary China.* Ithaca, NY: Cornell University Press.

14 Business and Global Governance

Marc Fudge

Chapter Contents

Case 14 Scenario

Zach and Zoey Discuss their Future

Zach wanted to share something with Zoey and invited her out to dinner at Tyler's uncle's restaurant on Main Street. As they leave Happy Paws and walk past the vet office, Splurge jewelers, and the U Scream Ice Cream shop, Zach begins talking. He mentions that he and Zoey are both busy running successful businesses. Zoey has opened two more Happy Paws stores, one across the state line and the other in Anyplace, the town next to the City of Somewhere. Zach has taken over all operations of the Double Z Beauty product line and the Double Z pet product line. His grandparents are enjoying their retirement years traveling and have even been able to visit Zoey's sister Zara in

DOI: 10.4324/9781003178620-18

China. Tyler is full time now at Good Buddy E-Solutions, watching over the websites and several employees himself. Between the three of them, they have been able to hire a number of people. Profits are up and life is looking pretty good. Zoey remarks that life is indeed good, and there's not much more she could ask for. But at the door of the restaurant, Zach acts unsettled and says things could be better. Upon hearing that, Zoey raises her eyebrows.

Tyler has been keeping stats on website traffic for both Happy Paws and the Double Z Beauty products. He mentioned to Zach that a number of repeat clients are from Asia and Europe and have increasingly expressed interest in Zach opening distribution facilities, perhaps in Tokyo and Madrid. One customer has even offered to work for Double Z in Japan. Tyler provides some reports from international finance institutions such as the World Trade Organization and International Monetary Fund on targeted countries, which are very informative and surprisingly easy to read. Zach never envisioned that the beauty and pet product lines would ever grow to the level they have and therefore had never considered opening any facilities overseas. Until now.

Zach is intrigued about the growth prospects of opening facilities in other countries. He recalled his former economics professor saying that recent global economic growth has risen substantially, and while the US had improved, it was Asia's developing nations where the greatest increase occurred, at something like 6+ percent.

As they make their way to their table, Zoey remarks that she supposes things could be better, but first they'd have to find out about the employment laws that are in place for each country into which they'd plan to expand. Maybe they could Skype Zara in China and she could help with that, Zoey suggests. She could even get them started on the tax implications of operating a business in a foreign country. Zoey also wonders how the industry standards and policies differ between Japan and Spain and the US. She asks why the growth rate has increased so much in Asia in comparison, and how long before Zach thinks it may level off or decline. Was that what was on his mind, or was it some other issue related to international trade?

Then Zoey looks around. There, in the restaurant, are her sister Zara and her parents. And over there are Zach's grandparents and parents. And Tyler, her best friend, is here too! Zach looks at Zoey and says that yes, all those things are concerns they will have to deal with if they seriously want to expand the business overseas. But they can talk about business–government relations tomorrow. Then Zach reaches deep into his pocket, takes out that pink diamond ring Zoey had admired in the Splurge jewelry shop window ages ago, and gets down on his knee.

Introduction

As discussed in Chapter 11, globalization refers to the increasing interdependence, integration, and interaction between people and companies in disparate locations. Everyday examples of globalization include the advance of worldwide technologies and higher levels of travel. Another important aspect is the strong trend toward global governance. Global governance is the voluntary integration of political and economic systems through intergovernmental organizations (IGOs) composed of sovereign states. Another group of international organizations, whose members are individuals and associations rather than sovereign states, are called non-governmental organizations (NGOs); they are not the focus of this chapter although they do contribute in important ways to international civil society and thus indirectly to global governance.

IGOs can have a regional focus, as we saw in the last chapter when discussing regional trading blocs such as the EU. In this chapter, we focus on IGOs that have a global scale, ultimately focusing on some IGOs that have either a trade or economic focus. While some IGOs only have an ad hoc commission, as is the case in many regional trading blocs (e.g., NAFTA), the more important global IGOs all have a substantial permanent secretariat, a legislative body where all members will occasionally convene, and often have branch offices around the world.

Global Governance

Global governance operates when member countries sign treaties to join IGOs. Member states seek access to certain IGOs and have to accept a variety of conditions of membership, must be approved by members, and must ratify the treaties by their legislative bodies (e.g., Congress), in most cases after the head of state (e.g., the President) has initially signed the treaty. That means that some countries are not given access when they seek it or are unable to meet the conditions of membership, some treaties are not ratified by their legislative body, and sometimes countries pull out of the IGO. For example, although after World War I President Woodrow Wilson was a great proponent of the League of Nations, a predecessor of the United Nations, Congress refused to ratify it and the organization eventually disbanded. It is important to note that global governance is quite different from global or world government, a case in which the world would be run by a single sovereign state; however, the world today has over 200 nation states.

Similar to regional IGOs, global governance through IGOs has been promoted because IGOs provide a multilateral forum for discussion and consensus building, they provide a structure for shared authority to allow detailed cooperation across national boundaries, and they have more permanence than simple treaties.

Global governance was weak or nonexistent for the most part until the nineteenth century. Multilateral treaties and alliances were made, but such agreements were generally highly limited to joint security issues. In the nineteenth century, with the advance of travel and technology, organizations began to be established to coordinate navigation of common rivers such as the Rhine, or to coordinate technology that required cooperation and critical standardization such as the telegraph. For example, the ITU, today called the International Telecommunication Union, began in 1865 as the International Telegraph Convention. Since World War II, IGOs have proliferated, with estimates of about 5,000 when counting regional and global organizations (Yearbook 2021–2021). Their success is based on the various types of benefits that countries desire, from military protection to human rights. The reasons include sovereign protection or security arrangements such as military alliances; political influence such as the effect of small countries joining larger collectives; economic rewards such as increased trade; and/or international well-being such as in environmental or wildlife protection or humanitarian principles. With the rise of global governance, the "rise of the market" has occurred and international trade has boomed under its mantle. Since 1950, for example, global trade has increased about 25-fold (WTO website); however, the growth of global trade has slowed considerably since the Great Recession (Statistica 2021).

Of course, IGOs have drawbacks as well. First, there is always some loss of sovereignty, even though such agreements are voluntary. IGOs can be very demanding, as is the case in joining the EU, and countries may not feel the benefits are worth the costs. IGOs often have dues, which can be substantial in some cases. Finally, the network of global governance today is complex, overlapping, and often confusing to citizens and newly elected officials despite some alignment and consolidation with the United Nations (UN).

Global governance, operating through IGOs, can occur in at least seven different functional areas. Some IGOs operate in multiple areas. Below is a list of IGO purposes with representative examples:

1. *Diplomatic, security, peace, and political cooperation*: UN (General Assembly, Security Council), Interpol (an international police organization).
2. *Resolution of political grievances*: UN (Security Council and International Court of Justice).
3. *Environmental well-being*: The United Nations Environmental Program (UNEP), the International Atomic Energy Agency (IAEA).
4. *International trading systems*: WTO.
5. *International financial system*: International Monetary Fund (IMF).
6. *Social and economic well-being*: UN (Economic and Social Council), World Bank Group, the World Health Organization (WHO), the World Food Program, UNESCO, and UNICEF.
7. *International standardization*: ITU discussed above, International Organization for Standardization (ISO).

We first briefly discuss three examples of IGOs whose aims are not directly related to the business world—the UN, Interpol, and the IAEA. Then we will discuss in more detail three examples of IGOs whose functions include regulating trade, finance, and international development—the WTO, IMF, and World Bank.

Three Important IGOs *Not* Directly Related to Business

The most widely known IGO is the United Nations, or UN. Actually, the UN itself is a large organization, and it acts as a coordinating body for many other organizations as well. Its purposes are to keep the peace, develop friendly relations among nations, improve the quality of life for citizens of member states, and to be a center for harmonizing global actions. The UN headquarters is in New York, but it has additional offices in Geneva and Vienna. The core of the UN has five primary bodies today. The Secretariat performs the day-to-day functions of the UN. The General Assembly provides a forum for all 193 members. The Security Council is responsible for world peace and security; it has five permanent members (China, France, Russia, the UK, and the US) and ten non-permanent members. In some cases the Security Council authorizes peacekeepers (aka "Blue Helmets"): in 2021, the UN was deploying soldiers loaned from member countries in 12 locations around the world. The Economic and Social Council coordinates commissions related to population, development, women, narcotics, forests, sustainable development, and numerous other cross-societal issues; it has 55 members. The International Court of Justice settles legal disputes and provides legal opinions to the constituent bodies of the organization; it has 15 judges. The UN system is very large, containing over 30 major organizations. Some of these were created in close concert with the UN, such as the Food and Agriculture Organization (FAO), the UN Educational, Scientific, and Cultural Organization (UNESCO), the World Food Program, the United Nations Environmental Program (UNEP), and the World Health Organization (WHO). These organizations receive much or all of their funds from sources other than the UN. Other organizations that were created before, or separately from, the UN but have close ties to the UN system, include the International Labor Organization (ILO), the ITU, and several others that we will examine in detail later in this chapter.

Another example of an important IGO is the International Criminal Police Organization, or Interpol, which facilitates international police cooperation. Established in 1923, it has 192 member countries and a budget of around €142 million, most of which is provided through annual contributions. The organization's headquarters is in Lyon, France, and it has a small staff of approximately 1,050. Its current Secretary-General is Jürgen Stock, a former German police officer and academic. Interpol is particularly important in capturing murderers, human traffickers, smugglers, pirates, terrorists, and drug lords, among other criminals, who cross national boundaries. It maintains a huge criminal "wanted" data base and provides the standard "most wanted" lists as well.

Yet a third example of an important IGO not directly related to business is the International Atomic Energy Agency (IAEA), whose current head is Rafael Grossi, an Argentine diplomat. The IAEA is headquartered in Vienna, Austria. The IAEA was created in 1957, has 173 members, and has a staff of 2,500. It encourages the peaceful use of nuclear energy and provides standards for safeguarding nuclear safety, for instance in power plants. The IAEA advises the international community after nuclear disasters such as at Chernobyl, Ukraine in 1986 and Fukushima, Japan in 2011. It also assists the monitoring of non-proliferation of nuclear weapons in places like North Korea and Iran, whose programs have been subjected to sanctions by the international community and Security Council.

Three IGOs Related to Business

The three largest business IGOs are the World Trade Organization (which was built on the GATT), the International Monetary Fund, and the World Bank Group. Although there are many IGOs, the dominance of these three in setting up world business regimes, bringing order to trade, sovereign finance, and development, is hard to overstate. We examine each below.

General Agreement on Tariffs and Trade (GATT): Predecessor to WTO

In the mid-1940s, the United Nations oversaw four conferences on trade—a Preparatory Committee in London (1946); a Drafting Committee in Lake Success, New York (1947); the Geneva Conference (1947); and the Havana Conference (1947–1948). At the Geneva Conference, a measure called the General Agreement on Tariffs and Trade (GATT) was created. GATT regulated trade on physical commodities using agreed-upon principles of trade liberalization, equal market access, reciprocity, non-discrimination, and transparency.

> The basic idea behind GATT was to eliminate protectionism and discrimination, allowing the trade in goods to flow smoothly from one country to another, without disruption or distortion, supposedly permitting all countries to achieve larger output levels and ultimately increasing the level of economic growth everywhere.
>
> (Hartwick and Peet 2003)

Following the neoliberal principles that had been emerging, the basic purposes of GATT were stated as:

Raising living standards
Ensuring full employment

> Increasing real income and effective demand
> Assuring the full use of the resources of the world by expanding the production and exchange of goods through reducing tariffs and other barriers to trade.
>
> (Hartwick and Peet 2003)

Furthermore, the purpose of GATT was to substantially reduce tariffs and trade barriers while eliminating trade preferences from nation to nation. Thus, in 1947, a broad set of commercial principles regarding international trade were promulgated and a multilateral agreement regulating trade among the 23 original signatory countries ensued. Although the US Congress did not approve of the GATT framework, President Truman put the framework in place by executive order, essentially bypassing congressional approval. Overall, countries endorsed GATT principles as they saw fit, most commonly as flexible trading principles that aimed to help contain domestic pressure for protectionism. Between 1986 and 1994, GATT trade negotiations (when there were 128 members), termed the Uruguay Round, established the World Trade Organization (WTO) to enforce GATT and to expand trade provisions beyond raw materials and manufactured goods.

World Trade Organization (WTO)

The World Trade Organization (WTO) was established in 1995, to provide a trade forum and to administer the world trade agreements approved at the end of negotiation rounds. Originally an ad hoc commission-style organization, since 1995 it has become one of the most important IGOs, despite being quite small, because of its importance in managing the world trading system. Currently, there are 164 nation members, which now include all major economies of the world, since the accession of China in 2001 and Russia in 2012. It is located in Geneva, Switzerland and is headed by Director-General Ngozi Okonjo-Iweala, the first woman and African to hold the position.

The WTO is driven by its member states, and all major decisions are made by members as a whole. Members are represented by government ministers, ambassadors, or delegates. The Secretariat of the WTO plays an integral function in terms of coordinating the activities of the member countries. The Secretariat is comprised of a staff of over 625, which includes experts in the areas of law, economics, statistics, and communications. The Secretariat staff assist member nations in ensuring trade negotiations progress smoothly and that international trade rules are correctly applied and enforced. In particular, the WTO follows the Most-Favored Nation (MFN) clause, which requires all members to treat one another equally. In practice, this has several implications. First, countries cannot unilaterally retaliate against one another by raising tariffs. Since tariffs protect domestic industries and workers, and raise money for governments, this clause is important for preventing frequent tariff and quota adjustments. However, whatever the MFN rate or conditions are for various products and services, countries may reduce them further in trading bloc agreements, such as free trade agreements. Second, while broad exceptions may be negotiated, this requires consensus and an extensive amount of time. Third, because countries are often perceived to manipulate trade rules, countries often use organizational mechanisms to dispute the practices of other countries.

The current round of negotiations is called the Doha Round, because the initial meeting was held in Doha, Qatar in 2001. While previous rounds increasingly focused on developed countries and issues surrounding services and intellectual property, the Doha Round was a result of developing countries expressing an interest in having more concessionary options. The Doha Round still has not been completed, because of disputes over protection of subsistence farmers in developing countries and the contention that agriculture in many developed countries is highly subsidized. A partial deal (called the Bali Package) was reached in the Ninth Ministerial Conference of the round in 2013. It provided highly concessionary terms toward agriculture in the least-developed countries, expanded assistance in meeting trade rules, and supplied a series of agreements to provide greater access to most developing countries, depending on their economic status. While the length of time taken to reach agreement had some critics wondering about the viability of the WTO, it is now hoped by WTO supporters that future negotiations will not be so contentious and long.

The WTO does more than just assist in the creation of a stable set of worldwide trade agreements: it also handles trade disputes, monitors trade policies, and provides technical assistance and training for developing countries. Part of the impetus for becoming a full IGO was the development of a dispute settlement mechanism. The Dispute Settlement Body sets up dispute panels that have binding authority of determination, although appeal within the WTO is possible. The US and EU are the most frequent complainants and respondents of trade disputes, although China is increasingly a party to disputes. "For its part, the United States filed more complaints than any other country, prevailing in 91 percent of these cases" (Hillman 2020). When this happens, like other countries, it must either change its trade practices or be subject to WTO sanctions on non-related products (generally tariffs on popular export items). The WTO also provides trade surveillance reports on all countries on a rotating basis; the executive summary of these reports is an invaluable tool for business people wanting to gain insight into the overall trade environment in various countries. Portions of the sixth trade policy review for Brazil are summarized in Exhibit 14.1.

Exhibit 14.1

Excerpts from the 2013 Trade Policy Review by the WTO for Brazil

Summary

1 Brazil weathered the global economic crisis well, supported by strong domestic and foreign demand and sound macroeconomic policies. Brazil has also contributed to global economic recovery by substantially increasing imports. Solid economic growth and active incomes policies have allowed Brazil to make progress toward reducing poverty, unemployment, and income inequality.

2 Further action is required to address long-standing structural shortcomings affecting the Brazilian economy's competitiveness, such as inadequate infrastructure, insufficient access to credit, and high taxes. The government has taken measures to deal with these problems but in its quest to support sectors affected by a loss of competitiveness it has also adopted some measures that may have a restrictive impact on trade. Given the size and importance of Brazil's economy, it is important for it to continue to open its market to trade and investment flows and for its policies to be conducive to growth.

Economic Environment

3 The Brazilian economy recorded a strong performance during most of the 2007–2012 period, with real GDP growth averaging 3.6 percent a year, albeit with important fluctuations. ... Sustained economic growth over almost a decade and active income policies have allowed Brazil to make important progress toward reducing poverty and income inequality, while employment figures have improved.

4 Since the second half of 2011, however, growth has decelerated significantly and the average real growth rate for 2012 was just 0.9 percent. This loss of dynamism may be partly attributed to the appreciation of the Brazilian real and the global economic slowdown, but it also reflects long-standing structural problems affecting the Brazilian economy's competitiveness such as inadequate infrastructure, insufficient access to credit, and a very high tax burden. To address these problems, the government has adopted measures aimed at removing infrastructure bottlenecks, expanding concessions and private–public sector partnerships, and reducing the tax

burden on certain manufacturing industries. However, to support sectors affected by a loss of competitiveness, the government has also taken some measures that have a restrictive impact on trade, including increasing tariffs temporarily, and using preferential margins for domestic goods and services in government procurement, and has increased export credits. The authorities have also taken measures to increase the availability of credit and the low level of financial intermediation. In mid-2011, the Central Bank lowered the policy interest rate (SELIC) to record low levels by Brazilian standards. On the fiscal side, the government was able to provide stimulus while maintaining a primary surplus throughout the review period. ...

5 9 Brazil is one of the WTO's most active participants, individually, and within the BRICS group of leading emerging economies. ... From October 2008 to October 2012, Brazil initiated three complaints under the WTO dispute settlement mechanism. ...

6 13 Brazil's 2012 applied MFN customs tariff is entirely *ad valorem*, with rates ranging from zero to 55 percent. The simple average MFN tariff applied in 2012 was 11.7 percent, up from 11.5 percent in 2008. ...

7 21 Brazil maintains a policy of free-trade zones for imports and exports, by which fiscal and other incentives are granted to promote production in, and the development and regional integration of, border areas in the north region. Eight free-trade zones have been created. ...

8 22 One of the Brazilian authorities' key concerns remains the availability and cost of credit. In this respect, the authorities consider that their policy of targeting credit is necessary to correct a market failure. To this end, Brazil maintains several official credit programs aimed at different sectors and types of producers.

International Monetary Fund (IMF)

In 1944, a conference was convened in Bretton Woods, New Hampshire. The purpose of the conference was "international concern over the competing currency devaluations and inflationary tendencies that characterized the interwar years and the fear of a post-war economic depression" (Boskey 1956). The conference at Bretton Woods included 44 governments (see Exhibit 14.2) and conceived two international financial organizations (IFIs)—the IMF and the World Bank (WB). Therefore, these two IFIs are also known as Bretton Woods Institutions. The IMF was initiated from these discussions, and was formally created the following year with 29 initial countries.

The IMF is essentially the central bank to the world. It is now comprised of 190 member countries. Some of the functions of the IMF include tracking global economic trends and performance, alerting its member countries when it sees problems on the horizon, providing a forum for policy dialog, and providing loan programs for countries experiencing economic distress. The current Managing Director is Kristalina Georgieva of Bulgaria; by tradition, the Managing Director is always a European.

The IMF has 24 executive directors representing individual countries if they have large economies, or groups of countries in the case of smaller economies. Countries contribute the financial resources that can be loaned to other countries in need. For example, during the Asian recession in 1997, the IMF helped out Thailand, Indonesia, and South Korea, among others, which led to weakness in Brazil and Argentina, who also needed bailouts. During the Great Recession starting in 2008, the biggest borrowers were the European countries of Greece, Portugal, Romania, and Poland, but others lined up, too, such as Mexico and Colombia. The largest borrowers currently are Argentina, Egypt, Ukraine, and Pakistan. It is important to note that the IMF has traditionally required strong conditions in order to qualify for lending, such as cutting services, increasing taxes, and adjusting interest rates. These conditions can cause such short-term pain and suffering for the public that both the IMF and the government of the day can be much decried. So while the IMF provides a sometimes necessary antidote to countries that fall victim to excessive public service and debt, this medicine more often than not hits the vulnerable members of a society harder, and many of those involved in financial manipulation or outright corruption are often less affected.

Yet the advice of the IMF has also been useful to many countries in handling global challenges. Examples include the economic turmoil caused by the oil shocks in the 1970s, the inflationary challenges in the 1980s, and the restructuring of the eastern European economies after 1989. IMF surveillance also tracks monetary policy, and in particular, currency manipulation.

Exhibit 14.2

The 44 nations represented at the Bretton Woods Conference were:

Australia, Belgium, Bolivia, Brazil, Canada, Chile, China, Colombia, Costa Rica, Cuba, Czechoslovakia, Dominican Republic, Ecuador, Egypt, El Salvador, Ethiopia, France, Greece, Guatemala, Haiti, Honduras, Iceland, India, Iran, Iraq, Liberia, Luxembourg, Mexico, The Netherlands, New Zealand, Nicaragua, Norway, Panama, Paraguay, Peru, the Philippines, Poland, South Africa, the USSR, the UK, the US, Uruguay, Venezuela, and Yugoslavia.

Exhibit 14.3

IMF "Headquarters 1" in Washington, DC

Source: Wikimedia Commons (2006).

World Bank (WB)

A global development bank, the World Bank was established in 1944 for the purpose of facilitating post-war reconstruction and development. If the IMF is the head of the international system, the World Bank is its heart. "The [World] Bank Group uses financial resources and its extensive experience to partner with developing countries to reduce poverty, increase economic growth, and improve the quality of life" (The World Bank 2011, p. 3). It was initially known as the International Bank of Reconstruction and Development (IBRD), and given the vast need to rebuild Europe after WWII, from roughly 1945–1955 much of the World Bank's focus was on reconstruction. Currently, the mission of the World Bank is to alleviate poverty around the globe.

The World Bank itself is divided into the IBRD and the International Development Association (IDA). However, the World Bank Group consists of five institutions, as seen in Exhibit 14.5. The World Bank is headquartered in Washington, DC, but has nearly 100 global offices. It employs approximately 10,000 staff and its annual lending is generally around $18–20 billion.

Exhibit 14.4

Headquarters of the World Bank, Washington, DC

Source: Wikimedia Commons (2008).

Exhibit 14.5

The five institutions of the World Bank Group

World Bank Group Institution	*Function*
The International Bank for Reconstruction and Development (IBRD)	IBRD lends to governments of middle-income and creditworthy low-income countries
The International Development Association (IDA)	IDA provides interest-free loans—called credits—and grants to governments of the poorest countries
The International Finance Corporation (IFC)	IFC provides loans, equity, and technical assistance to stimulate private-sector investment in developing countries
The Multilateral Investment Guarantee Agency (MIGA)	MIGA provides guarantees against losses caused by non-commercial risks to investors in developing countries
The International Centre for Settlement of Investment Disputes (ICSID)	ICSID provides international facilities for conciliation and arbitration of investment disputes

Source: The World Bank (2021).

Exhibit 14.6

Structure of the IMF and WB

International Monetary Fund (IMF)	*World Bank (WB)*
• Oversees the international monetary system	• Seeks to promote the economic development of the world's poorer countries
• Promotes exchange stability and orderly exchange relations among its member countries	• Assists developing countries through long-term financing of
• Assists all members—both industrial and developing countries—that find themselves in temporary balance-of-payments difficulties, by providing short- to medium-term credits. development projects and programs	• Encourages private enterprises in developing countries through its affiliate, the International Finance Corporation (IFC)
• Draws its financial resources principally from the quota subscriptions of its member countries	• Acquires most of its financial resources by borrowing on the international bond market

The IBRD aims to reduce poverty in middle-income and creditworthy poor countries by promoting sustainable development through loans, guarantees, risk-management products, and analytical and advisory services. The IDA aims to reduce poverty by providing interest-free credits and grants for programs that boost economic growth, reduce inequalities, and improve people's living conditions in the world's poorest nations.

The World Bank has a similar administrative structure as the IMF—24 directors and proportional voting (see Exhibit 14.6 for a comparison). However, because a number of loan projects in the past had negative ramifications for the recipient countries or citizens, World Bank decisions take a higher level of agreement and the process is more cautious in terms of not merely accepting the government of the day's intentions. The President of the World Bank has always been an American; David Malpass, a former US Treasury official, was nominated by the US and elected in 2019.

Criticisms of International Trade and Financial Organizations

Despite their noble goals, the three international trade and financial organizations have often been the targets of criticisms, which mainly focus on the problem of accountability resulting from their nondemocratic operation.

One accountability issue points to unequal representation in the three organizations. That is, wealthy countries are over-represented in the IMF and World Bank and overly powerful in the WTO. For example, the IMF operates a shareholder-controlled organizational system in which each member is assigned a quota, reflecting its relative size in the global economy. A member's quota determines the amount of its financial contribution, its access to IMF financing, and its relative voting power in the organization. A member country cannot unilaterally increase its quota. The increase must be approved by the Executive Board. In the past, China has attempted to increase its quota multiple times, but has been restrained by the board from getting what it wished. In 2015, modest reform was finally allowed, but it maintained the overwhelming dominance of Western nations (including Japan). As of 2020, the US had by far the largest voting rights, amounting to over 17 percent of the total, followed Japan, China, Germany, France, and the UK. China only has 6.4 percent of the voting power. The top 20 shareholders account for over 70 percent of the voting power, leaving the rest of the members, primarily developing economies, less than a 30 percent say in matters.

Another accountability problem comes from secretive operations in the organizations. For example, the WTO is notorious for its Green Room process. The term "Green Room" has its roots in British theater and refers to the room where performers wait before they go on stage. The WTO Green Room process starts with meetings of representatives of a limited number of WTO members specifically selected and invited by the host (often the WTO Director-General) to work out an agreement among themselves, and then present such agreement to the broader WTO membership for general acceptance. In the GATT era, the quad (which refers to the US, the European Union, Japan, and Canada) would act as an informal steering committee for the system. The quad, along with a few active members such as Australia and New Zealand, and strong members of transition economies and developing countries such as Brazil, India, and Mexico, took part in the Green Room meetings. The process worked negatively to reach a consensus—when none of the members present in the negotiation disagreed, there was consensus. Many developing countries voiced concern over the lack of transparency of the process. In addition to the Green Room process, the WTO was also criticized for its secretive discussions and reviews, such as dispute proceedings.

The WTO top-down approach to decision-making, lacking input from those affected by its policies and projects, has made the World Bank a target for criticism concerning accountability, especially when it involves a specific development project. For example, the Pak Mun Dam in Thailand was a project sponsored by the World Bank in the 1990s. The concept of the dam was proposed and approved without local involvement. The project resulted in the flooding of a vast area of land, including villages, farms, and forests, the destruction of fishing, the loss of navigation, the stagnation of water, and the displacement of thousands of indigenous people, who eventually lost their way of life (Friedrichs and Friedrichs 2002). Friedrichs and Friedrichs, in their Pak Mun Dam case study, argued that when international and national governments ignore local constituencies, it is a form of criminal conduct (2002).

As symbols of global governance, the WTO, IMF, and World Bank have also been blamed for the faults of globalization, such as the enlarged social gap between rich and poor, frequent and pervasive economic crises, immense ecological and environmental damages, the callous displacement of indigenous people, and the declining power of nation states. They have been often protested by environmentalists, human rights activists, labor unions, anti-capitalists, and anti-globalization activists. For example, on November 30, 1999, thousands of protesters blocked entrance to the WTO meetings in Seattle, Washington, forcing the cancellation of the opening ceremonies and eventually deadlocking the Seattle round of trade negotiations (see Exhibit 14.7) (Gillham and Marx 2000). The following April, more demonstrations were held at the IMF and World Bank meeting in Washington, DC, leading to mass arrests of protesters (Griswold 2000).

Exhibit 14.7

WTO protests in Seattle, November 30, 1999

Source: Wikimedia Commons (1999).

In recent years, all three organizations have been striving for improvements in accountability. The WTO publishes most of its important documents online for both public and member countries who might not be present at all committee meetings. It also improved the reporting of Green Room sessions and other meetings. The IMF has been pressing its members to make public all surveillance reports, and posts any self-evaluation of operations as well as outside reviews of operations. It also is attempting to reform the voting system, allowing bias in favor of developing countries. The World Bank is now more careful about obtaining local input, implementing a complaint mechanism for people who live in a project area, with inspection panels used for fact finding. It also requires a higher consensus of support for projects, by improving an approval vote from 50 to 80 percent.

Although the debate of disproportionate representation is not easily resolved, overall transparency and staff accountability have improved significantly in the three organizations during the past 20 years.

Factors of Economic Growth and the Role of Governments and Governance

Throughout this book, we have examined various angles about the useful and not-so-useful roles of government (and world governance) as it interacts with business in a market-based system. We began with the debate about the size of government (Chapter 1), moved on to theories about the relationships of business, society, and government (Chapter 2), reviewed the historical role of government with business (Chapter 3), and looked at the various economic policies of American government (Chapter 4). We examined proactive government models of support via economic development (Chapters 9–11), and finally surveyed international aspects of national and global governance related to business (Chapters 12–14). At this time, we summarize those discussions.

Broadly speaking, this book promotes the idea that the market economy has provided a vastly enhanced quality of life for Americans and much of the world in modern times. Simultaneously, it promotes the idea that governments and governance vehicles are critical to modern society and necessary for the long-term health of the market itself. This begs two questions regarding quality and quantity of government and its relationship with business. First, *how do you ensure that the private and public sectors balance each other to create wholesome synergies*, rather than (1) opposing one another in dysfunctional ways such as misrepresentation, obfuscation, and red tape, or (2) working together in unholy alliances that privilege elites? This book does not provide specific answers, but it does point to a wide range of strategies likely to enhance cooperative relations in general, and to increase the utility at an individual level in particular.

The second question becomes, *what is the right amount of government and in what areas?* The "reasonable" range is very large in advanced democracies today, where "successful" models range from relatively lean governments such as Japan (which nonetheless has had a large national debt for a long time) and the high-tax Scandinavian countries where complaints about government are relatively rare. There is nothing innately wrong with either advocating a much reduced governmental budget and role, nor is there anything inherently wrong with promoting a more robust government role. What this book has tried to do is get beyond the simplistic arguments that ignore the problems government can create, or paint it as the source of all problems. For example, it is unrealistic to suggest that cuts in government do not require realistic assessments about what is being sacrificed over the long-term; it is equally simplistic to suggest that any additional government outlays can all come from the rich. This is particularly important in terms of government outlays, which are much more likely to be long-term investments in the future of society rather than wealth creation for the more affluent.

In order to make a realistic assessment of the types of contributions of governments and governance mechanisms, it is necessary to have one last review of the determinants of economic growth, but to do so with the full range of factors that have been discussed over the course of the book. In all, we suggest 12 determinants of economic growth in which government's role in maximizing these factors varies considerably, from relatively modest to quite substantial.

As we have discussed, classical economic theory, the foundation of microeconomics, focuses on how the interplay of the important factors of labor, capital, and land can lead to competition—and thus efficiency and innovation—in an ideal market. We examine each of these factors in relation to government in light of contemporary economic demands.

Labor is not homogenous in most modern industries, and uneducated, low-quality labor is fine for subsistence and maintenance cultures. Even in Adam Smith's day, however, long apprenticeships were the substitute for formal education in Britain and ensured a high-quality workforce in the world. Later, formal education was introduced in order to keep the quality of the workforce high (among other reasons). In comparison, Eastern Europe and Russia elected to keep labor cheap and prevented widespread education. While a short-term cost saving back in the eighteenth century, this frugality ensured that over the long haul, those countries would remain at the bottom of the value chain for centuries. On the other hand, the US, like Great Britain, augmented its apprenticeship programs with compulsory public education in the nineteenth century. Going beyond Britain, however, the US created an extensive array of land grant universities for the "common man," the most ambitious educational initiative of its day. Not surprisingly, within decades the US became the scientific center of the world. While the system (probably better called a network) of higher education in the US continues to this day, the breakdown of the K-12 structure is, and will increasingly become, a drag on the American economy in the decades ahead

(Finn 2009). The role of government in education has been, and will remain, very extensive, even if ever changing.

Private capital sufficiency allows a market economy to operate efficiently because it allows effective redeployment of resources (i.e., investment), especially for large operations. Classical economics points out that taxes deflate private capital and therefore provide a small to large drag on short- and long-term capital effectiveness. Yet while lower taxes are always better in order for this factor to be maximized, all things being equal, the fact remains that it is impossible for all things to be equal because of the positive and often necessary products of taxes, such as national security. More realistically, it is critical for taxes to be a good-value exchange for a service society wants. For example, while the US military machine is a worthy reason for pride, its value for service is much reduced because Congress routinely requires purchases of unnecessary military equipment, keeps unnecessary facilities open, and adds earmarks to the budget that are not defense related (Negin 2020). Some countries have extraordinarily good and comprehensive services, including various types of insurance, and have virtually eliminated poverty, a good value (because of policy integrity and administrative competence) despite higher tax levels. Some countries have infrastructures that are in complete disrepair and social services that are largely lacking, so even though taxes may be low, they are still a poor value. American opinion seems to be that there is considerable policy and administrative waste in American government, and that by cutting it we could avoid painful choices such as increased taxes or spending cuts on important programs (Swanson and Blumenthal 2013), but that is hard to square with the thinking of serious economists today (Samuelson 2009), especially reducing taxes at a time when wealth disparity is growing and the rich are in fact getting richer (Hope and Limberg 2020). While it is important for the modern administrative state not to overwhelm the private sector for a robust capitalist economy (e.g., not to let mindless accretion of responsibilities prevent the thinning out of programs and services as the economy evolves), it is even more important for governments to provide value for service because of both civically wise and ethical policy-making, as well as administrative competence.

Substitution of public capital for private capital is another issue regarding capital sufficiency. Again, the picture is more nuanced than commonly portrayed. On one hand, there are few cases where government capital can completely substitute for private capital, as the fall and/or transition of the communist bloc countries demonstrate. However, there are numerous examples, including the US, where governments have helped infant industries or aided industries in times of crises. Infant industries can be assisted as they gear up their technology and work against economies of scale (Krugman 1979); the East Asian countries are clear examples. However, the more nuanced issue is how to keep government strategic, and not allow them to become structural and/or perverse. For example, while America's first major export industry, tobacco, was neither infant, small, nor strategic, it received large agricultural subsidies during the period from the Great Depression until 1982, and moderate subsidies through 2015, when all direct support and subsidies were finally phased out (FSA 2013). Supporting an unhealthy product in the first place is dubious (being classified as an agricultural good rather than a non-essential or luxury good); and continuing even modest, indirect support through 2015 seems remarkably non-strategic. On the other hand, the US government subsidy of transcontinental railroads accelerated the development of the West by approximately 20 years (Ambrose 2001), and there were numerous subsidies, both strategic and short-term, to the tech industry when it started. The failure to keep local economic development strategic and stripped of "pork" projects resulted in the Governor of California rescinding state support for municipal and county efforts (Dolan, Garrison, and York 2011).

Monetary trustworthiness is an issue when dealing with capital. When wars have occurred within domestic borders, it is common for money to be drained from banks and stored as precious metals and gems, which are portable and easily hidden, and for people to require them for larger purchases because printed money is no longer trusted. Similarly, the markets punish industries in countries that print too much money or that cannot manage their interest rates. Trade in the Roman Empire expanded massively because the system was both consistent and backed by precious metals. When the Roman Empire collapsed and its monetary system fell apart, so, too, did international trade for hundreds of years. Immediately after the American Revolution, when many called for the depreciation or default on US government debt accrued to pay for the war, Alexander Hamilton insisted on full repayment. That tradition of trustworthiness has generally protected markets from governmental causes of depressions, as have sometimes occurred in more unstable or untrustworthy economies. The major exception was during the Civil War when soldiers on both sides were paid with excessive currency, leading to hyperinflation; the Union greenback was restored after the war but the Southern Confederate dollar collapsed even before the end of the war (Thornton and Ekelund 2004). Thus, monetary trustworthiness created by governments is enormous in providing a stable platform for capital to be saved and used in domestic and trade pursuits.

Land, as discussed by Adam Smith, is really a metaphor for both land itself and its physical resources such as minerals and timber; we divide our discussion accordingly. Capitalism envisions the relatively rapid conversion of land for different uses in some areas, generally leading to land intensification; this is facilitated in a market economy when the "invisible hand" operates relatively freely. In turn, this means private possession must be protected in a system of secure ownership through trustworthy contracts and legal processes. The US is a model in this regard, ensuring that exceptions to property rights are minimized. Examples where property is devalued and less likely to be developed occur in countries in which nationalization is likely, abrogation of contracts is common, and manipulation of the legal system by powerful interests is frequent. Further, historically, the US has increased land resources by opening up the West through public land sales and land rushes, through conquest, and by allowing the private use of public lands in many cases. Nonetheless, there are exceptions in the US in which property rights are curbed (in addition to acquisition of land for public purposes such as roads and common amenities). The primary exception is the long-term degradation of land. Examples are not hard to find in an age where large industries can easily pollute their own and neighboring land. For example, the Hooker chemical company graciously ceded its former factory site to the Niagara Falls School District for $1, who, in turn, sold it to a developer whose tract homes were called Love Canal, after a canal that long before had been filled in with chemical waste. The 21,000 tons of toxic waste seeped into basements and infiltrated the local aquifer used for drinking. The level of birth defects, chromosome damage, and cancer in the area skyrocketed, requiring the eventual condemnation and purchase of the 36-block area by the federal government (Blum 2011). Another common example includes communities downwind of smokestack industries. Today, therefore, governments must assiduously protect property owners' rights to intensify land (to some degree modified by zoning ordinances), while carefully monitoring properties for their environmental effects, as an important exception to private ownership theory.

Availability of natural and physical resources is a concern of the classical dimension of growth. Lush resources include minerals, oil and gas, timber, waterways, access to water for drinking and agriculture, and so on. A single factor, such as spices in the Middle Ages or oil today, can bring wealth to a country rich in a scarce resource. Governments can assist with the exploration of resources, or the extraction of expensive ones. For example, Saudi Arabia has not only one of the largest oil reserves in the world, but it has the largest capacity to create fresh water, with over 30 oil- and gas-powered desalination plants. Yet the current power sources are so expensive that Saudi Arabia is looking to the future, when its oil reserves may run low, and is now also building solar desalination plants (Todorova 2014; Ghaithan et al. 2021). This example points to the need for countries to be forward looking in terms of resource conservation. For example, there are many historical cases of island and tropical cultures becoming impoverished after cutting down all their forests, or agricultural societies exhausting their soil because of poor conservation. Desertification is an enormous environmental problem in the world today, most notably in Africa, Australia, the western US, the Middle East, and Central Asia (Imeson 2012). While some desertification is caused by natural cycles, it is almost always exacerbated, and sometimes completely caused, by human activity and unsustainable population (Huang 2020). Human causes include overgrazing, stripping vegetation, and overharvesting ground-water supplies. Ground-water depletion today causes sinkholes in Florida, land subsidence of up to 10 feet in areas of Texas, and a 300-foot drop in the water table in most of southern Arizona.

Turning to an ocean example, an important source of food for the planet, fish are being caught at such an alarming rate that many species are close to extinction, and scientists predict the collapse of ocean fishing in the next 30 years (Hilborn 2012). Here, international governance structures will need to work together to ensure that this valuable resource is protected, but that many species are not fished to extinction. Governments and governance vehicles are needed to monitor resource extraction and depletion as the planet looks ahead to a population of at least eight billion people in the next 20 years, and at the current rate, ten billion by 2050.

Competition is a pillar of the classical growth model. It creates a dynamic that forces producers to pay attention to market demands, to be as efficient as possible, and to innovate. However, as much discussed in this book, there are several threats to "perfect" competition. One such threat comes from monopolies, so governments create anti-competition laws and rules to prevent single companies from manipulating the market and crushing incipient competition, as well as rules to prevent competitors from engaging in price collusion. Such regulation has been indispensable in producing a competitive environment in the US and in keeping the US at the top of the world economy. Countries that do not maintain competitive markets—and allow oligopolies, monopolies, and hyper-wealthy power elites—are much more prone to economic declines as the economy shifts over time.

Innovation is a critical product of growth for modern economies. Some experts think that innovation is the single most important factor in the current global economy (Fagerberg 1988, 1997; Cantwell 1989). Innovation comes at many different levels. Adaptation is the process of taking existing technologies or others' ideas and adjusting them for current needs, and is sometimes known as refinement. Invention is the creation of entirely new technologies or radically new uses. In the last 50 years, many countries have been good at adaptation, especially the rising Asian countries, but the US has led in true creation. Creation takes education, experimentation, and a willingness to re-create (Wolff 1995). The US has traditionally had a robust and relatively inclusive educational system, a penchant for experimentation going back to Edison, and a willingness to give up past technologies for things that are new, fresh, or simply have the potential to be the "next wave." The US government has invested heavily in research, with the annual budgets of the National Science Foundation and the National Institute of Health reaching $8.5 billion and $43 billion, respectively, in 2021. Other agencies that assist in basic research include the Department of Defense and the National Aeronautics and Space Administration (NASA), among others. Local governments have been instrumental in attracting top talent, creating technology centers, and fostering innovation incubators. Indirectly, but importantly, anti-competitive rules have greatly aided in keeping the US at the cutting edge in a world whose competitive spirit has increased exponentially since World War II, when the US easily dominated with its economic engine fully intact.

Infrastructure refers to the basic physical structures needed for the operation of a country, or the facilities necessary for an economy to function. Some infrastructure has more to do with internal national functions, such as the water system, sewers, the electrical grid, hospitals, and so on. Particularly important to both domestic and international commerce traditionally have been roads, canals, rail, bridges, sea ports, airports, and tunnels, which largely focused on the movement of physical goods. Wired communications infrastructure was less important as a critical trade factor, but that has dramatically changed in the last generation as commerce has moved into the age of the Internet. All great empires of the past have excelled at the infrastructure of their day. The Romans built roads to ensure quick military movement, but they were also an enormous boon to trade; they were built to last and some are still in use today. The conqueror Genghis Khan installed a postal system for his great sprawling Asian empire, which by the time Marco Polo visited his grandson, who consolidated and refined it, had expanded to 1,400 stations. The British built their great sea empire of the late nineteenth century on the excellently provisioned ports they had acquired such as Gibraltar, Hong Kong, Singapore, the Falklands, Bermuda and the Bahamas, and multiple locations in Africa, India, Australia, and the Pacific. The US government has been very forward thinking in this regard throughout its history, and has focused on unifying the country. It nationalized the postal service in 1775 and made it a Cabinet position in 1792; the transcontinental railways were initially federally sponsored; airports across the country were initially postal service centers; and the US federal highway system was completely overhauled under President Eisenhower to be the envy of the world. There are many other examples. A comparison between India and China provides a prime demonstration of the difference that infrastructure can make: India's infrastructure continues to be old, fragmented, and overburdened (Chilkoti 2014), while China's has been vastly upgraded, contributing greatly to its export-driven economic model (Dangra 2016). In addition to physical infrastructure, governments manage the airwaves and the Internet so there is orderly and fair access, standardization, and regulation to minimize fraud, copyright infringement, and other criminal activity.

The *consumer base* itself, on which commerce and trade depend, can often be assumed or ignored, jeopardizing the market's fundamental health, as the focus is often miscast on the specifics of marketplace mechanics. Yet when the market or consumers suffer, overall economic growth will also suffer, as will most individuals in society. A key assumption today is the existence of sufficient customers to drive the competitive marketplace and encourage efficiency and innovation. As a single factor, slow and steady population growth is the easiest to manage and use for economic prosperity when other factors are in place, the pattern for the US for most of its history. Elsewhere, rapid population growth has frequently been a problem, as is the case in many developing countries whose infant mortality rates have dropped since 1950, but whose birth rates have not. The most densely populated country in the world, China, instituted a repressive one-child policy in 1982 to curb population growth. While China will have many economic issues to contend with in the future, such as increasing dependence on the state by the elderly because of fewer children, this has been a considerable factor in concentrating resources on the young and on the state, rather than on unsustainable family expansion patterns. On the other hand, another immensely populated country, India, has yet to get a strong handle on its teeming population, and Africa's most populous country, Nigeria, is just beginning to see its population explode (Exhibit 14.8). These countries have severe economic hurdles to overcome because of this factor. Conversely, governments have special responsibility to prevent or mitigate unexpected population declines. The Black Plague in Europe decimated a third of the population and pushed the European recovery from the Middle Ages back a century. The US has worked to improve health through the reduction of a vast array of diseases such as the flu, the measles, pertussis, mumps, rubella, smallpox, diphtheria, a variety of semi-tropical diseases (e.g., yellow fever), polio, tuberculosis, AIDS, and the coronavirus variants. Another aspect of market protection by governments is the organization or support of risk reduction programs that provide assistance to consumers in old age, because of disability, or because of immediate job loss. This helps individuals in times of need, but also reduces potential wide economic swings in the economy. Yet another aspect of government assistance in maintaining healthy markets is ensuring that foreign competitors do not unfairly encroach in domestic markets and that domestic competitors are aided in the quest to expand abroad.

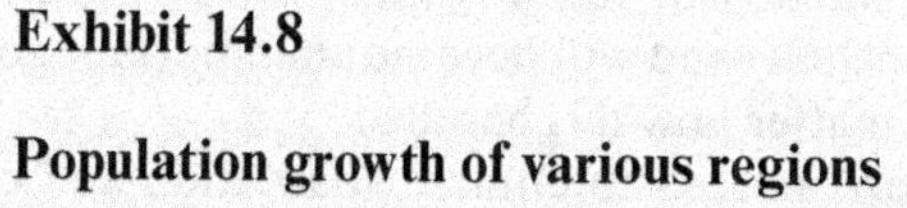

Exhibit 14.8

Population growth of various regions

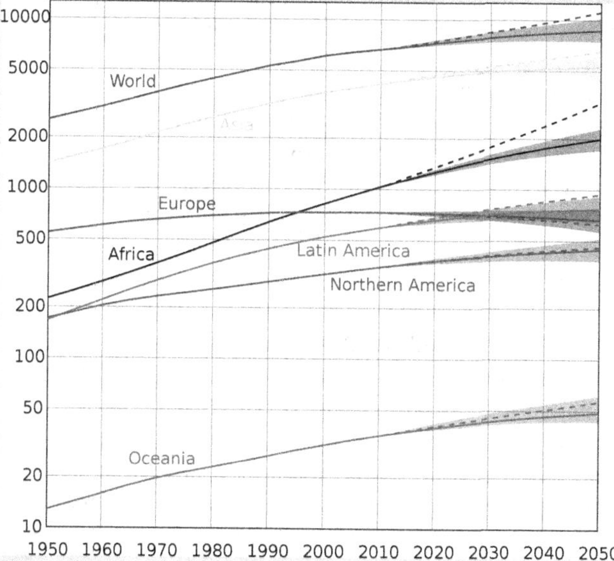

Source: BBC (Based on United Nations data) 2015.

Consumers who have the means to purchase goods is not the same as having a sufficient number of consumers. During the twentieth century, there was a worldwide push in democratization, for not only the ability to participate in the governance process, but also for economic access and opportunity. Therefore, there has been an interest in policies that ensure a healthy and broad middle class, as opposed to the aristocratic models of the past or the economic divides between rich and poor still found in developing countries. For the purpose of this discussion, economic growth has been most visible and sustained in countries with a large middle class. There are many policies that can be enacted to encourage a middle-class-driven economy, such as universal access to cheap but high-quality education, minimum-wage laws (i.e., the prevention of economic serfdom), and income redistribution through a progressive tax structure. The preferred responsible business model has become that of Henry Ford, who proudly paid above the prevailing wage, rather than that of the Robber Barons who preceded him, who were known for low wages despite the vast profits of their companies. Following the Ford model, the tech industry has not only produced incredible fortunes (e.g., Gates via Microsoft, Ellison via Oracle, and Bezos via Amazon.com), but has provided widespread lucrative employment even among lower echelons of employees. This has not been common in most other industries, where income contraction has been experienced. As a result, concerns about the increasing concentration of wealth in the US and the world at large, leading to what many have dubbed a second Gilded Age, has become a more and more debated issue recently (Schoen 2013; Piketty 2014; Hubmer, Krusell, and Smith 2021) and will become an important governmental issue in the future, no matter how it is handled.

Climate is our final factor and is related to climate adaptation and climate change. Like other species, humans have been remarkable at adapting to climates that are exceptionally cold, such as the Inuit in the north, and exceptionally high places, such as the Tibetans, the Peruvians, and the Amhara Ethiopians. Their climate adaptation is both cultural and physiological. The Inuit have culturally learned how to cope with hunting and the ice, and their physiology has adapted to a high-protein/high-fat diet. Likewise, those living in high altitudes are physiologically dissimilar from "lowlanders" because of genetic evolutionary changes in their respiratory systems allowing them to process oxygen differently. As a negative historical example, the large Norse settlement in Greenland started in 986, and thrived for a while during a Medieval warm period (hence the name, Greenland); a mini ice age started in 1275, driving the population, who did not adapt, into extinction by 1450 (Diamond 2005). Current positive examples of climate change are the use of the air conditioner in the US in hot deserts and the humid American South, the successful dike building of the Dutch against rising sea levels, and the irrigation of former deserts around the world. One negative example of climate change is the massive amount of desertification occurring around the world in dry regions where the effects

Exhibit 14.9

The major factors affecting growth, and government's roles

Growth Factor	*Explanation*	*Government's Role*
Labor		
Low-quality or unproductive labor	Low-quality labor works fine for subsistence and maintenance cultures	Little role
High-productivity labor	A competitive culture needs labor to be skilled in cutting-edge technology; this requires a highly sophisticated education system	Large role • provides access to basic and higher education
Capital		
Sufficiency	Savings required for growth, and one factor is moderate taxes. Alternatively, sometimes government "savings" are used in lieu of private savings	Large role • ensures taxes are good value in terms of services provided • selectively chooses what government should boost
Monetary trustworthiness	For commerce to expand beyond crude barter and metal-backed monetary systems, monetary system must be relatively stable over time	Large role • provides responsible printing and backing of money despite economic disruptions • moderates interest rates
Land		
Usable land	Use of land for the most productive purpose (intensification). However, when land is fundamentally degraded, future growth will slow	Large role • provides a secure system of private ownership • ensures land is not unnecessarily degraded
Availability of resources	Availability of natural and physical resources encourages growth. Loss or exhaustion of natural resources slow growth	Moderate role • assists with acquisition of new resources • ensures resources are not exhausted prematurely

Growth Factor	*Explanation*	*Government's Role*
Competition		
Multiple sources of competition and consumer knowledge	Lack of monopolistic conditions that curtail competition	Large role • provides rules to break up or prevent monopolies • provides regulations to enhance competition
Innovation allowed and/or encouraged	Simple adaptations need little assistance. A culture of modern innovation often takes a series of factors: education, experimentation, and a willingness to re-create	Moderate role • provides a high-quality educational system • facilitates competition • directly promotes R&D
But also Infrastructure		
Roads, bridges, air spectrum, etc.	Commerce requires a means to transport goods and services by roads, ports, airports, airwaves, etc.	Large role • owns most basic transportation platforms, e.g., roads • regulates and partners with private infrastructure for access and safety
Healthy Market		
Sufficient consumer base	There must be customers to buy products. A rapid decline in customers decreases growth	Moderate role • provides national security • provides public health, risk protection, and safety nets • reduces unfair trade practices • assists with expansion to foreign markets
Consumers have the means to purchase goods	Creates a broad pool of wealth in the population	Large role ensures that policies encourage a large middle class
Climate adaptation	Adaptation to climate is critical for growth	Small but growing role • assists with new behavioral patterns • discourages human-induced climate change

of human causes cannot be mitigated by mechanical and cultural measures. Other examples are very low regions such as Bangladesh, where most land is less than 10 feet above sea level and whose large population cannot adapt to land loss and frequent flooding that often affects 75 percent of the country. However, the list is long of those countries whose glum prospects regarding future flooding are extensive including China, the Netherlands, Germany, the Philippines, Nigeria, India, Vietnam, numerous Islands, and so on (Buchholz 2020). As the earth heats up (no matter what the causes), the polar ice caps melt, and the oceans rise, governments and world governance will need to address global warming if growth is not to be adversely affected, leaving our grandchildren in a considerably less fortunate position than we have inherited. See Exhibit 14.9 for a summary of the factors.

Analytical Case: The BRICS Development Bank

BRICS refers to the association of the five fastest-growing developing economies—Brazil, Russia, India, China, and South Africa. The term BRIC, coined by British economist Jim O'Neil, represents the four rapidly developing economies (before South Africa became part of it in 2010) that symbolize the shift in global economic power away from the developed G7 (Canada, France, Germany, Italy, Japan, the UK, and the US) countries. The shared demand for economic development and political interest have drawn the BRICS countries to closer cooperation.

On June 16, 2009, as a response to the US-originated global economic crisis of 2008, the BRIC countries held their first formal summit in Yekaterinburg, Russia. The summit focused its discussion on ways to improve the global economy, reform financial institutions, and enhance cooperation among themselves, as well as how developing countries could become more involved in global affairs. Following the summit, the four countries called for a new global reserve currency other than the US dollar.

With their increased economic power, the BRICS countries also demanded more say in international institutions. For example, in 2012, BRICS pledged to contribute $75 billion to the IMF to boost its lending power, on the condition that the IMF reform its voting system.

Seeing unpromising signs in the IMF, the BRICS countries started to seek their own ways. Such demands rarely went through IMF's voting system, which is dominated by developed countries.

On July 15, 2014, BRICS held its sixth summit, in Fortaleza, Brazil. The five nations announced the creation of the BRICS Development

Bank with $100 billion contributions (equally shared by each participating nation) as well as another $100 billion reserve (of which China contributes over 40 percent). The bank will be headquartered in Shanghai, China, with its first President, Chairman of the Board of Directors, and Chairman of the Board of Governors from India, Brazil, and Russia, respectively.

The BRICS Development Bank aims at offering an alternative to the existing IMF and World Bank for financial resources for development purposes. Unlike the IMF and World Bank, who assign votes based on capital share, the BRICS Development Bank assigns each participating country one vote, and no veto power from any single country.

Currently the BRICS represents 42 percent of the world's population and 26 percent of the land mass, and a shared 18 percent of the global GDP. The five countries' average growth rate is more than twice that of the developed world. The fast economic growth in these developing countries creates enormous demand for capital infrastructure investment. The BRICS financial pool could potentially better meet the needs for developing countries seeking loans outside the Bretton Woods Institutions.

Questions for Discussion and Analysis

1 What are the driving forces to the formation of the BRICS Development Bank?
2 What are the factors that may potentially enhance or undermine the cooperation among the BRICS members?
3 What are the economic and political implications of the BRICS Development Bank to global governance?
4 Currently the US dollar is the primary reserve currency used by other countries. Some economists anticipate that the BRICS Bank could potentially create a new reserve currency (e.g., RMB Yuan) for the world. If that happens, how will it affect international business?

Sources: Bryanski, G. (2009); Euronews (2009); Reuters (2012); Lewis, J., and Trevisani, P. (2014)

Practical Skill

Leveraging International Resources

Your team has been asked to provide a report for your corporation on the economic viability of placing a factory for your company in another country, which would be the shipping point for the rest of the continent. The comparison is between Argentina and Brazil. While others were assigned to look at possible cities in those countries, you were asked to provide a macroeconomic picture of the two countries. Since you want to use original research rather than secondary sources, you will be using WTO, IMF, and WB data. For example, in the case of Brazil, you would want to examine the annual WTO Country Profile and 2013 Trade Policy Review (these are only done every five to eight years), the IMF annual Staff Report for the Article IV Consultation, and a selection of the many economic forecasts and reports that the World Bank supplies.

If asked to do this as an exercise, provide a description of the types of macro-level data to be found using the information in these three important IGOs. How would you structure such a report? What other sources (IGOs, NGOs, or other) might you need for a country-level background analysis of these two countries?

Summary and Conclusion

1 Not only does business work in the context of national, state, and local governments, it also works through global governance structures, which is the voluntary integration of political and economic structures via treaties. Those structures are provided by international governmental organizations (IGOs) whose members are composed of sovereign states. Most IGOs have a substantial permanent secretariat, a legislative body where all members will occasionally convene, and often have branch offices around the world. IGOs operate in multiple areas. While several examples of (non-business) IGOs related to diplomatic, political grievances, and environmental purposes were mentioned, a major focus of this chapter was three (business-related) IGOs that concentrated our attentions on trade, finance, and economic well-being.

2 The current world order of trade management was started with the General Agreement on Tariffs and Trade (GATT) in 1947. It was composed of a series of trade rounds whose goal was to reach a number of member-wide agreements about increasingly low tariff levels. The World Trade Organization replaced and subsumed GATT in 1995, when

it became a permanent organization and assumed a binding trade dispute settlement function. Today, world tariffs are at an all-time low and trade is at an all-time high.

3 The International Monetary Fund (IMF) functions as the central bank to the world. Some of the functions of the IMF include tracking global economic trends and performance, alerting its member countries when it sees problems on the horizon, providing a forum for policy dialog, and providing loan programs for countries experiencing economic distress.

4 The World Bank is not a conventional or central bank: it is a global development bank. The World Bank uses its financial resources and expertise to partner with developing countries to alleviate poverty, increase economic growth, and improve the overall quality of life. It was initially known as the International Bank of Reconstruction and Development (IBRD). The World Bank itself is divided into the International Bank of Reconstruction and Development (IBRD), which focuses on middle-range countries, and the International Development Association (IDA), which focuses on the least-developed countries.

5 Finally, the chapter reviews 12 factors commonly associated with growth, and the associated roles of governments and governance structures in facilitating those growth factors in partnership with business. The classically identified macrofactors are labor, land, and competition. However, our discussion divides those more narrowly (as is common in contemporary economics) into low- and high-productivity labor, private and public capital, monetary trustworthiness, usable land, availability of resources, multiple sources of competition, and innovation. Infrastructure, a sufficient consumer base, the breadth of the consumer base, and climate adaptation were discussed as important additional factors. Government has at least a small role in all factors, but a large role in many, such as monetary trustworthiness and guaranteeing a fair playing field for true competition to occur.

6 The challenge in a modern capitalistic system is how to keep government (and governance structures) as modest as possible, while ensuring that they are large enough and well resourced enough to carry out the numerous roles assigned to them, for both the well-being of society and for building good business–government relations.

Key Terms

- BRICS
- IGO
- NGO
- GATT
- IMF
- Tariff
- Global governance
- Infrastructure
- UN
- IAEA
- Innovation
- World Bank
- IBRD
- Interpol
- WTO

Study Questions

1. What is global governance? How is it different from nation-state governance?
2. What is an intergovernmental organization (IGO)? What are the major purposes of IGOs?
3. Discuss the differences between the International Monetary Fund and the World Bank.
4. International trade and finance institutions have clearly provided many benefits to the global economy. Nonetheless, they have critics too, some of whom are very fierce about aspects of what these organizations do and stand for. Discuss some of the criticisms. Be sure to provide examples.
5. Discuss fully, with examples, the major factors affecting growth and government's roles.
6. What do you think are the top five challenges facing the global governance in the twenty-first century? Discuss fully with examples.

References

Ambrose, S. E. (2001). *Nothing Like It in the World: The Men Who Built the Transcontinental Railroad 1863–1896*. New York: Simon & Schuster.

BBC (Based on United Nations data) 2015. https://www.bbc.co.uk/news/world-asia-33720723.

Blum, E. (2011). *Love Canal Revisited: Race, Class, and Environmental Action*. Lawrence: University Press of Kansas.

Boskey, S. (1956). Bretton Woods Recalled. *International Bank Notes*, July. http://documents.worldbank.org/curated/en/370191468914668853/International-Bank-notes

Bryanski, G. (2009). BRIC Demands more Clout, Steers Clear of Dollar Talk. *Reuters*, June 26.

Buchholz, K. (2020). Rising Sea Levels Will Threaten 200 Million People by 2100. *Statistica*. February 11. https://www.statista.com/chart/19884/number-of-people-affected-by-rising-sea-levels-per-country/

Cantwell, J. A. (1989). A Classical Model of the Impact of International Trade and Production on National Industrial Growth. *Technological Innovation and Multinational Corporations* (chapter 8). Oxford: Basil Blackwell.

Chilkoti, A. (2014). Now for the Hard Part: India's Infrastructure Challenge. *Financial Times*, London, June 4.

Dangra, A. (2016). The Missing Piece in India's Economic Growth Story: Robust Infrastructure *S&P Global*. August 2. https://www.spglobal.com/en/research-insights/articles/the-missing-piece-in-indias-economic-growth-story-robust-infrastructure

Diamond, J. (2005). *Collapse: How Societies Choose to Fail or Succeed*. New York: Viking Press.

Dolan, M., Garrison, J., and York, A. (2011). California High Court Puts Redevelopment Agencies Out of Business. *Los Angeles Times*, December 29. https://www.latimes.com/local/la-xpm-2011-dec-29-la-me-redevelopment-20111230-story.html

Euronews (2009). BRIC Wants More Influence Archived, from the original on June 21.

Fagerberg, J. (1988). International Competitiveness. *Economic Journal, 98(391)*:355–374.

Fagerberg, J. (1997). Competitiveness, Scale, and R&D. *Technology and International Trade*. Brookfield, VT: Edward Elgar.

Finn, C. E., Jr. (2009). The End of the Education Debate. *National Affairs*, Winter:63–74.

Friedrichs, D. O., and Friedrichs, J. (2002). The World Bank and Crimes of Globalization: A Case Study. *Social Justice, 29(1–2)*:13–36.

FSA (Farm Service Agency) (2013). *Tobacco Transition Payment Program ("Tobacco Buyout")*. Website: United State Department of Agriculture.

Gillham, P., and Marx, G. T. (2000). Complexity and Irony in Policing and Protesting: The World Trade Organization in Seattle. *Social Justice, 27*:212–236.

Ghaithan, A. M., Al-Hanbali, A., Mohammed, A., Attia, A. M., Saleh, H., and Alsawafy, O. (2021). Optimization of a Solar-wind-grid Powered Desalination System in Saudi Arabia. *Renewable Energy*.

Griswold, D. (2000). In the Streets Around the IMF. *Workers World*, April 16. http://www.workers.org/ww/2000/diary0427.php.

Hartwick, E., and Peet, R. (2003). Neoliberalism and Nature: The Case of the WTO. *Annals of the American Academy of Political and Social Science, 590*, Rethinking Sustainable Government, November:188–211.

Held, D., and McGrew, A. (2003). *The Global Transformations Reader*. Boston, MA: Polity Press.

Hilborn, R. (2012). *Overfishing: What Everyone Needs to Know*. New York: Oxford University Press.

Hillman, J. (2020). A Reset of the World Trade Organization's Appellate Body. *Council on Foreign Relations*. January 14. https://www.cfr.org/report/reset-world-trade-organizations-appellate-body.

Hope, D., and Limberg, J. (2020). Here's Proof that Tax Cuts for the Rich Don't Boost the Economy. *The Conversation*. December 16. https://www.marketwatch.com/story/heres-proof-that-tax-cuts-for-the-rich-dont-boost-the-economy-11608136674.

Huang, J., Zhang, G., Zhang, Y., Guan, X., Wei, Y., and Guo, R. (2020). Global Desertification Vulnerability to Climate Change and Human Activities. *Land Degradation & Development, 31(11)*:1380–1391.

Hubmer, J., Krusell, P., and Smith Jr, A. A. (2021). Sources of US Wealth Inequality: Past, Present, and Future. *Nber Macroeconomics Annual, 35(1)*:391–455.

Imeson, A. (2012). *Desertification, Land Degradation and Sustainability*. Oxford: Wiley-Blackwell.

Krugman, P. R. (1979). Increasing Returns, Monopolistic Competition, and International Trade. *International Economics, 9*:469–479.

Lewis, J., and Trevisani, P. (2014). BRICS Agree to Base Development Bank in Shanghai. *Wall Street Journal*, July 15.

Negin, E. (2020). It's Time to Rein in Inflated Military Budgets: In an Era of Pandemics and Climate Change, We Need to Reconsider What "National Security" Means. *Scientific American*. September 14. https://www.scientificamerican.com/article/its-time-to-rein-in-inflated-military-budgets/.

Piketty, T. (2014). *Capital in the Twenty-First Century.* Cambridge, MA: Belknap Press/Harvard University Press.

Reuters (2012). Russia Says BRICS Eye Joint Anti-Crisis Fund. June 21.

Samuelson, P. A. (2009). *Economics: An Introductory Analysis*, 19th edn. New York: McGraw Hill.

Schoen, D. E. (2013). *The End of Authority: How a Loss of Legitimacy and Broken Trust Are Endangering Our Future.* Lanham, MD: Rowman & Littlefield.

Statistica (2021). https://www.statista.com/statistics/.

Swanson, E., and Blumenthal, M. (2013). "Wasteful Spending" Poll: Few Agree on What Government Waste Is, Most Want to Cut It. *Huffpost Plooster*, March 18. http://www.huffingtonpost.com/2013/03/18/wasteful-spending-poll_n_2886081.html.

The World Bank (2011). *A Guide to the World Bank*, 3rd edn. Washington, DC: The World Bank.

Thornton, M., and Ekelund, R. B. (2004). *Tariffs, Blockades, and Inflation: The Economics of the Civil War.* Wilmington, DE: Scholarly Resources, Inc.

Todovora, V. (2014). Reducing Energy Footprint of Water Desalination Is Priority, Say Experts. *The National*, Abu Dhabi, January 27.

Wikimedia Commons (1999). Steve Kaiser. https://commons.wikimedia.org/wiki/File:WTO_protests_in_Seattle_November_30_1999.jpg.

Wikimedia Commons (2006). IMF. https://commons.wikimedia.org/wiki/File:-Headquarters_of_the_International_Monetary_Fund_(Washington,_DC).jpg.

Wikimedia Commons (2008). AgnosticPreachersKid. https://commons.wikimedia.org/wiki/File:World_Bank_building.JPG.

Wolff, E. N. (1995). Technological Change, Capital Accumulation, and Changing Trade Patterns over the Long Term. *Structural Change and Economic Dynamics, 6(1)*:43–70.

The World Bank (2021). https://www.worldbank.org/en/home.

WTO (2020). Website. https://www.wto.org/.

Yearbook of International Organizations (2021–2022). Union of International Associations. https://uia.org/yearbook.

Index

Note: **Bold** page numbers refer to tables; *italic* page numbers refer to figures.

Printed in the United States
by Baker & Taylor Publisher Services